THE QUEST
REVEALING THE TEMPLE MOUNT IN JERUSALEM

LEEN RITMEYER
THE QUEST
REVEALING THE TEMPLE MOUNT IN JERUSALEM

Carta, Jerusalem
The Lamb Foundation

First published in 2006 by
CARTA Jerusalem
& The LAMB Foundation

Academic Consultant on Archaeology: Hillel Geva
Text and Art Editor: Barbara Laurel Ball

Reconstructions, Plans, Artwork & Photographs by the Author

Additional Graphics by Carta, Jerusalem
Maps: Lorraine Kessel
Artwork: Evgeny Vasenin, Vladimir Shestakovsky

All other credits appear next to images.

Systems Administrator: Daniel Wanoun
Production Manager: Shlomo Abergel

Cover art: Evgeny Vasenin
Cover photos: Temple Mount models — Philip Evans
Jerusalem — Garo Nalbandian

Copyright © 2006, 2015 by Carta Jerusalem, Ltd.

All rights reserved. No part of this book may be reproduced or transmitted in any form or by any means, electronic or mechanical, including photocopying, recording or by any other information storage and retrieval system existing now or in future, without permission in writing from the publishers.

ISBN: 978-965-220-628-2

Printed in Israel by Maor Wallach Press Ltd.
Bound by Weiss, Netiv Halamed Heh

Great care has been taken to cite all sources whenever known. If inadvertently such mention has been omitted but is called to our attention, due amends will be made in the following edition.
We shall also be grateful for pointing out any errors, omissions or incomplete information. Please address all comments to:

Carta Jerusalem, Ltd.
11 Rivka Street, POB 2500
Jerusalem 9102401, Israel
E-mail: carta@carta.co.il
www.carta-jerusalem.com

Contents

Preface 1
Introduction 7

Chapter One **The Herodian Temple Mount Walls**

Explorers before 1967 15
Excavations after 1967 18
The Western Wall 20
    The Western Wall Plaza (22) • Barclay's Gate (25) • Wilson's Arch (30) • The Western Wall Tunnels (32) • Warren's Gate (34) • The Rock-hewn Aqueduct (38) • The Strouthion Pool (42) • Robinson's Arch (44) • The Tyropoeon Valley Street (52) • The Trumpeting Stone (57)
The Southern Wall 60
    The Southwest Corner (61) • The Street and Plaza along the Southern Wall (63) • The Double Gate and Stairway (65) • The Double Gate Passageway (69) • The Triple Gate and Stairway (77) • The Underground Passageway of the Triple Gate (88) • The Royal Stoa (90) • The Single Gate Passageway (95) • Solomon's Stables and Ancient Vault (98) • The Southeast Corner (99)
The Eastern Wall 101
    The Straight Joint (Seam) (102) • The Tower (105) • The Double Entrance (107) • The Golden Gate Interior (107) • The Golden Gate Stairway (110) • The Northern Extension (113) • The Tower at the Northeast Corner (113) • The Pool of Israel (118)
The Northern Wall 119
    The Northern Façade of the Northeast Tower (119) • The Southern Wall of the Pool of Israel (121) • The Antonia Fortress (123) • The Northern Court (131)
Constructing Herod's Temple Mount 132

Chapter Two **The Pre-Herodian Square Temple Mount**

Historical Information 139
    Flavius Josephus (140) • *Middot* (144)
Previous Proposals for the Location of the Square Temple Mount 146
    Introduction (146) • Melchior de Vogüé (149) • Charles Warren (151) • Claude Reignier Conder (153) • Conrad Schick (154) • Charles Watson (155) • Carl Mommert (156) • Gustaf Dalman (158) • Frederick Hollis (159) • Jan Simons (160) • Louis-Hugues Vincent (161) • Asher Kaufman (162) • David Jacobson (164)
The Location of the Square Temple Mount 165
    The Discovery of the Pre-Herodian Western Wall—"The Step" (165) • The Fosse (168) • The Northern Rockscarp in Cistern 29 (169) • Five Hundred Cubits and the Length of the Cubit (170) • The Masonry near the Golden Gate (174) • The *Offset* North of the Golden Gate (177) • Ancient Gateposts inside the Golden Gate (177) • The *Bend* in the Eastern Wall (178) • The Eastern City

Wall (179) • The Southern Wall of the Square Temple Mount (184) • The Western Wall of the Square Temple Mount (184)

The Date of the Square Temple Mount 186
    The Literary Sources relating to Building Activities on the Temple Mount during the First Temple Period (186) • Hezekiah's Temple Mount (189) • The Literary Sources Relating to Building Activities on the Temple Mount during the Second Temple Period (194) • Post-Exilic Restoration (197) • The Identification of the Northeast Tower (198) • The Towers of Hananeel and Meah (200) • The Ptolemaic *Akra* (201) • The Sheep Gate and the Prison Gate (202) • The Tadi Gate (204)

Chapter Three The Hasmonean Temple Mount

The Location of the Seleucid *Akra* 207
The Cistern of the *Akra* 211
The Origin of the Triple Gate 212
The Vertical Joint *(Seam)* 213
The *Baris* 216
Solomon's Porch 219

Chapter Four The Underground Cisterns of the Temple Mount

Historical Information 221
Additional evidence for the location of the square Temple Mount 222
Key to the Underground Structures 230
The Cave al-Maghara below the "Holy Rock" (es-Sakhra) 231

Chapter Five Understanding Herod's Extension of the Temple Mount

The Drainage System in the Tyropoeon Valley 233
Warren's Gate 235
Barclay's Gate 236
The Double and Triple Gate Passageways 237
Summary 238

Chapter Six The Location of the Temple

The Temple Court 239
The Rock and the Temple 242
Description of the Rock 251
The Crusaders and the Dome of the Rock 256
The Location of the Holy of Holies 265
The Former Location of the Ark of the Covenant 268

Chapter Seven Reconstructing the First Temple

Introduction 279

Solomon's Temple in the Book of Kings 280
History of the First Temple 294
Hezekiah's Temple in the Book of Chronicles 303
Josiah and the Ark of the Covenant 308
Araunah's Threshing Floor and the Location of the Altar 312
Abraham and Mount Moriah 315

Chapter Eight **Reconstructing the Second Temple**

Rebuilding the Temple in the Post-Exilic Period—Introduction 317
   Jeshua and Zerubbabel (318) • The Altar and the Foundation of the Temple (320) • The
   Completion of the Temple (321) • Nehemiah and the *Birah* (322)
Changes in the Second Century B.C. 325
Pompey's Siege of the Temple Mount 332
Herod the Great and the Proto-Antonia 334

Chapter Nine **Reconstructing the Herodian Temple Mount**

The Herodian Porticoes and the Preserved Identity of the Square Temple Mount 339
The Gates of the Square Temple Mount 344
The *Soreg* 346
The *Ḥel* or Terrace 348
The Court of the Women 348
The Four Chambers of the Court of the Women 352
The Fifteen Semi-circular Steps 354
Levels of the Courts of the Temple 357
The Temple Court *(Azarah)* 365
   The Altar (365) • The Laver (368) • The Place of Slaughter (368) • The Court of the Israelites
   and the Court of the Priests (370)
The Buildings around the Temple Court 371

Chapter Ten **Reconstructing Herod's Temple**

Introduction 377
The Foundation of the Temple 381
The Porch *(Ulam)* 382
The Holy *(Heikhal)* 388
The Veil *(Parokhet)* 390
The Holy of Holies *(Debir)* 392
The Cells Surrounding the Sanctuary 395
The Inner Stairway *(Mesibbah)* 397
The Upper Chamber 398

Reference Section

Abbreviations 402 • Bibliography 403 • Notes and References 413 • List of Illustrations 423 • Index 435

Of Zion it is written:

Thy servants take pleasure in her stones and favor the dust thereof. (Ps. 102:14)

To John E. Mancini for sharing the vision to let the ancient stones tell their story and his unstinting support of *The Quest*.

Left: The Temple Mount today, looking west from the Mount of Olives.

Below: The land of Israel with Jerusalem at its heart.

TEMENOS: Enclosed sacred space.

Preface

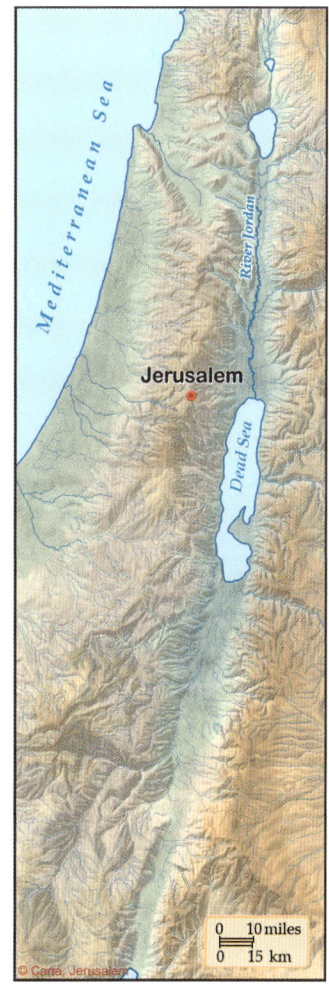

The Holy Temple was built on Mount Moriah, the central part of the eastern ridge on which Jerusalem was first founded. The Temple Mount in Jerusalem is for many people one of the most significant sites in the world. For me it is indeed the most fascinating structure ever built. This vast *temenos* has stirred up powerful emotions in people of varying religious beliefs and political backgrounds and has inspired artists and poets alike. Many books and articles have been written about the Temple Mount, but even after almost a century and a half of scientific research, this site is still, to paraphrase Winston Churchill in a different context, "a riddle wrapped in a mystery inside an enigma."

It had been my privilege to work from 1973 till 1976 as field-architect of the excavations south and southwest of the Temple Mount, under the direction of the late Professor Benjamin Mazar of The Hebrew University of Jerusalem. Mazar shared with me not only the ways and means to understand the archaeological and architectural remains of this vast area located adjacent to the Temple Mount, but also how to read and interpret the ancient literary sources that relate to the Temple Mount itself. Our frequent meetings were always stimulating and enriching. Generously he also allowed me to publish material from his excavations. It was these sessions that aroused my interest in the mysteries of the Temple Mount and its development, an interest that has only grown over the years.

Happily I was then, and still am, able to share this interest with my

Preface

Above: Benjamin Mazar (right) with author at the excavation site.

Below: Nahman Avigad with author during restoration work of the Palatial Mansion in the Jewish Quarter.

wife Kathleen, an archaeologist in her own right. We first met at the Temple Mount excavations and she has been part of this project every step of the way, helping in each aspect of its development. "Many daughters have done virtuously but thou excellest them all."

The impetus to construct the framework of the historical and architectural development of the Temple Mount in the Second Temple period evolved from my joint study with Professor Benjamin Mazar, done a few years after the official cessation of the Temple Mount excavations.

I am also indebted to the late Professor Nahman Avigad, director of the archaeological excavations in the Jewish Quarter of the Old City of Jerusalem, my employer at the time, for allowing me to simultaneously dedicate myself to the joint study with Professor Mazar.

The cornerstone of this study is the interpretation of the archaeological remains of a wall at the foot of the flight of steps at the northwest corner of the raised Muslim platform. Brian Lalor from Ireland, and my predecessor as the architect of the Temple Mount excavations, discovered these remains, and I am grateful to him for having pointed out to me the existence of this early wall.

The valuable comments and suggestions by Fr. Jerome Murphy O'Connor, O.P., Professor of the New Testament at École Biblique et Archéologique Française in Jerusalem, during the later stages of my research into the architectural development of the Temple Mount, were most helpful.

I am grateful to Dr. John Kane, my tutor at the University of Manchester. Our acquaintance goes back to 1974 when we first met in Jerusalem, where he was doing research for his own doctoral thesis. His wide-ranging knowledge of the archaeology of Jerusalem has been of great help to me as has his generosity in giving me access to his extensive private library.

The greater part of my doctoral research was supported by a grant from the *Biblical Archaeology Society* through the generosity of Joseph G. Hurley, Esq., and Ms. Davia Solomon of Hollywood, CA, both of whom are deeply committed to the study of the Temple Mount. I wish to extend to them my sincere thanks. A further grant from them enabled both Kathleen and me to dedicate ourselves to the writing of a more popular book on our findings. Research carried out for that volume is also included here.

Special thanks are due to the Rothschild Foundation for having

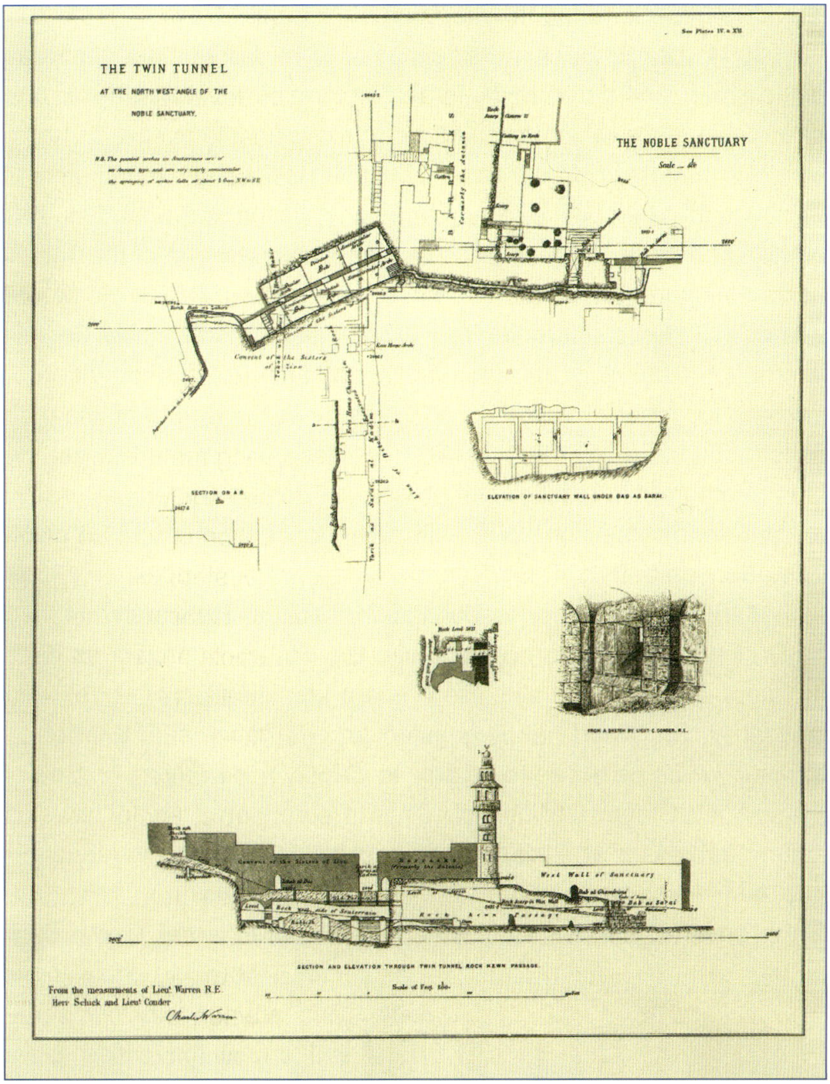

Preface

Left: Plate 37 of Warren's Atlas, published in 1880, containing a graphic account of his work in Jerusalem during the late nineteenth century.

Below: Sir Charles Warren.

sponsored a prolonged stay in Jerusalem in 1994, during which time a topographical survey of the Temple Mount was carried out, mainly of the rock formation inside the Dome of the Rock (Sakhra).

My appreciation to Hershel Shanks, founder and editor of *Biblical Archaeology Review*, for his interest and support. He was one of the first people to recognize the importance of this project.

The kind donation by Edgar and Marjorie Hall of Nottingham, U.K., of a complete set of Warren's plans, elevations, sections, etc., showing the results of the excavations at Jerusalem, 1867–1870 (on behalf of the Committee of the Palestine Exploration Fund, London, 1884)

Preface

Julie Lightburn, modelmaker, with author.

was a valuable asset to the research.

In 1994, the late Benjamin Adelman of Silver Spring, MD, chairman of the American Friends of the Israel Exploration Society, ordered one of our slide sets[1] which aroused his interest and led to the commission of a model of Herod's Temple Mount that he asked me to design. This was followed by the design and construction of five models, one of the Tabernacle in the wilderness and a detailed one of the Tabernacle itself, one of Solomon's Temple, one of Herod's Temple Mount and one of Herod's Temple. York Modelmaking and Display Co., an international architectural firm, built the models. The director Vic Roberts and his chief assistant Julie Lightburn were instrumental in their construction and my friend Philip Evans spared no effort to get the best photographic results. The process of design helped me greatly to comprehend sections of the Temple Mount to which I had given little attention before. This research too is part of the book.

In 1996 I joined the Associates for Biblical Research, headed by Dr. Bryant Wood, to help out with the Bethel–Ai project as field-architect. Not satisfied with the present identification of et-Tell with biblical Ai, Dr. Wood has suggested an alternative site, Khirbet el-Maqatir, which he hopes to be able to identify positively as Ai. One of the staff, Dr. Steven Collins, asked me to lecture on a regular basis as adjunct-professor at Trinity Southwest University (TSU) in Albuquerque, NM, which he heads.

For several years Dr. Collins and I led tours to Israel. One participant, John E. Mancini, who with his wife Chris attended all our seminars and tours, expressed great interest in my research and was keen to make this material publicly available. John had already set up the Lamb Foundation to help TSU and other projects, and during the fall of 1999 offered to help publish this book on the Temple Mount. I am delighted to thank him for the opportunity he gave me to devote myself to the presentation of my research carried out from the start of my archaeological career on the

Model of the Tabernacle in the wilderness. (photo: Philip Evans)

Preface

Model of the Herodian Temple Mount—overall view from the east. (photo: Philip Evans)

Temple Mount excavations in 1973. I would also like to acknowledge the editorial help of Latayne Scott of TSU during the early stages of the project.

Kathleen and I have experienced how pleasant it is to work with Carta, the Jerusalem publishers, on a number of publications. This book has, however, been a much more elaborate project. My thanks to all the people at Carta, their superb management and meticulous attention to the many details demanded by this title, especially to Barbara Laurel Ball for her sensitive editing and general supervision of the project. Their proficiency can be seen on every page.

In the concluding stages of publication, Hillel Geva, my friend and colleague from the time we worked together in the Jewish Quarter Excavations, agreed to become Scientific Editor to the archaeological parts of the book. His keen eye and sage comments helped give the book its final shape and style. Although we did not always agree on the date and interpretation of some of the archaeological material, I have benefited greatly from his candor and precision. The responsibility for any remaining errors is mine.

Thanks to John E. Mancini, to whom the book is dedicated, and all those who aided and accompanied me on this long and arduous journey. The public at large can now partake in the extensive documentation of Temple Mount history and archaeology provided by this volume and evaluate the proffered solutions to vexing questions.

Opposite page: Aerial view of Jerusalem and surroundings, looking northwest, early twentieth century.

Left: Model of Solomon's Temple. (photo: Philip Evans)

Below: Model of Jerusalem during the time of David (lower half) and Solomon's additions (upper half).

Introduction

The Temple Mount in Jerusalem is referred to by several names. In Hebrew it is called *har ha-bayit*, which means the Mountain of the House, and in Arabic its name is *haram al-sharif*, meaning the Noble Sanctuary. The history of the Temple Mount is a very long one. We first read about this place in Genesis 22:2, where God told Abraham,

> *Take now thy son, thine only son Isaac, whom thou lovest, and get thee into the land of Moriah; and offer him there for a burnt offering upon one of the mountains which I will tell thee of.*

According to internal biblical chronology, this must have been around the year 2050 B.C.—well over 4,000 years ago!

Approximately one millennium later King David built an altar on the threshing floor of Araunah, the Jebusite king. We read in 2 Samuel 24:25 that,

> *David built there an altar unto the LORD, and offered burnt offerings and peace offerings. So the LORD was intreated for the land, and the plague was stayed from Israel.*

David's son Solomon built the First Temple near the spot where David's altar stood. We are given an exact date for the beginning of this great work in 1 Kings 6:1:

INTRODUCTION

King Darius I (521–486 B.C.); relief from Persepolis.

FIRST TEMPLE: Built by Solomon and destroyed by the Babylonians.

SECOND TEMPLE: Built by Zerubbabel and Nehemiah and reconstructed by Herod, i.e., there were two structures during the Second Temple period.

And it came to pass in the four hundred and eightieth year after the children of Israel were come out of the land of Egypt, in the fourth year of Solomon's reign over Israel, in the month Zif, which is the second month, that he began to build the house of the LORD.

This Temple stood on Mount Moriah for some four hundred years, when it was destroyed by the Babylonians in 586 B.C.

Seventy years later a new temple, generally known as the Second Temple, was built under the direction of Jeshua the High Priest and Zerubbabel the son of Shealtiel. Ezra 3:2 tells us,

Then stood up Jeshua the son of Jozadak, and his brethren the priests, and Zerubbabel the son of Shealtiel, and his brethren, and builded the altar of the God of Israel, to offer burnt offerings thereon, as it is written in the law of Moses the man of God.

First the altar was built, then the foundation laid and, eventually, after some setbacks, the Temple *"was finished on the third day of the month Adar, which was in the sixth year of the reign of Darius the king,"* in c. 515 B.C.[1]

This Temple was in turn replaced by King Herod the Great, who began an ambitious building program in 19 B.C., but the Temple Mount was not to be completed by the time he died. He wished, in the words of Josephus,

…to undertake an extraordinary work, the reconstruction of the Temple of God at his own expense, enlarging its precincts and raising it to a more imposing height. For he

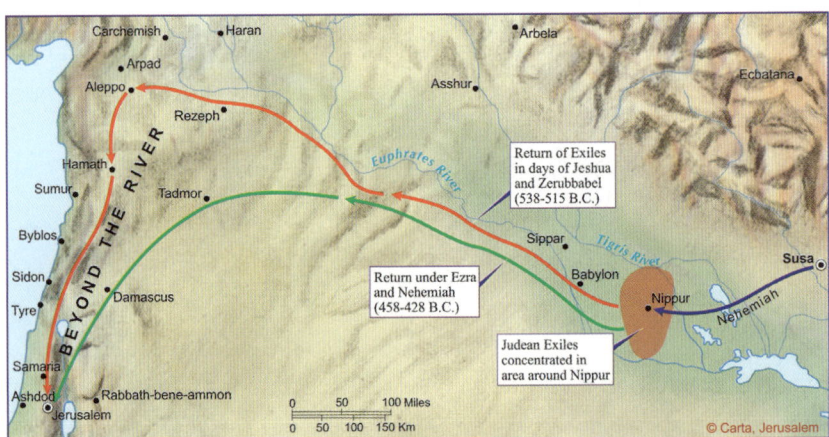

The return of the Jews from exile.

INTRODUCTION

believed that the accomplishment of this task would be the most notable of all the things achieved by him, as indeed it was, and would be great enough to assure his eternal remembrance.

(Ant. 15.380)

This magnificent new Temple was still called the "Second Temple." The term Second Temple generally relates to the period that commenced with the return from the Babylonian exile up to the destruction of the Temple in A.D. 70. Although Herod had built a new temple, it was referred to only by some as the Third Temple, a term reserved for the futuristic temple described in the prophecy of Ezekiel. Another reason for the retention of the name Second Temple is that there was, in fact, no interruption of the sacrifice while the new temple was being built. This temple was destroyed by the Romans in A.D. 70, less than a hundred years after the beginning of Herod's grandiose building program.

The walls of the Temple Mount were left lying in ruins throughout the Roman and Byzantine periods. Some 600 years after the destruction of the Temple, the Islamic invasion led to further eradication of Herod's glory. Although the outer walls were repaired under the Umayyad caliphs (A.D. 661–750), the entire area of the mount and its immediate surroundings were covered by an extensive religio-political complex. A new building was put up in the center of the Temple Mount, the Dome of the Rock, whose dome still graces the mount today.

The Crusaders erected a new city wall around Jerusalem, which necessitated the blockage of the southern and eastern gates to the

Above: Reconstruction of the Temple Mount based on Ezekiel's vision (chs. 40–44). (Chipiez, 1887)

Below: The Temple Mount during the Crusader period.

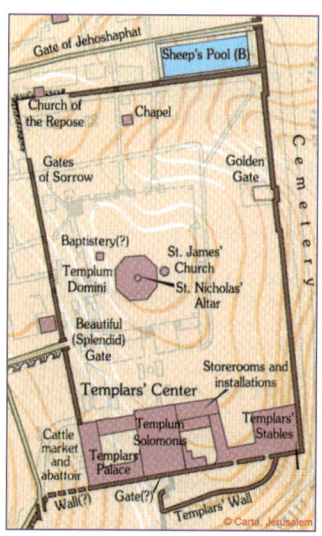

Introduction

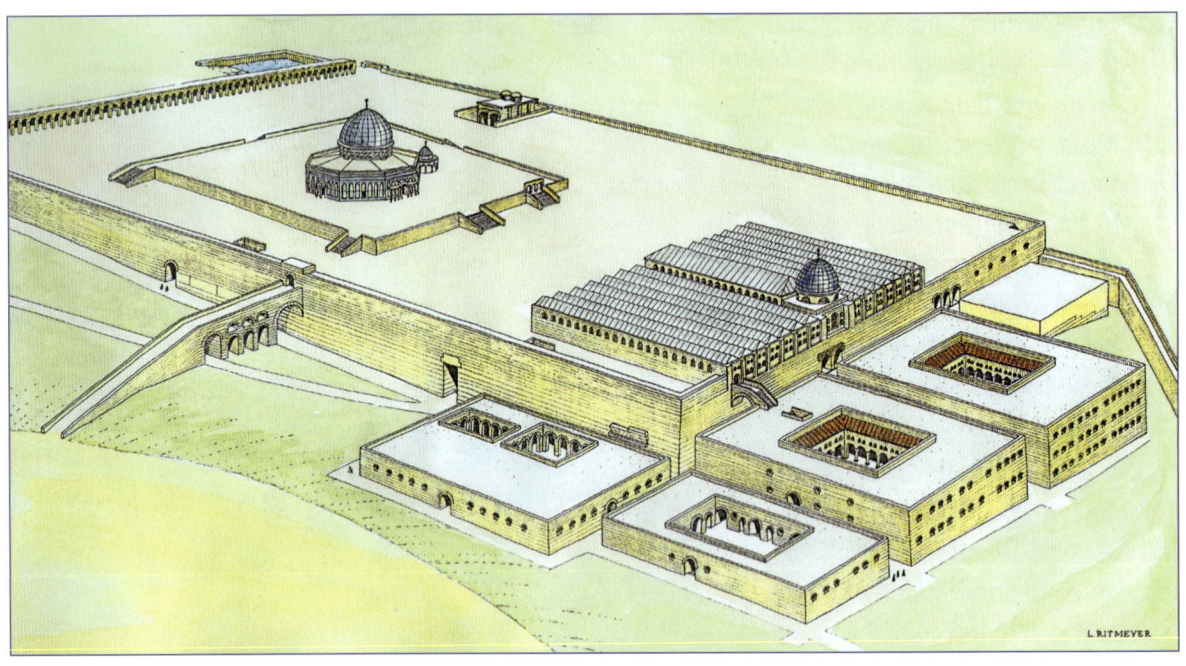

Above: Reconstruction of the Temple Mount and Umayyad palaces to the south. The Dome of the Rock stands on the raised platform.

Below: The Golden Gate (drawing by de Vogüé) in the eastern wall of the Temple Mount. The gate was closed already in the Crusader period, when it was opened only on two occasions annually. It was later closed permanently, apparently in the Ayyubid period.

Temple Mount. Under Mamluk rule, Jewish prayer at the Western Wall was restored, yet the Islamization of the Sultans wrought such a change on the character of Herod's Temple Mount as to make it virtually unrecognizable. Small wonder then, with only the outline of Herod's Temple Mount to go on and the literary sources inaccessible to all but the educated few, that the imagination of many artists throughout the ages had free rein to produce reconstruction drawings of the Temple which can only be described as pure fantasy. Depictions can be dated as far back as the Late Roman period in the synagogue of Dura-Europos in Syria.

All this history is common knowledge, yet the fact that both Solomon and Herod's temples had been razed completely (incidentally, on the same day of the year, the 9th of the Jewish month of Ab) has made it very difficult to locate the precise spot where these magnificent buildings once stood. Indeed, the words of Jesus concerning Herod's Temple, that *"there shall not be left here one stone upon another, that shall not be thrown down"* (Mt 24:2), have become an archaeologist's nightmare.

Although there is general agreement among scholars that the successive temples of Solomon, Jeshua and Zerubbabel, and Herod stood on the same middle part of the eastern ridge[2] now dominated by the Dome of the Rock, the problems raised when considering how

INTRODUCTION

the Temple Mount actually developed to its present-day form have never been solved satisfactorily. This is partly due to the apparently conflicting information in the historical sources and the differing interpretations of the archaeological evidence.

On the surface, the biblical account of Solomon's Temple in 1 Kings chapters 6 and 7 appears to be straightforward, but when comparing the description of this First Temple with that in 2 Chronicles chapters 3 and 4, there are so many disagreements that one almost gets the idea that two different buildings are being described.

It is not any easier to understand the Herodian Second Temple. The root of the problem lies in the fact that the two major historical sources we have at our disposal, namely the writings of Josephus and *massechet middot* (the tractate called *Middot* or "measurements" of the Mishnah), seem to contradict each other.

Josephus describes the Temple as situated on a hill that was enclosed completely by walls. This enclosure was first square and later enlarged to twice its size, having four gates in the west, two in the south and probably one in the north. *Middot*, on the other hand, refers to a square Temple Mount with only five external gates: two in the south and one in each of the other walls. The subject becomes even more complicated if one tries to impose the conflicting measurements given in these works onto the Temple Mount as we know it today.

Roman bust thought to be that of Josephus Flavius.

In the past, eminent scholars such as Watson,[3] Mommert,[4] Dalman,[5] Hollis[6] and many others have wrestled with these "three apparently irreconcilable sources"—Josephus, *Middot* and the archaeological data of the Temple Mount in Jerusalem, as characterized by Oesterly in his foreword to the doctoral thesis of Hollis.

None of these scholars, however, was able to positively date any of the archaeological remains on the Temple Mount to a pre-Herodian period, apart from the northern wall of the raised platform. Their various proposals as to the historical and architectural development of the Temple Mount during the Second Temple period, therefore, have not been fully convincing.

In the absence of any archaeological data (apart from the rockscarp below the northern boundary of the raised platform), the general approach to the problem has been to draw a plan of the square Temple Mount according to the individual's interpretation of *Middot*, having first chosen a certain length for the cubit. There are those who identify the site of the Altar with the Rock and those that view the

THE MISHNAH: A collection of Jewish oral laws, compiled in c. A.D. 200. The individual sections are called tractates.

RAISED PLATFORM: The elevated part of the Temple Mount, on which stands the Dome of the Rock.

11

Introduction

Limestone, four-horned altar from the Iron Age, found at Megiddo. (NEAEHL)

Rock as the site of the Holy of Holies.

The difference between those early theories and that offered here is that the former had begun by first proposing a certain location for the Temple and then trying to fit the courts around it, whereas the Temple location is in fact dependent on the position of the surrounding courts of the Temple Mount. I believe that only after the position of the square pre-Herodian Temple Mount has been firmly established should one look for the exact location of the Temple itself, not the other way around.

The research presented in this book began in 1981, when Professor Mazar asked me to undertake a project with him to research the meaning and location of the "palace" (Hebrew: *birah*) mentioned in Nehemiah. In Nehemiah 2:8, he asks Artaxerxes for a letter to Asaph, the keeper of the King's forest, *"that he may give me timber to make beams for the gates of the palace (birah) which appertained to the house...."*

According to Mazar, the Hebrew term *birah* was generally used during that period to describe a royal acropolis or administrative center. My suggestion to equate the *birah* with the 500-cubit-square Temple Mount mentioned in *Middot* 2:1, coupled with the discovery of the archaeological remains of the pre-Herodian western Temple Mount wall at the northwest corner of the raised Muslim platform, led eventually to the establishment of the outlines of this pre-Herodian square Temple Mount.

The conclusions of our joint study[7] were announced by Professor Mazar during the International Congress on Biblical Archaeology held in Jerusalem in April 1984.[8] The square was promptly dubbed the "Ritmeyer Square."[9] At this defining moment in my life, I realized that the unraveling of the mysteries of the Mount had become my personal quest. I had to seek and find them out.

Thereafter I continued to study the architectural development of the Temple Mount during the Second Temple period in much greater detail on my own, using all the information which could be gleaned from the observations below the Temple Mount made by Captain Charles Warren and others.

Although the hypothesis presented here also needs to be verified by archaeological excavations, it is we believe the first kind based entirely on archaeological evidence, made possible by working to a defined methodology that was centripetal in nature, i.e. working from

INTRODUCTION

the outer frame towards the center.

Thus I first analyzed the outer walls of the Temple Mount, both inside the excavations and outside. The next step was to discover more of the archaeological evidence of the square pre-Herodian Temple Mount. Once that was accomplished, information recorded in the Mishnah made it possible to locate the actual site where the Temple stood. An unexpected bonus was the discovery of the emplacement of the Ark of the Covenant.

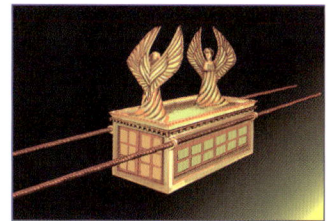

The Ark of the Covenant.

This book, designed as a textbook on the archaeology of the Temple Mount, will follow a similar methodology. In our comprehensive study of the Temple Mount, we will first look at the four walls of the Herodian Temple Mount and provide a brief history of archaeological investigation in the area. Then we will look at the architectural features of each of these walls.

Once we have the walls and their features well in mind, we will look at the square Temple Mount that antedated the Herodian temple—its history as recorded by Josephus and *Middot*, and the various theories which have been advanced by scholars about the location of the square mount and Temple.

At that point I will describe new and exciting discoveries that have literally re-written all those theories, most notably the discovery of a section of the pre-Herodian western wall (the "Step"). Here we will put in perspective all the literary and archaeological evidence to fix a date of the square Temple Mount.

Then we will investigate features of the Hasmonean Temple Mount, examine the significance of the underground cisterns of the Mount, and look at the way King Herod expanded the Temple Mount in the first century B.C.

With that quite literal foundation, you will be able to understand the reasons behind my proposed solution to Jerusalem's oldest archaeological controversy, namely the actual location of the Temple. On the way, we shall build up, in our imagination, the remains of three millennia and learn about and consider almost thirty years of intensive Temple research.

Join me and the witnesses of thousands of years on the quest to reveal what can be known about the most sacred place on this earth.

Coin of Herod.

Opposite page: Map of Jerusalem and the Temple Mount by Charles Wilson (1864–65), adapted by Carl Zimmermann, late 19th century.

Below: American biblical scholar Edward Robinson (1794–1863).

Bottom: Image of Frederick Catherwood, c. 1840.

Chapter One
The Herodian Temple Mount Walls

EXPLORERS BEFORE 1967

There was no such thing as exploration of the Temple Mount from the Crusader period that ended in the thirteenth century until the middle of the nineteenth century. Thus, for over six hundred years, its secrets were hidden from all but the Islamic faithful and the birds and beasts of Jerusalem.

During most of the centuries of the Ottoman period, Jews and non-Muslim visitors were banned from the Temple Mount. A small number of westerners did succeed in gaining access to the mount by disguising themselves as Muslims. The first European who managed to investigate the mount since Crusader times was Frederick Catherwood, an English architect-artist. His visit and survey of the area in 1833 produced the first plan of the *haram*.

A few years later, the American scholar Edward Robinson carried out a survey of the Old City, but was only allowed a view of the Temple Mount from the Antonia Fortress. He identified the arch in the Western Wall near the southwest corner of the Temple Mount as the remains of an original entrance. In the early 1850s another American, Dr. James Barclay, gained access to the Temple Mount for a few weeks for the purpose of advising a Turkish architect who was charged with repairs to the Dome of the Rock. The lintel, which can still be seen in the southern part of the Herodian wall at the Western Wall Plaza, was discovered by Barclay and the gate which lay beneath it was named after him.

In 1862, the French scholar and diplomat, Marquis Charles Jean

Chapter One: The Herodian Temple Mount Walls

Above: Sir Charles Wilson.

Below: Cross-section drawing of Warren's Shaft. (S. Cohen)

Melchior de Vogüé, was able to study the outer walls of the Temple Mount and to make important observations inside it. His ideas about the development of the Temple Mount are described in Chapter 2.2.

In 1865, an English officer, Charles Wilson, supervised the first mapping of the Temple Mount with the Royal Engineers as part of the Ordnance Survey of Jerusalem. This was the first time in history that westerners were allowed to use surveying equipment on the Noble Sanctuary and to map the city. This work resulted in a plan of the *haram* with all its underground structures at scale 1:500. It is still the most widely reproduced map of the platform in use today.

In the same year the Palestine Exploration Fund (PEF) was established with the aim of investigating the archaeology, geography, geology and natural history of the Holy Land. Captain Wilson was sent out again, this time by the PEF, to find sites in what was then known as Palestine, which would be suitable for further exploration.

In the wake of his report and due to limited financial resources, the PEF decided to focus on Jerusalem only. A team headed by Charles Warren set out in 1867 and for over three years explored the Old City of Jerusalem and the Temple Mount. These records of Warren's investigation of the Temple Mount area were of considerable help in the planning of the modern excavations by Benjamin Mazar. The many shafts and horizontal tunnels dug by Warren and his team yielded invaluable data on the lay of the bedrock and the subterranean stone courses of the Herodian walls.

During the course of excavations some of his tunnels were rediscovered, and they showed how daring and courageous Warren's digging methods were. The set of fifty plans that were published in 1884, together with the Jerusalem Volume of the *Survey of Western Palestine*, was consulted on an almost daily basis in the architect's office of our Temple Mount excavations. Although further work was carried out later by researchers such as Claude Conder, Charles Clermont-Ganneau, Conrad Schick, Frederick Bliss and Archibald Dickie, Stewart Macalister and others, the results of the explorations of Wilson and Warren stand out as milestones in the investigations of the Temple Mount.

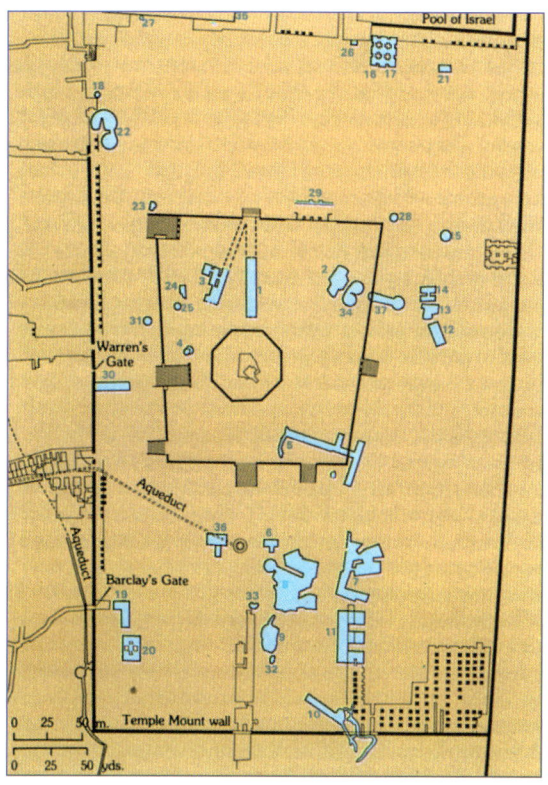

Plan showing the water system on the Temple Mount, indicating the location of 37 water cisterns examined in the nineteenth century, mainly by Warren and Conder.

The explorations in Jerusalem came to an abrupt end in 1911, when the debacle known as the "Parker Mission" jeopardized the position of all foreign archaeologists in Jerusalem. Attempting to locate the lost Temple Treasures, one Montague Brownslow Parker, the 30-year-old son of the distinguished Earl of Morley, organized an expedition, being spurred on by a Swedish mystic. This mystic, Walter Juvelius, had been excited by the results of Warren's underground excavations near the Temple Mount. In his belief that the treasures to be found would include the golden ark of the covenant and Solomon's crown and ring, Juvelius convinced Parker to raise funds for an archaeological expedition to Jerusalem.

The mission was legitimized by Père Vincent, a respected scholar of the École Biblique, who used the opportunity of this well-funded excavation to research the ancient water-systems, the results of which he published in his classic *Underground Jerusalem*. From

Chapter One: The Herodian Temple Mount Walls

Parker's point of view, however, the mission proved fruitless. In desperation, he bribed the governor Azmey Bey with $25,000 to allow them to excavate on the Temple Mount itself. Disguised in Arab dress, Parker and a small group of excavators excavated every night for a week in the southeast corner of the Temple Mount, in the area of Solomon's Stables where they had assumed the treasure lay. This again proved fruitless. When Parker and his men entered the Dome of the Rock on the night of April 17th, a Muslim guard discovered their presence and the group had to flee Jerusalem, as the ensuing disturbances and rioting put their lives in danger. The sad result was that all exploration of the Temple Mount was prohibited until the Old City of Jerusalem was conquered by the Israelis in 1967.

EXCAVATIONS AFTER 1967

A realistic reconstruction of Herod's Temple Mount became possible only when systematic excavation of the area south and west of the Temple Mount began in 1968, soon after the Six-Day War. The excavation was directed by the late Professor Benjamin Mazar,

Aerial photograph showing the beginning of the excavations in 1968.

CHAPTER ONE: THE HERODIAN TEMPLE MOUNT WALLS

Reconstruction of the Temple Mount complex during the time of Herod.

on behalf of the Hebrew University of Jerusalem and the Israel Exploration Society, and continued without a break until 1978.

As the dig progressed, our team surveyed each wall and stone and examined and recorded each architectural element until a complete plan of the multi-period site (from Iron Age to Turkish) was achieved. Though all measurements were originally taken in meters and centimeters (the metric system is used in Israel), for the convenience of readers who are used to the imperial system, in this book imperial measurements (feet and inches) are given first, followed by the metric.

In order to achieve a reconstruction of the area in the time of Herod the Great, we did three things: 1) separated the Herodian elements from the rest of the periods; 2) searched the ancient sources again and again for illumination; and 3) sought parallels with other monumental Hellenistic buildings. To our great satisfaction, a plausible picture of the magnificent Temple complex eventually emerged.

Let us in our mind's eye go in circuit around the Temple Mount and trace the remains that tell the tale of Herod's greatness as a builder and make such an accurate reconstruction possible.

We shall begin at the Western Wall, that fragment of masonry that became the focus for the longing of the dispersed Jews throughout the centuries, and which is now a center of worship and a site of national celebration. Perhaps no place on earth has had as many

19

Chapter One: The Herodian Temple Mount Walls

Reconstruction of the Herodian Western Wall.

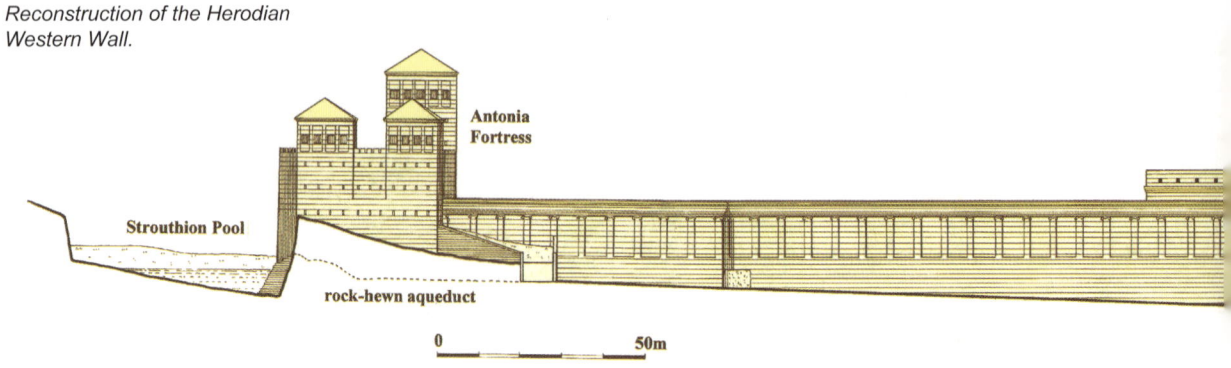

tears shed on its stones; thus it is a fitting place to begin to try to understand the solemnity and magnificence of this site.

THE WESTERN WALL

Contrary to tradition, the Western Wall is not a remnant of the Solomonic Temple, but rather a section of the massive retaining walls that Herod built almost a thousand years later in order to support the enormous substructure needed to extend the Temple platform. In so doing, he doubled the original area of the Temple podium and wrought a complete change in the area's topography. He filled in the part of the Tyropoeon Valley which used to lay to the west of Mount Moriah on which Abraham had prepared to sacrifice Isaac and where Solomon had built his Temple, and filled in a small valley to the north as well. The Southern Wall called for the filling in of the upper slope of the Kedron leaving only the Eastern Wall with its line unchanged.

To complete the Herodian extension, this wall was extended both to the north and to the south. Josephus, the Jewish historian, describes Herod's retaining walls as *"the greatest ever heard of by men"* (Ant. 15.396)[1]. Josephus further tells us that,

> *In the western part of the court (of the Temple) there were four gates. The first led to the palace by a passage over the intervening ravine, two others led to the suburb, and the last led to the other part of the city, from which it was separated by many steps going down to the ravine and from here up again to the hill.* (Ant. 15.410)

In the light of historical and archaeological evidence, this passage could be understood today as saying the following: "In the Western

QUICK STATS ON THE HERODIAN TEMPLE MOUNT WALLS

Northern Wall 1038 ft. (316 m);
Southern Wall 914 ft. (278.60 m);
Western Wall 1590 ft. (485 m);
Eastern Wall 1530 ft. (466 m).

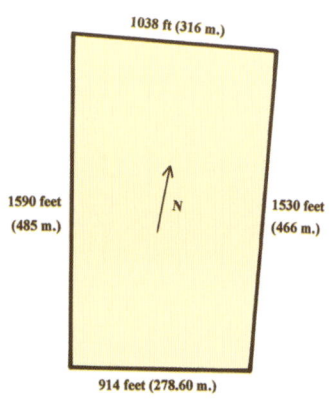

CHAPTER ONE: THE HERODIAN TEMPLE MOUNT WALLS

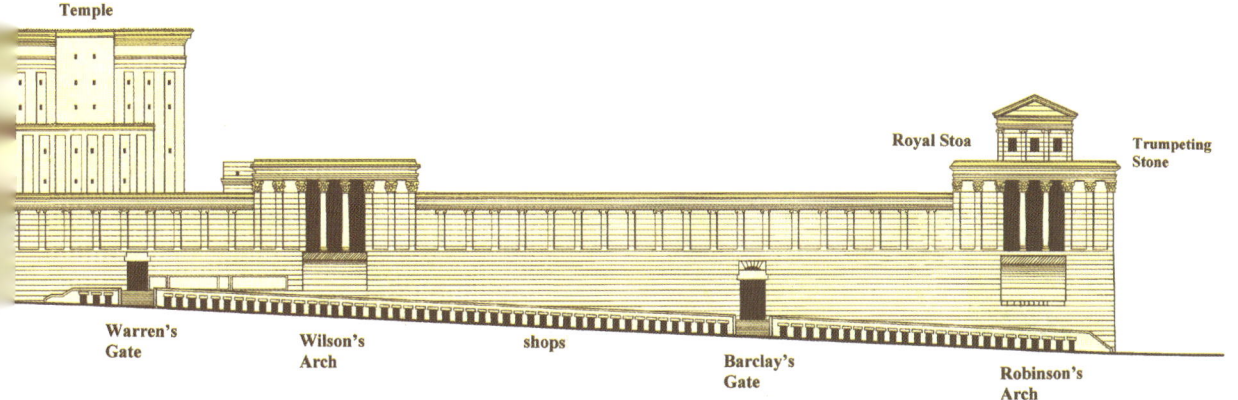

Wall of Herod's Temple Mount there were four gates. The first one led to the Hasmonean palace by a bridge which began at Wilson's Arch over the Tyropoeon Valley. Two others, the lower Warren and Barclay's Gates, led to the suburb. The last one above Robinson's Arch led to the other part of the city from which it was separated by many steps going down to the Tyropoeon Valley street, and from here ran alongside the northern wall of the stairway construction up again to the Upper City."

We will now examine in detail the various elements that make up the western wall. We begin at the Western Wall Plaza and then examine Barclay's Gate, part of the lintel of which can be seen there at its southern end in the place reserved for women's prayer. Wilson's Arch is located just to the north of the plaza and can be seen by entering through the arch at the northern end of the men's prayer area. Visitors to the Western Wall Tunnels can also see the arch from a platform built at its southern end.

As you continue walking through the tunnel, Warren's Gate is visible just to the north of a group of four massive Herodian stones that form part of the Western Wall to the

Close-up view of the Western Wall Plaza.

Chapter One: The Herodian Temple Mount Walls

north of Wilson's Arch. Herodian stones can be seen along the entire course of the tunnel. Near the end, the Herodian street surfaces and from this point onward, the tunnel becomes rock-hewn and ends in the Strouthion Pool, which is located to the immediate north of the Antonia Fortress.

To investigate Robinson's Arch, we must retrace our steps and enter the excavations near the Dung Gate. Three courses of arch stones can be seen jutting out from the Western Wall near the southwest corner. Below these curved stones, a stone course projects out from the wall. These are the surviving remains of a huge vault that supported a stairway leading from the Herodian street to the Temple Mount.

The Western Wall Plaza

Prior to the Six-Day War of 1967, the prayer area in front of the wall consisted of a narrow street. As soon as the Old City was taken by Israel, the empty hovels that stood near the wall were bulldozed and the whole area lowered, revealing more of the Herodian stone courses.

The picture below showing bulldozers at work on an archaeological dig may be a surprising sight, but A. Mazar assured me that they were only allowed to remove the soil after several archaeological test areas were dug. These tests showed that the layers to be removed contained no antiquities of any great historical value.

Lowering the area in front of the Wailing Wall in preparation for the construction of the Western Wall Plaza, as this area was subsequently known. This photo was taken by Amihai Mazar, a nephew of the late Benjamin Mazar, who was then a student of archaeology and supervised this project.

CHAPTER ONE: THE HERODIAN TEMPLE MOUNT WALLS

Above: Narrow street in front of the Wailing Wall where Jewish men and women were allowed to pray—1894.

Left: Complex of houses adjacent to the Western Wall—1894.

Chapter One: The Herodian Temple Mount Walls

The Western Wall Plaza plays an important role in the life of the Jewish people today. The site also attracts many tourists.

The whole area in front of the Western Wall was paved after the area was lowered and the newly named Western Wall Plaza plays a vital role in the life of the Jewish people today. Day and night people pray at the wall, which is the closest point to the Temple area where orthodox rabbinical authorities allow Jews to go. Most religious Jews do not enter the Temple Mount for fear of treading on the site of the

CHARACTERISTICS OF THE HERODIAN STONES IN THE WESTERN WALL PLAZA

The Herodian stones are characterized by their finely cut margins and flat bosses (right). The margins are about 4 inches (10 cm) wide and have been worked by an eight-toothed comb pick. The upper margins are usually a few centimeters wider than the other three margins. As each Herodian stone course is set back above the one below by about an inch (2–3 cm), looking up, the upper margin would appear to be of the same dimension as the others. The setbacks of the courses makes the wall narrower on top than at the bottom, giving the wall a batter. This was necessary as these walls are basically retaining walls and therefore have to withstand the great pressure exerted upon it by the fill on the inside. The bosses were finished with a fine pick. Great care was taken by the masons to make the stones perfectly square, so that no mortar was used in this great dry-stone construction. The stones of this part of the wall are so beautifully made that they became the standard to which other Herodian masonry could be compared.

Close-up view of a Herodian stone in the walls of the Temple Mount. Note the "letters" by supplicants stuffed into the crevices.

Chapter One: The Herodian Temple Mount Walls

Holy of Holies whose location has not yet been identified. The prayer area is divided into two sections with women praying on the right-hand side and the men on the left.

The lowest seven stone courses seen in the wall are Herodian, but there are another nineteen courses below the modern pavement! There the wall rests on the bedrock, some 70 feet (21 m) down. Geophysical examination[2] has established that the wall is 15 feet (4.60 m) thick in this area and the thickness is made up of several stones.

Directly above the Herodian masonry we see repairs of the wall made with stones of equal height to the Herodian stones. However, they are shorter than the latter stones and appear to be part of a general reconstruction of the Temple Mount during the Umayyad period.

Barclay's Gate

All that visibly remains of this gate is the massive lintel stone discovered by James Barclay in the early 1850s subsequently named after him.

> **SOME STATS ON BARCLAY'S GATE**
>
> *The 6-foot-10-inch- (2.08 m) high lintel is partly visible at the southern end of the Western Wall Plaza just above the steps leading into a small chamber below the ramp. Inside this chamber another lintel section can be seen.*
>
> *Assuming that the lintel projects as much over the southern jamb as it does over its visible counterpart, the total length has been calculated as 24 feet 8 inches (7.52 m)[3]. Before the 1967 excavations, the lintel was at ground level, showing an empty space just below it. The original gate was almost three times as high as the space visible below the lintel today. Warren, who in 1869 dug a shaft down to the bedrock along the northern jamb, found the sill-stone in such a poor state of preservation that he found it difficult to determine whether the gate was eight or nine stones high, but assumed that his first estimate was correct. Barclay's Gate was therefore probably 28 feet 9 inches (8.70 m) high, made up of eight stone courses, and was 18 feet (5.49 m) wide. There are an additional 14 stone courses below the level of the sill. Here the foundation stones are laid on the bedrock itself. At this point then the original Herodian wall stands up to a height of 26 courses, 22 below the lintel, which itself equals the height of two stone courses. To the immediate left of the lintel, at a higher level, are two courses of Herodian stones.*

The lintel of Barclay's Gate is visible just above the steps that lead into a small chamber below the ramp.

CHAPTER ONE: THE HERODIAN TEMPLE MOUNT WALLS

The lintel of Barclay's Gate in 1967 before the area was excavated. Note the empty space below the lintel and also the burning of candles, which was forbidden soon afterwards. *(photo: Amihai Mazar)*

A Vault below the Gate

In front of Barclay's Gate and below the level of the sill, Warren found,

> a heavy masonry wall, faced to the north with well-dressed stones in courses 9 inches to 18 inches in height, of malaki, without drafts; it is perpendicular, and abuts on to the Sanctuary wall, and is a retaining wall, as it has only a rough face to south: it is 6 feet thick, it continues down for 35 feet 6 inches, and its foundations are about 7 feet from the rock; they rest on rubbish.[4]

The stones of the Western Wall in the plaza area have finely-cut bosses all the way down to the bedrock, unlike those at the southwest corner where the stones below street level have very rough bosses that project at least one foot from the margins. Because of this, Warren initially thought that the section of the Western Wall to the south of Barclay's Gate was of a later date, and that the building of it had only commenced after the Tyropoeon Valley began to fill up. He

Below: Drawing of the visible Herodian remains near Barclay's Gate. The sketch shows the original size of the lintel and the gate.

Right: Sketch of Warren's shaft at Barclay's Gate, showing the remains of the vault and its northern retaining wall built on bedrock.

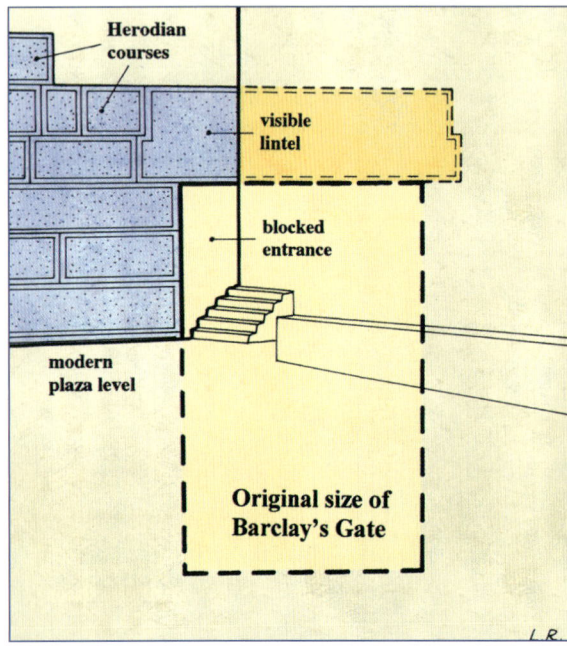

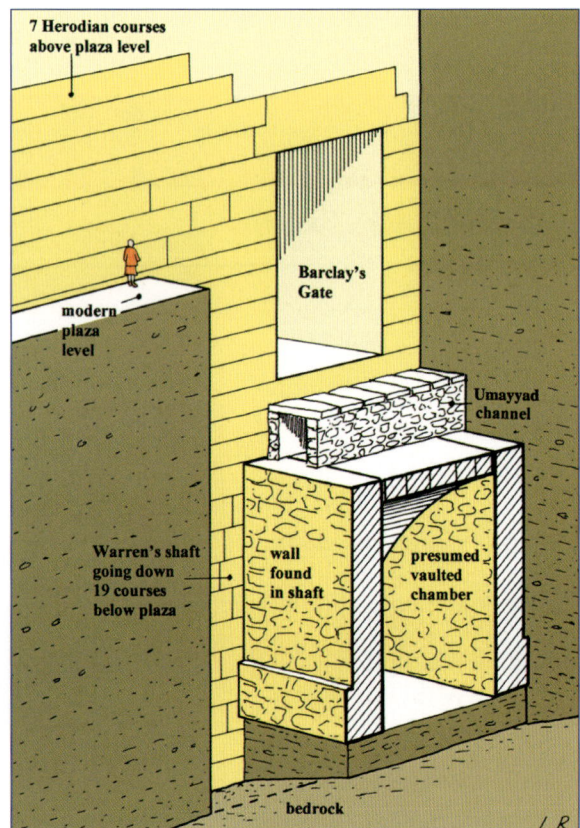

26

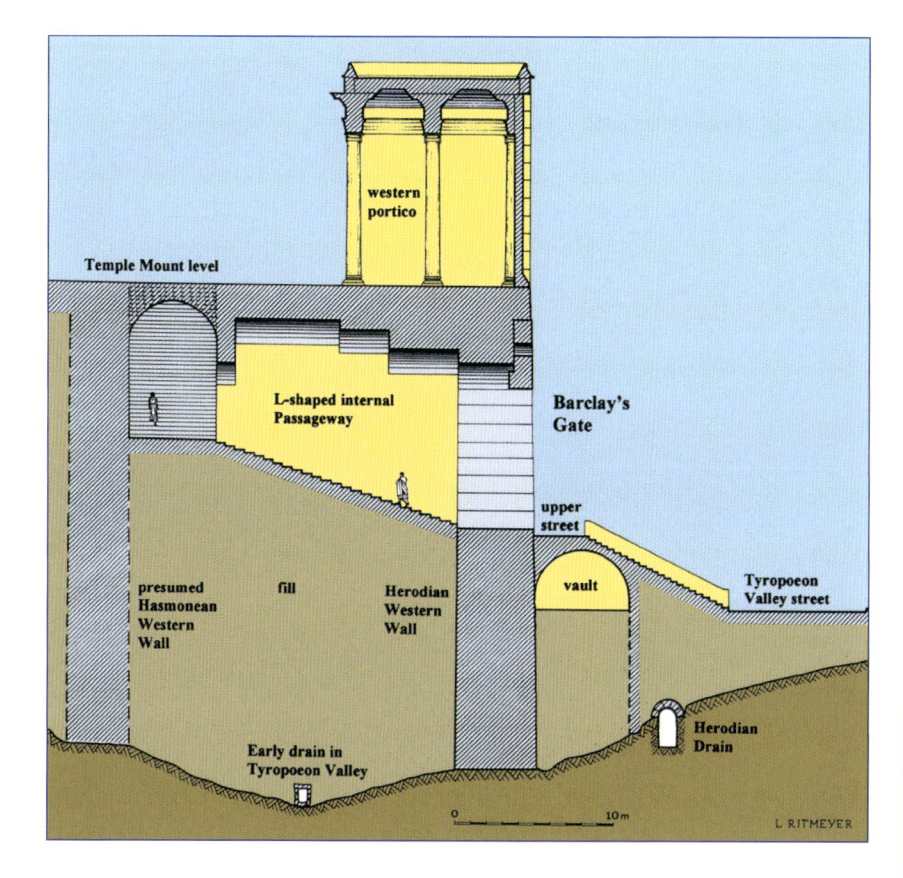

CHAPTER ONE: THE HERODIAN TEMPLE MOUNT WALLS

East-west section looking south through Barclay's Gate showing the internal stairway and the upper and lower street levels connected by steps built over a vault. The Western Wall is built on bedrock.

Above: View of the remains of a row of shops at the southwest corner of the Temple Mount.

Below: Remains of the staircase at the southwest corner of the Temple Mount.

therefore surmised that a roadway was built above the retaining wall that led to Barclay's Gate.

A few pages earlier,[5] however, Warren seems to indicate that this retaining wall had something to do with an arch or vault below the sill of Barclay's Gate, which he believed still existed there. While investigating the aqueduct running below the Herodian street he even wrote about "the arch supporting the viaduct to Barclay's Gate."[6]

In view of the Herodian street levels found in the Temple Mount excavations, it appears that this main Tyropoeon Valley street would have passed in front of Barclay's Gate at a level of some 13 feet (4 m) below its sill. From these excavations we also know that a row of shops was built against the Western Wall with a narrow road built over their roofs. In 1972 the foundations of a shop were found at 208 feet (63.5 m) to the north of the southwest corner. At 44 feet (13.5 m) to the south of Barclay's Gate, this is actually very close. A couple of years later a narrow staircase was found at the southwest corner. This staircase had the same width as the shop, 10 feet (3.05 m).

27

Chapter One: The Herodian Temple Mount Walls

Right: Reconstruction of the Herodian remains along the Western Wall near Barclay's Gate, incorporating the shops found along the wall.

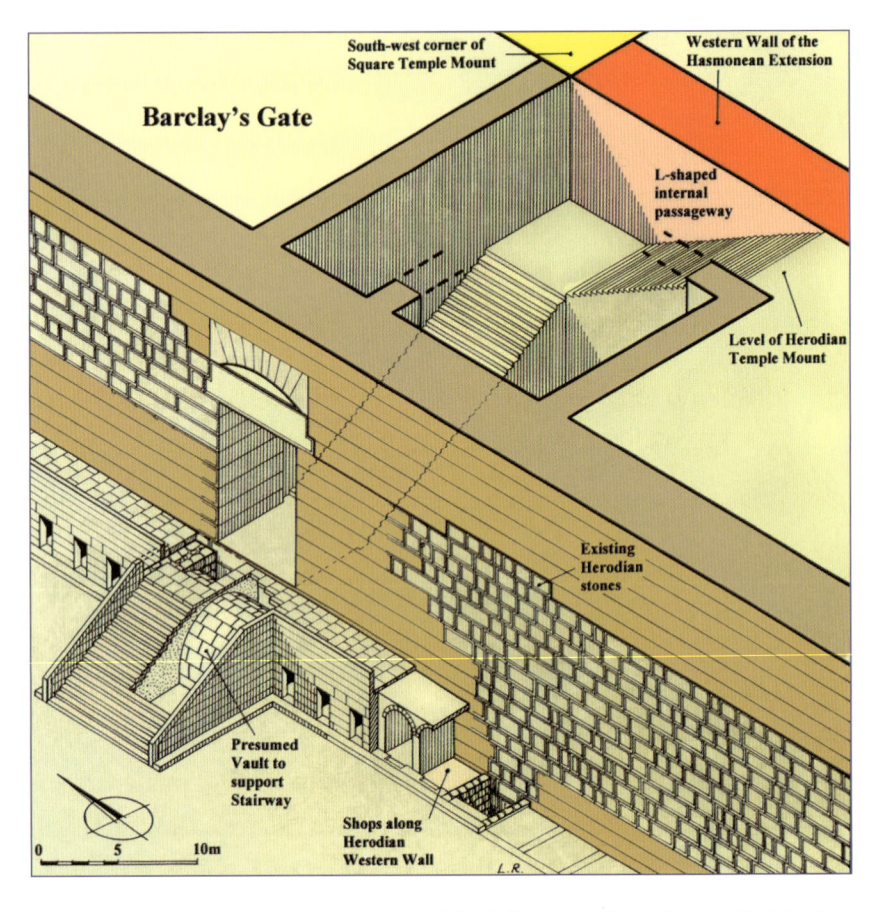

> **ONE SOLUTION TO THE VAULT QUESTION**
>
> *The purpose of this "masonry wall" has never been properly understood. Warren tried to explain, but his solution, as we saw, does not work. The problem with Barclay's Gate is how to get to it, as the sill of the gate is some 13 feet (4 m.) higher than the level of the main Herodian street which runs in front of it.*
>
> *Our solution to the problem of the vault in front of Barclay's Gate is that it carried a staircase from the lower main street to the level of the narrow street in front of the gate. Herodian vaults are usually closed off by side walls. The northern retaining wall discovered by Warren would therefore probably have closed the vault from the north; while the southern wall, which Warren had reason to believe also still exists, would have closed the vault to the south.*

Initially 6 steps were excavated, while it is now clear that a flight of at least 9 steps existed there. The most recent excavations uncovered the remains of many more shops. These cross walls were probably linked by vaults, so that the height of these shops would be at least 10 feet (3.05 m). This would necessitate a flight of at least 14 steps at the southwest corner, with possibly another smaller flight closer to Barclay's Gate. This high and narrow street would have given direct access to Barclay's Gate.

The Internal Passageway

It has been suggested that during the Herodian period an internal L-shaped staircase led up to the level of the Temple Mount. This was deduced from observation of the chambers that still exist in the interior of Barclay's Gate.

The area behind the gate has been filled in nearly up to the level of the lintel, but behind the lintel Warren[7] observed a 10 feet (3.05 m) deep and 19 feet 3 inches (5.86 m) wide segmental arch. The

Chapter One: The Herodian Temple Mount Walls

thickness of the lintel and the depth of the arch together is 15 feet (4.60 m), which corresponds to the average thickness of the Western Wall.

Behind this flat arch, a chamber opens up which is 47 feet (14.34 m) long and 18 feet (5.48 m) wide, covered over by an elliptical vault which Warren thought to be of later date. This chamber is separated into two parts by a dividing wall.

The area to the west is called the Mosque of al-Burak, after Mohammed's legendary steed. Prior to the famous night journey, the horse was said to have been tied to a metal ring, reportedly the one seen fastened in the southern wall of this chamber.

Above: Rare depiction of Mohammed mounted on his steed. Detail of Arab miniature, c. 1314/15.

A LOOK AT THE TWO CISTERNS IN THE CHAMBER (see plan, p.17)

The eastern remainder of this chamber in the interior of Barclay's Gate is part of the L-shaped Cistern 19. The corner of this cistern consists of a chamber roofed over by a dome that rests on walls and segmental arches. These form an 18 feet (5.48 m) square base on which the circular dome rests. A crude hole was made in the top of the dome, which rests on walls and segmental arches. These form an 18 feet (5.48 m) square base on which the circular dome rests. The dome was continued down to the square plan apparently by continuous spherical pendentives. From Warren's drawing it appears that these pendentives and the walls below the base of the dome are heavily plastered. The total distance from the Western Wall to the eastern side of the cistern is 86 feet (26.23 m).

The cistern continues to the south of the dome for 43 feet (13.12 m) in the form of another 18 feet (5.48 m) wide passage that runs parallel to the Western Wall. The roof of this southern branch of the cistern is a segmental vault rising to the south under an angle of 1 in 10. To the south of this cistern 19 is another cistern, Number 20. This cistern is 40 feet (12.20 m) wide and 54 feet (16.50 m) long and appears to be of post-Herodian date. However, the Western Wall of the cistern is in line with the western side of Cistern 19 and therefore may be its continuation. At the projected point where the continuation of the southern branch of Cistern 19 would have entered Cistern 20, there is an ancient covering arch.

FLAT ARCH: A flat arch is an architectural term for an arch without a curvature. It is constructed with voussoirs and a keystone, but the bottom of the arch is flat. It is also known in modern terms as a jack arch (in brick constructions, like lintels for windows and doorways).

ELLIPTICAL VAULT: An elliptical vault is a half ellipse from a centre on the springing line. However, judging from Warren's drawing of this arch on Plates 31, it looks rather like an segmental arch, because the arch looks like a segment of a circle drawn from a centre below the springing line.

Reconstruction of the Internal Passageway of Barclay's Gate

There is no doubt that some of the above-described remains belong to a Herodian gateway that had an internal underground L-shaped staircase. As the thickness of both lintel and flat arch corresponds to the average thickness of the Western Wall, it appears that this flat arch is an original Herodian construction. The 18 feet (5.48 m) wide L-shaped passageway appears to be Herodian also, especially as its width corresponds to that of other Herodian passageways like Warren's Gate and the Double Gate. The roof structure, however, may have been rebuilt at a later date.

As indicated on Warren's section of the Barclay's Gate passageway,

Chapter One: The Herodian Temple Mount Walls

Below: Wilson's Arch supported a bridge and aqueduct that crossed the Tyropoeon Valley, connecting the Temple Mount with the Upper City on the west. The present arch is possibly an Umayyad restoration of the original Herodian arch.

Opposite page (below): The remains of a stepped street found in the present-day Street of the Chain, which lies above Wilson's Arch.

> **DIMENSIONS OF THE ARCH AND THEIR IMPLICATIONS**
> *It has a span of 42 feet (12.80 m) and is 48 feet (14.65 m) wide. The arch is made up of 23 courses of voussoirs, 11 on both sides with a central keystone course, all of which have the same thickness. From this it may be assumed that the entire structure is contemporaneous.*

one would expect the floor inside the gate to be level for at least 15 feet (4.60 m) so that the wooden doors could be closed. From this point, a staircase rose for about 18 feet (5.48 m) to a landing, which must have existed below the dome. Another flight of steps would have continued southward until the level of the Temple Mount was reached.

Wilson already noted the difference between this bent passageway and the straight tunnels at the Double and Triple Gates. He proposed that this change of direction may have been caused by the rising bedrock levels; or alternatively, because of the existence of *"the original retaining wall of Solomon's Temple, which it was not thought necessary to remove when the area was enlarged by Herod."*[8] Later we will see that this latter proposal was not far from the truth.

Wilson's Arch

To the north of the Western Wall plaza is an underground space in which a huge arch can be seen. This area below the arch, which is actually part of the substructure of the Mahkame building above, is now used as a prayer hall. Tobler[9] first noted the existence of underground vaults below the area of the Gate of the Chain about the middle of the nineteenth century, but did not explore them. Warren

Chapter One: The Herodian Temple Mount Walls

named the arch after Charles Wilson, a British engineer who explored Jerusalem in the mid-nineteenth century and who, in 1864, was the first in modern history to have explored the arch.

Wilson noted that the first three courses on the east side of the arch were inserted into the Western Wall. Its western footing rests on a massive pier. However, although it is true that the southern end is keyed into the Western Wall, it appears that three original Herodian ashlars, one above the other, have been cut to receive the arch stones. The remainder of the arch above the first three voussoir courses merely abuts the wall, with the Herodian stones running behind them. On the north, only the springer can be observed, which is keyed into the wall and abuts a complete Herodian stone. This great arch appears to be a later rebuild of the original arch. This conclusion is based on the way the arch is joined to the wall and the fact that impost blocks are missing. These stone projections are typical of Roman arches and can still be seen at Robinson's Arch. The western pier on which the arch rests is, however, the original Herodian one.

The remains of a stepped street have been discovered[10] in the present-day Street of the Chain, which lies above Wilson's Arch. Potsherds, believed to be from the Late Roman period, were found below the pavement[11]. The common idea is that Wilson's Arch is Early

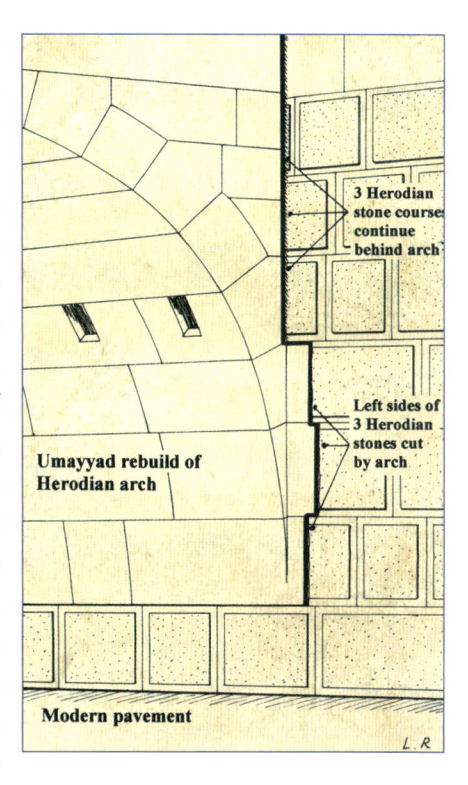

Sketch of the southern end of Wilson's Arch. The ashlars of the Herodian Western Wall have been cut to receive the springer and first two voussoirs.

A BRIDGE OF ARCHES

The original Herodian arch was the first of a series of arches that formed a bridge (see illustration, p. 34, on the right) spanning the Tyropoeon Valley below. It linked the Temple Mount with the Upper City, where the Hasmonean Palace was located and where most of the priestly families lived. The bridge was therefore known as the "Bridge of the Priests" (Heb: gesher hacohanim). In addition the bridge supported an aqueduct, bringing water from the so-called "Solomon's Pools" near Bethlehem to a huge cistern on the Temple Mount, known as "The Great Sea" (Cistern No. 8).

Chapter One: The Herodian Temple Mount Walls

Right: Section through Wilson's Arch and the stepped street found above.

Opposite page: Photo of the largest stone found in the Western Wall. It is 45 feet long and weighs 570 tons.

> **THE FOUR MASSIVE STONES FOUND IN THE TUNNEL**
>
> The height of these stones is approximately 12 feet (3.36 m). The northernmost is about 16 feet (4.88 m) long and weighs approximately 200 tons. Its northern edge forms the southern jamb of Warren's Gate. The largest stone is located next to this one. In the photo opposite two boys point to the two extremities of the largest stone, which is 45 feet (13.70 m) long and 11 feet 6 inches (3.19 m) high. Bahat estimated this stone to be 14–16 feet (4.20–4.90 m) deep and to weigh 570 tons.[13] However, this stone is probably not thicker than the other stones in the Temple Mount walls, i.e. 5 feet (1.5 m), and therefore is unlikely to weigh more than 175 tons. There are approximately twelve regular stone courses below these huge blocks, before bedrock is reached. To the south of the largest stone, there are two more stones with lengths of 7 feet (2.10 m) and 38 feet (12.05 m) respectively. The smaller stone weighs 27 tons and the larger 150 tons.

Islamic but new evidence shows that it might have been built as early as the Late Roman period (second century A.D.). Nevertheless, the arch and the street above it give us some idea of what the Herodian construction may have looked like.

The Western Wall Tunnels

To the north of Wilson's Arch an underground tunnel has been excavated[12] along the Western Wall up to the foot of the Antonia Fortress. Between Wilson's Arch and Warren's Gate to the north, four of the largest stones of Herod's Temple Mount have been found.

It appears that such large stones were occasionally available because of the thickness of the rock layers in the quarry. We believe that the stones in the so-called "Great" or "Master" course in the Southern Wall were also cut out of a rock layer which was thicker than usual. We do not believe that these stones represent an earlier phase in the wall construction as has been suggested by some 19th century scholars, especially as in both walls, normal Herodian stone courses can be seen below the "Great Course." The location of these large stones at street level may more likely be attributed to a desire by Herod to impress the pedestrians walking alongside. According to our calculations, these stones were level with the narrow street which

CHAPTER ONE: THE HERODIAN TEMPLE MOUNT WALLS

Chapter One: The Herodian Temple Mount Walls

Right: A model of Herod's Temple Mount shows the enormous size of the largest stones found in the Western Wall relative to the scale figures placed in front of them.
(photo: Philip Evans)

Below: View of Warren's Gate.

Opposite page (above): Warren's Gate and master course. The drawing (bottom) shows this portion of the Western Wall as it appears today. Above it is a reconstruction drawing of Warren's Gate and the master course with the beginning of the pilaster construction.

Opposite page (below): The Western Wall Tunnel. In between the concrete frames Herodian stones can be seen all along the tunnel.

Transversal Valley: The Transversal Valley runs from west to east in between the southwest and northwest hills of the Old City, more or less below the present David Street.

led above the roofs of the shops which ran along the Western Wall.

Walking along these large Herodian stones, one notices that at various levels holes have been cut into them. This was not done in the Herodian period, but at a later date when a cistern was built here against the Western Wall. To waterproof the cistern, the Herodian stones were covered with a thick layer of plaster, the remains of which can still be seen in the tunnel. The thick plaster apparently did not stick to the Herodian ashlars and therefore long peg-like stones were inserted into these holes. These pegs projected into the plaster layer and thus acted as ties to make the plaster adhere securely to the Herodian stones.

Warren's Gate

When Warren investigated the cisterns of the Temple Mount, he noticed that Cistern 30, which he examined from the inside, pierced the Western Wall. He therefore identified Cistern 30 as an early gateway, constructed in the same way as Barclay's Gate[14]. It was called Warren's Gate, after its discoverer.

This gate, located at 765 feet (233 m) north of the southwest corner and opposite the Transversal Valley, was the second suburban gate mentioned by Josephus. This location was probably chosen to give direct access to the Temple Mount from a street which may have run along this valley. The Transversal Valley runs just north of the First

CHAPTER ONE: THE HERODIAN TEMPLE MOUNT WALLS

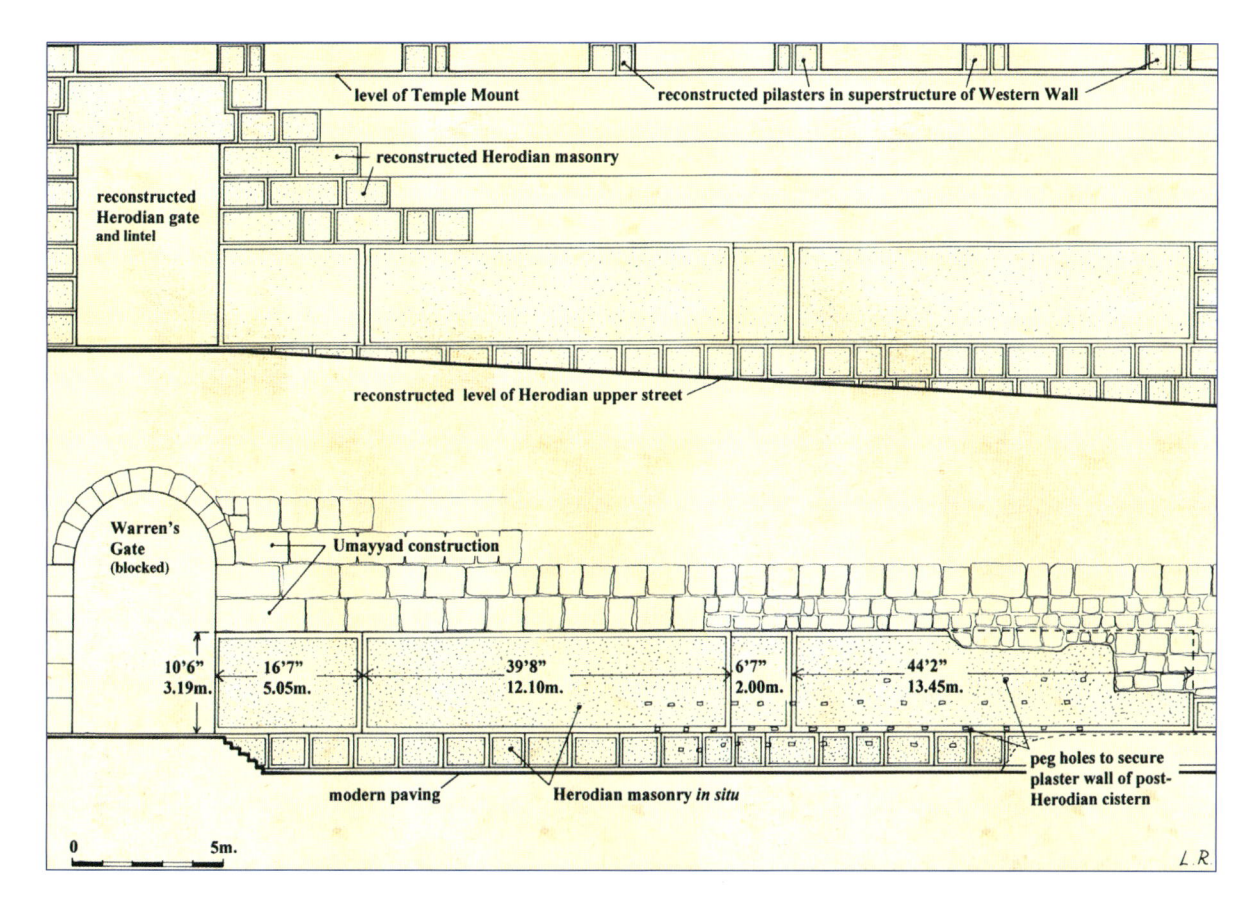

Diagram labels:
- level of Temple Mount
- reconstructed pilasters in superstructure of Western Wall
- reconstructed Herodian masonry
- reconstructed Herodian gate and lintel
- reconstructed level of Herodian upper street
- Warren's Gate (blocked)
- Umayyad construction
- 10'6" / 3.19m.
- 16'7" / 5.05m.
- 39'8" / 12.10m.
- 6'7" / 2.00m.
- 44'2" / 13.45m.
- modern paving
- Herodian masonry *in situ*
- peg holes to secure plaster wall of post-Herodian cistern
- 0 — 5m.
- L.R

Wall, which was Jerusalem's northern boundary during the First Temple period. However, in Herodian Jerusalem, this valley was incorporated into the city and may have been the prime location for a street (see illustration, p. 53 below). This street probably began at the Gennath Gate, remains of which have been found in the Jewish Quarter.[15] According to Josephus (*Ant.* 15.410), the Second Wall began its course at this point.

Today, Warren's Gate is blocked up and the arch visible at the top of the gate appears to date from the time when the Temple Mount was restored in the Roman period (see photo, opposite page below). The gate was apparently blocked by the Crusaders, who turned the interior passageway into a cistern.

The width of the passageway is 18 feet (5.50 m), identical to that of Barclay's Gate. The length of Warren's Gate is 84 feet (25.60 m) and its height 34 feet 6 inches

Chapter One: The Herodian Temple Mount Walls

CHAPTER ONE: THE HERODIAN TEMPLE MOUNT WALLS

(10.50 m). As we will see later on, this cistern, which has a vaulted roof, is, in our opinion, the first part of another L-shaped subterranean stairway, similar to that of Barclay's Gate.

Herodian masonry can be seen all along the Western Wall Tunnel, proving that the Western Wall is Herodian from beginning to end. The bedrock rises to the north and where it is located above street level, the rock was carved in Herodian times to look like stones of the period.

Towards the end of the Western Wall Tunnel, the Herodian paved street is again visible. Its level rises in a northerly direction and it terminates in a bedrock face. The northern part of this wall was already observed in the previous century beneath the Bab es Serai[16] (the name of the present gate at the northwest corner of the Temple Mount).

The base of the Western Wall is cut out of the rock itself. The wall continues at an angle behind a rock mass that was never removed (see opposite). The vertical quarry channel cut across the middle of this block shows that the process of removal was begun, but apparently never completed. It is interesting to note that the bedrock layer is very high. This may therefore have been the place from whence the huge stones north of Wilson's Arch were quarried .

As previously mentioned, the Western Wall abuts a vertical rockscarp that shows an entrance to a rock-hewn channel at a distance of several feet from the wall. We know that this channel was an aqueduct that brought water to Cistern 22 in pre-Herodian times, as the southern continuation was cut by the Western Wall of the Herodian Temple Mount. Above this point where the Western Wall cut the aqueduct, the wall appears to have two pilasters with a plinth between them.[17] This construction is similar to that of the pilasters on the Tomb of the Patriarchs in Hebron. The pilasters in the Western Wall have since been plastered and painted over, as the author was able to verify in 1973. As will be seen below, it is unlikely that these were original Herodian pilasters.

The northern part of the Western Wall is not exactly in line with the rest of the wall, being set forward by about 8 feet (2.44 m). This feature is

Opposite page: The Herodian street at the northern end of the tunnel. The Western Wall, which here is cut out of the rock, continues in an angle behind the large block of bedrock. The vertical quarry channel across the mass of rock shows that the quarrying process was never completed.

Below: Warren's sketch of the two pilasters found at the northern end of the Western Wall.

Chapter One: The Herodian Temple Mount Walls

reminiscent of the projection of the Herodian tower at the northeast corner of the Temple Mount, which was an integral part of the Eastern Wall. It is unlikely, however, that the projection in the Western Wall was part of a tower, as this projection is located approximately 260 feet (79 m) to the south of the northwest corner of the Herodian Temple Mount.

Having now reached the end of the Western Wall, we may conclude then that the Western Wall Tunnel excavations have proved that the Western Wall is one homogeneous wall of Herodian origin.

The Rock-hewn Aqueduct

The rock-hewn aqueduct mentioned in the preceding section is about 262 feet (80 m) long and ends in the north in the western pool of a large water reservoir, which was called the Strouthion by Josephus. The aqueduct is entirely cut out of the bedrock as a channel rather than a tunnel, i.e. its construction was begun on the surface and made deeper by cutting down into the rock. When the required depth was reached, the top of the channel was covered by stone slabs, presumably to prevent people from falling into it. The top of the channel is narrow, but its base is wider. The aqueduct is on average 86 feet (10 m) high, and 4 feet (1.20 m) wide near the bottom. As the aqueduct slopes down gently from north to south, we have to

View of the western pool of a large twin water reservoir, which was called the Strouthion by Josephus. (photo: Don Edwards)

CHAPTER ONE: THE HERODIAN TEMPLE MOUNT WALLS

View of the rock-hewn aqueduct.

remember that water used to flow in this direction, from the pool to the aqueduct, which is the opposite of the direction taken by present-day visitors to the aqueduct. The plan (p. 40) shows the location of the rock-hewn aqueduct and other archaeological remains.

Chapter One: The Herodian Temple Mount Walls

Right: Plan of Herodian and pre-Herodian remains at the northwest corner of the Temple Mount.

Below: Part of the stepped tunnel at Gibeon from the Iron Age. (NEAEHL)

Fosse: A rock-cut ditch or moat used in fortifications.

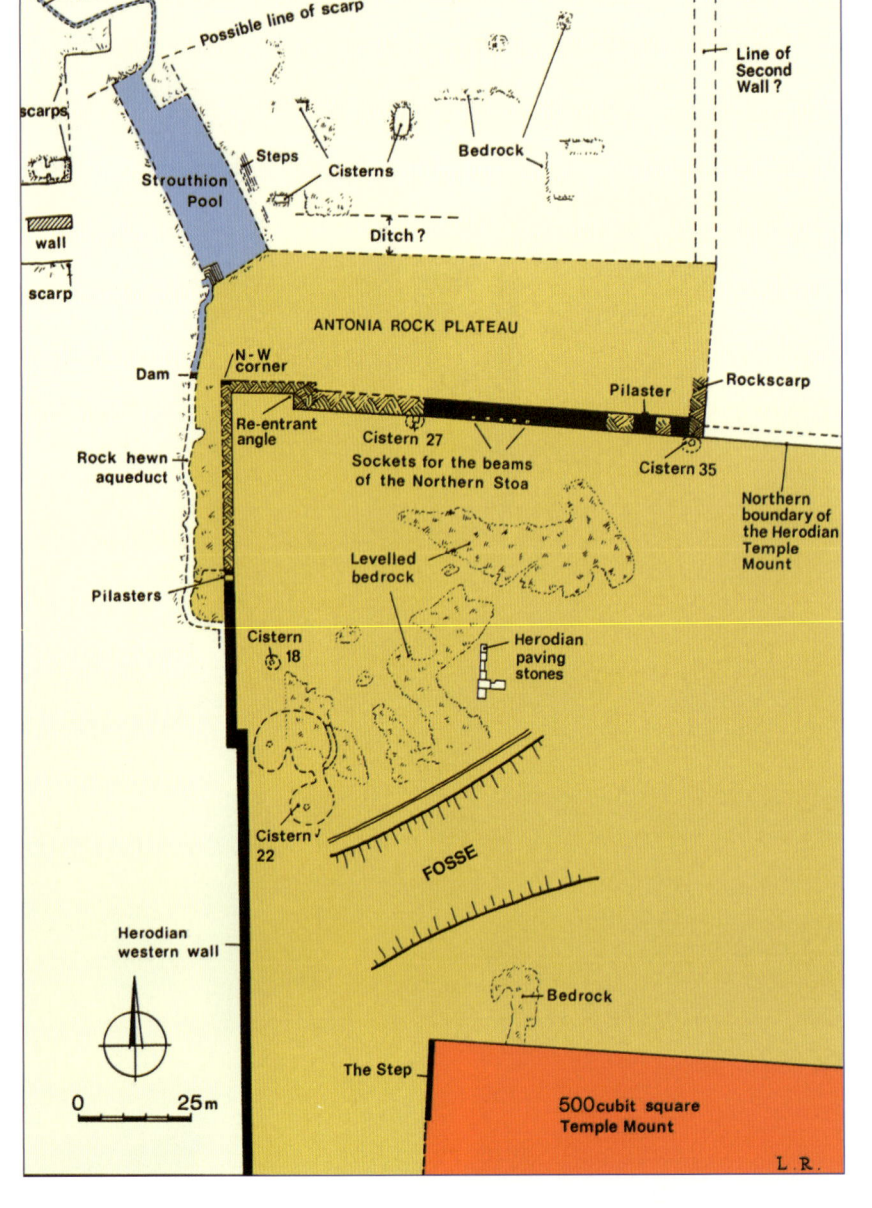

A flight of rock-hewn steps leads up from the bottom of the pool into the aqueduct. Here Warren first entered the channel in 1867 with his faithful assistant Sergeant Birtles. They used three old doors, two to stand on and one to place in front of them, to stay afloat above 6 feet of sewage. The exploration of this channel had to be carried out with great caution *"lest an unlucky false step might cause a header into the murky liquid."*[18] At about 28 feet from the entrance they encountered a ten-foot-high dam built across the channel. As mentioned above, the

Chapter One: The Herodian Temple Mount Walls

southern end was blocked off by the Herodian Western Wall.

Excavator Dan Bahat believes that this channel dates from the Hasmonean period.[19] There is no archaeological evidence, however, to prove that this is the case. Several archaeologists are of the opinion the channel is much older, one reason being that the construction as an open channel covered with slabs is reminiscent of the stepped tunnel at Gibeon,[20] which dates from the Iron Age.

Bahat's argument is based on his location of the *Baris,* which he believes stood on the Antonia Rock Plateau. Later on we will see that, in fact, the *Baris* stood at the northwest corner of the pre-Herodian Temple Mount (see below, p. 216), which is farther to the southeast. This whole area was therefore located not only outside the original Temple Mount but also outside the city walls of Old Testament Jerusalem.

As shown in the plan (opposite) both the aqueduct and Cisterns 18 and 22 are situated to the north of the Fosse. As will be explained in Chapter 2 (p. 168), this was an artificial moat or ditch cut across a narrow saddle which linked the Temple Mount with the natural elevation on which the Antonia was built. The natural northern defense line of the pre-Herodian Temple Mount consisted of the Bezetha Valley on the northeast and the Tyropoeon Valley on the west. The Fosse connected these two valleys and so the northern defense system was strengthened.

As it is conjectured that this channel is not connected with the

> **A POSSIBLE IDENTIFICATION FOR THE AQUEDUCT?**
>
> *An industry that used a lot of water and was often located outside the city was that of the fuller. A fuller was a launderer who made dirty clothes clean and soft by treading, kneading and pounding them in cold water. He also treated newly made cloth. He often used soaps and needed a lot of water to do his work and a large place or field to dry the clothes. The "soap" a fuller would have used was actually clay, known as fuller's earth, which could bleach and was used for scouring and cleansing wool and finishing cloth. This brings to mind a passage of the Hebrew Bible which is used three times, "the conduit of the upper pool, which is in the highway of the fuller's field" (2 Kgs 18:17; Isa 7:3, 36:2). This was the place from where Rabshakeh, who came from the north, addressed the men of Hezekiah.*
>
> **Is it possible that the "conduit" referred to in these verses is the rock-hewn aqueduct and that this area, then outside the city walls, was the field where the fuller would dry his clothes? If this identification is correct, then these water installations would date back to the Iron Age.**

Reconstruction of the large dam and reservoir near the Pool of Siloam, at the southeastern corner of the city. The outlet of the Siloam Channel can be seen at the top right.

Chapter One: The Herodian Temple Mount Walls

original Temple Mount or any fortress, it is possible to propose an earlier date for its construction. There must have been a reason why an aqueduct of such length was cut through the rock to bring water to two cisterns that were located to the north and outside of the pre-Herodian Temple Mount. Just to the north of the Fosse is a shallow channel cut in the rock, as if to catch the surface rainwater and prevent it from disappearing into the Fosse. All these elements—the long aqueduct, Cistern 18 (which may have served as a sump to catch dirt from the water before it entered the large Cistern 22) and this long surface ditch—may have been connected.

The Strouthion Pool

This pool, which Josephus called the "Strouthion," supplied the Antonia Fortress with water. It was located outside the Antonia, near its northwestern tower and received its water from the northern continuation of the Rock-hewn aqueduct described above. This aqueduct has been traced to the northern part of the Tyropoeon valley, which lies outside the present-day Damascus Gate. The floor of this upper aqueduct follows the same line as that of the Rock-hewn Aqueduct and they were therefore once connected. The Strouthion Pool was constructed later than the aqueduct and the dam mentioned

Composite section showing the northern end of the Herodian Western Wall, the Strouthion Pool and the northern and southern parts of the rock-hewn aqueduct.

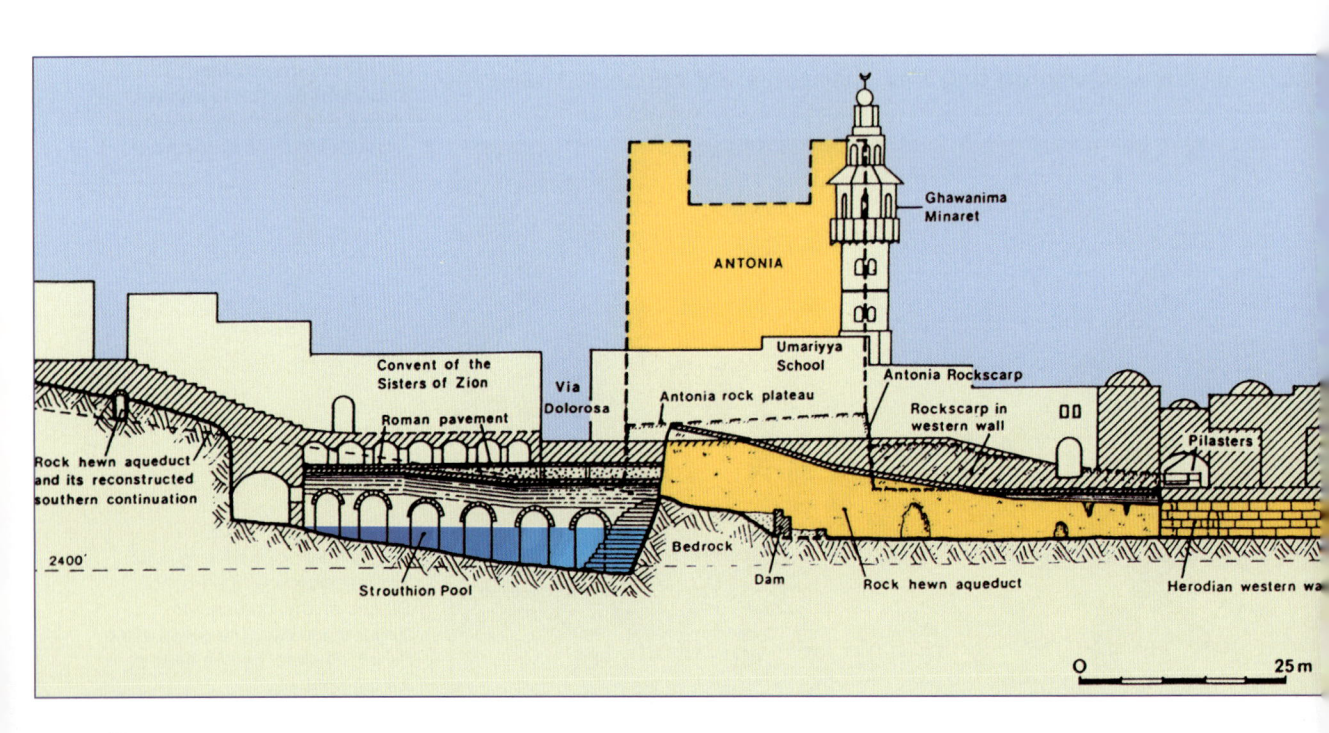

Chapter One: The Herodian Temple Mount Walls

Above: Roman battering ram.

Left: View of the northeast corner of the Antonia Fortress and the Strouthion Pool. The part of the fortress walls above the southern end of the pool, seen in the center of the picture, was the least protected and therefore chosen by the Romans as the easiest part to breach. (photo: Philip Evans)

Below: The so-called Lithostrotos, today under the Convent of the Sisters of Zion. (photo: Garo Nalbandian)

in the preceding section was built in the channel to prevent the waters from flowing out of the pool. In the Herodian period, the pool was an open reservoir.

During the capture of the Antonia in A.D. 70, the Romans built a siege ramp in the middle of this pool. After battering the walls of the Fortress, they gained access to the Antonia and were able to reach the Temple Mount *(War* 5.467). This spot was chosen as the most strategic to attack, since the rockscarp on which the northern wall of the Antonia Fortress stands bends here a little. This short section of the fortress walls above the southern end of the pool was the least protected and therefore the easiest part to breach.

Some sixty-five years after the capture of the Antonia, when Jerusalem was called Aelia Capitolina, this pool was covered over with twin vaults. The area above was paved and became part of the Forum. This pavement has erroneously been identified as the Lithostrotos, i.e. the pavement on which Jesus was condemned by Pilate (John 19:13).

Chapter One: The Herodian Temple Mount Walls

The excavations at the southwest corner of the Temple Mount.

Robinson's Arch

Let us now go to the southern end of the Western Wall of Herod's Temple Mount. This area and that to the south of the Southern Wall was extensively excavated for ten years following the Six-Day War, from 1968 to 1978. The bottom half of the western Temple Mount wall consists of the same beautiful Herodian ashlars we have seen earlier near the Western Wall plaza and inside the Western Wall tunnel. The top half is composed of stones from the Early Muslim and later periods.

The great skewback of an arch leading to the Herodian Temple Mount near the southwest corner was identified in 1838 by the American explorer Edward Robinson.[21] At that time, and up to 1967, the arch was at ground level with a vegetable plot in front of it.

Robinson noted four courses forming this arch, the lower one of which consisted of stones with projecting bosses; while the three higher ones formed the beginning of an arch that appears to have been destroyed in A.D. 70. From the first, Robinson identified this as

CHAPTER ONE: THE HERODIAN TEMPLE MOUNT WALLS

the bridge across the Tyropoeon Valley mentioned by Josephus in *Antiquities* 15.410.

About thirty years later, Charles Warren investigated this area and attempted to locate the piers that would have supported such a bridge. The pier closest to the Western Wall was found at a distance of 40 feet (12.80 m). His investigations to the west of this pier, however, did not result in the discovery of further piers. In Warren's words, *"If this [Robinson's Arch] was not the bridge stretching across the valley, and it is not, where was that bridge? It could be no other than that at Wilson's Arch."*[22]

Similarly, Conrad Schick[23] believed that there was only one stone arch, but then suggested that the remainder of the bridge was built of wood.

Hardly any researcher subsequently paid attention to the fact that in 1896 Watson had written that *"of these [four gates] one was doubtless the great flight of steps leading up to the Royal Cloister."*[24] As this cloister, or Royal Stoa, was built over the Southern Wall, the only candidate for the entrance gate into the cloister was the one built above Robinson's Arch, which would have necessitated a great flight of steps.

Gustaf Dalman also picked this up, writing in 1935 that the so-called *"Robinson's Arch to which an ascent, resting on several arches, seemed to have belonged, may have corresponded to the steps mentioned by Josephus."*[25]

Robinson's Arch as depicted in a 19th century engraving.

LONG-HELD THEORY DISPROVED BY EXCAVATIONS

By the 1960s the accepted opinon was firm: the immense Robinson's Arch was the first of a series of arches going west to form a bridge which connected the Temple Mount with the Upper City. Indeed, in the beautiful model of Jerusalem in the Second Temple period in the grounds of the Holy Land Hotel in Jerusalem designed by Professor Michael Avi-Yonah, a bridge was initially shown here leading to the Upper City.[26] This was a wealthy area of Jerusalem, located where the Jewish Quarter is today. There the excavations led by Professor Nahman Avigad[27] found richly decorated Herodian villas. Judging by the amount of mikvaot—ritual baths—present, these must have belonged to priestly families; and a bridge would have been very useful to them when going to the Temple. Because of this accepted opinion, Mazar's team took up the same quest of looking for the bridge in the late 1960s. However, all their efforts to locate the remains of the elusive bridge were unsuccessful. They opened several excavation squares at the foot of the Jewish Quarter's rockscarp, but found no traces of a bridge. It was then suggested that the pier belonged to a multi-storied monumental building and that the viaduct must have passed over its roof[28] to a Herodian gateway, of which the Romans left no remains.

Eventually, the excavators found the archaeological remains of a stairway leading up to Robinson's Arch, which put an end to all speculation.

45

Chapter One: The Herodian Temple Mount Walls

Right: View of Robinson's Arch.

Below: Drawings of the northern and southern ends of Robinson's Arch.

THE PROOF IS IN THE PROJECTIONS

Each of the southern arch stones of the first two courses has a small flat projection to the south (see right drawing). The projection on the lower stone has a margin and boss in the Herodian style and was therefore made to look like a wall stone. The top projection is too weathered to indicate if it once had a boss. These projections form a kind of key which bonds the arch into the wall.

On the north side of the arch, however, there are no such projections (see left drawing). This appears to indicate that Robinson's Arch was built as an integral part with the southwest corner construction, and that the continuation to the north followed after the arch was completed. **This would confirm my theory that the Herodian extension was built stone course after stone course from the inside, beginning at the south (see below, p. 132).**

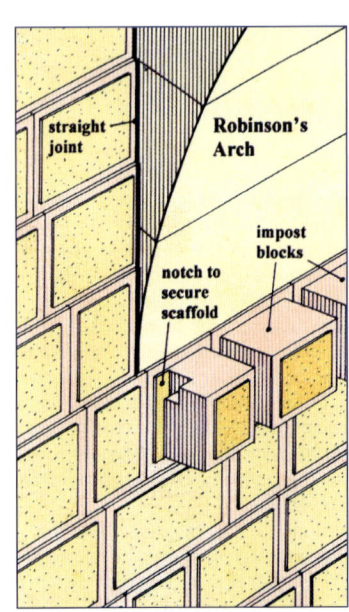

The Arch

An examination of the arch itself, located just over 39 feet (12 m) north of the southwest corner, shows that it is 50 feet 10 inches (15.50 m) wide. The arch stones (voussoirs) rest on a row of impost blocks that are stones with margins and large projecting bosses. Nine of these blocks are almost square and the southernmost block has

Northern end of Robinson's Arch

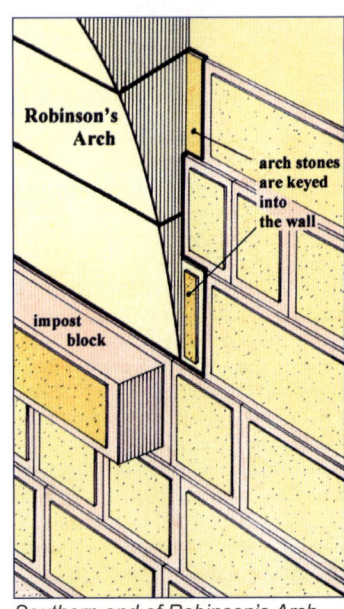

Southern end of Robinson's Arch

CHAPTER ONE: THE HERODIAN TEMPLE MOUNT WALLS

a long rectangular shape. The first course of the arch, in the form of five springers, rests on these impost blocks and is relatively well preserved. The next row of two enormous voussoirs and one smaller one is also complete, but shows signs of exposure to the elements. The topmost course, consisting of three voussoirs, is incomplete and badly damaged in places. At least one voussoir is missing.

The Pier

During the first three years of the excavations, between 1968 and 1970, a large area to the west of Robinson's Arch was cleared. The pier of the arch, which was already located in 1869 by Warren, was revealed at a distance of 42 feet (12.80 m) from the Western Wall. More recent excavations in this area by R. Reich and Y. Billig[29] have uncovered the pier in its entirety.

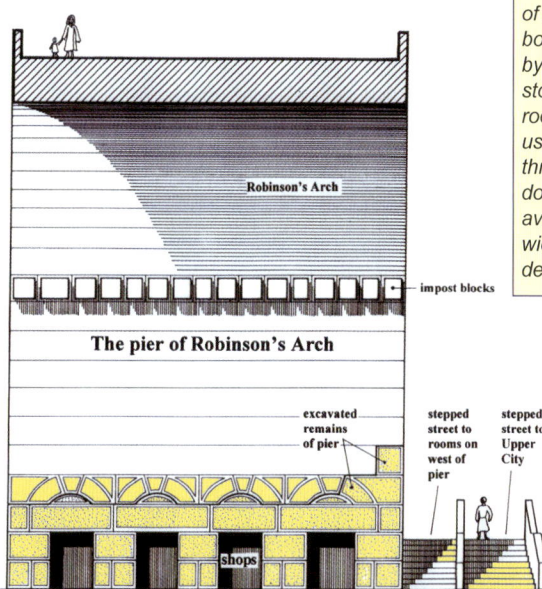

> **PIER STATS**
> *The pier is 50 feet 4 inches (15.35 m) long and 21 feet 4 inches (6.5 m) wide and has four rooms built into it at street level (illustrations, this page). This street has a curb on both sides and abuts the pier in the west. The pier is constructed of stones that resemble the ashlars of the Temple Mount walls, both in size and finish. Judging by the amount of coins and stone weights found in these rooms, it is clear that they were used as shops. The preserved thresholds show that they had double doors. The shops are on average 5 feet 5 inches (1.65 m) wide, 7 feet 10 inches (2.40 m) deep and 7 feet (2.15 m) high.*

Above: Reconstructed elevation of the Pier that supported Robinson's Arch, looking west.

Left: The Pier of Robinson's Arch.

47

Chapter One: The Herodian Temple Mount Walls

> **AN ARCH GETS SOME RELIEF**
>
> *All four lintel stones of the arch are preserved, and the construction of the pier demonstrates the function of a relieving arch.*
>
> *To prevent the huge weight of the pier and arch construction above pressing upon the lintel and causing it to crack and break, a relieving arch was built above the lintels. Relieving arches divert the pressure from above to the two side walls of the opening, thus "relieving" pressure from the lintels (see sketch below). Part of one relieving arch stone is preserved at the northern end of the pier. There would have been a similar stone on the other side, leaving room for a keystone to complete the arch. The preserved arch stone is not a single arch stone, but a wall stone that has been carved to make it look like two stones: a wall stone and a voussoir separated by a margin, which is an interesting construction. After the arches were built, the opening was closed off by a rounded stone, presumably to prevent birds or other small animals from entering and soiling the area. Two of these stones were found above the existing lintels.*

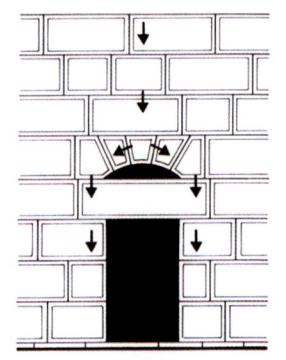

Elevation of a relieving arch. The pressure of the weight of the upper courses would break the lintel stone. The arrows indicate the diversion of the pressure away from the lintel to the sides of the door opening.

The Flight of Steps

After the first few years of excavations, it became apparent that the bridge theory had to be rejected, and several alternatives were suggested to explain the function of the arch. Some thought that it may have supported a balcony, making a kind of viewpoint. Others suggested that two staircases descended on either side down to street level. In 1971, after further examination, new evidence came to light. In front of the pier, above and in between the debris of the collapsed Robinson's Arch, many steps were found, some of which were still joined together. Another find was the discovery of walls topped by the remains of arches. The walls run east-west and are located to the south of and at right angles to the pier. Altogether four of these walls were found at a distance of 15 feet (5 m) from each other.

The first wall had the beginning of vaults on the top of both its faces, a higher spring to the north and a lower one to the south. It soon became clear to site architect Brian Lalor and archaeological supervisor Menahem Magen that a series of vaults existed to the south of the pier of Robinson's Arch. These had been built in order to support a flight of steps rising from the south towards Robinson's Arch. Calculating the angle of the vault construction and taking into consideration the height of the steps, many of which were found in between these walls, it became apparent that this flight of steps could not have been continuous since the angle of the steps was steeper than the uniform incline of the vaults. Intermediate landings

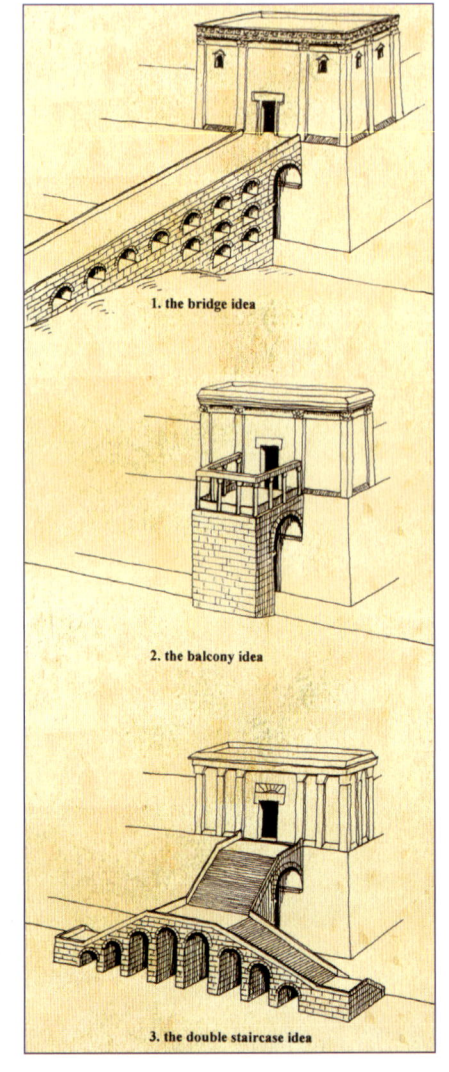

1. the bridge idea

2. the balcony idea

3. the double staircase idea

CHAPTER ONE: THE HERODIAN TEMPLE MOUNT WALLS

Opposite page (right): Several ideas of how to reconstruct Robinson's Arch were put forward before the foundations of the stairway were found.

Left: Pilaster stones found in the debris in front of the pier of Robinson's Arch. In lower center a Herodian wall stone can be seen. This is the bottom course of the pilaster construction of the Temple Mount walls. The right side of this stone is part of the sloping surface and the left side is the beginning of the pilaster with both elements cut out of the same stone. Another pilaster fragment with the typical Herodian margins can be seen lying on its side on top of the debris. This stone shows that part of the pilaster and part of the wall set back in between the pilasters were cut out of the same stone. This demonstrates that the pilasters were not separate wall elements, but were keyed in to the wall construction. A set of three steps still joined together is visible at lower left.

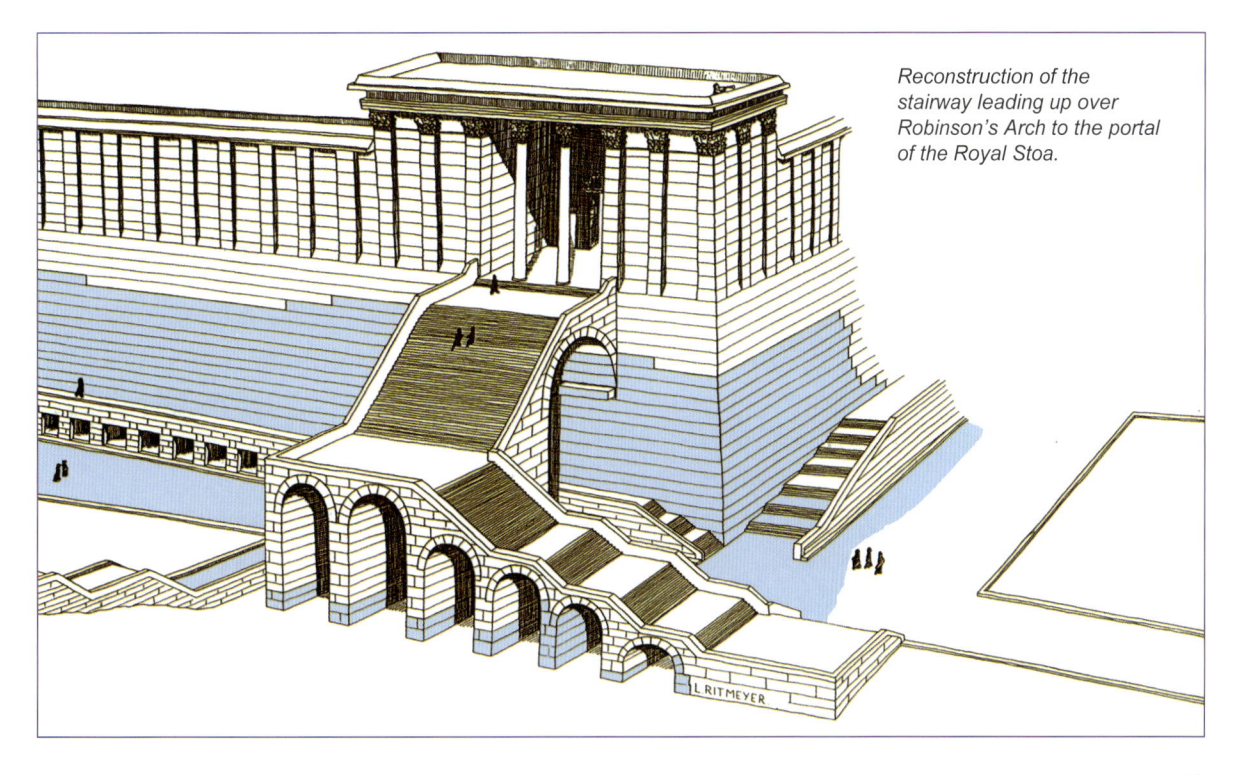

or platforms must therefore have been inserted above the tops of the vaults and also on top of the pier construction. From this latter platform the stairway must have turned east to continue over Robinson's Arch.

The construction of alternating steps and landings was already

Reconstruction of the stairway leading up over Robinson's Arch to the portal of the Royal Stoa.

49

Chapter One: The Herodian Temple Mount Walls

known from a flight of steps near the southwest corner that rises up towards the Double Gate. Eventually the southernmost wall of the series of vaults was discovered with two steps still remaining on top of the vault. This provided conclusive evidence for the stairway construction. The width of these walls is 36 feet (11 m). This is not as wide as the 50-foot 10-inch (15.50 m) wide Robinson's Arch, but it is wider than the 29 feet 6 inches (9 m) of the street below. This form of construction would accommodate a growing number of pilgrims ascending to the Royal Stoa, who undoubtedly would have wished to linger on the higher platforms to admire the view of the city.

Despite extensive efforts, the southern termination of this flight of steps was not found. There are two possibilities: either it continued south until the steps reached street level, or it made an angle toward the east to join up with the street. From an architectural planning point of view, the latter is the preferred solution.

Pilasters in the Herodian enclosure wall of the Tomb of the Patriarchs in Hebron. Note that the sloping surface of the lowest stone in between the pilasters is not the full height of a regular stone course.

Pilasters

The upper portion of the Temple Mount walls were decorated at regular intervals with rectangular engaged pillars, called pilasters. Some of these pilaster stones were found in the debris that was lying against the pier of Robinson's Arch and also along the Southern Wall of the Temple Mount.

This kind of construction is known to us from examples in and near Hebron. The Tomb of the Patriarchs in Hebron, also known as the Cave of Machpelah, was built by King Herod the Great over the cave-tomb where Abraham, Isaac and Jacob were buried with their wives. In nearby Elonei Mamre, known in Arabic as Haram Ramet el-Khalil, another Herodian enclosure was built apparently as a sanctuary for

CHAPTER ONE: THE HERODIAN TEMPLE MOUNT WALLS

the Edomites to whom Herod was related.[30] In both these structures, the characteristic pilaster construction is still preserved. The pilasters in Hebron[31] are still standing to their full height. The pilasters in Elonei Mamre are 35 inches (88 cm) wide and set apart at 6-foot (1.90-m) intervals, while those in Hebron are on average 3 feet 9 inches (1.14 m) wide, spaced at about 6 feet 9 inches (2.07 m).

In the Temple Mount excavations, only one complete pilaster stone was found. Its width was 59 inches (1.50 m), similar to the thickness or diameter of the columns inside the Double Gate passageway and other fragments of large Herodian columns found in the excavation. The intercolumniation could not be established on the basis of these remains alone. However, the distance between the pilasters in the Southern Wall of the Temple Mount was probably connected with the spacing of the columns of the Royal Stoa, which will be discussed below.

We have previously noted the presence at the northern end of the Western Wall of a set of pilasters. The height of these sloping plinths is about half the height of a Herodian stone course, a similar construction to those found in Hebron and Elonei Mamre. However, this is unlike the many plinth stones found in the Temple Mount excavations. The former plinths appear to be an anomaly in the context of the architecture of the Temple Mount, where the plinths are of the full-size of a Herodian stone course.

I conclude therefore that this must have been the prevailing style of construction in the upper parts of the Herodian Temple Mount walls.

> **THREE CASES OF PILASTER CONSTRUCTION**
>
> *In all three cases—Hebron, Mamre and here on the Mount—the pilaster construction is similar. The curtain wall in between the pilasters is set back and its lowest stone course has an outward sloping surface instead of a horizontal ledge, so that the rain falling on this part of the wall would continue to flow down smoothly to the lower part of the wall. The purpose of this construction is to make the wall as strong as the thickness of the pilasters, yet light, as the curtain wall in between was probably only 20 inches (0.50 m) thick.*

Above: Drawing by de Vogüé of pilasters in the outer walls of the Tomb of the Patriarchs in Hebron.

Left: Pilaster construction at Elonei Mamre.

Chapter One: The Herodian Temple Mount Walls

The stepped street ascending to the Upper City over a series of vaults.

Above: Section of the Herodian street excavated during Mazar's Temple Mount excavations at southwest corner of Barclay's Gate.

Opposite page: In the renewed excavations which were carried out between 1994 and 1996, the whole street had been laid open. Both curbstones lining the street are visible.

The Ascent

In *Antiquities* 15.410, after describing the four gates in the Western Wall, Josephus refers to the descending flight of steps as *"many steps going down to the ravine."* It has been calculated that there must have been approximately one hundred steps going down from the Temple Mount to the street below. Josephus then continues writing: *"and from here up again to the hill."* To the north of the pier a stepped street was found, built over small vaults, rising to the west. *These are undoubtedly the remains of the ascending street mentioned by Josephus and thus show the description of Josephus to be correct in many of its details*.

The Tyropoeon Valley Street

In the northern part of the excavation, below Robinson's Arch, R. Reich and Y. Billig uncovered a large section of a beautifully preserved Herodian pavement. In the photograph (opposite) curbstones lining both sides of the street can be seen. The paving stones are up to 4 feet (1.22 m) long and over a foot (0.31 m) thick. In the recent excavations by Reich and Billig the whole street had been laid open. A large pile of stones were left *in situ* to show the destruction in A.D. 70 of the Temple Mount walls (see opposite).

The street runs parallel to the Western Wall and the southern continuation was found in front of Robinson's Arch and near the southwest corner. In several places, the eastern curb was found at a distance of about ten feet from the wall. Cross walls belonging to

Chapter One: The Herodian Temple Mount Walls

Chapter One: The Herodian Temple Mount Walls

rooms that were 6 feet 7 inches (2 m) wide were found between the wall and the curb. We have already noted the existence of four shops in the pier of Robinson's Arch. Shops lining this street on both sides would have given the street the distinctive character of a market.

This street, which runs through the Tyropoeon Valley, probably began at the present-day Damascus Gate and certainly terminated at the southern city gate near the Siloam Pool. Bliss and Dickie in 1894–1897[32] traced long stretches of the southern part of this street and the drain that runs beneath it. They also discovered a branch of the street that descended by steps to the Siloam Pool. They wrote:

> *Assuming the identity of the two constructions, we have a street passing along the west of the old Temple, under Robinson's Arch, and running down the Tyropoeon with a fork above the Siloam Pool, one branch terminating at the pool and the other sweeping around the base of the western hill to the gate....*

As the street runs through the Tyropoeon Valley which intersects

Reconstruction drawing of the Siloam Pool and the adjacent stepped Herodian street.

Chapter One: The Herodian Temple Mount Walls

Reconstruction of Herodian Jerusalem. Note the street that begins in the north where the Damascus Gate now stands. It runs through the Tyropoeon Valley, passes under Robinson's Arch and descends into the City of David. A branch of the street leads down by steps to the Siloam Pool, while the street itself ends at the South Gate.

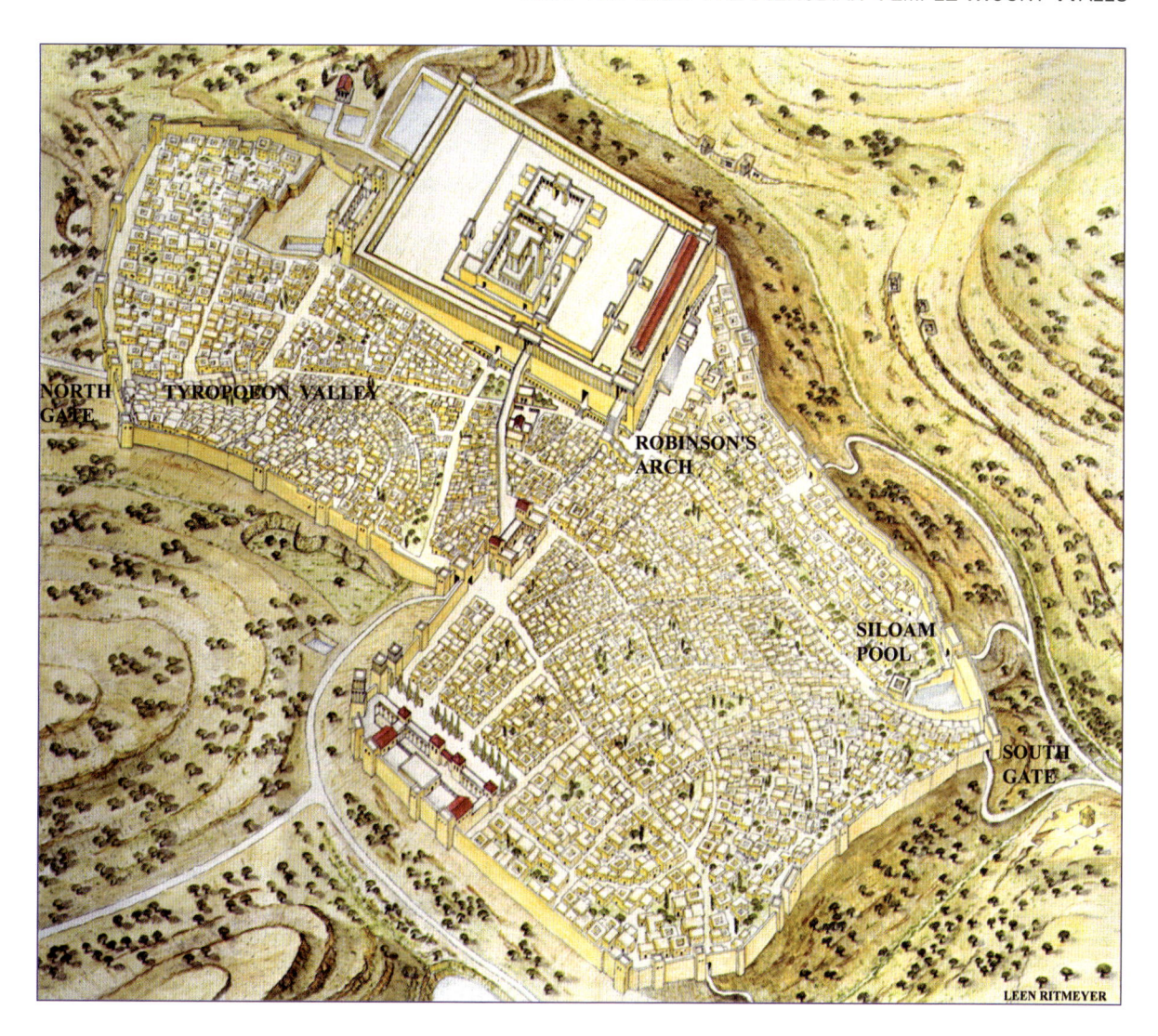

the city from north to south, the street (which we have dubbed the Tyropoeon Street) must have been the main thoroughfare of Jerusalem. It has been suggested that the northern section of this street was the Upper Market mentioned by Josephus in War 5.137.

The Tyropoeon Valley and Drain

During his explorations near the southwest corner of the Temple Mount, Warren discovered an almost 600-foot-long section of a drain which he called "The Old Aqueduct."[33] This drain has been partially excavated during the excavations headed by Mazar.[34]

A system of channels built below the paving stones conveyed the rainwater from the street together with the sewage of adjacent

55

Chapter One: The Herodian Temple Mount Walls

Plan of the drain at the southwest corner, as discovered by Warren.

DRAIN DIMENSIONS

The drain consists of three sections. The northern and southern parts are masonry-built and roofed with flat slabs. These two sections are identical in construction and belong apparently to the same drainage system.

The central section is, for most of its length, cut into the bedrock and passes through some bedrock-cut tombs, apparently from the First Temple period.[35] The roof is made of short sections (from 10 to 15 feet, 3 to 5 m long) of semi-circular vaulting, each section consisting of five to seven voussoirs. The southern part of the Herodian Western Wall was built to the west of the Tyropoeon Valley, and this construction must have cut through the pre-Herodian drain. A new section therefore had to be built to reconnect the two parts of the earlier drain. The drainage system is located at a depth of approximately 18 feet (6 m) below the Herodian street.

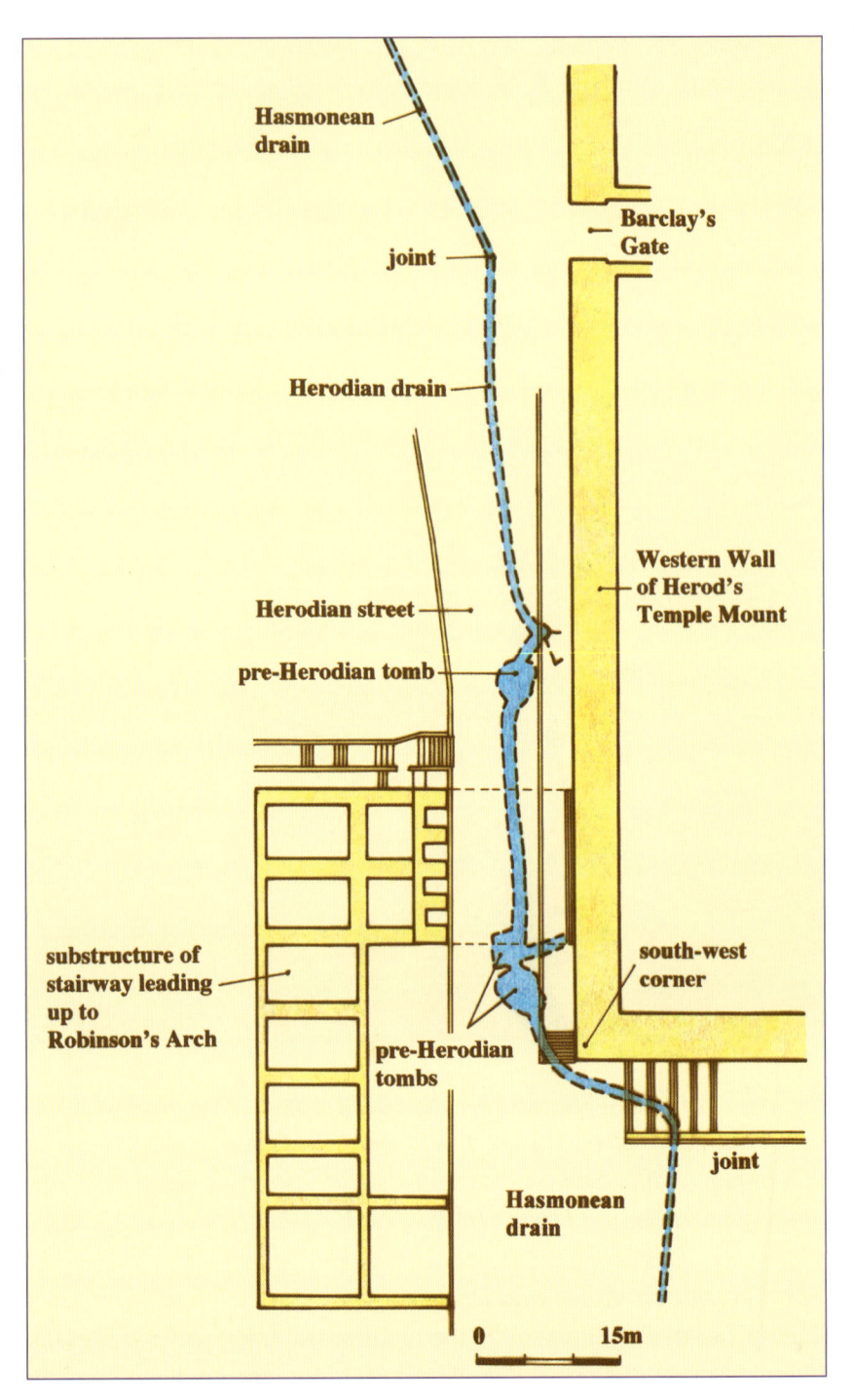

buildings to this drain. At the southwest corner narrow slits between pavers then conducted the rainwater to the drain below. One paving stone near the western curb had five slots cut into it, almost like a modern manhole, to convey water to the drainage system. This stone

CHAPTER ONE: THE HERODIAN TEMPLE MOUNT WALLS

could also have been an inspection cover. Seeing that the drainage system is connected with the Herodian street, it is reasonable to assume that the central vaulted part of the drain also dates to the Herodian period. The fact that the roof of the drain is made of short sections of vaulting would indicate that it was built by different groups of builders who were working simultaneously in order to replace the earlier drain as quickly as possible and also to prevent delays in the construction of the Western Wall. The repair followed a slightly different route as a section of the earlier (Hasmonean) drain had to be removed in order to build the new Herodian southwest corner; then the two sections were linked up again by the Herodian drain, which skirted this corner.

Manhole with five slots cut into it found near the western curb below Robinson's Arch.

It should be noted here, that at a point below Robinson's Arch, two large voussoirs interrupt the vaulting. Warren was of the opinion that these stones had broken the roof of the drain and therefore concluded that Robinson's Arch was a reconstruction of a much earlier arch. However on close inspection it became clear that the vaulting was built up to and slightly over the sides of these voussoirs. These arch-stones are identical in size and in style to the other voussoirs of Robinson's Arch that fell onto the Herodian street during the destruction of the Temple Mount in A.D. 70. It appears, therefore, that the drain was cut in the bedrock at the same time as the construction of Robinson's Arch. The voussoirs which apparently fell down during the construction phase must have been too heavy to move and were therefore incorporated into the roofing of the drain. In any case, they would not have been visible after the drain was covered.

The Trumpeting Stone as it was found lying on the street.

The Trumpeting Stone

One of the most interesting discoveries of the entire excavation was made at the southwest corner. This was a large corner parapet stone which was found lying on its side on the paving stones of the street.

The Mosaic commandment of Deuteronomy 22:8 reads: *"When thou buildest a new house, then thou shalt make a battlement for thy roof, that thou bring not blood upon thine house, if any man fall from thence."* In accordance with this, a battlement or parapet was built along the

Chapter One: The Herodian Temple Mount Walls

Above (left): Reconstruction drawing of a priest blowing the trumpet while standing in the niche that was cut into the Trumpeting stone.

Above (right): The inscription on the Trumpeting Stone, which reads, "to the place of trumpeting to...." The inscription is incomplete, but probably read, "to the place of trumpeting to announce."

Below: During preparatory work for the Jerusalem Archaeological Park, the corner parapet stone has been put right side up and a copy of the inscription has been attached to its original place. The original is on display in the Israel Museum.

edges of roofs to prevent people from falling if they came too close to the edge. Similarly, a parapet was constructed on the roofs of the porticoes all around the Temple Mount. Several stones with rounded tops and sloping sides were found amidst the fallen stones of the walls.

However, this stone was different, not only because it was a corner stone, but because a niche was cut out of the inner slope on its southern side. Above this niche was an inscription in Hebrew, which read *"l'bet hatqia l'hakh . . . "* The first two words *"l'bet hatqia"* mean "to the place of trumpeting," but the last Hebrew word is incomplete. Scholars have suggested completing the inscription with *l'hekhal* (to the Temple), *l'ha-kohn* (for the priest) or *"l'hakhriz,"* (announce). The latter suggestion, which would make the inscription read, *"to the place of trumpeting to announce,"* has the most support.

As it was found lying directly on the street and underneath other fallen Herodian stones, it must originally have been located at the top of the southwest corner whence it was the first stone to have been thrown down. High above this corner stood the Royal Stoa, so that the Trumpeting Stone was located some 138 feet (42 m) above street level. From this elevated position, a trumpet call could be heard all over the city. This would tie in with Josephus' description in *War* 4.582, where he speaks of a huge defensive tower built above a

CHAPTER ONE: THE HERODIAN TEMPLE MOUNT WALLS

…corner opposite the lower town [i.e. the southwest angle]. The last was erected above the roof of the priests' chambers at the point where it was the custom for one of the priests to stand and to give notice, by sound of trumpet, in the afternoon of the approach, and on the following evening of the close, of every seventh day, announcing to the people the respective hours for ceasing work and for resuming their labours.

This would also indicate that the tower at this corner contained chambers used by the priests who were in charge of blowing the trumpets.

Every day during the Temple services trumpets were blown at different places, according to Mishnah *Sukkah* 5.5. There were never less than 21 blasts per day, but not more than 48 altogether. Some of these would have been blown above the southwest corner, as the Mishnah notes: *"On the eve of the Sabbath they used to blow six more blasts, three to cause the people to cease from work and three to mark the break between the sacred and the profane."*

This inscription has been described as "monumental" and "finely executed" by B. Mazar and others; and it certainly appears so. However, traces of fine plaster inside the niche indicate that the inscription was, in fact, plastered over once the stone was securely put in its place. The inscription could therefore have been cut into the stone by the masons as a directive to the builders so that they would know where to place this special stone since hundreds of other

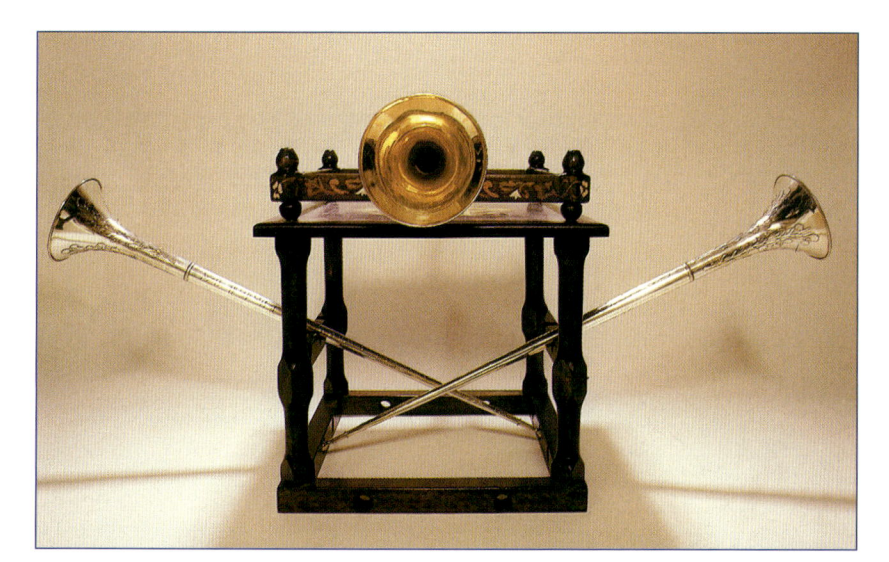

> **WHAT KIND OF TRUMPET?**
> *The drawing on the opposite page gives an idea of how the priest stood with his trumpet in the designated place made especially for him. The trumpet used was probably a silver trumpet such as was mentioned in Numbers 10.2 and depicted on the Arch of Titus in Rome, which portrays the capture of the Temple treasures by the Romans.*

Silver trumpets were used in the Temple to herald the arrival of the Sabbath, New Month, festivals, etc. The instruments shown here were reconstructed according to Talmudic sources and the Arch of Titus in Rome. (photo: The Temple Institute, Jerusalem)

CHAPTER ONE: THE HERODIAN TEMPLE MOUNT WALLS

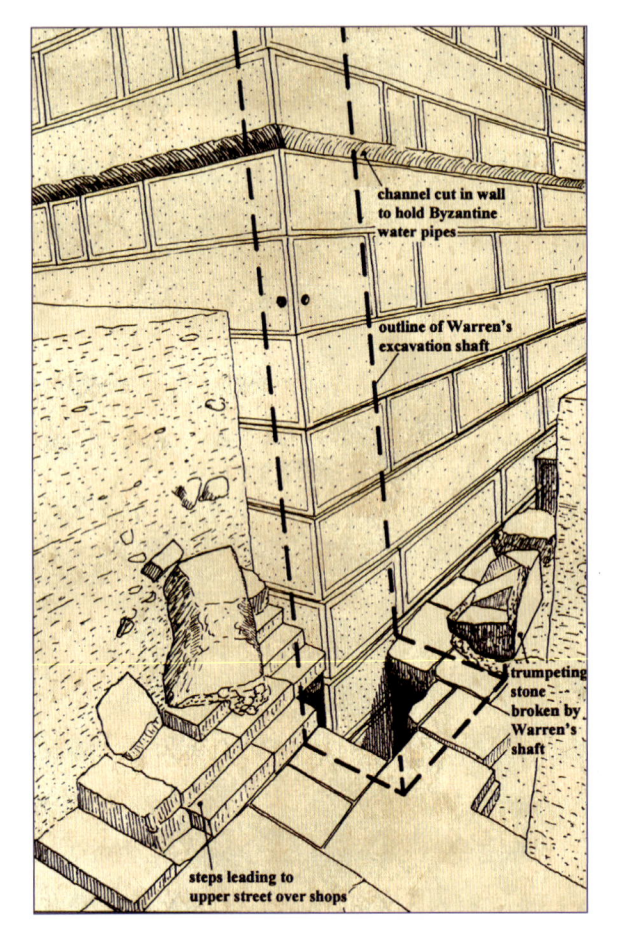

similar stones must have been hewn to complete the parapet around the roofs of the towers and porticoes that surrounded the Temple Mount.

The Trumpeting Stone and Warren's Shaft

This stone, falling from such a great height, would probably have been broken. However, there is a possibility that in this case the stone was not broken to its present extent by the Roman destruction of A.D. 70. In 1867, Charles Warren investigated this area and dug through the fallen debris down to the bedrock right beside the corner. When reconstructing the outline of Warren's shaft, it becomes clear that the stone would have protruded into the dark shaft. This raises the possibility that part of the Trumpeting Stone may have been accidentally smashed by Warren's workmen before they pierced the paving slabs in order to dig down to bedrock.

THE SOUTHERN WALL

All the lower courses of the Southern Wall are Herodian, including the "Great" or "Master" course that runs from the Double Gate to the southeast corner. The Double Gate is one of the

Above: The heavy dashed line indicates the outline of the excavation shaft Warren dug at the southwest corner. The workmen pierced the pavement to be able to dig down to the bedrock. The western side of the Trumpeting Stone protruded into the shaft and was most likely broken off by Warren's workmen who for most of the time worked in the semi-dark.

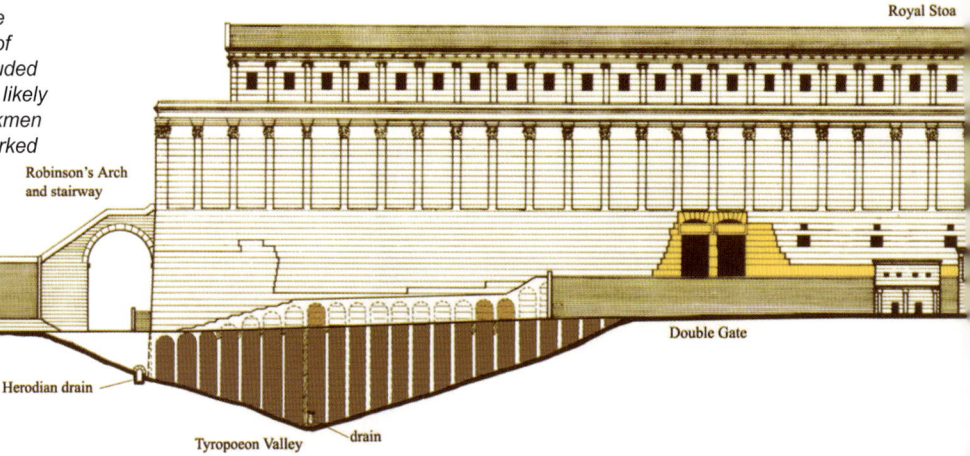

Chapter One: The Herodian Temple Mount Walls

two gates which are mentioned by Josephus (*Ant.* 15.411), *"The fourth front of this (court), facing south, also had gates in the middle."* The other gate is the Triple Gate. The southwest and southeast corners are integral parts of the Western and Eastern Walls, respectively. Above this wall, Herod the Great built the Royal Stoa. Therefore all the elements of the wall and the internal underground structures, the Double and Triple Gate passageways, Solomon's Stables, the ancient vault, the passage below the Single Gate and the southern part of the Eastern Wall will be described below in connection with the construction of the Royal Stoa.

The Southwest Corner

This corner has been preserved to a great height due to the enormous stones used in its construction. These large ashlars were laid so that when viewing one side of the corner their faces are alternately large and small. This construction is called a headers-and-stretchers or quoin construction (from the French *quoin*, i.e. corner).

Two small Herodian stones are visible at the top of the remaining corner construction. As the header and stretcher construction would have continued to the top of this corner, it is likely that these two small

> **WEIGHTY STONES OF THE SOUTHWEST CORNER**
>
> *Some of the largest stones are 39 feet 4 inches (12 m) long, 7 feet 10 inches (2.40 m) wide and 43 inches (1.10 m) high. The average weight of limestone is 2.5 tons per cubic meter. Therefore a stone with a volume of nearly 32 cubic meters weighs 80 tons! Since the Romans were unable to shift these heavy stones, all the corners of the Herodian Temple Mount have been preserved to a great height.*

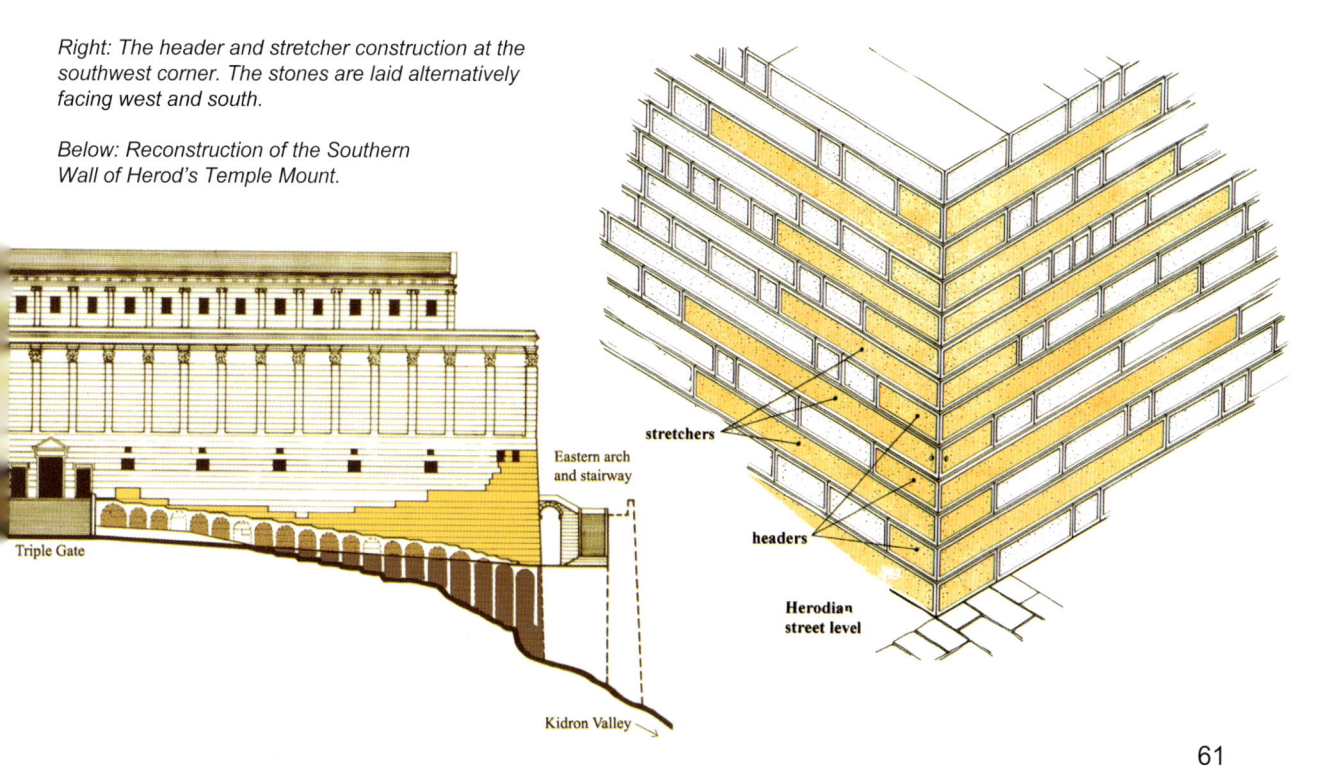

Right: The header and stretcher construction at the southwest corner. The stones are laid alternatively facing west and south.

Below: Reconstruction of the Southern Wall of Herod's Temple Mount.

Chapter One: The Herodian Temple Mount Walls

View of the western part of the Southern Wall. The top of the western part of the Southern Wall is dominated by a Crusader construction that today houses the Islamic Museum and the Mosque of the Women. The darker masonry below this lighter-colored building belongs to the Umayyad repair of the Southern Wall. The Herodian stone courses can be seen near the southwest corner.

Herodian stones were put there at a later date.

Only near the southwest corner has Herodian masonry survived in the upper parts of the wall. The nine highest surviving stone courses at the southern face of this corner continue east for some 75 feet (23 m), after which a vertical break appears.

The reason for the sudden termination of the Herodian stones at this point is usually attributed to the Roman destruction. However, in the Byzantine period, a groove was cut into a Herodian stone course. This groove begins at Wilson's Arch, where the main Herodian aqueduct coming from the Pools of Solomon near Bethlehem was tapped, and goes south to the southwest corner. It rounds the corner where the remains of a drainage pipe was found cemented in this groove. The vertical break mentioned above also cut the Byzantine drain.

The destruction of this part of the Herodian Southern Wall therefore must have occurred at the end of the Byzantine period. In A.D. 614 a Persian invasion of the Holy Land resulted in the destruction of many churches and monasteries, and probably also of the Southern Wall

CHAPTER ONE: THE HERODIAN TEMPLE MOUNT WALLS

The "high-level aqueduct" to Jerusalem in the Bethlehem area. This part was a pipe composed of interlocking stone segments. (NEAEHL)

of the Temple Mount. As the Byzantine drain was found again farther to the east, it is clear that this section had not been destroyed by the Romans. The resulting gap in the wall was repaired during the Umayyad period when the Aqsa Mosque was built over the Southern Wall.

The Street and Plaza along the Southern Wall

At the southwest corner, a stepped street, 21 feet (6.40 m) wide, was found rising in an easterly direction toward the Double Gate.[36] Two flights of three steps have been preserved at a total distance of 37 feet (11.20 m) from the corner. Eventually this street would have risen to the level of the remaining paving slabs in front of the Double Gate. The excavated remains along this stretch of the Southern Wall indicate that here as well a series of shops was built against the Temple walls and that the stepped street ran over its roof.

The imprint of burnt arches in the wall, such as those first identified by the author to the east of the Triple Gate (see below, pp. 99–101), made a reconstruction of this stepped street possible.

To the south of this narrow street described above, the remains of a wider street or plaza were found at approximately the same level as the street near the southwest corner. A line of curbstones is built along the northern edge of the paving stones where they are laid against the wall that supports the narrow street. The excavated paving slabs indicate that the plaza had a minimum width of 30 feet (9 m). No curbstone was found to the south of these stones.

At a distance of 36 feet (11 m) from the northern curbstones, the foundations of a massive 9-foot- (3-m) wide wall were found. A strong

> **RECONSTRUCTING FROM THE EVIDENCE OF BURN MARKS**
>
> *In this area, the first burnt arch was found at 98 feet (30 m) from the southwest corner. The height of the arch indicated by its burnt imprint indicated that the stepped street continued to rise to the east in the same pattern of three steps and landings in between, up to the point where the imprint was found. At 272 feet (83 m) from the corner, the imprint of two additional burnt arches could be identified. The difference in height between these burnt arches and the single one is only 2 feet (60 cm). This shows that the street between the two sets of imprints rose only slightly to allow for many shops to be built between the corner and the stairway leading up to the Double Gate.*
>
> *To complete the reconstruction of this stepped street, a steeply sloping flight of steps had to be inserted after the last burnt imprint to reach the level of the street at the top of the monumental stairway which led up to the Double Gate. No burnt imprints were found west of the first one and all the wall ashlars were in perfect condition. This indicates that no shops were built under the first flight of steps.*

63

Chapter One: The Herodian Temple Mount Walls

Right: Section through the Southern Wall plaza and middle supporting wall.

Below: Artist's impression of the pilgrimage to Jerusalem. (The Temple Institute, Jerusalem)

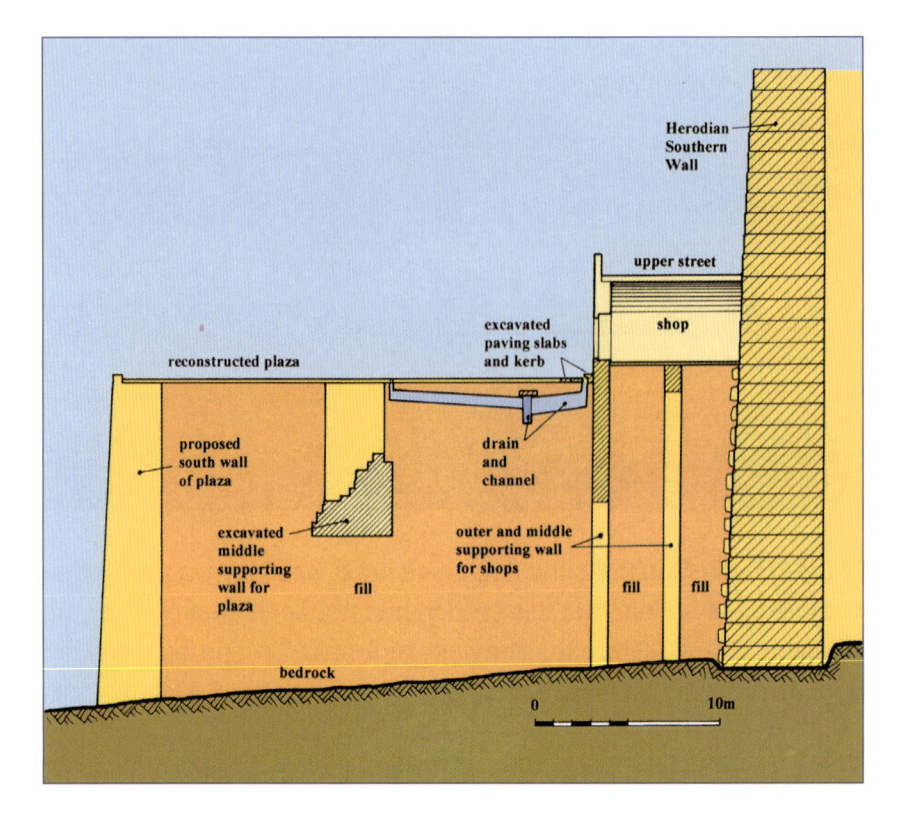

Chapter One: The Herodian Temple Mount Walls

foundation wall would have been necessary to support this street, as the deepest point of the Tyropoeon Valley runs some 55 feet (17 m) below.

As this pavement leads to the plaza in front of the huge stairway in front of the Double Gate and had to accommodate many pilgrims, B. Mazar proposed that this massive wall may have served as the middle underground supporting wall. If another stretch of 30 feet (9 m) existed at the other side of the 9 feet (3 m) supporting wall, then the total width of that plaza would have been approx. 81 feet (25 m). We will soon see that an even wider plaza existed to the south of the Double Gate and a wider approach would have been more in style with the grand architectural design for this area, enabling thousands of pilgrims to approach the Temple from the south.

The Double Gate and Stairway

A wide flight of steps was excavated in front of the Double Gate. The thirty steps, partly cut into the rock and partly built of large stones, were laid alternately as steps and landings, thus conforming to the slope of the mountain and assuring a reverent ascent. The total width

Below: The Double Gate as seen by the explorer Tipping in 1846.

Bottom: View of the excavated and restored remains of the steps leading up to the Double Gate.

Chapter One: The Herodian Temple Mount Walls

> **EVIDENCE OF A SPACIOUS PLAZA**
>
> *It is evident from the point of view of design and town-planning that a wide plaza must have existed south of the stepped approach to the Double Gate. At the foot of the steps a strip of approximately 16 feet (5 m) wide smooth bedrock has been found, which was part of the plaza. Only five original paving slabs, totaling some 172 feet square (16 m²), have withstood the ravages of time and the needs of post-Herodian builders for construction material. At a distance of 100 feet (30 m) from the bottom of the steps, a long foundation wall was found in the bedrock remains of some Hasmonean rooms. These rooms had been filled in with layers of stone and thus could not have continued to be used as such. This wall and the systematically layered stone fill would have formed an adequate foundation for the plaza, giving it the required dimensions, enabling it to be compared to similar plazas in the ancient world, such as those in Assos, Priene and Athens. Because of the topography, which falls away steeply in all directions but north, this 100-foot- (30-m) wide plaza probably extended only to the area opposite the steps. The location of a drainage channel and other preserved bedrock remains also indicate that the eastern continuation of the plaza would have been narrower.*

of the excavated stairway is 105 feet (32 m), which represents only half the original width based on a symmetrical layout of these steps in relation to the longitudinal axis of the Double Gate. In Roman architecture, a staircase would never have been built on only one side of a gate, unless the topography made a symmetrical layout impossible. The total width would therefore have been 210 feet (64 m). The missing steps have been restored on site to give the visitor a better understanding of the "feel" one would have had in the past of ascending up to this important Temple gate.

On top of the steps, a 21-foot (6.40-m) wide street had to be crossed in order to enter the gate. Enormous paving stones were used to pave the street. The largest surviving paving stone is 16.7 feet (5.10 m) long and 6.7 feet (2.05 m) wide and has a surface of approximately 112 square feet (10.45 sq. m). This paving stone has even one step of the stairway cut out of it, thus the stone itself is therefore actually 7.9 feet (2.40 m) wide. It rests on a double vault that was used as a water reservoir. This narrow street is the continuation of the stepped street found near the southwest corner and runs the entire length of the Southern Wall.

Reconstruction plan of the southern part of the Herodian Temple Mount and the adjacent street complex.

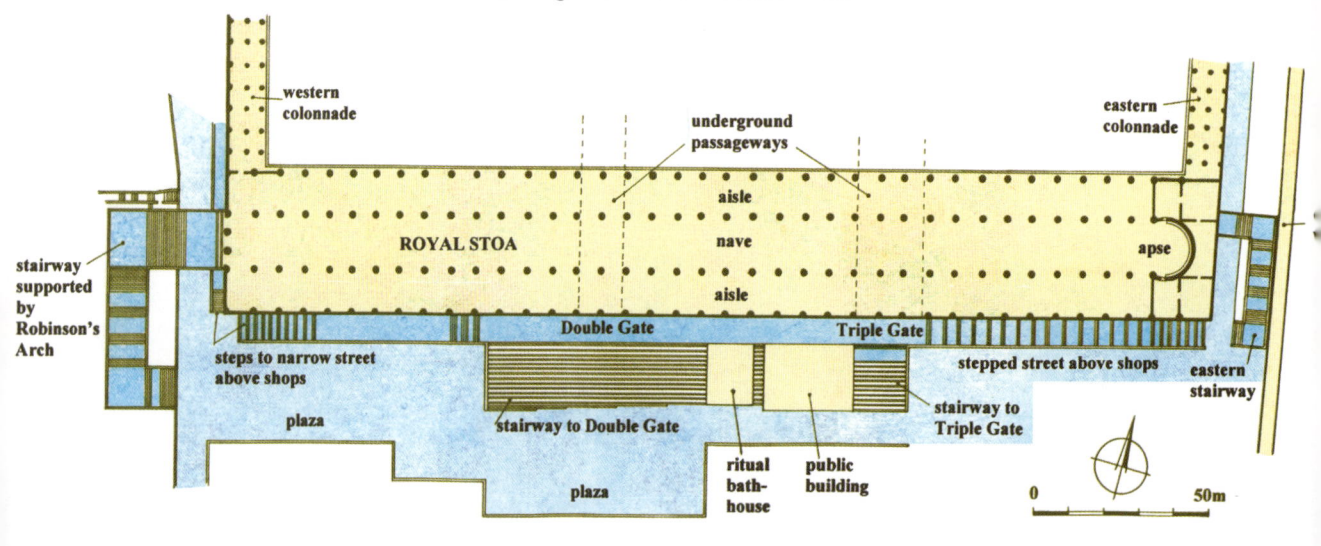

CHAPTER ONE: THE HERODIAN TEMPLE MOUNT WALLS

The Double Gate

The Double Gate[37] has well-preserved Herodian features. A close-up of the exposed part of the gate reveals a Herodian stone course at the bottom of the wall and the remains of a single block above it. The smaller stones above these original gate jambs appear to be an external repair to the damaged corner. This is also clear from the fact that the bottom of the first smaller stone does not sit on top of the Herodian stone below, but overhangs it a little.

> **DOUBLE GATE STATS**
>
> *The Double Gate with its underground twin passageway is located 331 feet (101 m) east of the southwest corner. The total exterior width of the gate is 39 feet (11.90 m), which is made up of two gates each 16 feet 5 inches (5 m) wide, divided by a 6 feet 3 inches (1.90 m) wide central pier. The two gates have been completely preserved in their Herodian form with their lintels and relieving arches virtually intact, although the eastern jamb has been partly patched up with Umayyad stones. The half of this gate opening which is visible on the outside has been blocked off with smaller stones in the Crusader period. The rest of the eastern gate and the western gate opening are not visible from the outside, being concealed by a Crusader tower (the so-called Zawiyya Khanthaniyya) which is built against the Southern Wall and has an internal zigzag passageway.*

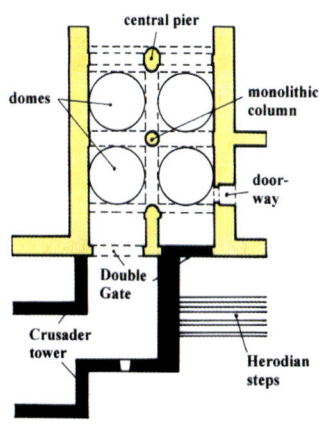

Above: Plan of the Double Gate passageway and the adjacent Crusader tower.

Left: View of the Double Gate from the outside.

67

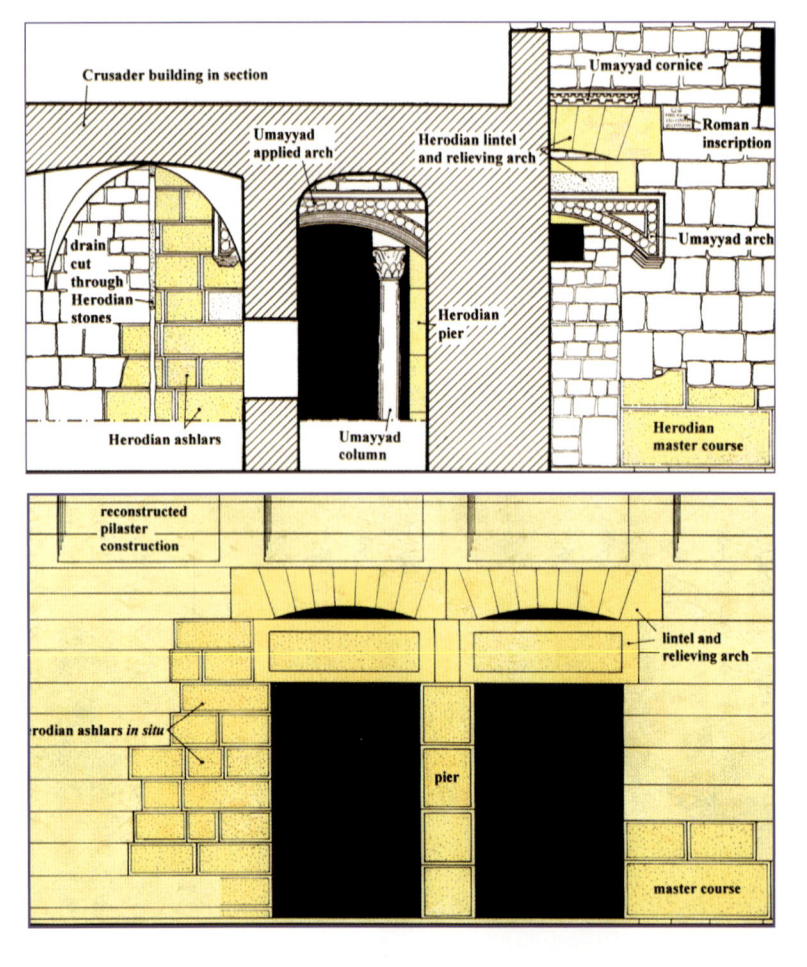

Chapter One: The Herodian Temple Mount Walls

Below: Close-up view of the Double Gate lintel.

Higher up, a decorative arch can be seen that was attached to the exterior and is situated in front of the lintel. Together with a decorative cornice, located a few feet above, these additions belong to the Umayyad period when the Double Gate passageway was used again to enter the Temple Mount. The arch is an applied one, that is, a hole was cut in the wall to insert the bottom stone, on which all the other arch stones rest.

Just behind the arch, the original Herodian lintel stone, which survived the Roman destruction, is visible. A relieving arch, which also appears to be Herodian, can be seen above the lintel. The top of this relieving arch is level with the Temple courts. On the inside, this large Herodian lintel rests on the central entrance pier and the Herodian side walls of the passageway. Both lintels are supported on the inside by small columns that were too short for this purpose and therefore smaller blocks have been laid on the Corinthian capitals to reach the bottom of the lintels. According to Burgoyne,[38] these post-Herodian elements stem from a repair of the gate prior to the building of the Aqsa Mosque in A.D. 691–692.

The western gate is still open and accessible but only from within the passageway, and can be seen inside the tower. The actual western jamb is not visible because of the later construction built against it. Just to the left, however, a stretch of Herodian masonry has been preserved, so it is fair to assume that the west corner of the gate still exists behind this later masonry.

Although only a small part of the façade of the pier is visible from the outside because of the Crusader construction, the rest of the pier can be seen inside the passageway.

Chapter One: The Herodian Temple Mount Walls

> **FEATURES OF THE PIER**
>
> *The pier of the Double Gate is built up of four large stones that are 16 feet 5 inches (5 m) long. The jambs of the gate openings are 3 feet 3 inches (1 m) wide and project 10 inches (25 cm) from the walls of the passageway. The central pier has a 9-foot- (2.75-m) long recess in which half of a double door could be folded away. The Double Gate, therefore, could be closed by two sets of double doors.*
>
> *The northern part of the pier is semi-circular. This round pilaster was topped by a capital that can no longer be seen because of a concrete construction that was built in the passageway to support the El Aksa mosque in the wake of the 1927 earthquake. A painting made in the 19th century shows a capital above the pier stones, but without enough detail to determine its style.*

Opposite page (above): Elevation of the exterior Herodian remains of the Double Gate inside the Crusader building and a reconstruction of the Double Gate. The extant Herodian remains are colored in.

Below: The vaults inside the western (top) and eastern (bottom) gateways of the Double Gate, viewed from north.

Behind the inner faces of the lintels, shallow vaults spring from the central pier to the side walls. The western vault is made up of five large courses (right, above), while the eastern vault appears to have been repaired at a later date, as only parts of the original springers are preserved and the middle section is made up of smaller stone courses (right, below).

The Double Gate Passageway

In 1976 I was able to investigate the area beyond this doorway. At the time, the area was partially excavated with a view to strengthening the foundations of the El Aqsa mosque. Behind the doorway, a section of the other side of the eastern wall of the passageway was uncovered that proved to be 7.2 feet (2.19 m) thick and 27.7 feet (8.45 m) long. At the southern end of the excavated area, the back of the Southern Temple Mount Wall could be seen and turned out to be 7.4 feet (2.25 m) thick.

On the opposite northern side of this area, at 10 feet 8 inches (3.25 m) from the doorway, a corner was formed between the passageway and a wall which went east at this point. The thickness of this wall could not be established, but its location on the plan showed that it was probably the remains of the foundation wall, or *stylobate,* for the southernmost row of free-standing columns of the Royal Stoa.

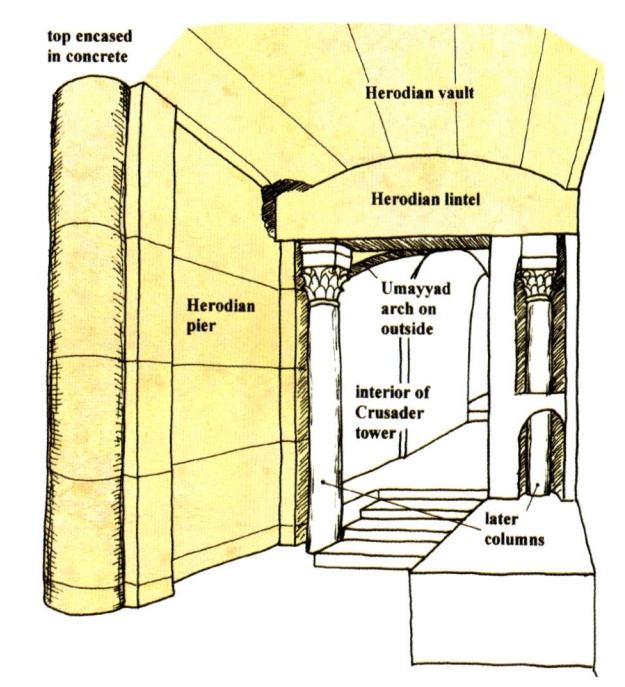

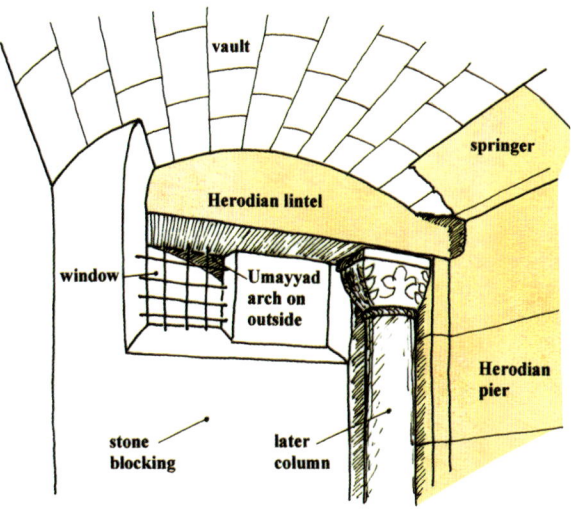

Chapter One: The Herodian Temple Mount Walls

Right (above): Plan of the Double Gate passageway and domes.

Right (below): View of the excavations to the east of the Double Gate passageway.

> **INSIDE THE DOUBLE GATE PASSAGEWAY**
>
> The first 66-foot (20-m) section of the southern part of the double passageway is preserved in its entirety and dates to the Herodian period, including the domes in the ceiling. The preserved part of this passageway is divided into four square bays (there were apparently six originally) that are separated from each other by four shallow arches that spring from a monolithic column. The southern sides of the two southernmost bays are formed by the shallow vaults emerging from the central entrance pier, while the preserved northern sides of the northernmost bays are formed by shallow arches that spring from the side walls and rest on the southern round pilaster of the large central pier. A vault of later construction continues to the north. This domed construction is undoubtedly connected with the colonnades of the Royal Stoa above.
>
> At 17 feet (5.25 m) from the Southern Wall there is a doorway in the eastern wall of the twin passageway that has a lintel and relieving arch. The door is 5 feet (1.52 m) wide and about 10 feet (3 m) high; its jambs are 18.5 inches (47 cm) wide and project about 6 inches (15 cm) from the inner wall, indicating that it could be closed. This doorway, which looked like a niche, was known as "Elijah's Standing Place."

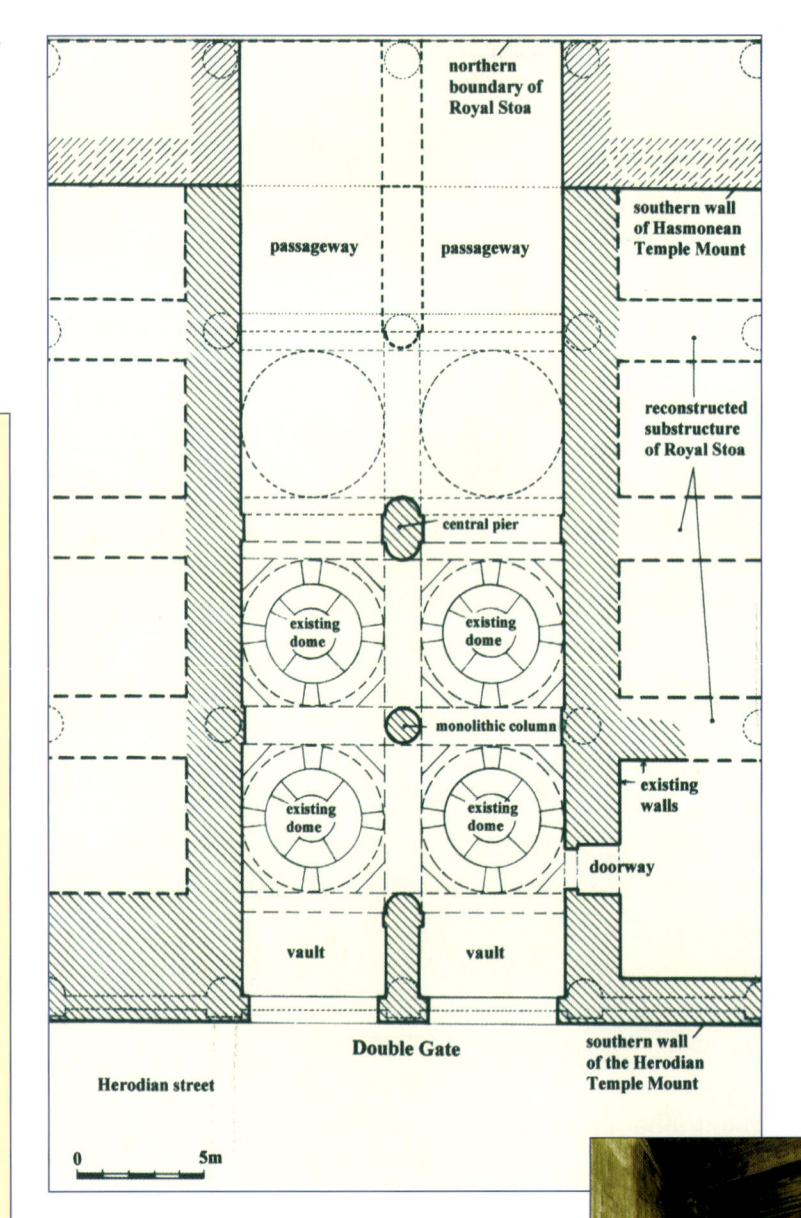

The substructure of the Royal Stoa between the Double and Triple Gates was thus formed by long walls, running from east to west, creating a solid foundation for the mighty columns of the stoa above. The preserved remains of this wall are not sufficient to determine if these walls had openings to connect the spaces in between these support walls.

CHAPTER ONE: THE HERODIAN TEMPLE MOUNT WALLS

The Dome Construction

The domes inside the Double Gate passageway are unique in their construction, as they are the earliest examples of shallow spherical domes with continuous spherical triangular pendentives. The structure of all four domes is identical.

As has already been noted by Spencer Corbett,[39] this construction technique differs from a later development in the construction of pendentive domes in which all the courses of the dome consist of concentric rings of stone that continue into the pendentives. In these later type of pendentives, all the stone courses are therefore part of the dome structure, while in the earlier examples such as the dome in the Western Thermae at Gerasa and the domed Mausoleum in Sebaste-Samaria (both of which date to the second century A.D.), the pendentives are independent architectural constructions.

On the basis of this construction, Corbett raised the possibility that the domes of the Double Gate may be Herodian. He was under the impression that the decorations were made of plaster, a sixth-century application that had been added to the domes later on.

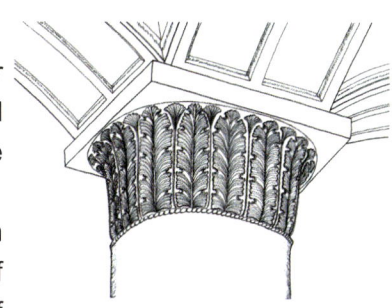

Above: Drawing of monolithic column in the Double Gate passageway and the four domes springing from its capital.

Below (left): Elevation of the eastern wall of the Double Gate passageway with a doorway, known as "Elijah's Standing Place"

Below (right):. Doorway in the eastern wall of the Double Gate passageway viewed from the east.

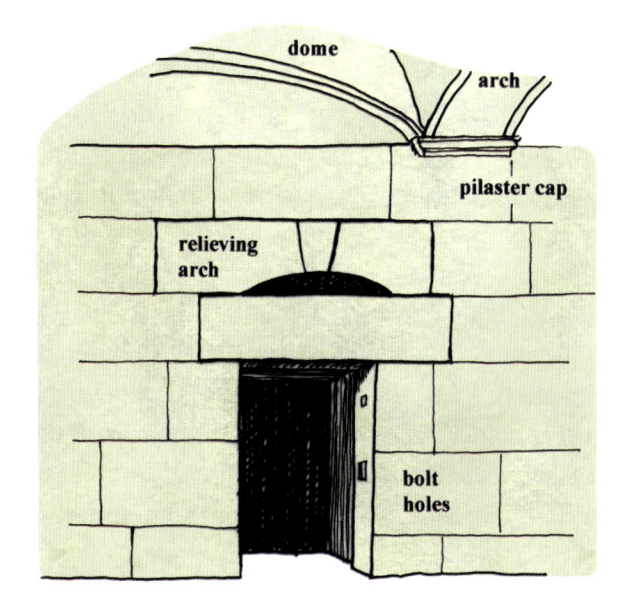

I was able to verify, however, that, apart from a small plaster repair, the decorations of the domes are in fact all carved in stone. Both the carving technique and the style of decoration proved to be typically Herodian and could be compared with many other Herodian fragments

Chapter One: The Herodian Temple Mount Walls

Domed roof of a burial chamber in the Roman Mausoleum at Sebaste (Samaria), late 2nd to early 3rd centuries A.D. (NEAEHL)

THE PENDENTIVES
The pendentive is made up of two stones, a small triangular stone at the base, and a large one placed above it (see plan, p. 70, and illustration on opposite page, left]. The two adjoining surfaces of these two pendentive stones are set in a plane surface that radiates from the center of the dome, while the top surface of the upper pendentive is curved. These four upper pendentive stones are locked together by four smaller wedge-shaped keystones. A circular base is thus created for the dome proper, consisting of six stones. The first and only course consists of five stones, one of which is a small keystone, while a large circular keystone completes the dome structure. Altogether 18 stones are used to build each dome. The only exception is the northeastern dome which has 21 stones. Whereas the circular course of dome stones on the other three domes consists of five stones, one of which is a small keystone, here four small keystones separate the four larger stones.

found in a corresponding stratigraphical context. *On the basis of these facts, it can now be stated with certainty that both the domes of the Double Gate and their decorations date from the Herodian period; and that they are therefore the first examples of this unique type of dome construction.*

The pier between the two openings of the Double Gate is 16 feet 5 inches (5 m) long, while the distance between this pier and the monolithic column is 18 feet 6 inches (5.64 m). The diameter of this column is 4 feet 9 inches (1.46 m). The distance between the monolithic column and the northernmost surviving Herodian pier (Central pier in plan, p. 70), which has two engaged columns, is 18 feet 4 inches (5.60 m).

The northernmost pair of shallow arches that support the northernmost domes spring from the side wall in front of a pilaster cap and rest on the southern engaged column of this, almost 8-foot- (2.40 m) long, northern pier. The center of this pier is therefore located at 5 + 5.64 + 1.46 + 5.60 + 1.20 m=18.90 meters, or 62 feet from the external face of the Southern Wall. This axis virtually coincides with the center of Robinson's Arch. *The axis going through the central pier of the Double Gate passageway was therefore the true axis of the Royal Stoa.*

The spacing of the columns in the Double Gate passageway is directly connected with that of the columns of the Royal Stoa, which was built above the Southern Wall. As will be discussed below, the center of the northern pier coincides with the longitudinal axis of the Stoa. The total width of the Royal Stoa would therefore be double the distance between the Southern Wall and the center of the northern pier, that is, 124 feet (37.80 m).

The Decoration of the Domes

Although all four domes are Herodian in construction, only the two western ones are fully decorated. The designs are cut an inch deep into the stones of the dome. Floral and geometric designs are interwoven in intricate patterns.

CHAPTER ONE: THE HERODIAN TEMPLE MOUNT WALLS

The southwest dome has a vine with leaves and grape bunches twined among eight decorated squares (above, left). Because of the curvature of the dome, these squares may appear to be diamond shaped; but in reality they are true squares, as I was able to verify in 1974 when the stones of the domes could be touched and measured from a scaffolding which was erected at that time for repair purposes. The eight squares are arranged in an eight-pointed star[40] and have four different designs, with one square of the same design located opposite its twin.

The squares are decorated with geometric designs and some have rosettes in between the raised bands. The vine and squares are bordered by two wreaths. The inner one enclosed a central design, which was difficult to discern because of the poor state of preservation of the circular keystone. The outer wreath has an inner decoration of interlocking waves, a central design of olive leaves designed in a triple pattern separated by four rosettes, and an outer band of rope molding. Scallops were used to decorate the four corners.

The main decorative feature of the northwest dome is a huge circular multi-petalled scallop arranged around a central design (above, right). In the center of the dome is a singular five-branched rosette surrounded by four layers of twelve-rayed stars with rosettes in the third layer. A wreath of rosettes surrounds the scallop. In the four corners there are sets of three acanthus leaves out of which vines

Above (left): Drawing of the southwest dome in the underground passage of the Double Gate. The black lines indicate the individual stones. (based on drawing by Nili Cohen and Martha Ritmeyer)

Above (right): Drawing of the decoration of the northwest dome. (drawing: Nathaniel Ritmeyer)

Below: View of the interior of the Double Gate. (photo: Garo Nalbandian)

Chapter One: The Herodian Temple Mount Walls

appear with leaves and grape bunches. This vine surrounds the whole of the scallop design.

Two decorated pendentive stones in opposite corners of the northeast dome survived. These corners were decorated with acanthus and lilies. A large wreath of inter-weaving vines in between two egg-and-dart motives surrounds a central design which, apart from a wave pattern, has not survived the passage of time. The remainder of the dome stones are very smooth, but not decorated. The southeast dome has no decoration whatever. It appears that the decorated domes fell down during the original construction or as a result of an earthquake and were built again during the same Herodian period but were left undecorated.

> **COULD THIS BE THE BEAUTIFUL GATE?**
>
> *Despite the imperfection of the undecorated domes, it must have been an impressive experience for pilgrims to go up to the Temple Mount through this beautifully decorated underground passageway (above). For this reason some researchers have proposed that this was the Beautiful Gate, mentioned in Acts 3, where the lame man was healed by the Apostles Peter and John.*

The lame man being healed by the Apostles Peter and John, 19th century engraving.

CHAPTER ONE: THE HERODIAN TEMPLE MOUNT WALLS

In Between the Double and Triple Gates

As can be seen above, the excavations in this area have proved that the bedrock between the Double and Triple Gates is practically level, although some deep natural depressions had to be covered over with vaults to support the street. We have already noted that the largest paving stone in front of the Double Gate is supported by a double vault that was used as a water cistern. It would appear that Warren measured the bottom of this vault and thought that he had found the top of the bedrock in this area. His topography of the bedrock in this area is therefore incorrect.[41]

In between the two southern gates, the "Great" or "Master" course is visible directly above the Herodian street which connected these gates. This course is the only one surviving in this area, a fact which

Opposite page (above): Reconstructed interior view of the underground passageway of the Double Gate..

Below: Reconstruction drawing of the buildings in between the Double and Triple Gates.

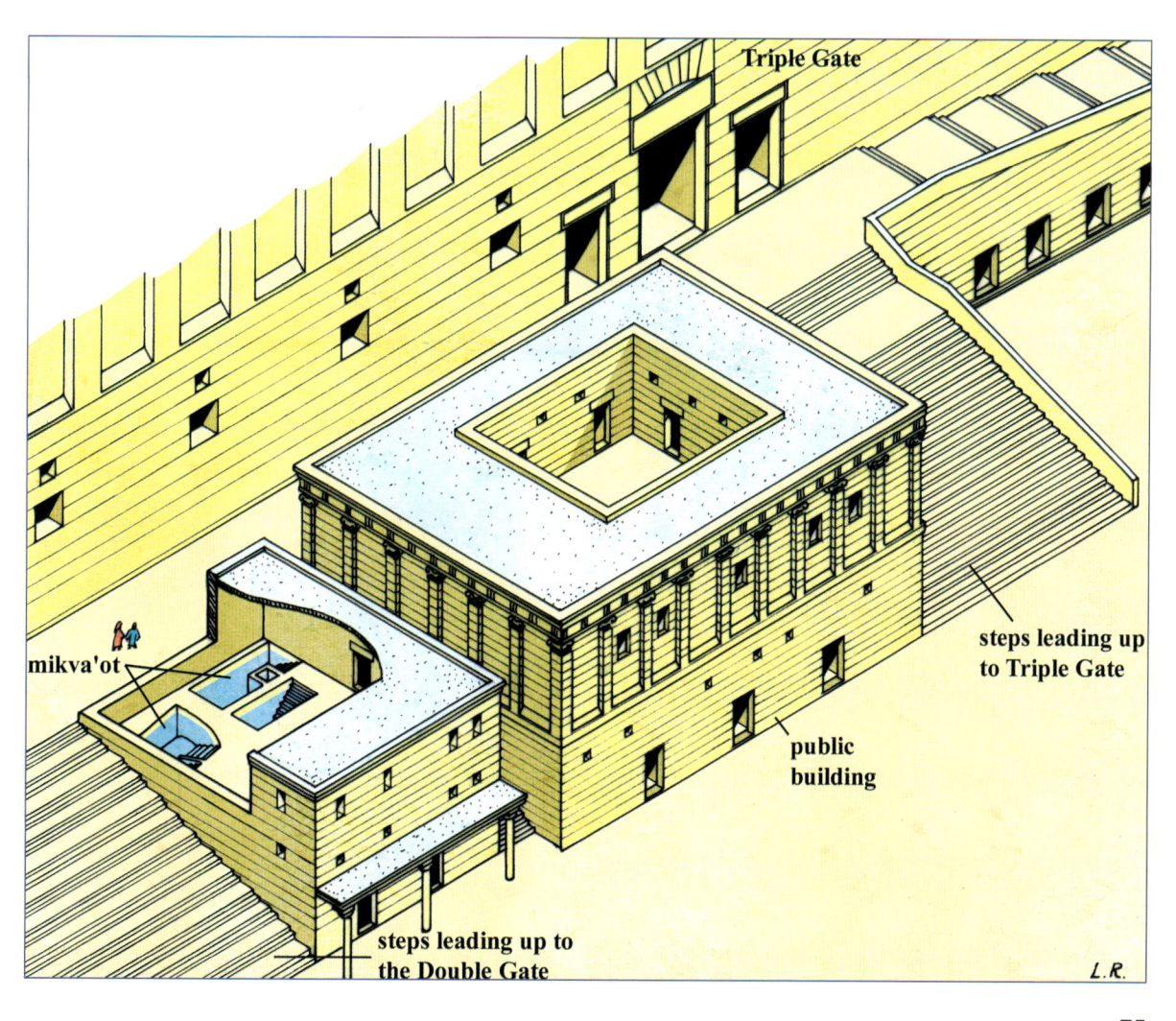

Chapter One: The Herodian Temple Mount Walls

Reconstruction drawing of the Council Chamber, generally identified with the Chamber of Hewn Stone mentioned in the Mishnah.

A Herodian mikveh found next to the Double Gate stairway.

is probably due to the large size of the stones, each of which is at least 6 feet (1.82–1.94 m) high. This course continues in an easterly direction, goes around the southeast corner and terminates 25 feet (7.60 m) to the north of this corner.

The remains of two buildings have been found in between the staircases leading up to the Double and Triple Gates. Several *mikva'ot* (ritual baths) were found cut into the bedrock there. The building on the east was probably a public building. The many rooms that were found inside this building were, of course, located at basement level. The upper rooms which would have formed the main part of the building would have been arranged around a central courtyard. The function of this large building, which is located in a prominent location between the Double and Triple Gates, is unknown. It was suggested that it may have been one of the three council houses that existed during that time according to Mishnah *Sanhedrin* 11.2: *"Three courts were there: one used to sit at the gate of the Temple Mount, one used to sit at the gate of the Temple Court, and one used to sit in the Chamber of Hewn Stone,"* with the last the most important of the three. However, these courts were situated on the Temple Mount itself and not on the outside.

This complex, comprising a ritual and a public building, had before been

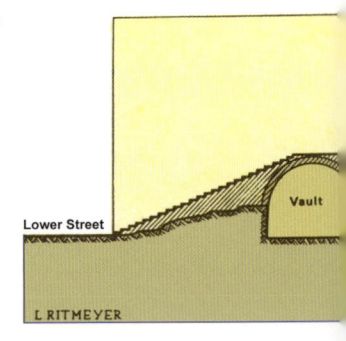

Chapter One: The Herodian Temple Mount Walls

reconstructed as a single building. However, with the discovery of a drainage channel which ran south through the complex, a consistent feature found under every Herodian street, I concluded that a stepped street must have separated the western from the eastern half of the complex. This drain is quite sizeable and was therefore most likely used to drain the *mikva'ot* when necessary.

The Triple Gate and Stairway

The Triple Gate, located 215 feet (65.60 m) to the east of the Double Gate, is 51 feet (15.50 m) wide and consists of three 13-foot- (4 m) wide openings that are separated by two 6-foot- (1.80 m) wide piers. The lowest stone of the western gate jamb is part of the Great Course and has a classical molding. This ashlar is the only *in situ* remains of the Herodian gate that undoubtedly stood on this spot. The length

Section through stairway of the Triple Gate, the underground passageway and the Royal Stoa above the Southern Wall.

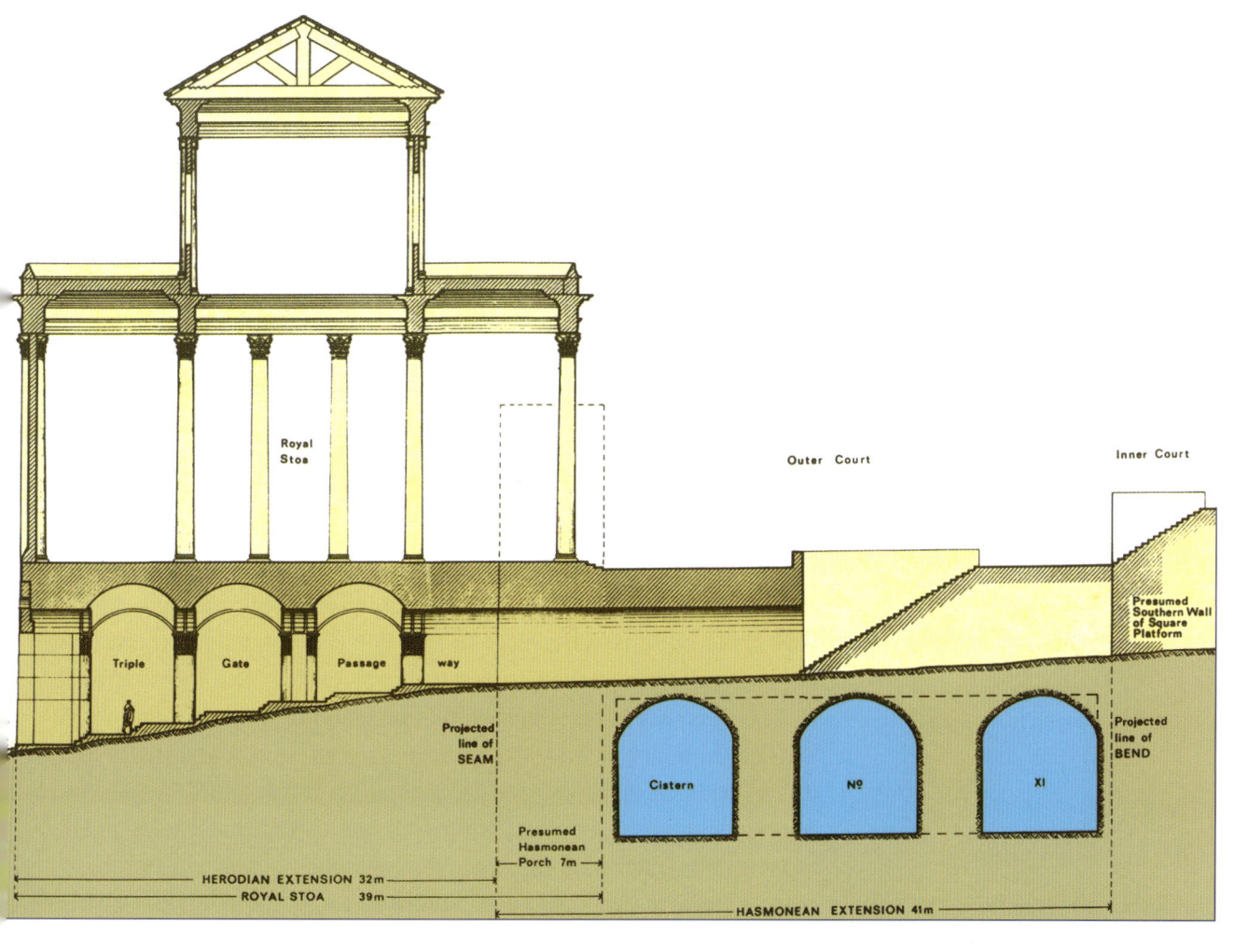

Chapter One: The Herodian Temple Mount Walls

View of the Triple Gate.

of the ashlar is 4 feet (1.22 m), of which 30 inches (76.5 cm) on the left have been carved as a regular Herodian Temple Mount wall stone and the remaining 18 inch (45.5 cm) section on the right has been decorated with a classical gate profile. The molding once went around the gate opening and consisted of a *cyma recta* profile flanked on either side by two flat bands. The outer band is a 3 inch (8 cm) wide separation band to distinguish between the ashlar and the molding, which in effect is only 15 inches (37.5 cm) wide.[42] The present-day gate with its three semi-circular arches was probably built in the Umayyad period and blocked up by the Crusaders when

CHAPTER ONE: THE HERODIAN TEMPLE MOUNT WALLS

they turned this part of the Temple Mount wall into a city wall. Its present width is greater than that of the Double Gate and may reflect, as we shall see, that of the original Herodian gate.

The factor which determines the original width of this gate lies in the remains of a vault which is situated some 23 feet (7 m) south of the gate's façade. A staircase ran up from the lower plaza area over this vault to the higher gate. This is attested by the fact that several steps have been found in the area, among which was one large stone with three steps carved out of it. The rock-cut vault is divided into two chambers by a 2 foot 4 inch (70 cm) wide wall that has a doorway linking the two rooms. The western chamber is 23 feet 8 inches (7.20 m) wide and is preserved intact, its west side lining up with the western jamb of the Herodian gate. Although the eastern side of the chamber on the east is broken, if we assume a symmetrical layout for this vault, this room presumably had the same width as the western chamber. This would make the original vault 50 feet (15.10 m) wide, identical to the width of the gates that once stood over the arches that today are named after Robinson and Wilson.

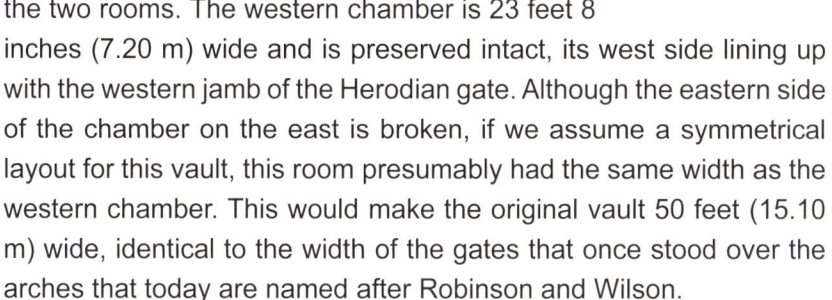

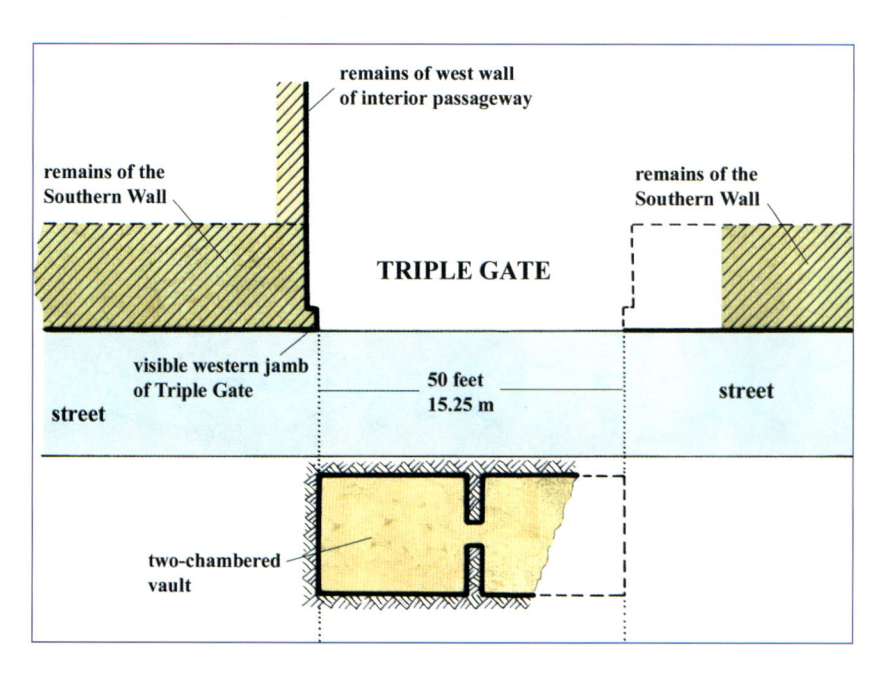

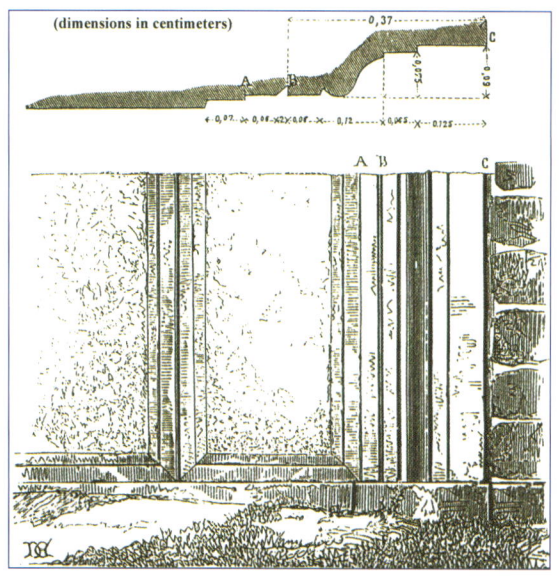

Top: Elevation and section of molding of west doorjamb of the original Triple Gate (after De Vogüé, with corrections).

Above: View of the west doorjamb of the Triple Gate.

Left: Plan of the Triple Gate showing the remains of the Southern Wall, the west wall of the interior passageway and the two-chambered vault.

Chapter One: The Herodian Temple Mount Walls

We have now established the width of the gate and this knowledge helps us to determine its original form. Classical gates, with few exceptions, were either single or triple. There are two surviving single gates, Barclay's and Warren's, which have respective widths of 18 feet 4 inches (5.60 m) and 15 feet (4.60 m). The Double Gate is 39 feet (11.90 m) wide. *The Herodian gate that stood at the site of the present-day Triple Gate was wider and therefore only could have been a triple gate.*

The Triple Gate and Aceldama

The beautiful molding which can be seen on the *in situ* western jamb of the Triple Gate is absent from any of the other surviving gates. Most of the gates could be used by secular visitors to the Temple Mount. Thus, the more elaborate decoration of the Triple Gate may have something to do with its special function.

This is indicated by the interesting parallel of a series of tombs dating from the same period and located in the Hinnom Valley. According to Josephus *(War* 5.506), the high priestly family of Annas (Ananias) built a tomb complex which was located at the mouth of the Hinnom Valley near the Siloam Pool. The context of the passage

Sketch of the walled compound of the Monastery of St. Onuphrius in the Hinnom Valley. Two first-century tombs, one called the "Refuge of the Apostles" and the other with a notable two-pillared porch (known as distyle in antis), located within the monastery grounds, are part of a lavishly decorated tomb complex. The most outstanding tomb—that of Annas the High Priest—lies outside the walls of the monastery.

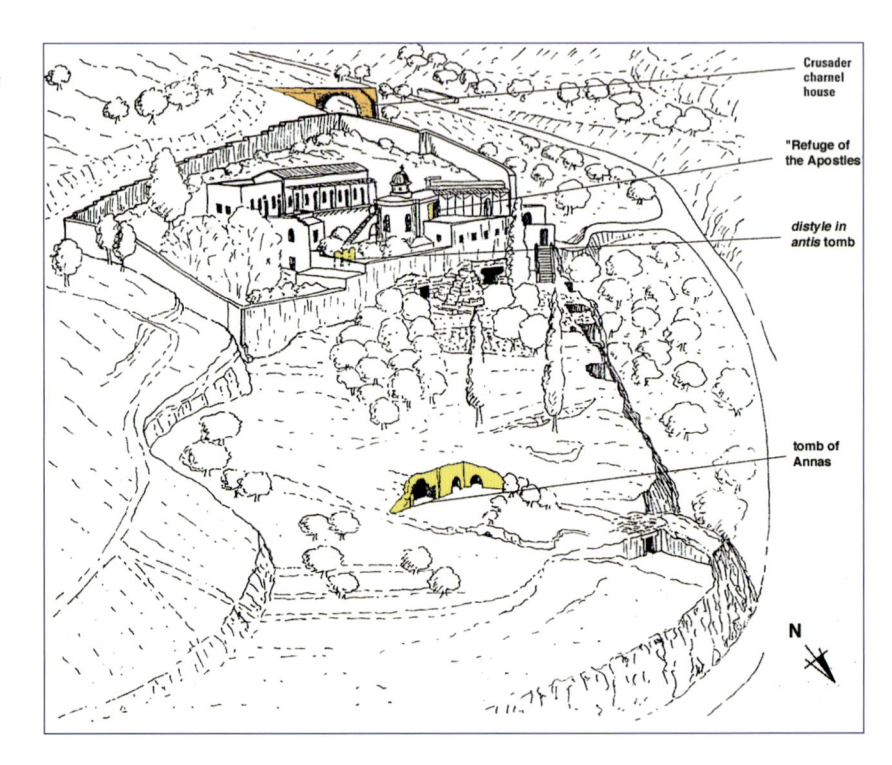

CHAPTER ONE: THE HERODIAN TEMPLE MOUNT WALLS

The Hinnom Valley today, looking southeast. In center, the Greek Orthodox Monastery of St. Onuphrius.

is a description of the circumvallation wall (siege dike) that the Romans built around Jerusalem to isolate the Jewish defenders of the city. From the Assyrian camp in the northwest of the city, the wall was directed to the Mount of Olives and from there it went to the hill opposite the Pool of Siloam. From there, says Josephus, *"inclining westwards, the line descended into the Valley of the Fountain [Siloam], beyond which it ascended over against the tomb of Ananus the high priest."* The investigations by MacAlister[43] and also by Gustaf Dalman and his son Knut Olaf[44], in the early part of the twentieth century, revealed the remains of a splendid tomb complex in the area described by Josephus, just below the Monastery of St. Onuphrius.

In the Temple Mount excavations, only fragments of architectural elements were found, but this rock-cut tomb, because of its distance from the Temple, escaped the Roman destruction and therefore these magnificent remains have survived to this day. The decorations used in the tombs closely resemble those seen on the fragments of the Temple Mount excavations.

81

Chapter One: The Herodian Temple Mount Walls

One tomb is especially noteworthy. Its anteroom had a triple gate façade cut out of the bedrock. This room led first into a porch and then into a domed chamber whose side walls have a rock-cut decoration in the form of beautiful Attic mock doorways, crowned by pediments. The entire tomb façade seems to have been a kind of miniature of the Triple Gate in the Southern Wall of the Temple Mount, which can actually be seen from the tomb looking due north. Furthermore, if you superimpose the proportions of the tomb's triple entrance on the remains of the 50 feet wide Triple Gate, its height is found to be identical to that of the still-existing Double Gate.

Additional confirmation that the Temple decoration was used as a model for these tombs was still forthcoming. The side molding used in some of the other tombs nearby was found to correspond closely with that of the western jamb of the Triple Gate. Thus, the

CHAPTER ONE: THE HERODIAN TEMPLE MOUNT WALLS

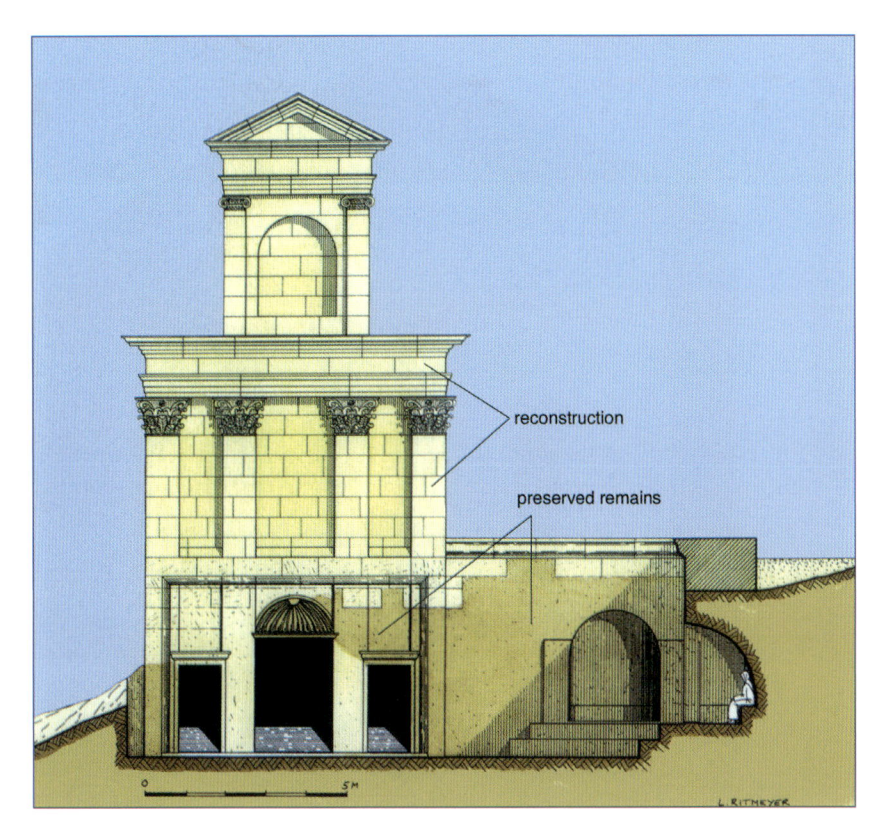

Opposite page (above): View of the Monument of Annas.

Opposite page (below): False doorway in the tomb chamber of Annas.

Left: Reconstruction of the triple-gated entrance to the tomb chamber of Annas.

reconstruction uses the tomb's façade to conclude that the gate had a triple form. While its conch decoration could not be superimposed on the Temple gate, the pediment used in the Attic doorway does seem to be compatible with the style of the Triple Gate, especially as such a molding has been found in the Temple Mount excavations below Robinson's Arch.

The remains of the tomb's façade indicate that the decorative frame would have continued upwards in stone. The form of the original superstructure is unknown, but since the Royal Stoa was located above the Triple Gate of the Temple Mount, we have reproduced a similar arrangement in the reconstruction of this tomb. A tomb with a superstructure is styled a "monument," and the only monument mentioned in this area (by Josephus in *Wars of the Jews* 5.506) is that of Annas the high priest.

The interior of the tomb is also highly decorated. The principal chamber has a completely preserved and magnificently decorated domed ceiling. The central feature of the dome is a deeply carved rosette of thirty-two petals, grouped around a whorl rosette of light

83

Chapter One: The Herodian Temple Mount Walls

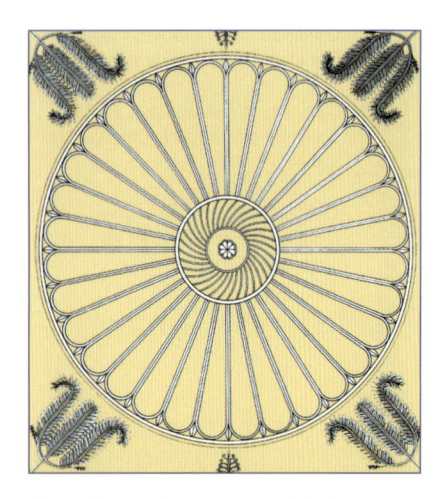

Right: Reconstruction of the interior of the tomb chamber of Annas and its domed ceiling (detail above).

Below: Reconstruction of the so-called Tomb (or Pillar) of Absalom in the Kedron Valley. Its circular roof is built of finely cut stone, topped by a conical structure with a rosette-shaped calyx.

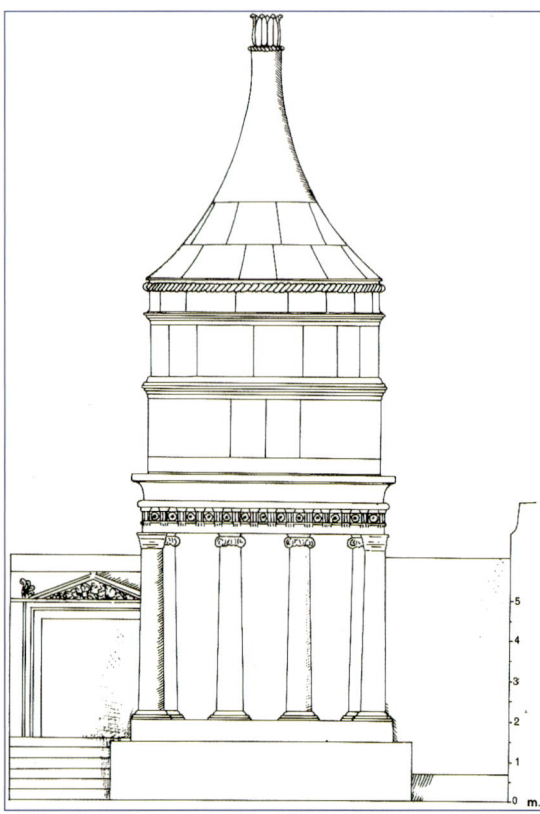

petals that can still be seen. Stylized acanthus leaves fill the four corners of the ceiling. This huge rosette distinguishes this tomb chamber from all other Second Temple tombs in Jerusalem, none of which have such sculpted ceiling decoration. (The only exception is a small rosette on the ceiling of the burial chamber of the so-called Tomb [or Pillar] of Absalom.)

The decoration of this dome closely resembles that of the northwest dome in the underground passageway of the Double Gate (see illustration, p. 73 [top right]). Three loculi *(kochim)* are cut into the east and west walls of this tomb chamber. The central one in the west wall has been framed by a mock Attic doorway. The loculus itself was closed off by a blocking stone that was carved in the same style as the false door. The false doorway marked therefore an elaborately decorated burial cavity for a very wealthy person. The opposite wall has been completely obliterated, but may have been a mirror image of this beautifully carved wall and could have been the burial place of the deceased's wife.

As to the reasons for the many parallels between the tomb and the Triple and the Double Gate of the Temple Mount, we can only conclude that the priestly family who had the tombs built, wanted to transfer some of the magnificence which they were accustomed to seeing while entering the Temple, to their last resting place. Although several other decorated tombs have been found in this area, one of which was called "The Refuge of the Apostles," we believe that this most beautifully decorated monument with its triple entrance and superstructure was most probably that of Annas, while his sons would have been buried in the nearby tombs.[45]

Given the similarities of the extant decorations, the façade of this tomb, therefore, was used to reconstruct the appearance of the Herodian Triple Gate.

The Relationship between the Double and Triple Gates

The question arises as to why the two gates in the Southern Wall differ in their form—one double and one triple? This is a puzzle that has long absorbed the archaeologists of Jerusalem. The Mishnah, which describes the earlier 500-cubit-square Temple platform which Herod enlarged, mentions the *"two Hulda Gates on the south, that served for coming in and for going out"* (*Middot* 1.3).

There has been arguing back and forth as to the meaning of this description. Did the pilgrims go in via the Double Gate and out by the Triple Gate or vice versa? Or did the mishnaic tractate *Middot* mean something else entirely? We now know that the Mishnah is concerned with the earlier Temple Mount and not with the Herodian extension. The name Hulda therefore relates to a pre-Herodian gate and cannot refer to the two gates in the Southern Wall.

Another way of resolving the question is to look at the architectural planning of the two gates. As mentioned before, a double gate is a rare phenomenon in classical architecture. When found, such as at the Porta Negra in Trier, Germany, or the gateway of Arles (also called

The double gate of Porta Negra in Trier, Germany.

Chapter One: The Herodian Temple Mount Walls

Reconstructed window frame based on excavated remains.

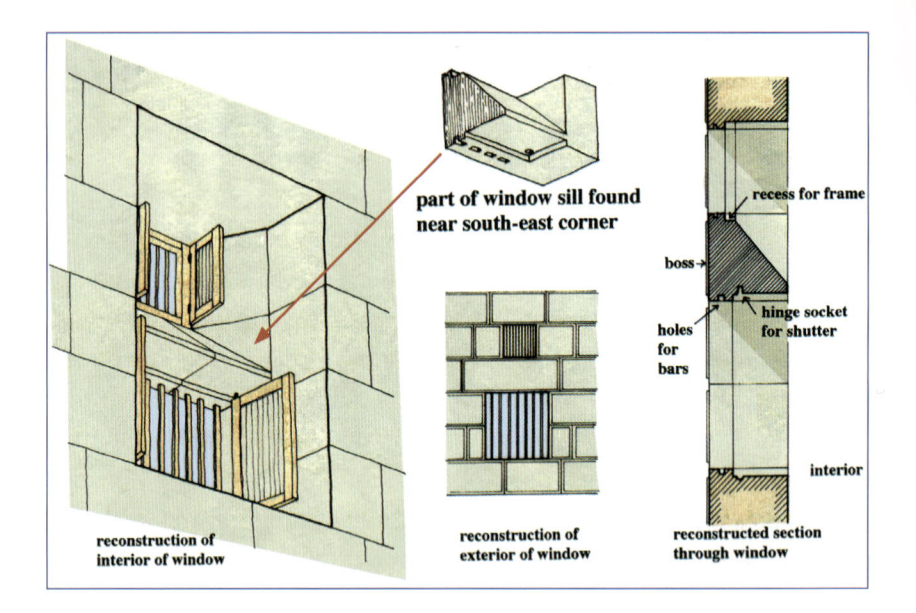

Porte d'Auguste) in Nîmes, France, such a gate is always associated with the circulation of two-way traffic, one side for going in and the other for going out. Several of the excavated ritual baths in Jerusalem and elsewhere also have double entrances, clearly designed as entrance and exit, with frequently a low wall built on the steps to separate the traffic.

Apart from their form, there are other dissimilarities between the two gates that may be crucial to our understanding of their original purpose. Firstly, their approaches differ in that the Double Gate has a very broad staircase and that leading up to the Triple Gate is much narrower.

Secondly, the Double Gate opens into an underground passageway that led directly onto the Temple platform, while the Triple Gate (although it also had a ramp which gave access to the court) seems to have been more directly connected with the underground vaulted structures which are today represented by the so-called Solomon's Stables. In the immediate area, a complete window frame was found which had grooves for metal bars to give light and air for the underground structure (see illustration above).

Thus, from the point of view of architectural planning, the description in *Middot* seems to refer to entry to the Temple court by the Double Gate only. *Middot* 2.2 sheds even more light on the circulation, recording that *"whosoever it was that entered the Temple Mount came in on the right and went round and came out on the left,*

CHAPTER ONE: THE HERODIAN TEMPLE MOUNT WALLS

save any whom aught befell, for he went round to the left." Although the Hulda Gates stood at the entrance to the pre-Herodian Temple Mount, it is reasonable to suggest that the Double Gate entrance and passageway were built to correspond with it. The pilgrims then would normally have entered through the right or east opening and come back through the left or west opening of the Double Gate. This also makes sense as regards the location of the ritual bathing complex which was located to the right or east of the Double Gate stairway.

The Triple Gate, however, had a narrow approach and would appear to have been used less by pilgrims and more by those members of the priestly order who needed access to the underground storerooms. From there, of course, they could also reach the Temple platform. An interesting alignment has been brought to my attention by a Swiss scholar, Roger Liebi. He pointed out that *"the western side of the underground passageway of the Triple Gate actually lines up with the south-east corner of the platform of the Dome of the Rock."* As we will see later (pp. 371–375), that is where I locate the Chamber of Hewn Stone, where the Sanhedrin used to assemble. Prior to the

Model of the Temple platform—overall view from the southeast. (photo: Philip Evans)

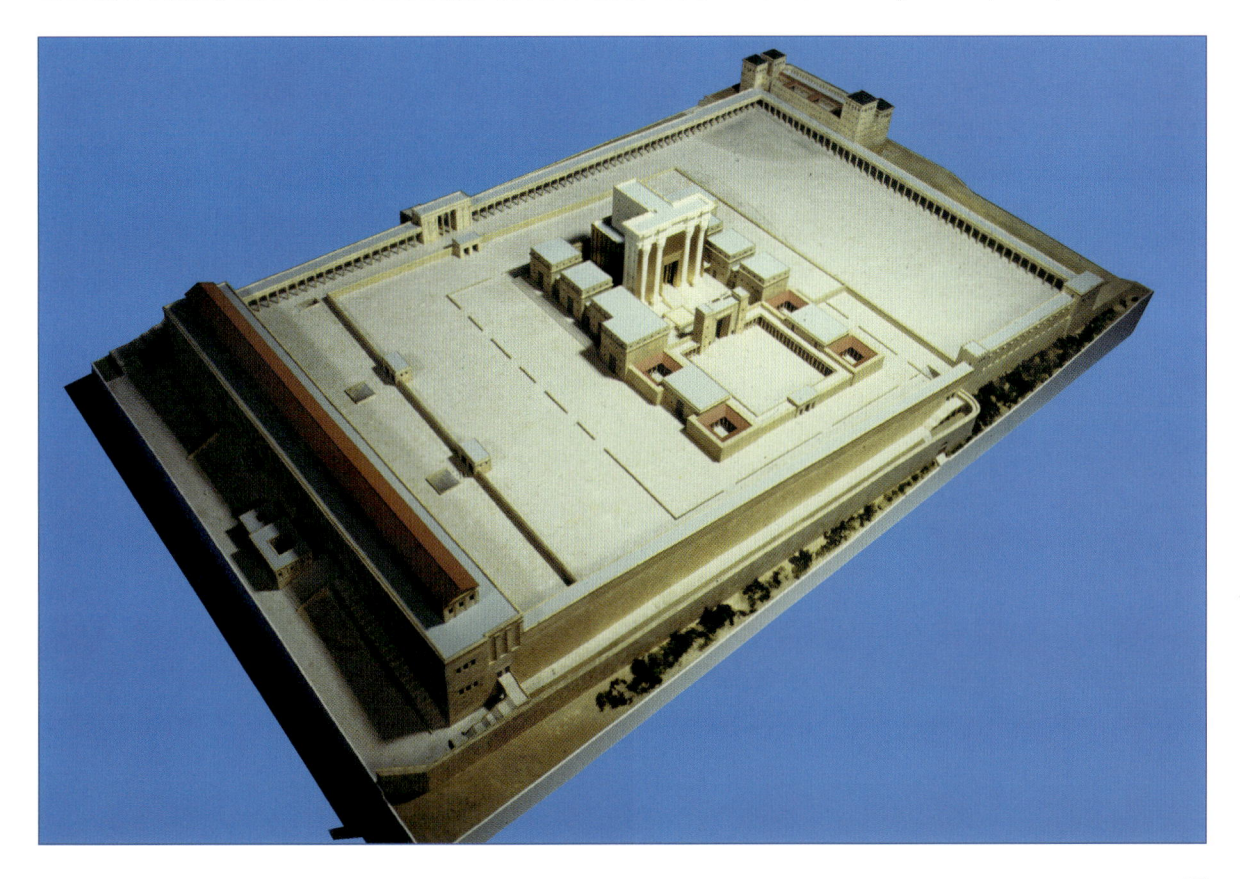

87

Chapter One: The Herodian Temple Mount Walls

Below: General view of the underground passageway of the Triple Gate.

Opposite page (middle): The west wall of the Triple Gate passageway. The pilaster stone is located to the right of the arrow.

Opposite page (bottom left): Close-up view of the pilaster stone in the west wall of the underground Triple Gate passageway, looking west.

Opposite page (bottom right): Detail of the pilaster, looking southwest.

construction of the Court of the Women, one would have passed by this building en route to the eastern gate of the Temple Court. *The Triple Gate passageway is therefore located on an important route used by the priests to reach the Chamber of Hewn Stone or the Temple Court itself. This may be another reason why only the outside of the Triple Gate was decorated and the other gates to the Temple Mount had plain façades.*

The Underground Passageway of the Triple Gate

Before it was blocked, the Triple Gate gave access to three underground tunnels. The walls between these tunnels have arched openings so that the whole construction is interconnected. The northern part of the eastern tunnel is filled up and a blocked-up opening in its Eastern Wall used to give access to Solomon's Stables. In the Western Wall of this underground passage Warren[46] noticed *"the remains of an engaged column, which is apparently* in situ, *at 60 feet from the south wall of the Sanctuary; there is only the lower course of it left, it rests on the rock and has no base moldings.*

CHAPTER ONE: THE HERODIAN TEMPLE MOUNT WALLS

LINING UP PILASTERS FOR AN AXIS

This particular pilaster has a flat surface, which is 3 feet 5 inches wide (1.04 m) and projects 1.5 feet (46 cm) from the wall. This flat part of the pilaster is flanked on both sides by two round, quarter-circular projections; the southern one of which is 2 feet (61 cm) long and the northern one 18.75 inches (48 cm). The length of this pilaster is therefore 7 feet 2.75 inches (2.20 m) while it stands probably to a height of 4 feet 6 inches (1.37 m). It is almost as long as the central pier in the Double Gate passage and is located at the same distance from the Southern Wall. On both sides of this pilaster are large ashlars, which are part of the same wall fragment. It can be seen that the western wall of this passageway is built on scarped rock, which is also part of this Herodian wall.

The center of this pilaster is located at a distance of 62 feet 7 inches (19 m) from the face of the Southern Wall. This measurement is virtually identical (with just a few inches in difference) to the distance between the center of the large northern pier in the Double Gate passageway and the Southern Wall. **The relevant position of this pilaster must therefore be identical to that of the northern pier in the Double Gate passageway, that is, its center coincides with the longitudinal axis of the Royal Stoa. This measurement confirms again the width of the Stoa as 124 feet (37.80 m).**

Chapter One: The Herodian Temple Mount Walls

Above: View of the model shows the layout of the 912-foot- (278-m-) long Southern Wall with the Royal Stoa above. (Photo: Philip Evans)

Below: A Corinthian capital found in the excavations of the Jewish Quarter. (NEAEHL)

The Royal Stoa

The description by Josephus of the Royal Stoa is recorded in *Antiquities* 15.411–415:

> The fourth front of this (court), facing south, also had gates in the middle, and had over it the Royal Portico, which had three aisles, extending in length from the eastern to the western ravine. It was not possible for it to extend farther. And it was a structure more noteworthy than any under the sun. For while the depth of the ravine was great, and no one who bent over to look into it from above could bear to look down to the bottom, the height of the portico standing over it was so very great that if anyone looked down from its rooftop, combining the two elevations, he would become dizzy and his vision would be unable to reach the end of so measureless a depth.
>
> Now the columns (of the portico) stood in four rows, one opposite the other all along—the fourth row was attached to a wall of stone—and the thickness of each column was such that it would take three men with out-

CHAPTER ONE: THE HERODIAN TEMPLE MOUNT WALLS

stretched arms touching one another to envelop it; its height was twenty-seven feet, and there was a double molding running round its base.

The number of all the columns was a hundred and sixty-two, and their capitals were ornamented in the Corinthian style of carving, which caused amazement by the magnificence of its whole effect. Since there were four rows, they made three aisles among them, under the porticoes. Of these the two side ones corresponded and were made the same way, each being thirty feet in width, a stade in length, and over fifty feet in height. But the middle aisle was one and a half times as wide and twice as high, and thus it greatly towered over those on either side.

This description contains conflicting information, because on the one hand, Josephus says that the Royal Stoa reached from the Eastern Wall to the Western Wall, which means that it was 914 feet (278.70 m) long. On the other hand, he writes that the Stoa was a stadium long (600 feet/180 m). Previous reconstruction drawings have therefore shown the actual Stoa located in between two courtyards and towers, making the Stoa short and yet having the whole of the Southern Wall filled with an interesting-looking complex.

However, we believe that it is possible that Josephus confused the length of the Royal Stoa with the length of the southern wall of the pre-Herodian square Temple Mount, which according to him also had a length of one stadium. Apart from this inaccurate measurement, we will see that the description of the Stoa by Josephus is fairly reliable. We found that the archaeological evidence indeed points to the fact that the Stoa occupied the entire length of the Southern Wall. Let us first examine how the north-south width of the Stoa was formed.

The southern aisle of the Royal Stoa would be located between the Southern Wall of the Temple Mount, which had pilasters built into it, and the row of columns which must have stood on a line that runs above the monolithic column in the Double Gate passageway and the wall that was found to the east of this passage. The distance between the Southern Wall, measured at the base of the pier of the Double Gate, and the monolithic column is 35 feet 3 inches (10.74 m). Allowing for a batter of approximately 4 inches (10 cm) for the four courses that make up the height of the pier, and presuming the width

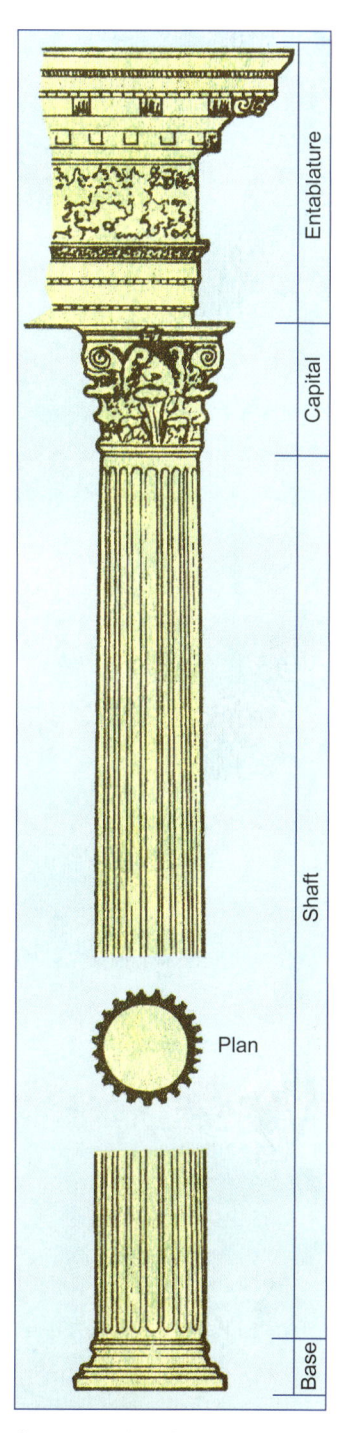

Reconstruction of a Corinthian-styled column. (Carta, Jerusalem)

CHAPTER ONE: THE HERODIAN TEMPLE MOUNT WALLS

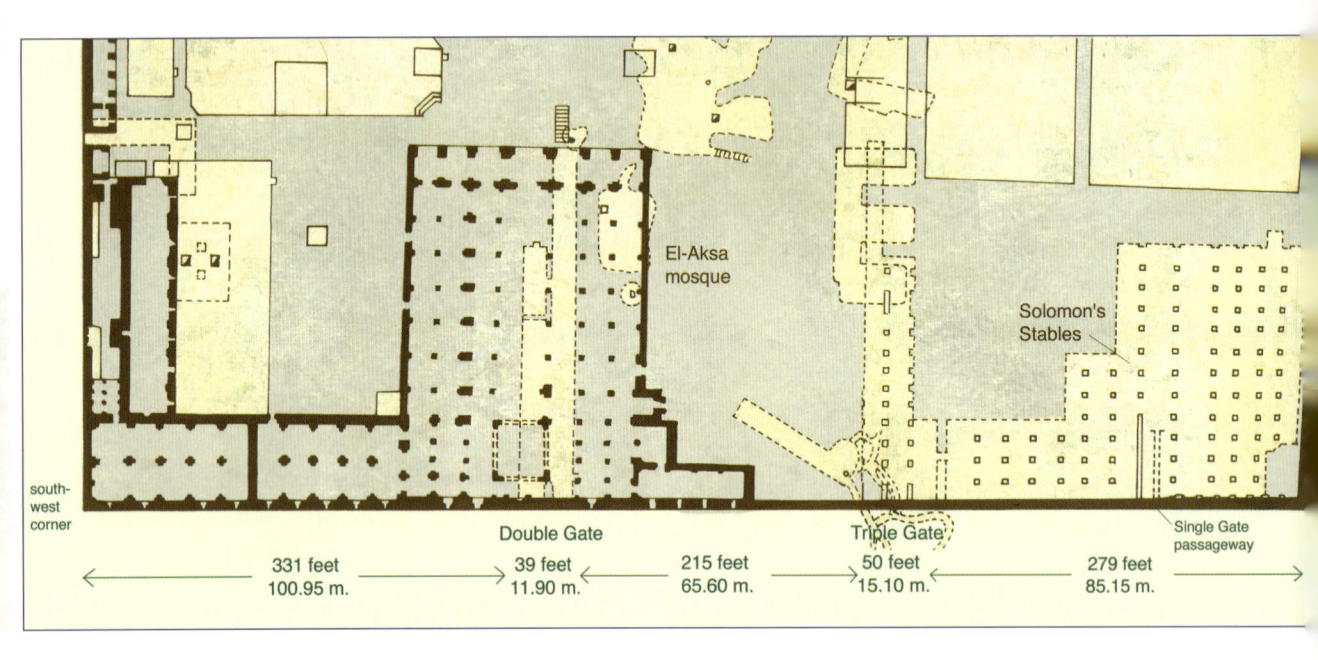

Map of Southern Wall area with dimensions.

> **DIMENSIONS OF THE SOUTHERN WALL**
>
> The distance from the southwest corner to the 39 feet (11.90 m) wide Double Gate is 331 feet (100.95 m). The wall in between the Double and Triple Gates is 215 feet (65.60 m) long. The Triple Gate used to be 51.5 feet (15.70 m) wide and the distance from this gate to the southeast corner is 277.5 feet (84.55 m). The total length of the Southern Wall is therefore 914 feet (278.70 m).

of the Southern Wall above the court level to be the same as the monolithic column, which is 4 feet 9 inches (1.45 m), the width of the southern aisle, as measured between the inner face of the Southern Wall and the column, is then 30 feet 2 inches (9.19 m)—which is the same as the figure given by Josephus, as the Roman foot was nearly identical.

The central aisle should be one and a half times as wide, that is, 45 feet (13.72 m). The almost 8-foot- (2.40-m-) long northern Herodian pier in the Double Gate passageway is located 18 feet 4 inches (5.60 m) north of the monolithic column. Based on symmetry, one would expect the southern row of columns of the northern aisle of the Royal Stoa to be positioned at the same distance of 18 feet 4 inches to the north of the central pier in the Double Gate passageway. The width of the central aisle would be twice 18 feet 4 inches (5.60 m) plus the length of the northern pier of 8 feet (2.40 m); that is, 44 feet 8 inches (13.61 m). This corresponds closely to the figure of one and a half times the width of the side aisles, as given by Josephus, which was 45 feet (13.72 m).

We have already seen that the centers of the central pier in the Double Gate passageway and the pilaster in the Triple Gate passageway coincide with the longitudinal axis of the Royal Stoa. This axis has already been established at a distance of 62 feet (18.90 m) from the Southern Wall. Thus, based on symmetry, the total width of the Royal Stoa has been calculated as 124 feet (37.80 m). It should be clear, of course, that there never existed a row of columns above the line connecting the central pier in the Double Gate passageway and the Triple Gate pilaster. This central pier with its adjacent domes merely supported the floor of the central aisle of the Royal Stoa.

To establish the east-west spacing of the Royal Stoa, we have proposed that it was as long as the whole of the Southern Wall, that is, 914 feet (278.70 m). As the floor level of the stoa was the same as that of the Temple Mount, and given the fact that the heavy columns needed a strong foundation, it follows that the Double and Triple Gates with their underground passageways and side chambers must be part of the substructure of the Royal Stoa. One would expect therefore to see a correlation between the spacing of the columns of the Stoa and the Herodian remains inside these underground structures.

Apart from the southwest and southeast corners of the Temple Mount, the side walls of the Double Gate passageway and its columns, together with the west wall of the Triple Gate passageway must all fit within the grid of the Stoa. The length of the stoa was made up of four rows of forty columns and therefore the distance between the centers of the columns should be 914 feet (278.70 m) minus the thickness of one wall (c. 4 feet 9 inches/1.45 m) divided by 39, which makes 23 feet 4 inches (7.11 m). This measurement equals the distance between the centers of two adjacent columns. To put it differently, this measurement is made up of two halves of a column (4 feet 9 inches or 1.45 m, equal to the diameter of a column) and 18 feet 7 inches (5.66 m) for the intercolumniation (the space in between two columns), which gives a ratio of 1:4.

This intercolumniation is virtually the same as the width of 18 feet of the underground passageways, and is therefore a remarkable confirmation of the east-west spacing of the forty columns of the Royal Stoa.

Measuring at the level of the Great Course, the 914-foot- (278.70 m) long Southern Wall of the Temple Mount is divided as follows: from the southwest corner to the Double Gate, 331 feet (100.95 m); width of Double Gate, 39 feet (11.90 m); 215 feet (65.60 m) in between the Double and Triple Gates; original width of the Triple Gate, 50 feet (15.10 m) and 279 feet (85.15 m) from the reconstructed gate to the southeast corner (see plan, p. 92). Working with an intercolumniation

Computerized depiction of the interior of the Royal Stoa. (Courtesy Slawek Jozwik)

Chapter One: The Herodian Temple Mount Walls

Reconstruction of the Royal Stoa.

of 18 feet 7 inches (5.66 m) we found that there were fourteen intercolumniations from the southwest corner to the Double Gate, two above the Double Gate, nine intercolumniations between the Double and Triple Gates, three intercolumniations above the Triple Gate and eleven for the remainder to the southeast corner.

From the description of Josephus, we were under the impression that the cloisters were part of the enclosures which Herod added to the Temple Mount. We expected, therefore, that the Herodian extension to the south of the Hasmonean Temple Mount would be at least that of the width of the Royal Stoa. However, this is not so. Whereas the width of the Royal Stoa is 124 feet (37.80 m), the Herodian extension at the southern end of Eastern Wall is less—only 105 feet 6 inches (32.16 m). This difference in measurement may point to the existence of porticoes on the Temple Mount during the Hasmonean period, a possibility we will discuss later (see illustration on p. 77).

CHAPTER ONE: THE HERODIAN TEMPLE MOUNT WALLS

The Single Gate Passageway

The Single Gate is a small blocked gate 9 feet 4 inches (2.85 m) wide which has a pointed arch and is located 105 feet (32 m) from the southeast corner. Its sill is located one Herodian stone course lower than that of the Triple Gate, but it nevertheless provided an entrance to the underground area which today is called Solomon's Stables. This arched gateway is believed to be a Crusader opening made to allow this underground space (which may have been constructed in the Umayyad period) to be used as stables for the horses of the Templars.

On October 18th, 1867, Charles Warren discovered an entrance into an underground tunnel five Herodian stone courses below the Single Gate. This entranceway is situated 111 feet 6 inches (34 m) west of the southeast corner, and the tunnel into which it led was fully excavated in 1973 by Mazar's team.

The general impression of this tunnel is that it was constructed simultaneously with the Herodian Southern Wall. The ashlars are of a slightly inferior quality, with many of the stones showing faults such as chipped corners and edges, irregular margins and indentations. It appears to me that these stones were rejected because of their faults but were still acceptable for the underground construction, where the

The Knights Templar.

View of the Single Gate.

95

Chapter One: The Herodian Temple Mount Walls

A LOOK AT THE TUNNEL

The passageway is built at right angles to the Southern Wall and is 69 feet (21.10 m) long and approximately 3 feet (1 m) wide. There are two openings at the southern end of the tunnel, one above the other. The lower opening is two stone courses high while the upper one is the height of one course. The two openings are separated by one stone, which is laid like a lintel. The soffit of this stone has been partially cut away to provide headroom. Warren noted that the first roof stone has a square cut on the inside of the tunnel:

> *A check 10 inches square, and of the same depth, is cut in one of the roof stones, and there is a mark of abrasion on one of the side stones (east), as though a metal gate has swung against it.*[47]

The internal passageway is constructed of three courses of large stones, each 3 feet 9 inches (1.15 m) high. Most have the typical Herodian margins and bosses. The roof stones too are made of similar Herodian stones. The stone courses of this tunnel are laid in courses, well bonded together, especially with those of the Southern Wall. The vertical joints, however, are not as close together as the Southern Wall stones, and some of the interstices have been filled up with small stones set in grayish-black mortar.

Interior view of the passageway below the Single Gate.

CHAPTER ONE: THE HERODIAN TEMPLE MOUNT WALLS

emphasis is on strength and not on beauty. Vitruvius, who wrote in the time of Augustus, actually recommended this procedure.[48] The fact that five Herodian stone courses remain *in situ* above this tunnel proves its Herodian construction date.

The northern end appears also to have been an entry point, as all the stones facing north are bossed and end in a straight line. It is interesting to note that this northern opening is exactly in line with the northern face of the central pier/pilaster of the Royal Stoa in both the Double and Triple Gate tunnels. Unfortunately, the nature of the fill made it too dangerous for further excavation.

It is a matter of speculation whether the northern exit of the passageway opens into an underground chamber or into a long underground passage that could have been built between the exit of the passageway and the southern wall of the Hasmonean Temple Mount. It is also possible that this tunnel was made during the construction of Herod's southern extension in order to provide the workmen with quick access to the building site from the south. From this point of view, it is possible that the southern part of the substructure of the Royal Stoa, up to the central pillars, was built first, with the space in between being used as a builders site. Once the building had progressed and this space was built up, the passageway was probably no longer used.

Some reconstruction drawings depict the southeast part of the Temple Mount constructed with rows upon rows of vaults.[49] This passageway appears to indicate instead that the area below the level of Solomon's Stables was filled up solidly with masonry and fill.

Above: Elevation of the entrance to the passageway below the Single Gate.

Below: Isometric section through Single Gate passageway showing its relationship to the Royal Stoa.

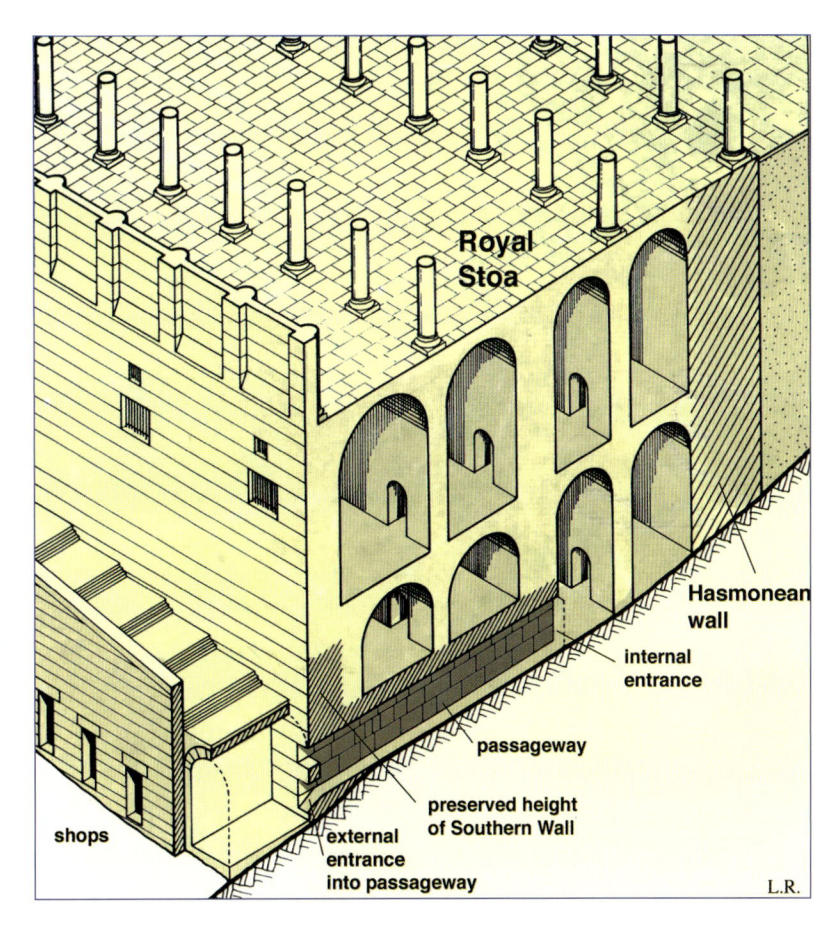

97

Chapter One: The Herodian Temple Mount Walls

Solomon's Stables and Ancient Vault

Below the platform at the southeast angle are huge underground vaults that are mistakenly called Solomon's Stables (see plan, p. 92). The only Herodian elements belonging to this construction are the outer walls of the Temple Mount at the southeast corner. In its middle northern part there are the conspicuous remains of a vault[50] which appears to be the oldest element of this underground construction. The eastern face of this vault is located 144 feet (43.90 m) to the east of the western wall of the Triple Gate passageway. It is approximately 39 feet (11.90 m) long, with a span of approximately 15 feet (5 m). Its southern end is 82 feet (25 m) from the face of the Southern Wall.

The construction date is difficult to determine, but there are two

View of the remains of an early vault in Solomon's Stables.

alternatives. The vault cannot be earlier than Herodian, as this vault crosses the projected southern wall of the Hasmonean extension. This leaves the possibility of a Herodian or post-Herodian date. If it is Herodian, then the Hasmonean wall was never higher than the base of the vault; or alternatively, the Hasmonean wall must have been lowered in the Herodian period.

I had previously advocated this last possibility, but it is more likely that this vault is post-Herodian. Herodian vaults usually follow the Roman construction with an impost course below the springer course.

CHAPTER ONE: THE HERODIAN TEMPLE MOUNT WALLS

This vault however has an unusual slanting stone course below the voussoirs: a most unclassical feature. It is therefore presumably of a post-Herodian date and may perhaps be the earliest surviving remains of Umayyad construction in this area.

The inside of the Herodian southeast corner of the Temple Mount is visible inside Solomon's Stables. Descending a staircase in the southeast corner, one enters a room with a little domed shrine, the so-called Cradle of Jesus. Near the southeast corner of this room a small window, two stone courses high, can be seen in the Southern Wall and two larger windows in the Eastern Wall. Their lintels are the springers of a vault, indicating that this underground area was vaulted in Herod's time.

The inner lintels over the windows in the Eastern Wall near the southeast corner.

The Southeast Corner

The street running along the Southern Wall is level between the Double and Triple Gates, but from that point descends to the southeast corner. The excavations revealed the foundations of a series of shops built at a lower level against the Temple Mount wall. These foundations were partly cut out of the living rock. The roofs of these shops apparently carried the stepped street that would have descended to the southeast corner.

Chapter One: The Herodian Temple Mount Walls

AN EXCITING DISCOVERY!

It was here at this corner that I had my first experience of the excitement generated by a chance find that suddenly illuminates the reconstruction. Assigned to the Southern Wall area in 1973, surveying these remains and pondering how these shops could have supported the street overhead, I noticed the imprints of a series of descending arches burnt into the wall. A close inspection of these arches showed not only that they were semicircular, but that also a semicircular line was scratched in the wall in order to help the builders construct the arches in the correct position. The burnt areas clearly corresponded to the exposed parts of the Southern Temple Mount Wall that were visible inside the shops. No burning was discerned where the walls of the shops and their vaults were built up against the Temple wall.

The only possible scenario that could have left such an indelible imprint on the Southern Wall brought the tragedy of the Roman destruction vividly to life. The limestone of which the Herodian construction is built and the bedrock itself can be reduced to powder when exposed to very high temperatures. (That is the way in which lime is produced, by burning blocks of limestone in a kiln).

In this case, the Roman soldiers must have put brushwood inside the still-existing shops. The large blaze thus created when this was set alight would have caused the vaults to collapse, along with the stepped street supported by these arches. However, before the arches collapsed, the fire burnt into the wall of the Temple Mount that formed the back wall of the shops—leaving the imprint of the arches as an evocative testimony to this dreadful inferno. Josephus writes that five days after having burnt the Temple, Titus "then gave his troops permission to burn and sack the city . . . on the next day they set fire to . . . the region called Ophlas, the flames spreading as far as the palace of Queen Helena" (War 6.353–355). The Ophlas, or Ophel in Hebrew, is the area in between the Temple Mount and the City of David.

While measuring these burnt remains, it became apparent that the apexes of the arches descending to the eastern corner were all 2 feet (60 cm) lower than the previous one. Taking the height of a typical Herodian step into consideration, three steps had to be built in between two arches to overcome the difference in height. The stepped street was therefore constructed of a series of three steps with landings between them. Our conclusion about these steps was confirmed when, in the western part of the Southern Wall, a section belonging to the same street that had already been excavated revealed in situ two flights of three steps on either side of a landing. In the wake of this find we discovered in this western part of the Southern Wall another three burnt imprints of arches, as mentioned above. Using all this information, a very accurate reconstruction could be made of this narrow street.

Above (left): View of the burnt arch east of the Triple Gate.

Above (right): View of burnt arches near the southeast corner.

The southeast corner has been preserved to a great height, owing to the enormous size of the corner stones. The largest corner stone, which is part of the Great Course, is estimated to weigh nearly

CHAPTER ONE: THE HERODIAN TEMPLE MOUNT WALLS

100 tons. Near the top of the Herodian stones, a small Herodian window can be seen, which we have already mentioned when we investigated Solomon's Stables. It is possible that another small window once existed west of it, as part of a tower that originally stood at this corner.

THE EASTERN WALL

The most ancient masonry of the Temple Mount can be seen in the central part of the Eastern Wall and it is therefore the most interesting of all the walls of the Temple Mount. As this chapter deals with the Herodian Temple Mount, we will describe only those sections of the Eastern Wall that belong to that period.

Some 130 feet (40 m) of the southern part of the ancient Eastern Wall was exposed by bulldozer during the time when the Jordanians controlled this area before 1967. About one hundred years prior to this, Warren explored this area deep underground, excavating shafts which went down to the bedrock (see illustration, p. 104).

Several of the Temple Mount stones near the bottom of the southeast corner had red painted letters on them, leading Warren to

View of the model showing the reconstructed eastern end of the Southern Wall. (photo: Philip Evans)

Chapter One: The Herodian Temple Mount Walls

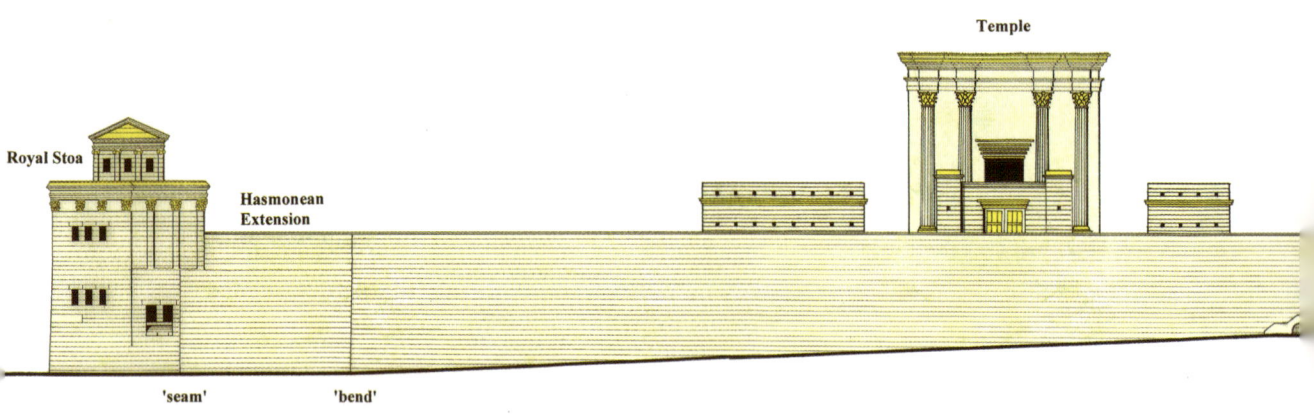

speculate that the letters were of Phoenician origin. He therefore concluded that this corner construction dated back to Solomonic times. Near the Pool of Israel next to the northeast corner of the Temple Mount, more painted letters were found on a stone. The drip marks of one of the letters show them to be painted on the stone before it was put in place.[51]

Comparing Warren's drawings of these stones with the typical Herodian masonry, which is now so well known, it is obvious that the stones that Warren investigated so deep underground are of Herodian and not Solomonic origin.

There are several features to be observed in this stretch of Herodian masonry that we will discuss below: namely a vertical joint (and its relationship to the Royal Stoa), the remains of a tower and a small gateway.

Top: Elevation of the Eastern Wall of the Herodian Temple Mount.

Above: View of the southern end of the Eastern Wall.

Opposite page (above): View of the Seam.

Opposite page (below): Elevation of the Seam.

The Straight Joint (Seam)

Above ground, Herodian masonry is visible from the southeast corner up to a vertical joint, called by Warren the "straight joint." This feature, also known as the *seam,* is located 105 feet 6 inches (32 m) north of the southeast corner. This stretch of Herodian masonry must therefore constitute the extent of Herod's southern addition to the Temple Mount. A close inspection of this seam shows that the stones on the north side of the seam had their margins cut for the later Herodian addition. The stones to the north of the seam are obviously part of a corner construction, as the ashlars are laid in the typical "headers and stretchers" formation. As we shall see later, this construction dates from the Hasmonean period.

CHAPTER ONE: THE HERODIAN TEMPLE MOUNT WALLS

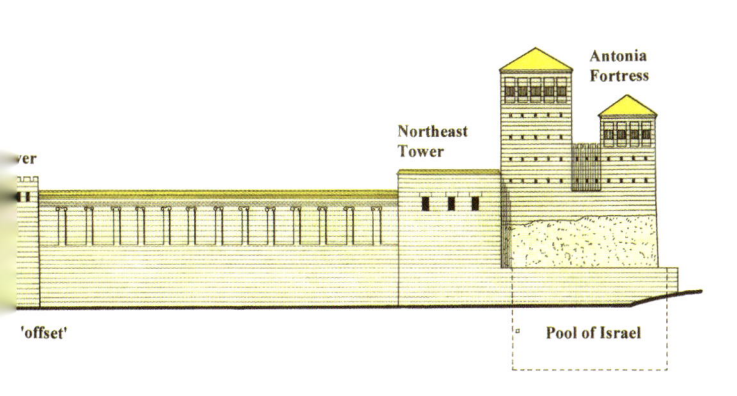

Wilson[52] noted that the distance of 105 feet 6 inches (32 m), from the southeast corner to the seam, is almost the same as the distance from the southeast corner to the passageway below the Single Gate. He speculated therefore that *"it is a question whether these two points may not possibly indicate the limits of the original structure, a corner tower unconnected with the walls."* In a footnote, however, he indicated that if such a tower existed, a straight joint would have to exist in the Temple Mount wall below the Single Gate. He did not see the wall at the underground passage, but Mazar's excavations have made it clear that no such joint existed. On the contrary, the whole of the Southern Wall is one homogeneous Herodian construction.

We have already noted that the Herodian southern addition to the Eastern Wall is 18 feet 6 inches (5.80 m) less than the width of the Royal Stoa (see p. 90). We suggest therefore that the space of 18 feet 6 inches to the north of the *seam,* which was incorporated within the Royal Stoa, was most likely the space previously occupied by the southern Hasmonean Stoa. This Hasmonean Stoa must, of course, have been dismantled by Herod, as our calculations have shown.

As previously mentioned, two pairs of domes exist in the Double Gate tunnel. On the north, the southern engaged column of the northern Herodian pier support these domes. This pier has also an engaged column on its northern side. The corresponding pilaster in

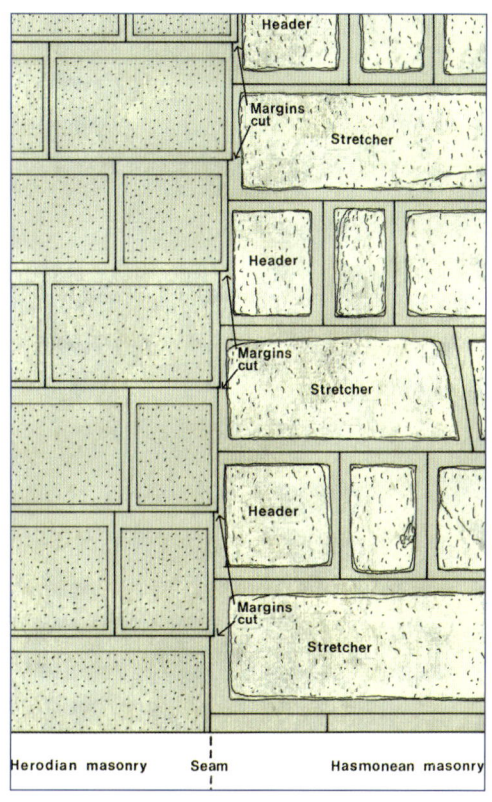

Chapter One: The Herodian Temple Mount Walls

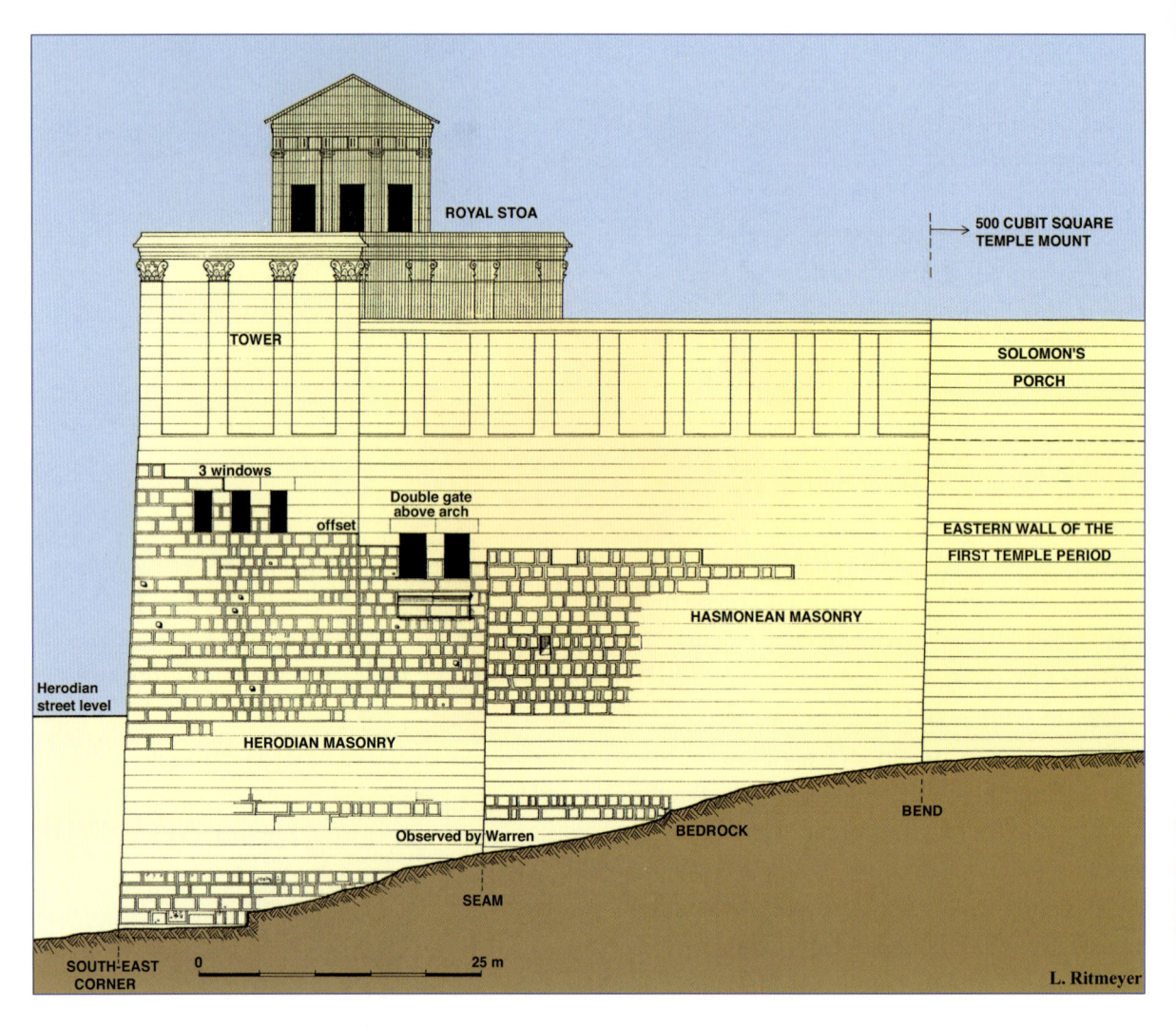

Reconstruction drawing of the southern part of the Eastern Wall of the Temple Mount.

the underground Triple Gate passageway has two engaged round pilasters as well. This indicates that at least another set of domes existed to the immediate north of the pier and pilaster. These northern domes must have been supported by another column that would be located below the rows of columns that divide the main aisle of the Royal Stoa from the northern one, at a distance equal to that between the central pier and the monolithic column in the Double Gate passageway.

Assuming that the Herodian Southern Wall was built parallel to the Hasmonean southern wall (basing our assumption on the direction of the east wall of the underground passageway of Barclay's Gate), there would not be enough space for a fourth, northernmost line of domes. In our reconstruction drawings of the Double and Triple Gate underground passageways (see illustrations on pp. 70 [plan] and 77), only three rows of domes are visible, followed by tunnels that must originally have existed in the Hasmonean extension. Herod may have incorporated these tunnels into his underground approach to the Temple Courts, or otherwise have rebuilt them.

It is interesting to note therefore that the position of the Seam would verify the historical sources that allude to the existence of Hasmonean porticoes around the Temple Mount.

The Tower

At 66 feet 7 inches (20.30 m) from the corner, a vertical line, or offset, appears in the eighth visible course above ground level. This line is created by small projections that are built into the ashlars. These projections gradually deepen in the higher courses. Although this southernmost part of the Eastern Wall projects from the remainder of the wall, it is not a separate feature, as the projections are frequently cut out of one and the same stone. The impression is that this projected part of the wall is the beginning of a tower that stood high over the southeast corner. In a forthcoming section we will discuss the remains of a large projecting tower at the northeast corner.

The tower at the southeast corner hardly projects from the wall, but nevertheless provides a visual balance to the whole of the Eastern Wall. Near the preserved top of the Herodian tower, the remains of three centrally located windows can be seen. The southernmost one has the original lintel still in position and the sides of the middle window are also complete, although the lintel is missing. Of the third window, only the southern side has been preserved. When describing the southeast corner (see above, pp. 98–99), we mentioned that the inner lintels of these windows are actually springers of a vault. It would appear that the tower here had chambers.

Reconstruction model of the southeast corner, showing the projecting tower, the three windows and the stepped entrance to the small double gateway. (photo: Philip Evans)

Chapter One: The Herodian Temple Mount Walls

CHAPTER ONE: THE HERODIAN TEMPLE MOUNT WALLS

The Double Entrance
At 13 feet 8 inches (4.20 m) north of this projecting line, the remains of a 22 foot 4 inches (6.80 m) wide double entrance gateway can be seen. Below this entrance, which is now blocked with small stones, two arch stones set on three impost blocks are visible. Although the bosses of the two large impost blocks have been badly eroded, they must have projected at least as far as that of the smaller and better preserved northern block.

The arch evidently supported a stairway, which may have mirrored its much larger western counterpart, namely that of Robinson's Arch. This eastern staircase could apparently be reached from the Herodian street below. As will be seen below, when we discuss the Golden Gate, a section of a massive wall was found by Warren at a distance of 46 feet (14 m) from the Temple Mount wall.[53] Given the fact that this wall was found running from south to north and turning toward the Temple Mount just to the north of the Golden Gate, it appears to be the eastern city wall of Jerusalem. It is therefore possible that the stairway under discussion was built against the eastern city wall which also may have supported it.

The Golden Gate Interior
With Herod's enlargement of the Temple Mount, the Eastern Wall now had two gates, the small one near the southeast corner and the other at the present-day Golden Gate. This well-known gate was in

Opposite page: View of the Golden Gate from the east.

Below: View of the remains of the double entrance gateway, located between the offset of the tower (left) and the seam (right).

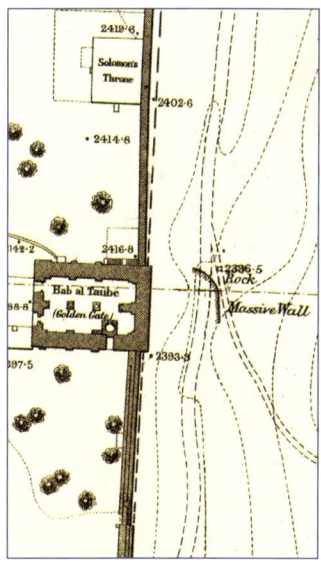

Above: Detail of Warren's Plate IV, showing the location of the massive wall.

Left: View of the Golden Gate from the Temple Mount.

Chapter One: The Herodian Temple Mount Walls

Artist's impression of the Yom Kippur ritual of sending the scapegoat into the wilderness. Here, the High Priest is seen presenting the scapegoat to the one responsible for leading the animal into the wilderness. The two stand under the Shushan (i.e. Golden) Gate on the eastern side of the Temple Mount. (The Temple Institute, Jerusalem)

> **WHAT SETS THIS GATE APART FROM ALL OTHERS?**
>
> *Intriguing details about this gate are given in the Mishnah. Middot 1.3 mentions it as one of the five gates to the original Temple Mount and relates that the Palace of Shushan, so real in the memories of the builders of this wall after their return from exile in Babylon, was portrayed on it. The tractate Kelim 17.9 states that in a chamber above this gate the standard measures of the cubits were kept.*
>
> *This gateway also has strong associations with the sacrifice of the Red Heifer, outlined in Numbers 19:1–10. In Parah, another of the mishnaic tractates, the complete Temple ritual concerning this sacrifice is related. In chapter three, we learn that the Red Heifer was brought over an arched causeway leading from the Temple Mount to the Mount of Olives. The heifer was then burnt and its ashes collected. These ashes, when mixed with water, were used as a purification for sin.*
>
> *There was no need to change this system during the Herodian period, so it can be safely assumed that it would have been through this gate that the Red Heifer was led out to the Mount of Olives during that time period as well. On the Day of Atonement (Yom Kippur), it was through here also that the scapegoat (azazel) was led away into the wilderness (Leviticus 16, Mishnah, Yoma).*

fact built in the Umayyad period, but on the foundations of an earlier gate.

According to the Mishnah, there was only one gate in the Eastern Wall. We must remember that the small gate near the southeast corner gave access only to the Herodian underground areas that are now occupied by Solomon's Stables. The Mishnah concerns itself mainly with the Temple Mount which existed before Herod's extension; thus the small Herodian gate near the southeast corner would have been irrelevant and would certainly not be considered as a Temple Mount gate. The Jewish tradition that the Golden Gate was the original eastern gate of the Temple Mount is probably correct.

CHAPTER ONE: THE HERODIAN TEMPLE MOUNT WALLS

FEATURES OF THE GATEPOSTS

Inside the gateway, two large monolithic gateposts have survived. The northern one is 15 feet (4.5 m) high while the height of the southern one is 12 feet (3.5 m). The top of the southernmost post is level with the top of an ancient stone course that can still be seen in the Eastern Wall to the immediate south of the Golden Gate. The second post is one stone course higher.

As the monoliths line up with the adjoining masonry in the eastern wall, they appear to have been constructed contemporaneously, although they may have been inserted at a later date, i.e. Hasmonean or Herodian. We shall see later that this masonry dates from the First Temple period (see pp. 174–176). The distance between the two surviving gateposts is approximately 29 feet (8.5 m). This is too wide for a single opening and therefore a central post would have had to be inserted in the middle of the gate.

As Herod left the line of the original East Wall untouched, this gate would have been in use during his time, as no other Herodian eastern gate has been found.

Above: Drawing by de Vogüé of southern monolithic gatepost inside the Golden Gate.

Left: Section through the Golden Gate looking north and showing the large northern monolithic gatepost.

Below: Ancient masonry visible in the northern part of the Eastern Wall of the Temple Mount and (below) a proposed reconstruction of this part of the wall during the Herodian period.

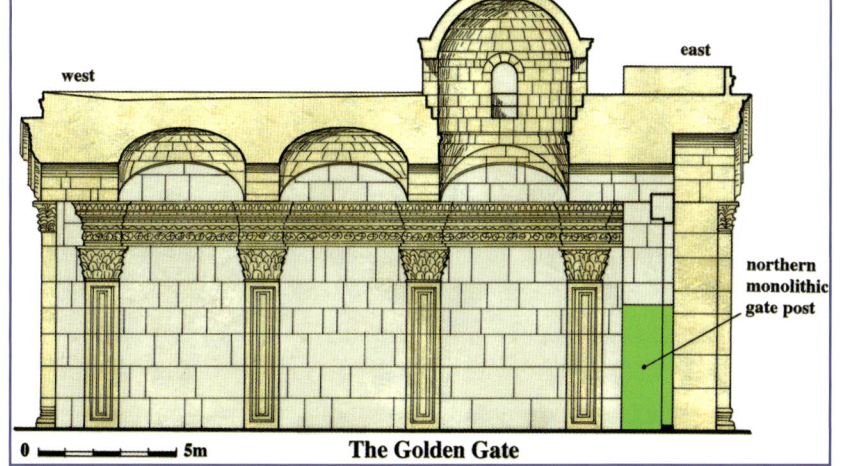

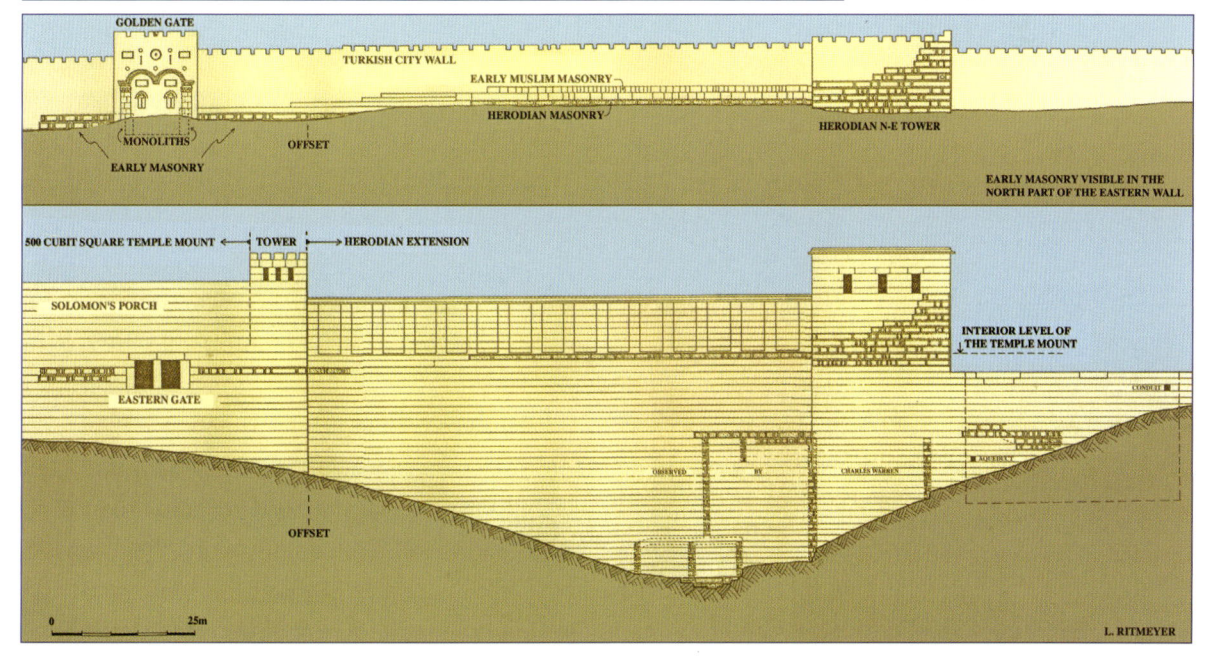

Chapter One: The Herodian Temple Mount Walls

Arch found in grave in front of the Golden Gate. (photo: Obe Hokansen)

The Golden Gate Stairway

In 1969 James Fleming, then a student at the American Institute of Holy Land Studies in Jerusalem, fell into a modern grave in front of the Golden Gate while exploring the area. Looking up he saw the remains of an arch.[54] It was suggested then that this arch might have been part of a pre-Herodian or possibly Solomonic gateway. This is impossible, however, as the bedrock rises so steeply in this area that there wouldn't be sufficient room for an underground passageway to lead up to the Temple platform. It must be noted here that the lay of the bedrock in the sectional drawing published by James Fleming is quite inaccurate.

In addition, the voussoirs and stone courses of this arch appear to be Herodian and do not resemble earlier masonry. The sill of the Golden Gate is situated 44 feet (13.41 m) above the bedrock. It is more reasonable therefore to suggest that this arch was part of a Herodian staircase leading up from the street below to the sill of the original gate. How, otherwise, could one reach the level of this gate which was built so high into the wall? The arches supporting this stairway would have been similar to those in the Herodian stairway construction of Robinson's Arch. As the top of the arch is still intact, it is interesting to contemplate that this stairway may still exist, although covered over by the debris of the destruction of the Temple in A.D. 70.

Right: Reconstruction of stairway leading up to the Eastern Gate of Herod's Temple Mount. (photo: Philip Evans)

Opposite page: General view of the reconstruction model showing the stairway leading up to the Eastern Gate. (photo: Philip Evans)

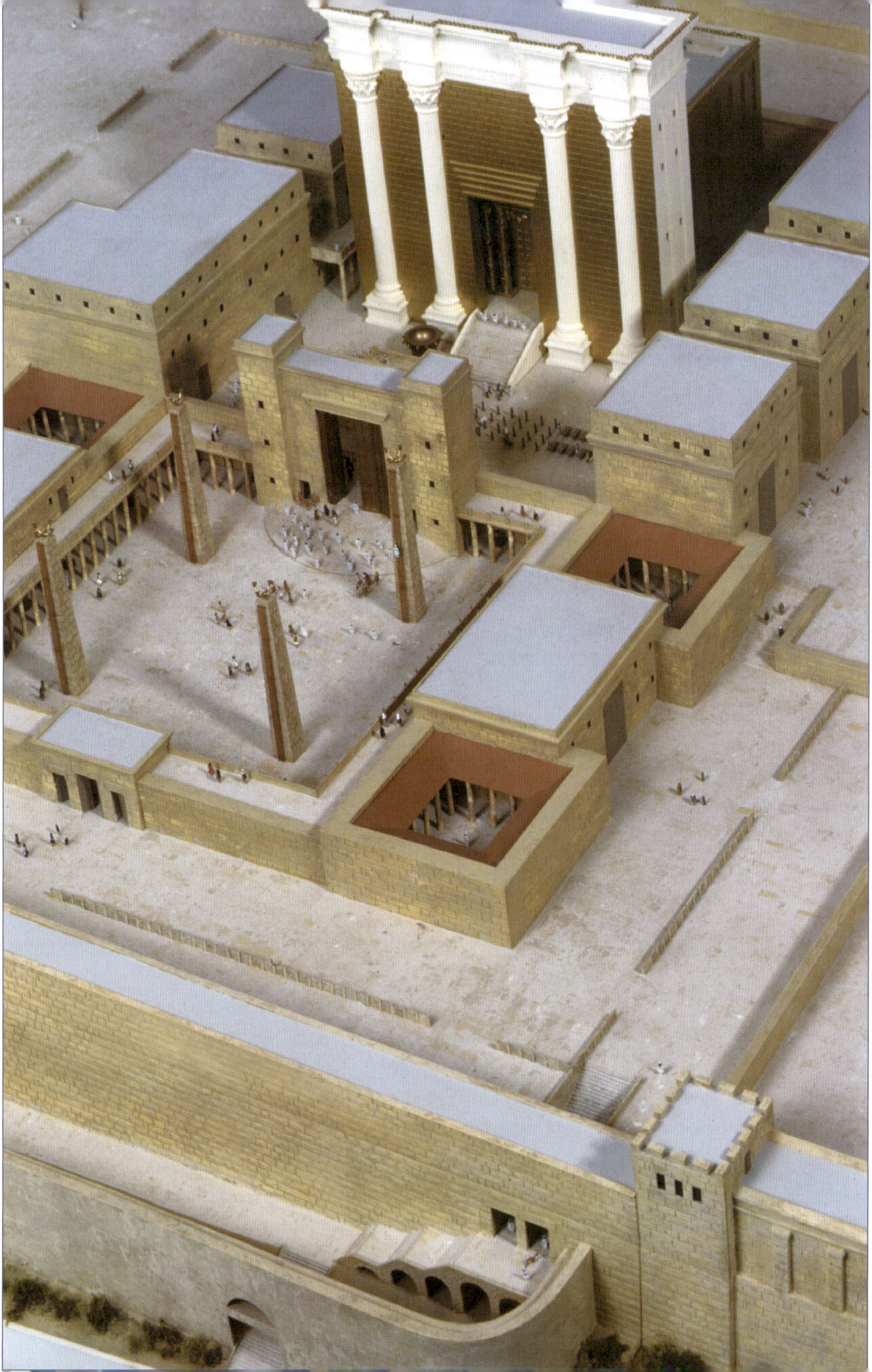

CHAPTER ONE: THE HERODIAN TEMPLE MOUNT WALLS

Artist's impression of the sacrificial ceremony of the Red Heifer and the "causeway" described in the Mishnah. (The Temple Institute, Jerusalem)

Many reconstructions show a bridge leading from the Eastern Wall to the Mount of Olives. This is based on the description of the ceremony of the sacrifice of the Red Heifer as recorded in the Mishnah. According to *Parah* 3.6,

> They made a causeway from the Temple Mount to the Mount of Olives, an arched way built over an arched way, with an arch directly above each pier [of the arch below], for fear of any grave in the depth below.

This causeway was used for the Red Heifer and the scapegoat and was built by the high priests at their own expense *(Shekalim* 4.2). *Yoma* 6.4 gives a different reason for the building of this causeway: "And they made a causeway for it [the scapegoat] because of the

CHAPTER ONE: THE HERODIAN TEMPLE MOUNT WALLS

Babylonians who used to pull its hair, crying to it 'Bear [our sins] and begone!, Bear [our sins] and begone!"

The city wall to the east of the Temple Mount is reconstructed on the basis of a curved section of the wall found by Warren in the previous century, as mentioned above (p. 107). Josephus also writes that the city wall *"joined the eastern portico of the Temple" (War* 5.145). The eastern portico stood directly over the eastern wall of the earlier Temple Mount and was therefore older than the other, Herodian porticoes. This ancient portico was referred to as "Solomon's Porch" in the New Testament (John 10:23; Acts 3:11). The sources state clearly that whilst the eastern wall remained in place, the mount was extended in the other three directions.

The Northern Extension

Very ancient masonry can be seen on either side of the Golden Gate. This masonry appears to continue underground. North of the Golden Gate, it continues for 68 feet (20.70 m) to the point which we have called the "offset" and to which we will return in Chapter 2 (p. 174). From the "offset" northward, one course of Herodian stones can be seen above ground continuing to an integrally built Herodian tower which still exists at the northeast corner of the Temple Mount.

In the following sections, we will see that substantial archaeological remains of the northern boundary of the Herodian Temple Mount still exist today. The Herodian remains of the tower at the northeast corner, the Pool of Israel and the Antonia Fortress will be discussed, together with remaining Herodian paving slabs in the court to the north of the Temple.

The Tower at the Northeast Corner

All four corners of the Herodian Temple Mount have partially survived the Roman destruction. As already mentioned, this was due to the very long stones used in the corner constructions. The northeast corner of the Temple Mount, mistakenly called in Warren's time "The Tower of Antonia" or "The Castle of Antonia,"[55] is no exception.

This tower and the stretch of wall between it and the Golden Gate is the part of the Temple Mount that is least understood. Very little has been written about it, and several scholars followed Conder,[56] who believed that this part was post-Herodian. Hollis[57] and Simons[58] identify this wall as part of the Third Wall built by Agrippa, and the

> **RAMP OR BRIDGE?**
> The Hebrew word for causeway is kevesh, which is usually translated as 'ramp' and not bridge, which is gesher. I suggest therefore that the stepped approach to the Golden Gate, just described, was the beginning of this arched ramp that continued down into the Kedron Valley and up again to the Mount of Olives. There is therefore no reason to suggest that an actual bridge was built over the Kedron Valley. Such a bridge would have had to span an enormous distance, as the valley is located some 180 feet (55 m) below the level of the sill of the Golden Gate. The so-called bridge thus would have been 20 feet (6 m) higher than the famous Pont du Gard in France, which is 160 feet (49 m) high!

View of the Pont du Gard in France.

113

Chapter One: The Herodian Temple Mount Walls

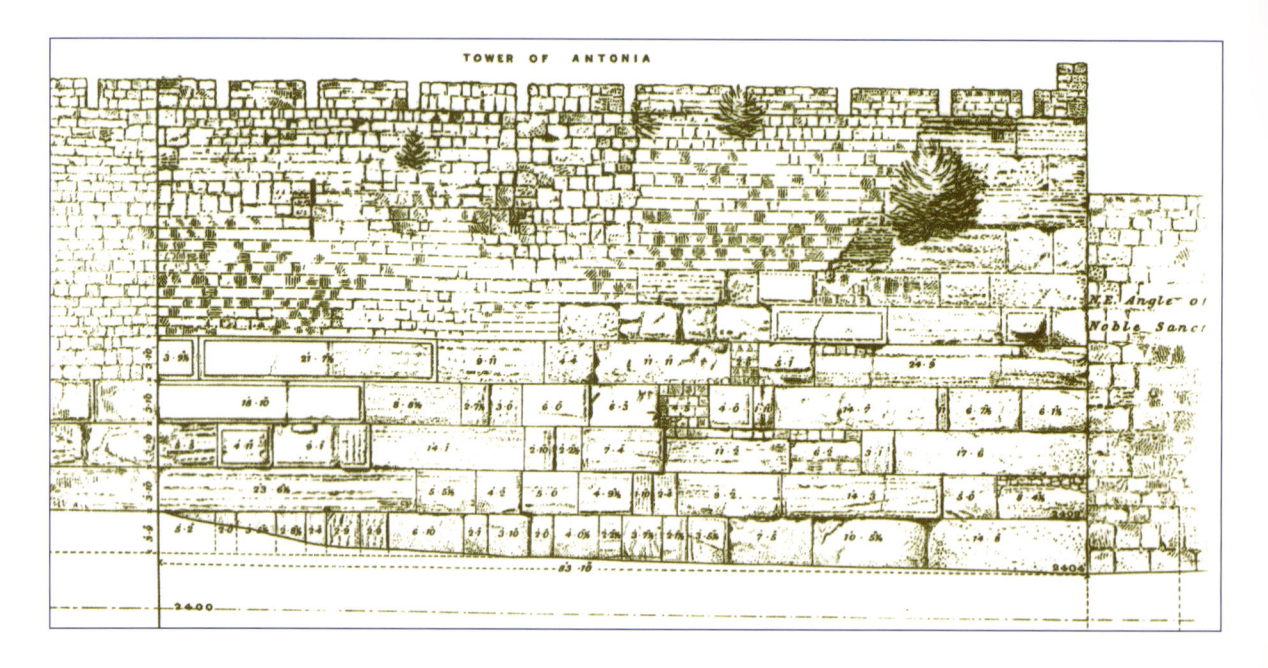

Warren's drawing of the east face of the Herodian tower at the northeast corner of the Temple Mount.

tower at the northeast corner of the Temple Mount as one of the towers of this city wall.

Parts of the eastern and northern faces of this tower are still preserved. The typical Herodian margins and bosses are still clearly visible on most of these large stones, which are on average 3 feet 10 inches (1.15 m) high.

The eastern face, whose above-ground section projects about 7 feet (2.14 m) from the Eastern Wall of the Temple Mount, has been well documented by Warren,[59] who noticed that the stones of this tower were similar to those at the *"Wailing Place."* Underground, Warren observed that these stones, which have a smooth Herodian boss, go down as far as one or two courses above the level at which the tower starts to project from the wall below. The course at which the tower begins to project is 17 courses below ground level. There are another 15 stone courses below the start of the projection of this tower (see p. 109 [bottom]), where the wall is founded on the bedrock.

At the northern corner of the eastern face of this tower, 11 Herodian stone courses are visible above ground. This means that altogether 28 courses of the tower are preserved from the point at which it starts to project. The top of the preserved southern corner is six courses lower; thus at this point there are 22 courses standing above the level where the tower begins to project. As there are another 15 courses below this point, this means that at the southern corner of this tower a

CHAPTER ONE: THE HERODIAN TEMPLE MOUNT WALLS

total of 37 stone courses are preserved.

Above ground, it can be seen that the tower is an integral part of the wall in which it is set. Warren's description[60] of how the northeast corner was formed confirms this: *"Though the stones of the tower were like those at the Wailing Place, and those to south of it had rough projecting faces, yet at this point these two different faces were cut on one and the same stone, the stone being cut back from 2 to 4 feet, at the angle of the tower."* This construction is, of course, reminiscent of the remains of the tower at the southeast corner, where a similar offset has been observed in the Eastern Wall. The stones on either side of the offset considered here show that this masonry had been clearly intended to be seen above ground.

Warren examined the masonry below ground to the south and north of the tower. He noticed that while the stones of the tower are smoothly finished almost from the point at which it begins to project, those flanking the lower 6 courses all had rough faces. Warren[61] remarks concerning the two types of masonry:

> *The wall of the tower above course P is similar in many respects to that at the Jews' Wailing place, but the roughly faced wall below the course P and to the south of the tower is not similar to the roughly faced portion at the southwest angle of the Sanctuary, although it would be difficult to specify exactly how it differs.*

The stones with rough faces at the southwest angle that were discovered in the Temple Mount excavations are located immediately below the Herodian street. This type of Herodian masonry (Fig. B, below) differs from the smoothly-finished Herodian stones (Fig. A, below) only in that the bosses of the stones of type B, which were not intended to be seen, were never finished. In fact, the rough face represents the original rockscarp from which the stone was quarried.

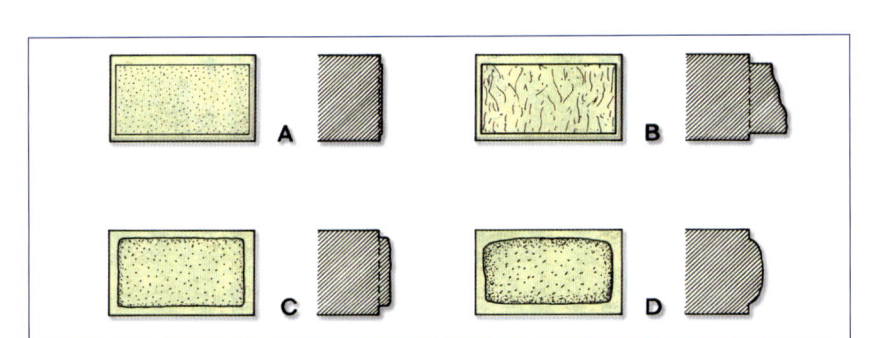

Masonry types in the Eastern Wall:
A. *Herodian masonry with flat, smooth boss;*
B. *Herodian masonry with unfinished boss;*
C. *Hasmonean masonry with projecting boss;*
D. *Early masonry with bulging boss.*

115

Chapter One: The Herodian Temple Mount Walls

Top: View of the junction of the south corner of the Herodian tower and the Eastern Wall at the northeast corner of the Temple Mount.

Above: Close-up view. Note that only the lowest course is bonded with the tower.

As the stones came from varying places in the quarries, this would account for the difference in size and shape of the projecting bosses. Only the margins were cut in the typical Herodian fashion, using the eight-toothed comb pick, to ensure the correct fitting of one stone to the other. Some of these stones have no side margins. The same applies to the stones of the tower at the northeast corner of the Temple Mount, as they were not on view—there was in fact no difference between the stones underground at both corners, despite Warren's feeling.

The absence of pilasters in the wall remains of the northeast tower has been used by some scholars as a point in favor of a post-Herodian date for this part of the boundary of the Temple Mount.[62] However, the following must be borne in mind. First, from an aesthetic point of view, pilasters are not always continued right into a corner. Corners are often treated differently to give an impression of strength. This can be seen, for example, in the Herodian walls surrounding the Tomb of the Patriarchs in Hebron, where the corners are substantially wider than the pilasters. It is quite obvious that there the corners have been treated to make them look like towers, just as in the Temple Mount.

Secondly, this tower (together with the Antonia) had a defensive function to fulfill, which is not the case with the Southern and Western Walls. Pilasters would weaken a wall, while defensive corners were built for fortification. Indeed, the small stone repair in the northern face of the northeast tower may actually mark those parts of the wall which were badly damaged during the Roman siege of A.D. 70.

Warren failed to see the difference between the stones with unfinished bosses in the tower at the northeast corner of the Temple Mount and the *"large stones, with marginal drafts 3 inches to 6 inches wide, with rough projecting faces"* to the north and south of the Golden Gate.[63] We believe that this type of masonry (see illustration, p. 115 D) dates from Hezekiah's time, as we shall see later (pp. 174–176).

It must be noted also that contrary to Warren's drawing of this

CHAPTER ONE: THE HERODIAN TEMPLE MOUNT WALLS

tower and the adjacent Eastern Wall of the Temple Mount, the three courses in the wall immediately south of the tower are not properly bonded, except for the lowest one. Simons[64] was also of the opinion that there was no break between the tower and the three lower courses of this wall, but this is clearly not so.

Wilson[65] observed that the lowest visible course of the Eastern Wall in this location (see below) *"projects beyond the others, and seems never to have had the dressing of its face completed."* Both these features are also characteristic of the stones below and to the side of the point at which the northeast tower begins to project deep below ground. The lowest course, which is visible above ground between the tower and the *offset,* would therefore actually be the topmost remaining course of the Herodian wall in this area.

The two courses that are built above this Herodian course do not follow the coursing of the tower, and these stones have no marginal drafts at all. This type of masonry which can be seen in the Wailing Wall area above the Herodian courses and also in the western part of the Southern Wall, dates from the Umayyad period when the walls of the Temple Mount were repaired. The Golden Gate was also constructed during this period and the stones, which are devoid of margins in the wall between this gate and the northeast tower, also date from this time.

General view of the masonry to the south of the northeast tower of the Temple Mount. Note the projecting bosses of the lowest course, which is Herodian.

CHAPTER ONE: THE HERODIAN TEMPLE MOUNT WALLS

The Pool of Israel

Although the northeast corner of the Temple Mount is clearly defined above ground, the Eastern Wall does not stop here completely as one would expect, but rather continues below ground to the north for another 126 feet (38.4 m). Warren clearly expected to see a break in the wall underground in the gallery that he began to explore on June 5th, 1869. He wrote,

> A gallery was driven along the wall (level 2,363 feet 3 inches) to north, past where the straight joint between the Castle of Antonia [i.e. the northeast tower] and city wall should occur; but no straight joint was found to exist. The wall runs on without a break of any kind, and there is no projection. [66]

It should be noted that although the Herodian ashlars continue northward without a break, the wall changes its character, as the width of the wall is far greater than the usual 16 feet (5 m). In fact, the wall here is a staggering 46 feet (14 m) wide!

Reconstruction of the Pool of Israel. As can be seen, its location and depth afforded protection for the Temple Mount from attacks coming from the north. (photo: Philip Evans)

SOLVING THE DILEMMA OF THE POOL

The only possible explanation for this is that this part of the wall served as the eastern dam of the large water reservoir called the Pool of Israel. This reservoir is not mentioned by Josephus. It was first mentioned by its Arabic name, Birket Isra'in, in the writings of Muqadassi, an Arab geographer who lived in Jerusalem in the 10th century A.D. This pool, built as an integral part of the Herodian Temple Mount, was strategically placed in what is now known as the St. Anne's Valley with the purpose of providing an abundant supply of water. The Pools of Bethesda were also built in this valley. The dimensions of the Pool of Israel are 126 feet (38 m) from north to south and 360 feet (110 m) from east to west. The western side of the Pool of Israel slopes down towards the east, where its depth is about 69 feet (21 m) below the level of the Temple Mount.

The pool must also have served as a kind of "moat," protecting the northern wall of the Temple Mount, as it would have been impractical to launch any attack on the Temple Mount from its enormous depth. Warren also found the overflow channel of the Pool of Israel, at about one stone course above the level at which the northeast tower starts to project from the wall. This was apparently the ground level during the Herodian period. This ground level has been built up from the bottom of the valley with fills taken from different areas as attested by the description of the soil in the shafts dug by Warren. Some mosaic cubes were even found close to the bottom of his shafts.

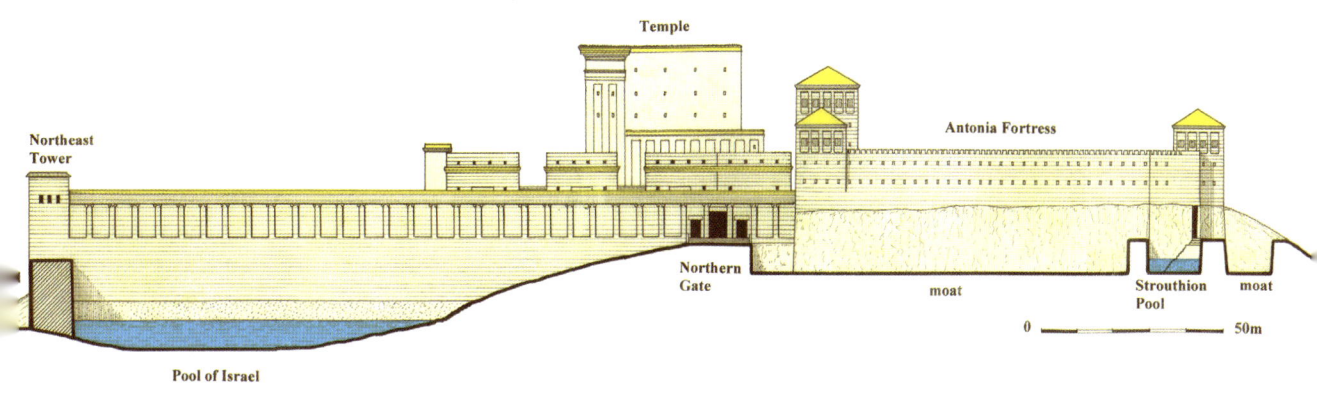

CHAPTER ONE: THE HERODIAN TEMPLE MOUNT WALLS

Above: Elevation of the Northern Wall of the Herodian Temple Mount.

Below: Reconstruction drawing of the northeast corner of the Temple Mount, indicating the Herodian remains in situ.

THE NORTHERN WALL

We have noted above that the remains of the eastern face of the Herodian tower at the northeast corner of the Temple Mount have survived to a height of approximately 30 feet (9 m) above ground. As the northern face of this corner is in line with the southern wall of the Antonia, we may assume that they were once connected. The Northern Wall of the Herodian Temple Mount was therefore protected by the tower at the northeast corner, the northern face of which we will describe more fully, the Pool of Israel, and the Antonia Fortress at the northwest corner of the Temple Mount. In addition, we shall see that this Northern Wall may have had a gate.

The Northern Façade of the Northeast Tower

The northern face of the northeast tower is the least known. As the Turkish city wall abuts this angle, it has been proposed that this angle is not a corner at all.[67] Indeed, Wilson[68] writes of *"the sudden termination of the large stones"* of the tower, and Wilkinson[69] calls the northeast corner a *"false corner"* because it *"is not matched by any corresponding corner in the Herodian wall below."*

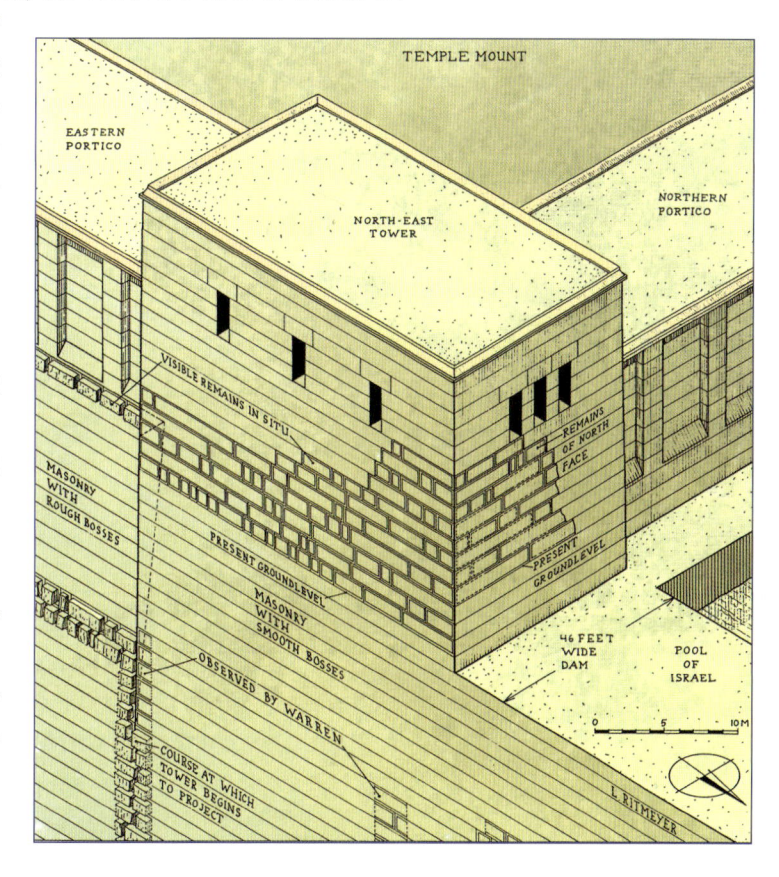

119

Chapter One: The Herodian Temple Mount Walls

Right and below: Drawing and view of the northern face of the Herodian tower at the northeast corner, indicating the Herodian ashlars only and showing where the later repairs were made with smaller stones.

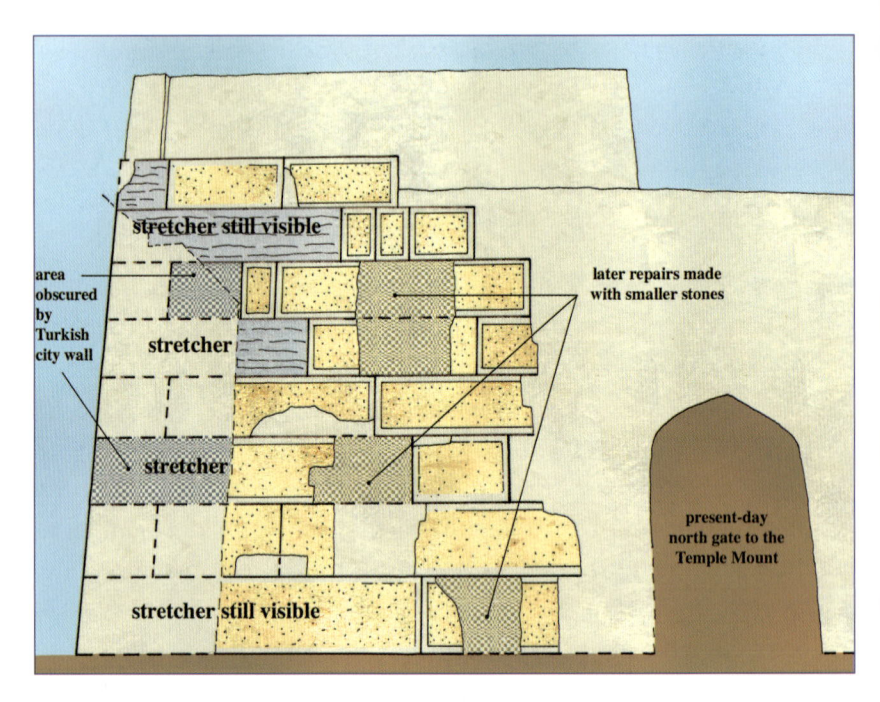

stretcher still visible

area obscured by Turkish city wall

stretcher

later repairs made with smaller stones

stretcher

present-day north gate to the Temple Mount

stretcher still visible

However, the fact that the northern part of the Herodian Eastern Wall below ground is also the external wall of the Pool of Israel does not exclude the possibility that this corner is also the northeast corner of the Temple Mount.

In our opinion, the original northern face has been preserved, although its stones are in a poor state of preservation. As many missing front parts of the obviously eroded and damaged ashlars have been filled in with small stones, the overall effect is such a patchwork that it can hardly be recognized as the northern façade of the Temple Mount. The two visible stones at the top of the Herodian tower are laid in the usual corner construction of headers and stretchers.

Viewed from the north, the top stone is a header and the one below is a stretcher. Although partially obscured by the Turkish city wall, another stretcher can be seen at the bottom of this northern face with two others in the alternating courses in between. As the joints

CHAPTER ONE: THE HERODIAN TEMPLE MOUNT WALLS

between the courses of the northern face of this tower line up with those of the eastern face, it is clear that both faces belong to one corner construction. This observation was also made by Burgoyne, a British architect, who wrote[70] that *"the coursing of the Herodian masonry continues on both east and north faces of the wall where the distinctive ashlar long and short work is indisputable evidence of Herodian construction (as may be seen at the southwest and southeast corners)."* It is therefore beyond doubt that this northern face is indeed part of the northeast tower of the Herodian Temple Mount.

Few scholars have correctly identified this face as Herodian and many were apparently unaware of Merrill's warning[71] that, *"An examination of the stones of which it is composed would have saved many writers from falling into serious error."* We again agree with Burgoyne[72] that, *"the intriguing variety of masonry types scattered among the Herodian stones belongs to later repairs and is not, as has been suggested, evidence that the Herodian stones are in secondary use."* The northern face of this tower represents therefore the northern boundary of the Herodian Temple Mount at this point.

The Southern Wall of the Pool of Israel

Below is a copy of a rare photograph taken in 1894[73] that shows the Pool of Israel before it was filled in during the 1930s. Warren investigated the bottom of the pool, and found the plastered floor 75

Old photograph of the Pool of Israel taken in 1894, before the pool was filled in.

Chapter One: The Herodian Temple Mount Walls

View of the south wall of the Pool of Israel. The rough stones can be seen below the two windows.

feet (23 m) below the level of the Temple courts. The pool is so deep that from the angle this photograph was taken, the bottom cannot be seen. Four large windows are visible in the Northern Wall of the Temple Mount. The large stones below these windows belong to the southern wall of the Pool of Israel, which corresponds to the Northern Wall of Herod's Temple Mount.

On first examination, it would appear that two different kinds of stones were used in this wall, separated by the line of vegetation. The stones above this line are rough and the ones below, at the lower right of the picture, are smoother. Thick walls like this one were built by placing two rows of stones with their faces outward and filling the center with rubble and mortar. Only the outer face of the stones was dressed and never the back, as they would not have been seen and the rough surface also provided a better grip for the mortar.

Thus when looking at the rough upper stones, what we actually see is the back of the stones that face southward towards the Temple Mount. The vegetation grows in the softer core of the wall and below

CHAPTER ONE: THE HERODIAN TEMPLE MOUNT WALLS

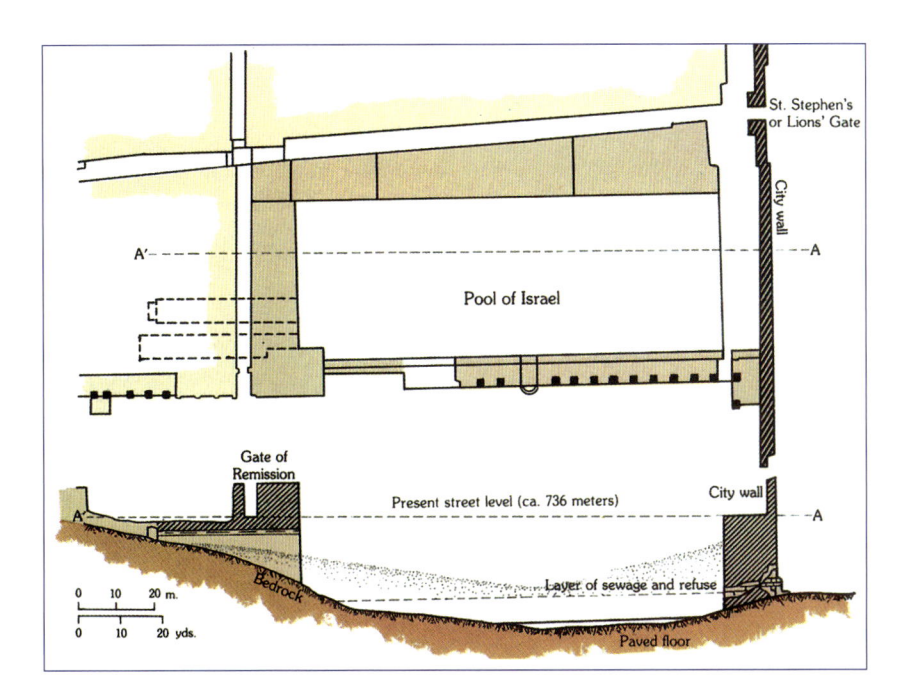

Plan (top) and cross section (bottom) of the Pool of Israel.

that we see the smoother stones that face the pool.

It is interesting to note that the Mamluk buildings and porticoes, located along the northern boundary of the Temple Mount, are built on the line between the northeast tower and the southern rockscarp of the Antonia Fortress. This indicates that the remains of the Herodian northern retaining wall are still preserved below ground. Although the upper part of the Northern Wall in between the two surviving northern corners of the Herodian Temple Mount did not survive the Roman destruction, we may nevertheless assume that the present northern boundary wall of the Temple Mount still follows the same line as that of the Herodian period.[75]

The Herodian Northern Wall can therefore be traced by following a line drawn between the corner of the northeast corner of the Temple Mount and the elevation of the southern rockscarp of the Antonia.

According to the description by Josephus of an attack on the northern quarter of the Temple Mount, it appears that a gate once existed in this wall *(War* 2.537; 6.222). The gate could only have been situated between the Antonia and the Pool of Israel.

The Antonia Fortress

The extension to the north of the square Temple Mount, as designed by Herod, called for a partial cutting away of the high hill that was

---

DATING THE POOL

The northern Temple Mount wall was built above this southern wall of the Pool of Israel. As the eastern wall of the Pool of Israel is clearly Herodian, we conclude that the pool must date from the Herodian period.

The date of the Pool of Israel has been the subject of scholarly debate, with some scholars favoring a later date because of the small stones found in the northern face of the southern wall of the pool.[74] *However, it must be considered that plaster would not have adhered easily to the smooth surface of Herodian limestone blocks, while small stones would have provided a better "grip" for the hydraulic plaster.*

Chapter One: The Herodian Temple Mount Walls

View of the northwest corner of the Temple Mount, showing the rockscarp on which the Antonia was built.

located to the north of the Fosse. The bedrock, which projected high above the level of the outer courts of the Temple Mount, was cut away, primarily to make this area more or less level with the rest of the northern court. This quarrying left vertical rockscarps standing almost 30 feet high in certain places. These rockscarps formed an almost unassailable foundation for the Antonia Fortress that dominated the Temple Mount from this high elevation.

That the Antonia was located near the northwest corner of the Temple Mount corresponds, of course, with Josephus' description (*War* 5.238–246):

> *The tower of Antonia lay at the angle where two porticoes, the western and the northern, of the first court of the Temple met; it was built upon a rock fifty cubits high and on all sides precipitous. It was the work of king Herod and a crowning exhibition of the innate grandeur of his genius.*
>
> *For, to begin with, the rock was covered from its base upwards with smooth flagstones, both for ornament and*

CHAPTER ONE: THE HERODIAN TEMPLE MOUNT WALLS

in order that anyone attempting to ascend or descend it might slip off. Next, in front of the actual edifice, there was a wall three cubits high; and behind this the tower of Antonia rose majestic to an altitude of forty cubits. The interior resembled a palace in its spaciousness and appointments, being divided into apartments of every description and for every purpose, including cloisters, baths and broad courtyards for the accommodation of the troops; so that from its possession of all conveniences it seemed a town, from its magnificence a palace. The general appearance of the whole was that of a tower with other towers at each of the four corners; three of these turrets were fifty cubits high, while that at the southeast angle rose to seventy cubits, and so commanded a view of the whole area of the Temple. At the point where it impinged on the porticoes of the Temple, there were stairs leading down to both of them, by which the guards descended; for a Roman cohort was permanently quartered there, and at the festivals took up positions in arms around the porticoes to watch the people and repress any insurrectionary movement. For if the Temple lay as a fortress over the city, Antonia dominated the Temple, and the occupants of that post were the guards of all

Left and below: Two interior views of the Antonia Fortress. (photos: Philip Evans)

Chapter One: The Herodian Temple Mount Walls

three; the upper town had its own fortress—Herod's palace.

The hill Bezetha was, as I said, cut off from Antonia; the highest of all the hills, it was encroached on by part of the new town and formed on the north the only obstruction to the view of the Temple.

This description has caused much debate among scholars. Most of them would of course agree that the Antonia was located at the northwest corner of the Herodian Temple Mount, at the junction of the western and northern porticoes; and that the rockscarps formed part of it. It is also understood that a rock-hewn moat existed to the north of the fortress, cutting it off from Bezetha. This is recorded by Josephus elsewhere, for example in *War* 5.149–150:

This hill, which is called Bezetha, lay opposite Antonia, but was cut off from it by a deep fosse, dug on purpose to sever the foundations of Antonia from the hill and so to render them at once less easy of access and more elevated, the depth of the trench materially increasing the height of the towers.

Above: View of the re-entrant angle formed at the northwest corner of the Temple Mount.

Below: Coin of Mark Antony after whom the Antonia was named.

Finally, it is also clear that the Second Wall of Jerusalem terminated at this fortress, as Josephus records in *War* 5.146, *"The second wall started from the gate in the first wall which they called Gennath, and, enclosing only the northern district of the town, went up as far as Antonia."* No remains of this wall, however, have ever been found in this area.

The problem in identifying the location of the Antonia Fortress lies in its relation to the previous Temple fortress called the *Baris* (see below, p. 216). This was a Hasmonean fortress located at the northwest corner of the square Temple Mount. Herod apparently rebuilt the *Baris* between 37 and 31 B.C. and called it Antonia after his friend Mark Antony *(Ant.* 15.403–409; 18.92). Some scholars have proposed therefore that the *Baris* stood outside and to the north of the Hasmonean Temple Mount.[76] We cannot agree with this proposal and, in Chapter 8 (p. 322), will look more closely at the historical context of this problem.

Chapter One: The Herodian Temple Mount Walls

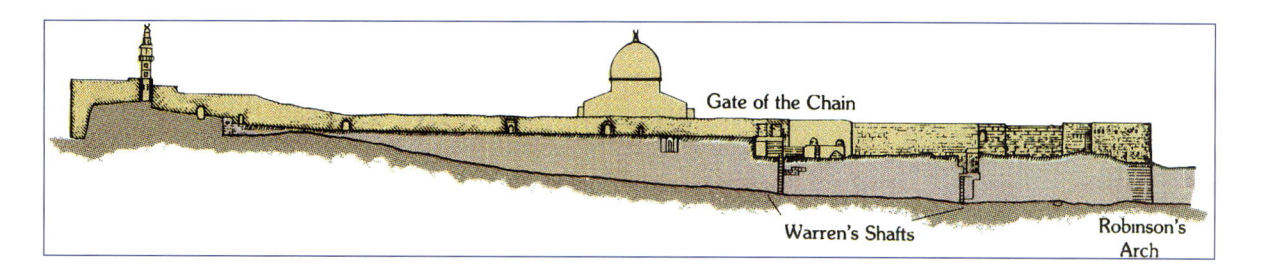

Cross section of the Temple Mount from north to south, after Warren. Viewed from the west, it is evident that quarrying from the Herodian period in the natural bedrock in the northwest corner of the Temple Mount was required for construction of the Antonia Fortress. The Ghawanima minaret now stands in the center of this elevated rocky plateau.

For now, we will concentrate on the fortress which stood above the rockscarp at the present northwest corner of the Temple Mount and, architecturally, being very closely linked to the Herodian Temple Mount. This new fortress-palace formed an integral part of the latter, as did the Pool of Israel.

This view is further supported by the identification by Burgoyne[77] of the archaeological remains of the northwest corner of the Herodian Temple Mount. He identified a corner stone by the typical Herodian drafting on its western and northern sides, which according to him is located *in situ* 13 feet (4 m) north of the Ghawanima minaret. This corner must therefore be the original northwest corner of the Herodian Temple Mount.

The northern and western sides of the two lower stories of this minaret are built against the internal northwest corner of the Temple Mount, which is located where the scarped western and northern rockfaces meet.[78] Burgoyne noted that a recess 30 feet (9 m) long and 8 feet (2.50 m) wide had been cut into the northern rockface, forming an inward pointing, or re-entrant, angle (see plan, p. 40, and photo, opposite). This would have been an ideal place for a staircase to be inserted to go up from the Temple Mount to the Antonia platform.

If the Antonia were already standing here when Herod started to enlarge the Temple Mount, there would have been no need to build a separate northwest corner, because the Antonia would have served as such. The Western and Northern walls would have been built against the southern and eastern sides of this fortress. However, the discovery of this Herodian northwest corner indicates that this new fortress was built following the enlargement of the Temple Mount.

Some theories as to the extent of the Antonia, such as those of De Vogüé,[79] Warren,[80] Schick,[81] Watson,[82] Hollis,[83] and even as recent as that of Simons,[84] showed the Antonia projecting onto the Temple Mount area. By now, however, such ideas have been virtually abandoned.

Other scholars such as Barnabé,[85] Vincent,[86] Marie-Aline de Sion[87] and

> **COULD PAUL HAVE STOOD HERE?**
>
> *If there was indeed such a staircase, its existence would bring to life in our minds the event recorded in Acts 21: 37–40. When the Apostle Paul was captured on the Temple Mount and was about to be led into the Antonia Fortress, he stood on the steps and asked the Roman captain if he could address the Jewish people. As this location is also the place where the northern and western porticoes met (War 5.238), we can imagine Paul climbing the staircase and then standing on the roof of the porticoes to give his stirring defense in Hebrew from this elevated spot.*

Chapter One: The Herodian Temple Mount Walls

Benoit[88] agree that the Antonia was situated above and to the north of these rockscarps that are still visible near the northwest corner of the Temple Mount, where the Umariyya School is now located. This school building is constructed on a mass of rock, defined to the north by a rockscarp and measuring approximately 120 feet (36.50 m) from north to south and 400 feet (122 m) from east to west.

It was Benoit who suggested that the location of the Antonia was restricted to this rocky plateau. He criticized the theories of Barnabé, Vincent and Marie-Aline de Sion, all of whom incorporated into their plan of the Antonia Fortress various archaeological elements that have been excavated to the north of the Umariyya School. These elements include the so-called Lithostrotos pavement, the Strouthion Pool, the double gate to the west of the Ecce Homo arch and some rockscarps. Benoit pointed out that his colleagues' designs were untenable, as the Lithostrotos pavement, the Ecce Home arch and the double vault over the Strouthion Pool are all contemporary and date to the period of Hadrian (A.D. 132–135). He also proved that the proposed gates, galleries and towers are entirely without foundation. Bagatti[89] has also proved that the so-called stylobate, which was the basis for the reconstruction of the galleries of the Antonia by Marie-Aline, is actually the remains of a staircase. Other elements of Marie-Aline's theory have been refuted by Wightman,[90] so that there is no need to discuss them here.

The location of the Antonia on the rocky plateau, as suggested by Benoit, has gained wide approval. However, this proposal still needs further refinement.

Above: Close-up view of one of the sockets for the beams of the northern stoa.

Below: Photograph taken in the nineteenth century, showing the holes, or sockets, for the beams of the northern stoa.

That the rockscarp is the southern limit of the Antonia has recently been confirmed by Burgoyne, who was able to identify the sockets for the beams of the northern portico, or stoa.[91] These sockets, which are 19 inches (48 cm) square, are located in this rockscarp at about 29 English feet (8.84 m) above the level of the Temple Mount. The horizontal beams would have rested on top of an architrave which ran above

CHAPTER ONE: THE HERODIAN TEMPLE MOUNT WALLS

Drawing of the Antonia rockscarp with the present-day Umariyya School.

the capitals of the columns; and so the height of the columns would have been shorter, approximately 27 feet (8.23 m).

Burgoyne[93] identified the remains of an ancient wall, which ran all along the top of this southern rockscarp and which was more than 13 feet (4 m) thick. Because of its size and location, he identified this as the southern wall of the Antonia Fortress.

Parts of this wall are visible in the southern rooms of the Umariyya School. Some of these rooms are actually carved into this wall, further traces of which have been found as far east as the Is'ardiyya, a building that once housed a library. Inside this building, the remains of a Herodian pilaster have been found, preserved *in situ* to a height of 6.5 feet (2 m). Further investigations have shown that the north wall of the Temple Mount is made of scarped bedrock as far as the al-Farisiyya, where it stands to a height of over 8 feet (2.50 m).[94] The length of this rockscarp, measured from the east side of the bedrock remains of the Herodian Western Wall near the Ghawanima minaret, where we have identified the internal northwest corner of the Herodian Temple Mount, is about 394 feet (120 m).

The wall of three cubits in height that Josephus mentioned in the above-quoted description of the Antonia may have enclosed an

> **AN ANCIENT CONFUSION**
>
> *Josephus in* Ant. *15.413 indeed gives a measurement of 27 Roman feet for columns on the Temple Mount (the Roman foot[92] is approximately 11.65 inches [0.296 m]). However, Josephus in this context is speaking here of the columns of the Royal Stoa, which have always been known to be higher than those of the other porticoes. Indeed, in* War *5.190, he describes the columns of the Royal Stoa as being 25 cubits high, which, according to the cubit of 20.67 inches would be 43 feet (13 m). The remains of columns found in the Temple Mount excavations indicate that the columns of the Royal Stoa were approximately 38 feet (11.58 m) high. It appears therefore that Josephus in* Ant. *15.413 must have confused the height of the columns of the Royal Stoa with those of the porticoes that surrounded the Temple Mount.*
>
> *The rockscarp on which the Antonia stood is at present only 32 feet (9.75 m, c. 19 cubits) higher than the court of the Temple, although when measured from the bottom of the Strouthion Pool, the rockscarp is 60 feet (18.29 m, c. 35 cubits) high. It is doubtful whether the rock was ever higher; therefore Josephus' figure of 50 cubits must be an exaggeration. This perhaps shows that his measurements, when given in Roman feet, are more reliable than those given in cubits.*

Chapter One: The Herodian Temple Mount Walls

A PLAUSIBLE RECONSTRUCTION OF THE ANTONIA FORTRESS

Having investigated the Herodian remains in the vicinity of the Antonia, we can now suggest a reconstruction of this fortress. It had four towers, three of which were 50 cubits (86 feet or 26.25 m) high, while that on the southeast was 20 cubits higher than the other three, i.e. 70 cubits (120 feet or 36.75 m) high. The towers would have had loopholes and windows for defense purposes. The roof itself may have been covered with lead sheeting to prevent it from being set alight by flaming arrows. Strong walls, fortified with battlements, would have connected these towers. On the inside the fortress had several courtyards surrounded by porticoes, shops and barracks. A reconstruction of the Antonia Fortress must take into consideration the bedrock salient to the south and west of the Ghawanima minaret. It is possible that the southwest tower of the Antonia was partly located above this scarp. We suggest that the southern part of this western scarp may have carried an L-shaped approach road. This would have ran from the west over the western salient up to the line of the Western Wall of the Temple Mount. From there it would have first turned north through the basement of the southwest tower of the Antonia and then, turning east, enter the inner courtyard.

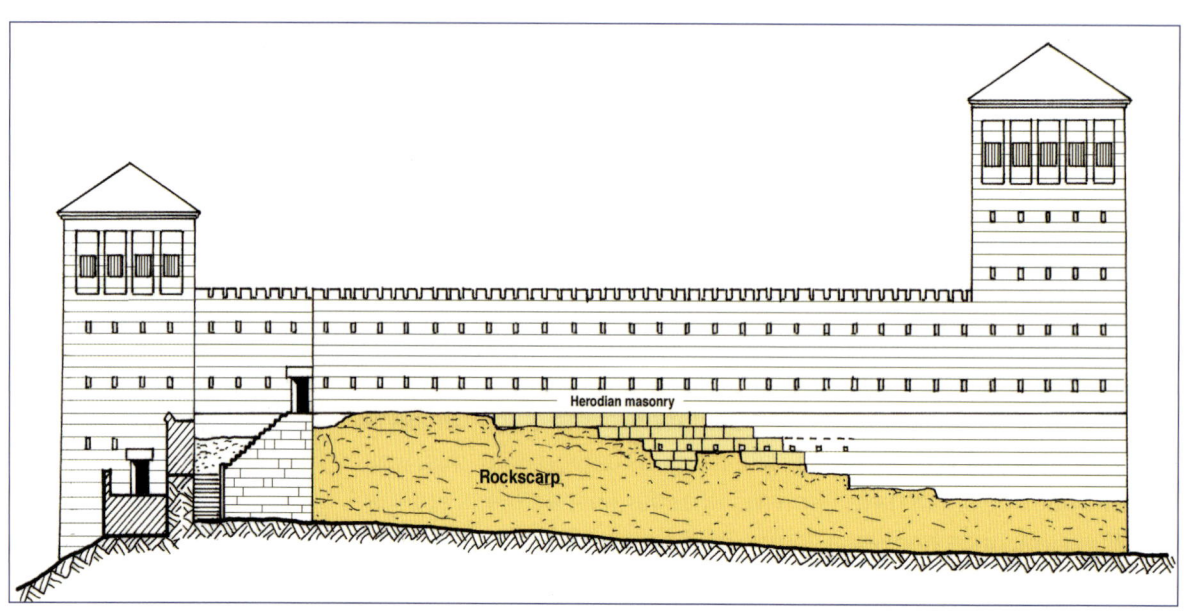

Top: View of the L-shaped approach to the Antonia Fortress. (photo: Philip Evans)

Above: Reconstruction drawing of the southern wall of the Antonia Fortress.

area larger than the actual fortress, and may have included not only the Strouthion Pool, but also the moat itself, which was apparently a large area to the north of the fortress. The scanty bedrock remains to the north of the Antonia plateau make it difficult to establish the exact width of the moat that separated the Antonia from Bezetha. The high rockscarp at the northern end of the Strouthion Pool may have extended to the west and to the east, in which case the moat would have been approximately 160 feet (48 m) wide.[95] We propose

CHAPTER ONE: THE HERODIAN TEMPLE MOUNT WALLS

The Northern Part of the Temple Mount Courtyard

In order to create a level area in the northern part of the Herodian Temple Mount, Herod's workers found it necessary to fill in that part of St. Anne's Valley that was located to the south of the Herodian Northern Wall, including its western branch, the Bezetha Valley and the Fosse (for plan, see p. 168). The bedrock of the natural hill on which the Antonia Fortress was built was partly cut away to form steep rockscarps.

This part of the court was paved and some of the large paving slabs still survive to the present day, though they have recently been

Above: Reconstruction model of the Antonia and the northern stoa. (photo: Philip Evans)

Below: Herodian paving slabs between the Fosse and the Antonia.

Cedars of Lebanon, used in the construction of the Temple.

covered up with garden soil. Bagatti[96] gives the dimensions of the two largest paving stones as 7 feet (2.14 m) and 8.5 feet (2.59 m) by 5 feet 8 inches (1.74 m). He also mentions another that is 2 feet 11 inches (0.88 m) long.

The Herodian Eastern Wall between the *offset* north of the Golden Gate, along with the northeast tower and the southern wall of the Pool of Israel, form in fact a huge retaining wall that was built to counteract the pressure of the enormous amounts of fill that had to be dumped there to raise this area to the level of the Temple court.

CONSTRUCTING HEROD'S TEMPLE MOUNT

So far we have discussed the great Herodian constructions. Let us now consider how these magnificent buildings were erected and what techniques were used to accomplish the work.

The main building material used in constructing the Temple Mount was local limestone. Even today, most buildings in Jerusalem are made of or faced with local limestone. Different types of wood were also used for ceiling beams, doorframes, doors and furniture. Certain trees such as cedar had to be imported from Lebanon.

The building stones were quarried out of the mountains around Jerusalem, which are composed of Turonian and Cenomanian limestone. Several types of limestone were and still are used in the building trade. They are called *mizzi yahudi, mizzi hilu, mizzi ahmar* and *meleke*.

The top layer of conglomeratic limestone, called *nari (*which means firestone*)*, is found at the top of the Mount of Olives and on other mountaintops surrounding the Jerusalem basin on the east and south. It is a soft, fire-resistant limestone. Because of its light weight, it is often used to make arches or vaults in smaller buildings.

The next limestone layer in the region of the Old City is *mizzi hilu* (which means sweet limestone), so named because it is an easy stone to carve. It is a hard stone, non-granular, and can be polished to a high degree. The Rock, for example, is part of this limestone range which can reach depths of 82 feet (25 m). Many of the decorative elements found in Mazar's excavations were made of this limestone, as were load-bearing stones such as columns and capitals.

Below this *mizzi hilu* lies the much softer granular stratum called *meleke* (meaning "royal"). This rock is soft underground, but hardens on exposure and is therefore an ideal building material. Many stones

CHAPTER ONE: THE HERODIAN TEMPLE MOUNT WALLS

Bedrock layers in the Jerusalem mountains near Yad Vashem.

of the Temple Mount walls are made of this *meleke* limestone. An interesting example of how the different qualities of limestone were exploited can be seen at Robinson's Arch, where all the voussoirs are made of the lighter and easier-to-quarry *meleke,* but the keystone—which had to withstand the strongest stress forces—was made of the much harder *mizzi hilu.*

The lowest geological layer in the Jerusalem area which can be quarried is *mizzi yahudi,* an extremely hard limestone used mainly where resistance to wear is needed, such as for thresholds and door sockets. Because of its hardness it is difficult for water to penetrate these underground layers. Thus water collects in cavities in the softer *meleke* layer that lies above it, flows from one cavity to another and pours out into the Gihon Spring.

A large workforce was necessary for the construction of the Temple Mount and the buildings that were designed to be built on this artificial platform. According to Josephus *(Ant.* 15.390), Herod

> ...prepared a thousand wagons to carry the stones, selected ten thousand of the most skilled workmen, purchased priestly robes for a thousand priests, and trained

133

Chapter One: The Herodian Temple Mount Walls

HOW LIMESTONE WAS QUARRIED

The different geological strata are all made up of horizontal layers that vary in depth from 18 inches (45 cm) to 5 feet (1.50 m). This natural horizontal layering determined the quarry method that has been employed since Iron Age times.

Most of the stones used in the outer walls of the Herodian Temple Mount range in height from 40 to 47 inches (1.00 to 1.20 m). The height of each course is dependent on the height of the bedrock layer from which the stones are cut. Great care was taken to ensure that the individual stones in each stone course had the same height. Each stone course would therefore have its own individual height, but occasionally a stone course is stepped up a little, presumably because one rock layer was completely quarried away and another was started with a slightly different height.

In the quarries, the stone-cutter would use chisels to straighten the vertical face of the stone and to flatten the top surface. Examining the stone formation for possible cracks, he would then choose and set out the size of the stone he was going to extract. The length of the stone was dependent on the quality of the rock and that is the reason why all the stones have different lengths.

Using a pick-axe, he would then dig narrow channels of approximately 4 to 6 inches (10 to 15 cm) wide around the new stone and all the way down to the next bedrock layer. The three sides of the incipient stone would then be free, but still attached to the bedrock at the bottom.

Two methods were used to free the stone, using either wooden or iron implements. In the former case, the channels that were cut around the stone would have had a consistent width all the way down. Wooden beams were inserted into two of these grooves at right angles and hammered in tightly. The quarry-men would then pour water over the wood, causing it to swell. The resulting pressure was strong enough to cause the stone to split off from the rock layer below. If the extraction tools were made of iron, the channels would be V-shaped. Long metal strips would be placed opposite each other inside the grooves. Workmen hammered iron wedges down in between the strips, creating pressure that separated the stone from the natural rock.

The next stage was the squaring-off of the stone and preparation for transportation. The smaller stones were placed on wagons pulled by oxen, while larger ones would be encased in round wooden wheel-like constructions and rolled down by oxen from the quarry to the building site. Columns were rolled down in a frame that was fixed around them. The frame was made of two long beams, which were placed along the two long sides of the column, and two short beams which were placed opposite the ends of the column. Rings were fixed in the center of these short beams. The two ends of the columns had holes drilled in their centers into which iron dowels were fitted and affixed to the stone with lead. These dowels were then placed into the rings of the frame. The column inside this frame could now be rolled like a bicycle wheel. Oxen would pull at one of the long beams of this contraption and the column would roll gently down to the site.

Large stones were lifted on one side by cranes and placed on wooden rollers. While the stones were being shaped in the quarry, the masons left small square projections of about 4 inches (12 cm) sticking out on either side of the stones. Ropes were placed around them, so that cranes fitted with pulleys could lift them and place them on rollers. Several teams of oxen would pull the stones with ropes placed around the same projections. Once the stones were lowered into place, these projections were removed. Yet a few have survived and left us evidence of how the stones were lifted and transported. It is still a mystery, however, how the very large corner stones, some weighing over 75 tons, were moved at the time.

Close-up view of one of the small square projections left by stonemasons.

some as masons, others as carpenters, and began the construction only after all these preparations had diligently been made by him.

The quarries were located about a mile away from the Temple Mount, near today's Russian Compound north of the Old City, where a 40-foot (12.50 m) long column can still be seen (see photo, p. 136). Quarrying was discontinued and the column was left still attached to the bedrock when a defect in the stone was detected. Transporting such stones was facilitated by a slope of 2.5 percent down to the 130-foot (40 m) lower Temple Mount. Because the surface area to the north is higher, the stones for the construction of the Temple Mount came thence.

CHAPTER ONE: THE HERODIAN TEMPLE MOUNT WALLS

We have seen how the stones were quarried and transported. Now we must ask how these stones were placed in the walls, especially corner stones that weighed 75 tons or more and which can still be seen high above the level of the Herodian street. Some of the more pious of the local workers at the Temple Mount dig, who were constantly handling large stones in their work, were so awed by the size of these corner stones that they attributed their placement to angels. In their eyes, it would have been impossible for mere men

Quarrying stone. The stone cutter at right uses a pickaxe to cut a channel in the rock. The other worker pours water over the wooden beams that have been tightly wedged in the channels. The water makes the wood swell and the resulting lateral pressure causes the stone to split off from the rock to which it is attached at the bottom.

Transporting stones. At top left the bedrock shows its natural horizontal layering. At top right the quarried stones are waiting to be moved to the stone-cutter at bottom left who dresses the stone and leaves a projection so that the stone can be lifted by the crane at bottom right. In the middle of the picture oxen are pulling a very large stone. The men move the rollers from the back of the stone to the front to ease the movement of the stone.

135

Chapter One: The Herodian Temple Mount Walls

Large column found in situ *in the Russian Compound.*

to move such stones, let alone lift them up to such a great height. In a sense they were right, for no person could have lifted such large stones to such a great height, despite the sophisticated Roman engineering techniques which were current at the time of building.

In fact, the stones did not have to be hoisted up from below or rolled up a ramp. I believe that they were instead lowered into place by cranes similar to those that had lifted them up in the first place at the quarries. Let us remember that the 15-foot- (5 m) thick Temple Mount walls are essentially retaining walls built to retain the huge pressure of the fill which was dumped behind the new walls and in between the old Temple platform. This is why every stone course is set back an inch or so from the course below, giving the wall a batter, which is characteristic of retaining walls.

As no records have been preserved to inform us exactly how the walls were constructed, we have to make an educated guess. We must keep in mind that a kind of hardcore fill had to be deposited between the old and new Temple Mount walls and that the manner in which Robinson's Arch is set in the wall indicates that the construction began with the southern wall. The most logical way for Herod's engineers to have solved this construction problem would have been to build the foundation course on the bedrock first. This would have involved the clearing of the site down to bedrock and then setting out the line of the wall. Next the bedrock had to be cut in order to create level areas for placing the foundation stones. After the first row was built, fill was laid in the area behind it up to the top of that first stone course. A level work surface was thus created on which, from the inside of the Temple Mount, the second row of stones could be transported to their final destination above the foundation course. A crane would have lowered the stones to their places on the wall. Again, after filling in the inside, the third stone course could be built. By repeating this process over and over again, building stone course upon stone course and simultaneously filling up the inside, the whole of Herod's extension was raised up to the level of the old platform. The original southern retaining wall was 130 feet (40 m) high at its highest point and in the east, the highest part of the wall was 160 feet (48 m) high!

At the northwest corner where the Antonia Fortress was located, the rocky mountain was higher than the platform. That is why, as we have previously seen, part of the mountain had to be quarried away in

Chapter One: The Herodian Temple Mount Walls

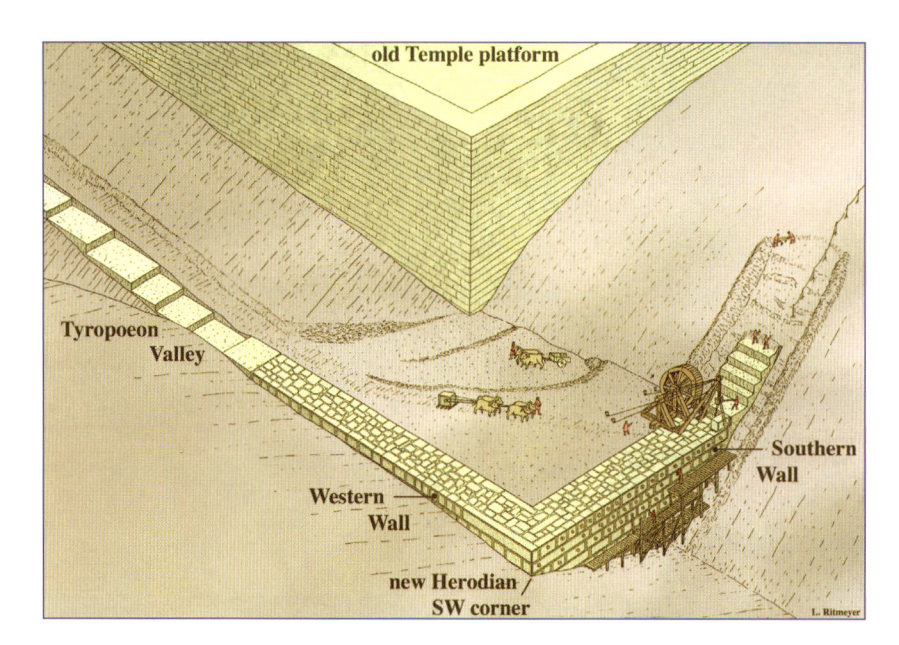

The process of building the Herodian Temple Mount walls.

order to make the platform level. Even so, one can still detect a slight rise in the rock, sloping up to the southern rockscarp of the Antonia. As Mount Moriah slopes down from north to south, it is reasonable to suggest that the stones of the retaining walls were brought in from the north and that the construction of the first stone courses commenced in the south.

It has not been possible to determine the nature of the fill behind the Herodian Temple Mount walls. It would not have consisted only of a homogeneous fill of hard core, but would also have had a grid of foundation walls, such as the walls of the passage below the Single Gate, built into it to support the walls of the projected buildings above. The large retaining walls, with stones weighing up to 570 tons and the massive fill behind them, had to be planned and constructed meticulously to form a solid substructure on which the magnificent Herodian buildings could be built.

Stones belonging to the superstructure of the Temple and its surrounding buildings had collapsed during the destruction of A.D. 70. Most of these stones were removed later for other building purposes, and the few stones that were found in the dig were not very large in comparison to the stones of the retaining walls. To hoist up stones which weigh no more than two or three tons to the top of the buildings on the Temple Mount would not have posed a great problem for Herod's skilled engineers and builders.

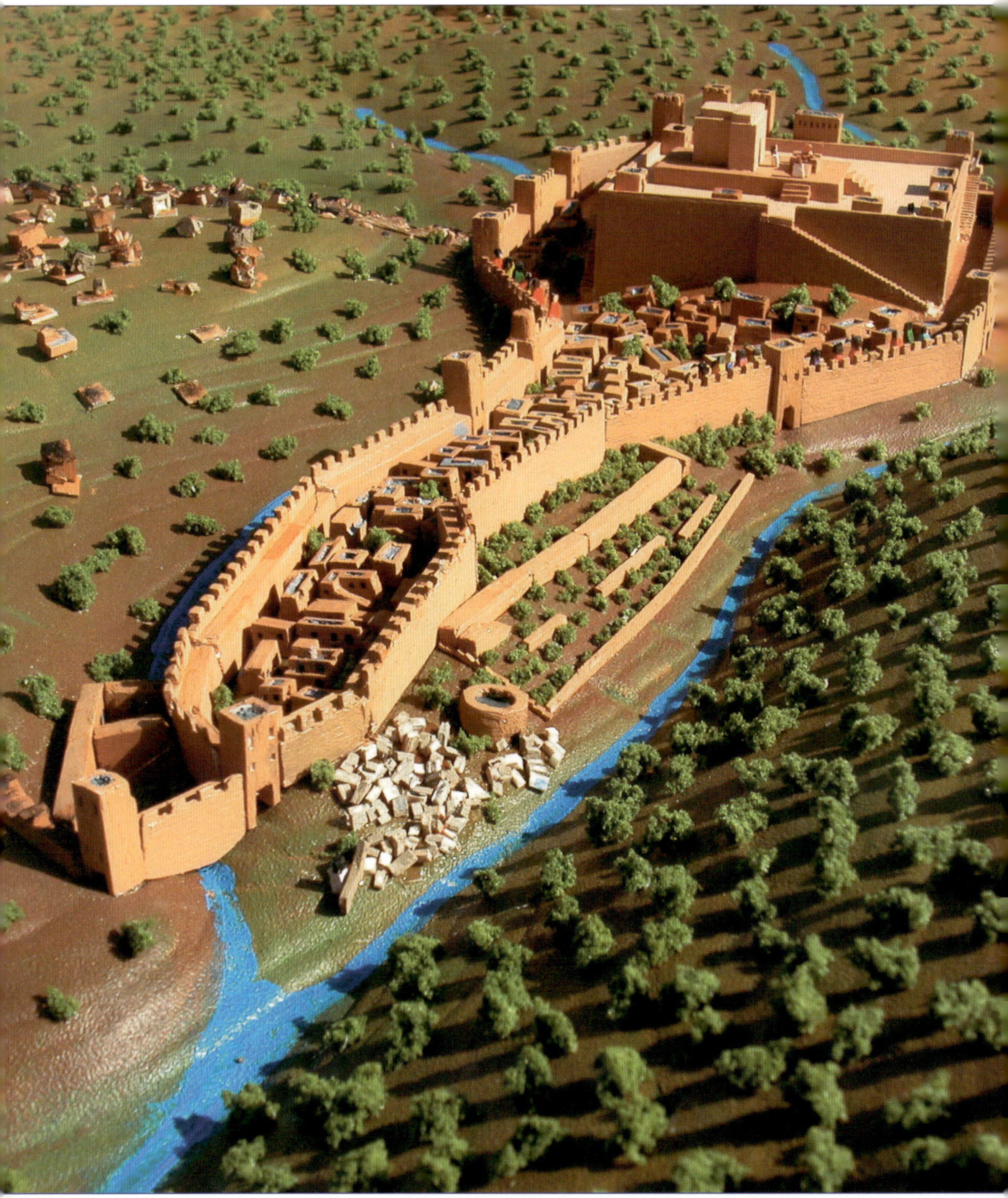

Opposite page: Reconstruction model of Jerusalem and the square Temple Mount in the time of Nehemiah.

Below: William Makepeace Thackeray (1811–1863), translator of some of Josephus' works.

Chapter Two
The Pre-Herodian Square Temple Mount

HISTORICAL INFORMATION

The major historical sources which are referred to in this book are the works of Flavius Josephus and the tractate *Middot* of the Mishnah. Although additional historical works, such as the Bible, the *Letter of Aristeas,* the *Books of Maccabees, Ecclesiasticus* and other writings are also quoted in the later chapters, only Josephus and *Middot* contain the vital information upon which our research is based.

In the past, the descriptions of the Temple in Josephus and *Middot* were thought to be difficult to understand and appeared to contain many discrepancies. These were summed up by Thackeray[1], who translated some of the works of Josephus:

> *For comparison with this [Josephus'] account of Herod's Temple we possess a second partial description in the tractate of the Mishnah entitled* Middot(h) *(= "measures" sc. of the Temple), written c.* A.D. *150. The two accounts are in many particulars inconsistent.* Middoth *on some points usefully supplements Josephus; but its author, whose information comes to him at second hand, writes without the strict regard for accuracy of a mere antiquarian. Like Ezekiel, he has before him a picture of the ideal Temple of the future. Of the two accounts, that of Josephus, who had seen the Temple, is the more trustworthy; but the discrepancies between Josephus,* Middoth*, and archaeological discovery are so great that in*

Chapter Two: The Pre-Herodian Square Temple Mount

the opinion of the most recent editor[2] of the tractate "the true picture of the Herodian Temple can no longer to-day be drawn."

This view has had to be revised since Mazar's excavations at the Temple Mount and our subsequent research. We believe that our research shows conclusively that Josephus is concerned mainly with the Herodian Temple Mount, although he makes a few remarks about the previous "Solomonic" sanctuary which, according to him, was a square having sides of a stadium in length.

The subject of *Middot*, on the other hand, is exclusively the 500-cubit-square "Mountain of the House," as the Temple Mount is referred to in this historical document. We propose that this square "Mountain of the House" of *Middot* is the same as the square "Solomonic" (or rather pre-Herodian) sanctuary mentioned occasionally by Josephus; and refers basically to the area occupied by the Temple Mount as it existed at the end of the First Temple period. Despite the expansions of the Temple Mount during the Hasmonean and Herodian periods, this square platform retained its separate entity. Indeed, this area alone is the subject of the tractate *Middot*. We will first examine the description of Josephus.

Flavius Josephus

Josephus' account is of vital importance, as he saw the Herodian Temple complex with his own eyes. However, the measurements given by him are not always easy to understand. His first references to the square Temple Mount are in *Antiquities*:

> *Outside of this [sacred precinct] he [Solomon] built another sacred precinct in the form of a quadrangle and erected great and wide porticoes.* (Ant. 8.96)

> *This hill our first king, Solomon, with God-given wisdom surrounded with great works above at the top....Such was the whole enclosure, having a circumference of four stades, each side taking up the length of a stade.*
> (Ant. 15.398, 400)

Josephus Flavius, as pictured in a 19th-century illustration.

From these two statements it could be understood that the Temple Mount was already a square in the time of Solomon. However, Josephus' other record of Solomon's building activities, that in *War* 5.184–185, gives a different picture:

Chapter Two: The Pre-Herodian Square Temple Mount

Model of the so-called "Porch of Solomon," or eastern portico which faces the Temple façade. (photo: Philip Evans)

Though the Temple, as I said, was seated on a strong hill, the level area on its summit originally barely sufficed for shrine and altar, the ground around it being precipitous and steep. But king Solomon, the actual founder of the Temple, having walled up the eastern side, a single portico was reared on this made ground; on its other sides the sanctuary remained exposed. In course of ages, however, through the constant additions of the people to the embankment, the hill-top by this process of levelling up was widened.

From these apparently contradictory statements it may be inferred that Solomon built the actual Temple, while the four-stadia-square Temple Mount was constructed by the later kings of Judah.

It also appears that Josephus, in describing Solomon's Temple, used Herod's Temple as a model. As the building of a separate eastern portico is not recorded elsewhere, it seems plausible that "the Porch of Solomon," as the eastern portico in Herod's time was referred to, was an integral part of the post-Solomonic square Temple Mount, rather than an independent structure built by him.[3]

Chapter Two: The Pre-Herodian Square Temple Mount

After mentioning this square structure in *Antiquities* 15.400, however, Josephus continues to describe the outer enclosures. He can only be referring to the outer courts which Herod added to the north, south and west of the pre-Herodian Temple Mount. This would agree with the paragraph in which, after having described the court or enclosure which surrounded the inner court of the Temple and the Court of Women, Josephus writes,

> *Into none of these courts did King Herod enter since he was not a priest and was therefore prevented from so doing. But with the construction of the porticoes and the outer courts he did busy himself, and these he finished building in eight years.* (Ant. 15.420)

The walls of these outer enclosures, added by Herod the Great, can be none other than the existing Western, Southern and Northern walls and parts of the Eastern Wall of the present-day Temple Mount. As we have seen earlier, the excavations to the west and south of the Temple Mount have proved indisputably that these walls were originally built by Herod the Great.

The fact that the Temple Mount was enlarged in three directions only is also confirmed by Josephus in *War* 5.186–187, which presumably refers to the Herodian additions which were made to the earlier Temple Mount:

> *They further broke down the north wall and thus took in an area as large as the whole Temple enclosure subsequently occupied. Then, after having enclosed the hill from its base with a wall on three sides, and accomplished a task greater than they could ever have hoped to achieve.*

As will be seen below, the extension in three directions, as designed by Herod, made the Temple Mount exactly twice its original size. Again, this enlargement was referred to by Josephus in *War* 1.401: "Thus, in the 15th year of his reign, he [Herod] restored the Temple and, by erecting new foundation-walls, enlarged the surrounding area to double its former extent."

It is worth mentioning here that some researchers, such as de Vogüé, Warren, Conder and Hollis, have tried to circumvent the above difficulty by adopting the measurement of 400 cubits (600 feet/ 183 m), mentioned elsewhere by Josephus, as a dimension of length

Lt. C. R. Conder (1848–1910). (photo: Palestine Exploration Fund)

Chapter Two: The Pre-Herodian Square Temple Mount

> ### Reconciling Josephus and the Mishnah
>
> It is clear then that most of Josephus' text refers to the Herodian Temple Mount. The measurements in his text (War 5.192), however, are difficult to comprehend: "The complete circuit of them [i.e. the porticoes of the outer court], embracing the tower of Antonia, measured six furlongs (stadia)." A surface with a compass of six stadia is, of course, twice as large as one with a compass of four stadia, if one square is placed next to another. However, that was not the way the Temple Mount was enlarged according to Josephus. In addition, it must be considered that the length of a stadium (c. 607 feet or 185 m) does not equal the length of 500 cubits mentioned in Middot (see below, pp. 170–173).
>
> It would appear that the only way to understand these figures is to assume that Josephus' length of a stadium refers to the sides of the pre-Herodian (though not necessarily Solomonic) square Temple Mount, which, as we will attempt to prove in this book, were in reality 861 feet (262.50 m) or 500 cubits long. The stadium was chosen by Josephus, presumably, because it was the nearest Roman unit of measurement which approximates 500 cubits, although a stadium is in effect 30 percent shorter.
>
> The perimeter of the present-day Temple Mount is about 5,120 to 5,150 feet and its surface 35 to 36 acres.[4]
>
> This figure is about twice as large as the surface of the 500-cubit-square pre-Herodian Temple Mount, which is 17.2 acres. A square stadium, however, has a surface of 8.6 acres, which is only 25 percent of the present surface. This discrepancy would in itself prove Josephus' measurements wrong.
>
> The only way in which the square "Solomonic" (which must be understood to mean pre-Hasmonean) Temple Mount of Josephus can be equated with that mentioned in the Mishnah would be to assume that Josephus gave a rough estimation only of the measurements of the Temple Mount.

for the sides of the square Temple Mount. This would be especially attractive, as a length of 600 feet approximates that of a stadium. However, an examination of the two texts where this measurement occurs makes it quite clear that Josephus is speaking of the height of the outer walls of the Temple Mount and especially that of the Eastern Wall.

The first passage is *Antiquities* 8.97:

> *But wonderful and surpassing all description, and even, one might say, all sight, was the (third) sacred precinct which he made outside of these, for he filled up with earth great valleys, into which because of their immense depth one could not without difficulty look down, and bringing them up to a height of four hundred cubits he made them level with the top of the mountain on which the Temple was built; in this way the outer precinct, which was open to the sky, was on a level with the Temple.*

The second passage, which is taken from Whiston's translation (*Ant.* 20.9.7 ‖ *Ant.* 20.221 [Thackeray, ed.]) reads, *"These (eastern) cloisters belonged to the outer court, and were situated in a deep valley, and had walls that reached four hundred cubits [in length] and were built of square and very white stones."*

The first quote refers to a *"bringing up,"* in other words, up to the internal level of the Herodian Temple Mount. This was achieved by building massive retaining walls and simultaneously filling up the interior until it was level with *"the top of the mountain."*

The second quote refers to the supporting walls, which had to be of the same height at least as the internal fill in order to retain the outward pressure. It is clear then that both quotes refer to a vertical measurement. The insertion by Whiston of the words *"[in length]"* after *"four hundred cubits"* in the second quote is therefore, in our opinion, unjustified.

The figure of four hundred cubits must, of course, be an exaggeration given the fact that the height of the internal level of the Temple Mount above the lowest point in the Eastern Wall, excluding the porticoes, is 160 feet (48 m)—which is equivalent to 91 cubits.

Middot

As mentioned above, the subject of *Middot*[5] is the "Mountain of the House," or *har ha-bayit*, as the Temple Mount is called in Hebrew. The size of the Temple Mount is given in *Middot* 2.1: *"The Temple Mount measured five hundred cubits by five hundred cubits."*

Despite the fact that the Mishnah, including *Middot*, was compiled some time after the Roman destruction of the Temple in Jerusalem (probably during the second century A.D.), this measurement of 500 cubits was found to be correct for the sides of the square pre-Hasmonean Temple Mount.[6] The fact that Herod's outer enclosures are not referred to at all indicates that *Middot* refers only to the area occupied by the Temple Mount as it existed at the end of the First Temple period. Only this original, square "Mountain of the House" seems to have been "holy" according to the author(s) of *Middot*[7]. This would agree with the description of the inner enclosure by Josephus in *Antiquities* 15.417–419, from which King Herod was barred.

In consequence, the gates mentioned in *Middot* must necessarily belong to this square Temple Mount, as *Middot* 1.3 says:

> There were five gates to the Temple Mount: the two Huldah Gates on the south, that served for coming in and for going out; the Kiponus Gate on the west, that served for coming in and for going out; the Tadi Gate on the north which was not used at all; the Eastern Gate on which was portrayed the Palace of Shushan. Through this the High Priest that burned the [Red] Heifer, and all that aided him went forth to the Mount of Olives.

Later on in this chapter we shall try to locate these gateways. We have shown above that the gates mentioned by Josephus were built in

Rare title page of the mishnaic tractate Middot(h), *printed in Latin in 1630.*

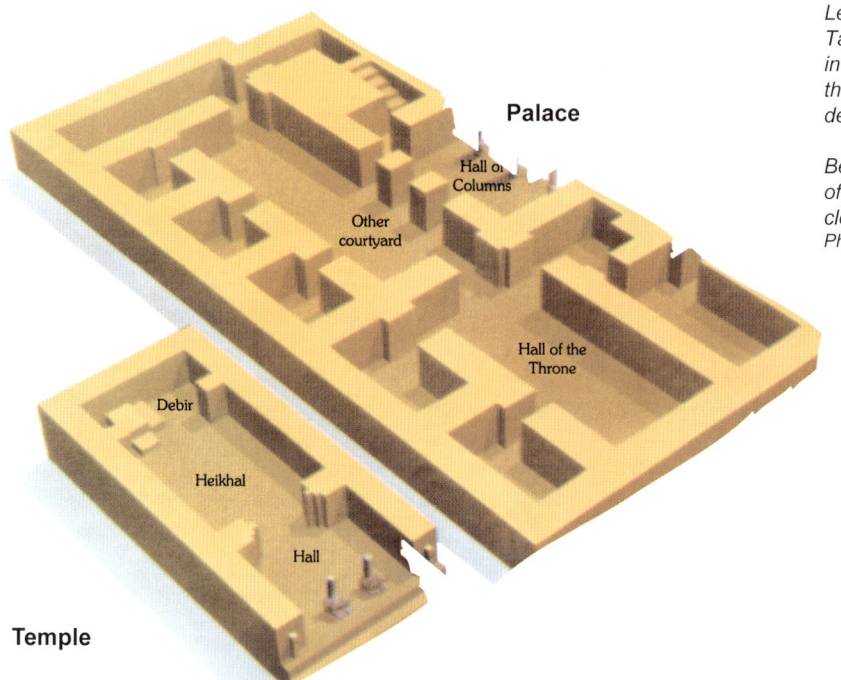

Chapter Two: The Pre-Herodian Square Temple Mount

Left: Plan of the temple at Tell Ta'yinat in northern Syria (today in Turkey), which resembles that of the Solomonic temple as described in the Bible.

Below: Reconstruction model of the Temple Mount showing a close-up view of the soreg. *(photo: Philip Evans)*

the outer walls of the outer enclosures that were added by Herod the Great during a building project that lasted eight years. The five gates mentioned in *Middot* cannot be the same as those Herodian gates, of which there were at least seven and probably eight, according to Josephus. The fact that the "Mountain of the House" of the Mishnah refers only to this square area is also supported by the fact that the Herodian porticoes and the Antonia fortress are not mentioned in this tractate.

From the exclusive reference to the earlier square made in *Middot*, which was written after the construction of the Herodian platform, it would appear that the gates mentioned in this tractate belong specifically to this earlier square Temple Mount. After Herod's additions, the earlier square Temple Mount became a kind of walled inner court or enclosure. *Middot* further mentions that inside this walled compound there was another barrier, called in Hebrew the *soreg*. This was a low barrier which had inscriptions placed at certain intervals forbidding Gentiles to proceed any farther. Beyond this barrier and above a flight of steps was a narrow terrace, called the *hel*. This terrace surrounded the inner Temple complex with its elaborate gates and courtyards. This complex will be described in Chapter 9.

145

CHAPTER TWO: THE PRE-HERODIAN SQUARE TEMPLE MOUNT

Opposite page: Schematic plans of various proposals for the location of the square Temple Mount.

SAKHRA: Arabic for Rock, particularly the rock-mass inside the Dome of the Rock.

View of the northeast corner of the raised platform. The northern wall is to the right of the corner.

PREVIOUS PROPOSALS FOR THE LOCATION OF THE SQUARE TEMPLE MOUNT

Introduction

The results of the 1968–1978 excavations around the present-day Temple Mount have added immensely to our knowledge of the outer walls. The latest investigations into how the Temple Mount developed have also shown many of the conclusions of previous researchers to be in error. An examination of some of these theories is a valuable exercise, however, as it forces one to examine aspects of the subject one might have overlooked and confirms that our proposal satisfies all the necessary criteria.

As can be seen (opposite), where the proposals concerning the location of the square Temple Mount by some of the best known researchers have been tabulated, there is no consensus about any feature on the Temple Mount.

Most of the researchers began with the preconceived idea that the rock *es-Sakhra* is the site of the altar or the Holy of Holies. As a rule, this position was adopted owing to a lack of any other archaeological data. Some of these researchers, like Conder, Watson and Hollis, place the Holy of Holies over the Rock; while others like Schick, Mommert, Dalman and Vincent believe that the Rock is the place where the Altar of Burnt Offerings was located.

De Vogüé places the square Temple in the northern part of the Temple Mount while Fergusson would locate it in the southern part. The other researchers each propose a different location, with some of them incorporating one or two walls of the raised platform into their plan.

De Vogüé advocates a Herodian date for all of the monumental masonry of the outer walls of the Temple Mount, whether above or below ground, as do Conder and Vincent. Others, like De Saulcy, Warren, Schick and Mommert believe in a Solomonic origin for at least part, if not all, of these walls.

The principal error made by most researchers is to equate the square Temple Mount, described both by Josephus and Middot*, with that built by Herod the Great. Such a position cannot be maintained, as neither of the measurements given in these two sources can be reconciled with the dimensions of the present-day Temple Mount.*

We have seen that the measurements given by Josephus and

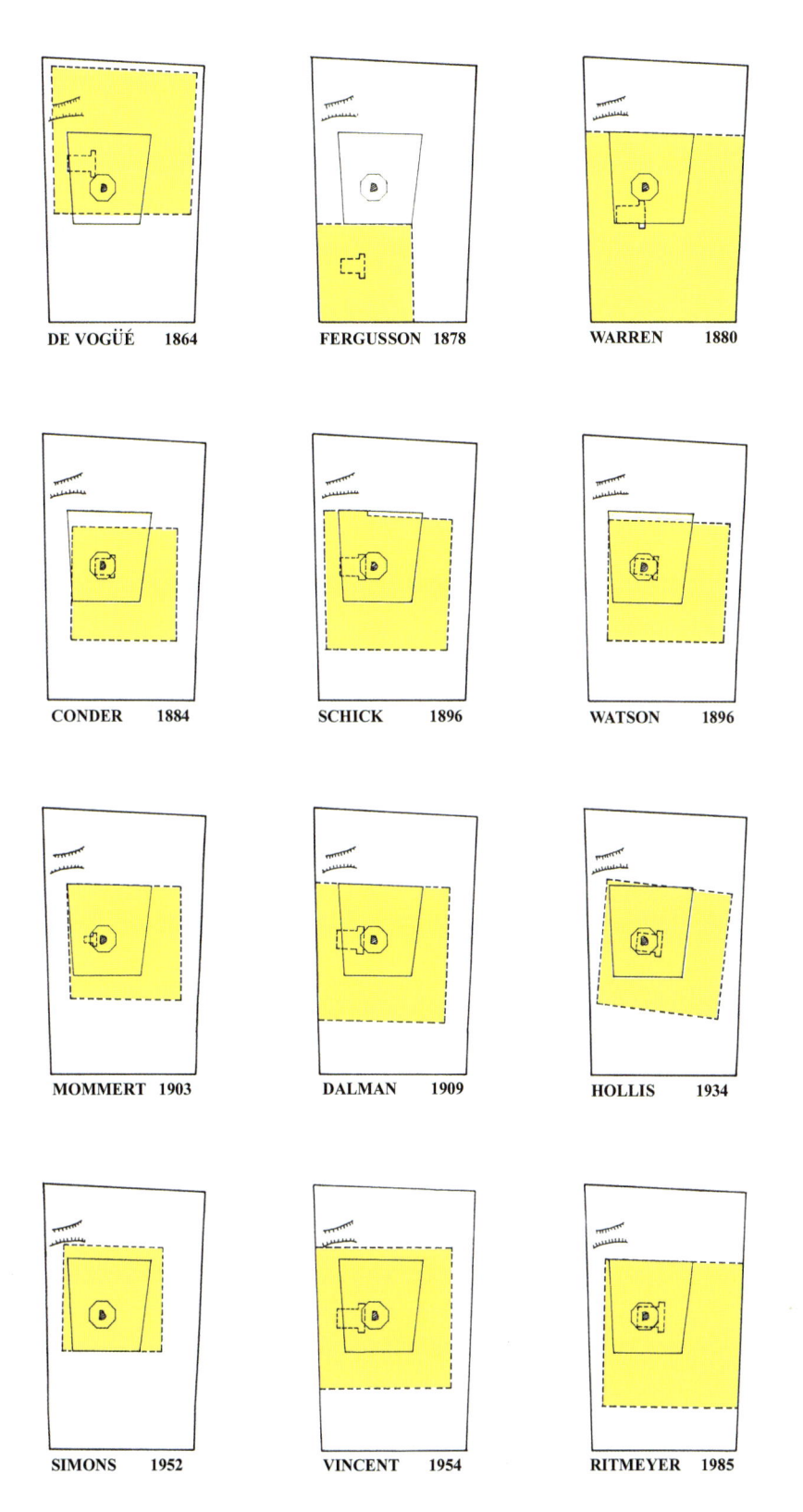

CHAPTER TWO: THE PRE-HERODIAN SQUARE TEMPLE MOUNT

DE VOGÜÉ   1864

FERGUSSON   1878

WARREN   1880

CONDER   1884

SCHICK   1896

WATSON   1896

MOMMERT   1903

DALMAN   1909

HOLLIS   1934

SIMONS   1952

VINCENT   1954

RITMEYER   1985

Chapter Two: The Pre-Herodian Square Temple Mount

> **ONE SOURCE OF DISPARITY: DIFFERING CUBIT LENGTHS**
>
> The length of the cubit employed by the various scholars differs greatly. De Vogüé, for example, uses a length of 20.67 inches (525 mm) for the cubit. Warren, Watson and Hollis base their plans on an 18-inch (457 mm) long cubit, while Conder uses a unit of 16 inches (406 mm). The choice of the measurement for the cubit was made occasionally, as in the case of Watson, for the sake of convenience.

Tosafot Yom Tob: A commentary on the Mishnah written by Yom Tob Lipmann Heller (1579–1654).

View of the entrance to el-Aksa Mosque on the Temple Mount.

Middot are incompatible. Some researchers (such as Mommert and Schick) have tried to reconcile them by adopting unusual units of measurement, while others have suggested interpretations which do not take the sources fully into consideration. However, most researchers, apart from Simons and Holtzmann, accept the measurements of *Middot* as the correct ones for the square Temple Mount.

Let us examine the above-mentioned proposals in greater detail. For the sake of clarity, we shall confine ourselves to those descriptions which are accompanied by a plan.

Regretfully, Chaplin did not accompany his article[8] with a plan. Relying on the measurements given by *Tosafot Yom Tob* for the free spaces between the Temple courts and the outer boundaries, he arrives at the following interesting location for the square Temple Mount (Chaplin 1875, p. 26):

> …reckoning the cubit at 20 inches (arbitrarily chosen), we find (1) that if the center of the Sakhra be regarded as the center of the Holy of Holies, the northern boundary of the mountain of the house would come to within a few feet of the northern limit of the present platform, where is the scarped rock discovered by Captain Warren; (2) that the southern boundary would come to within a few feet of the entrance of El Aksa, a point near which other considerations would lead to the supposition that the mountain of the house terminated; (3) that the western boundary would fall a few feet west of the foot of the present western ascent to the platform; and (4) that the eastern boundary would fall within a few feet of the present eastern wall.

Had Chaplin chosen the real cubit of 20.67 inches (525 mm), his location of the Mountain of the House would have coincided with the one presented in this book.

We will be examining in particular the date given to the outer walls of the present-day Temple Mount, the historical context assigned to the descriptions of Josephus and *Middot*, the methodology used to arrive at the different locations for the square Temple Mount, and the points on which the various theories are unconvincing.

A different proposal as to the area and shape of the mishnaic

Chapter Two: The Pre-Herodian Square Temple Mount

Mountain of the House has been advocated in recent years by Kaufman. Although we shall examine his proposal below, we have not included it on page 147, as his plan of the Temple Mount is the only one which is not square.

Melchior de Vogüé

De Vogüé (1864) believed that the masonry of the present-day Temple Mount belonged to the Herodian period and explained the difference in style between ashlars with smooth and rough bosses as "finished" and "unfinished" specimens of the same architectural style (de Vogüé 1864, p. 5).

De Vogüé stated that the measurements of four and six stadia for the circumference of the Temple Mount, as mentioned by Josephus in *Antiquities* 15.400 and *War* 5.192, referred respectively to the ancient Temple Mount and to that enlarged by Herod (de Vogüé 1864, p. 24).

According to de Vogüé, the description of the Temple in *Middot* referred to the Temple Mount as enlarged by Herod, as it mentions that the southern court is the largest. This, according to him, must have been due to Herod's building activities. De Vogüé contended that the measurement of 500 cubits was erroneously applied by the compilers of *Middot* to Herod's Temple Mount, while he believed that the compilers took this measurement from the prophet Ezekiel, whose descriptions de Vogüé interpreted as referring only to Solomon's Temple (de Vogüé 1864, p. 21, n. 6).

According to de Vogüé, the stadium square Temple as described by Josephus referred to the Solomonic Temple, having sides of 500 cubits according to Ezekiel. In order to compensate for the inaccuracies in the measurements and attempting to fit them in with the dimensions of the present-day Temple Mount, de Vogüé suggested that these measurements were taken along the inside of the porticoes which were added later by Herod.

De Vogüé represented the extension from four to six stadia in a simple plan (de Vogüé 1864, p. 22) showing the placing of an additional square to the south of the original one. The original square Temple Mount including the porticoes, which had a width of 30 cubits each, measured thus 560 cubits—which agrees with the present width of the Temple Mount. Having noted that the distance from the northeast corner to the Golden Gate measures 147 meters, which corresponded to 280 cubits, de Vogüé then laid out his square

> **ASSESSING DE VOGÜÉ'S THEORY**
>
> Evaluating de Vogüé's theory, we agree that there is "unfinished" Herodian masonry in the Temple Mount walls. However, he is wrong in his belief that the heavy-bossed masonry in the Eastern Wall to the north of the seam and the masonry near the Golden Gate belong to this category. Neither types of masonry are Herodian but belong to earlier periods. De Vogüé was apparently not completely aware of all the topographical aspects of the Temple Mount and did not realize that his original square Temple Mount is to a great extent located over the Bezetha Valley, which Herod was supposed to have filled in, according to *War* 5.186. In addition, there is no break in the Western Wall near Wilson's Arch, his point X, where he believed Herod's extension would have begun. Although he understood correctly that Josephus indicated that the enlarged Temple Mount with a perimeter of six stadia was built by Herod, he is wrong in suggesting that *Middot* also refers to the same extended Herodian Temple Mount. The recorded doubling of the Temple area by Herod could have been achieved in many different ways, not just by simply placing one square to the south of the original one. That this was not the method used, is clear from the words of Josephus, who wrote: "Then, after having enclosed the hill from its base with a wall on three sides…they built around the original block the upper courts and the lower Temple enclosure" (*War* 5.187).

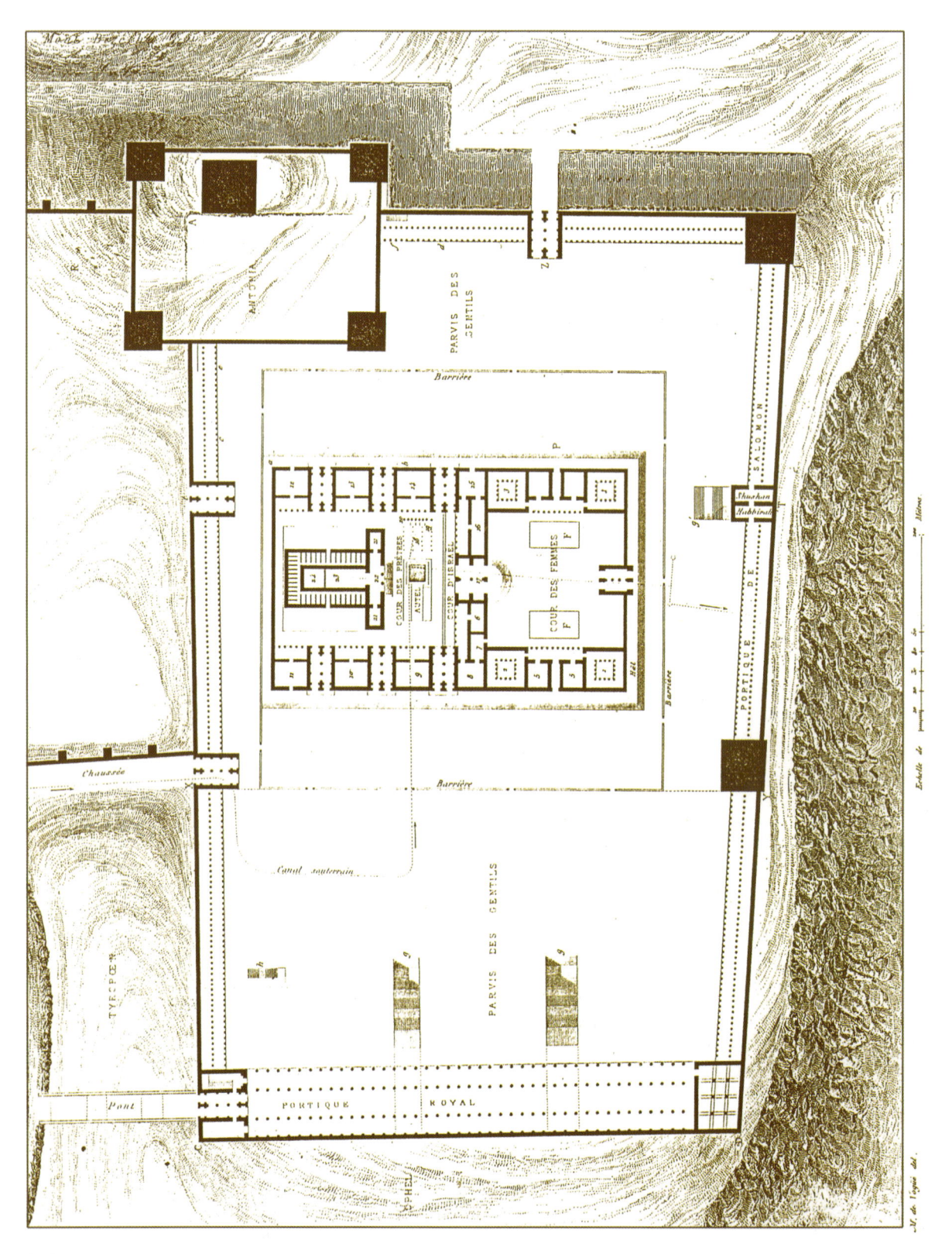

Chapter Two: The Pre-Herodian Square Temple Mount

CHAPTER TWO: THE PRE-HERODIAN SQUARE TEMPLE MOUNT

(AGYX on Pl. XV, see opposite page) by doubling this distance along the Eastern Wall. Herod's extension is therefore located to the south of line XY, i.e. south of Wilson's Arch; and this constituted the Court of the Gentiles.

Charles Warren

Two of Warren's works (1880 and 1881) were written essentially to refute the theories of Fergusson,[9] who located his 600-foot-square Herodian Temple Mount at the southwest corner of the present-day Temple Mount and identified the Dome of the Rock as the Constantinian Church of the Resurrection. However, these two works of Warren do contain some information on Warren's own ideas concerning the development of the Temple Mount.

Opposite page: De Vogüé's plan of the Temple Mount.

Below: Warren's plans of the Solomonic (left) and Herodian (right) Temple Mount.

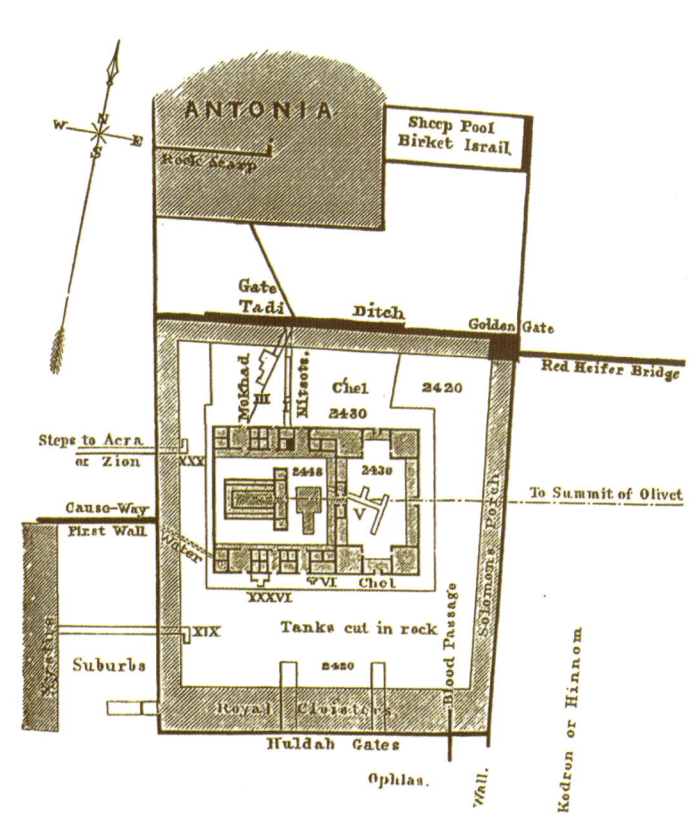

Chapter Two: The Pre-Herodian Square Temple Mount

Details from Warren's Plate XXI, illustrating (top) a drawing of a stone on which were painted two characters (Hebrew letters) Kuf and (above) one of the characters (also the letter Kuf) that was found on one of the stones on the south side of the southeast corner of the Solomonic Temple Mount.

Warren believed that the masonry in the southern wall below the Great Course was Solomonic, along with the lower portions of the Eastern Wall south of the Golden Gate. The masonry of the southern wall to the west of the Double Gate belonged to the Herodian period, as did all of the Western Wall.

From Josephus, Warren understood that Solomon's Temple court was a rectangle, having sides of a stadium or 400 cubits (600 feet or 182.88 m). The width was equal to the width of the Haram, or 900 feet (274.32 m). Herod enlarged this Temple to form a square of over 900 feet. Although Warren relied on Josephus' descriptions that Herod's Temple was square, he believed that the measurements used by Josephus *"contradict each other very much"* (Warren 1880, p. 85) and therefore dismisses them. Warren used the description of the Mountain of the House from *Middot* to reconstruct Herod's Temple Mount, especially the information concerning the gates and the buildings of the courts, but he ignored the dimension of 500 cubits.

According to Warren, the doubling of the area by Herod was achieved by first including the area of Solomon's palace, which measured 600 by 300 feet (182.88 by 91.44 m) and which was located near the southeast corner where Warren found the *"Phoenician characters"* (Warren 1881, p. 9, fig. facing p. 4), and then adding the remaining square of 300 feet (91.44 m) near the southwest corner (see plan, p. 151, left).

ASSESSING WARREN'S THEORY

Evaluating Warren's theory, we note that his solution would perhaps result in an approximate square having a circumference of six stadia, excluding the Antonia. However, Josephus did not mention that the enlarged Temple Mount remained a square. From Warren's plan (above, right), it is clear that his Temple Courts are rather larger than the intended square, as Warren also took the northern edge of the raised platform as the northern limit of Herod's Temple Mount.

We agree with Warren that the northern edge of the raised platform constituted the northern limit of the square Temple Mount. He came to this conclusion after his discovery of the Fosse and the valley that is located to the east of it. However, his choice of this line for the northern limit of the Herodian Temple Mount appears also to be connected with his remarks concerning the date of the masonry to the north of the Golden Gate. Warren noted that the masonry of the northeast tower is similar to that of the "Wailing Wall" and although the lower masonry in the Eastern Wall with the rough bosses was thought to be slightly different from that near the southwest corner, he also wrote that, "it would be difficult to specify exactly how it differs" (1884, p. 141). For this reason, Warren excluded the northern part of the present-day Temple Mount from the Herodian Temple Mount. As we have shown in Chapter 1 (pp. 113–117), we believe the masonry in this area to be Herodian; therefore the Herodian Temple occupied all of the present-day Temple Mount.

The principal flaw in Warren's theory is in his application of the measurement of 400 cubits to the sides of Solomon's Temple Mount when it is obvious, especially from Ant. 8.97, that this measurement referred to the height (see discussion on pp. 140–144). He also did not realize that the square Temple Mount of Josephus referred to the pre-Herodian one, and that of Middot only to part of the Herodian Temple Mount. Warren's theory was therefore based mainly on the results of his own explorations rather then on the measurements given by Josephus and Middot which he failed to interpret correctly.

CHAPTER TWO: THE PRE-HERODIAN SQUARE TEMPLE MOUNT

Claude Reignier Conder

According to Conder, all the walls of the Haram were Herodian with the exception of the masonry to the north of the Golden Gate, which he dated to the time of Agrippa, A.D. 41 (Warren and Conder 1884, p. 245).

Many of his conclusions were reactions to theories proposed by Warren. For example, Warren thought that the red-painted characters that he found on the stones near the southeast corner were Phoenician and therefore concluded that the southeast corner construction was built by Solomon. Conder, however, interpreted them as Semitic-Aramaic (Conder 1909, pp. 118–119) and therefore contemporary with the building of the Herodian Temple Mount. On the basis of his interpretation he concluded that the southeast corner was Herodian and not Solomonic as Warren thought.

Conder understood, like Warren, that Josephus' measurements for Solomon's Temple courts were 400 cubits in length. These courts were rebuilt by Herod, who also increased the size of the Temple platform from four to six furlongs with the building of Antonia. He believed that the dimensions of Herod's outer enclosures were *"nowhere given by ancient writers"* (Conder 1909, pp. 123–125).

According to Conder, the measurements of *Middot* referred to the same Herodian square Temple Mount that lay within the *soreg* (Conder 1878, vol. 1, p. 356). He believed that the measurement of 500 cubits (666 feet or 203 m according to 16 inches or 406 mm to the cubit) was more exact than the stadium (600 feet or 182.88 m) of Josephus.

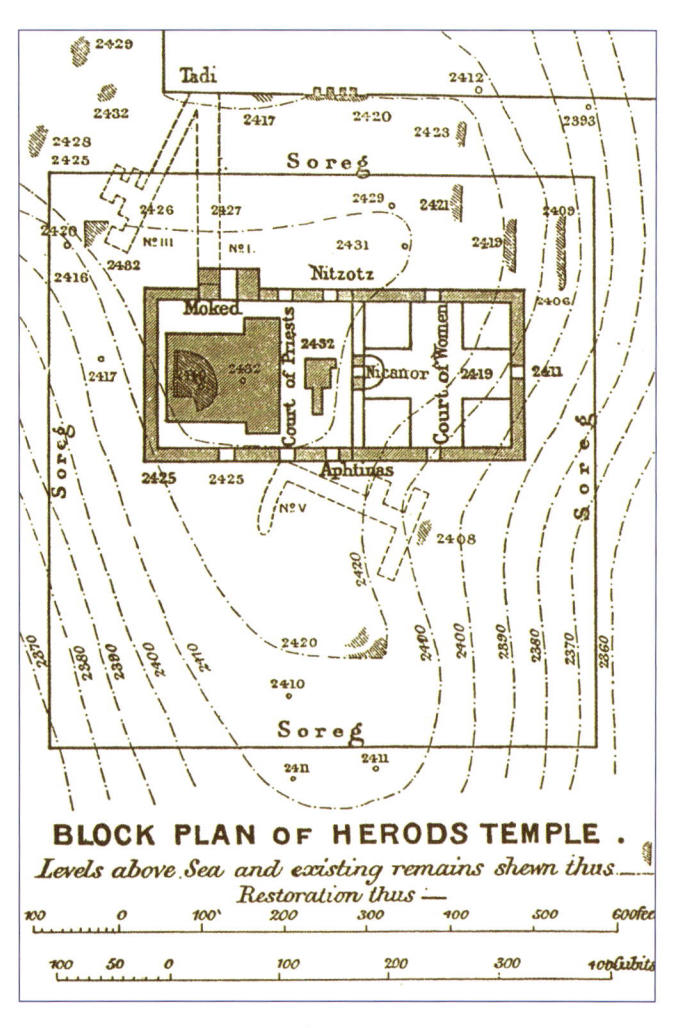

Conder's block plan of Herod's Temple.

ASSESSING CONDER'S THEORY

Like Warren, Conder also incorrectly interpreted Josephus' 400 cubits as a measurement of length. He also wrongly equated the Mishnaic "Mountain of the House" with the Herodian "outer rampart" (Conder 1909, p. 129), despite the discrepancy in the number of gates; although earlier (Conder 1909, p. 124) he had suggested that the measurement of 500 cubits given in the Mishnah may refer to the "space inside the dividing balustrade." Conder was correct in placing the Holy of Holies over the Rock, although he did not give any consideration other than established traditions for his choice. Had he not chosen 16 inches for the length of the cubit but the one of 20.67 inches (525 mm; see pp. 170–173), he would have arrived at a more satisfactory solution.

153

Chapter Two: The Pre-Herodian Square Temple Mount

In order to establish the position of the square Temple Mount (see plan, above), Conder relied on religious traditions that placed the Holy of Holies on the Rock. Using the rock levels of the Temple Mount, he then proceeded to lay out the courts so that these levels agreed with those mentioned in the historical sources.

Conrad Schick

According to Schick (1896), most of the walls of the present-day Temple Mount dated to the Solomonic period except the southwest corner and the masonry north of the Golden Gate, both of which he asserted are Herodian (Schick 1896, p. 320).

He believed that *Middot* describes the Solomonic Temple, which

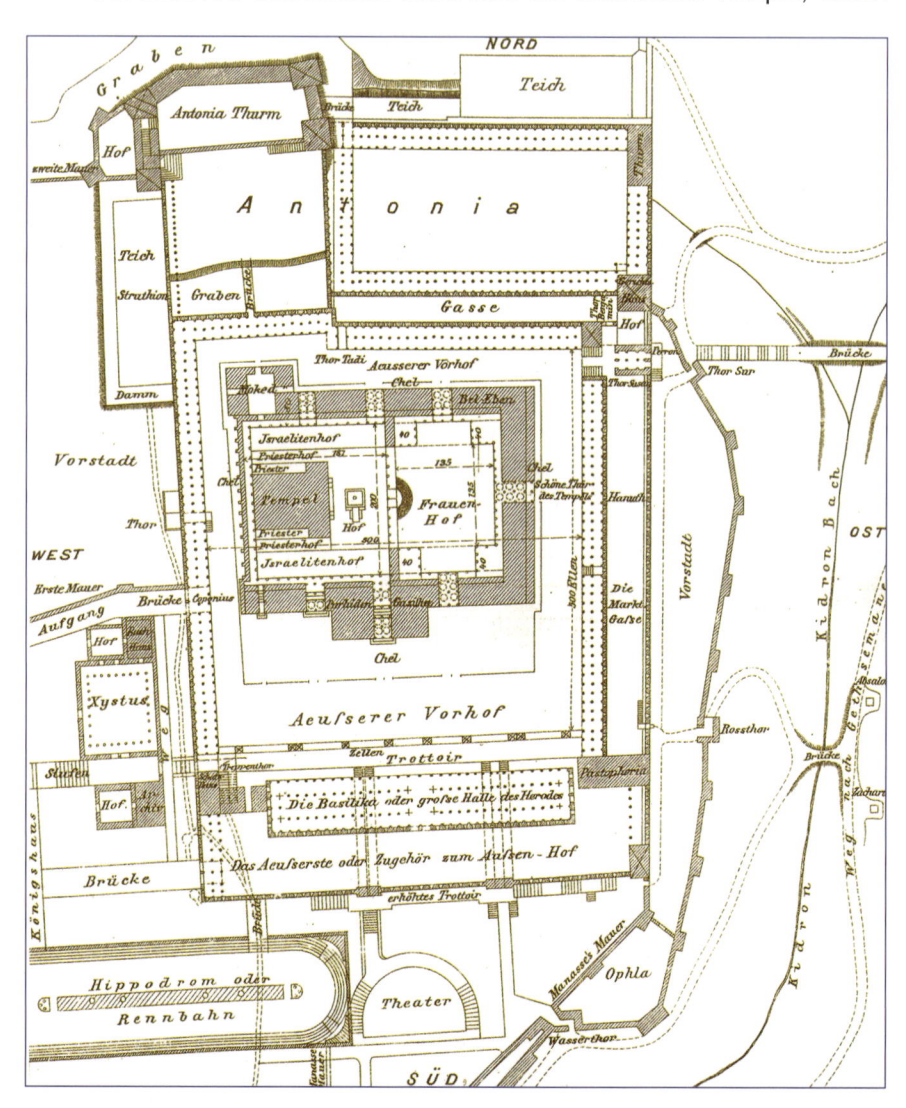

Schick's plan of the Herodian Temple Mount.

CHAPTER TWO: THE PRE-HERODIAN SQUARE TEMPLE MOUNT

corresponded to the stadium square sanctuary of Josephus. In order to achieve this agreement, Schick adopted a stadium of 900 feet, which is supposed to equal 600 cubits. Deducting the widths of the two surrounding porticoes of 50 cubits, he then arrived at 500 cubits for the outer court of the Temple (Schick 1896, pp. 159–160). The extension of the square Temple by Herod the Great, he believed, was described by Josephus.

In order to arrive at a plan of the Temple Mount, Schick first studied the plan of the Tabernacle, noting that as the Tabernacle was located in the western part of the court, so must have been the Solomonic Temple, which he believed *Middot* described.

Shifting this square plan around on the expanse of the current Temple Mount, Schick concluded that the arrangement would only work if the Altar of Burnt Offerings were placed over the Rock. The northern wall of Schick's Temple Mount corresponds to the northern edge of the raised platform, while the western portico coincides with the Western Wall (Schick 1896, p. 156, Tafel VI; see plan, opposite).

Herod the Great enlarged the Temple Mount to the north by adding the Antonia, which according to Schick, occupied all the area between the northern boundary of the raised platform and the present-day northern limits of the Temple Mount. The southern extension was constructed on the remaining foundation walls of the Royal Palace and other buildings erected by Solomon near the southeast corner.

> **ASSESSING SCHICK'S THEORY**
>
> *The fact that the southern wall, including the southeast corner, is Herodian invalidates most of Schick's proposals. The adoption of the unusual length of the stadium is most unconvincing in explaining that the square Sanctuary of Josephus is the same as the 500-cubit-square Mountain of the House of the mishnaic tractate Middot. Finally, the interpretation of the Rock as the Altar of Burnt Offerings appears to be based on convenience, rather than on evidence.*

Charles Watson

Watson made a clear distinction between the Mountain of the House, or the Sanctuary, and all the buildings which stood within its boundaries, i.e., the Temple and the Inner Court, the Court of the Women to the east and the Outer Court within, and including the *Soreg* on the one hand, and the Court of the Gentiles with its Outer Cloisters on the other (Watson 1896, p. 49).

Like Warren,[10] Watson believed that the southern Haram wall east of the Double Gate from the Great Course down and the Eastern Wall up to the Golden Gate belong to the Solomonic period; while the southern wall west of the Double Gate and the western wall up to the Antonia fortress belong to the Herodian extension of the Temple Mount (Watson 1896, p. 59).

Although Watson did not provide a historical analysis of the descriptions of the Temple Mount by Josephus and in *Middot,* he

CHAPTER TWO: THE PRE-HERODIAN SQUARE TEMPLE MOUNT

Watson's plan of the Temple of Jerusalem.

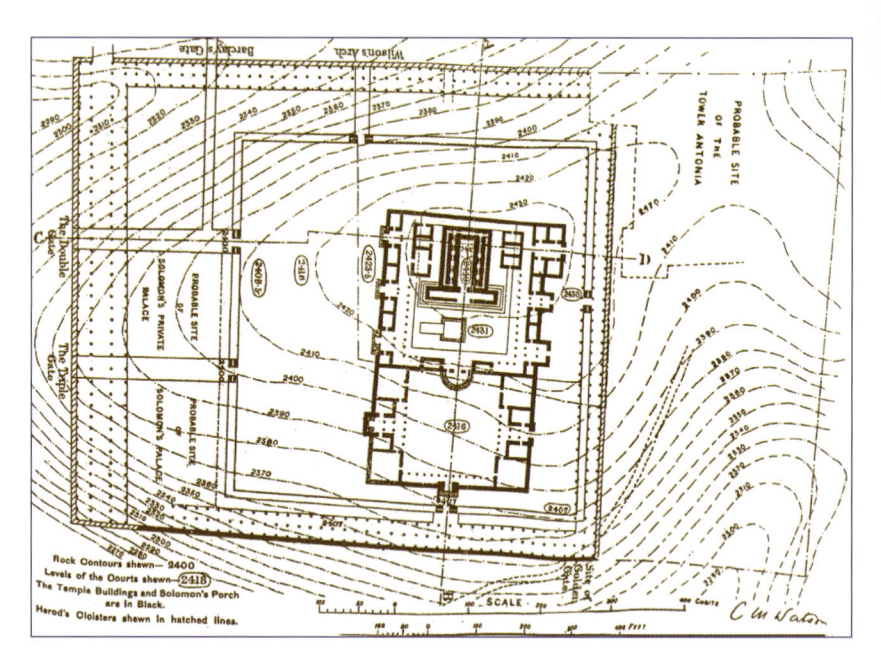

> **ASSESSING WATSON'S THEORY**
>
> *Watson's analysis of the different descriptions given by Josephus and those in* Middot *is basically correct. However, his lack of understanding of the different types of masonry in the Eastern Wall, his unsatisfactory choice for the length of the cubit and his disregard of Josephus' statement that the eastern line of the Temple Mount was never changed are the main reasons why, in our opinion, Watson's location of the square Temple Mount is incorrect.*

believed that, despite the different dimensions given in these two texts, the mishnaic Mountain of the House is essentially identical to the Sanctuary as described by Josephus (if the Court of the Gentiles added by Herod is excluded). According to him, this square platform dates originally to the Solomonic period (Watson 1896, p. 57). This is further supported, he believed, by the fact that the authors of Middot "cared only for the Sanctuary" (Watson 1896, p. 50).

His methodology consisted of first preparing a plan of the Mountain of the House based on the measurements of *Middot,* using a cubit of 18 inches (457 mm; Watson 1896, Plan 2; see above). Taking into consideration that the foundations of the Temple were six cubits, he placed the Holy Place of the Temple on the site of the Dome of the Rock.

Carl Mommert

According to Mommert (1903), the ancient masonry visible in the Haram walls belonged to the Solomonic period. The difference between ashlars with smooth and rough bosses he attributed merely to different styles of decoration (Mommert 1903, p. 112). According to him, only the ashlars without marginal drafts, those seen lying above the drafted masonry in many places, were Herodian repairs.

As Mommert believed that Herod built only the new Temple, the Stoa and the Antonia (Mommert 1903, p. 117), he subsequently

CHAPTER TWO: THE PRE-HERODIAN SQUARE TEMPLE MOUNT

interpreted the descriptions of Josephus as referring solely to Solomon's Temple. Inside the Haram walls not only did the Temple with its courts stand, measuring 500 cubits square, but also the Solomonic summer and winter palaces (Mommert 1903, p. 247), the outer walls of which he equates with the Haram walls. According to him, these areas were later paved by Herod and thus added to the Temple Mount.

The Mountain of the House of *Middot* was understood to be a special part of the enclosed area containing the Solomonic Temple and its courts. Mommert therefore correctly understood that the gates of *Middot* belonged to this square of 500 cubits and not to the Haram walls. He attempted to reconcile the measurements of *Middot* with those of Josephus by adopting a cubit of 16 inches, based on the scale of Gudea (500 cubits = 199.5 m = 655 feet) and an Olympic stadium (192.27 m = 631 feet).

Mommert suggested that the Rock was the place of the altar, around which the Temple and the courts were laid out. According to his Tafel II (see plan), the northern limit coincided with the northern edge of the raised platform. He relied on the measurements given by Rabbi Abraham Ben David Arie for the dimensions of the different courts (Mommert 1903, p. 213 ff.).

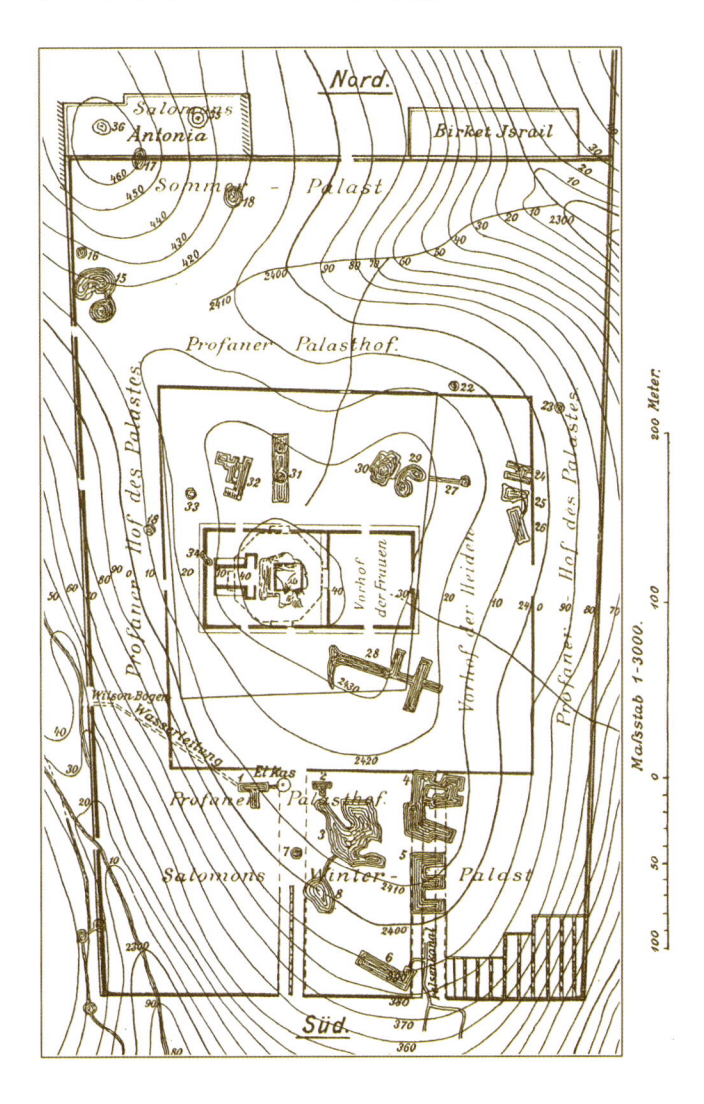

Mommert's plan of the Solomonic Temple and the Palace Court.

RABBI ABRAHAM BEN DAVID of Posquieres (known as RaBaD) was the talmudic authority in Provence at the end of the 12th century. RaBaD studied both Talmud and the philosophic/scientific learning coming out of Spanish Jewry. He opened a yeshivah in Posquieres (France).

> **ASSESSING MOMMERT'S THEORY**
>
> *In the light of our present understanding of the existing masonry and its chronology, especially since Mazar's excavations, Mommert's Solomonic date for the Haram walls is untenable, also his interpretation of the texts of Josephus, especially his explanation of the manner in which Herod doubled the size of the Temple Mount. The courts to the south and north of the Temple are equal in size in his plan, whereas according to Middot 2.1, the southern court was larger than the northern one. Finally, his choice of the Rock for the altar is adopted arbitrarily and his length of the cubit is not based on relevant archaeological evidence.*

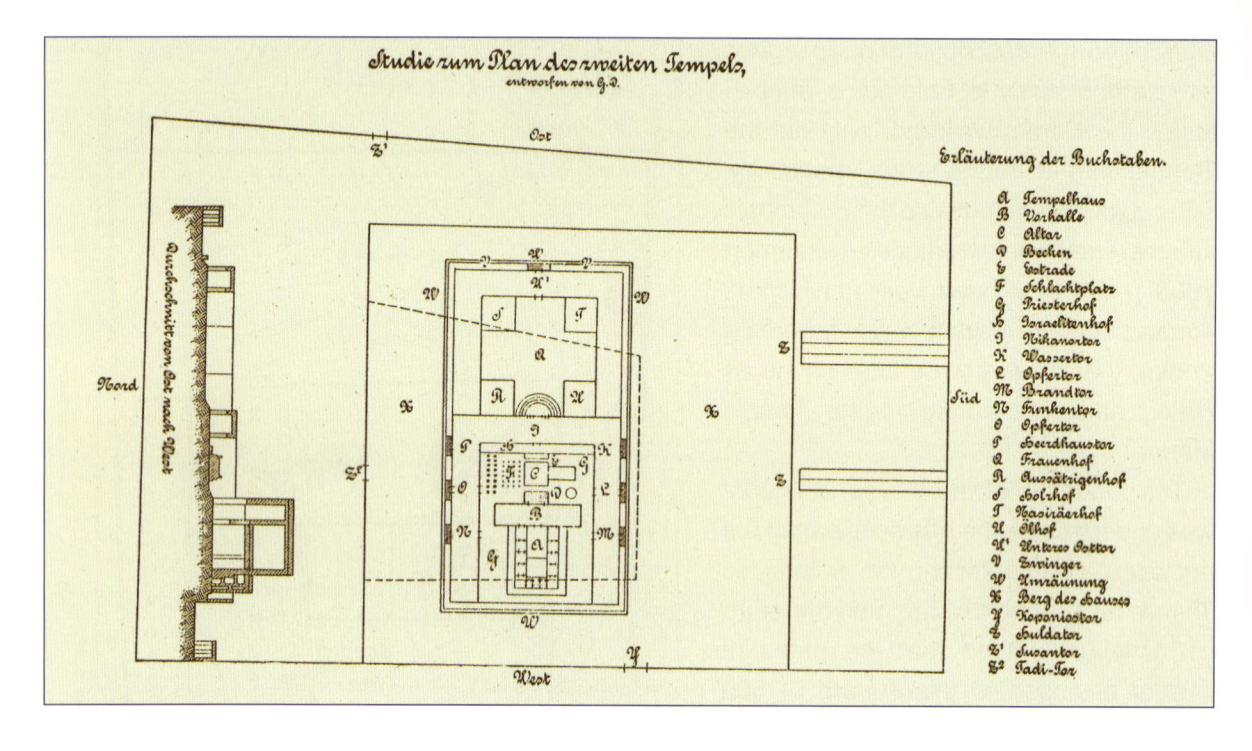

Chapter Two: The Pre-Herodian Square Temple Mount

Dalman's plan of the Second Temple.

Gustaf Dalman

Concerning the date of the Temple Mount walls, Dalman believed that *"the middle part [of the eastern wall] was, at the earliest, a remnant of the Temple of Zerubbabel, but the rest, with its substructure, may have originated in pre-exilic times"* (Dalman 1935, p. 296).

According to Dalman, both the Mishnah and Josephus describe the Second Temple as rebuilt by Herod the Great, although the dimensions of the Temple of Ezekiel's prophecy were also incorporated into the Temple plan (Dalman 1909, p. 31).

Dalman placed the square Temple so that the north wall of the outer court fell on the line of the northern edge of the present-day raised platform. He noted also that the width of 500 cubits for the outer court, as given by the Mishnah, would have reached from this northern edge almost to the northern end of the Double and Triple Gate passageways (Dalman 1909, p. 54). At this point, according to him, the southern extension of Herod began.

Although Dalman noticed that the distance between the Western Wall of the raised platform and the eastern wall of the Temple Mount was 500 cubits (ibid. 1909, p. 56), he found the information contained in the Mishnah insufficient to make *"the exact placing of the inner, higher-lying terraces"* (Dalman 1935, p. 297) possible.

> **ASSESSING DALMAN'S THEORY**
>
> In his sketch (above), Dalman placed the Western Wall of the square Temple Mount at the present-day Western Wall, although he stated that the Sanctuary undoubtedly reached as far as the Eastern Wall. As previously mentioned, the Western Wall can be proven to be Herodian, and therefore no part of it could have belonged to the earlier Mountain of the House described in the Mishnah.
>
> It is a pity that Dalman did not follow up his observation of the distance of 500 cubits between the Western Wall of the raised platform and the Eastern Wall. Had he done so, he would have arrived at a very satisfactory positioning of the mishnaic Mountain of the House.

CHAPTER TWO: THE PRE-HERODIAN SQUARE TEMPLE MOUNT

He initially suggested that the Rock was the place of the altar, although he also raised the possibility that the rock may have been located between the Porch of the Temple and the steps leading up to it.

The plan presented (Dalman 1909, p. 55; see opposite page) is basically a sketch designed more to focus on the existing problems rather than to propose a solution which, in his opinion, would be misleading; he believed that only archaeological excavations could provide a definite answer to the problem.

Frederick Hollis

In dating the Haram walls, Hollis (1934) followed Warren and Conder in his belief that the masonry of the southern wall below the Great Course was Solomonic, as he believed was the Eastern Wall up to the Golden Gate. The masonry to the north of the latter was dated by Hollis to the time of Agrippa.

Hollis applied the measurement of 400 cubits given by Josephus to the Solomonic Temple Mount and the square of a stadium to that of Herod. Noting that the stadium was smaller than any of the Haram walls, Hollis suspected Josephus of *"confusing the older Temple with the new"* (Hollis 1934, p. 112), or alternatively suggested that Josephus referred to a specially marked-off pavement.

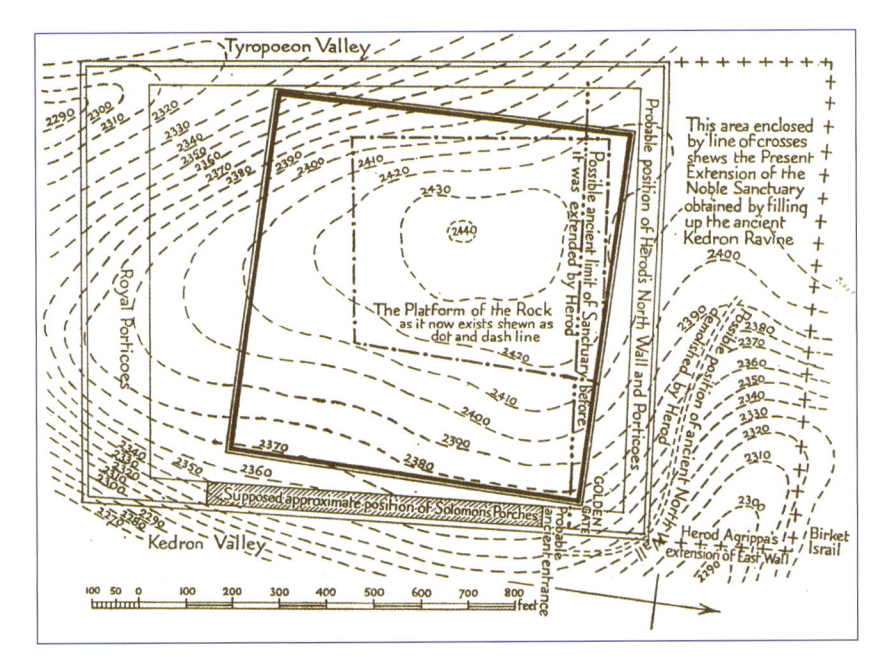

Below: Hollis's plan of the Mount of the House.

> **ASSESSING HOLLIS'S THEORY**
>
> Dr. Oesterly, in his foreword to Hollis's book, said that the thesis of Hollis was *"a genuine effort to reach a reconciliation between these three irreconcilable sources"* (Josephus, Middot and the archaeological data of the Temple Mount). However, Hollis himself was not fully convinced that his solution was correct, for he wrote, following his interpretation of Middot and Josephus' Antiquities, that *"Somewhat along the lines here suggested it may be possible to find a solution of the insoluble riddle"* (Hollis 1934, p. 117). The idea that Josephus confused the older Temple with the new one has no foundation in the text, as is quite clear from War 5.184–187. Furthermore, to claim that the square refers to a paved area only is contradicted by the fact that the whole of the Temple Mount was paved: *"the entire courts that were exposed to the air were laid with all sorts of stones"* (War 5.192). An overriding factor in Hollis's thinking is that he believed that *"the measurements given had a significance ceremonial rather than architectural"* (Hollis 1934, p. 16). A final factor in rejecting Hollis's plan is his view on the orientation of the Temple due east and west. Though previously Shaw Caldecott[11] advanced the theory that such an orientation could indicate *"a disavowal of sun-worship,"* there is no foundation in the historical sources that would allow Hollis to sustain such a claim.

Chapter Two: The Pre-Herodian Square Temple Mount

The so-called Throne of Solomon, built against the inner face of the eastern wall.

The 500 cubits of *Middot* he also referred to Herod's Temple Mount, and this measurement supposedly reconciled with the stadium of Josephus by referring it to an area excluding the porticoes and that part of the southern court where the ramps of the Double and Triple Gates are located (ibid. p. 116). This area, *"measuring 770, 870, 770, 845 ft."* is then equated with the 500 cubits of *Middot*.

After choosing to place the Holy of Holies over the Rock, he then lays out a court of 750 feet (228.60 m) square, giving certain distances between the Rock and the walls as they best fit the rock contours (Hollis 1934, p. 122). The exact north-south orientation of his square may have originally been chosen, according to him, *"as a disavowal of sun-worship"* (Hollis 1934, p. 125 ff.; see plan, p. 159).

Jan Simons

Simons (1952, pp. 381–436) gives an excellent though brief overview of most of the research on the relationship of the present-day Temple Mount and the historic Temple that had been carried out up to 1940 (Simons 1952, p. 406, n. 2). He believed the Western Wall to be of Herodian origin, although maintained that the northern part of it was designed only to screen off the area in front of the Antonia. The southern wall was mainly Herodian apart from the parts below the Great Course. The eastern wall was Solomonic from the *"seam"* up to the so-called Throne of Solomon (a structure built against the inner face of the eastern wall, approximately 110 feet or 33.53 m north of the Golden Gate) and was actually at first a city wall, which was later incorporated into Herod's eastern Temple Wall.

Simons' sketch of the relative positions of Antonia and the northern part of the Herodian Temple area.

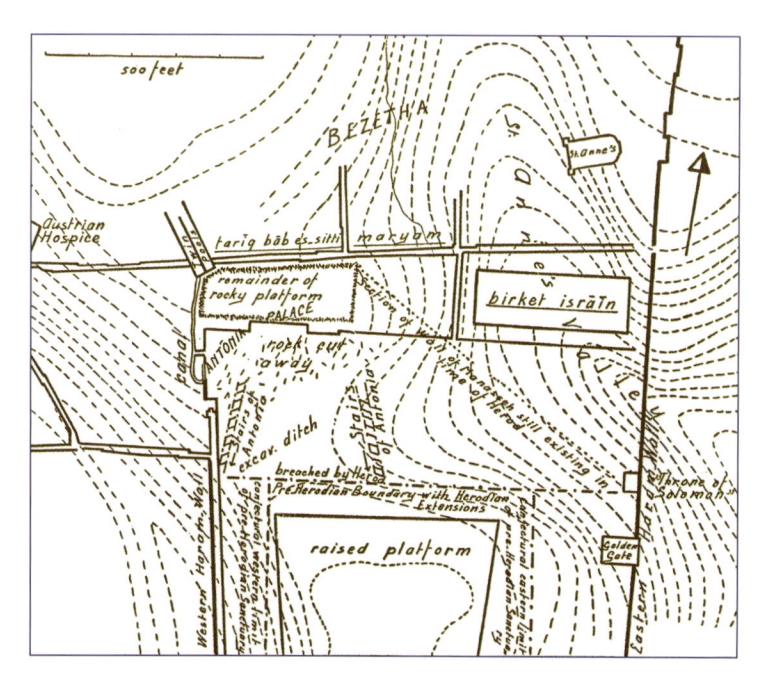

The area with a circumference of 4 stadia, as described by Josephus, *"has to be interpreted as referring to the outer wall of the pre-Herodian Temple"* (Simons 1952, p. 395). The Herodian extension, inclusive of the Antonia, was 6 stadia. However, Simons said, the uncertainty as to the

Chapter Two: The Pre-Herodian Square Temple Mount

location of the Antonia and the lack of information concerning the northern boundary of Herod's Temple make it *"extremely risky,"* if not impossible, to calculate the extent of Herod's Temple and to check it against Josephus' measurements, which Simons suspected to be understated.

The Temple described in *Middot* referred to the Herodian Temple, although Simons wrote (1952, p. 406) that *"the confrontation of Middot and Josephus is frankly perplexing."* Rejecting the view that *Middot*'s square of 500 cubits is the same as Josephus' square stadium, he then preferred the description of Josephus, mainly because he was an eye-witness and also because Simons believed that *Middot*'s measurements were influenced by Ezekiel.

Louis-Hugues Vincent

Vincent basically followed de Vogüé's Herodian theory for the date of the walls of the Temple Mount, although he preferred to explain the duality of the marginally drafted masonry (blocks with smooth and rough bosses) as different forms of the same type. The Herodian date was also based on his structural analysis and comparison of the northern section of the western Temple Mount wall, which was discovered by Conder, with the outer walls of the Tomb of the Patriarchs in Hebron (Vincent and Stève 1956, p. 544 ff.; Vincent and Mackay 1923, p. 103 ff.). He pointedly remarked that "it is regrettable that the nature of a large stretch of the eastern wall to the south of the Golden Gate remains unknown, the exact knowledge of which would be of the greatest interest in determining the chronology of the walls" (Vincent and Stève 1956, p. 557).

Vincent believed that Josephus described Solomon's Temple as a square, in order to facilitate his explanation that Herod later doubled the Temple Mount by means of adding two stadia, rather than by laying out a new design. The reason for this, according to Vincent, was that Josephus wanted to show that Herod's Temple was essentially an imitation of Solomon's (Vincent and Stève 1956, p. 441).

According to Vincent, the measurement of 500 cubits square for the Mountain of the House was reminiscent of Ezekiel's Temple and used in *Middot* to express the separation of the entire sacred area from the profane (Vincent and Stève 1956, p. 497). Vincent believed that the description was very precise in illuminating the Jewish concept of the eschatological Temple, but was of little usefulness for

> **ASSESSING SIMONS' THEORY**
>
> *The northern line of Herod's Temple Mount, according to Simons, coincided with a line running west from a bend in the Turkish city wall near the Throne of Solomon and measured a stadium in length, but the location of the other walls was conjectural (Simons 1952, Fig. 55; see plan, opposite page). Although he only presented the northern half of his proposed square, upon completion, its southern line is found to coincide with the southern wall of the raised platform! There are, of course, no ancient remains visible there to warrant the adoption of this line.*

Vincent's placing of the mishnaic Temple on the Temple Mount.

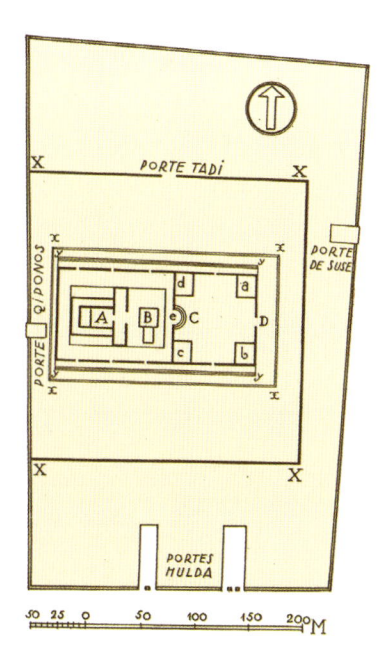

Chapter Two: The Pre-Herodian Square Temple Mount

> **ASSESSiING VINCENT'S THEORY**
>
> *Despite his detailed description of the walls of the Temple Mount, we believe that Vincent failed to distinguish between the different types of masonry with rough bosses. For example, this is the reason why he denied that the "seam" in the Eastern Wall represents a change in construction. He also failed to understand that the gates of Middot were located in the outer wall of the square Mountain of the House, and not in the Herodian walls, which in turn led him to suppose that the Temple of Middot did not represent a description (or part) of the existing Temple Mount.*

an archaeological reconstruction; especially given the fact that the gates mentioned in *Middot* were in reality located in the outer walls of the present-day Temple Mount. Vincent's plan (Vincent 1954a, Fig. 1; see plan, previous page) is therefore only a schematic representation, as he does not believe a realistic plan to be feasible.

Asher Kaufman

Kaufman's proposal for the area and shape of the mishnaic Mountain of the House is the only one which is not square. He reached his conclusion by proposing that, in the Second Temple period, the area measuring 500 cubits by 500 cubits excluded the Temple and its immediate courts. Therefore, said Kaufman, the 500-cubit-square Temple Mount could not have had a surface of 250,000 square cubits. Based on the occurrence of the term *har ha-bayit* in the Old Testament, Kaufman concluded, however, that, during the First Temple period, it did refer to the area that included the Solomonic Temple and Royal Palace. According to him this "precise topographical meaning" was

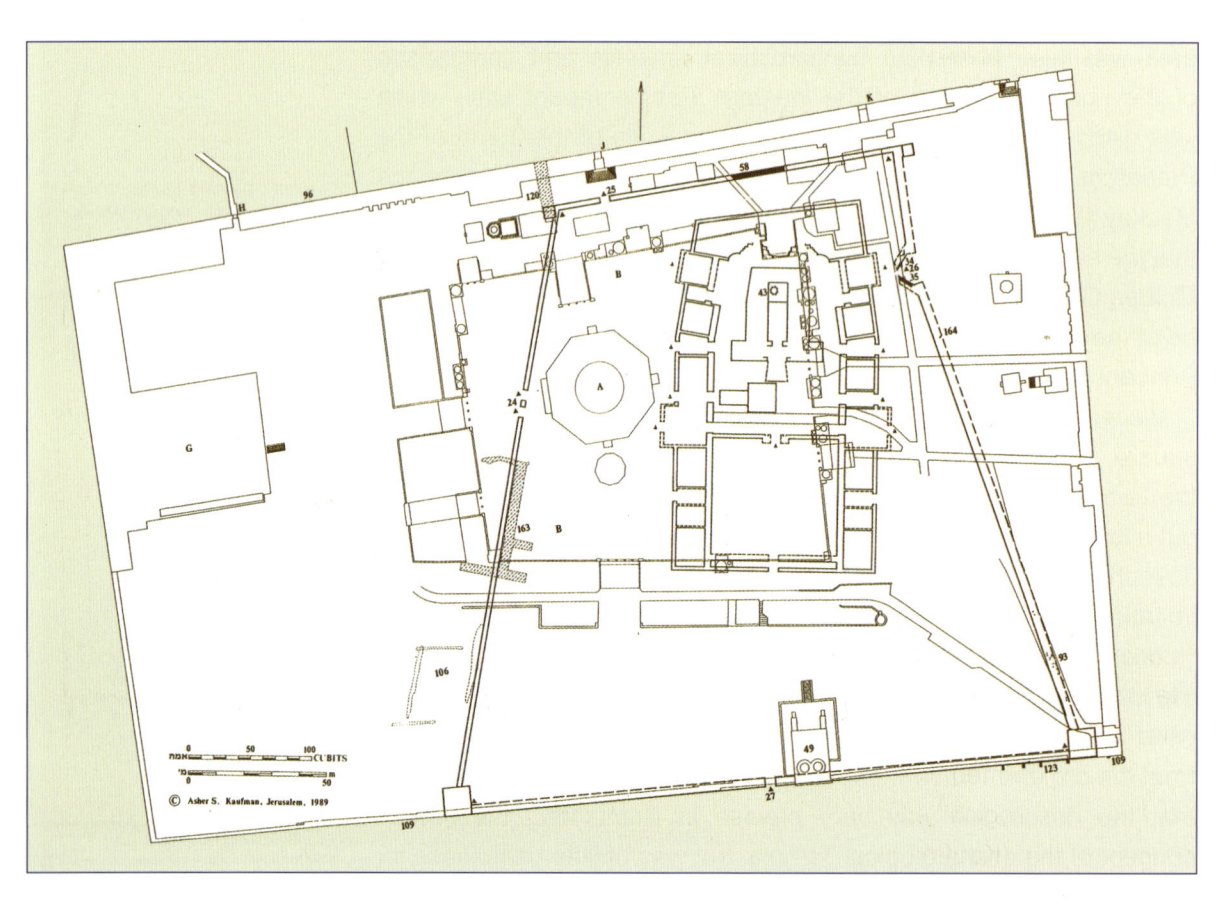

Kaufman's plan of the Temple Mount.

CHAPTER TWO: THE PRE-HERODIAN SQUARE TEMPLE MOUNT

> **ASSESSING KAUFMAN'S THEORY**
>
> The centerpiece of Kaufman's theory is the identification of the large stone under the Dome of the Spirits, which he claimed is the bedrock Foundation Stone of the Holy of Holies. However, the bedrock contour map made by Warren[12] indicates that the bedrock is located at least 10 feet below the floor of this small monument; thus, this location conflicts with Josephus' testimony that the Temple was built on top of the hill. The Rock is about 15 feet higher than the bedrock in Kaufman's location for the Temple. This discrepancy alone makes his theory untenable.[13]
>
> The stone below this little dome appears to be a Herodian paving stone, as its size approximates that of other paving slabs found in front of the Double and Triple Gates (see illustrations below). The purpose of the rectangular projection at its northeast corner allowed a smaller paving slab to be laid next to it.
>
> Kaufman ignored the most important topographical data of the area to the north of the raised platform, i.e. the existence of the Fosse, the Bezetha Valley to the west of this ditch and the rockscarp under the northern edge of the raised platform. The northern court of Kaufman's Temple would fall into the Bezetha Valley, which near the Eastern Wall is 160 feet lower than the Rock.
>
> His identification of a sill as belonging to the Tadi Gate is speculative, as the date of this wall fragment[14] cannot be established without archaeological investigation. The size of this sill is also too small to qualify as that of a Temple Mount gate. Furthermore, Kaufman neither discussed the architectural development of the Temple Mount nor the two different masonry styles that are represented in the eastern wall of his proposed mishnaic Temple Mount.
>
> Kaufman derived the small cubit he uses in his Temple Mount design from the mishnaic tractate Kelim. However, Kelim means "vessels." Herbert Danby[15] in his translation of the Mishnah explains that
>
> "…this word has, however, the wider sense of 'articles of utility', including clothing, implements, and utensils of all kinds. The tractate deals with every kind of vessel's susceptibility to uncleanness, at what stage in their manufacture they become susceptible, and how damaged they must be to be regarded as insusceptible to uncleanness."
>
> Kelim 17.10 contains two different opinions about the size of the cubit that was used for certain installations of the sanctuary:
>
> "Rabbi Meir says, all the cubits were of the middle size, apart from the golden altar and the horn and the circuit and the base [of the altar]. Rabbi Yehudah says, the builders' cubit was six handbreadths and that of vessels five [handbreadths]."
>
> The objects under discussion are obviously installations, such as altars, tables, benches and perhaps certain dividing walls, all constructed long after Herod's Temple was completed. The Temple itself is not the object of Kelim, and therefore the cubit mentioned here cannot be the one used in the Temple Mount construction referred to in tractate Middot.

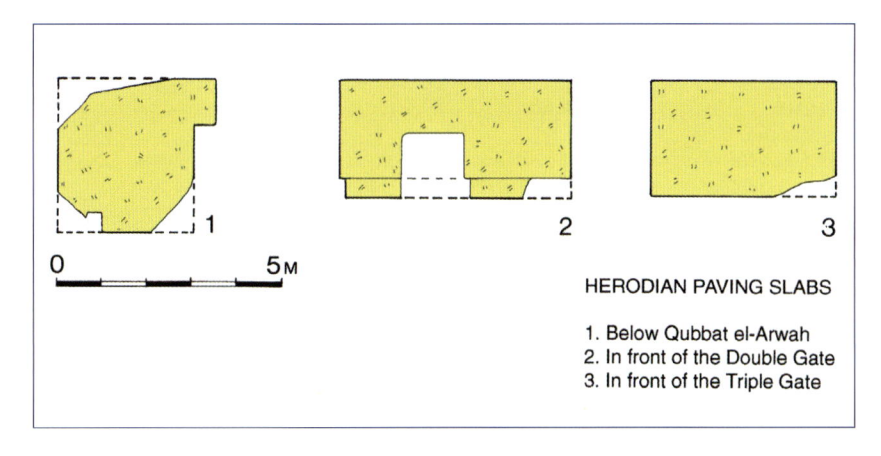

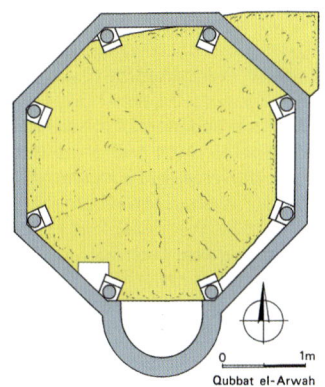

HERODIAN PAVING SLABS

1. Below Qubbat el-Arwah
2. In front of the Double Gate
3. In front of the Triple Gate

Qubbat el-Arwah

later lost (Kaufman 1984/5, p. 97). Kaufman did not refer to Josephus stating that the Temple Mount before Herod's expansion had the shape of a quadrangle.

Kaufman claimed to have identified several bedrock features and other archaeological elements on the Temple Mount, on which he bases his plan (Kaufman 1991, p. 40; see plan, opposite page).

Above (left): Plan comparing the size of the paving stone below the Dome of the Spirits with similarly sized paving slabs in front of the Double and Triple Gates.

Above (right): Plan of the Dome of the Spirits and the paving slab on which it rests.

Chapter Two: The Pre-Herodian Square Temple Mount

David Jacobson

Jacobson believes that the Herodian *temenos* was set out according to a geometrical order based on angles of 60 degrees with the altar at the center of the Temple Mount. In order to accommodate this design, Jacobson proposes a location for the Northern Wall of Herod's Temple Mount which runs through the middle of the Pool of Israel (Jacobson 1990/91, Fig. 1, line B-C; see plan here). At the center of this design is the altar, which he locates at the Dome of the Chain.

ASSESSING JACOBSON'S THEORY

The main problem[16] with this design is the location of the Northern Wall. Jacobson took Warren's notation on Pl. 13, "possible termination of Old Wall with marginal drafts," as an indication that the Northern Wall met the Eastern Wall at this point.
Examining Warren's drawing (opposite), it is clear that at this point he is referring to the preserved top of this wall and not to its northern end, which is located 125 feet to the north of the northeast corner. Here Warren drew a vertical line from the preserved top of the wall down to bedrock and labeled it "probable termination of Old Wall." Jacobson's "northeast corner" is only half the true distance indicated by Warren. We have shown (see p. 158) that the northern boundary of the present Temple Mount is indeed the North Wall of the Herodian Temple Mount and that it cannot be located elsewhere. This alone, of course, would invalidate this design as his point R lies well to the north of the Herodian Temple Mount. Jacobson also does not recognize that the present northeast corner is Herodian. The fact that stones from later periods are interspersed with the Herodian ashlars in the northern face of the northeast angle of the Temple Mount (see p. 119) is incorrectly understood to "signify that the ancient masonry is here in secondary use" (Jacobson 1990/91, p. 38).
Jacobson's symmetrical layout of the Temple Mount has the altar at its center. However, apart from one or two disputed opinions in the Talmud,[17] there is no ancient source that says that the altar was located in the center of the Temple Mount. Indeed, if this were the case, the people standing in the Court of the Women would not have been able to see the blessing of the priests that was pronounced each day from the Porch of the Temple because the great height of the altar would have obscured their view.
Jacobson selects a cubit of just over 18 inches (0.464 m), though he chooses a length of 205 meters (672.5 feet) for the sides of the soreg, which actually constitutes 442 cubits of 0.464 meters. The location of this square temenos is more or less identical to that proposed by Mommert (see plan, p. 157).
This symmetrical layout, however, contradicts Middot 2.1, which states that the spaces around the Temple court were unequal. Jacobson recognizes this shortcoming. His explanation, that the unequal distances may have been caused by the existence of certain buildings inside this area, is unsatisfactory.
Jacobson's layout of the Herodian Temple Mount according to the principles of Roman imperial architecture does not take into consideration the historical development of this ritual complex. We see in the plan of the Temple Mount rather an asymmetrical development of an oriental building, the maximum extension of which was achieved as far as was physically possible.
In reality, the southwest corner was built across the Tyropoeon Valley, while the Western Wall was not built parallel to the previous one. The northwest corner necessitated the cutting away of a large part of a hill. The topographical conditions made an extension to the east impossible. Only the southern extension was minimal, actually less than the width of the Royal Stoa. It is difficult to imagine that in such circumstances the ideal geometrical design proposed by Jacobson could have been utilized.

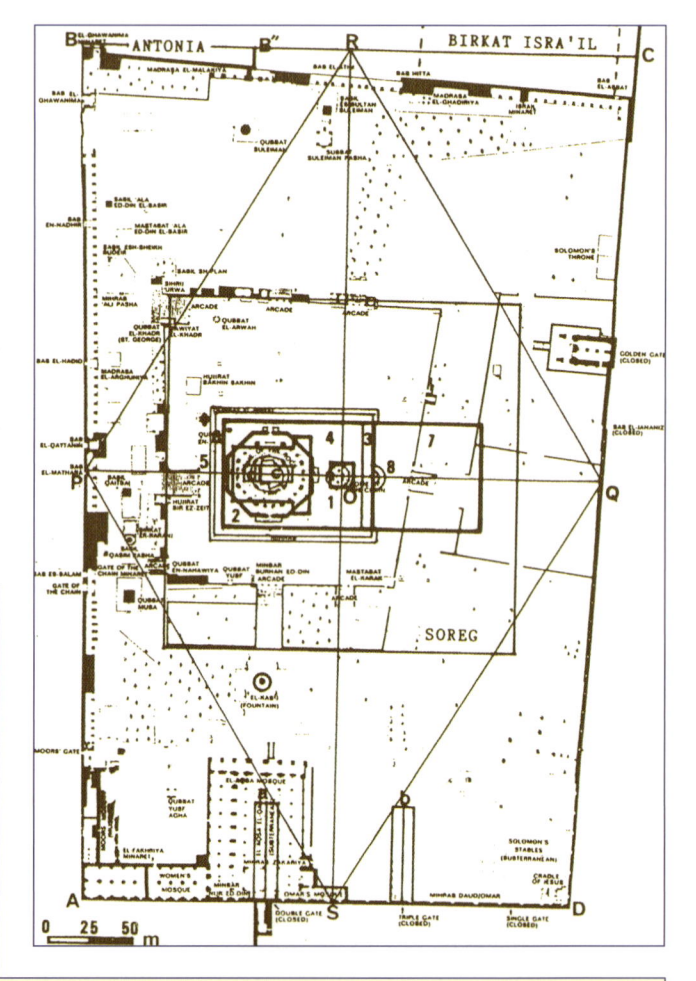

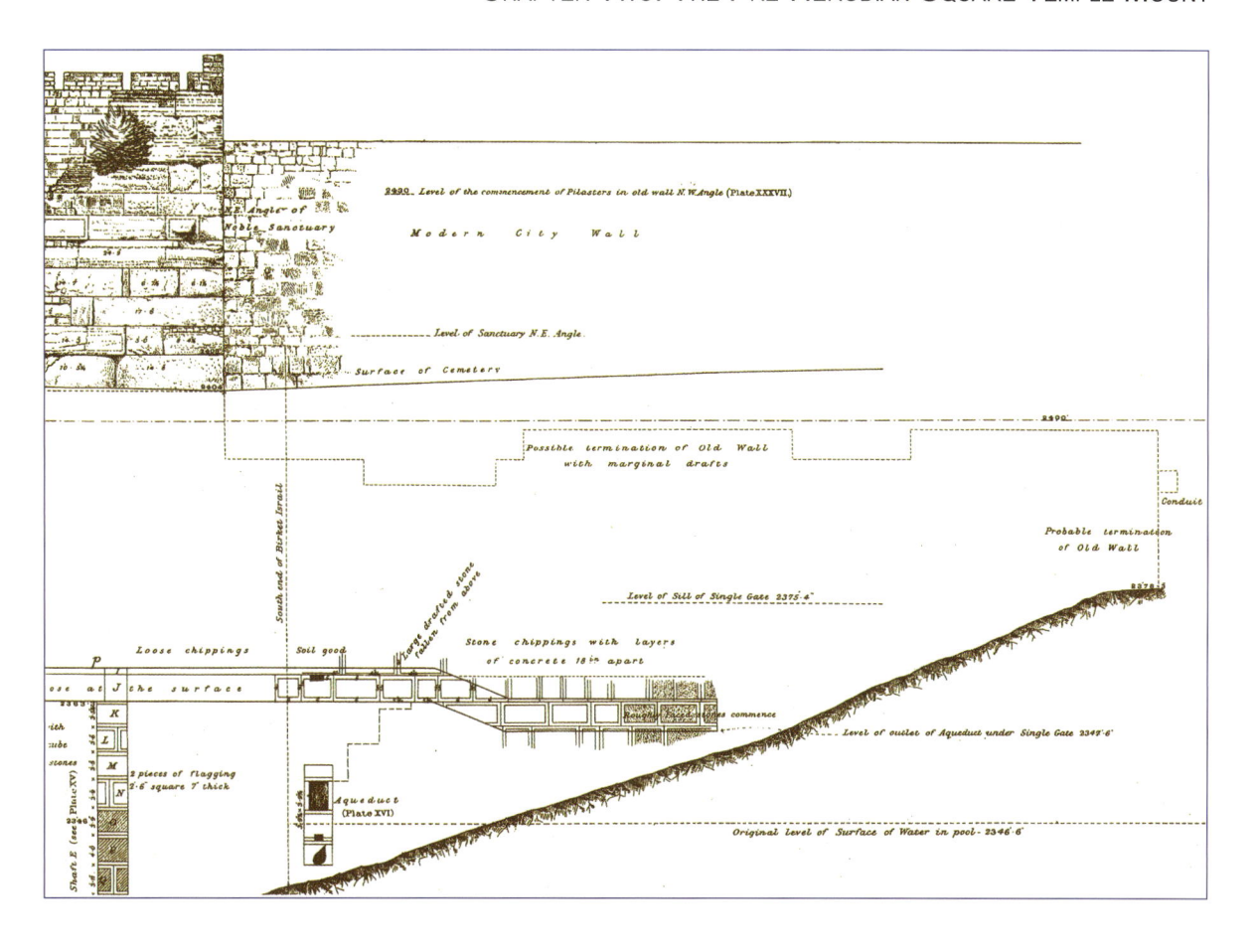

CHAPTER TWO: THE PRE-HERODIAN SQUARE TEMPLE MOUNT

Opposite page: Jacobson's plan of Herod's Temple.

Above: Detail of Warren's Plate 13.

THE LOCATION OF THE SQUARE TEMPLE MOUNT
The Discovery of the Pre-Herodian Western Wall — "The Step"

Having examined some of the early and contemporary proposals for the location of the square mishnaic Temple Mount, we will now present the archaeological evidence which forms the basis for my discovery of the actual location of the 500-cubit-square Temple Mount.

The Crucial Step

The starting point of the research that led to the establishment of the location of the 500-cubit-square Temple Mount was the odd angle of the *step* at the northwest corner of the raised platform.[18] Eight flights of steps topped by arcades lead up to the platform of the Dome of the Rock. The steps near the *Qubbat el-Khadr* are the only ones not built parallel to the walls of the platform, their direction being derived from the angle of the bottom step.

Overleaf: Flight of steps at the northwest corner of the raised platform, the lower step of which formed part of an ancient wall.

Chapter Two: The Pre-Herodian Square Temple Mount

Chapter Two: The Pre-Herodian Square Temple Mount

Part of this step appears, in effect, to be the remains of an ancient wall, being composed of a long (56 feet or 17 m) line of single ashlars. This is in contrast to the other steps of this flight, which are made up of many smaller stones. Another remarkable feature of this line of stones is that, unlike the present-day Western Wall, it lay parallel to the central section of the Eastern Wall, which is generally accepted as being of pre-Herodian origin.[19]

Ashlar with protruding boss in the flight of steps at the northwest corner of the raised platform.

Although the level of the adjoining pavement has since been raised and conceals the evidence, a photograph taken in 1972 (above) shows the rough boss of the southernmost ashlar of this *step*. These ashlars have a westward-projecting boss of just over 3 inches (7.62 cm), the margins being 4 inches (10.16 cm) wide, giving an impression of pre-Herodian masonry, comparable to that seen in the central section of the Eastern Wall near the Golden Gate. The fact that we had a wall of early masonry parallel to the ancient Eastern Wall made the conclusion that this was part of the original Western Wall of the pre-Herodian Temple esplanade irresistible[20] (see plan, following page).

The adjacent bedrock levels indicate that this stone course rests immediately on the bedrock, making this point the actual foundation course of the northern part of the pre-Herodian Western Wall. If this is so, the archaeological evidence had revealed both the western and eastern lines of the pre-Herodian Temple Mount.

The literary sources in the form of *Middot* inform us that the Mount was 500 cubits square. How could we find out how far north the western line extended? An understanding of the topography of the area was essential to try to determine the course of the northern wall. Again we turn to the records of Charles Warren.

Chapter Two: The Pre-Herodian Square Temple Mount

Plan of the Temple Mount with indications of the pre-Herodian square Temple Mount.

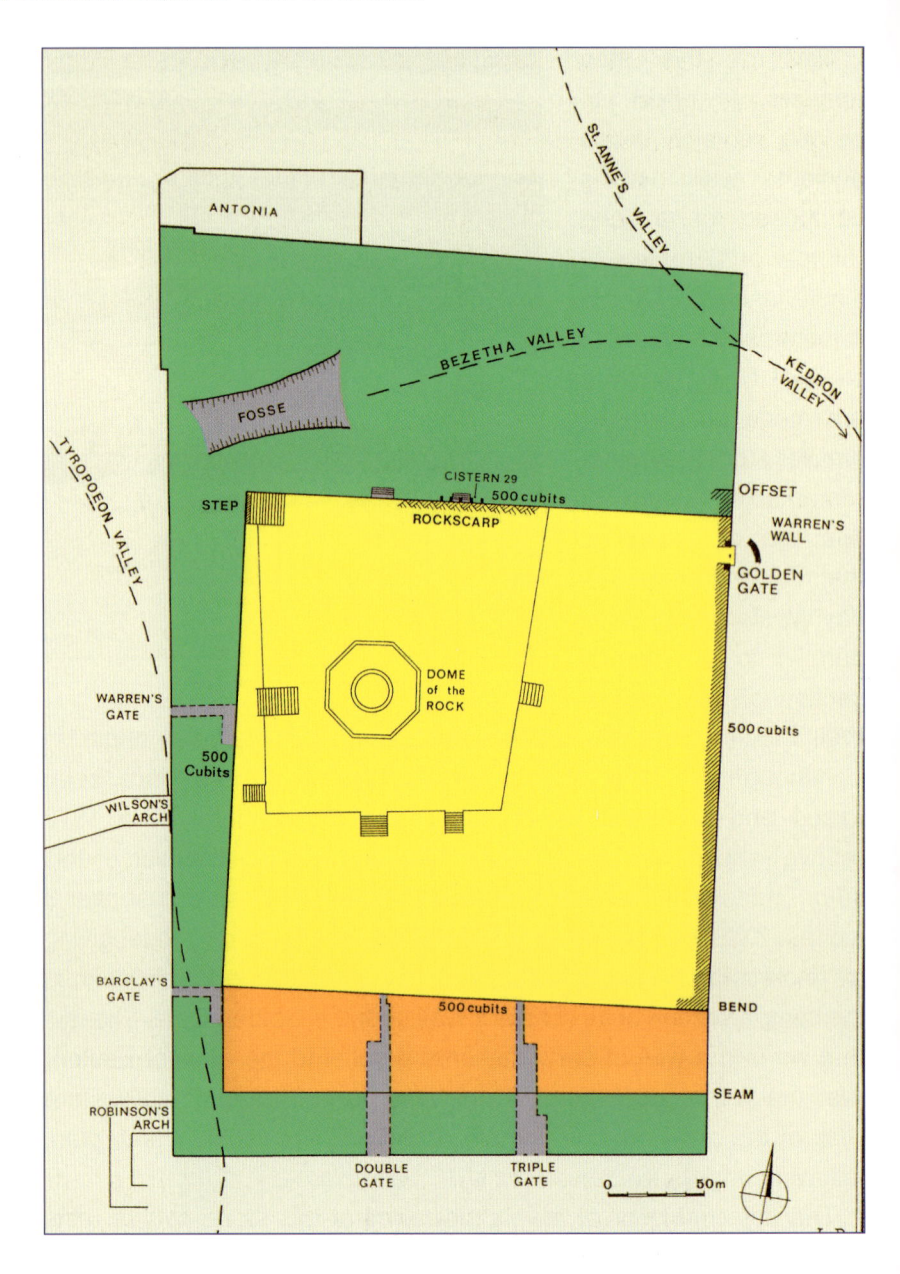

The Fosse

Warren reported the uncovering of an *excavated ditch* or *fosse* (see plan, above), 52 feet (15.85 m) north of the staircase.[21] The importance of this *fosse*—apparently the same as that described by the Greek historian and geographer Strabo *(Geography* 16.40), who gives its measurements as 60 feet deep and 250 feet broad—was immediately obvious. Natural valleys protected the Temple Mount on

CHAPTER TWO: THE PRE-HERODIAN SQUARE TEMPLE MOUNT

its western, southern and eastern sides, but this was not the case on the north where it was connected by a narrow saddle to the hill on which later the Antonia was built. By cutting away this saddle, the approach to the Temple Mount from the north was thus effectively cut off. This artificially cut *fosse* therefore completed the natural boundary of the pre-Herodian Temple Mount, linking the Tyropoeon Valley on the west with the Bezetha Valley, which is the western branch of St. Anne's Valley[22] that runs eastward into the Kedron Valley.

This same *fosse*, together with part of the small Bezetha Valley, is undoubtedly the one recorded by Josephus (*Ant.* 14.61) as having been filled in by Pompey's soldiers in 63 B.C., thereby enabling them to storm the great towers that stood at the northwest corner of the Temple Mount. As we shall see later (pp. 216–219), these towers belonged to the Hasmonean fortress called the *Baris*. As the location of this fortress is still being discussed in archaeological circles, it is important to remember that the northwest corner of the square Temple platform, where these great towers stood, could not have been located beyond this *fosse*.

Head of Pompey, from a coin.

The Northern Rockscarp in Cistern 29

Having limited the northern extent of the pre-Herodian Western Wall to not more than 52 feet north of the raised platform, the natural direction to turn now was eastwards, in order to trace any possible remains of the pre-Herodian northern wall.

When I had first examined the *step*, I noted that the northern end of the northernmost large stone in the *step* was exactly in line with the northern edge of the raised platform. But this was a surface observation. We looked to the reports of Warren's explorations to know what was happening underground. A natural subsidence along the central part of the northern edge of the raised platform had enabled Warren to examine Cistern 29 (see plan, opposite). This is, in fact, a vaulted passageway built against the northern edge of this platform. The southern wall of this chamber, which also comprises part of the northern wall of the raised platform, was described by Warren as a *quarried rockscarp*. (The chamber, incidentally, may have been part of the Monastery of the Temple, built by the Crusaders.)[23] This *rockscarp* features prominently on Warren's drawings (Warren 1884, Pls. 2, 6)[24] and it gives a definite impression of having been squared off in order to provide the foundation for a fortified wall.

View of the northernmost large stone in the Step *which is precisely in line with the northern edge of the raised platform.*

169

Chapter Two: The Pre-Herodian Square Temple Mount

Close-up view of the flight of steps at the northwest corner of the raised platform.

In the first chapter (p. 123 ff.), we described how the rockscarps quarried out of the hill that was located to the north of the Fosse provided a strong base for the Antonia Fortress. Here, rock had been cut to heighten and accentuate the defensive nature of the boundary wall to the north of the Temple. As no other wall to the north of the Temple was known, apart from the Herodian northern wall of the Temple Mount described in Chapter 1 (p. 119), the possibility of this being the northern wall of the square Temple Mount appeared more and more likely.

By projecting lines westward from this *rockscarp* and northwards from the *step,* a right-angled corner is formed which would fulfill the requirement for the northwest corner of the pre-Herodian Temple Mount to have been located north of the *step* and south of the Fosse.

It is interesting to note that, with this projection of the northwest corner, the northernmost ashlar of the *step* actually "fits" exactly into this corner. The northwest corner of this ashlar (see photograph, lower right corner) constitutes therefore the northwest corner of the square Temple Mount.[25] As the photograph shows, in the next step up to the raised platform there is an additional ashlar continuing this line to the east, which may also belong to the same northern boundary of the early platform.

The fact that just enough space—about 52 feet (15.85 m)—is left between this corner and the *fosse* for the location of towers such as those described by Josephus confirms that this location of the northern wall of the square Temple Mount fits in well with the information given in the historical sources.[26]

Five Hundred Cubits and the Length of the Cubit

For the latter identification of the northern wall of the square Temple Mount to be correct, the distance, measured along the northern *rockscarp,* between the *step* and the present-day eastern wall of the Temple Mount, must be 500 cubits.

Therefore, continuing the line of the *rockscarp* eastward, the northeast corner of the pre-Herodian Temple would be located at

CHAPTER TWO: THE PRE-HERODIAN SQUARE TEMPLE MOUNT

> **DEFINING A CUBIT**
>
> There is much confusion as to the length of the cubit, especially as we know that more than one cubit was in use in antiquity. Different lengths for these cubits have been suggested by scholars.[27]
>
> That more than one cubit was in use in biblical times is clear from 2 Chronicles 3:3, where it is stated that Solomon was instructed to build the house of God using cubits "after the first measure." This implies, of course, that there was another "measure" and that at least two different cubits must have been in use during the First Temple period. The prophet Ezekiel (40:5, 43:13) indeed refers to two cubits, one of which was a handbreadth longer than the other. The long or Royal Cubit of seven handbreadths was that used in Ezekiel's description of the Temple, and is therefore the Temple Cubit. Although so far no rods or inscribed lengths of cubit have been found in Israel, a beautiful specimen of an Egyptian Cubit 20.67 inches long is on display in the Egyptian Gallery of the British Museum (no. K136542, see photograph) together with a rod which is exactly twice as long. In the Egyptian Museum of Torino there is a golden cubit exhibited of the same length and two rods of a span (half a cubit) each. This long or Royal Cubit (20.67 inches or 525 mm) and the Short Cubit of about 18 inches (450 mm) were in use in Egypt since about 3000 B.C. and were widely used in the ancient world. The small cubit was divided into 24 fingerbreadths or 6 handbreadths and the Royal one into 28 fingerbreadths or 7 handbreadths. There is increasing archaeological evidence to show that both these long and short cubits were used simultaneously in Israel since the tenth century B.C. The determination of the length of these cubits is based on the units of measurements found in excavated tombs and other buildings, as we will see in later discussion. From these excavations it can be established with increasing certainty that the length of the longer cubit is 20.67 inches (525 mm) and that of the shorter cubit 17.7 inches (450 mm).

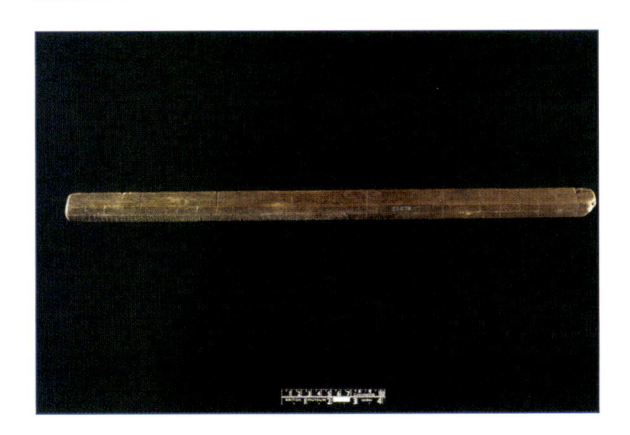

Above (left): Egyptian cubit. (British Museum)

Above (right): Golden cubit exhibited in the Egyptian Museum of Torino. (photo: Francesco Cordero di Pampatarato)

the point where it meets the eastern wall. Here again, it would form a right-angled corner, just north of the Golden Gate, at about 1,101 feet (335.60 m) north of the Herodian southeast corner. The actual distance between the *step* and this postulated corner is 861 feet (262.50 m).

As we have already mentioned (see p. 143), this distance of 861 feet is approximately 30 percent longer than the stadium of Josephus. On the other hand, if this length represents the 500 cubits of *Middot*, then the cubit must be one five-hundredth part of this measurement, that is, 20.67 inches (525 mm). The problem is to establish whether this represents the length of a cubit or whether it is just an arbitrary measurement.

In the nineteenth century, Flinders Petrie[28] was the first to establish that several tombs in Jerusalem were cut according to the former unit

171

Chapter Two: The Pre-Herodian Square Temple Mount

The Great Pyramid of Khufu (center) in Giza.

of measurement writing that *"six tombs show 20.57 inches, which is the regular Egyptian cubit, varying from 20.5 to 20.7"* (Petrie 1892, p. 30). He also records that other tombs were cut according to a longer cubit of 22.62 inches (575 mm).

Writing in 1908, Smith,[29] in describing the size of the Inner Sanctuary of the Temple, uses the sacred cubit of 20.67 inches (525 mm) which according to him was the one *"most probably"* used. Although he does not give the sources from which he deduced this measurement, it is nevertheless worth noting that this outstanding scholar of the history of Jerusalem came to this conclusion.

Scott, in his well-researched article,[30] refers to the Egyptian Royal Cubit of 20.6 to 20.7 inches (524–527 mm) and the Egyptian common cubit of 17.4 to 17.7 inches (444–450 mm).

Ben-David[31] states:

> The Egyptian "short" cubit of 450 mm is thus called to differentiate it from the Egyptian "long" or Royal Cubit of 525 mm [20.67 inches]. The existence of such a Royal Cubit is to be found in Egypt as early as the end of the fifteenth century B.C.E. in connexion with a certain Amonemapet who lived during the reign of King Horemhib (Horos in Greek) (Hultch 1882: pp. 349, 355). But Petrie states that there is evidence that this cubit of 525 mm existed as much as one thousand years earlier, during the Third Dynasty, c. 2700–2650 B.C.E. The first accurate calculation of this cubit was based on the pyramid of Snefru (Third Dynasty). Research into the measurements of the pyramid of Khufu (Petrie 1967: p. 377) has proved that this cubit was in reality 524 mm long. This Egyptian "long" cubit has been throughout history termed the Royal Cubit. Much later it came to be known as the Philaeterian-Ptolemaic cubit.

Jeremias[32] suggests that the Philaeterian Cubit of 525 millimeters was widely used in Palestine during the first century A.D. He quotes Didymus (end of first century A.D.), *"who calculates the Egyptian cubit of Roman times as 1.5 Ptolemaic feet."*

CHAPTER TWO: THE PRE-HERODIAN SQUARE TEMPLE MOUNT

Ussishkin,[33] in his research into the Siloam Tunnel, found that *"the length of the reconstructed tunnel is c. 643 m while 1,200 cubits of 52.5 cm are 630 m...the longer cubit could have been somewhat shorter or longer, and in that case the measurements would vary accordingly."* The same author also states[34] that,

> ...it seems that it is possible to prove in a most convincing manner that all the gable-roofed tombs [in the village of Silwan east of the City of David] were hewn using the long cubit; the half cubit was used extensively too. It seems also that the long cubit was used in the hewing of tombs no. 1, 2 and 3 ("the Tomb of Pharaoh's Daughter") and of the monolithic tomb no. 34.

According to Barkay[35], the square palace-fort A at Lachish (tenth century B.C.) measured *"60 cubits of the standard of the longer or Royal Cubit."* One of the two large burial caves at St. Etiénne is also cut according to this cubit.[36]

Eshel[37], who examined a late Iron Age cemetery north of Jerusalem, records that *"at Gibeon three tombs (3, 4 and 9) were hewn using the long cubit. It has already been shown that these tombs can be dated to the seventh-sixth centuries B.C.E. on typological grounds."*

These examples prove that both the Egyptian long or Royal Cubit and the Egyptian short cubit were units of measurement employed in Israel during the First Temple period. The measurement of 262.50 meters or 861 feet for the northern side of the mishnaic Temple Mount turns out to be exactly 500 cubits of this long or Royal Cubit. As this is identical to the measurement given in *Middot* for all the sides of the Mountain of the House, we therefore conclude that the dimensions of *Middot*, are, in fact, based on actual measurements of the square Temple Mount in Jerusalem. *Thus we believe that we have positively identified the northern wall of the square Temple Mount.*

Above: Reconstruction of the Tomb of Pharaoh's Daughter in the village of Silwan.

Below: Reconstruction of the burial caves in the courtyard of the St. Etiénne Monastery, Jerusalem.

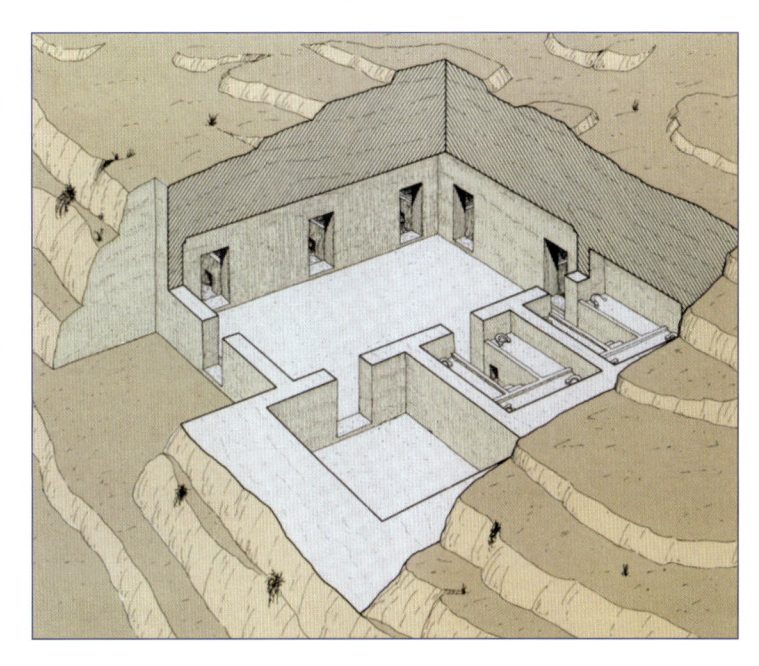

173

The Masonry near the Golden Gate

The next step in our research was to investigate the Eastern Wall at the point where it meets the northern boundary. We did expect to find the northeast corner of the square Temple Mount in the form of a vertical joint at that meeting point. The discovery of the northeast corner of the ancient square Temple Mount would have provided further confirmation of our theory. This, however, was not the case. Further discussion in subsequent chapters explains why such a discovery is not needed in order to confirm our theory and why, on the contrary, one should not expect to find evidence of a corner in this particular spot.

Examining the masonry of the Eastern Wall of the Temple Mount, we noticed that there were four different types of ancient masonry in the wall, which dated to three different periods (see illustration, p. 115). We have already described the Herodian masonry at the two ends of the Eastern Wall, where we saw ashlars with finished and unfinished bosses. Hasmonean stones, with their rough projecting bosses, can be seen north of the *seam.* Two stretches of the most ancient masonry (see illustration, p. 115 [D]) in the Temple Mount walls can be viewed on both sides of the Golden Gate. This masonry is located in the middle part of the Eastern Wall. The southern stretch is visible up to 51 feet (15.50 m) south of the Golden Gate. Wilson describes the southern part of this masonry as follows: *"From the Golden Gate to the so-called postern, a distance of 51 feet, there are three courses of large stones with marginal drafts 3 inches to 6*

Stretch of ancient masonry south of the Golden Gate.

CHAPTER TWO: THE PRE-HERODIAN SQUARE TEMPLE MOUNT

Detail of ancient masonry south of the Golden Gate.

inches wide, and extremely rough faces, projecting in many cases as much as 9 inches."[38]

To the north of the Golden Gate, this same type of masonry is again visible for a distance of about 68 feet (20.73 m), at which point an *offset* is exposed (see photo, p. 177). We have called it an *offset* because just to the north of it, the Herodian masonry is set back about two feet, giving the impression that this is a corner which sticks out from the wall. Additionally, it is clear that the line of this wall, from the Golden Gate to the *offset*, follows a slightly different direction from the line of the later Turkish city wall above. Yet both these stretches of early masonry located on either side of the Golden Gate are in one line and therefore belong to one and the same wall.

It is not easy to date this wall on the basis of its masonry alone. Most of the stones, which have margins on all four sides and rough, bulging bosses, are somewhat eroded. The stones to the north of the Golden Gate are more eroded than those to the south. As the Temple Mount was extended from the center outwards over a long period of time, the central section, especially as seen in the Eastern Wall, must be the oldest and the sections farthest away from the center the latest additions.

Comparing This Masonry with That between the Seam and the Bend
There is a superficial similarity between these stones and the eroded upper ones north of the *seam* near the southeast corner, which have always been exposed.[39] However, after the clearance by

Chapter Two: The Pre-Herodian Square Temple Mount

Stretch of ancient masonry north of the Golden Gate.

bulldozer carried out in 1966 by the Jordanian Department of Antiquities, many more such courses were exposed. The lower stones were less eroded and in a far better state of preservation than the upper ones. They show a craftsmanship of higher quality (see photo, p. 103) than those near the Golden Gate. The arrisses or edges of the bosses, and consequently the margins, are straighter and better executed; while the bosses have as a rule a flat surface and a smoother finish (see illustration, p. 115 [D]). The margins have been worked by a tooth-edged chisel. Special features such as a slanted vertical joint occur occasionally in both types of masonry.

The masonry to the south of the *bend*, as will be discussed further in Chapter 3, in our opinion belongs historically to a Hasmonean extension to the south of the Temple Mount. The Hasmonean masons probably copied the style described above as accurately as possible when they extended the Temple Mount to the south.

The dentate tool marks visible on the margins of these Hasmonean stones are, however, absent from the rougher masonry near the Golden Gate. The difference in the manner of execution of the bosses and the margins indicates that the two masonry styles belong to different periods. Chapman, in his doctoral thesis,[40] discounts the widespread use of a dentate tool before the sixth century B.C. The lack of these tool marks indicates therefore that the oldest masonry of the Temple Mount may date from a time before the sixth century B.C.

Similar types of masonry, though on a slightly smaller scale, can be seen in the retaining walls of sixth-century B.C. Phoenician temple sites such as at Byblos and the later temple of Eshmoun near Sidon in Lebanon.[41] Another parallel may be found in the masonry of the retaining walls of the Achaemenid palaces at Pasargadae.[42] These examples provide further support of an early date for the masonry under discussion.

CHAPTER TWO: THE PRE-HERODIAN SQUARE TEMPLE MOUNT

The *Offset* North of the Golden Gate

Having examined the Hasmonean masonry of the southern end of the Eastern Wall and established its date, we return to the question of the northeastern corner of the pre-Herodian Temple Mount. As indicated above, we expected to find a seam roughly in the middle of this stretch of masonry between the Golden Gate and the *offset*.

There was, however, no indication of a corner construction preserved in this section of wall. On the contrary, the early masonry continued in an unbroken line to the *offset*. However, the *offset* itself gave every appearance of forming the corner of the early masonry, with the Herodian wall built against it, but slightly set back.

It seemed obvious that the corner could have been positioned here, at 39 feet (11.90 m) to the north of our projected corner, only if a tower had been built at this corner of the Temple Mount. If so, it must have been an integrally built tower, otherwise we should have found a vertical joint where we expected to find one. And, if this was the case, we would have to conclude that the 500-cubit-square Temple Mount of *Middot* referred exclusively to the platform proper, excluding any towers that may have projected from it.

So was the presence of towers built along the northern wall attested to in the sources? Chapter 3 of the Book of Nehemiah, which details the building of the city's walls after the Exile, mentions towers built along the northern wall in the first verse. As will be discussed below (pp. 197–203), archaeological remains in the northern wall of the raised platform indicate that a gate and several towers existed in the northern boundary of the square Temple Mount.

Ancient masonry north of the Golden Gate. Note the deviation in direction from the Turkish city wall above. The offset *is visible in the foreground. (photo: Alexander Schick)*

Ancient Gateposts inside the Golden Gate

Before leaving this area, we will examine the evidence of remains inside the Golden Gate of the early eastern wall of the square Temple Mount. In Chapter 1.5.4 we already described the two enormous monolithic gate jambs located at the eastern end of the interior of the Golden Gate. The top of these monoliths does not line up with

Chapter Two: The Pre-Herodian Square Temple Mount

Below (left): View along the Eastern Wall showing its "bend" at the place where the pillar sticks out from the wall.

Below (right): Model of Nehemiah's Jerusalem and the square Temple Mount, viewed from the southeast.

Opposite page (above): Schematic plan of the Temple Mount showing the change in direction in the Eastern Wall at the bend.

Oppostie page (below): Close-up view of the so-called Mohammed's Pillar.

the stone courses of the gate; thus we must conclude that these gateposts are older than the gate itself. The eastern faces of the monoliths appear to be set in the same line as the ancient stone courses on either side of the Golden Gate.

We have also pointed out that the level of the top of the southern monolith coincides with that of the ancient masonry on the south side of the Golden Gate, while the top of the northern monolith is one stone course higher than the stones to the north of the gate (see illustration, p. 109). These monolithic gateposts may have been part of the earliest wall section of the Temple Mount walls. Even if they were inserted at a later date, it follows that as no remains of any other pre-Herodian eastern gateway are known, the site of the Golden Gate is the only possible location for the earlier Shushan Gate.[43] The location of this early gate in the Eastern Wall does not line up with the axis of the Temple. However, as we will see later, this does not disqualify it as an original gate of the Temple Mount.

The *Bend* in the Eastern Wall

If the position of our projected northern wall of the square Temple Mount is correct, then the southeast corner of the square should be located 861 feet (262.50 m) south of the projected northeast corner.

Warren made an important observation about the Eastern Wall that appears to support the position of the square platform. Starting at the southeast corner of the present-day Temple Mount, the Eastern Wall

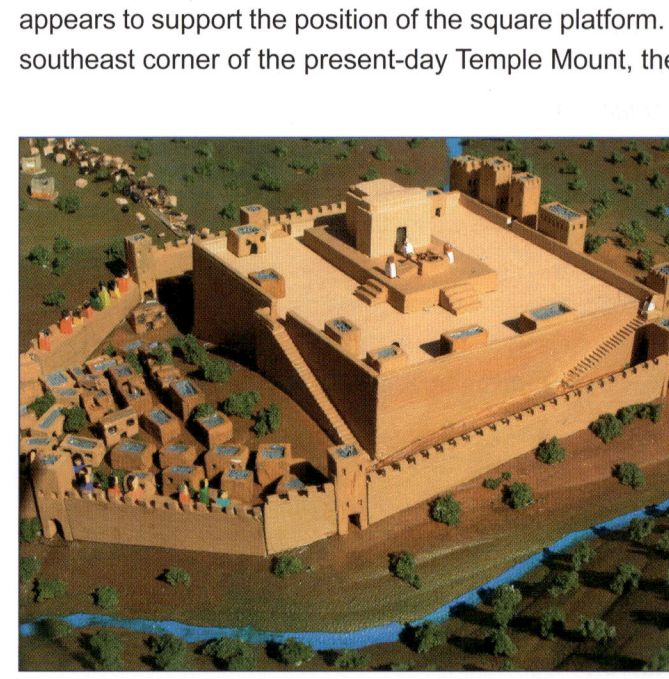

Chapter Two: The Pre-Herodian Square Temple Mount

shows Herodian masonry for 105 feet 6 inches (32 m) above ground (108 feet below ground). At that point a "straight joint" or *seam* is visible, north of which appears Hasmonean masonry that Warren traced underground for about 53 feet (16 m) north of the *seam* (see drawing on p. 104). Unfortunately, because of the dangerous nature of the debris, he could not continue his tunneling efforts farther north, so we don't know how far this Hasmonean masonry continues underground. However, Warren did note that *"it is probable that below the surface the first 260 feet of wall [from the southeast corner] are in a straight line."*[44]

At this point, which was later adjusted by Simons[45] to 240 feet (73.20 m) from the southeast corner, the wall changes slightly in direction. Warren continues,

> At this point there is a small postern on about the same level as the Single Gate on the south side. From this postern the wall takes a slight bend to northeast, so that at 650 feet from the southeast angle it is about 8 feet to east of a line in production of the first 260 feet.

The cause for this slight deviation in direction (see plan, above) is, in our opinion, a change in masonry deep below ground. As this point is located exactly 861 feet (262.50 m), or 500 cubits south of the projected northeast corner, we believe it comprises indirect archaeological evidence of the southeast corner of the square platform, which is probably still in existence underground.

The bend in the wall can be seen by standing close to the southeast corner and looking north along the top of the wall. The bend is located at the point where a column, known as Mohammed's Pillar, projects from the wall.

The Eastern City Wall

Given that towers are usually defensive features, it is instructive to examine the nature of the walls of the pre-Herodian Temple Mount in

Chapter Two: The Pre-Herodian Square Temple Mount

View of the eastern wall of the Temple Mount today. (photo: Garo Nalbandian)

this area. The existence of a separate northern city wall is not attested to in the historical sources. Because of the existence of a deep valley located to the north of the square Temple Mount, which together with the Fosse and the towers would have provided sufficient protection against any attack from the north, it would appear that the northern wall of the Temple Mount was also the northern city wall.

The situation on the eastern side of the Temple Mount, though, was different. Josephus, when writing about the first (or most ancient) wall, described it as terminating where it *"joined the eastern portico of the Temple."*[46] This indicated a separate eastern city wall. Again Warren's records provide illumination.

Warren wanted to examine the masonry of the Eastern Wall, but because the whole area in front of it is occupied by a Muslim cemetery and therefore off-limits to excavations, he tried to reach the wall from a shaft which he began at a distance of 143 feet (43.50 m) from the Temple Mount wall. Warren did not succeed in reaching the masonry below the Golden Gate. His way was blocked by a massive masonry wall. Accidentally discovered, at 46 feet from the Temple Mount, Warren described[47] it as follows:

> *This wall is composed of large quarry-dressed blocks*

Chapter Two: The Pre-Herodian Square Temple Mount

of missae, so far similar to the lower course seen in the Sanctuary wall near the Golden Gate, that the roughly dressed faces of the stones project about 6 inches beyond the marginal drafts, which are very rough. The stones appear to be in courses 2 feet 6 inches in height, and over 5 feet in length. On trying to break through the wall a hole was made 5 feet 6 inches, without any signs of the stones terminating. The horizontal courses are not close, but appear to be about 12 inches apart, and filled in with stones 6 inches cube, packed in a very curious cement, which now looks like an argillaceous stone and has a conchoidal fracture.

In this wall, the horizontal joints between the courses are about 12 inches (30 cm) apart, which is rather unusual for large free-standing walls. We don't know if these curious joints occur also in the higher courses; it is possible that this feature only exists at the bottom courses as a result of levelling operations given that the wall is built on a steep slope.

As small, marginally drafted stones were widely used in Hasmonean constructions, this apparently unusual construction may represent

Chapter Two: The Pre-Herodian Square Temple Mount

Reconstruction model of the eastern city wall in the time of Nehemiah.

the repair to the eastern city wall under Jonathan, as recorded in First Book of Maccabees[48] 12.37: *"They gathered together to rebuild the city. Part of the wall over the eastern ravine had fallen, and he restored the quarter called Chaphenatha."*

In any case, the location of the massive wall found by Warren east of the Golden Gate, and the fact that it turns in a northwesterly direction, would qualify this wall as a candidate *par excellence* for Jerusalem's eastern city wall of the First Temple period.[49]

According to our reconstruction (below), the eastern city wall would join the eastern wall of the square Temple Mount near its northeast corner, a little to the north of the present-day Golden Gate.

Furthermore, a city wall in this position would also provide protection and support for a staircase which must of necessity have been built here in order to reach the higher sill of the Eastern Gate. As shown earlier, in Chapter 1 (p. 110), a Herodian arch found in a grave in front of the Golden Gate was probably part of a stairway. This Herodian stairway probably replaced an earlier ramp or flight of steps, without which the great difference in height between the foot of the wall and the sill of the gate could not be overcome.

Chapter Two: The Pre-Herodian Square Temple Mount

The wall that abuts the southeast corner of the Temple Mount at present[50] is not built on bedrock, unlike the wall found by Warren, and has been dated to the Byzantine period. It therefore has no connection with the eastern city wall of the Herodian or earlier period. The results of Warren's excavations near the southeast angle of the Temple Mount[51] show that during the construction of the Herodian Temple Mount walls, a 21-foot (6.40 m) deep foundation trench was cut here through the *"solid red earth."* This must have been *terra rossa,* which in Jerusalem always represents the virgin soil.

These explorations have therefore proven that no other city wall ever joined the Temple Mount at this corner. This is further proof that the eastern city wall, which undoubtedly co-existed with the square Temple Mount, must therefore have been located farther to the east. The same wall was apparently still in use in the Herodian period and it would also have provided an excellent support for a staircase descending from the small double gate near the Seam located near the southeast corner.

Detail of Warren's Plate 19, showing the "solid red earth."

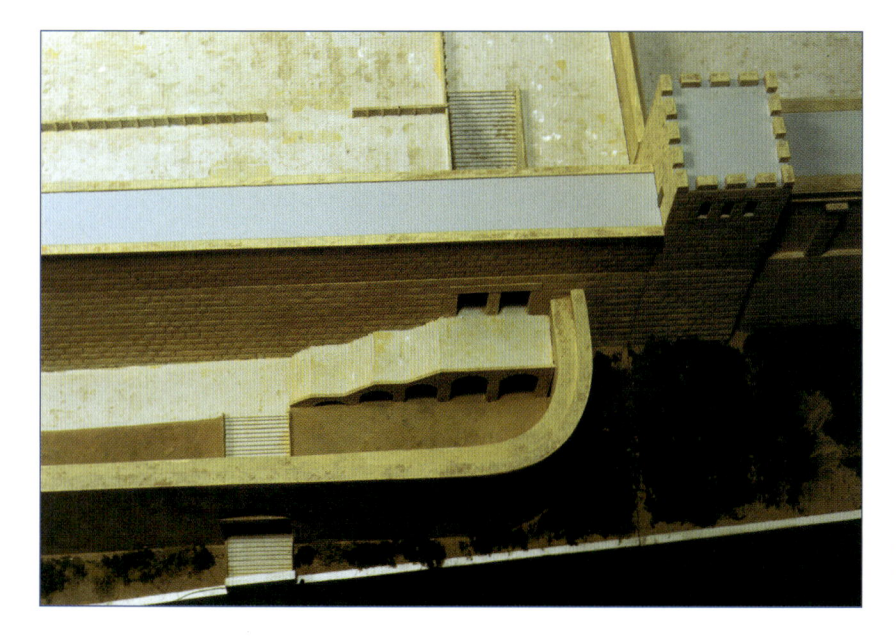

Reconstruction model of the northeast angle of the square Temple Mount. (photo: Philip Evans)

CHAPTER TWO: THE PRE-HERODIAN SQUARE TEMPLE MOUNT

Opposite page: Pompey's siege of Jerusalem in 63 B.C.

The Southern Wall of the Square Temple Mount

The southern wall of this square platform should be parallel to the northern wall. The southeast corner is located at the *bend,* and the southwest corner would be formed at the intersection of this line of the southern wall with the southern continuation of the *step,* the only archaeological remains visible of the pre-Herodian Western Wall (see photo, p. 164).

As will be seen later (p. 236) during our discussion of Barclay's Gate, the southern wall was probably only 853 feet (260 m) or 495 cubits long. This may have been due to the fact that when setting out the southern wall, the two corners could not be seen because of the high elevation of the mountain in between. Such differences are quite common in building sites of this magnitude. In any case, this irregularity constitutes less than 1 percent, and is therefore negligible.[52]

The two Hulda Gates, mentioned in the Mishnah, were located in this southern wall of the square Temple Mount and must not be confused, as they often are, with the Herodian Double and Triple Gates.

The Western Wall of the Square Temple Mount

The remains of this western wall, as already described above, are visible near the northwest corner of the raised platform. As will be discussed later in Chapter 5 (pp. 235–236), further confirmation that this is indeed the line of the square Temple Mount can be derived from the two suburban gates, named after Barclay and Warren.

The location of the Kiponus Gate, the western gate of *Middot*, is a matter of conjecture as no archaeological remains can be identified. The name *Kiponus* according to Simons[53] *"very likely stands for Coponius, the name of the first Roman procurator of Judea."*

Josephus records that during the siege of Pompey there existed a bridge that reached from the Temple to the city.[54] The Herodian bridge, of which Wilson's Arch is part, may have replaced or strengthened a pre-Herodian bridge. There is no doubt that a gate would have existed at the point where the bridge joined the outer Western Wall of the square Temple Mount. Following Herod's extension of the Temple Mount, this gate would have been located on the Temple Mount itself, to the east of the later gate which would have been built in the Herodian western wall, above Wilson's Arch. The Herodian bridge

Coin of Coponius (A.D. 6–9).

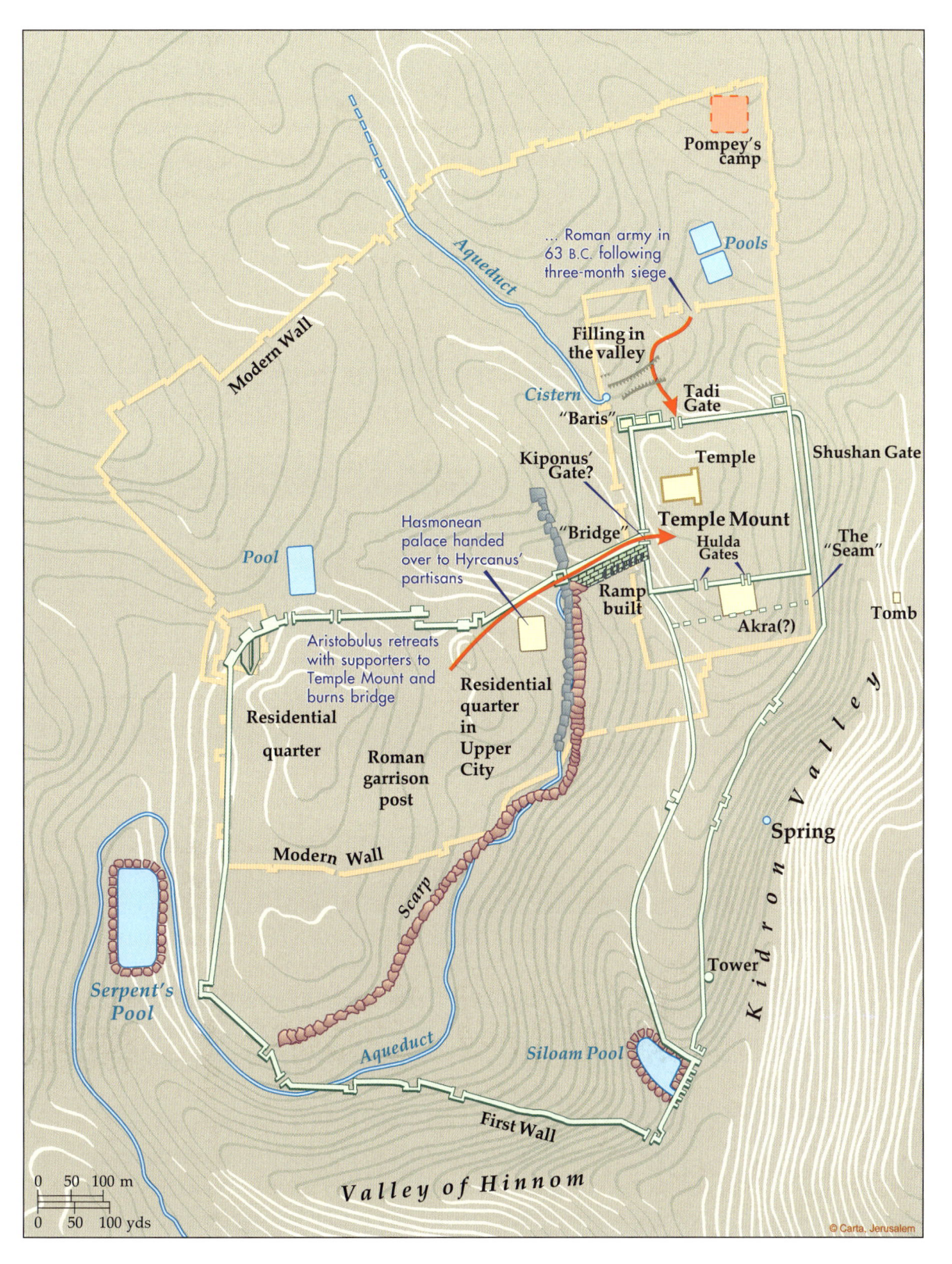

Chapter Two: The Pre-Herodian Square Temple Mount

would therefore have been shorter than its predecessor.

The fact that the name of Coponius (c. A.D. 6–9) is attached to this gate does not mean to say that this gate was necessarily a new gate built by him. However, it is interesting to note that Josephus mentions that a couple of years before Coponius was sent to Judea, some of the cloisters of the Temple were burnt during a fight between the Jews and the soldiers of Sabinus.[55] The original western gate of the square Temple Mount was possibly rebuilt under Coponius' rule, and therefore his name may have been given to this gate by the authors of the Mishnah.

THE DATE OF THE SQUARE TEMPLE MOUNT

The date of the construction of the 500-cubit-square Temple Mount can be established with certainty only by scientific archaeological excavation. This at present is impossible because of the political situation.

The date of the square Temple Mount's extension to the south, from the *bend* to the *seam*, indicates that the construction of the square Temple Mount proper must have taken place earlier. As will be discussed below, in Chapter 3, we propose that the extension was made in the Hasmonean period, probably after 141 B.C.

Although no conclusive evidence concerning a pre-Hasmonean date for the construction of the square Temple Mount can be gleaned from the literary sources, it is worthwhile to briefly review the relevant passages.

The Literary Sources Relating to Building Activities on the Temple Mount during the First Temple Period

In *Antiquities* 15.400, Josephus appears to suggest that the Solomonic Temple Mount was a square having sides of a stadium in length. It is also recorded in 1 Kings 7:12 that Solomon built a "Great Court" round about the Temple and the Royal Palace: *"And the great court round about was with three rows of hewed stones, and a row of cedar beams, both for the inner court of the house of the LORD, and for the porch of the house."*

This passage, however, gives no indication as to the layout or size of this court. In this context it is interesting to note that the excavations at Tel Dan[56] have revealed a temple complex from the ninth century B.C. which indeed had a square platform, measuring 36 cubits (62

Chapter Two: The Pre-Herodian Square Temple Mount

Reconstruction of the high place at Dan.

feet, 19 m) square, with evidence of wooden beams incorporated into the masonry. Does this represent a miniature replica of the Jerusalem Temple, as Jeroboam, who was the apparent builder, tried to lure Israel away from Jerusalem (1 Kgs 12:28)?

The square has often been used in the biblical literature of both the Old and New Testaments. The Holy of Holies in the Temple was a square,[57] as was the side elevation of the ark,[58] the altar of burnt offerings,[59] the altar of incense,[60] the breastplate[61] and the *"great city, holy Jerusalem"* described in the Book of Revelation.[62] The camp of the tribes of Israel during their wanderings in Sinai appears to have been organized in the form of a square.[63] The symbolism of the square, with its four sides of equal dimensions, would appear to indicate totality.[64]

It is therefore theoretically possible that the platform on which Solomon's Temple stood was a square, although not as large as 500 cubits. However, despite the obvious symbolic importance of the use of the square, it would be somewhat speculative to attribute the building of the early square platform in Jerusalem to Solomon in the light of Josephus' statement in *War* 5.185, that after Solomon had built the Temple, *"In course of ages, however, through the constant additions of the people to the embankment, the hilltop by this process of levelling up was widened."* In the sentence before this, though, Josephus had written of Solomon's Temple that *"the sanctuary*

Artist's reconstruction of the breastplate of the High Priest.

187

CHAPTER TWO: THE PRE-HERODIAN SQUARE TEMPLE MOUNT

THE KINGS OF JUDAH	
Rehoboam	928–911
Abijam	911–908
Asa	908–867
Jehoshaphat	867–846
Jehoram	846–843
Ahaziah	843–842
Athaliah	842–836
Joash	836–798
Amaziah	798–769
Uzziah	769–733
Jotham	758–743
Ahaz	733–727
Hezekiah	727–698
Manasseh	698–642
Amon	641–640
Josiah	639–609
Jehoahaz	609
Jehoiakim	608–598
Jehoiachin	597
Zedekiah	596–586

Above: Sucessors of Solomon and their regnal years (B.C).

Below: Signet ring inscribed "(Belonging) to Jotham," thought to be that of Jotham, king of Judah. Found at Tell el-Kheleifeh (biblical Ezion-geber). (NEAEHL)

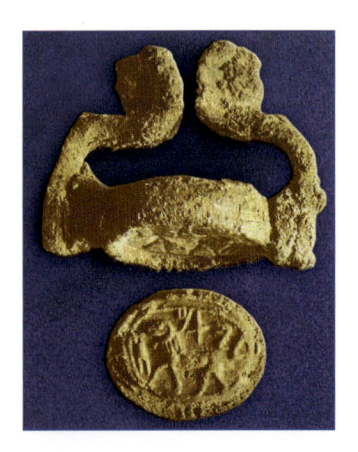

remained exposed," indicating that the building was not protected by a fortified court.

This latter quote, however, does not seem to take into consideration the above-quoted biblical account in 1 Kings, where the Temple is portrayed as surrounded by a Great Court. We must also consider that when Josephus mentions *"Solomon"* it is sometimes clear from the context that he actually refers to his successors, specifically, the predecessors of Herod the Great.

Later on, in 2 Chronicles 20:5, we read about a *"New Court"* that was probably built by Jehoshaphat. Was this a new and enlarged square court, measuring 500 cubits each side and replacing the Solomonic outer court that surrounded both the Temple and the Royal Palace? Or did he only repair and fortify the existing Solomonic court, while also raising the level of the outer court, the Temple always remaining higher than the Royal Palace?[65] In any event, it could not have been an additional third court as it is recorded that in the beginning of Manasseh's reign there were only two Temple courts (2 Chr 33:5), just as there were in the time of Solomon (2 Chr 4:9).

Josephus (*Ant.* 9.237) records that Jotham *"erected porticoes and gateways in the Temple area, and set up those parts of the walls that had fallen down, and built very large and impregnable towers."* In addition, 2 Chronicles 27:2 records concerning this same king that *"he built the High Gate of the House of the LORD."*

There are other passages which hint at building activities on the Temple Mount during the latter part of the First Temple period, passages we will examine in greater detail in Chapter 7.2 on the history of the First Temple. These passages, combined with the results of the archaeological excavations conducted around the Temple Mount in the Jewish Quarter and the City of David, caused Mazar[66] to write:

> *The period between the reign of Uzziah, King of Judah, in the mid 8th century B.C.E., and the destruction of Jerusalem and the exile at the beginning of the 6th century, is depicted in numerous biblical sources as a time of renaissance in the city of Jerusalem, which served as the capital of Israel since the days of David and Solomon. These sources record the ascendancy of Jerusalem as the site of the royal sanctuary and the seat of the monarchy, namely of the Davidic dynasty.... By synthesizing*

Chapter Two: The Pre-Herodian Square Temple Mount

the abundant and varied [archaeological] information now available, we should be able to trace the stages in the development and ascendancy of Jerusalem, a process which continued unabated for more than 150 years until the very eve of the disaster which befell it in 586 B.C.E.

The greatest builder in the First Temple period after Solomon was undoubtedly Hezekiah. We will next examine building activities that can most likely be attributed to his reign.

Hezekiah's Temple Mount

Major building activities took place in Jerusalem during the reign of Hezekiah. The archaeological remains in the Jewish Quarter and in the City of David allow us to visualize the words of Isaiah 22:8–11, which refer to the construction of Hezekiah's Tunnel, the Siloam Pool and the Broad Wall[67] (the latter mentioned by name in Neh. 3:8, 12: 38). In the light of these building activities, it appears reasonable to suggest that the Temple area would not have been neglected.

Second Chronicles 33:15 may indicate that an artificially created Temple Mount already existed in the time of Manasseh when the Temple Mount is referred to as *har bayit-Yahweh*. Manasseh was an

Aramaic inscription on stone tablet commemorating the reburial of King Uzziah's remains. (NEAEHL)

Reconstruction of the cities of David, Solomon and Hezekiah.

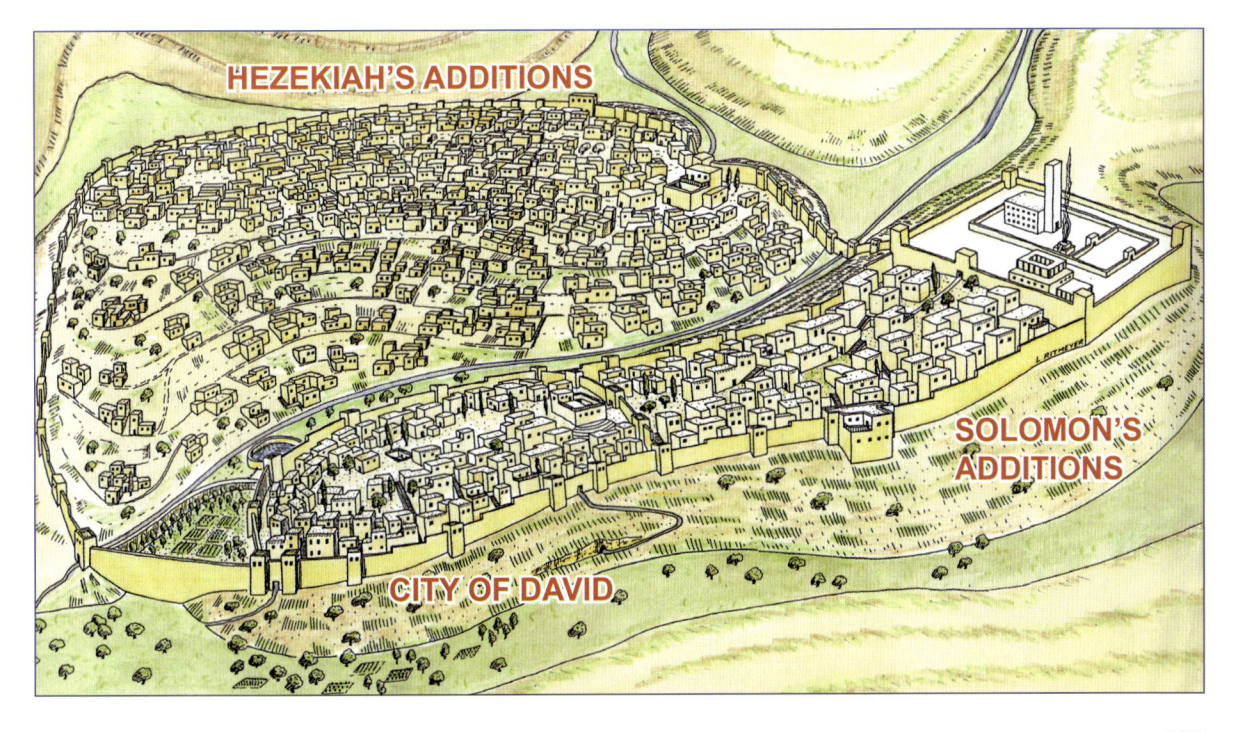

HEZEKIAH'S ADDITIONS

SOLOMON'S ADDITIONS

CITY OF DAVID

CHAPTER TWO: THE PRE-HERODIAN SQUARE TEMPLE MOUNT

Right: "And all nations shall flow unto it" (Isa 2:2). Artist's impression of pilgrims approaching the Holy Temple of Jerusalem. (The Temple Institute, Jerusalem)

Below: View of the excavated remains of the Middle Gate located in today's Jewish Quarter of the Old City.

Bottom: Reconstruction of the Middle Gate.

idol worshiper and therefore unlikely to have improved the Temple Mount. Thus, it is most likely that his father, Hezekiah, actually constructed this mount which surrounded the Temple. The prophets Isaiah (2:2) and Micah (4:1) who lived during the time of Hezekiah looked forward to a glorious future for the Temple Mount, as it says in Isaiah: *"and it shall come to pass in the last days, that* har bayit-Yahweh *shall be established in the top of the mountains, and shall be exalted above the hills; and all nations shall flow unto it."*

It is generally understood that Solomon built his palaces to the immediate south of the Temple. It would be logical to assume that the construction of a large 500-cubit-square Temple Mount would have obliterated these palaces. But, as Mazar[68] pointed out, only two palaces are mentioned as having been destroyed in 586 B.C. First to be destroyed was the relatively new palace near the Middle Gate,[69] and one month later the old palace in the City of David (2 Kgs 25:9–10). There is no mention of the destruction of Solomon's palace adjacent to the Temple. It is possible that Solomon's palace complex had fallen into disrepair by the time of Hezekiah and was included in the new Temple Mount.

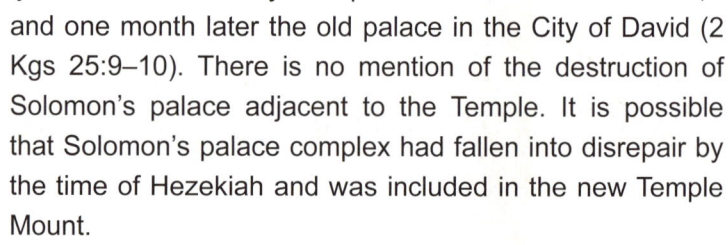

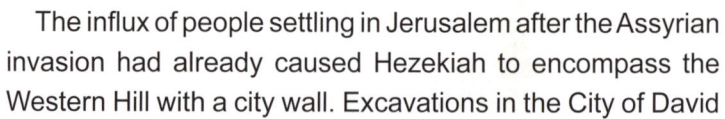

The influx of people settling in Jerusalem after the Assyrian invasion had already caused Hezekiah to encompass the Western Hill with a city wall. Excavations in the City of David have also shown that this part of the eastern slope was enclosed by the new city wall built by Hezekiah.[70] He may therefore also have felt the need to enlarge the existing Temple Mount to accommodate the larger number of new worshipers. It would have been necessary to dismantle one of Solomon's buildings, namely, the House of the Forest of Lebanon (1 Kgs 7:2), which served as an armory (2 Kgs 10: 16–17) and may have been alluded to in Isaiah 22:8: *"thou didst look in that day to the armour of the House of the Forest."*

The Temple Mount was referred to as a citadel, called the *Birah*, at the end of the First Temple and beginning of the Second Temple periods. The reference in the Bible is 1 Chronicles 29:1–2, 29:19:

> *Furthermore David the king said unto all the congregation, Solomon my son, whom alone God hath chosen, is yet young and tender, and the work is great for the palace (birah) is not for man, but for the Lord God. Now I have prepared with all my might for the House of my God the gold for the things of gold....*
> *(Then David asks God to) give unto Solomon a perfect heart, to keep thy commandments, thy testimonies, and thy statutes, and to do all these things, and to build the palace (birah), for the which I have made provision.*

Mazar[71] explains the meaning of *Birah* as follows:

David instructing Solomon as to the erection of the Temple in Jerusalem, after 19th-century engraving.

Chapter Two: The Pre-Herodian Square Temple Mount

Aerial view of the mound of ancient Susa (biblical Shushan). (photo: Oriental Institute, University of Chicago)

A fundamental assumption is that the Birah of the biblical sources of the Persian period was the citadel of Jerusalem on 'Mount Zion' (that is, the Temple Mount), including in its fortifications the Second Temple complex. The Hebrew term birah, Aramaic birta, derived from Assyrian birtu (castle, fort, citadel), was used in that period to describe a royal acropolis (as at Susa or Ecbatana) and administrative citadels at the centers of the western provinces, including Jerusalem, Samaria and Tyre of the Tobiads. In the anachronistic story in 1 Chronicles 28–29, David presents Solomon with a plan for the Birah (verse 19), including the sanctuary and its adjacent courts and structures. The following (29:1) is noteworthy: "The work is immense, for the birah is not for men but for Yahweh God." The author had in mind the Birah on the Temple Mount, including the sanctuary and its fortifications, just as Nehemiah did in his request to the king to supply him with timber from Lebanon for the gates of the birah of the Temple (ha-birah asher la-bayit), as well as for the gates of the city and his own palace (Nehemiah 2:8). It seems that in the Hellenistic period, too, the citadel

CHAPTER TWO: THE PRE-HERODIAN SQUARE TEMPLE MOUNT

was separated from the city, but included the Temple in its fortified enclosure.

As the Book of Chronicles was written after the exile, it is evident that the square Temple Mount was already in existence at the time of writing. The reference to a Solomonic *Birah* is therefore anachronistic indeed, as Mazar mentioned—the Chronicler would have been familiar only with the Temple Mount as it existed at the end of the First Temple period.

We therefore suggest that the construction of the square Temple Mount took place during the reign of Hezekiah, a time of extraordinary architectural activity towards the end of the eighth and at the beginning of the seventh century B.C.

Further support for this date can perhaps be derived from the fact that the Temple described by Ezekiel also measured 500 cubits square. In chapters 40 and 41 we read about three outer lower gates, each of which is 50 cubits long (Ezek 40:21). Inside these lower gates is a court, 100 cubits wide (verse 19). Farther inward there are three inner gates, each of which is identical to the lower ones and therefore also 50 cubits long. In between these gates there is therefore a distance of 100 cubits. In front of the Temple, and in between the inner façades of the three inner gates, there is an inner court which is 100 cubits foursquare (verse 47). Going along the north-south axis, we arrive at the following measurements:

Ezekiel's vision of Jerusalem (Ezek 48:30–35).

lower north gate	50 cubits
lower north court	100 cubits
higher north gate	50 cubits
inner square court	100 cubits
higher south gate	50 cubits
lower south court	100 cubits
lower south gate	50 cubits
Total north-south length	**500 cubits**

This Temple complex, which comprises the Temple and two sets of three gates, measures 500 cubits square, like the one built by Hezekiah. In addition, however, this 500 cubits square inner complex described by Ezekiel is surrounded by a massive court, measuring 500 reeds, or 3,000 cubits, square. This court has an outer wall that measures a reed high and wide (Ezek 40:5).

Chapter Two: The Pre-Herodian Square Temple Mount

Although Ezekiel's Temple is usually interpreted as futuristic, it is possible that his measurements of the inner 500-cubit-square platform were based on those of the pre-exilic Temple Mount that Ezekiel would have known.

Rebuilding the walls of Jerusalem in the time of Nehemiah, 19th-century engraving.

The Literary Sources Relating to Building Activities on the Temple Mount during the Second Temple Period

It is generally assumed that the Temple built in the days of Zerubbabel the son of Shealtiel and Jeshua the son of Jozadak followed the pattern of Solomon's Temple, though it did not approach the latter in magnificence, as Ezra 3:12–13 says:

> *But many of the priests and Levites and chief of the fathers, who were ancient men, that had seen the first house, when the foundation of this house was laid before their eyes, wept with a loud voice; and many shouted aloud for joy: So that the people could not discern the noise of the shout of joy from the noise of the weeping of the people: for the people shouted with a loud shout, and the noise was heard afar off.*

While this seems to refer to the rebuilding of the Temple proper, Nehemiah, who came much later to Jerusalem, was more concerned with fortifying the outer walls and gates of the square Temple Mount

Chapter Two: The Pre-Herodian Square Temple Mount

on which the Temple itself stood. The Scriptural references are:

Nehemiah 1:1, where we read that Nehemiah was in "Shushan the palace." In the Books of Nehemiah and Esther, the word for palace is always *Birah*. As Mazar already pointed out, this *Birah* was the fortified royal acropolis in Persia. The same word has been used to indicate the Temple Mount complex in Jerusalem.

Nehemiah 2:8. Nehemiah asks for *"a letter unto Asaph the keeper of the king's forest, that he may give me timber to make beams for the gates of the palace which (appertaineth) to the house* (ha-birah asher la-bayit)*, and for the walls of the city, and for the house that I shall enter into."*

Nehemiah 7:2: *"Now it came to pass, when the wall was built, and I had set up the doors, and the porters and the singers and the Levites were appointed, that I gave my brother Hanani, and Hananiah the ruler of the palace* (birah)*, charge over Jerusalem: for he was a faithful man, and feared God above many."*

Smith[72] has already indicated several times that the name *Birah* was applied to the entire Temple area, although once or twice he conveyed the idea that this name applied to the outer court only. We cannot quite agree with the latter suggestion, as *Middot* 1.9 mentions a certain passageway (to which we will refer later), which was located inside the *hel* and led "under the *Birah*." The whole of the square Temple Mount was therefore called the *Birah,* but practically speaking, it is the surface of the Temple Mount that is referred to in this quote. The *hel* was a terrace on the Temple Mount, which was part of the consecrated area adjacent to the Temple gates. The *mikveh,* in which the unclean priests had to wash, was located outside the *hel* and below the *Birah*, the surface of the Temple Mount.

There is a theoretical possibility, of course, that the actual construction of the square Temple Mount may have taken place long after the restoration of the Temple Mount by Nehemiah. A major reconstruction

Artist's impression of the High Priest sanctifying himself in the mikveh before changing vestments. (The Temple Institute, Jerusalem)

Chapter Two: The Pre-Herodian Square Temple Mount

Right: Jerusalem in the time of the Maccabees.

Below: Antiochus III, king of Syria.

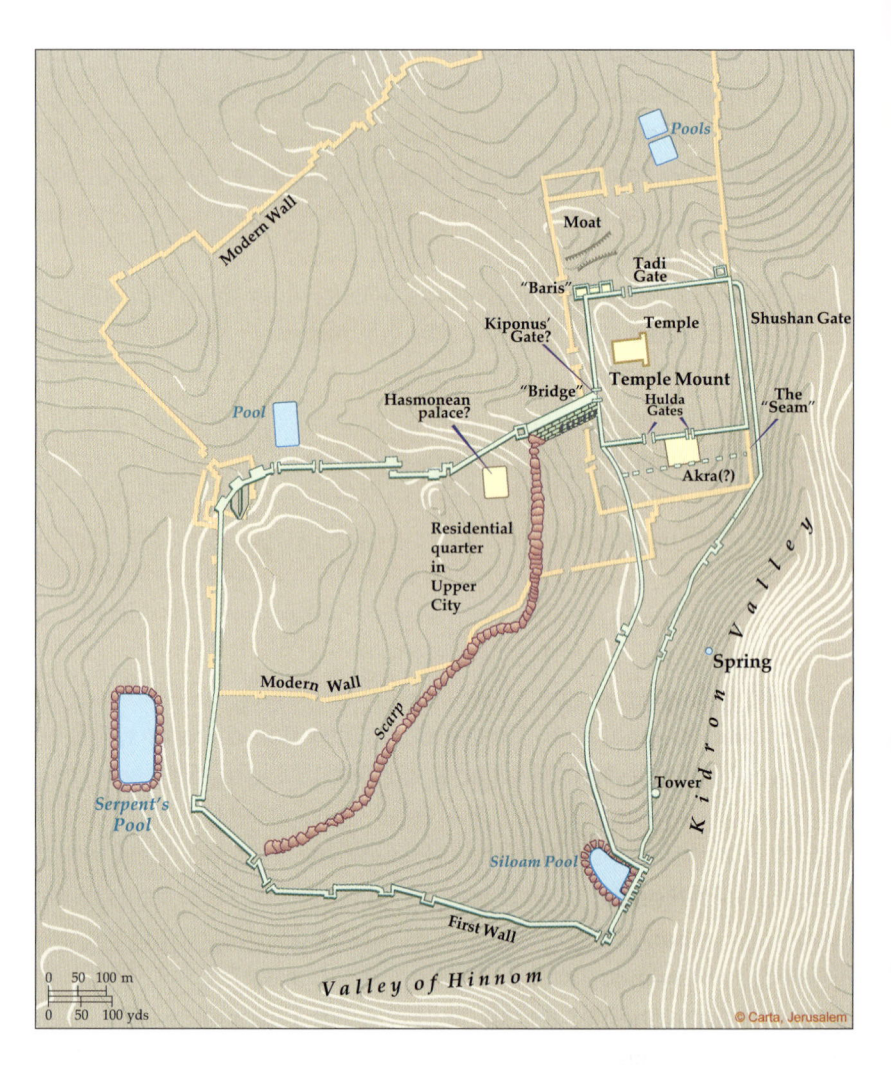

must have taken place in the Hellenistic period in the wake of the edict of Antiochus III (*Ant.* 12.141), which says *"that the work on the Temple be completed, including the porticoes and any other part that it may be necessary to build."* However, the text states that this would refer to a completion or reconstruction only.

Large building projects were also undertaken during the Maccabean period. Indeed, it has also been suggested that the square Temple Mount was created during the early Maccabean period. This was the view of Jerome Murphy-O'Connor, OP, who wrote in a private communication, dated 2 December 1990,

> The common impression is that Judas simply tidied up the area and brought the Sanctuary back into use, but

Chapter Two: The Pre-Herodian Square Temple Mount

this is contradicted by the texts. Serious physical damage to the sanctuary is attested in 1 Macc. 3:45 and 4:38 and major restoration work is mentioned under Judas: "they restored the gates and the chambers for the priests …they fortified Mount Sion with high walls and strong towers all around" (1 Macc. 4:57–60) and under Jonathan who repaired "part of the wall on the valley to the east had fallen" (1 Macc. 12:37). In the light of such evidence I would suggest that your square Temple is essentially a Maccabean construction.

The works undertaken during this period were undoubtedly of a large scope. However, to us the record in the Books of Maccabees indicates that the walls of the Temple Mount were only repaired and fortified—that is, made stronger and perhaps higher—rather than constructing a completely new Temple Mount, one that measured 500 cubits square.

An enlargement of the Temple Mount to this exact size, which would make it identical to the inner Temple complex described by Ezekiel, would certainly have been recorded, especially in the light of the religious importance of such an enterprise.

Post-Exilic Restoration

However, we had initially suggested that the early masonry visible in the lower courses of the Eastern Wall near the Golden Gate dated to the time of Nehemiah.[73] The fact that this masonry can be dated to at least the sixth century B.C. could support this. According to the biblical record, Zerubbabel and Jeshua built the altar in 535 B.C., and twenty years later, in 515 B.C., the Temple was completed (Ezra 3:2, 6:15). In the next century (around 444 B.C.), Nehemiah repaired the city walls and the walls of the Temple Mount (see below).

If this earliest masonry did indeed date back to the time of Nehemiah, and considering that Nehemiah mainly repaired existing

The returning exiles from Babylon construct the altar of the Second Temple—an artist's impression. (The Temple Institute, Jerusalem)

Chapter Two: The Pre-Herodian Square Temple Mount

walls, then it would be conceivable that beneath this masonry, near the Golden Gate and below the level of the Muslim cemetery, there exists an even earlier wall of the First Temple period. This is the view of Kathleen Kenyon[74]:

Dame Kathleen Kenyon.

> There were certainly a number of vicissitudes in the history of the immediately pre-Herodian Temple, but basically it was the Temple restored by Zerubbabel after the return from the Babylonian exile. It is inconceivable that Zerubbabel, with his very exiguous resources, should have increased the size of the Solomonic platform. It is reasonably certain that he built upon the basis of surviving foundations, and restored the platform as best as he could.

We now believe that this masonry dates from the First Temple period and our previous proposal that the early masonry near the Golden Gate may have represented Nehemiah's repair. Nevertheless, the study of the post-exilic building activities as recorded by Ezra and Nehemiah has led to a better understanding of the appearance of the Temple Mount at the end of the First Temple period.

Our location of the square Temple Mount has led to the possible discovery of the remains of a tower at its northeast corner. As mentioned before, certain other towers and a gate are known to have existed along the northern wall of the Temple Mount during the First Temple period. Identifying the location of these structures would also further strengthen our suggestion that the construction of the square Temple Mount took place during the First Temple period.

The Identification of the Northeast Tower

The possible discovery of the remains of a tower at the northeast corner of the square Temple Mount has been described above (see above, section 2.3.6). The Book of Nehemiah (chapter 3) describes the building and the restoration of the city walls of Jerusalem. At the end of chapter 3, while describing the northern part of the eastern city wall, Nehemiah mentions that certain merchants repaired a stretch of wall, *"over against the gate Miphkad and the going up* (aliyah) *of the corner"* (Neh 3:31–32). As a rule, *aliyah* is translated as *"chamber"* in the Old Testament, and in one case (2 Sam 18:33), *aliyah* refers to the upper chamber of a gate. It could, therefore, also refer to an

Chapter Two: The Pre-Herodian Square Temple Mount

Reconstruction model of Nehemiah's Jerusalem, from the east, showing the northeast corner of the Temple Mount and the gate Miphkad.

upper chamber or turret[75] of a tower, located at a corner between the gate *Miphkad* and the Sheep Gate, the last structure mentioned in this chapter.

The sources do not give the location of the gate *Miphkad*. In the prophecy of Ezekiel's Temple *"the appointed place of the house" (mipqad ha-bayit)*, where the sin offering is burnt, is located outside the Temple. This may be an indication that the gate *Miphkad* of Nehemiah's time could have been located outside the Temple, and may therefore have been a gate in the eastern city wall, near the approach to the eastern gate of the Temple Mount.

The text does not indicate whether the corner referred to was the northeast angle of the square Temple Mount or a corner of the city wall. The archaeological remains in the area of the Golden Gate indicate that the city wall found by Warren (see plan, p. 166) was curved and had no corner built into it, and that the only tower found in this area was part of the square platform. Our suggested reconstruction of this area (see above, also p. 181) shows that the city wall linked up with the Eastern Wall near the northeast corner of the square Temple Mount and that the tower belongs to the square platform. Although this tower is architecturally an integral part of the

199

Chapter Two: The Pre-Herodian Square Temple Mount

Temple Mount, its location near the termination of the Eastern Wall closely associates it with this city wall. Additionally, the northern wall of the square Temple Mount would have effectively doubled as a city wall, as there was no independent city wall skirting the north of the Temple Mount. This then is most probably the reason why the northeast tower is mentioned in the description of the city walls.

We propose therefore that the remains of this tower be identified with the "going up of the corner," which was located near the gate Miphkad, *according to Nehemiah's record.*

The Towers of Hananeel and Meah

The existence of defensive towers in the northern wall of the square Temple Mount during the siege of Pompey in 63 B.C. was recorded by Josephus (*Ant.* 14.61). According to his narrative, some towers must have stood close to the southern side of the Fosse to which we have already referred (see above, pp. 168–169), that is, the northwest corner of the mishnaic Temple Mount. Because of the limited space between the northern wall of the square Temple Mount and the Fosse, it seems reasonable to assume that these towers were attached to the square Temple Mount. If this was the case, they could be identified with the Hasmonean *Baris*, which according to Josephus stood at the northwest angle of the Temple (*Ant.* 15.403).

It is interesting to note that the Tower of Hananeel, according to

Reconstruction model of Nehemiah's Jerusalem from the north, showing the Towers of Meah and Hananeel, and the Sheep and Prison Gates.

CHAPTER TWO: THE PRE-HERODIAN SQUARE TEMPLE MOUNT

Nehemiah's description of the city wall,[76] also stood at or near the northwest corner of the Temple Mount. This tower already existed at the end of the First Temple period, according to the biblical record of Jeremiah 31:38 and Zechariah 14:10. Hananeel's Tower must have been destroyed during the Babylonian conquest of 586 B.C., and later rebuilt by Nehemiah. The *Baris* was apparently the successor of the Tower of Hananeel, as it occupied the same location at the northwest corner of the square Temple Mount. This would indicate that at least the northwest corner of Nehemiah's Temple Mount coincided with that of the pre-exilic period.

Continuing this line of thought, we dare suggest that this fortress at the northwest corner may have had twin towers, the eastern one of which may have been the Tower Meah, or the "Tower of the Hundred" (Neh 3:1, 12:39), as this tower is always mentioned together with the Tower of Hananeel. It is possible, as already suggested by Simons,[77] that these two towers are respectively the eastern and the western tower of a fortress located at the northwest corner of the pre-exilic Temple Mount that was later superseded by the Hasmonean *Baris*.

The Ptolemaic *Akra*

Before the *Baris* was constructed at the northwest corner of the square Temple Mount by Hyrcanus in c. 134 B.C., another fortress or citadel is mentioned by Josephus (*Ant*. 12.133, 138). He refers to a citadel, or *Akra,* from which a Ptolemaic garrison was ejected by the forces of Antiochus III in 198 B.C. As Wightman suggested,[78] this citadel was probably built soon after the Ptolemaic invasion of the Land of Israel at the beginning of the third century B.C. A citadel near the Temple Mount would have consolidated the Ptolemaic hold over Jerusalem against the threat of the Seleucids. In this context, one would expect this citadel to be located on the north side of the Temple Mount, where it could best serve against Syrian attacks from the north.

Seleucid war elephant.

In the Second Book of Maccabees (4.12, 4.27–28, 5.5–6), an *acropolis,* or citadel, is described that served as an administrative center for the Seleucid commander, whose responsibility it was to collect taxes. The historical background indicates that this citadel existed before the construction of the Seleucid *Akra* to the south of the Temple Mount in 168 B.C. (see below, p. 207).

This is supported by another historical document, the *Letter of*

Chapter Two: The Pre-Herodian Square Temple Mount

Aristeas,[79] although there are some doubts as to its authenticity. According to this letter, the author visited a citadel adjacent to the Temple Mount in Jerusalem during the reign of Ptolemy II Philadelphus (285–246 B.C.). He describes his ascent to a strongly fortified citadel that was situated on an elevated place, from which it was possible to view the offering of the sacrifices. His description would certainly fit a citadel located at the northwest corner of the pre-Herodian Temple Mount.

Silver tetradrachm of Ptolemy II Philadelphus.

We suggest that the remains of the ancient towers of Hananeel and Meah probably still existed at the beginning of the Ptolemaic domination of the Holy Land, although by then their names may have been forgotten. These towers, situated at the strategic northwest corner of the Temple Mount, may have been rebuilt as the Ptolemaic Akra.

The Sheep Gate and the Prison Gate

Archaeological evidence for another tower in the northern wall of the square Temple Mount may be found in the so-called Cistern 29, investigated by Warren. It consists of a 70-foot (21 m) long passage going east to west with four bays on the south that have medieval pointed vaults resting on piers attached to the northern wall of the platform. The southern parts of these piers are cut out of the rock and project from the northern end of the raised platform. Warren[80] wrote about these southern bays: *"The bays are from 11 feet to 13 feet span, and about 16 feet deep. The piers are 3.5 feet thick."* We are especially interested in his descriptive account of this area, where he writes[81]:

> The southern side of these bays is scarped rock, and on it the wall supporting the northern edge of the Mosque platform is built. Portions of the piers are also scarped from the rock, which appears to shelve down rapidly to the north; so that, if the earth and these vaults were removed, the northern end of the Mosque platform would present the appearance of a perpendicularly scarped rock with excrescences on its face 3 feet 6 inches thick, 12 feet apart, and projecting about 6 feet.

Warren was able to investigate only the visible area, but noted that both ends were blocked by fill. There may therefore be more cells cut

CHAPTER TWO: THE PRE-HERODIAN SQUARE TEMPLE MOUNT

out of the bedrock than the four he saw. These bedrock projections are apparently part of the substructure of a building that once stood above them and could be accessed from the Temple Mount.

In the record of Nehemiah 12:39, the Sheep Gate and the Prison *(Matarah)* Gate are mentioned after the Towers of Hananeel and Meah. Could these bedrock cells discovered in Cistern 29 have been used as a prison? If this feature indeed points to the former location of the Prison Gate, and we follow the circuit described in Nehemiah 12, where the Sheep Gate is mentioned just before the Prison Gate, then the latter and the twin towers of Hananeel and Meah would have flanked this same Sheep Gate.

Below: Dedication of the wall of Jerusalem as described in Nehemiah 12:27–43, after 19th-century engraving.

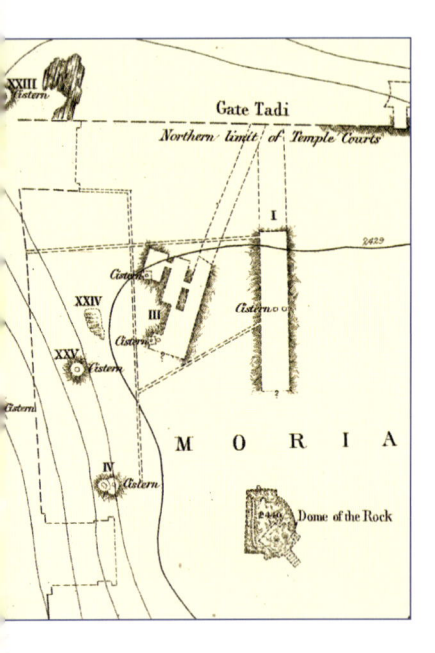

CHAPTER TWO: THE PRE-HERODIAN SQUARE TEMPLE MOUNT

The Tadi Gate

According to the Mishnah *Middot* 1.3, there was a gate in the north wall of the 500-cubit-square Temple Mount called the *Tadi* Gate, which apparently was never used. *Middot* 1.9 indicates that this gate had a subterranean passage, and 2.3 states further that the gate had a lintel composed of two stones that leaned against each other. An interesting example of such a construction was found in the passageway at the top of the stepped tunnel that leads down to Warren's Shaft in the City of David. The roof of the entry tunnel is made of stone slabs whose tops lean against each other, forming a continuous gable. We propose that the lintel construction of the Tadi Gate was probably also gabled in similar fashion.[82]

Warren already suggested that this Tadi Gate of *Middot* may have been located in the northern wall of the raised platform[83] and was connected with Cistern 1. This cistern is a tunnel-like passageway, 130 feet (39.5 m) long, 24 feet (7.30 m) wide, with its floor located 30 feet (9.10 m) below the surface of the platform. The side walls are cut out of the bedrock and the roof is a stone vault. The northern end is closed with a rough stone wall and the passageway may also have extended farther to the south. It appears therefore that this structure, originally built as an underground passageway, as its shape suggests, was plastered over and turned into a cistern much later, probably during the Early Muslim or Crusader period. When Herod the Great extended the platform to the north, any gate at the end of this passageway would have been buried underground, thus rendering it useless, as *Middot* 1.3 indeed indicates.

Another cistern complex nearby, Cistern 3, also has a passageway on its east side, concerning which Warren[84] wrote:

The production of the main gallery of No. 3 cuts the production of the gallery of No. 1, if both are produced northward, just at the north wall of the platform, where the subterranean gate Tadi appears most probably to have been placed, as shown on the plan (Pl. 6). The ground in this vicinity has a hollow sound.

Above: Detail of Warren's Plate 6, showing the Tadi Gate.

Below: Reconstruction of the Tadi Gate with leaning lintel stones.

CHAPTER TWO: THE PRE-HERODIAN SQUARE TEMPLE MOUNT

Left: The only indication above ground of the Tadi Gate is the well head of Cistern 1, photographed here in the 19th century by the Russian photographer Narinsky.

Below: The Cistern today.

The northern parts of both these passages are blocked by similar-looking walls that made it impossible for Warren to investigate their relation to the northern wall of the raised platform. Warren had suggested that this cistern may have been the bathhouse of the Temple. Schick, who also investigated this cistern,[85] discounted this possibility as he found no remains of steps leading to the surface. Later, in Chapter 9, we shall see that this cistern is indeed located below the Chamber of the Hearth, from which priests could descend into the bathhouse. The entrance would have been a short distance to the north of the blocked passageway.

The location of Cistern 1 is of interest because it forms part of a clear north-south axis through the Rock and the underground passageways of the Double Gate. From an architectural point of view, this shows that both passageways were designed at the same time, and that both are related to the Rock.

It is tempting to speculate that the mishnaic Tadi Gate stood in the same place as the pre-exilic Sheep Gate. The meaning of *Tadi* remains unknown. It has been suggested[86] that *Tadi* is a misreading of *Tali* or *Taleh,* which means *Lamb* in Hebrew. In that case, it would not be difficult to see the connection between the Sheep and the "Lamb" Gate.

205

Rock hewn aqueduct
St. Anne's Valley
Bezetha Valley
Kedron Valley
Fosse
Baris
Tadi Gate
Shushan Gate
Tyropoeon Valley
Temple
Gate
Bridge
West Gate
Council House
Transversal Valley
Proposed Street above Drain
Hulda Gates
Bend
Hasmonean
Extension
Seam
0
50m
L.R.

Opposite page: Plan of the square Temple Mount and the Hasmonean extension.

Below: Tetradrachma of Antiochus IV Epiphanes.

Chapter Three
The Hasmonean Temple Mount

The square Temple Mount was extended to the south during the Hasmonean period (see opposite page). We will first examine the location of the *Akra* and a cistern on the Temple Mount known as the Cistern of the *Akra*. We will then discuss the main elements that helped us determine the layout of the Hasmonean Temple Mount. These elements are the masonry in the Eastern Wall between the *seam* and the *bend*, the location of the *Baris* and the evidence for porticoes.

THE LOCATION OF THE SELEUCID *AKRA*

As the location of the Seleucid *Akra* is connected with the location of the square Temple Mount, we will only examine those passages in the historical sources which cast light on this subject, without going into all the historical implications. Although Josephus sometimes refers to the Lower City as the *Akra*, we are here mainly concerned with the fortress by that name.

In 168 B.C. Antiochus IV Epiphanes built the *Akra*, a fortress for his Macedonian garrison from which the Jewish population could be controlled. Josephus records that it stood *"in the lower portion of the town"* (*War* 1.39) and that it commanded or overlooked the Temple. Josephus writes in *Antiquities* 12.252 that Antiochus

> … built the Akra in the Lower City; for it was high enough to overlook the Temple, and it was for this reason that he fortified it with high walls and towers, and stationed a Macedonian garrison therein. Nonetheless there re-

Chapter Three: The Hasmonean Temple Mount

mained in the Akra those of the (Jewish) people who were impious and of bad character, and at their hands the citizens were destined to suffer many terrible things.

This is confirmed later by Josephus (*Ant.* 12.362):

At this time the garrison in the Akra of Jerusalem and the Jewish renegades did much harm to the Jews; for when they went up to the Temple with the intention of sacrificing, the garrison would sally out and kill them—for the Akra commanded the Temple.

This description agrees with that given by the author of the Books of Maccabees, who, when referring to the event mentioned above, puts the *Akra* in the Lower City, which he calls the City of David.

They fortified the City of David with a great and strong wall, with strong towers, and it became unto them an Akra. There they installed an army of sinful men, renegades, who fortified themselves inside it, storing arms and provisions, and depositing there the loot they had collected from Jerusalem; they were to prove a great trouble. It became an ambush for the sanctuary, an evil adversary for Israel at all times. (1 Macc 1.33–36)

Coin with a Seleucid king (unknown) on obverse and Apollo on reverse.

Among scholars, there is less disagreement about the historical interpretation of the Books of Maccabees and Josephus than about the topographical problems connected with the location of the Seleucid *Akra*, which are styled the *"most debated," "most enigmatic,"* and *"thorniest"* by Simons,[1] Avigad[2] and Wightman,[3] respectively.

There are many theories as to the location of the *Akra*.[4] Some scholars such as Robinson, Warren, Vincent and Avi-Yonah would place the *Akra* on the western hill of Jerusalem. However, since the term *"Lower City"* as used by Josephus is always understood to refer to the southeastern hill of Jerusalem, one would expect the *Akra* to be situated to the immediate south of the square Temple Mount, on a spot sufficiently elevated to overlook the Temple,[5] This would, of course, fit the City of David, where the author of the Books of Maccabees places the *Akra*.

The fact that the *Akra* overlooked the Temple Mount does not necessarily mean that the rocky mountain on which the *Akra* was built was itself higher than the Temple Mount, but rather that the Temple Mount could be overlooked by someone standing on the

CHAPTER THREE: THE HASMONEAN TEMPLE MOUNT

highest parts of this fortress. The fact that the southeast hill slopes away rapidly in all directions to the south of the square Temple Mount excludes all but the highest rock levels near the southern wall of the square Temple Mount as a possible location for the *Akra*.

As can be seen from the section through the bedrock on which the Herodian Southern Wall is built (see illustration, pp. 60–61), the area between the Double and Triple Gates is relatively flat. The topography of the area between the respective passageways (see p. 206) shows that this too is a fairly flat area that consequently would have been a suitable site for the construction of the *Akra* fortress. The flatness of this ground could be ascribed to the leveling operations of Simon the Maccabee, who, after after having razed the *Akra*, *"thought it would be an excellent thing and to his advantage to level also the hill on which the Akra stood, in order that the Temple might be higher than this"* (Ant. 13.215).

The average level of the bedrock here, according to Warren's maps, is 2,400 feet, while the courts of the Temple Mount directly above are 20 feet (6 m) higher. Thus it is not difficult to imagine the construction here of a fortress high enough to overlook the Temple.[6]

It is also clear from Josephus and the Books of Maccabees that the *Akra* controlled the main approach to the Temple, presumably the road leading from the City of David to the Hulda Gates. This approach, from the Lower City to the Temple Mount, traced the route of the later Herodian Double Gate passageway. Thus the *Akra* could not have been located far away. *We suggest, therefore, that the* Akra *was built to the immediate south of the square Temple Mount, with its*

View of the excavation areas in the City of David, looking north towards the Temple Mount. (NEAEHL)

Chapter Three: The Hasmonean Temple Mount

Plan of the square Temple Mount and the site of the Akra and Cistern 11.

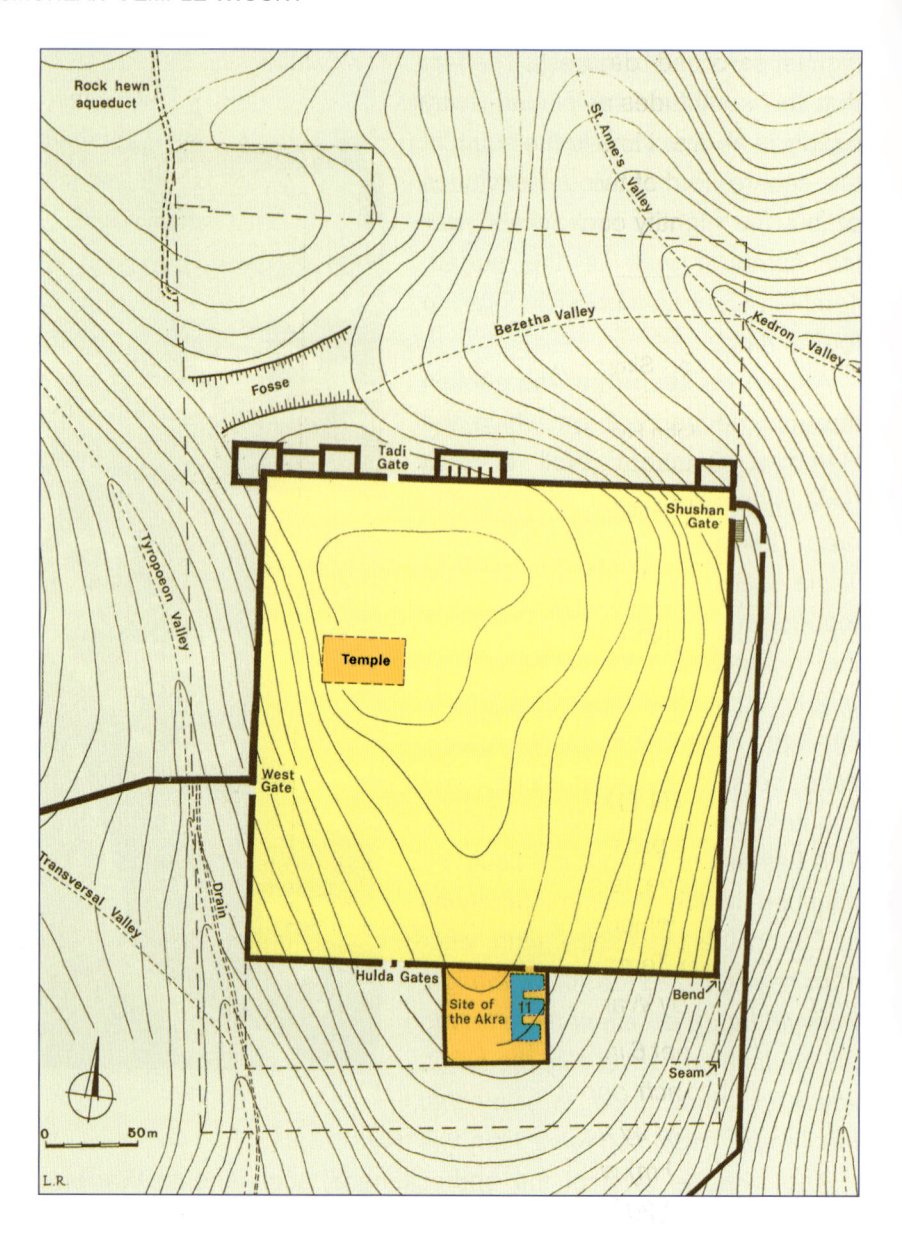

main gate facing west, from which the road leading to the southern Hulda Gates of the square Temple Mount could be controlled (see plan, above).

Our placement of the *Akra* would also confirm that a wall, between a western entrance of the *Akra* and the eastern side of the approach to the Hulda Gates, must have separated the *Akra* from the road linking the City of David to the Temple. It is recorded that Jonathan *"decided…to erect a high barrier (wall) between the Akra and the city, to separate it from the city and isolate it"* (1 Macc 12:36).

CHAPTER THREE: THE HASMONEAN TEMPLE MOUNT

The recorded destruction of the *Akra*, followed by quarrying activities, precludes any hope of ever finding archaeological remains of its existence. However, as we shall see in the following chapter, Warren's record of the cisterns below the Temple Mount has made it possible to identify one of them with the *Akra* fortress.

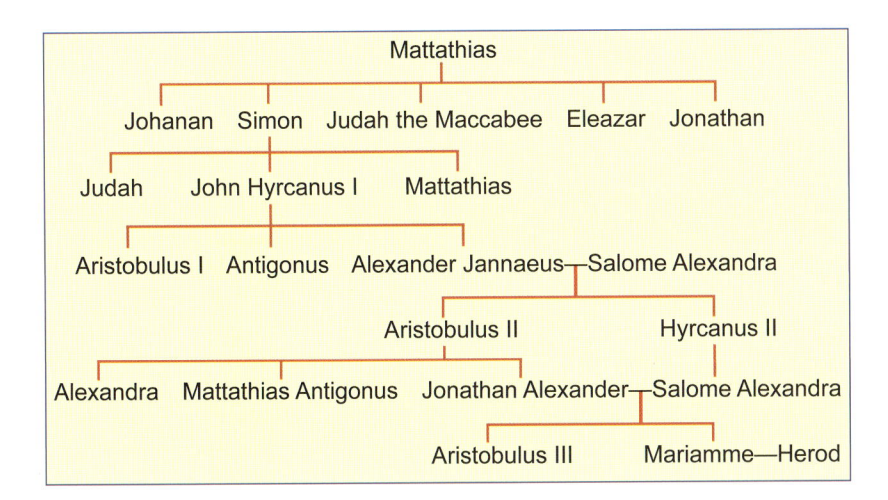

Genealogical table of the Hasmonean family.

```
                              Mattathias
         ┌──────────┬──────────┼──────────┬──────────┐
      Johanan     Simon   Judah the    Eleazar   Jonathan
                          Maccabee
         ┌──────────┼──────────┐
      Judah   John Hyrcanus I  Mattathias
         ┌──────────┬──────────┬──────────────────┐
   Aristobulus I Antigonus  Alexander Jannaeus─Salome Alexandra
                                   ┌──────────┬──────────┐
                               Aristobulus II      Hyrcanus II
         ┌──────────┬──────────┐        ┌──────────┐
   Alexandra  Mattathias Antigonus  Jonathan Alexander─Salome Alexandra
                                        ┌──────────┬──────────┐
                                    Aristobulus III    Mariamme─Herod
```

THE CISTERN OF THE *AKRA*

Adjacent to the projected southern wall of the square Temple Mount, as outlined above, is a curiously shaped cistern. Its plan is in the form of the letter E, which is unlike all the other mainly irregularly shaped cisterns of the Temple Mount. This Cistern 11 (see plan, opposite) was explored by Warren and described by Conder[7] as follows,

> *It is 61 feet 6 inches (18.75 m) deep and consists of three tanks, each about 26 feet (7.9 m) by 40 feet (12.2 m) connected by a passage running north and south and 14 feet (4.30 m) wide. The total contents are about 700,000 gallons (3,200 m³). The roof is of rock cut out into arches. Steps on the west ascend to the mouth of the tank and west of these are foundations of a massive wall on the rock. The passage from the Triple Gate is continued, so as to run over this tank (see illustrations, pp. 77, 212).*

This cistern is located just south of the projected mishnaic Temple Mount and its position suggests that it was specially cut to provide the Macedonian garrison stationed in the *Akra* with a water supply ample enough to withstand a long siege. Stones quarried from this cistern may initially have provided building material for the *Akra*.

Chapter Three: The Hasmonean Temple Mount

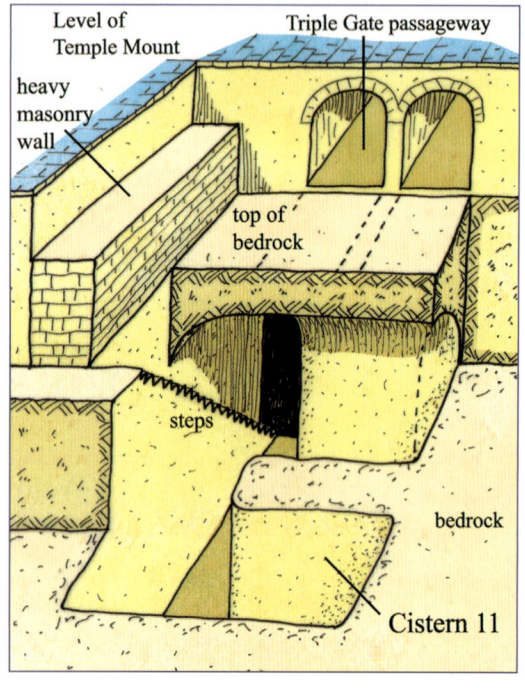

Top: Drawing of a Macedonian phalanx.

Above: Sketch of Cistern 11.

Interestingly, the tractate *Erubin* of the Mishnah calls one of the cisterns of the Temple Mount *be'er haqqer*.[8] This name, which means "The Cistern of the Akra," suggests that one of the cisterns of the Temple Mount was named after the fortress that lay on top of it. In addition, the presence of the foundations of a massive wall in this cistern, described by Warren, together with the cistern's peculiar E-shape, suggest a design that could support a large building.

The literary evidence, combined with the unusually shaped Cistern 11, provides the first tangible evidence for the location of the Akra in the northern part of the area between the Double and Triple Gate passageways.

THE ORIGIN OF THE TRIPLE GATE

A direct entrance from the *Akra* to the Temple Mount was recorded by Josephus (*Ant.* 12.406): *"Nicanor was coming down from the Akra to the Temple"* (more evidence, incidentally, that the *Akra* was built adjacent to the Temple Mount).

With the western entrance of the *Akra* close to the Hulda Gates, one would expect the other gate to be located at the opposite end of the fortress. This gate may have been the forerunner of the Triple Gate, as its passageway runs directly above Cistern 11. It is interesting to note in this context that a production of the lines of the passageways of the Double and Triple Gates would divide the southern wall of the

CHAPTER THREE: THE HASMONEAN TEMPLE MOUNT

square Temple Mount into three portions of more or less equal size to the casual observer. The extension of the Temple Mount to the west by Herod the Great destroyed this symmetry, when he extended the western section from the Double Gate to the southwest corner.

THE VERTICAL JOINT (*SEAM*)

As we have already suggested in Chapter 1 (pp. 102–105), the masonry in the eastern wall of the Temple Mount, to the north of the vertical joint (popularly known as the *seam*), which is visible above ground, 105 feet 6 inches (32 m) from the southeast corner, appears to have been part of an enterprise to enlarge the square Temple Mount to the south.

There is no doubt that this masonry is earlier than the Herodian masonry seen south of the *seam*. Although these stones are slightly smaller and shorter than the Herodian ones, they have been cut very precisely. Their margins are narrow and straight, tooled with a broad chisel unlike the tooth-comb pick used by the Herodian masons. The bosses are flat and project much more than the Herodian ones. A careful examination of the stones to the immediate north of the *seam* will show that parts of their southern margins have been cut away in several places in order to create a better key for the Herodian stones that adjoin them to the south of the *seam* (see illustrations, p. 103).

The stones to the north of the *seam* were built as headers and stretchers, which is always indicative of a corner construction. In an underground shaft, Warren followed this masonry to the north for some 55 feet (17 m). It is a pity that he did not continue excavating this tunnel further. We believe that he would have found that this masonry extended 134 feet (40.84 m) north of the *seam* to the previously mentioned *bend* in the Eastern Wall. There, according to our theory, is located the southeast corner of the square Temple Mount.

It is difficult to determine the date of this masonry (see illustrations, right), and widely varying dates have been suggested. Some, like Laperrousaz,[9] have suggested a Solomonic date for this type of masonry. Both Dunand[10] and Kenyon[11] date this wall section to the Persian period, comparing it with other sites of the sixth century B.C. On the basis of comparable masonry of buildings in Greece and Asia Minor, Tsafrir[12] has tentatively suggested that this wall section may belong to the Hellenistic period.

We suggest that, historically, this type of masonry could best

Above: View of the Seam in the Eastern Wall. (photo Alexander Schick)

Below: Drawing of Hasmonean stone with projecting boss.

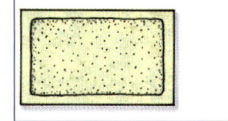

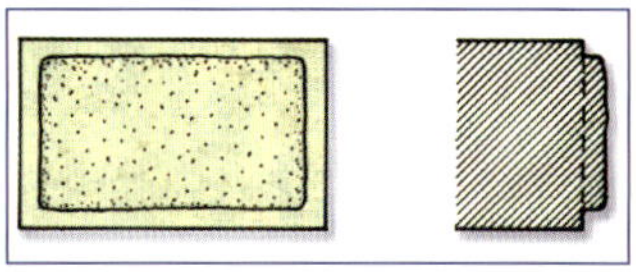

213

CHAPTER THREE: THE HASMONEAN TEMPLE MOUNT

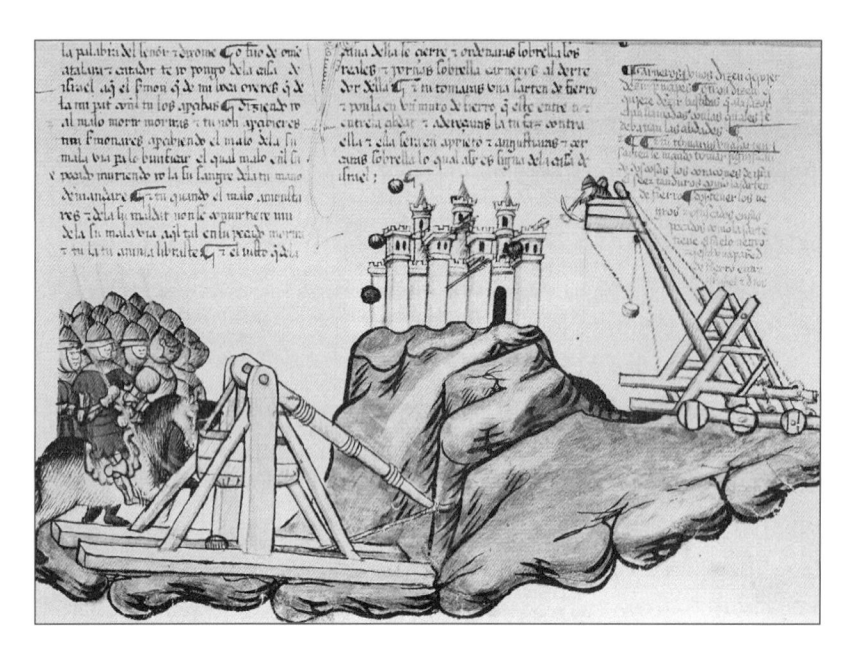

Judah's attempt to storm the Akra fortress, as illustrated in the Alba Bible, 15th century.

be ascribed to the building activities during the time of Simon Maccabee. Avigad[13] pointed out that the fortification of the Upper City carried out during the Hasmonean period was probably initiated by Jonathan and completed by Simon.

In 141 B.C. Simon starved the garrison of the *Akra*, occupied the fortress and razed it to the ground. Following that, 1 Maccabees 13.52 and 14.37 tell us that,

> *He strengthened the fortifications of the Temple Mount by the side of the Akra, and took up residence there with his men.... He settled Jewish soldiers in it and fortified it as a protection for the country and city, and heightened the walls of Jerusalem.*

This seems to indicate that a large area, previously occupied by the *Akra*, was built adjacent to, or perhaps incorporated in, the Temple Mount.

The preserved upper part of the Hasmonean section of the Eastern Wall of the Temple Mount stands only two stone courses higher than the internal level of the so-called Solomon's Stables. To our knowledge, no remains of the western continuation of the corner construction at the *seam* are visible at this level. It seems likely that the upper part of this southern Hasmonean wall was destroyed in A.D. 70, together with the Herodian Temple complex, or otherwise dismantled and reused during later generations.

Between October 1999 and January 2000, the *Waqf*, or Islamic authorities, conducted an illegal dig on the Temple Mount without any archaeological supervision. It opened up an area of about 100 square feet (30 x 30 m), with the aim of inserting a wide staircase from the north down to the floor level of Solomon's Stables, which had been converted into an underground mosque, called the Marwani Mosque.

CHAPTER THREE: THE HASMONEAN TEMPLE MOUNT

Hundreds of truckloads of archaeological fill were removed by bulldozers. In my estimation, these removal operations extended some 100 feet (30 m) northward of the eastern end of Solomon's Stables and descended to a depth of about 30 feet (9 m). According to my calculations, the eastern part of the southern wall of Hezekiah's square Temple Mount was located in this dig, as was a substantial part of the Hasmonean extension.

I had initially hoped that remains of the pre-Herodian Temple Mount would be found. However, the Hasmonean masonry in the Eastern Wall stands only one or two stone courses above the floor level of the stables, which was the deepest point of the earth removal operations. As the digging sloped down from north to south to this level, the remains of the southern wall of the square Temple Mount, which are situated farther to the north, would not have stood high enough to have possibly been uncovered.

The earliest date to which one could attribute the construction of Solomon's Stables is the Umayyad period. Later the Crusaders used these vaults indeed as stables. The excavated fill immediately north of the stables would therefore not have contained much material from before this time, and any earlier remains would have been located below the floor of the stables.

Construction near the Southern Wall of the Temple Mount; these arches lead to Solomon's Stables. (photo: Sam Michelson)

215

CHAPTER THREE: THE HASMONEAN TEMPLE MOUNT

From the *seam*, the southern wall of the square Temple Mount continued west and probably extended the full width of the Temple Mount of that period (see p. 206). This assumption is based on the position of the inner walls of the L-shaped underground passageway of Barclay's Gate, which, as will be discussed in Chapter 5 (p.236), was built against the western wall of the square Temple Mount during the Herodian period.

There must also have been tunnels to give access to the original gateways in the southern wall of the square Temple Mount, the westernmost of which was known in the Mishnah as the Hulda Gates. These tunnels would have been extended farther to the south during the expansion of the Temple Mount under Herod the Great.

THE *BARIS*

The Hasmonean extension to the south of the square Temple Mount initially had a military function and was probably later incorporated in the Temple Mount itself. This would have been possible when the *Baris*[14] was built by Hyrcanus I (134–104 B.C.) at the northwest corner of the Temple Mount, presumably to take over this military function. At that time, there was no longer any need to control the local population, which had been the purpose of the southern Seleucid *Akra*. Given the new political situation there was again a need to protect the Temple Mount from external enemies, who traditionally attacked the Temple Mount from the north.

According to *Antiquities* 14.61, the *Baris* had several towers, one of which was called *Straton's Tower* (*Ant.* 13.307–313), which had an underground passage *(hypogeion)* where Antigonus was murdered. This *hypogeion* linked the fortress with the Temple courts. The only underground passageway in this vicinity is the one called Cistern 1. Warren surmised a connection with the Tadi Gate[15] and one may propose, therefore, that Straton's Tower was built against the northern wall of the square Temple Mount, incorporating the Tadi Gate in the *Baris* fortress.

This citadel was rebuilt by Herod shortly after his capture of the Temple Mount in 37 B.C., and called Antonia (see discussion in Chap. 1, pp. 123–130), which, according to Josephus (*War* 5.238), stood at the junction of the northern and western cloisters. It should be remembered that this construction took place almost twenty years before Herod began to enlarge the Hasmonean Temple Mount.

Coin of John Hyrcanus I.

CHAPTER THREE: THE HASMONEAN TEMPLE MOUNT

Plan of the Temple Mount at the beginning of Herod's reign and the location of the original Antonia.

Several scholars locate the *Baris* at the northwest corner of the present-day Temple Mount at the place where the Herodian Antonia Fortress stood.[16] If correct, the *Baris* must have stood to the north of the Fosse, isolated from the Temple Mount. This is difficult to accept given the fact that in Josephus' record of the siege of Pompey, no reference is made to such a fortress, which his soldiers would have had to capture in order to reach the Fosse, nor would it correlate with *Antiquities* 14.60, which states that the north side of the Temple was open to attack:

Chapter Three: The Hasmonean Temple Mount

Reconstruction model of the Antonia Fortress (in foreground) at the northwest corner of the Herodian Temple Mount, and Solomon's Porch (in background), on the south. (photo: Philip Evans)

And at dawn Pompey pitched his camp on the north side of the Temple, where it was open to attack. But even here stood great towers, and a trench had been dug, and the Temple was surrounded by a deep ravine.

Additionally, there is no tunnel to the north of the Fosse that could have linked a fortress with the square Temple Mount.

As both the Hasmonean *Baris* and the Herodian Antonia, as described by Josephus, were located at the northwest corner of their respective Temple Mounts, we suggest that the two fortresses must have stood in different places. The *Baris* would have been located at the northwest corner of the square Temple Mount and the Antonia at that of Herod.

As these fortresses stood at the northwest corner of their respective

CHAPTER THREE: THE HASMONEAN TEMPLE MOUNT

Temple Mount, we have suggested that the *Baris* was built on the site of the earlier Ptolemaic *Akra* (see Chap. 2, p. 201). The importance of this latter fortress probably declined when the Seleucid *Akra* was built. The need for another fortress at the northwest corner presented itself again during the Hasmonean period, hence the construction of the *Baris* described by Josephus:

> *At the angle on the north side there had been built a citadel, well fortified and of unusual strength. It was the kings and high priests of the Hasmonean family before Herod who had built it and called it Baris.* (Ant. 15.403)

SOLOMON'S PORCH

The Hasmonean Temple Mount was most likely embellished, under Hellenistic influence, with porticoes all around. This is borne out by the fact that Josephus (*Ant.* 14.476) relates that after Herod was made king, he captured Jerusalem and the Temple Mount and *"some of the porticoes round the Temple were burnt."*

It is interesting to note that apparently not all the porticoes were burnt, but presumably only those in the front line of Herod's attack. Because the steepness of the Kedron Valley would have made it impossible to direct the attack from the east, it seems likely that the eastern portico of the square Temple Mount could have escaped destruction (see illustration, opposite and on p. 141).

This eastern portico was apparently never rebuilt by Herod the Great, for during the rule of Agrippa II (A.D. 50–c. 93), when it was proposed to rebuild the portico, its construction was attributed to Solomon, not Herod (*Ant.* 20.220 ff.). The fact that this portico was named after Solomon does not necessarily mean that it was originally built by him, but by Herod's predecessors.

We propose, therefore, that Solomon's Porch of the New Testament (John 10:23, Acts 3:11) refers to that part of the eastern stoa that stood on the original square Temple Mount, which was of Hasmonean origin.

Coin of Agrippa II.

220

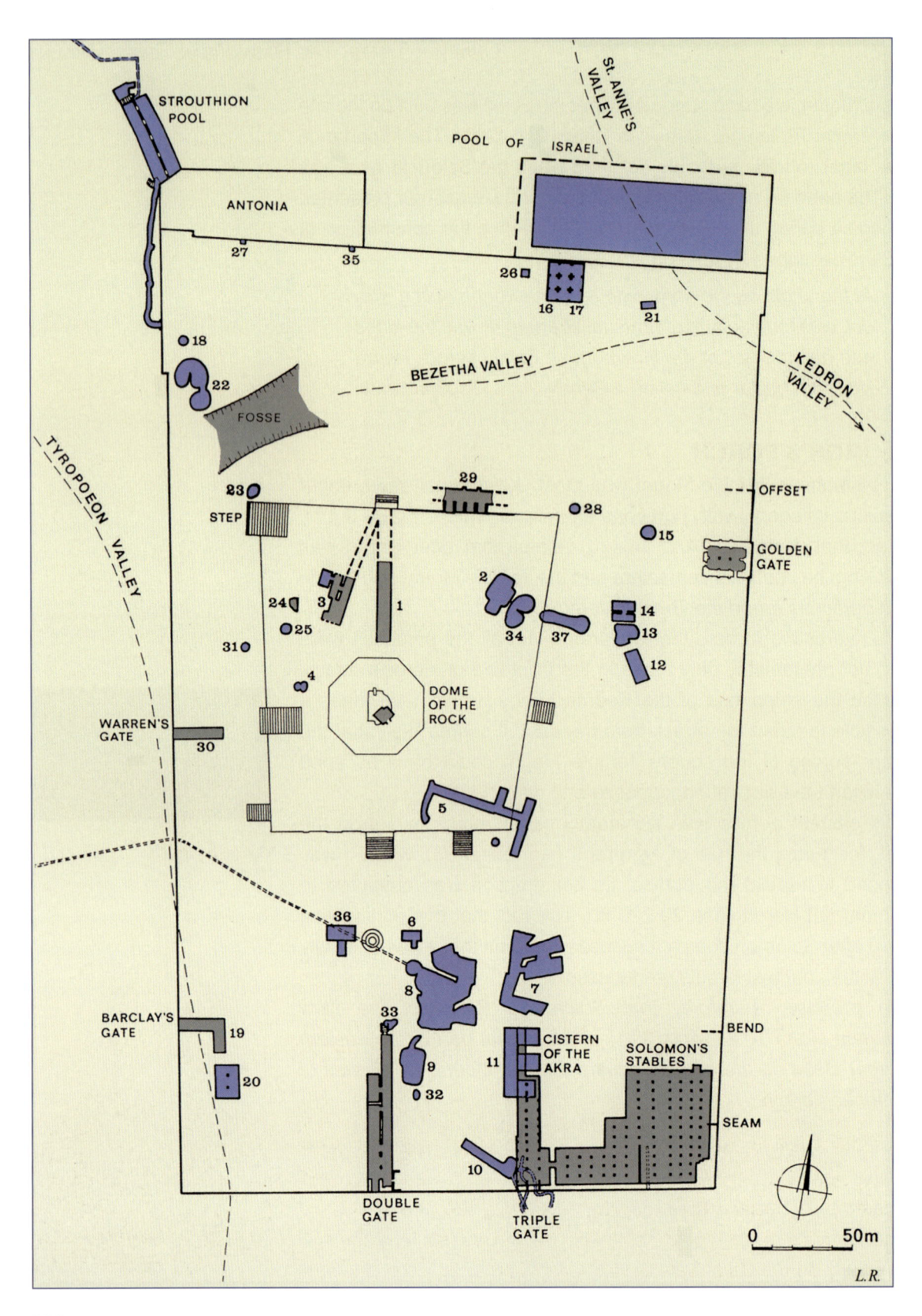

Opposite page: Plan of the cisterns and underground structures of the Temple Mount according to the numeration of Warren.

Below: Charles Clermont-Ganneau.

Bottom: Philo of Alexandria.

Chapter Four
The Underground Cisterns of the Temple Mount

HISTORICAL INFORMATION

The vast network of reservoirs beneath the Temple Mount (see opposite page) is well preserved, although at present inaccessible for research. We therefore have to rely on the records of Wilson and Warren, who were able to investigate and measure most of the cisterns. Warren's investigations in Jerusalem between the years 1867 and 1870 followed the comprehensive survey and mapping of Jerusalem by Charles Wilson, who subsequently collaborated with Warren to produce the book *Recovery of Jerusalem*, published in 1871. A complete account of these studies was published in 1884 and contains the observation of explorers such as Clermont-Ganneau, Chaplin, Schick, Guthe and others.[1]

The existence of these cisterns has been known for a long time and they are mentioned in many historical documents such as the Books of Maccabees, Ecclesiasticus, the description by Philo,[2] the *Letter of Aristeas*,[3] the tractate *Erubin* of the Mishnah, the Pilgrim of Bordeaux, and other works.

It is clear that not all of the underground structures were originally reservoirs. Some of the Herodian underground passageways, such as those belonging to Barclay's and Warren's Gates, were later used as cisterns, especially after the destruction of the Temple Mount by the Romans in A.D. 70. Other earlier passages, such as the two converging on the Tadi Gate and that of Cistern 5, were probably

Chapter Four: The Underground Cisterns of the Temple Mount

Opposite page: Plan showing the development of the Temple Mount with the cisterns and underground structures.

Below: Deep in the bowels of the Temple Mount, the author looks at the inspection tunnel of Cistern 10, at the right of the picture.

adapted in the same way. It has also been suggested that some of the cisterns, including the cave below the Rock, may have belonged to a Middle Bronze Age I cemetery.[4]

Most of the cisterns collected rainwater from the vast esplanade and diverted to the various reservoirs by means of channels. Others were replenished by an aqueduct leading from Solomon's Pools near Bethlehem to the Temple Mount.[5] The very slight difference in height (approximately 100 feet or 30.48 m) between the springs near Solomon's Pools and the aqueduct's final destination, mandated a meandering route of 13 miles (21 km)—twice the actual distance between the two points—which means an average descent of less than one percent, a remarkable piece of engineering in itself.

Another aqueduct that has been traced back as far as the Damascus Gate, apparently filled Cisterns 18 and 22 in the northwest corner of the Herodian Temple Mount. Cut by the Herodian western wall, it must therefore be of pre-Herodian origin.

ADDITIONAL EVIDENCE FOR THE LOCATION OF THE SQUARE TEMPLE MOUNT

Further evidence for the placing of the square Temple Mount can be derived from the position of some of the underground cisterns (see opposite page).

Three of these cisterns are located just inside the perimeter of the proposed square Temple Mount. Cistern 15 is located along the northern edge of the platform and could conveniently catch the run-off rainwater from that part of the Temple Mount. Cistern 31 could fulfill a similar function in the west and Cistern 33 in the south.

Cisterns 23 and 28 are located just outside the northern wall of the platform, probably inside towers that were built along the northern wall, such as the towers of Hananeel and Meah and the Prison Gate. It is possible that additional cisterns not yet discovered exist along this alignment.

Two very large cisterns, Numbers 7 and 8, called respectively "*The Sea*" and "*The Great Sea*," are also aligned along the inside of the southern wall. These, the largest cisterns on the Temple Mount, are located in the southern court of the mishnaic Temple Mount, which was the most spacious of the four courts surrounding the Temple (*Middot* 2.1).

The painting of Cistern 8, the "Great Sea," made in 1872 by William

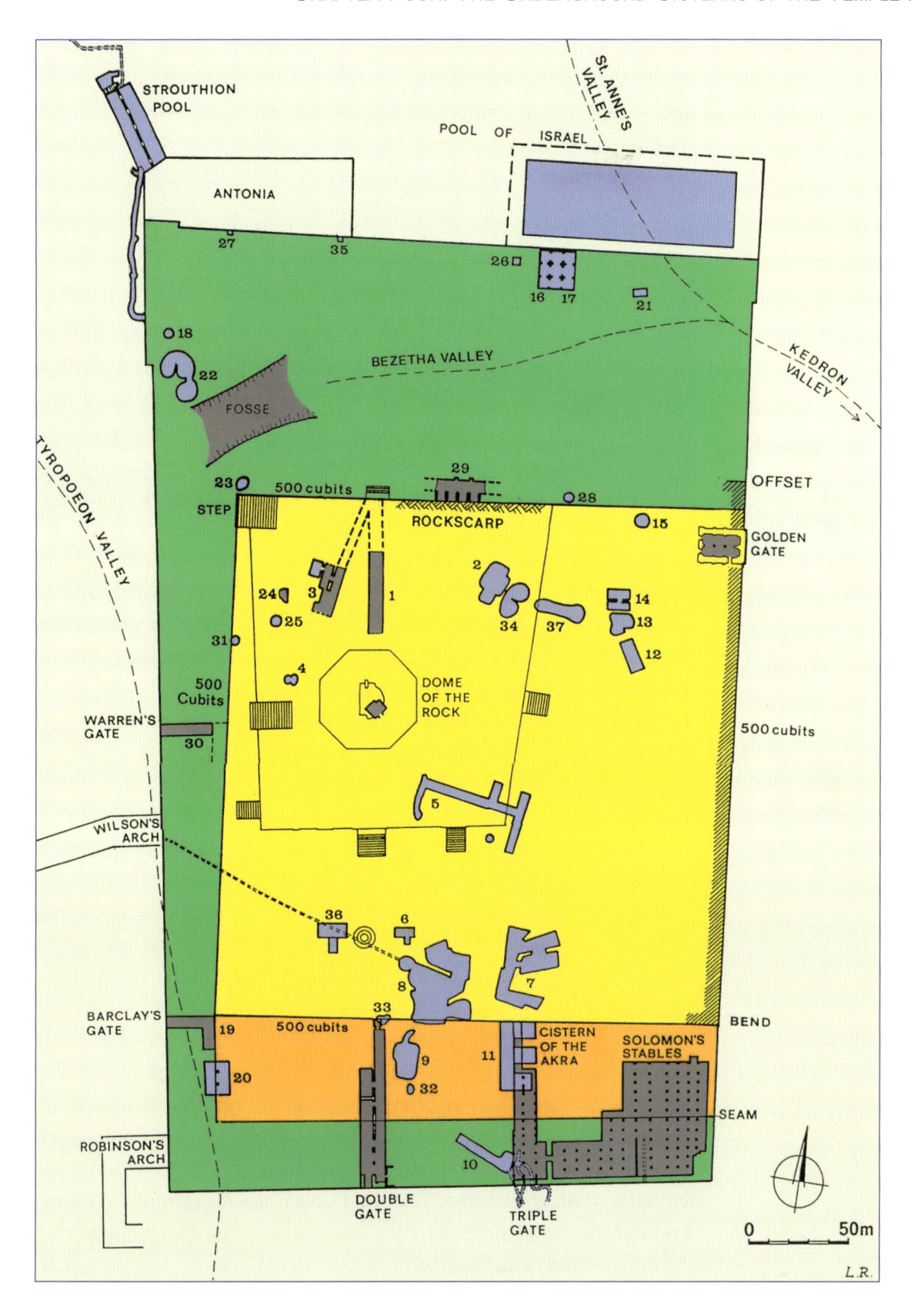

Chapter Four: The Underground Cisterns of the Temple Mount

Chapter Four: The Underground Cisterns of the Temple Mount

Painting of the "Great Sea" by William Simpson, 1872.

Simpson,[6] shows a view to the north, inside this gigantic cistern, known in Arabic as *bahr al-kebir*, which held 2 million gallons of water. The cistern was accessed from the south by a staircase, with the stepped entrance to the cistern just south of our square Temple Mount and inside the proposed site of the *Akra*.

If this cistern was already in existence at the time of the building of the *Akra*, it would have been unnecessary to cut Cistern 11, which (as mentioned before) was intended to supply water to the Macedonian garrison. *We suggest therefore, that Cistern 8 was dug following the destruction of the* Akra *and before the subsequent Hasmonean extension of the Temple Mount to the south.*

In this context we would like to tentatively identify this and some of the other large cisterns of the Temple Mount with those mentioned in the historical sources. In the mishnaic tractate *Erubin* 10.14, three cisterns are mentioned: *"They* [the priests] *may draw water with a wheel on the Sabbath from the Golah-cistern and from the Great Cistern, and from the Cistern of the Akra on a Festival-day."*

As the Mishnah only acknowledges a Temple Mount of 500 by 500 cubits, it follows that these cisterns were located on the square Temple Mount in the large courts that surrounded the Sanctuary. *As we have already identified Cistern 11 with "the Cistern of the Akra," we propose the identification of Cistern 8 with "the Great Cistern" of the above-mentioned source.*

Chapter Four: The Underground Cisterns of the Temple Mount

As Cisterns 5, 7, 8 and 11 are the largest on the Temple Mount and are all located in the southern court, one would expect that the second largest cistern, Number 7 (called in Arabic *al-bahr* or "the Sea") would also have been mentioned in the historical sources. The southern court is located nearest to the Lower City and the *"Hill of Ophel,"* or *Ophlas* as Josephus called the area south of the Temple (*War* 5.145). There the bulk of the population resided in the time of Zerubbabel and Nehemiah. Therefore, most of the people going to the Temple would approach it from the south and a large portion of the activities connected with the Temple service, including the drawing of water, would take place there.

In the apocryphal work Ecclesiasticus, the author Ben Sira extols the work of the High Priest Simon son of Onias, who

> *repaired the Temple during his lifetime and in his days fortified the sanctuary. He laid the foundations of the double height, the high buttresses of the Temple precincts. In his day the water cistern was excavated, a reservoir as huge as the sea.* (Ecclesiasticus 50.1–3)

The Temple and its precincts referred to are the same as those built by Jeshua and Zerubbabel and were probably in need of repair after three centuries of service.

Simon being installed as High Priest, from the Book of Maccabees, 17th century engraving.

Chapter Four: The Underground Cisterns of the Temple Mount

Artist's impression of the water-libation ceremony during the festival of Sukkot and the celebrants reaching the Water Gate at the Holy Temple. (The Temple Institute, Jerusalem)

Although Cistern 8 has been identified by some as the one mentioned by Ben Sira, we (for reasons set out above) believe that Cistern 8 was dug after the destruction of the *Akra*, and therefore cannot be identified with that mentioned in Ecclesiasticus. We would suggest that Cistern 7 is a better candidate, for the following reasons.

The "excavation" of cisterns is in fact a quarrying operation, supplying large amounts of stones. Being surrounded by steep valleys, it is naturally very difficult to transport stones from the surrounding mountains to the Temple Mount. It is thus reasonable

Chapter Four: The Underground Cisterns of the Temple Mount

to assume that most of the building material would have come from underground quarries located on the Temple Mount. When all the stones needed were extracted, the resultant hollow area would be plastered and used as a cistern.

This could explain the rough, rock-hewn staircase of 44 steps in Cistern 8, which was probably used only to bring up the quarried stones. Simpson,[7] who depicted this cistern in a painting, actually wrote about these steps, which were worn away to such a degree that "*it is difficult to understand what was the original object for which the steps were cut.*" Water was actually hauled up through shaft openings in the ceiling of the cistern and not up the steps. Other large cisterns, such as 5, 11 and 22, also have rock-cut steps, while Cistern 7 shows evident signs of unfinished quarry activities.

As the passage quoted above from Ecclesiasticus, concerning the excavation of a reservoir, is preceded by a record of the building activities on the Temple Mount by the High Priest Simon (c. 220–195 B.C.), it seems logical to connect these quotes and conclude that the stones needed to repair the Sanctuary in Simon's time came from a large cistern. In our opinion, this can only be Cistern 7, which was located in the southern court of the square Temple Mount.

*In accordance with the layout of the Herodian Temple and its surrounding buildings (see below), we propose the identification of Cistern 5 with the Golah Cistern (*bor ha-gola*), mentioned in* Erubin *(10.14).* The large Cistern 5 would be situated next to the Water Gate near the Altar, thus providing a convenient source of water for the Temple service. This Water Gate was the easternmost of the three gates in the southern wall of the inner courtyard, located apparently next to the Golah Chamber, the middle of the three chambers that were located to the south of the inner courtyard (*Middot* 5.3,4):

> *There were six chambers in the Temple Court…those to the south were the Wood Chamber, the Golah Chamber, and the Chamber of Hewn Stone…the Golah Chamber—the Golah Cistern was there, and a wheel was set over it, and from thence they drew water enough for the whole Temple Court.*

These references show that the Golah Cistern was located near the Golah Chamber, in the southern

Artist's impression of the Wood Chamber, one of the chambers in the Temple Court. (The Temple Institute, Jerusalem)

CHAPTER FOUR: THE UNDERGROUND CISTERNS OF THE TEMPLE MOUNT

This photo shows the two wellheads of Cistern 1. They are in line with the Rock inside the Dome of the Rock.

wall of the inner courtyard. It can be seen in the plan on page 232 that Cistern 5 adjoins this southern wall. As *Golah* in Hebrew means "exile" or Diaspora, the historical context may hint at a reference to the exiles who returned from Babylon. We suggest therefore that the stones needed to repair the Temple would have come from this cistern. The quarrying of Cistern 11 probably supplied stones for the construction of the *Akra*, and that of Cistern 8 for the Hasmonean extension to the south of the square Temple Mount.

Chapter Four: The Underground Cisterns of the Temple Mount

The remaining cisterns are nearer the center of the Temple Mount and are probably associated with the Temple and its courts (see below). To complete our analysis of the cisterns, we will add the following.

As mentioned above, *Middot* 1.3 describes the Tadi Gate as being *"on the north, which was not used at all."* An underground passage leading to a *"Chamber of Immersion,"* or *mikveh*, was apparently used by priests who had a nocturnal emission. This underground passage was the same as that which led to the Tadi Gate.

Both Warren and Conder[8] concluded that if Cisterns 1 and 3 were extended farther to the north, they would meet exactly at a point in the rockscarp where they supposed the Tadi Gate was located (see detail of Warren's plan, p. 206). Cistern 1 was probably the passageway which could be reached from the Chamber of the Hearth, which was the name of one of the three gates on the north of the inner court of the Temple. Cistern 3 was probably the immersion room itself. *Middot* 1.6 continues to tell us that there were *"four rooms in the Chamber of the Hearth...by that to the northwest they went down to the Chamber of Immersion."*

Although the Tadi Gate was made obsolete by Herod's northern extension, the underground pas-sage was apparently still used by the priests to visit the immersion room. In Chapter 9, we will see that the northwest room of the Chamber of the Hearth would have been located directly above Cistern 3.

As already mentioned in Chapter 2 (pp. 204–205), it is also interesting to note that this passageway (Cistern 1) is exactly in line with the rock inside the Dome of the Rock, as well as the passageways of the Double Gate. Entering the Temple courts through either the northern Tadi Gate or the southern Hulda Gates, the eyes of the pilgrim of yore would be fixed directly on the Holy of Holies. In our opinion, that most sacred of spots was built over the Sakhra, an indication of the importance of this architectural alignment which also shows that these gates were built according to a uniform plan.

This southern route passes between Cisterns 6 and 36, which, according to Reich, may have been *mikva'ot*.[9] It is interesting to note that these *mikva'ot* were located south of the *soreg* (see Chapter 9, p. 346, and plan, p. 338) in the southern court of the early square Temple Mount, where the Court of the Gentiles was located in the time of Herod.

Close-up view of the wellhead over Cistern 1.

Plan showing the north-south alignment of Cistern 1 with the Sakhra and the passageway to the Double Gate.

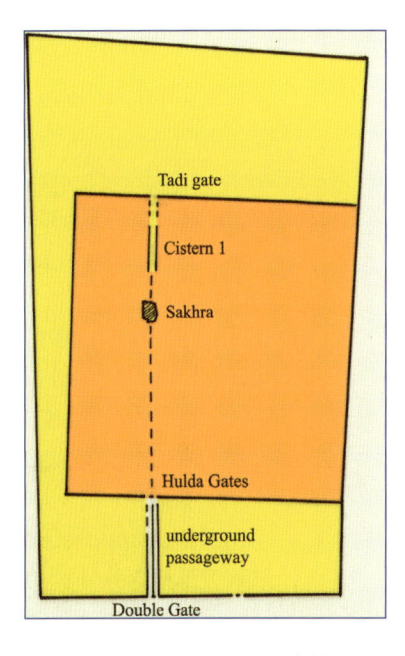

Chapter Four: The Underground Cisterns of the Temple Mount

KEY TO THE UNDERGROUND STRUCTURES

Cisterns 1 to 37, according to the numeration of Warren and showing their position in relation to the square Temple Mount (see pp. 220, 223):

1. Tadi Gate passageway and *hypogeion* of the Hasmonean *Baris*
2. Cistern located in the northern court of the square Temple Mount.
3. Bathing complex used by the priests, including at least one *mikveh*, probably located in the westernmost chamber.
4. Retort-shaped cistern, located in the western court of the square Temple Mount.
5. Passageway-shaped cistern, probably used in ceremonies connected with the Altar, now called *The Well of the Pomegranate*. May be identified with the *"Golah Cistern"* of *Erubin*.
6. T-shaped cistern east of *El-Kas* (The Cup). May have been used as a *mikveh* in the southern court of the square Temple Mount.
7. Very large cistern known as "The Sea," probably that mentioned by Ben Sira in *Ecclesiasticus*. Located in the southern court of the square Temple Mount.
8. Largest cistern called *"The Great Sea"* or *"The Black Well,"* probably the *"Great Cistern"* mentioned in *Erubin*. Located to the west of Cistern 7.
9. Cistern called *"The Well of the Leaf."* Located in the Hasmonean extension of the square Temple Mount.
10. Passageway-shaped cistern near the Triple Gate. Connected with rock-cut channels that run under the Herodian Southern Wall below the Triple Gate. Located below the Herodian Royal Stoa.
11. Large E-shaped cistern. May be identified with *"The Cistern of the Akra."*
12, 13, 14. Cisterns located in the northern court of the square Temple Mount.
15. Cistern located just inside the northern boundary wall of the square Temple Mount.
16, 17. Vaulted cistern with two well-heads, of medieval construction.
18. Cistern which in pre-Herodian times received water from a recently rediscovered rock-hewn aqueduct. Located in the northern extension of Herod's Temple Mount.
19. Barclay's Gate passageway.
20. Continuation of Barclay's Gate passageway.
21. Small cistern, probably of medieval construction.
22. Large pre-Herodian cistern with domed roof and rock-cut staircase running around the wall, which probably also received water from the rock-hewn aqueduct (see Cistern 18).
23. Cistern located at the northwest corner of the square Temple Mount, presumably inside a tower.
24. Relatively modern chamber, the eastern wall of which is a rockscarp.
25. Cistern in the western court of the square Temple Mount.
26. Small cistern, probably of medieval date.
27. Small cistern south of the Antonia fortress.
28. Small cistern just outside the northern boundary wall of the square Temple Mount, known as *"The Well of the Abyssinian."* It may have been located inside a tower.
29. Masonry chamber, built against the northern rockscarp of the square Temple Mount,

CHAPTER FOUR: THE UNDERGROUND CISTERNS OF THE TEMPLE MOUNT

> probably part of the Crusader *"Monastery of the Temple."* May be identified with the Prison Gate.
> 30. Warren's Gate passageway. Probably part of an L-shaped construction similar to Barclay's Gate passageway. Here, however, the second leg has later been filled in.
> 31. Cistern which falls just inside the western wall of the square Temple Mount.
> 32. Small cistern beneath the el-Aksa mosque.
> 33. Small cistern north of the el-Aksa mosque located, under the steps leading down to the Double Gate passageway. This cistern is located inside the Hasmonean extension to the square Temple Mount.
> 34. Cistern located in the northern part of the Temple Court.
> 35. Small cistern located near the eastern side of the Antonia Fortress.
> 36. T-shaped cistern west of el-Kas. Like Cistern 6, this cistern may have been used as a *mikveh* in the southern court of the square Temple Mount.
> 37. Cistern located in the northern court of the square Temple Mount (explored by C. Schick).

THE CAVE AL-MAGHARA BELOW THE "HOLY ROCK" (ES-SAKHRA)

The Dome of the Rock on the Temple Mount.

Typologically, this cave belongs to the same group of underground tanks as the cisterns but was never included in the numeration of Warren, presumably because of its unique location. This cave, which is not plastered, lies beneath the Rock inside the Dome of the Rock building. There is a circular shaft in the roof of the cave.

Another cave, known as *bir el-arwah*, or Well of Souls, is said to lie underneath this cave, although its existence has never been verified. On the contrary, Bagatti[10] relates that while witnessing restoration works in the cave, he saw no entrance to such a lower cave in the floor of the rock-hewn cave, al-Maghara.

The Rock is an important piece of archaeological evidence in an area where remains associated with the Temple are very sparse. The precise function of this rock, which stands about 7 feet (2 m) above the level of the platform, will be discussed in Chapter 6.

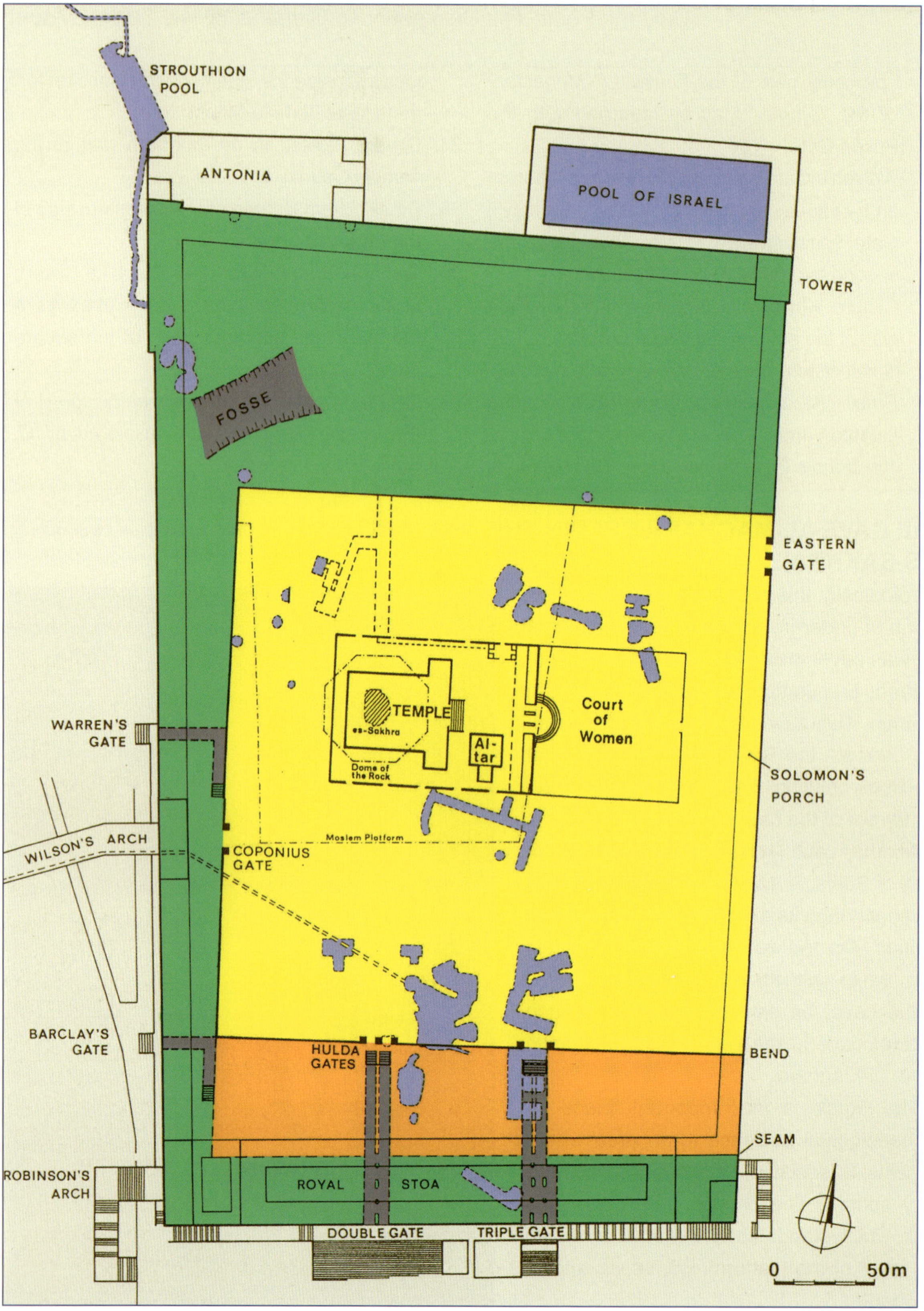
STROUTHION POOL
ANTONIA
POOL OF ISRAEL
TOWER
FOSSE
EASTERN GATE
TEMPLE
es-Sakhra
Dome of the Rock
Al-tar
Court of Women
SOLOMON'S PORCH
Moslem Platform
WARREN'S GATE
WILSON'S ARCH
COPONIUS GATE
BARCLAY'S GATE
HULDA GATES
BEND
SEAM
ROBINSON'S ARCH
ROYAL STOA
DOUBLE GATE
TRIPLE GATE
0
50m

Opposite page: Plan of the Temple Mount, showing the location of the 500-cubit-square Temple Mount and the Herodian Temple complex.

Below: Topographical map of Jerusalem showing location of the Tyropoeon Valley.

Chapter Five
Understanding Herod's Extension of the Temple Mount

Our positioning of the square Temple Mount and the location of the Hasmonean extension make it possible to understand the way in which Herod the Great extended the then existing Temple Mount to its present size.

Looking back on the research, one might argue that theoretically the location of the early square Temple Mount could have been deduced merely from the study of the remains of Herod's Temple Mount, both above and below ground; but we strongly believe that without the discovery and interpretation of the *step,* this would have been virtually impossible.

We are by now familiar with the fact that Herod extended the Temple Mount to twice its previous size, by adding new courts to the north, west and south (see plan, p. 168, and opposite). In extending the platform he had to take into consideration the existing structures, especially the entrances to the old Temple Mount and the drainage system which runs on the west through the Tyropoeon Valley. We will briefly examine those Herodian constructions that support the proposed location of the pre-Herodian square Temple Mount and the subsequent Hasmonean extension to the south.

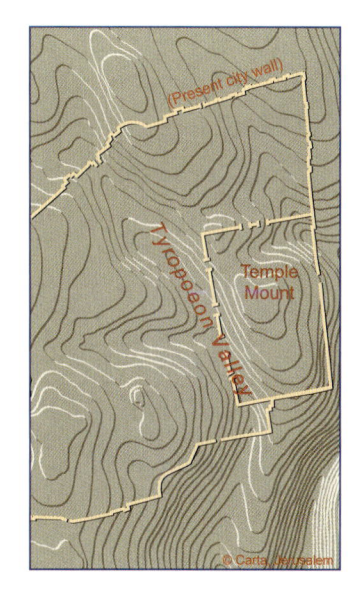

DRAINAGE SYSTEM IN THE TYROPOEON VALLEY
The Herodian southwest corner was built on the western side of the Tyropoeon Valley, cutting through a pre-Herodian drain as we have

Chapter Five: Understanding Herod's Extension of the Temple Mount

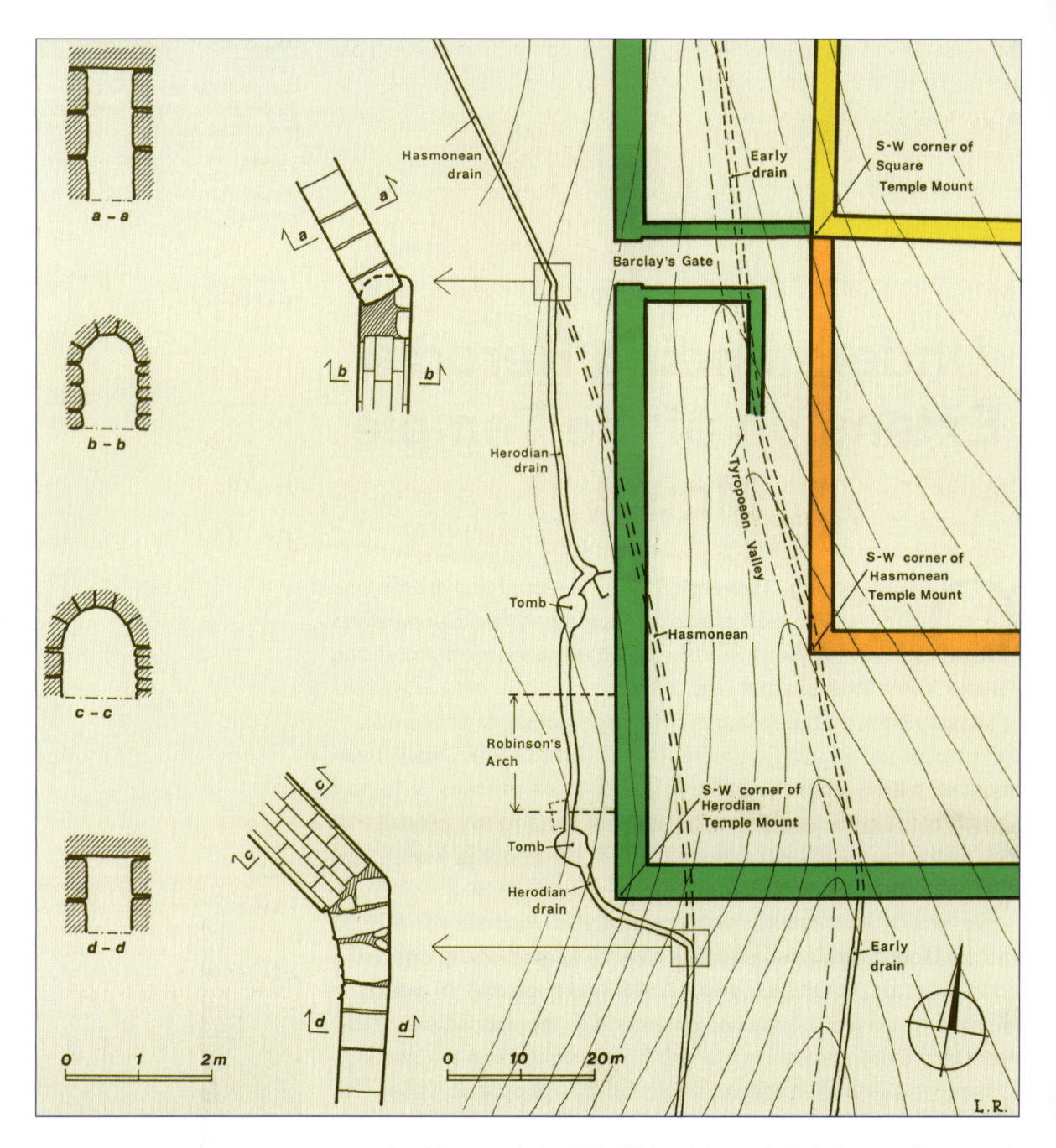

Plan of the drains at the southwest corner, as discovered by Warren, and their relationship to the square Temple Mount and the subsequent extensions.

seen in Chapter 1 (p. 52). This slab-roofed drain ran from north to south through the Tyropoeon Valley, parallel to the valley bed approximately 60 feet (18 m) to the west. Before it was diverted by Herod, it would have passed close to the southwest corner of the Hasmonean Temple Mount at the same distance of 60 feet (18 m) from the valley bed. That is in accord with our proposed location of

CHAPTER FIVE: UNDERSTANDING HEROD'S EXTENSION OF THE TEMPLE MOUNT

the Hasmonean extension showing that this corner was built almost in the valley bed itself (see plan, above). This close relationship suggests that the drain was built during the Hasmonean period and was probably connected with the reorganization of the street complex to the west of the extended Temple Mount in this period.

At 90 feet (27.50 m) east of the southwest corner, in the bed of the Tyropoeon Valley, Warren found another drain, built of small stones and covered with flat slabs, cut by the Herodian Southern Wall. Warren cleared this 4-foot (1.20 m) high and 2-foot (0.60 m) wide drain for a distance of 600 feet (183 m). The drain's northern continuation would also have been cut by the Hasmonean extension, but it would have run to the west of the square Temple Mount. Its position relative to the early square Temple Mount may indicate that this drain existed prior to the one described above. In fact, it could be the earliest drain in the Tyropoeon Valley.

Another interesting speculation: the three different drainage systems may have been connected to the three stages of the Temple Mount. As drains are usually constructed below streets, these drains may also point to the existence of three successive streets in the Tyropoeon Valley—not surprising, as the main north-south route ran through the valley.

View of the Herodian drainage channel under the street running along the western wall of the Temple Mount. (NEAEHL)

WARREN'S GATE

From the Herodian street, the level of the Temple Mount could be reached by two gates, according to Josephus *(Ant.* 15.410). Today they are known as Warren's and Barclay's Gates.

Warren's Gate is the northern of these two suburban gates. During his investigations of Cistern 30, Warren identified the area underground as the internal passageway of a gate. As this passage pierced the western wall, he decided that this was the site of a gateway. As noted in Chapter 1 (p. 34), this gate and its underground passageway were probably the same design as Barclay's Gate.

Both passageways are 18 feet (5.50 m) wide. The length of Warren's Gate is 84 feet (25.60 m) and its height, 34 feet 6 inches (10.50 m). In our opinion this cistern, which has a vaulted roof, is the first part of another L-shaped subterranean stairway. There is a space of approximately 18 feet (5.50 m) left between the eastern end of Cistern 30 and the projected western wall of the square platform. Ample space for a square chamber, like the domed chamber in

Sir Charles Warren (1840–1927).

Chapter Five: Understanding Herod's Extension of the Temple Mount

Barclay's passage, from which another passageway would have led up to the Temple courts. This second, or eastern, continuation could have turned to the south or to the north. A southern extension of the internal stairway is more logical, as this exit would be close to the gate that once stood over Wilson's Arch. A parallel can be seen at the southwest corner, where the exit of the passage of Barclay's Gate would be close to the gate located over Robinson's Arch. This eastern part of the internal stairway was probably filled in after the destruction of the Temple and the western part turned into a water tank at a later date.

Reconstructing the passageway by relying on Barclay's internal stairway, we see that this stairway would have been built against the projected western wall of the pre-Herodian Temple Mount. If this reconstruction is correct, it reconfirms our location of the square Temple Mount.

BARCLAY'S GATE

From Barclay's Gate, which we have already described, a subterranean internal stairway led up to the Temple Court. Unlike the underground passageways of the Double and Triple gates which are straight, the underground stairway of Barclay's Gate is L-shaped and passes through Cisterns 19 and 20 (see plan, p. 220). The first part begins at the gate and passes through the al-Burak Mosque in an easterly direction until it reaches a distance of 84 feet from the western wall inside Cistern 19. The passageway then turns south under a flat dome, and its continuation is found in Cistern 20 that probably leads to the surface.

A section through this gate[1] shows that the eastern wall under the flat dome has a distinct batter, just like that of all other Temple Mount walls. This is apparently the earlier western wall of the Hasmonean Temple Mount built when the square platform was extended to the south following the destruction of the *Akra*.

The reason then for the L-shape of the underground stairway was that Herod's builders built the southern part of this stairway alongside the existing Western Wall (see illustrations, pp. 27, 28) instead of piercing through it, which would have been very difficult.

Again we find confirmation of the location of the square Temple Mount and its Hasmonean extension, which extended

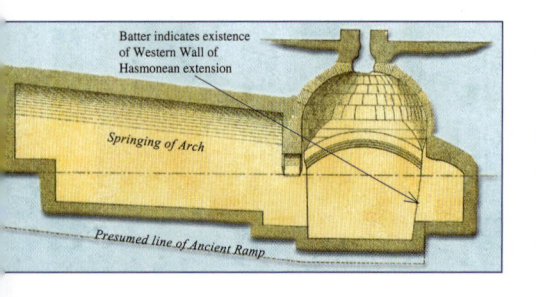

Above: Dr. James T. Barclay (1807–74).

Below: Detail of Warren's Plate 31, showing section through Barclay's Gate.

CHAPTER FIVE: UNDERSTANDING HEROD'S EXTENSION OF THE TEMPLE MOUNT

the full length of the southern wall of the square platform.

THE DOUBLE AND TRIPLE GATE PASSAGEWAYS

The full extension, including the Hasmonean one, to the south of the square Temple Mount measures about 240 feet (73.15 m) at the southeast corner and approximately 270 feet (82.30 m) at the southwest corner. The problem of the southern extension is closely linked with the construction of the Royal Stoa built above the southern wall, as explained earlier (see p. 102).

Warren reported a break in the masonry of the Double Gate passageway at 190 feet from the Southern Wall. A similar break exists in the Triple Gate tunnel. Although the masonry at these points is certainly not Herodian, this break may nevertheless indicate the original length of the underground tunnels. A staircase leading up to the southern Temple court from this point would exit a short distance before the southern wall of the square Temple Mount where the original Hulda Gates stood, leaving enough space in front of these gates to be accessible from other directions.

The placing of the Hulda Gates in the southern wall of the square Temple Mount may resolve a problem concerning the meaning of the name *"Hulda."* It has been suggested that *"Hulda"* may refer to the prophetess of the Old Testament (2 Kgs 22:14; 2 Chr 34:22) who lived in Jerusalem during the time of King Josiah, the great-grandson of Hezekiah. Alternatively, some researchers, among them Schick,[2] believe that this name refers to the special construction of the underground tunnels, which they associated with those made by moles (*huldah* being the Hebrew word for a "mole").

Since the construction of the Hulda Gates preceded that of the tunnels, it is clear that the name Hulda can only refer to the prophetess and not to the mode of construction. This, of course, still leaves the question of the connection of the name Hulda to the southern gates of the square Temple Mount.

Theories as to the existence of a monument that may have been erected in her honor in the vicinity of these gates cannot be proven. However, the fact that the name of an Old Testament prophetess is attached to a gate of the square Temple Mount prompts the suggestion that this gate was named at the end of the First Temple period, and may therefore indicate the existence of the 500-cubit-square Temple Mount at that time.

Above (top): Hilkiah, Ahikam, Acbor, Shaphan, and Asaiah seek advice from the prophetess Huldah, 17th century engraving.

Above: Josiah orders the Book of the Law read aloud to the elders, 17th century engraving.

Chapter Five: Understanding Herod's Extension of the Temple Mount

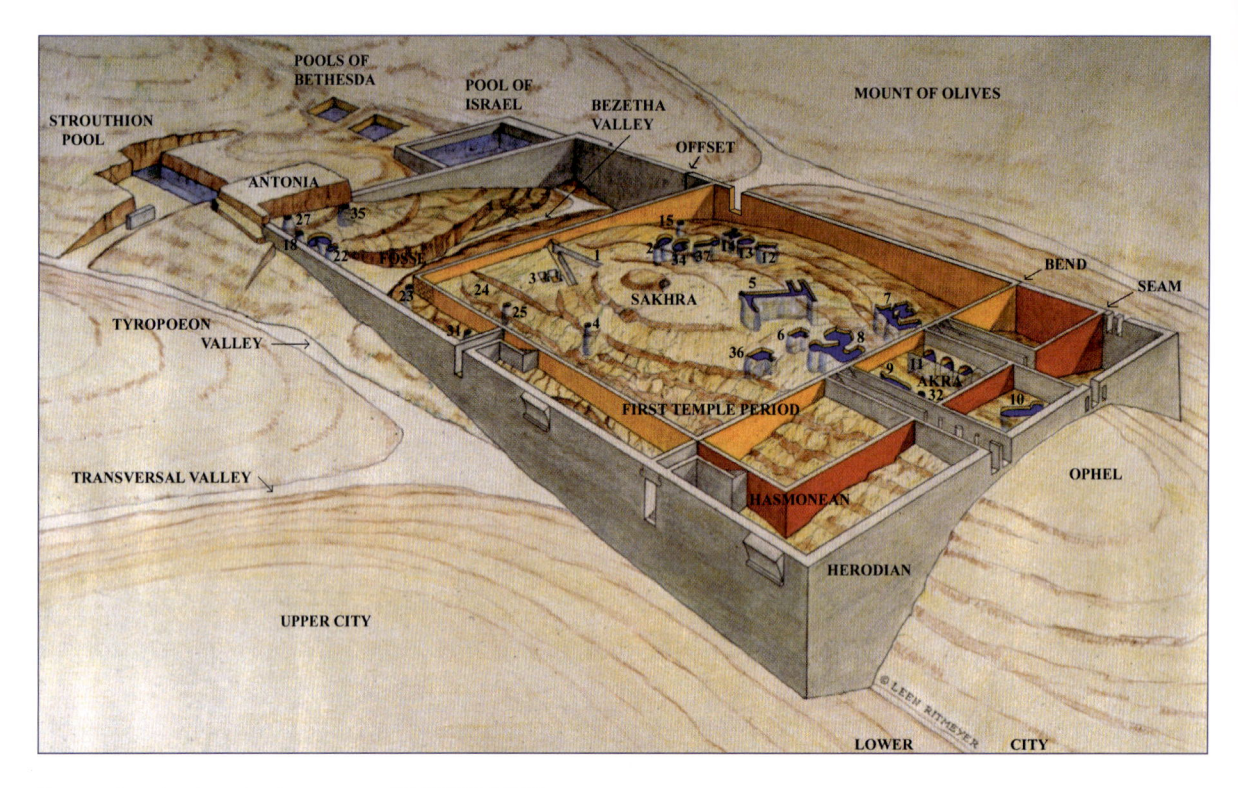

Perspective drawing showing the stages in the historical development of the Temple Mount.

SUMMARY

Before continuing our research into the location of the Temple, let us summarize the results of our research so far. We have shown that the square Temple Mount in Jerusalem dates back to the First Temple period. Despite later Hasmonean and Herodian additions, the outline of the early, square, platform was always preserved. This square *temenos* is the subject of *Middot*, which refers to it as the "Mountain of the House." The measurement of 500 cubits given in *Middot* was found to be correct, rather than the stadium of Josephus.

The first clue as to the architectural development of the early square Temple Mount (see illustrations, p. 166, above) lay in the odd angle of the lowest step of the staircase at the northwest corner of the raised platform. This *step* appears to be the remains of an early wall composed of a row of single ashlars. Furthermore, the *step* is virtually parallel to the eastern wall, which is generally accepted as being of pre-Herodian origin. The style of masonry used in this *step/wall* resembles that found in the central section of the same eastern wall. We have therefore identified it as the western wall of the pre-Herodian square Temple Mount.

The Fosse found by Charles Warren 52 feet (15.55 m) north of

Chapter Five: Understanding Herod's Extension of the Temple Mount

this stairway was probably the valley which was filled in by Pompey's soldiers in 63 B.C. so that they could take the northern wall of the Temple Mount. Warren found the remains of a *quarried rockscarp* below the edge of the northern wall of the raised platform. Lines projecting from this *rockscarp* form right angles with both the *step/wall* and the Eastern Wall, so we have identified it as part of the northern wall of the square Temple Mount. The length of such a northern wall would be 861 feet, or 500 cubits according to the Royal Cubit of 20.67 inches (525 mm).

Measuring 500 cubits along the eastern wall from the point where it intersects with the line of the *rockscarp*, there appears a change in the wall's direction. This *bend*, we suggest, points to the existence of the southeast corner of the square platform, deep below ground.

The southern wall of the square platform should be parallel to the northern wall. The southwest corner of this platform would be formed at the intersection of the southern wall with the southern continuation of the *step/wall* mentioned earlier.

The *seam* in the Eastern Wall represents the extent of the Hasmonean addition to the south of the square platform. This extension was built after the destruction of the Seleucid *Akra*, which stood, we believe, above Cistern 11, probably the "Cistern of the *Akra*" mentioned in the mishnaic tractate, *Erubin*.

In the first century B.C., King Herod the Great enlarged the Temple Mount to twice its original size by adding new courts to the north, west and south. In order to create a level court, the *fosse* was completely filled in and the bedrock of the natural hill on which the Antonia Fortress was built was partly cut away.

Confirmation for the location of the square Temple Mount and the Hasmonean extension can be derived from the special construction of some of the Herodian gates.

The L-shaped underground passageways of Warren's and Barclay's Gates in the Herodian Western Wall were apparently built against the pre-Herodian western wall. The underground tunnels of the Double and Triple Gates in the Herodian southern wall still reflect in their length of approximately 240 feet (73.20 m), the size of the southern extension of the square Temple Mount.

We believe that this new concept integrates all the factors—e.g., topography, archaeology and historical sources—and that everything appears to slide neatly into place.

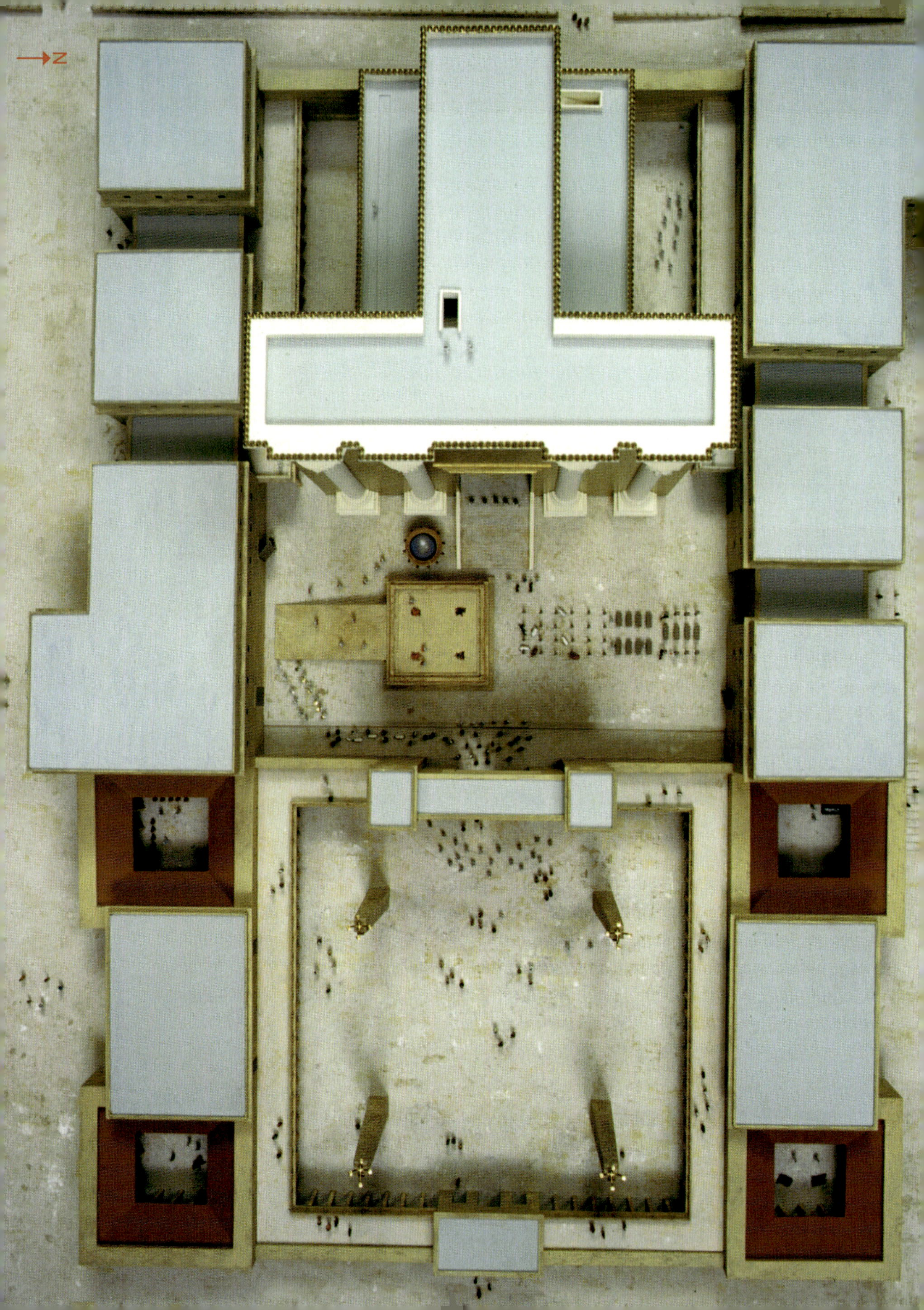
Z

Opposite page: Bird's-eye view of a model of the Temple court (center) and the courts surrounding it. (Photo: Philip Evans)

Below: Model of the Herodian Temple Mount showing the space of 11 cubits between the western wall of the Temple and its courtyard. (Photo: Philip Evans)

Chapter Six
The Location of the Temple

THE TEMPLE COURT

Having analyzed the historical development of the Temple Mount, the search for the location of the Temple can now begin. First, we must place the 500-cubit-square Temple Mount in order to apply the available information to the location of the Temple itself.

According to Mishnah *Middot* 2.6 and 5.1, the Temple was located inside the Temple Court, which measured 187 by 135 cubits. The Temple (100 x 100 x 100 cubits) was placed symmetrically within the court, which included an 11-cubit-wide Court of the Israelites and a similar-sized Court of the Priests (see plans on pp. 345, 362).

Behind the Temple, at the western end of the court, there was a space of 11 cubits and therefore the location of the Temple inside its court can be determined accurately on the Temple Mount. Although this in itself does not help determine the location of the Temple, *Middot* contains information about the dimensions of the courtyards surrounding the Temple Court. Once we determine the location of this inner court, then we can place the Temple.

Middot 2.1 provides specific information regarding the relative areas of the courts that surrounded the Temple Court:

> The Temple Mount measured five hundred cubits by five hundred cubits. Its largest [open] space was to the south, the next largest to the east, the third largest to the north, and its smallest [open space] was to the west; the place where its measure was greatest was where its use was greatest.

Chapter Six: The Location of the Temple

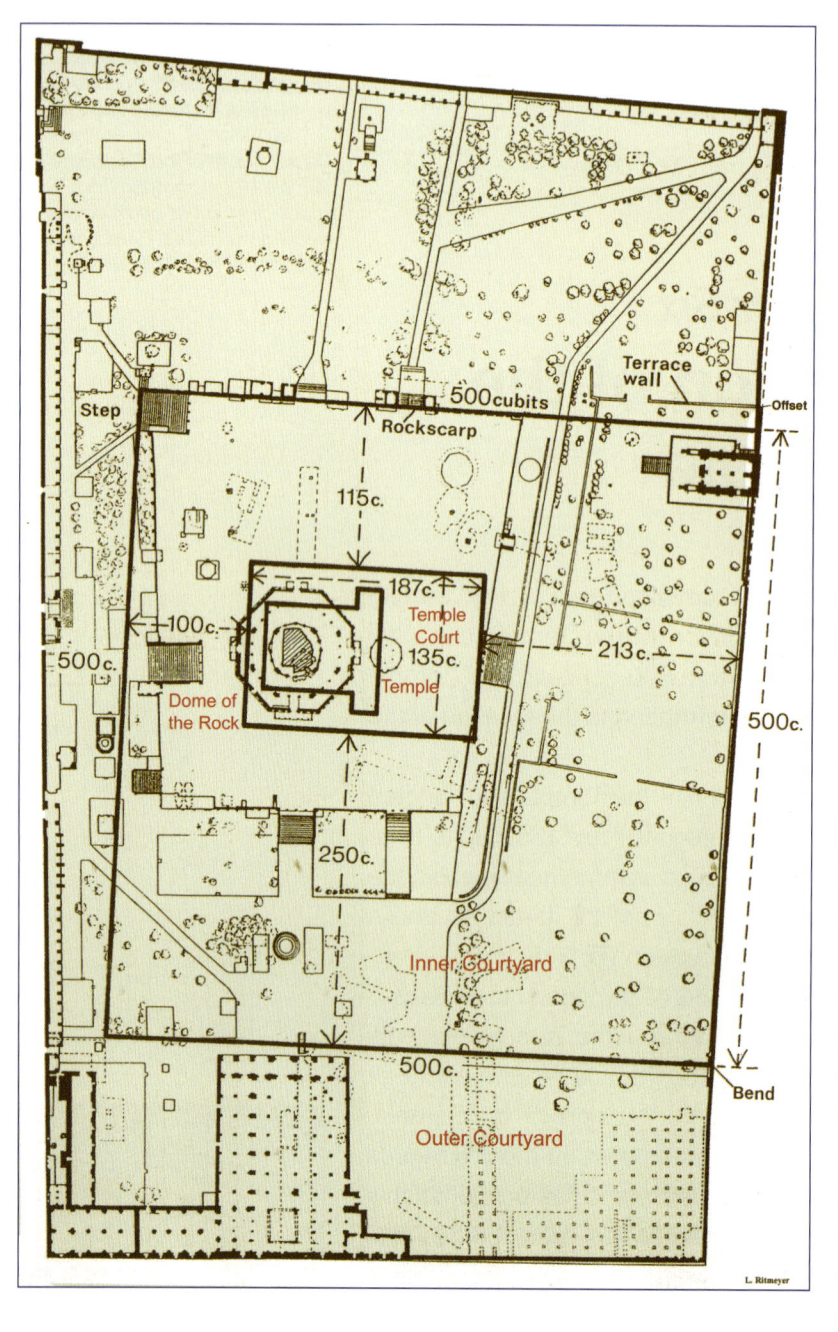

Plan of the Temple Mount, looking north, showing the proposed location of the Temple and the Temple courts, with measurements in cubits.

And, most conclusively of all, Josephus had told us that Herod's Temple was built on the top of the mountain.[1]

Using this information and placing the Temple Court on the 500-cubit-square platform, it soon becomes obvious that the Holy of Holies of the Temple has to be located over the Sakhra, the rock-mass inside the Dome of the Rock, in order to conform to the requirements of the unequal sizes of the courts. *Middot* 4.6 also tells us that the foundation of the Temple was 6 cubits (10 feet or 3.05 m) high. If the Temple was placed anywhere else, higher foundations would have been needed to create a level platform for the Temple.

The size of the courts can be measured on the plan shown here. Going counterclockwise, from south to west, they are 250, 213, 115 and 100 cubits, respectively—all of which surprisingly agree with those given by Tosefot Yom Tov in his commentary on the mishnaic tractate *Middot* 2.1 dating from the sixteenth century.

To refine this proposal, it was necessary to analyze the Rock.

THE ROCK AND THE TEMPLE

To research and analyze the Rock down to its minutest detail was no easy task, as no one before had conducted a systematic archaeological

CHAPTER SIX: THE LOCATION OF THE TEMPLE

research of this rock, which is actually the summit of Mount Moriah. Indeed, the Rock is so little known in archaeological circles. Israeli archaeologists, who had uncovered much of ancient Jerusalem in nearby excavations, avoided the Rock like the biblical plague that fell on the city during the reign of David. The political sensitivities of the area and the seemingly intractable problems involved in its interpretation made it a veritable scholarly *terra incognita* despite its being the focus of the three major world religions.

The rocky mass inside the Dome of the Rock is surrounded by a wooden fence that makes examination difficult. However, on a visit to the shrine in 1992, I was able to make a crucial observation. I noticed certain flat areas to the west of the hole that goes down to the ceiling of the cave below the rock. Standing on the east of the Rock and looking west over this hole, these flat areas could easily be discerned. It looked as if a channel with a step in it had been cut across the rock from east to west. These flat areas proved to be the

View of the Rock.

SAKHRA: Arabic for Rock, particularly the rock-mass inside the Dome of the Rock.

Chapter Six: The Location of the Temple

View of the cave beneath the Holy Rock, 19th century engraving.

key in researching the problem of the relationship between the Rock and the Temple.

In many archaeological sites, bedrock is leveled to create horizontal bases for square or rectangular foundation stones. A series of such flat spaces is called a foundation trench. Without such a trench, the first tier would not be level. It is impossible to erect a stable building when the stone courses in its walls are sloping down. The same would have been true for the walls of the Temple.

But why would one of the walls of the Temple be built on the Rock? Asking the question was almost the same as providing an answer. The visible rock measures 43 by 56 feet (13 by 17 m) and is larger than the Holy of Holies, which measured 20 cubits (34 feet 6 inches or 10.50 m) square. This is one of the reasons why some researchers have rejected the Rock as a possible location for the Holy of Holies. However, if this was indeed the place of the Holy of Holies, then it is logical to conclude that at least one of its walls must have been built on the Rock. *If so, the Rock, also called the Foundation Stone or Even ha-Shetiyah, would truly live up to its name.*

Some proposals would have put the Altar, which according to *Middot* 3.1 was 32 cubits or 55 feet (16.80 m) square, on the Rock—but then the Rock, being smaller than the Altar, would have been completely covered. Another problem in placing the Altar over the Rock is that it would put the well-known cave, which laid beneath the Rock and supposedly drained off the blood to the Kedron Valley, in the wrong place. According to *Middot* 3.2, this original drain was located at the southwest corner of the Altar, while the cave would be at its southeast corner if the Altar was placed over the Rock. Incidentally, during restoration work in the Dome of the Rock in 1959, when the paving stones in the cave were lifted, Bagatti[2] observed bedrock less than a foot below the floor of the cave. He saw no signs of a drain.

Another problem: if we place the Altar over the Rock, the Temple would have stood far to the west of the Rock. If that were so, then, according to the line of the bedrock, the western foundations of the Temple would have to be 50 feet (15.24 m) deep, while according to *Middot* they were only 6 cubits (10 feet 4 inches or 3.15 m) deep. This by itself is sufficient reason to reject the Rock as the location of the Altar.

The Bible tells us that the altar was built on the threshing floor of Araunah (2 Sam 24:18; 1 Chr 21:18). The flat top of the Rock would

CHAPTER SIX: THE LOCATION OF THE TEMPLE

Araunah the Jebusite offering his threshing floor to David (2 Sam 24:18), 19th century engraving.

be far too small for a threshing floor and the high scarps would have posed a danger to the oxen. Threshing floors are usually round and on a relatively flat area. It is known that the diameters of threshing floors range from 40 to 46 feet (12 to 14 m).³ The flat top of the Rock measured no more than 21 by 50 feet (6.5 by 15 m), too narrow and therefore inadequate for the task. Finally, threshing floors are not usually located on the top of mountains, but a little below so that the wind will carry away the chaff only and leave the grain.

In 1994, I was able to continue researching the relationship between the Rock and the Temple.⁴ I wanted to determine if the flat areas I had noticed in 1992 and which I had identified as being the foundation trench for a wall really comprised part of the southern wall of the Temple. I experimented on an enlarged photograph of the Rock (above), drawing over the flat areas the line of this southern wall of the Holy of Holies, which is the part of the Temple that we had concluded stood over the Rock. In order to trace the other walls, it was necessary to take some measurements by "pacing."⁵

Chapter Six: The Location of the Temple

View of the Rock showing the location of the Holy of Holies.

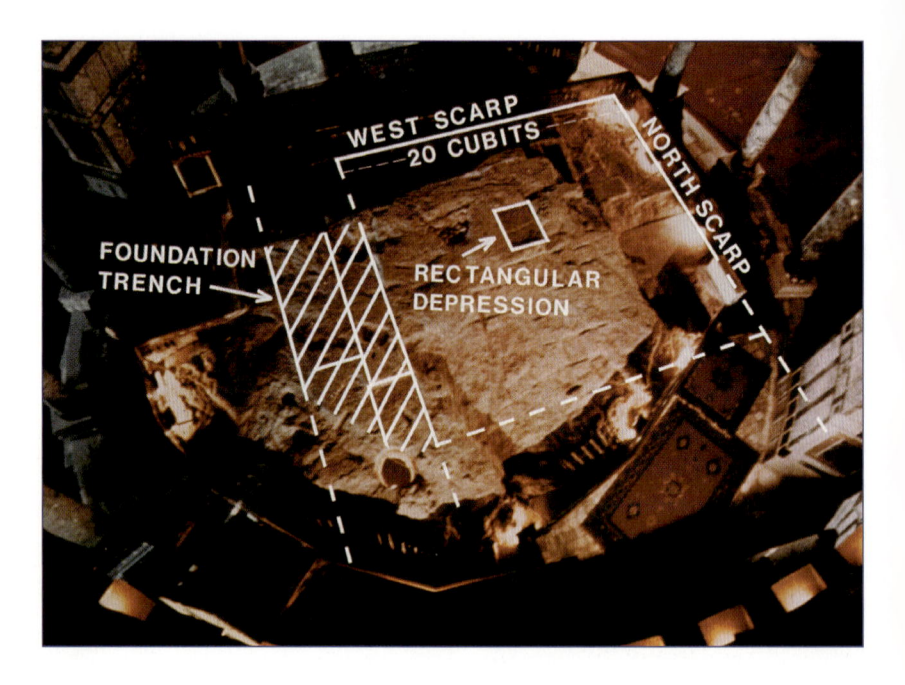

First, I stood on the western side of the Rock and tried visually to determine the exact point where the inner (that is, the northern) line of the flat areas would cross the natural western rockscarp. The importance of this rockscarp is obvious: its vertical face would have provided a good support for a wall built against it. From that point, I paced northward along the western fence to the corner of the scarp, measuring a distance of 34 feet 5 inches (10.5 m). Converting this into Royal Cubits gave us a size of 20 cubits. This is in accordance with the measurement given in 1 Kings 6:20 as the inner measurement of the Holy of Holies of Solomon's Temple. Although expected to be in line with the inquiry I was following, the thrill of discovery was electrifying when I added this western line to the photograph.

Thus encouraged, I continued the experiment. If the southern wall of the Holy of Holies was actually built on the Rock and the western wall stood at the foot of the western scarp, then the northern wall had to be drawn at the northern end of the exposed rock. In order to locate the eastern end of the Holy of Holies, 20 cubits were measured from the western scarp. No evidence of a wall could be expected here because Solomon's Temple had a wooden partition (1 Kgs 6:31; see photo, p. 288); and in the later Temple, a veil divided the Holy of Holies from the Holy (Mishnah *Shekalim* 8.4,5; *Yoma* 5.1ff.; Mt 27:51). Thus, on the photograph we drew a

CHAPTER SIX: THE LOCATION OF THE TEMPLE

dotted line to indicate where the partition would have been.

Outlined on the photograph of the Rock was the interior of the Holy of Holies, appearing to fit all the requirements. Knowing the sweep of history that had passed over it, I resolved to study and examine the Rock until it lay open like a textbook and I could verify my proposal with hard facts.

The next development, however, was totally unexpected. Before I put away the now very-much-used photograph and headed once more for the Temple Mount, I noticed a dark rectangle right in the center of my 20-cubit square. This came as a surprise because its location was plainly related to the square I had just traced. The only object I knew that had been placed in the middle of the Holy of Holies was the Ark of the Covenant and the measurement I estimated for the indentation was 1.5 by 2.5 cubits—the same as the measurement of the Ark.

Anything as phenomenal as this identification is usually met with massive skepticism. The more extraordinary the find, the greater the demand for its verification. Retracing the Temple's history, I turned over all sorts of scenarios as to when an indentation such as this one might have been cut into the rock.

Artist's impression of the High Priest making his way through the Sanctuary, walking between the curtains that divided the Holy area from the Holy of Holies during the Second Temple period. (The Temple Institute, Jerusalem)

Going back to the origins of the Temple, I knew from the biblical account that Solomon had prepared a special place for the Ark of the Covenant where it was laid under the wings of the great cherubim. But Manasseh had set up a graven image of Asherah (a full-sized female figure carved out of a tree trunk) apparently in the Holy of Holies itself—otherwise the Ark would not have been moved from its original place. That the Ark was removed is certain, because the Bible recounts its return in the time of Josiah (2 Chr 35:3). The priests, being afraid that the Ark might be damaged or even destroyed by Manasseh, must have moved it from the Temple to a safe place.

The question I was asking myself was, could the depression have been the base for this statue? Picturing this, however, I realized that such a large statue would not have had sufficient room under the wings of the cherubim, which were not recorded as having been removed in the time of Manasseh. Thus it could not have been placed in the center of the Holy of Holies.

After the Babylonian destruction of the Temple, the Temple was

Chapter Six: The Location of the Temple

The High Priest offering incense on Yom Kippur before the rectangular depression which marked the original emplacement of the Ark of the Covenant. (Photo: Philip Evans)

rebuilt under Jeshua and Zerubbabel with no mention of the Ark of the Covenant. Had anything been placed in the Holy of Holies, it would surely have been mentioned. As before, the Holy of Holies was entered only once a year by the High Priest on the Day of Atonement.

It is also well recorded that when Pompey, the Roman general who besieged the Temple in 63 B.C., entered the Holy of Holies, he was astonished to find it completely empty. The source of this information is Tacitus[6], who wrote about Pompey's visit to the Temple:

> *Invoking the right of conquest, he entered the Temple. It was in this manner that it became common knowledge that the place stood empty with no likeness of gods within, and that the shrine had nothing to reveal.*

Retracing the time of the building of Herod's Temple, it seemed to me that if this depression did indeed mark the original emplacement of the Ark, then it would have continued as the place for the High Priest to place his firepan on the Day of Atonement (see illustration on p.391), as Herod's Temple (and the preceding one) were merely reconstructions of the First Temple.

I focused my attention on the early Roman period because it

CHAPTER SIX: THE LOCATION OF THE TEMPLE

did appear to provide the only likely alternative to my instinctive interpretation. Early Christian pilgrims had found two statues on the site of the former Temple.[7] Could the rectangular depression have been the base for one of these statues? But according to Roman classical proportions, column bases for statues are always square and, for a statue of any considerable height, would need to be much bigger than the allowed space. If a Roman statue did stand in this area (and the sources alleging this are not believed to be fully reliable), then it would probably have been large and impressive to proclaim Roman victory over Judea.

Apart from the reference to these statues, the historical record has shown that the Temple Mount had been all but ignored during the Roman period. During the Byzantine period the Rock had been deliberately concealed, as the early Christians considered that God had abandoned the Jewish people and that the site had no further relevance. When Caliph Omar conquered Jerusalem in A.D. 638, the place was used as a dung heap that took much labor to clear. During that time, at least, the Rock could not have been tampered with.

Then with the construction of the Dome of the Rock and the reverence accorded to it by the Muslims, its protection was assured until the Crusaders took Jerusalem. It is well known that the

Judaea Capta engraved on a gold coin minted in Rome in honor of the Roman victory over Judea. (Reuben and Edith Hecht Museum, Haifa)

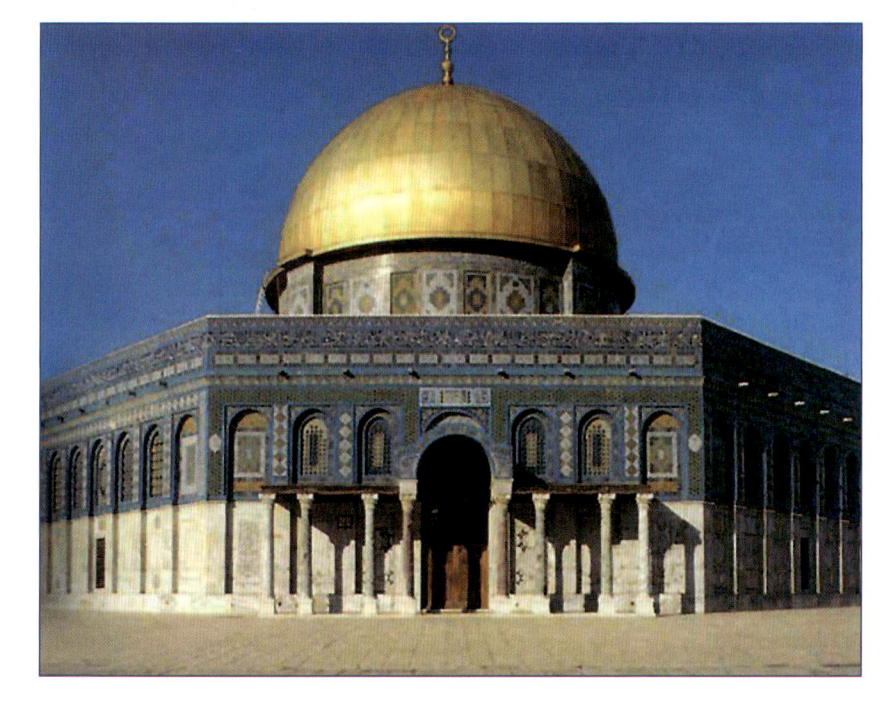

The Dome of the Rock, viewed from the southwest.

Chapter Six: The Location of the Temple

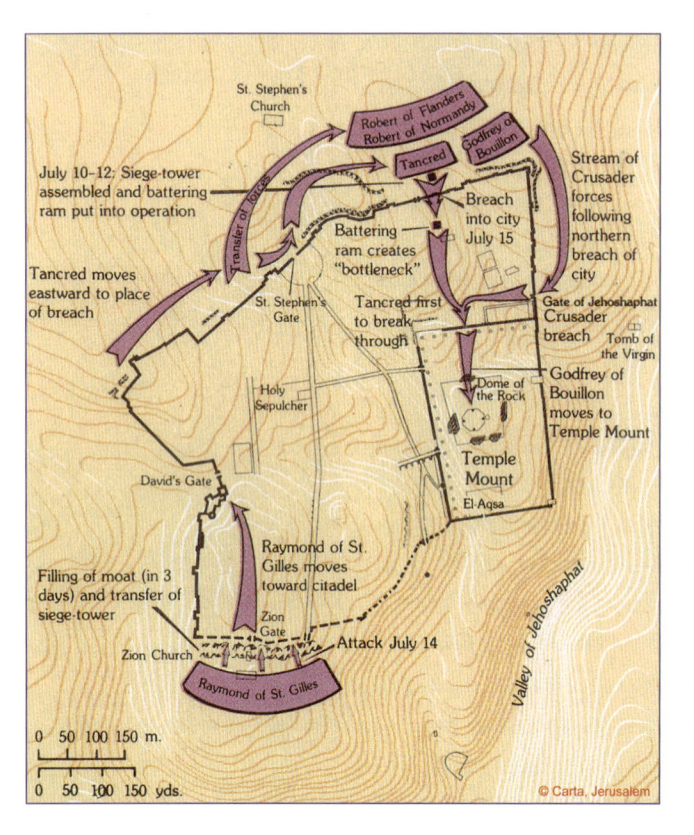

The last stage of the Crusader siege of Jerusalem, 10–15 July 1099.

Crusaders wrested the Dome of the Rock from the Muslims in 1099 and converted it into a church called Templum Domini. Their intervention in this area proved to be more devastating to the Rock than all the earlier destructions. Apart from their building activities, the Crusaders were reputed to have sold chunks of the Rock for their weight in gold.

I asked myself if the rectangular depression could possibly be a quarry mark for one of those pieces of rock which was sold to pious Christians back in Europe. But looking up Peters' book on Jerusalem[8] which I carried about with me, I found that a Muslim historian recorded that during the period when the Crusader church was built over the Rock, only a small part of the back of it was exposed and the rest was paved over.[9] This "small part of the back" obviously referred to the eastern side of the Rock that sloped like a ramp and had obvious quarry marks still visible on its surface. The top of the Rock would have been submerged and therefore been protected by the marble slabs that supported the Crusader altar. Thus, the possibility that the depression was a Crusader quarry mark appeared less and less likely.

From the time that the Muslims reconquered the Dome of the Rock in 1187, throughout the Turkish period and that of the British Mandate until today, the Rock has been safe behind its fence, protected by strict Islamic law.

I realized that if this rectangular depression was indeed the "Mark of the Ark," the sanctity of the Temple Mount could have ensured its survival up to the present day. It certainly was the most extraordinary piece of archaeological evidence I had ever come across in all my years of experience on excavating and measuring ancient buildings. I knew, however, that I would have to acquaint myself with the turbulent history of the Rock before the Temple plan that I saw unfolding before my eyes could be reliably demonstrated.

CHAPTER SIX: THE LOCATION OF THE TEMPLE

DESCRIPTION OF THE ROCK

To begin with, an accurate plan of the Rock, based on the description and measurements given by Gustaf Dalman,[10] Hans Schmidt[11] and others, had to be made. Dalman's plan was quite accurate. In 1910 the Rock was temporarily deconsecrated for repair work and Dalman was actually allowed to walk on it. In a series of subsequent visits to the Dome of the Rock he was able to make further measurements by stretching tapes over the rock with the help of a mosque attendant who stood within the fence. Opportunities such as these did not recur following the disastrous Parker Mission, which was forcibly aborted in April 1911 and which engendered much hostility among the local Muslims toward all archaeologists (see Chapter 1, p. 17).

To the existing plans I added new features, based on my own observations and measurements taken by pacing out during several visits to the Dome of the Rock. I modified other details with the help

Detailed cross section of the Dome of the Rock, drawn by de Vogüé, 19th century.

Chapter Six: The Location of the Temple

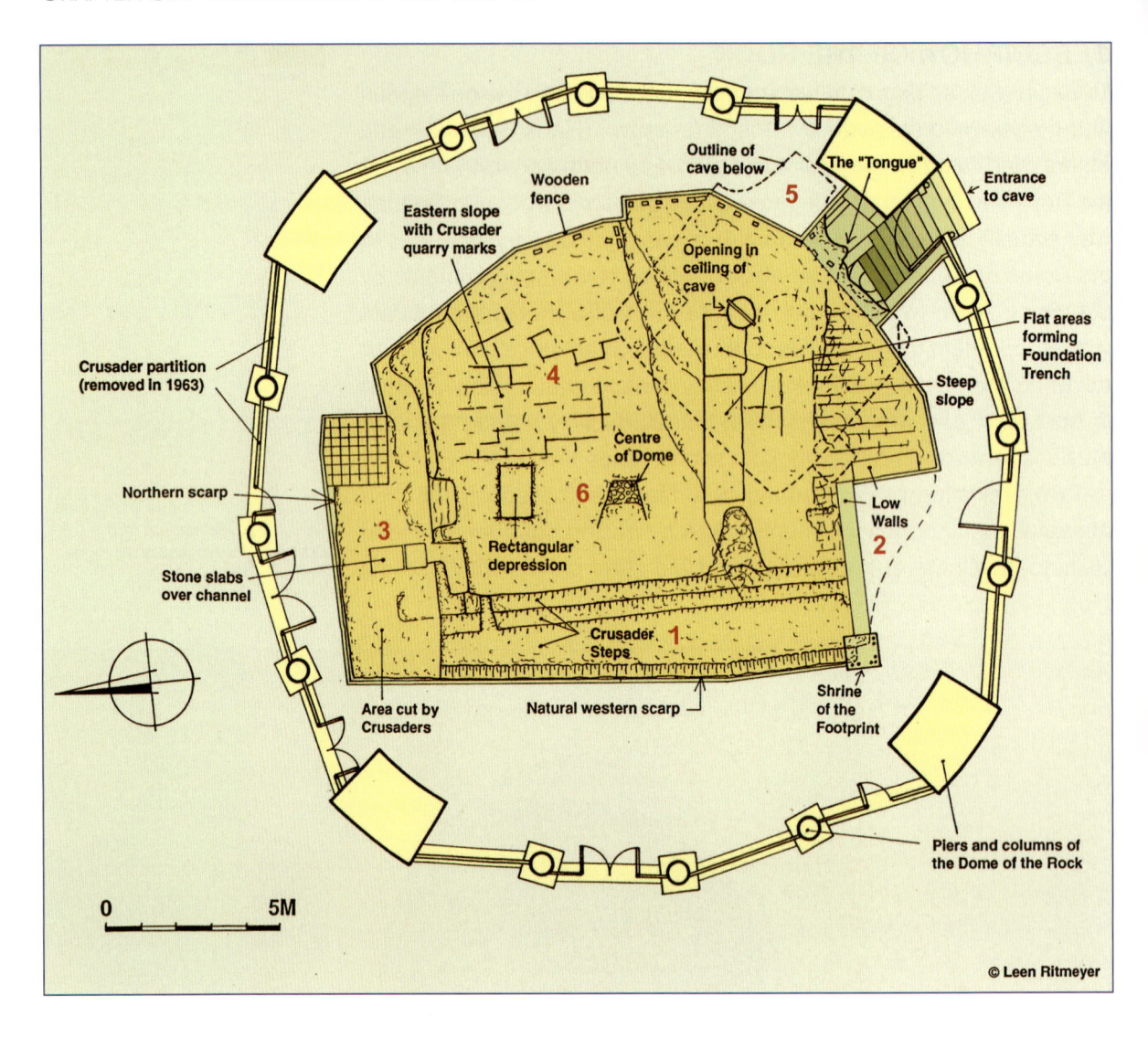

Plan of the Rock.

of photographs taken from the ambulatory below the dome (see plan, above). I had first visited the Dome of the Rock in 1967 and many times since, but the relevant observations made during 1992 and 1994 made sense only after having first established the location of the 500-cubit-square Temple Mount.

Six major features characterize the Rock: (1) the western steps; (2) the cut on the south; (3) the northern shelf and the mysterious drain; (4) the eastern slope; (5) the cave below the Rock; and (6) the upper level with the rectangular depression we have identified as the former location of the Ark of the Covenant.

We will now examine these features of the Rock in that order:

CHAPTER SIX: THE LOCATION OF THE TEMPLE

1) *The Western Steps*

Vision is partly obstructed by the wooden fence that surrounds the Rock on all sides, yet we see immediately that the western face of the Rock, which stands 3 feet 7 inches (1.09 m) above the pavement, is a natural rockscarp with many deep grooves running down from the top. The bottom of the scarp, being close to the fence, is more difficult to see. There are some twenty-seven grooves in the western face of the Rock. In its southern part there are eight grooves that Muslims hold to be the fingers of the angel Gabriel, who they believe held down the rock when it wanted to follow Mohammed during his ascent to heaven. Although the line of the rockscarp is slightly broken, the major direction is approximately 3.5 degrees east, which is virtually identical to the direction of the *step* and the eastern wall of the Temple Mount.

Above the western scarp is a flat area, some 38 feet (11.55 m) long by 5 feet (1.52 m) wide in the south and narrower in the north. It has the appearance of a broad landing, somewhat similar to the landings of the monumental staircase which leads up to the Double Gate in the Southern Wall of the Herodian Temple Mount. There are two more parallel but much narrower steps to the east. If allowed to climb them, one would reach the flat upper level of the Rock.

Above: View of the natural western scarp inside the Dome of the Rock. (photo: Garo Nalbandian)

Below: Isometric view of the Rock with part of the floor of the Dome of the Rock removed to show the full height of the western and northern scarps.

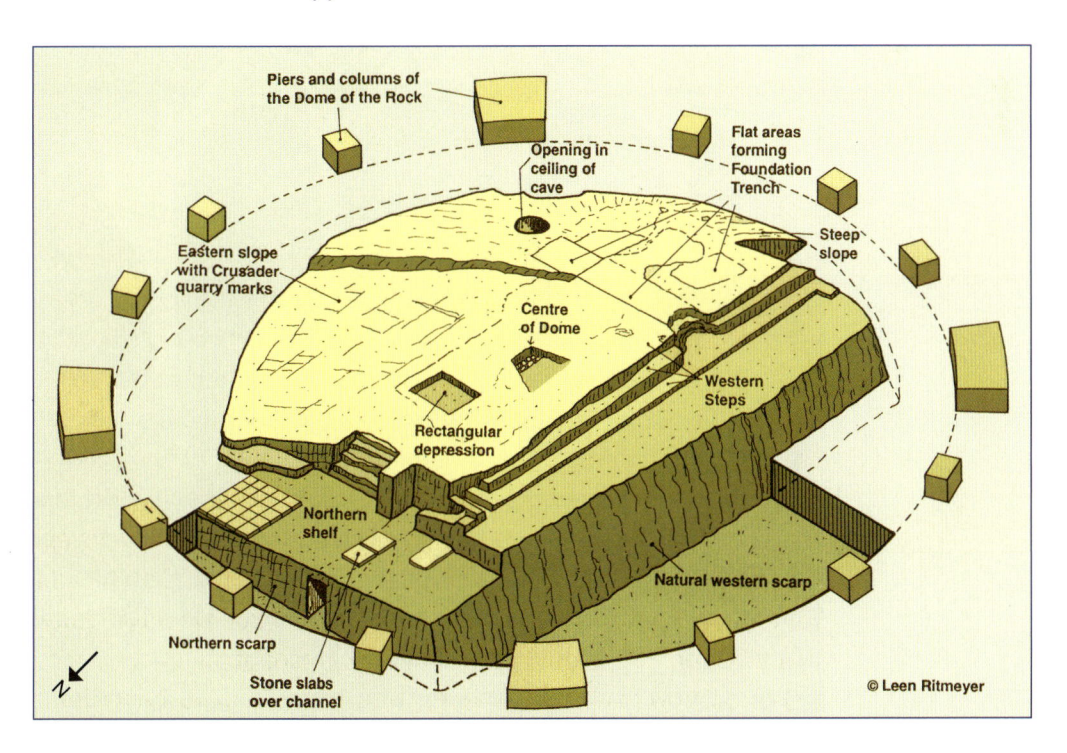

253

Chapter Six: The Location of the Temple

The ascent of the Prophet Mohammed on his steed, Buraq, guided by Jibra'il and escorted by angels. A miniature painting from a sixteenth-century Persian manuscript.

2) The Cut in the South

At the southern corner of the western scarp an ornate chest stands on small marble columns that are obviously from the Crusader period and in secondary use. Inside the chest is a stone, supposedly bearing the imprint of a foot. Through a semicircular hole in the marble front panel you can indeed touch the stone which has an irregular depression which slopes down and narrows from front to back. People throng in front of this chest to touch the stone, with obvious delight. I tried it myself, but I seemed to lack the lively imagination necessary to recognize a footstep in this indentation.

Many legends are connected with this footstep. One holds that it was Mohammed's last footprint before ascending to heaven[12] or the place where Jesus stood when he drove out the money changers.[13] When Kaiser Theodoric II visited this place in 1229 he was so offended by a priest who took money from pilgrims in exchange for the privilege of touching the stone, that he slapped his face!

It has been suggested that this stone with the footprint was originally located on the Rock near the southern slope. This was

Expulsion of the money changers from the Temple. Fresco by Giotto, 1304–06.

recorded by Ibn el-Arabi[14] in 1091 and by Saewulf[15] in 1102. Earlier, in 1047, Nasir i-Khusrau[16] apparently saw seven footprints on the rock. The first time that a separate stone with a footprint is mentioned is in 1173 by Ali of Herat[17]. Comparing these records, it seems most likely that this stone with the footprint was removed from the Rock during the Crusader period.

Going around the corner, we see two walls at right angles to each other. The longest wall (13 feet 9 inches or 4.20 m) faces south and is decorated with marble panels. Looking over the top of this wall and behind the Shrine of the Footprint, one can see a multi-shafted column on its side, with a single column below it. Under this shrine can be seen the bedrock, which, at its lowest point, comes within one inch of the marble facing of the long wall. This means, of course, that the rock behind the chest has not been cut vertically, but has a steep natural slope.

The long wall makes a corner with a shorter wall, which is 7 feet 2 inches (2.20 m) long. It appears that the Rock has been cut here, as though someone had taken a small wedge out of a round cake. The cut could not have been continued eastward as that would have destroyed the cave. As it is, the wedge-like cut stopped an inch short of breaking through the ceiling of the cave below! Who had done this and when? We will attempt to answer this question after we have examined an even larger cut in the northern part of the Rock.

Philosopher, poet and traveler, Nasir-i-Khusrau (1004–1088).

3) The Northern Shelf

Retracing our steps and going to the northern side of the western steps, we see that the whole northern part of the Rock has been lowered. This northern shelf, as I call it, is about 20 feet long and 10 feet wide (6 by 3 m) and stands only a few inches higher than the pavement of the Dome of the Rock. The long scarp—or, more properly, scar—is clearly visible toward the south of this shelf and is on average 4 feet (1.20 m) high.

Remembering the wedge-shaped cut in the south, the artificially cut western steps and now the lower northern shelf, the question of "whodunit" reverberated in my head. Was there a pattern to these three major cuts in the Rock? Were they all made at the same time and why? Looking at the Rock from the western entrance of the Dome of the Rock, while mentally eliminating the wooden fence, it appeared that the shape of the Rock had been changed to look like

Chapter Six: The Location of the Temple

Opposite page: Dalman's plan of the Rock.

a square block, to fit exactly in the middle of the four major piers that support the majestic dome above. Before that the rock must have looked much larger.

THE CRUSADERS AND THE DOME OF THE ROCK

According to the records of John of Würzburg[18] in 1170, there was in this northern part of the rock, during the time of the Latin Kingdom, a portrayal of the Presentation of Jesus in the Temple. Here, the Crusader kings used to place their crowns after their coronation. Another description, this time by Theodoric,[19] shows that this place was surrounded by a separate iron grille. He also records that a cubit away there was the rock on which Jacob was reputed to have slept when he had the vision of the ladder reaching up to heaven. Ali of Herat[20] states that here was the only place where the rock was visible at the time of the Franks.

This is supported by the records of Joannes Phocas[21] (1185). According to him there were two vaulted chambers in the northern part of the church (as the Dome of the Rock was referred to by the Crusaders), in one of which was portrayed the Presentation of Christ and in the other the wondrous ladder of Jacob. This is what he wrote:

Jacob's Ladder by William Blake, 18th century.

> *Towards the eastern side of the city is a church, which is the Holy of Holies. This church is most exceedingly beautiful, having a vaulted roof, and standing upon the ancient foundation of the renowned Temple of Solomon, decorated both within and without with variegated marbles and mosaics. On the left [north] side of this church are two vaulted chambers, in one of which is depicted the Presentation of our Lord Christ, because in that place the just man Simeon received our Lord Christ into his arms, and in the other the wondrous ladder which Jacob saw reaching up to heaven, with the angels of God ascending and descending it; and beneath the picture of this ladder is to be seen the stone upon which Jacob laid his head.*

On the plan of Dalman[22] (opposite), made in 1912, I studied the iron grille that was erected between the pillars surrounding the Rock during the Crusader period. It was removed only in 1963 but a small part of the iron fence has been preserved

Chapter Six: The Location of the Temple

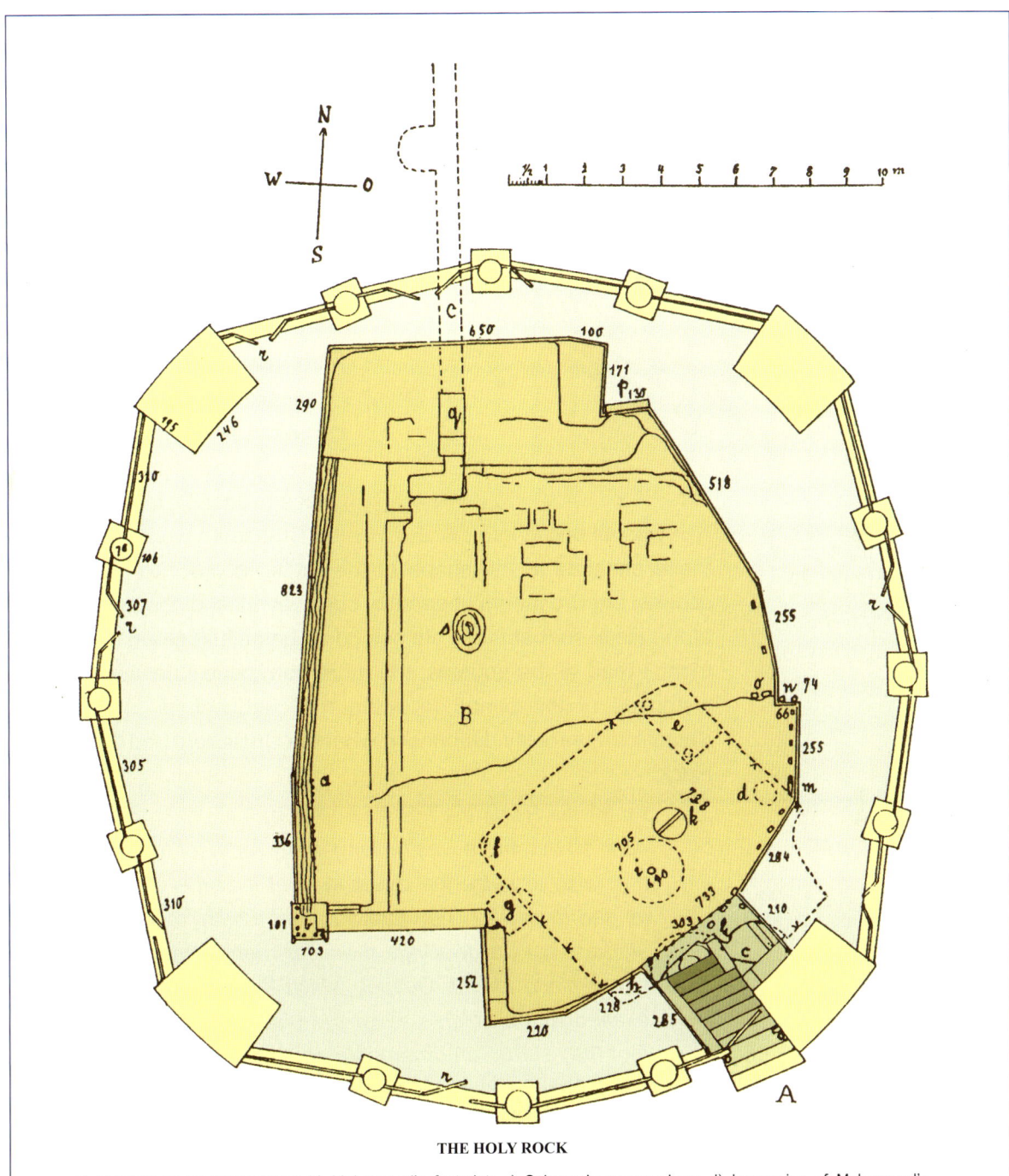

THE HOLY ROCK

a) Gabriel's finger impressions; b) Mohammed's footprint; c) Solomon's prayer place; d) Impression of Mohammed's head; e) Khadr's prayer place; f) Gabriel's seat; g) Abraham's prayer place; h) David's prayer place; i) Round marble slab on top of the "Well of Souls"; k) Air vent of cave; l) Rock tongue; m) Idris' footprint; n) Idris' prayer place; o) Mohammed's footprints; p) The prophet's prayer place; q) Stone slab over channel; r,r,r,r,r) Entrances in use; s) Longish-round depression

CHAPTER SIX: THE LOCATION OF THE TEMPLE

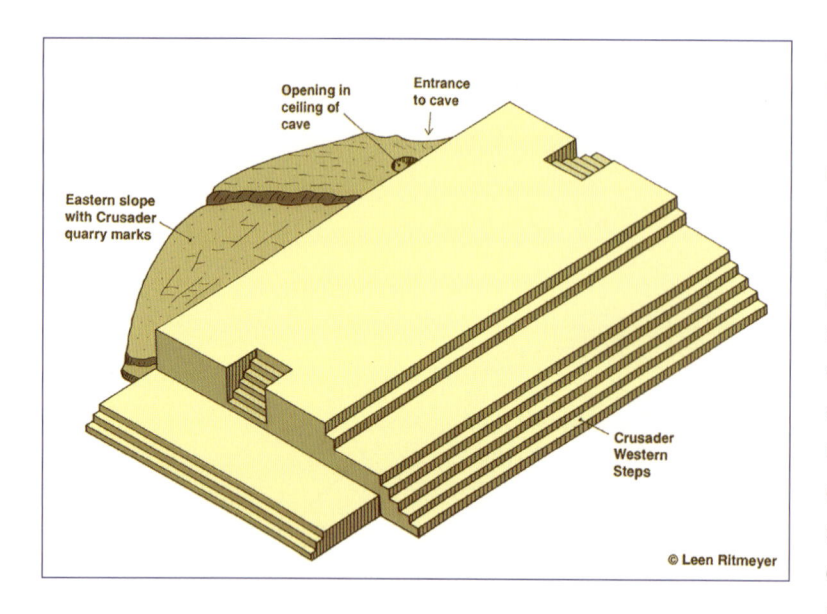

The foundation for the Crusader Church built over the Rock. After having reduced it to size, the Crusaders covered the Rock with stone slabs and built a flight of steps on the west.

and can be seen in the Islamic Museum near the el-Aqsa Mosque. The rest was used to cover drains in the Old City. The northern side of the grille had two openings, a very wide double gate and a smaller single one. It seems logical that the large gate was located opposite the place of the Presentation, where the Crusader kings deposited their crowns; and that the smaller, single door to the immediate east was used for visiting the place of Jacob's ladder.

It was all falling into place. Only the Crusaders would have made these changes to the shape of the Rock. In order to obtain easy access, the Crusaders apparently cut away most of the northern part of the Rock so that these shrines could be built at ground level. The more I read of the sources, the more convinced I became. Muslim historians of the period following the conquest of Jerusalem to Saladin clamorously denounced what the Crusaders had done to the Rock[23]:

As for the Rock, the Franks built over it a church and an altar, so that there was no longer any room for the hands that wish to seize the blessing from it or the eyes that longed to see it. They had adorned it with images and statues, set up dwellings there for monks and made it into a place for the Gospel, which they venerated and exalted to the heights. Over the place of the Prophet's foot they set up an ornamental tabernacle with columns of marble, marking it as a place where the Messiah had set his foot; a holy and exalted place, where flocks of animals, among which I saw a species of pig, were carved in marble. The Rock, the object of pilgrimage, was hidden under constructions and submerged in all this sumptuous building. So that the Sultan ordered that the veil be removed, the curtain raised, the concealments taken away, the marble carried off, the stones broken,

CHAPTER SIX: THE LOCATION OF THE TEMPLE

the structures demolished, the covers broken into. The Rock was to be brought to light again for visitors and revealed to observers, stripped of its covering and brought forward like a young bride. Before the conquest only a small part of the back of it was exposed, and the Unbelievers had cut it about shamefully; now it appeared in all

Interior of the Dome of the Rock, as pictured in Wilson's Picturesque Palestine *in 1880.*

Chapter Six: The Location of the Temple

Below: A reconstruction of the Crusader Church inside the Dome of the Rock.

Opposite page (above): Clermont-Ganneau's drawing of the section of the passage just north of the Rock.

Opposite page (below): View of the northern side of the Rock, showing its thin horizontal layers of rock.

its beauty, revealed in the loveliest revelations. Candelabra gleamed upon it, light on light, and over it was placed an iron grille.

The Franks had cut pieces from the Rock, some of which they carried to Constantinople and Sicily and sold, they said, for their weight in gold, making it a source of income. When the Rock reappeared to sight the marks of these cuts were seen and men were incensed to see how it had been mutilated. Now it is on view with the wounds it suffered, preserving its honour forever, safe for Islam, within its protection and its fence.

The reason the Crusaders had so mutilated the rock was that in their eyes the Rock *"disfigured the Temple of the Lord."*[24] When they transformed the Dome of the Rock into a church, the Crusaders probably cut the Rock down in size, to make it more aesthetic for westerners, and covered it with stone slabs. As we have seen, the northern part was lowered to make space for the two shrines at

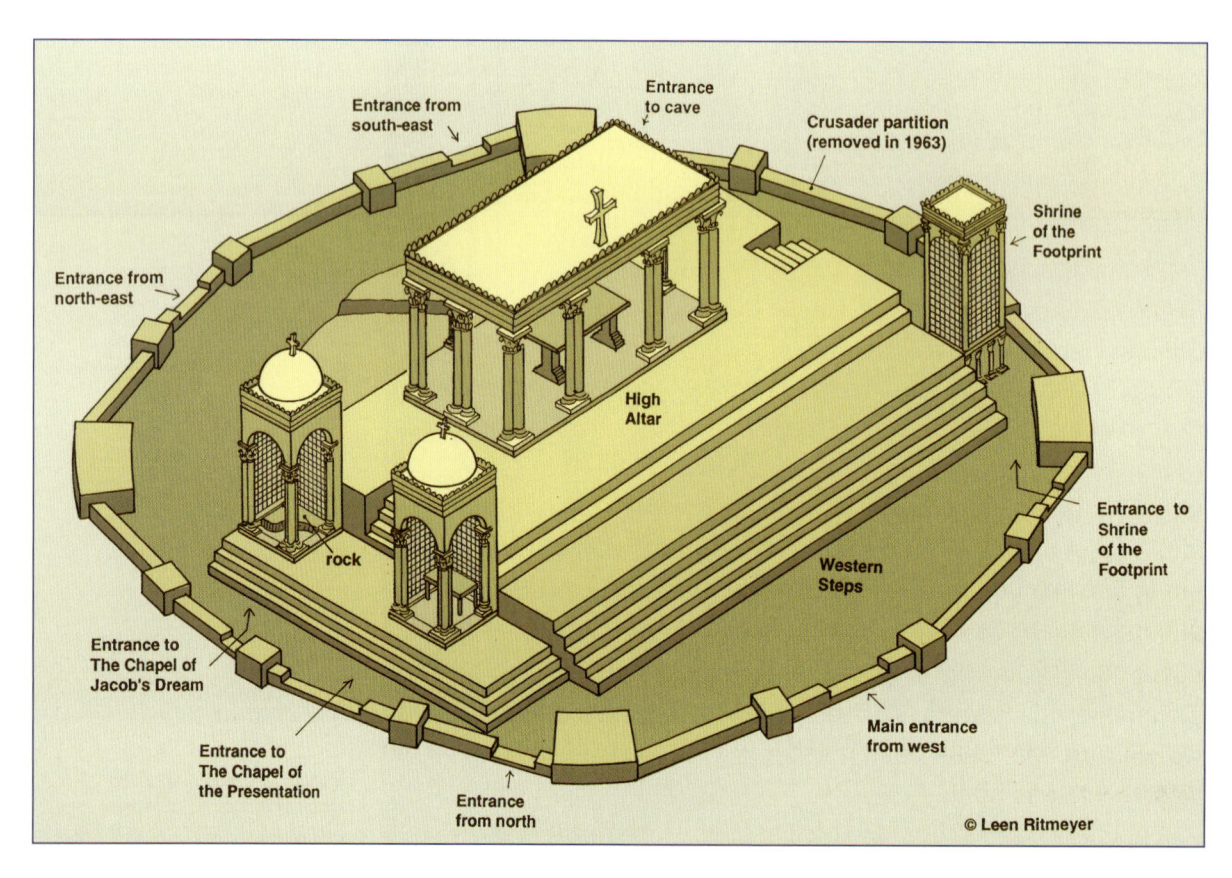

260

CHAPTER SIX: THE LOCATION OF THE TEMPLE

> **A MYSTERIOUS DRAIN — REMNANT OF THE TEMPLAR'S SEARCH FOR THE ARK OF THE COVENANT?**
>
> Conspicuous in the western part of this northern shelf are two stone slabs which are cemented together on the rock (see illustrations, pp. 252 and 253). They are 25 inches (62 cm) wide, the northernmost is 3.5 feet (1.10 m) long and the other 22 inches (55 cm). They cover an opening which was investigated in 1869 by Warren,[25] who reported seeing an empty space, apparently the beginning of a channel, 5 feet long, 2 feet wide and 3 feet deep (1.52 m x 61 cm x 91 cm). The northern extension of this channel is cut in the rock, but the bottom was covered with soil and Warren did not see the bedrock below. Some years later, Clermont-Ganneau[26] saw the extension of this channel to the immediate north of the rock, outside the fence. Here, it was not cut in the rock, but made of stones and plaster. The place where the channel entered the rock was filled in.
>
> The compelling conclusion to be drawn from these observations is that the northern edge of the Rock continues down perpendicularly for at least 3 feet 3 inches (1 m) below the floor of the Dome of the Rock, while the top of the Rock stands on average 5 feet 7 inches (1.70 m) above the floor. If this area could be excavated down to the bedrock, we would see that the top of the Rock rises to a total height of approximately 8 feet 10 inches (2.70 m) above its immediate surroundings. The perpendicular scarp would have added dramatically to the visual effect of this rock formation, which rests on top of the mountain.
>
> This channel was cleared by Captain Parker when seeking the Temple treasure.[27] He apparently followed the channel for a distance of 29 feet (8.80 m) to the north (see plan, p. 257). After 20 feet (6 m) he found a circular plastered installation to the left of the channel. Parker believed that this channel continued up to a black paving slab, situated between the two pillars opposite the northern gate. This slab is called the "Flagstone of Paradise" because, according to Muslim tradition, it covers the entrance to paradise.[28] Muslims also believe this to be the burial place of Solomon. John of Würzburg thought that this was the location of the Temple spring mentioned by Ezekiel.[29]
>
> In the south, the channel is connected to the 2-foot- (58 cm) wide opening cut in the rockscarp. Here the bottom of the channel slopes upward and after 8 inches (20 cm) turns to the west, where its width is 2 feet 4 inches (70 cm). After almost 3 feet 3 inches (1 m) the channel comes to an end near the western steps. The purpose of this channel is unclear. It has been suggested that it may have been the drain for the Altar. The difficulty with this interpretation is (as already mentioned in section 6.2) that the drain is recorded as being located at the southwest corner of the Altar (Middot 3.2), while here we are at the northwest corner of the Rock.
>
> In our reconstruction, we place the Holy of Holies on the Rock. It would follow that this channel, if it were Herodian or earlier, would have drained this square inner room of the sanctuary. However, there is no reference in the sources to any such installation. Furthermore, as the Temple was roofed over, there would in fact have been no need for such a drain, especially since a very large drainage system was located in the southern part of the building.
>
> **It is possible that this channel was cut by the Crusader Templars, who are known to have dug tunnels on the Temple Mount in search of the Ark of the Covenant. If so, this must have taken place early in the time of the Latin Kingdom before the northern shelf was cut.**

ground level, and the southern wedge was cut away to make the rock fit more symmetrically inside the Dome of the Rock. Having thus reduced the mass of rock to a more manageable size, they then built a broad staircase in the west leading to the High Altar, which stood on the top of the Rock (see illustration, opposite).

4) The Eastern Slope

Before walking around to the eastern part of the Rock and still looking at the scarp at the southern end of the northern shelf, we see clearly that the thin rock layers of which the mountain is made are horizontal at the top, but toward the east they dip down until the level of the pavement, near the balustrade. On this slope, which we see when we walk around to the east, no scarps are visible as they are in the west, south and north.

It appears that the bedrock continues to slope down in an easterly

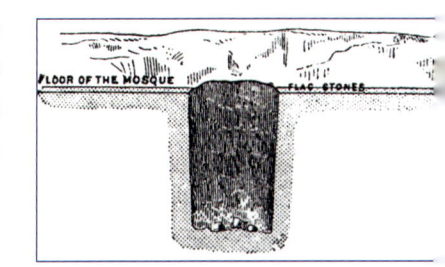

261

Chapter Six: The Location of the Temple

Royal Crusader seal with inscription: "the city of the king of all kings," and depictions of (left to right) Church of the Holy Sepulcher, "David's Tower," and the Dome of the Rock. (NEAEHL)

Entrance to the cave inside the Dome of the Rock. (photo: Garo Nalbandian)

direction below the pavement. If so, then after approximately 11 feet 2 inches (3.4 m) it would reach a depth of 3 feet 3 inches (1 m) below the pavement of the Dome of the Rock. This was the depth recorded by Clermont-Ganneau[30] in 1873, when he witnessed a small excavation near the eastern door of the Dome of the Rock. He actually saw *terra rossa*, the typical red earth found immediately above the bedrock, at a depth of 23 inches (57 cm) below the paving in this area. After excavating to a depth of 36 inches (90 cm) below the paving slabs, no bedrock was encountered, though the feeling was that it could not have been much farther down. In 1959, Bagatti[31] saw the bedrock at several places below the floor during repairs conducted at that time. According to his observations, the rock on the whole appeared level, but dipped down toward the outer walls of the Dome of the Rock. From these and Clermont-Ganneau's other observations in the northern part of the Dome of the Rock, we learn that the bedrock in general is located 3 feet 3 inches (1 m) below the floor of the Dome of the Rock.

On the sloping surface in the east of the Rock, many quarry marks are visible, showing that slabs have been extracted here at some time, possibly as a result of a Crusader practice of raising money by selling pieces of the rock for their weight in gold, as mentioned before. Remembering the narrow bedrock layers which we saw at the northern scarp, it would appear that only a thin layer of stones was removed—not more than 10 to 12 inches (25 to 30 cm) thick. The original bedrock slope would therefore have been that much higher.

The discovery of these quarry marks on the eastern slope confirms the source that records the removal of slabs of rock from the Rock by the Crusaders. This observation makes it highly unlikely that the rectangular depression on the flat top of the rock resulted from such a practice, particularly since the thickness of the rock removed from the slope is much more than the depth of the shallow depression.

5) The Cave

Walking around to the south, we see the entrance to the cave, cut entirely out of the rock near the southeast corner of the Rock. Fourteen steps, about 5 feet (1.50 m) wide, descend into the cave. The lowest three steps are semicircular. The cave has an irregular square shape, with a width varying from 22 feet 7 inches to 24 feet (6.90 m to 7.33 m) and a maximum depth of 24 feet 3 inches

CHAPTER SIX: THE LOCATION OF THE TEMPLE

(7.40 m). The bedrock is visible on either side of the steps. While descending into the cave, one can see in front, a vertical stretch of rock, measuring approximately 3 feet 3 inches by 6 feet 6 inches (1 by 2 m) wide. On the right of it is a projection, the so-called Tongue, which can be touched on the right side when descending into the cave. This projection indicates the original width of the entrance to the cave. The widening of the entrance to the right was probably the work of the Crusaders, who used the cave for ritual purposes. It is possible that the Crusaders also enlarged the cave in order to use it as a crypt.

The ceiling of the cave looks natural. Its height varies from approximately 4 feet 11 inches (1.50 m) at the side walls to 8 feet 7 inches (2.62 m) at the middle of the end wall. In the central part of the cave's ceiling is a hole, 2 feet 7 inches (80 cm) in diameter, cut through the bedrock that is here 5 feet 7 inches (1.70 m) thick. There are no signs of rope marks, as found on wellheads of cisterns.

Some researchers thought that this hole, first mentioned by Ali of Herat[32] in 1173, served to drain the Altar waste into the cave. Others connect this feature with the *lapis pertusis* ("pierced rock") where the Jews used to assemble to mourn the loss of their Temple. This term was first used by the Pilgrim of Bordeaux.

However, we think that the Crusaders may have cut this hole and called the cave the Holy of Holies. Here they venerated the angel's announcement to Zacharias that he would have a son (Lk 1:13.). The many candles and lamps, which are usually lit at such shrines, would have made a ventilation system imperative. *Thus, the Crusaders may have cut the hole in the ceiling of the cave to create a chimney!*

Angel appearing to Zacharias by Ghirlandaio, 1486–90 (detail).

6) The Upper Level

Ascending the steps leading out of the cave we turn left again, back to the eastern slope. If you let your eyes skim over the upper level of the Rock in front and to your left, you will see that it is practically horizontal.

The upper level of the Rock, however, can actually better be appreciated by examining a picture taken from high up under the dome (see photo, p. 243). The top of the rock is approximately 10 feet (3 m) wide on the north but widens out to approximately 20 feet (6 m) on the south. The level on the south is a bit lower and is located at 4 feet 3 inches (1.30 m) above the floor; in the middle it is 5 feet 3

263

Chapter Six: The Location of the Temple

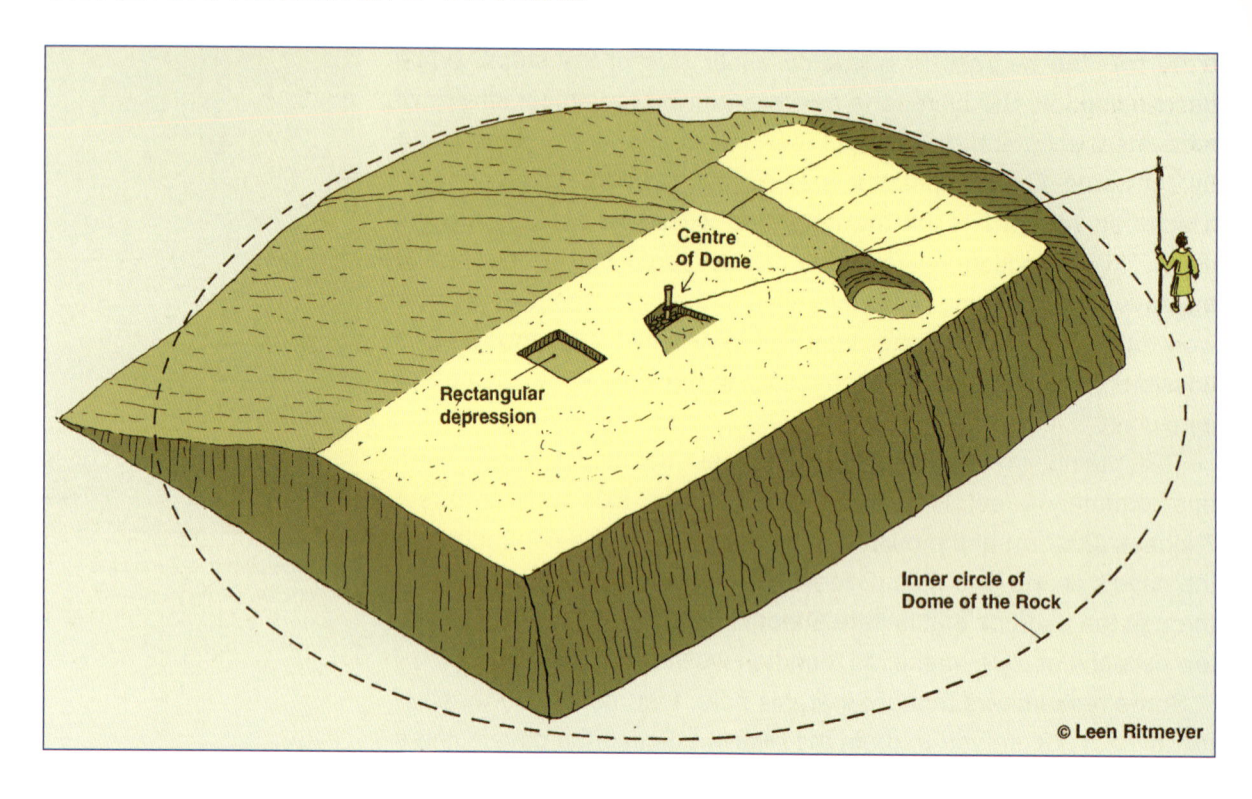

The Rock during the Early Islamic period, showing how the inner circle of the Dome was set out. In the drawing, the Crusader cuttings have been eliminated.

inches (1.60 m) in height with the highest point being 5 feet 10 inches (1.77 m). A rocky ledge runs over the Rock from east to west with the higher side on the south. This ledge became more pronounced after the Crusaders quarried the eastern slope.

Two depressions are visible in the northern part. At 13 feet (4 m) from the northern scarp and 4 feet 7 inches (1.40 m) from the western scarp is an apparently artificially-cut trapezoid indentation with two ledges spreading out toward the west. At the deepest point no rock is visible, only small stones and mortar. It has been suggested[33] that this place may have been the spot where a tree for Asherah (i.e., a full-sized female figure carved out of a tree trunk) was planted. We suggest, however, that as this place is located at the very center of the Dome of the Rock, it may have played a role as the pivot from which the ground plan of the Dome of the Rock was laid (see illustration, above).

Just to the north is the now familiar rectangular depression. The sides of this indentation vary from half an inch to 6 inches (1 to 15 cm). This can barely be seen from the east, if you are over 6 feet (1.80 m) tall, otherwise you must stand on your tiptoes. In my estimation the depression measures 4 feet 4 inches (1.30 m) from east to west

CHAPTER SIX: THE LOCATION OF THE TEMPLE

and about 3 feet 3 inches (1 m) from north to south, and located 15 feet 7 inches (4.75 m) south of the northern edge of the Rock and 13 feet 9 inches (4.20 m) from the western edge. Below, we will see that this depression is of great antiquity and played an important role in the Temples of Jerusalem. To the east of this rectangle is a horizontal ledge, 11 to 12 inches (25 to 30 cm) wide, the high point of the eastern slope.

Farther to the south, the upper surface of the rock widens out toward the east. Near the hole in the ceiling of the cave there are two flat areas. The smaller of the two lies to the immediate west of the hole and the other, which is longer and about 10 cm higher, is located farther west. Dalman[34] noticed these areas, but could not understand their purpose nor did he think that the near surroundings indicated their function. He cites Rudolf Kittel, who thought that the lower one (because of its close proximity to the hole) was a receptacle for blood, to channel it into the cave below.

Standing to the east of the Rock and looking west, the flat areas and especially their northern edge appear very clearly and remind us of a foundation trench for large stones. In our estimation, the lower, eastern one measures 3 feet 3 inches by 4 feet 11 inches (1 by 1.50 m) and the western one, 3 feet by 8 feet 2 inches (90 cm by 2.50 m). The length of the latter may have reached 13 feet 2 inches (4 m) but for the natural depression in the rock mentioned earlier. The distance between the northern edge of this foundation trench and the northern edge of the Rock is 34 feet 5 inches (10.50 m).

Going around now to the south and passing by the entrance to the cave, we stand near the 9-foot-3-inch-long paneled wall mentioned earlier. Looking over the top, we see in front of us some more flat areas which are not so well defined. Nevertheless, together with the flat areas to the west of the hole in the ceiling of the cave, they appear to form a wide foundation trench for a broad wall that would have run from east to west. The thickness of this wall, based on the measurements of this southern foundation trench, is well over 10 feet (3 m) from north to south. The bedrock slopes down steeply from these level areas in a southerly direction, as previously described.

View of the flat areas of the Rock.

THE LOCATION OF THE HOLY OF HOLIES

We have now completed our tour and the time has come to put together all we have seen and match it with the historical records.

Chapter Six: The Location of the Temple

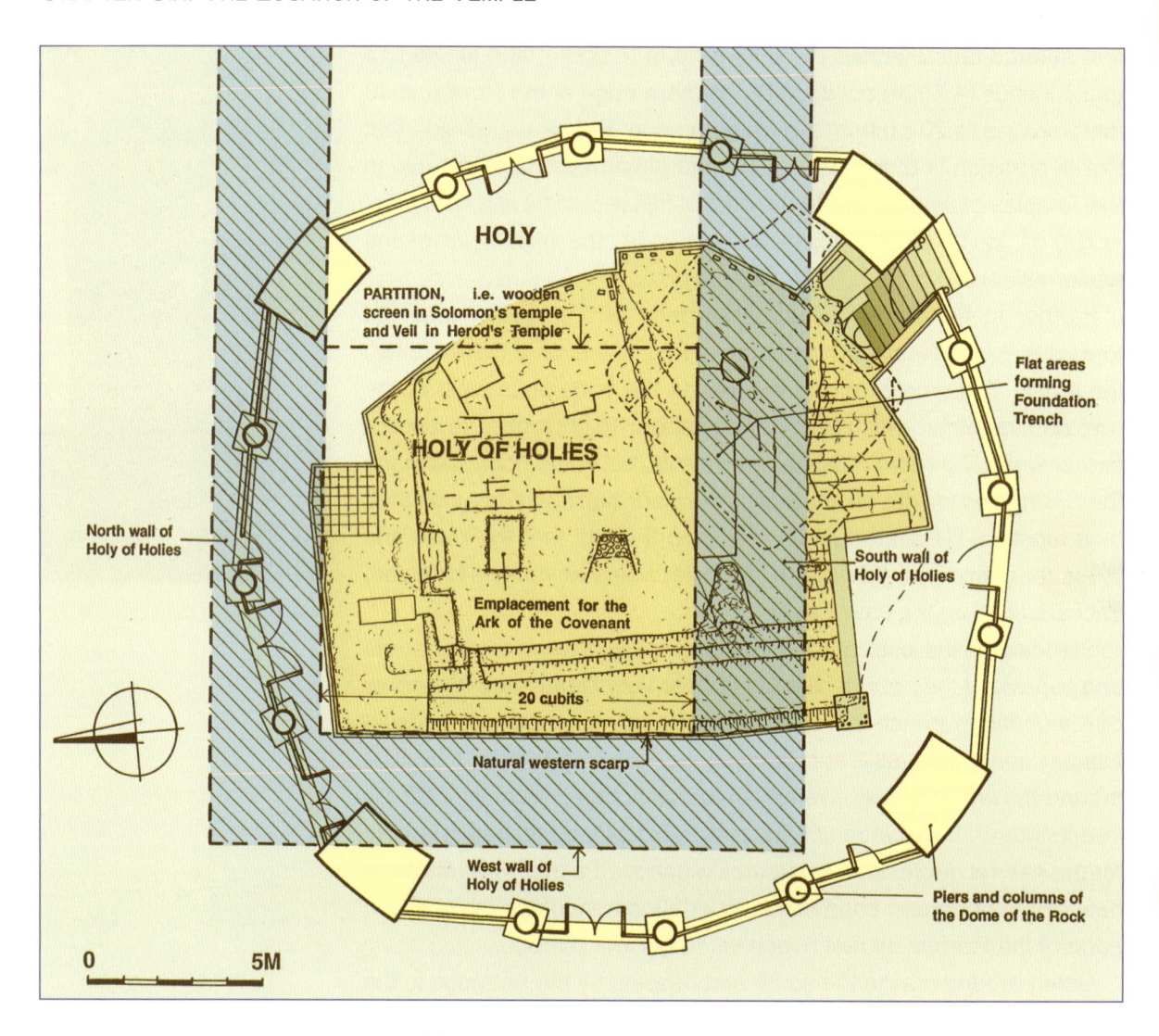

The location of the Holy of Holies in Solomon's Temple.

The original appearance of the Rock can be deduced by visually eliminating all the changes made to it throughout the ages. Since the time of Saladin, however, the Rock appears to have remained untouched.

As explained before, I attribute the northern and southern cuts to the Crusaders, also the cuts in the west. Before the Crusaders transformed the Rock, the upper level therefore would have been much larger and the flat rock would have filled most of the Holy of Holies. The slope leading up to it from the Holy would have been a little higher and probably smoother.

The thickness of the Temple walls in the Second Temple period measured 6 cubits or 10 feet 4 inches (3.15 m) according to *Middot*

Chapter Six: The Location of the Temple

4.7. The dimensions of the combined flat areas in the southern part of the Rock are in perfect agreement with this information. I propose therefore that this is the place where the southern wall of the Holy of Holies stood. Just outside the southern wall of the Holy of Holies, the rock sloped down sharply.

The western wall would have stood at the foot of the natural western scarp. As the direction of the scarp is virtually identical to that of the *step* and of the eastern wall of the Temple Mount, both the First and Second Temples would have had the same orientation, i.e. the longitudinal axis of the Temple would have been at right angles with the eastern wall. As the western scarp is a natural one and its direction unchanged, there are no grounds to believe that the axis of the First Temple would have been different from the Second Temple.

The continuation of this axis is aligned with the top of the Mount of Olives, where the Red Heifer was sacrificed. According to *Middot* 2.4, *"the [High] Priest, that burns the [Red] Heifer and stands on the top of the Mount of Olives should be able to look directly into the entrance of the Sanctuary when the blood is sprinkled."* Given that the line between the Rock and the highest peak of the Mount of Olives crosses the eastern wall of the Temple Mount at right angles, it appears that the Temple axis was set out from this line and that the walls of the square Temple Mount were arranged parallel to or at right angles with this line. *The fact that there is a topographical design to the alignment of the Temple and the Temple Mount is yet another confirmation of our location and direction of the Temple.*

Line of vision between the Temple and the highest peak of the Mount of Olives.

The distance between the southern foundation trench and the northern edge of the Rock is 34 feet 5 inches (10.50 m), which is exactly 20 cubits. The northern wall of the Holy of Holies would have been built exactly here, at the foot of the northernmost scarp, which was cut originally for that purpose.

As already mentioned, there never was a stone wall between the Holy of Holies (or *debir*) and the Holy (also called

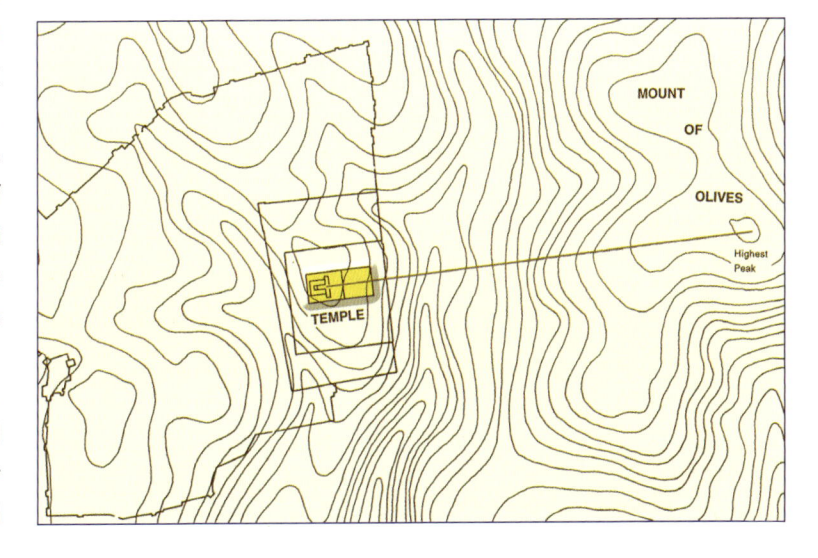

CHAPTER SIX: THE LOCATION OF THE TEMPLE

heikhal). Therefore no foundation trench would have been visible on the sloping surface on the east of the Rock. Nevertheless, on the plan we can plot the dividing line between the two chambers of the Sanctuary so that the whole area occupied by the Holy of Holies can be set out.

THE FORMER LOCATION OF THE ARK OF THE COVENANT

The most intriguing question in this archaeological analysis of the Rock is the purpose of the rectangular depression, mentioned above. According to Josephus, the inner chamber was completely empty: *"In this stood nothing whatever: unapproachable, inviolable, invisible to all, it was called the Holy of Holy"* (*War* 5.219). He was apparently unaware of the existence of this most interesting feature.

According to my plan, this depression falls exactly in the center of the Holy of Holies. The dimensions of this level basin appeared at first to agree with those of the Ark of the Covenant which were 1.5 by 2.5 cubits (2 feet 7 inches by 4 feet 4 inches or 79 by 131 cm), with the longitudinal axis coinciding with that of the Temple. These measurements were based on viewing a commercially available photograph taken from high up in the ambulatory under the Dome.

In 1996 Fr. Jerome Murphy O'Connor of the École Biblique d'Archéologique in Jerusalem, during a search through the photographic archives of the school for material for one of his own publications, came across a set of photographs of the Rock he thought I might find useful. They were the work of two different photographers, both pre-1914. The smaller ones were the work of A. Jaussen and were marked with his characteristic J. The remainder were by the better-known Père Raphael Savignac and appeared to have been taken to illustrate the book *Jérusalem Nouvelle*, a work

Photograph of the Rock taken directly above the emplacement of the Ark of the Covenant.

CHAPTER SIX: THE LOCATION OF THE TEMPLE

written by another eminent Dominican scholar, Père L. H. Vincent with Père F. M. Abel. These photographs were taken from the ambulatory below the Dome, but this time from at least six different angles. One was especially valuable, as it was taken looking directly from above the depression. The rectangular depression did not appear to be quite so rectangular. It definitely was not a square, but was closer to being one than I had previously thought.

This was tantalizing. I was convinced that all the other elements of my identification of the Holy of Holies were correct, so what did this mean? A photogrammetric survey of the Rock appeared to be the only way to proceed from this point forward. Photogrammetry, simply put, is the science of measurement and analysis from stereoscopic photographs. The word was introduced by the architect Albrecht Meydenbauer in 1867 and is most commonly associated with topographic mapping. I now had in my possession photographs that were of good enough quality to give results by this method. A photogrammetrist, having access to different views of the same object, would be able to create an accurate plan. Clive Boardman of Photoarc Surveys in Harrogate thus completed a photogrammetric survey of the Rock, from these photographs.

I explained what I wanted done and awaited the results eagerly. I was given a computer-rendered drawing showing that the length of the depression was exactly the same as that of the Ark of the Covenant (1.31 m or 4 feet 4 inches). However, the width was more

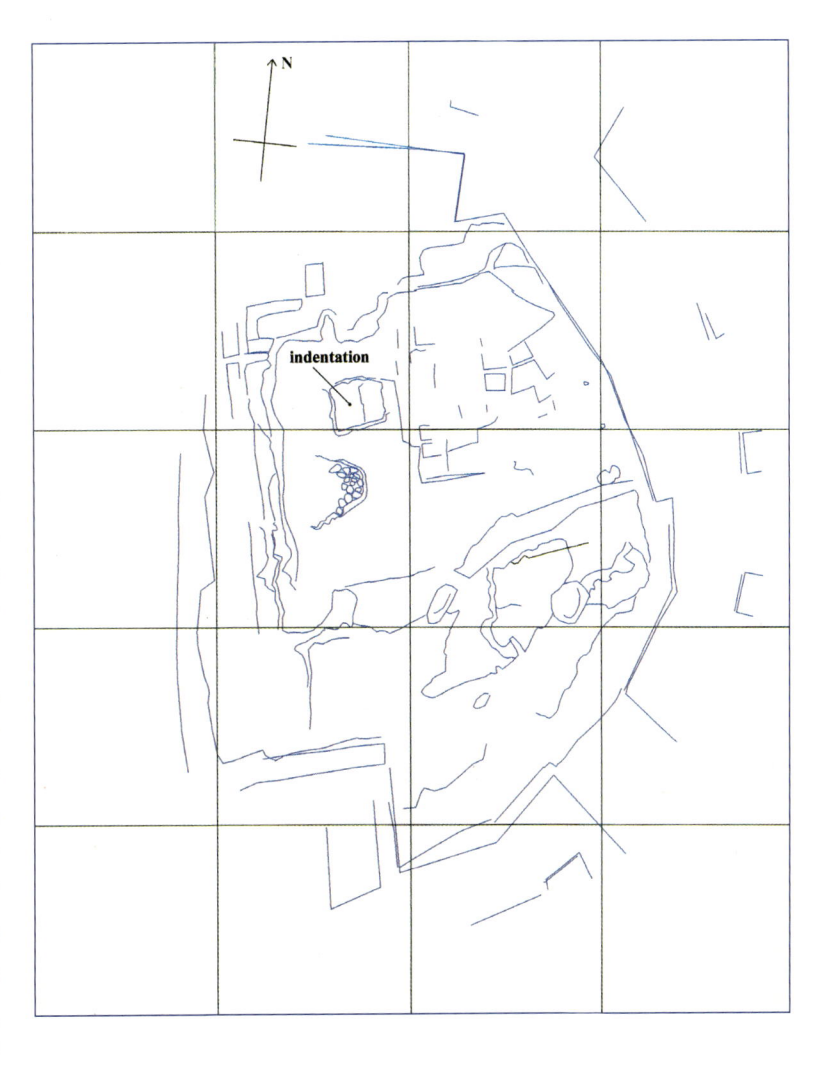

Above: Photogrammetric plan of the Rock.

Below: The author sitting with a photogrammetrist to create the plan, above, of the Rock.

Chapter Six: The Location of the Temple

Right: View of the rectangular depression (marked by blue rectangle) of the Rock. (Courtesy World of the Bible Ministries)

Below: Moses delivering the Law into the hands of the priests (Deut 31:26), 19th century engraving.

than I had originally thought it to be (1.00 m or 3 feet 3 inches, instead of 80 cm or 2 feet 7 inches).

On the one hand, this was wonderful confirmation, but the width threw me off balance as I tried to understand why the depression, which I believed to be the place where Solomon prepared for the Ark of the Covenant after all its years of journeyings with the Children of Israel, was actually too wide for it.

The answer was in a Bible passage I came across while reading Deuteronomy 31:26. Here Moses tells the Levites that bore the Ark, *"Take this book of the Law and put it in the side of the Ark of the Covenant of the LORD your God that it may be there for a witness against thee."*

CHAPTER SIX: THE LOCATION OF THE TEMPLE

Was the scroll of the Law placed inside the Ark together with the two tablets of stone inscribed with the Ten Commandments, the golden pot which had manna and Aaron's rod that budded? Some rabbinic authorities are of this opinion.[35] Or was the scroll meant to lie outside and alongside the Ark? Only if it was outside and accessible could it be a witness.

The Hebrew text reads *mezad aron habrit* which means: "from the side of the ark of Yahweh," and not "inside." The Jerusalem Bible translates *mezad* as "beside" and has an interesting note to this verse in Deuteronomy (p. 257), *"The Law mediated by Moses, 4.14+, is thus placed beside the Decalogue uttered by God himself; both possess the same divine authority; cf. 28.69 and 5.24,27."*

Deuteronomy 28:69 in the Jerusalem Bible is actually Deuteronomy 29:1 in other versions and reads:

> *These are the words of the covenant, which the LORD commanded Moses to make with the children of Israel in the land of Moab, beside the covenant which he made with them in Horeb.*

Chapter 5 of Deuteronomy describes the giving of the Ten Commandments, but concludes with the Israelites asking Moses to go up to God and to receive from Him the commandments, statutes and judgments and to tell them so that they could observe them.

So it would appear that the Book of Deuteronomy (Hebrew, *Devarim*) was regarded as a teaching scroll and vitally important to preserve beside their most important ceremonial object, the Ark of the Covenant. Roland de Vaux, in his magisterial work, *Ancient Israel*, mentions some most interesting extra-biblical parallels to this practice in his chapter on the Ark of the Covenant. He writes that a rubric (or section of a legal code) of The Egyptian Book of the Dead reads, *"This chapter was found at Khmun on an alabaster brick, under the feet of the Majesty of this venerable place (the god Thoth), and it was written by the god himself."*[36] So it would appear that this particular section was deemed to be of such importance that it was kept at the feet of Thoth. De Vaux also writes in the same place that

> *Hittite treaties stipulate that the text shall be placed in a temple at the foot of an image of a god. A letter from Ramses II about his treaty with Hattusil is most explicit: "The writing of the oath (pact) which I have made to the*

Above: Moses and the burning bush, from a wall painting in the synagogue at Dura Europos, Syria, 3rd century.

Below: Thoth, the Egyptian god of writing, as depicted on a papyrus from the New Kingdom, c. 1550–1090 B.C.

Chapter Six: The Location of the Temple

Great King, the king of Hattu, lies beneath the feet of the god Teshup: the great gods are witnesses of it. The writing of the oath which the Great King, the king of Hattu, has made to me, lies beneath the feet of the god Ra: the great gods are witnesses of it."

I had seen drawings portraying a shelf attached to the side of the Ark on which the scroll was carried.[37] However, such a ledge was nowhere described in the minute specifications given for the construction of the Ark and it would seem to be a highly precarious way of carrying a precious scroll. We must remember that this scroll was actually written by Moses, as the words of Deuteronomy 31: 9 testify: *"And Moses wrote this law and delivered it unto the priests the sons of Levi, which bare the ark of the covenant of the LORD and unto all the elders of Israel."*

The careful preservation of this scroll would have been the job of the Kohathites. This was the Levitical family entrusted with looking after and carrying the Ark and all the other furniture inside the Holy

King David bringing the Ark of the Covenant to Jerusalem. (The Temple Institute, Jerusalem)

CHAPTER SIX: THE LOCATION OF THE TEMPLE

Place (Num 3:31). They would have borne the scroll with the rest of their "most holy things" all those years in the Wilderness. Whenever the Ark rested, they would have placed the Ark inside the Holy of Holies with this scroll, perhaps in a protective wrapping or receptacle such as Jewish scrolls today are kept, lying beside it.

It would appear therefore that during the First Temple period a special place was prepared for the Ark and the Deuteronomy Scroll by cutting this flat basin in the rock. It is clear that without such a flat area the Ark would have wobbled about in an undignified manner and the scroll could have rolled away—which could not conceivably have been allowed.

Several texts in 1 Kings 6 and 8 may actually refer to a specially prepared place for the Ark. In 1 Kings 6:19 it says that Solomon prepared the *debir* in the midst of the house from within *"to place there the Ark of the Covenant of Yahweh"* and in 1 Kings 8:6, *"the priests brought in the Ark of the Covenant of Yahweh unto His (or Its) place, into the debir of the house, to the most holy, under the wings of the Cherubim."* This means that a special place was prepared or assigned to the Ark. This is further emphasized in verses 20 and 21 of the same chapter, where Solomon says that he has *"built an house for the name of Yahweh God of Israel. And I have **set** [my emphasis] there a place for the Ark...."* The Hebrew verb *sim* which is translated here as "set" can also mean "put" or "make." In the light of this discovery, I suggest to translate this verse as *"I have **made** there a place for the Ark."*

This small basin which Solomon had made has been preserved until today. Of course, its orientation mystified me at first, as most pictures show the Ark standing in the Tabernacle or in the Temple with its long side facing the veil. If this depression marked the place of the Ark, it was clear that it must have stood the other way around. Thinking about this, it became obvious that this was the only way it could have stood—otherwise it would have been impossible for the priests to withdraw the staves (1 Kgs 8:8) because of the position of the two large cherubim under whose wings the Ark was placed. In addition, the staves, being 10 cubits long, would have hit the walls of the Holy of Holies, which was only 20 cubits square. On the other hand, if the Ark was placed with its short side facing the veil, then, on withdrawing the staves, they would have projected 1.25 cubits (half

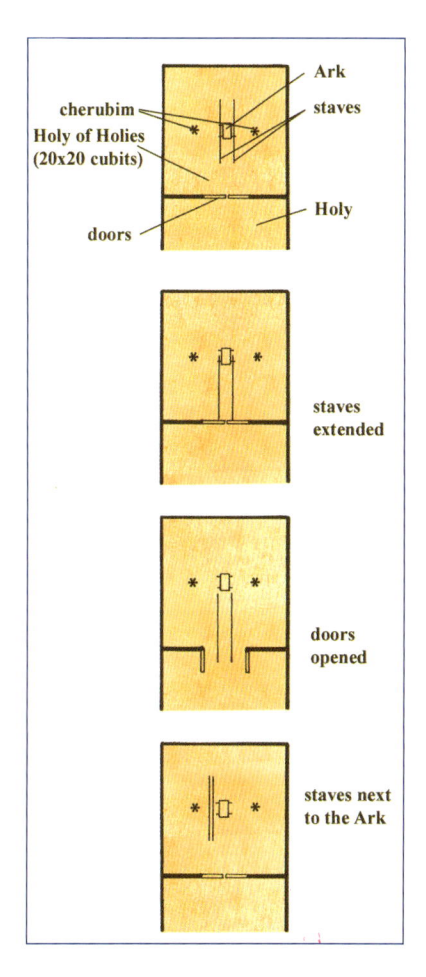

Schematic plan of the Holy of Holies in Solomon's Temple and the removing procedure of the staves from the Ark of the Covenant, as mentioned in 1 Kings 8:8.

Chapter Six: The Location of the Temple

The harp-playing King David and the High Priest kneeling before the Holy Ark. Painting in the Church of Our Lady of the Ark of the Covenant in Kiriath-jearim.

the length of the Ark) into the Temple's Holy, the main hall in front of the Holy of Holies. The doors, made of olive wood, would therefore have had to be opened.

This is my explanation of 1 Kings 8:6-8, which reads:

> And the priests brought in the ark of the covenant of the LORD unto his place, into the oracle of the house, to the most holy place, even under the wings of the cherubim. For the cherubim spread forth their two wings over the place of the ark, and the cherubim covered the ark and the staves thereof above. And they drew out the staves, that the ends of the staves were seen out in the holy place before the oracle, and they were not seen without: and there they are unto this day.

A superficial reading of this passage may appear to contradict the Mosaic prohibition on the removal of the staves (Ex 25:15). However, I believe that the staves remained in place only until the Ark of the Covenant reached its final resting place in Solomon's Temple. Did the Ark not go before the children of Israel in the three-day journey *"to*

CHAPTER SIX: THE LOCATION OF THE TEMPLE

search out a resting place for them" (Num 10:33); and did King David not say, *"Arise, LORD, into thy rest; thou and the Ark of thy strength"* (Ps 132:8)?

Once placed in the Temple, the Ark had reached its final resting place; therefore it is written in 1 Kings 8:8 that the staves were drawn out. King Josiah commanded later to *"put the holy Ark in the house which Solomon the son of David king of Israel did build; there is no burden upon your shoulders"* (2 Chr 35.3)—implying that only when the Ark was being carried from place to place (as in the wilderness wanderings or in times of danger, or during the reign of Josiah's predecessor, Manasseh), the staves needed to be attached to the Ark.

According to the information given in Exodus 26, the staves could have been no longer than 10 cubits, as that was the size of the Holy of Holies in the Tabernacle, in which the Ark was placed.

In some representations, the staves are depicted as having been fixed along the two short sides of the Ark. Not only is this an unnatural way of carrying long objects, but it would have also made it impossible to carry the Ark of the Covenant into the Tabernacle. It had first to pass the curtain, which was supported by five pillars. The four gaps between these five pillars therefore each measured less than two and a half cubits (a fourth part of the width of the Tabernacle, which was ten cubits), taking the width of these pillars into consideration. It is clear therefore that the Ark could only have been carried into the Holy of Holies with its narrow side first, with staves placed on the long side.

Although the Talmud (*Menahot 98*) states that the Ark was positioned with its long side facing the partition with the staves fitted along the short sides, this clearly cannot be the case. To get around this problem, it has been suggested that the Ark was first placed in the Holy of Holies and that the pillars were erected afterwards. This, however, would be in contradiction to the record in Exodus 40:18 which says that Moses first raised up the Tabernacle and the pillars and afterwards (verse 20) put in the Ark.

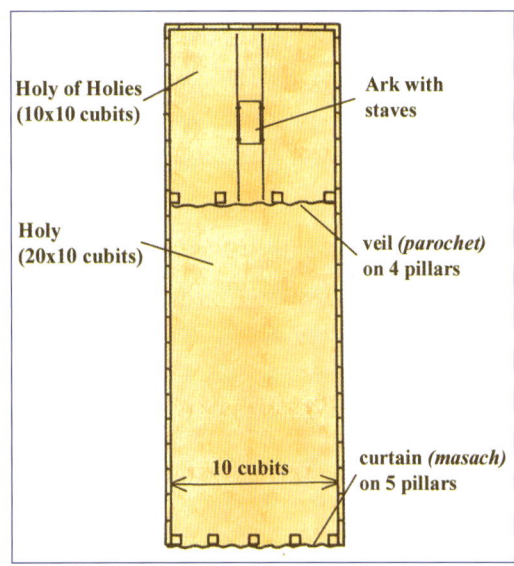

Above: Plan of the Tabernacle.

Below: Reconstruction of the Ark of the Covenant.

275

Chapter Six: The Location of the Temple

The Holy of Holies in Solomon's Temple.

In the First and Second Temples, the eastern slope would have served as a ramp for the High Priest to ascend once a year on Yom Kippur to the Holy of Holies (see illustration, following page). This would conform to the record of the vision the prophet Isaiah had in chapter 6, where in verse 1 he saw *"the Lord sitting upon a throne, high and lifted up."* In which part of the Temple would the Lord have been sitting in this vision? We are told in Exodus 25:22 that the Lord said to Moses: *"I will commune with thee from above the mercy*

Chapter Six: The Location of the Temple

seat, from between the two cherubims which are upon the ark of the testimony." As the Ark was located in the Holy of Holies, that must have been the place where Isaiah saw the Lord, in the highest place in the Temple. This record of Isaiah's vision would agree with our location of the Holy of Holies built on the Rock, the highest point of Mount Moriah.

Later, Herod created a six-cubit-high foundation for his Temple (*Middot* 4.6), which almost completely buried the rock. Only the very top of the Rock remained visible inside the Holy of Holies. Instead of the ramp inside the Temple, the level of the Temple floor was reached by a staircase of twelve steps outside the Temple, in front of the Porch (see illustration, below). According to *Yoma* 5.2, the new floor was a little lower than the top of the Rock:

> *After the Ark was taken away a stone remained there from the time of the early Prophets, and it was called Shetiyah. It was higher than the ground by three finger-breadths. On this he used to put [the fire-pan].*

We believe that during the Second Temple period, the High Priest on Yom Kippur placed his censer or fire-pan in this depression, which was the same place where the Ark of the Covenant stood during the First Temple period.

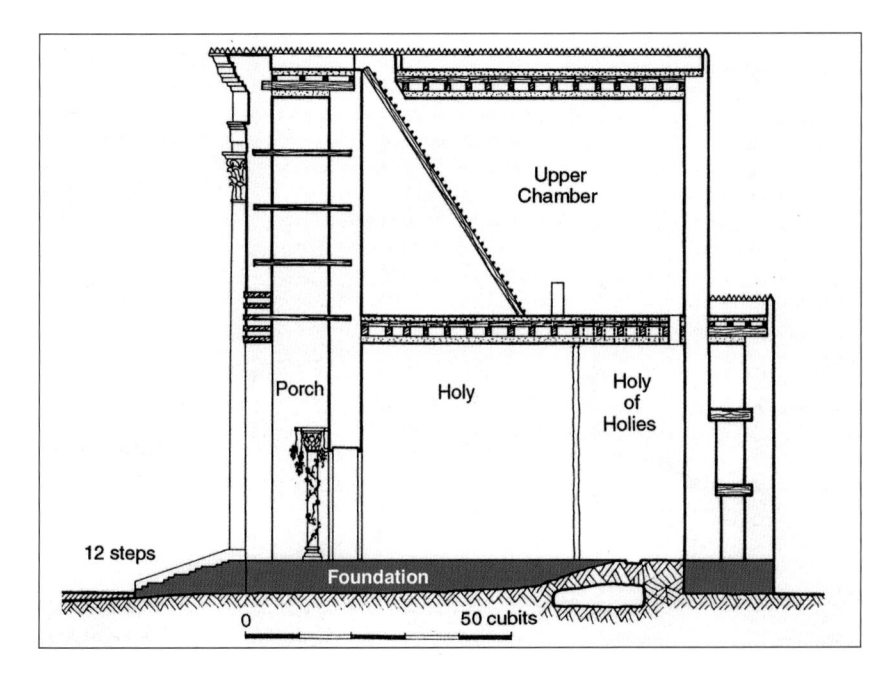

Section through Herod's Temple.

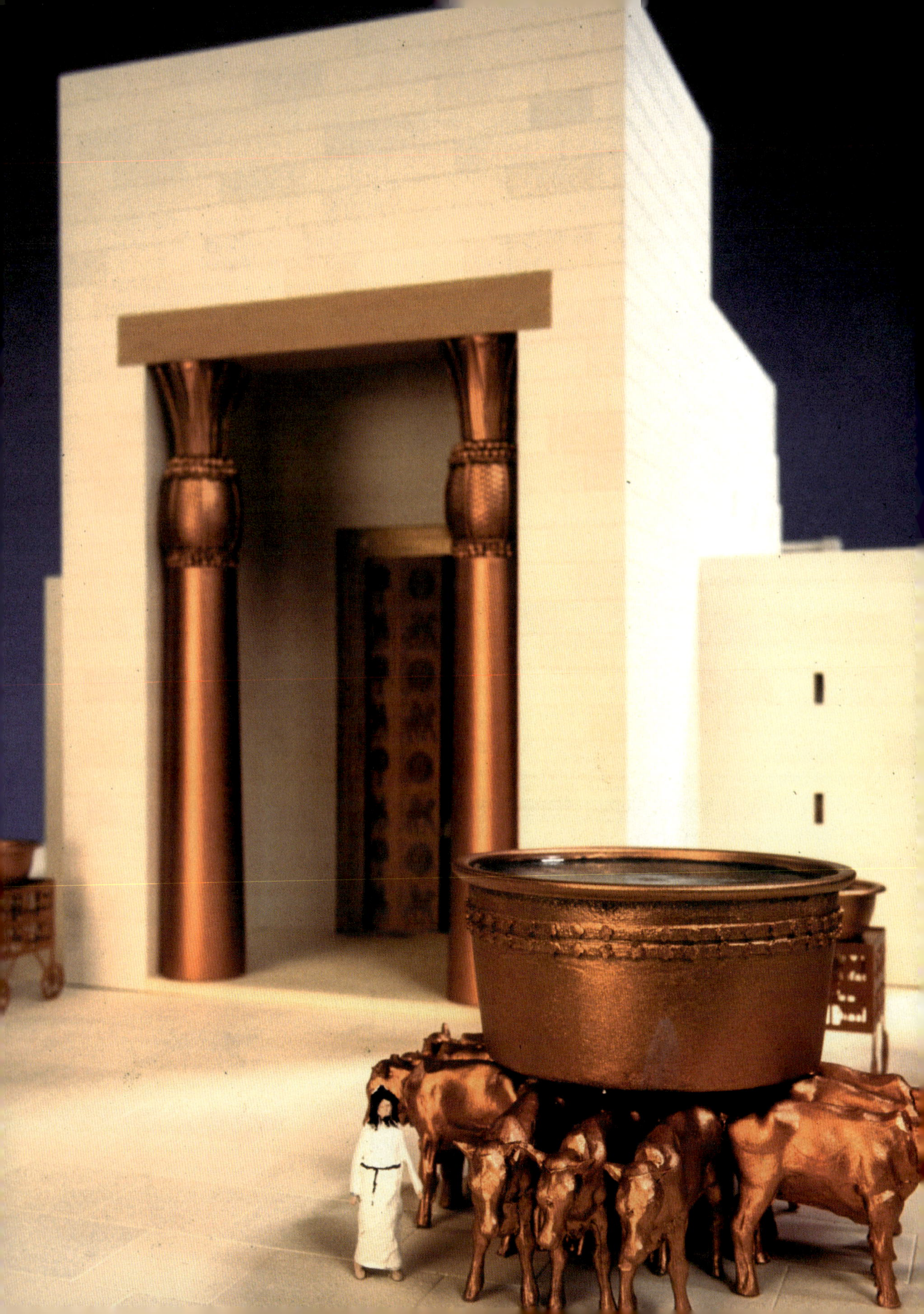

Opposite page: Model of the First Temple, showing the Temple façade and the so-called Sea of Solomon in the foreground. (photo: Philip Evans)

Below: Reconstruction of the Ark of the Covenant. (photo: Vic Roberts)

Chapter Seven
Reconstructing the First Temple

INTRODUCTION

The many reconstruction drawings which have been made of Solomon's Temple are usually based on the artist's personal interpretation of the biblical text. Some designs are more fanciful than others and often use contemporary architectural styles for the decoration of the building.[1]

The reconstructions we will attempt here are the first based on archaeological evidence. We believe that we have found the negative impressions of the walls of the Holy of Holies of Solomon's Temple and also the emplacement of the Ark of the Covenant. These two discoveries could make an accurate reconstruction possible.

The problem with making reconstruction drawings of Solomon's Temple, for researchers who knew no Hebrew, is twofold: first of all, the English text is not always an accurate translation of the original Hebrew, and secondly, the two descriptions of Solomon's Temple in the Hebrew Bible—the one in the First Book of Kings and the second in the Second Book of Chronicles—do not agree with each other. We will deal first with the latter problem and will examine the Hebrew text where necessary during the account of our reconstructions.

According to the Hebrew Bible, the Books of Kings are considered part of the pre-exilic historical books called "The Early Prophets." These Books of Kings are thought to have been written by the prophet Jeremiah. The Books of Chronicles are part of a post-exilic work that includes also the Books of Ezra and Nehemiah. This is based on a similarity of style in these books and also on the fact that

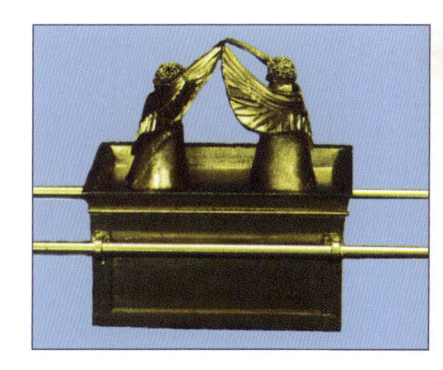

279

Chapter Seven: Reconstructing the First Temple

the last verses in Chronicles are identical to the first verses in the Book of Ezra.²

It is therefore our premise that in the older First Book of Kings we have a description of the Temple as it was indeed built during the reign of King Solomon, while the Temple described in the Second Book of Chronicles was probably that which was extensively reconstructed at a later date, probably during the reign of King Hezekiah.

This two-Temple theory is not illogical. Hardly any building survives in its original state for four hundred years, even today. One possible cause for structural damage to the Temple building is a major earthquake which, according to Isaiah 6, happened in the last year of King Uzziah's reign (approximately 736 B.C.). It appears that the main building was damaged and that the side buildings had collapsed. Again, in 2 Chronicles 2:21–24 we read that King Ahaz took away a portion of the Temple, cut in pieces the vessels and shut the doors.

The evidence of these records leads to our suggestion that two different Temple buildings are described in the books of Kings and Chronicles, although the main inner core may have survived. This will become clear when we look at the history of the First Temple.

SOLOMON'S TEMPLE IN THE BOOK OF KINGS

The main description of Solomon's Temple is found in the Book of Kings. Large amounts of stone and wood were necessary for its construction. Limestone is freely available in the Jerusalem mountains, but large timbers had to be imported from Lebanon. King Solomon therefore enlisted the help of Hiram, King of Tyre. Josephus refers to the correspondence between the two kings, letters that in

Above: The traditional tomb of King Hiram at Tyre. (photo École Biblique et Archéologique Française, Jerusalem)

Below: Inscription on a bronze bowl at Limassol in Cyprus: "merchant of Carthago, servant of Hiram, king of the Sidonians."

CHAPTER SEVEN: RECONSTRUCTING THE FIRST TEMPLE

Cedars of Lebanon by James Harding, 19th century.

his time were apparently still preserved in the archives of Tyre *(Ant. 8.50–55)*.

According to Josephus, King Hiram was glad to have received a letter from King Solomon, to which he replied,

> *King Eiromos [Hiram] to King Solomon. It is proper to praise God for having given to you, who are a wise man endowed with every virtue, your father's royal power. As for me, I am very glad of this and I will assist you in all the things mentioned in your letter. I will have my men cut down many great cedars and cypresses and send them down to the sea, and will order my servants to put together a raft and sail and deliver them at whatever place in your country you may choose, and then your men shall carry them to Jerusalem. And take care, on your part, to furnish us in return for them with grain, of which we are in need because we live on an island (or peninsula).*

To arrive at a satisfactory reconstruction we need to read the biblical record accurately. Below is the description of Solomon's Temple as given in the King James Version of the Hebrew Bible, beginning with 1 Kings 6:1. To clarify the terms used for the architectural components of the sanctuary, we have given their Hebrew equivalent in parentheses.

281

Chapter Seven: Reconstructing the First Temple

THE FIRST BOOK OF KINGS — CHAPTER 6

1 And it came to pass in the four hundred and eightieth year after the children of Israel were come out of the land of Egypt, in the fourth year of Solomon's reign over Israel, in the month Zif, which is the second month, that he began to build the house *(bayit)* of the LORD.

2 And the house *(bayit)* which king Solomon built for the LORD, the length thereof was threescore cubits, and the breadth thereof twenty cubits, and the height thereof thirty cubits.

3 And the porch *(ulam)* before the Temple *(heikhal)* of the house *(bayit)*, twenty cubits was the length thereof, according to the breadth of the house *(bayit)*; and ten cubits was the breadth thereof before the house *(bayit)*.

4 And for the house *(bayit)* he made windows of narrow lights.

5 And against the wall of the house *(bayit)* he built chambers (the *yatsia͑*) round about, against the walls of the house *(bayit)* round about, both of the Temple *(heikhal)* and of the oracle *(debir)*: and he made chambers *(tsela͑ot)* round about:

6 The nethermost chamber *(tsela͑)* was five cubits broad, and the middle was six cubits broad, and the third was seven cubits broad: for without in the wall of the house *(bayit)* he made narrowed rests round about, that the beams should not be fastened in the walls of the house *(bayit)*.

7 And the house *(bayit)*, when it was in building, was built of stone made ready before it was brought thither: so that there was neither hammer nor axe nor any tool of iron heard in the house *(bayit)*, while it was in building.

8 The door for the middle chamber *(tsela͑)* was in the right side of the house *(bayit)*: and they went up with winding stairs *(lulim)* into the middle, and out of the middle into the third.

9 So he built the house *(bayit)*, and finished it; and covered the house *(bayit)* with beams *(gebim)* and boards *(sederot)* of cedar.

10 And then he built chambers (the *yatsia͑*) against all the house *(bayit)*, five cubits high: and they rested on the house *(bayit)* with timber of cedar.

11 And the word of the LORD came to Solomon, saying,

12 Concerning this house *(bayit)* which thou art in building, if thou wilt walk in my statutes, and execute my judgments, and keep all my commandments to walk in them; then will I perform my word with thee, which I spake unto David thy father:

13 And I will dwell among the children of Israel, and will not forsake my people Israel.

14 So Solomon built the house *(bayit)*, and finished it.

15 And he built the walls of the house *(bayit)* within with boards *(tsela͑ot)* of cedar, both the floor of the house *(bayit)*, and the walls of the ceiling (Heb.: from the *karkah* [ground] of the *bayit* up to the walls of the ceiling): and he covered them on the inside with wood, and covered the floor *(karkah)* of the house *(bayit)* with planks *(tsela͑ot)* of fir.

16 And he built twenty cubits on the sides of the house *(bayit)*, both the floor and the walls (Heb.: from the *karkah* up to the walls) with boards *(tsela͑ot)* of cedar: he even built them for it within, even for the oracle *(debir)*, even for the most holy place *(kodesh hakodashim)*.

Chapter Seven: Reconstructing the First Temple

17 And the house *(bayit)*, that is, the Temple *(heikhal)* before it, was forty cubits long.

18 And the cedar of the house *(bayit)* within was carved with knops and open flowers: all was cedar; there was no stone seen.

19 And the oracle *(debir)* he prepared in the house *(bayit)* within, to set there the ark of the covenant of the LORD.

20 And the oracle *(debir)* in the forepart was twenty cubits in length, and twenty cubits in breadth, and twenty cubits in the height thereof: and he overlaid it with pure gold; and so covered the altar which was of cedar.

21 So Solomon overlaid the house *(bayit)* within with pure gold: and he made a partition by the chains of gold before the oracle; and he overlaid it with gold.

22 And the whole house *(bayit)* he overlaid with gold, until he had finished all the house *(bayit)*: also the whole altar that was by the oracle he overlaid with gold.

23 And within the oracle *(debir)* he made two cherubim of olive tree, each ten cubits high.

24 And five cubits was the one wing of the cherub, and five cubits the other wing of the cherub: from the uttermost part of the one wing unto the uttermost part of the other were ten cubits.

25 And the other cherub was ten cubits: both the cherubim were of one measure and one size.

26 The height of the one cherub was ten cubits, and so was it of the other cherub.

27 And he set the cherubim within the inner house *(bayit)*: and they stretched forth the wings of the cherubim, so that the wing of the one touched the one wall, and the wing of the other cherub touched the other wall; and their wings touched one another in the midst of the house *(bayit)*.

28 And he overlaid the cherubim with gold.

29 And he carved all the walls of the house *(bayit)* round about with carved figures of cherubim and palm trees and open flowers, within and without.

30 And the floor *(karkah)* of the house *(bayit)* he overlaid with gold, within and without.

31 And for the entering of the oracle *(debir)* he made doors of olive tree: the lintel and side posts were a fifth part of the wall.

32 The two doors also were of olive tree; and he carved upon them carvings of cherubim and palm trees and open flowers, and overlaid them with gold, and spread gold upon the cherubim, and upon the palm trees.

33 So also made he for the door of the Temple *(heikhal)* posts of olive tree, a fourth part of the wall.

34 And the two doors were of fir tree: the two leaves of the one door were folding, and the two leaves of the other door were folding.

35 And he carved thereon cherubim and palm trees and open flowers: and covered them with gold fitted upon the carved work.

36 And he built the inner court with three rows of hewed stone, and a row of cedar beams.

37 In the fourth year was the foundation of the house *(bayit)* of the LORD laid, in the month Zif:

38 And in the eleventh year, in the month Bul, which is the eighth month, was the house *(bayit)* finished throughout all the parts thereof, and according to all the fashion of it. So was he seven years in building it.

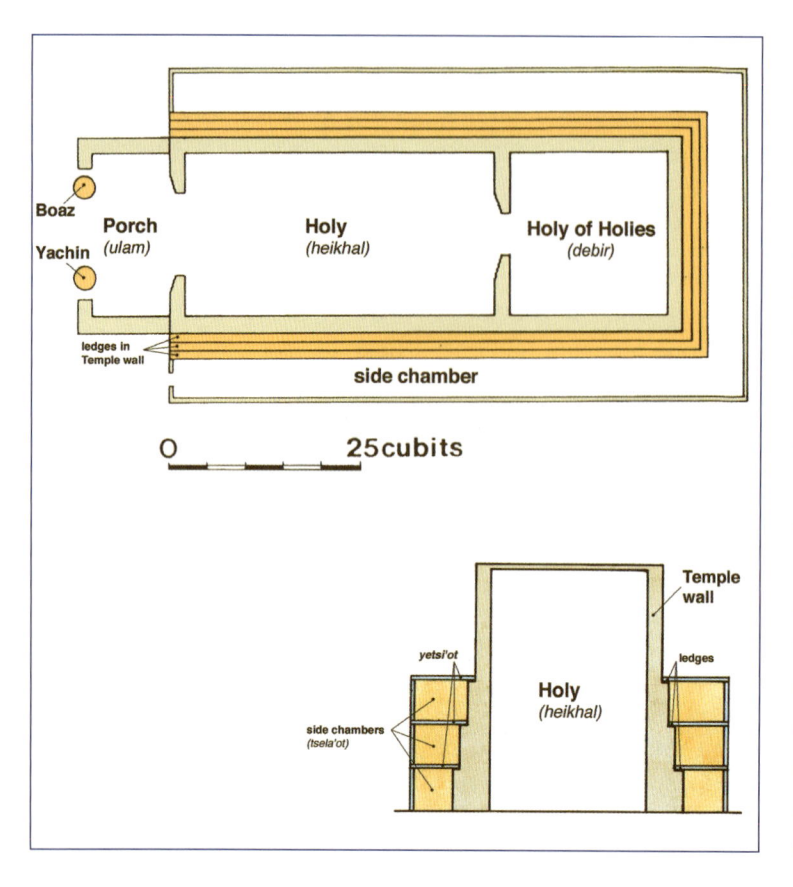

Chapter Seven: Reconstructing the First Temple

Plan and E–W section of Solomon's Temple.

From this description, it is obvious that the whole building was called "The House *(bayit)* of the LORD." The word "Temple" *(heikhal)* is reserved for the Holy alone—although in the English language the term "Temple" refers to the whole building. This is perhaps derived from verse 17 where the two terms appear to be synonymous.

Approaching the front of the building, which faced more or less east toward the highest peak of the Mount of Olives, one would first encounter the *ulam,* or Porch, then the *heikhal,* which is the first chamber of the *bayit,* also called the Holy, and lastly the inner chamber, which is referred to as the *debir,* or Holy of Holies.

Chapter 6 of the First Book of Kings opens with the historical setting of the commencement of building Solomon's Temple, which the records say took place 480 years after the Exodus from Egypt. Most biblical scholars agree that Solomon began to rule in about 971 B.C. and began to build the Temple in his fourth year, 967 B.C. This would place the Exodus in 1447 B.C. and the Conquest at the end of the fifteenth century B.C., all of which is in harmony with the biblical chronology.[3]

The general dimensions of the *bayit* and the *ulam* are given in verses 2 and 3. These dimensions refer to the inner measurements, while the thickness of walls and other architectural elements, such as doors and partitions, are not given. The length of 60 cubits (103 feet 2 inches or 31.50 m) excludes that of the *ulam,* which is 10 cubits (17 feet 2 inches or 5.25 m) from east to west. The total inner dimensions, including the *ulam,* were 70 cubits (120 feet 7 inches or 36.75 m) long, 20 cubits (34 feet 5 inches or 10.50 m) wide and 30 cubits (51 feet 7 inches or 15.75 m) high.

Verse 4 tells us that there were "windows of narrow lights" *(halonei*

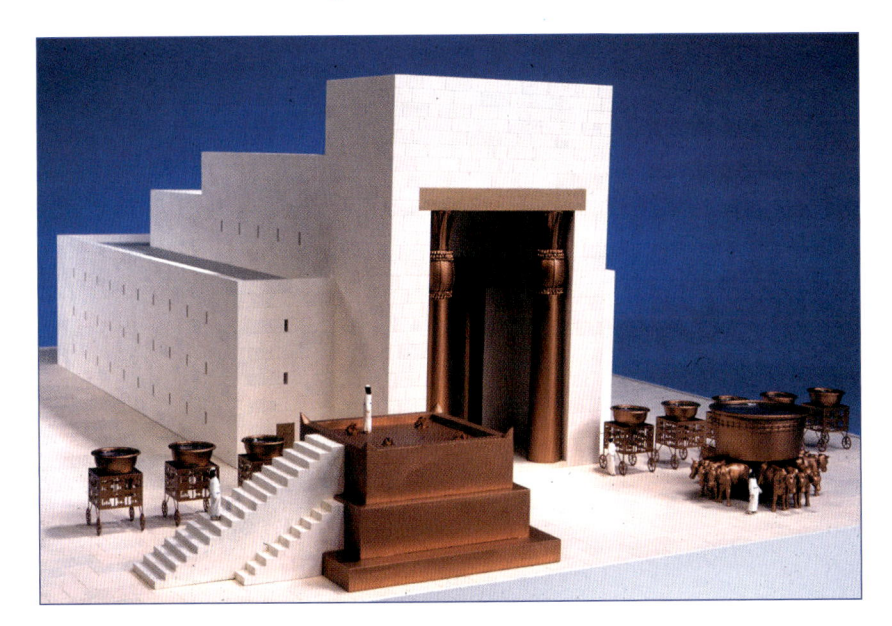

CHAPTER SEVEN: RECONSTRUCTING THE FIRST TEMPLE

Model of Solomon's Temple—an overall view from the east. (photo: Philip Evans)

shequfim 'atumim) in the building. These openings were most likely restricted to the *heikhal,* where the priests needed light during their daily administrations. That the *debir* had no windows may be deduced from 1 Kings 8:12, which informs us that *"The Lord said that he would dwell in the thick darkness."* The Hebrew for window *(halon)* means an aperture, *shequfim* indicates that light could penetrate through the windows, while *'atumim* actually means that they could be closed. Usually, this is interpreted as windows which are narrow on the outside, to let the light in and keep the heat out, and broad on the inside, so as to maximize the amount of light that can enter the building. Windows of this type are well known in warmer climates. It is also possible that these windows could be closed somehow, or that they had some kind of grille to let light in and keep animals such as rodents and birds out.

The *bayit* was surrounded by a wooden, three-story-high structure. The general name for this wooden encasement is the *yatsia^c*, which only occurs in the singular, and is made up of three *tsela^cot*. This latter term is derived from the Hebrew for ribs, while

Reconstruction drawing of Solomon's Temple.

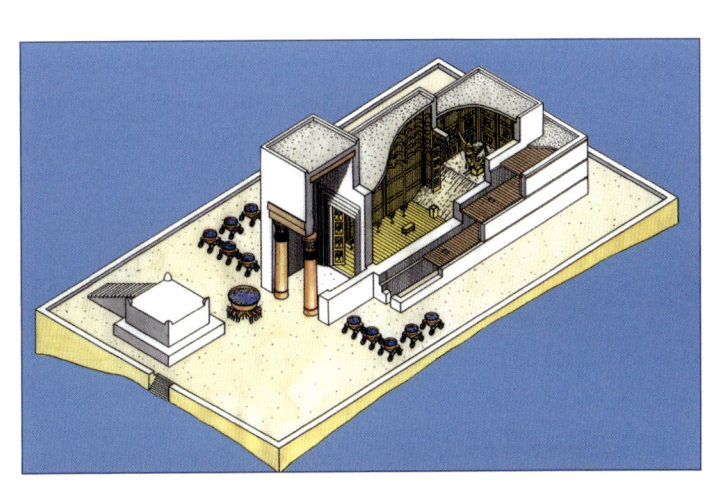

Chapter Seven: Reconstructing the First Temple

Opposite page: Interior view of the Holy in Solomon's Temple, looking east. (photo: Philip Evans)

Above: View of the three stories of the yatsi'a, the trapdoors (lulim) and the ladders connecting the different floors in the model of Solomon's Temple. (photo: Philip Evans)

Below: The so-called Solomon's Quarries underneath the Damascus Gate of the Old City. Tradition has it that this is where Solomon extracted the stones for the Temple.

yatsia^c means spreading out and is closely related to *yatsua^c*, which means a bed. The whole wooden construction therefore extended from the *bayit* and was built around it like a ribcage of three layers, each of which was five cubits high.

This structure, made from cedars, was built against the outer wall of the *bayit*, which had one-cubit-wide ledges on which the *tsela^{c}ot* rested. To keep the outer wall of the *yatsia^c* straight, we are told that the width of the bottom story was 5 cubits, the middle one 6 cubits and the one on top, 7 cubits. To prevent this construction from collapsing, a stone wall may have been built on the outside. The entrance at the right-hand side of the building and the three stories were connected by *lulim,* a term usually interpreted as trapdoors rather than winding staircases. Simple ladders would have been used to climb from floor to floor.

According to 1 Kings 6:7, the walls of the *bayit* were built of whole stones *(even shlema)* and no sound of hammer or axe or any other metal tool was heard whilst the *bayit* was built. According to some scholars the *bayit* was built with unhewn stones. However, the word "whole" can also mean "perfect." The fact that no iron tools were heard when the building was erected does not necessarily mean that no iron tools were used to cut the stones. It is more likely that the stones were dressed to perfection in the quarries, using the usual stonecutters' tools. Only after all the stones were beautifully squared were they transported to the building site, with no further need for iron tools. There was time only for assembling the perfect stones. If an imperfect stone reached the construction site, it was probably rejected by the builders. King Herod the Great followed a similar procedure when he built the Second Temple many centuries later.

The roof of the *bayit* was made of cedar wood (verse 10) with cross beams *(gebim)* running from wall to wall and boards *(sederot)* intersecting from beam to beam.

In verse 15, we read that the inner stone walls of the *bayit*, from ground to ceiling, were covered with boards of cedar wood and that the floor was made of planks of fir wood (cypress). According to verse 30, these planks were coated on both sides with gold. One might suggest that the whole of the Temple had a wooden floor. However, the next verse, 16, which describes the *debir,* mentions only the wall boards and no planks for the floor. This would be in harmony with our finding of the emplacement of the Ark of the Covenant, which King

Chapter Seven: Reconstructing the First Temple

Chapter Seven: Reconstructing the First Temple

Solomon had to prepare by cutting a horizontal basin in the rock (see 1 Kgs 6:19, 8:6, 8:21). Only the *heikhal* had a wooden floor. It was made of fir wood, as were the doors leading into this chamber.

The *debir* or *kodesh ha-kodashim* (Holy of Holies) itself is described in verses 19 to 32. It is a cube of 20 cubits, separated from the 30-cubit-high *heikhal* by a wooden partition made entirely of olive wood. There was no stone partition between the *debir* and the *heikhal,* so that the whole house was in essence one long chamber with doors facing east. The stone walls were covered with boards of cedar from the rocky ground up to the ceiling and decorated with cherubim, palm trees and open flowers, just like the rest of the walls and doors. The designs were carved in the cedar wood and then overlaid with gold.

View of the wooden partition in front of the debir. *(photo: Philip Evans)*

The problem with the height of the *debir* and the *heikhal* is the ten-cubit difference between the two. Some have suggested that there was a secret chamber above the *debir,* while others said that it was built on a raised platform with steps leading up to it. Both proposals rest on the belief that the roof of the Temple building was level. However, this need not be so and this form of construction is certainly not mentioned in the sources. Our proposal puts the *debir* over the

CHAPTER SEVEN: RECONSTRUCTING THE FIRST TEMPLE

View of the wooden partition from inside the debir. *(photo: Philip Evans)*

Rock, which is about 5 cubits higher than the area to the east. Given that the *debir* was 20 cubits high, its roof must have stood 25 cubits above the floor level of the *heikhal*. The height of the *heikhal* was 30 cubits, and therefore the roof of the *debir* must have been 5 cubits[4] lower than the roof of the *heikhal* (see illustration, p. 287).

Inside the *debir* stood the two large cherubim (singular *cherub*, Heb. plural *cherubim*) made of olive wood and covered with gold. They were ten cubits high with a wingspan of ten cubits, and would thus touch the walls with their outer wing tips and one another's inner wing tips. We are not told what they looked like, only that they had wings. Josephus was not willing to speculate on the subject, for he wrote in *Antiquities* 8.73, *"As for the cherubim themselves, no one can say or imagine what they looked like."*

The two cherubim were placed over the Ark of the Covenant, undoubtedly the holiest furnishing ever made, if it even can be referred to as such. It consisted of a rectangular chest made of *shittim* (or acacia) wood and was covered with gold (see illustration, right). The word Ark, *aron* in Hebrew, simply means a chest and has been translated as "coffin'" in Genesis 50:26. God had commanded Moses to make the Ark of the Covenant (Ex 25:10–22) and inside it Moses placed the two tablets of the law. Later Aaron's rod that budded was placed in it (Num 17:10) together with the golden pot that held the manna (Ex 16:33; Hebrews 9:4).

Above: The acacia or shittah *tree is one of the most common species found in Sinai.*

Below: A reconstruction of the Ark of the Covenant.

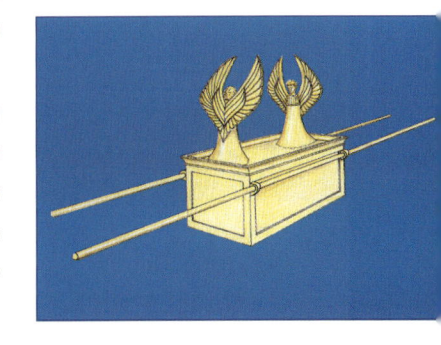

Chapter Seven: Reconstructing the First Temple

Phoenician remains of an ivory carving of winged sphinxes with human faces, reminiscent of cherubim. (British Museum)

The two cherubim standing over the Ark of the Covenant in the Holy of Holies of Solomon's Temple. (photo: Philip Evans)

> **CHERUBIM**
>
> The prophet Ezekiel, in his vision of the cherubim in chapters 1 and 10, described composite creatures that had four wings and four faces: namely those of a man, a lion, an ox and an eagle. Many ancient ivories have been found in Israel, Egypt, Phoenicia and Mesopotamia, portraying composite figures having a human head, a body (usually of a lion, but sometimes of an ox) and eagles' wings. Scholars usually refer to these representations as cherubim. As these are the only prototypes dating from about the time of the building of Solomon's Temple, we have applied elements of these figures in our portrayal of the large cherubim in the debir. We did not fill in the outlines as we can only guess their exact appearance. Cherubim are first mentioned in the Book of Genesis 3:24, where it says that "he placed at the east of the garden of Eden cherubim." It is interesting to note that the verb "placed" (vayisken) in the Hebrew is closely related to the word for tabernacle (mishkan). Is it possible that here we encounter the very first tabernacle, to which Abel and Cain brought their sacrifices? Perhaps it was the cherubim, who as divine representatives either accepted or rejected certain offerings and protected the way to the tree of life.
>
> The mishkan in the wilderness was built to house the Ark of the Covenant, which also had cherubim on the kaporet, or mercy seat. We see then that cherubim are always present in biblical sanctuaries. Several texts, such as Psalm 80:2, 1 Samuel 4:4, 2 Samuel 6.2, 2 Kings 19:15 and Isaiah 37:16, indicate that cherubim are the dwelling place of God. The Hebrew cherub (kerub) may be a composite word made up of ke and rub or rob, where ke means "as," and rob a "multitude." This would fit with Isaiah 66:1–2:
>
> "Thus saith the LORD, The heaven is my throne, and the earth is my footstool: where is the house that ye build unto me? and where is the place of my rest? For all those things hath mine hand made, and all those things have been, saith the LORD: but to this man will I look, even to him that is poor and of a contrite spirit, and trembleth at my word."
>
> Thus God makes His dwelling with people who fear His name, and the cherubim may be representative of those people.

The mercy seat was a kind of lid that covered the top of the chest. Made of pure gold, it was held in place by a golden ridge or crown. Two cherubim overshadowed the mercy seat with their wings. The cherubim were beaten out of the same piece of pure gold as the mercy seat.

The Ark was built in Sinai by *Bezaleel ben Uri*, whose name appropriately means, "In the Shadow of *El* (God), the Son of my Light." After a long journey, the Ark was eventually placed inside the *debir,* the Holy of Holies of Solomon's Temple.

Chapter Seven: Reconstructing the First Temple

The inner walls of the sanctuary were covered with planks of cedar wood on which were carved images of cherubim, palm trees and rosettes. The carved planks were then covered with gold leaf.

Solomon's Temple had two sets of doors. The first set, made of fir wood, opened into the *heikhal*. Each door had two leaves and was decorated with carved figures of cherubim, palm trees and rosettes, overlaid with gold leaf.

In verse 33, we are told that the door frame was made of olive wood, of a fourth part. This latter phrase is difficult to understand. Does it mean that the door frame took up a fourth part of the width of the wall, which would make the door very small, or do we have here a description of a recessed door frame made of four stepped frames? This is the opinion of some scholars[5] and we have incorporated this idea into our reconstruction. The door into the *debir* had five frames. The whole partition between the *heikhal* and the *debir* was made of olive wood, including the carved doors. There was no veil in Solomon's Temple; only the tabernacle and Herod's Temple contained veils.

In the following chapter, 1 Kings 7, we read about the construction of the two pillars of bronze, which were 18 cubits (31 feet or 9.45 m) high and had elaborate double capitals. The first capital, 5 cubits high, was apparently round in shape and surrounded by nets in which pomegranates were set. Above, another capital, 4 cubits high, had

Proposal for the decoration of the inner walls of Solomon's Temple (east-west section).

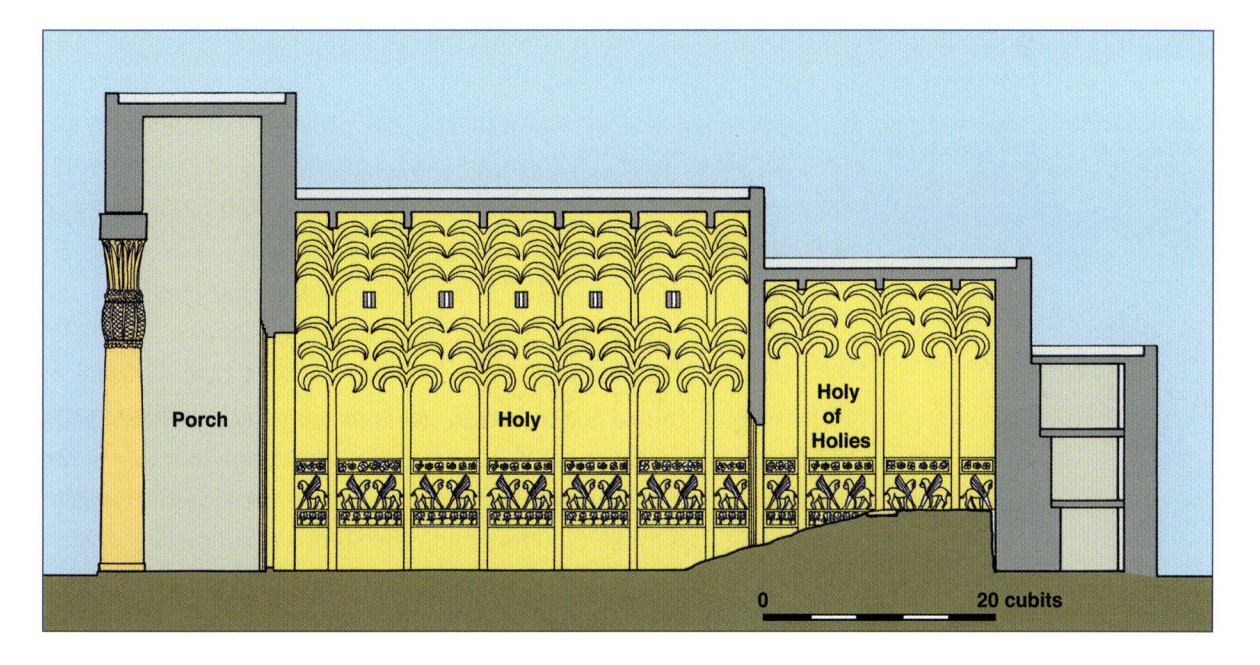

Chapter Seven: Reconstructing the First Temple

View of Solomon's Temple with the two pillars, Yachin and Boaz. (photo: Philip Evans)

the appearance of a lily. The names of the pillars are *Yachin* ("He will establish") and *Boaz* ("in strength"), indicating that God himself is the one who will establish the Temple, just as he indicated to David in 2 Samuel 7:25:

> And now, O LORD God, the word that thou hast spoken concerning thy servant, and concerning his house, establish it for ever, and do as thou hast said.

The height of these columns was 18 cubits, although in 2 Chronicles 3:15 the height is given as 35 cubits. Later we will see that this is not a mistake, but a later development in the construction of the Temple. We are told that these columns and other bronze items were cast in clay ground in the Jordan Valley (1 Kgs 7:46) under the supervision of a certain Hiram, who belonged to the tribe of Naphtali.

CHAPTER SEVEN: RECONSTRUCTING THE FIRST TEMPLE

Usually these pillars are thought to have been free-standing, but I have always understood, as did Fritz[6], that they supported the lintel of the *ulam.* The height of this porch is not given. However, it must have been at least 30 cubits high, as the columns with the capitals already reached 27 cubits. A large lintel resting on the capitals must minimally have been one cubit high and therefore the roof of the porch could have been level with the roof of the *heikhal.* From an architectural point of view, however, it would be more pleasing for the porch to be a little higher than the main building, more so since the roof of the *kodesh hakodashim* was low.

This sanctuary was set in a courtyard within walls constructed of successive layers of three courses of hewn stone and beams of cedar wood. Remains of such constructions have been found at Megiddo[7] and Tel Dan[8]. Recesses in the stones of the platform at Dan show that these beams were about 4 inches (10 cm) high and 8 inches (20 cm) wide. These wooden beams probably served to stabilize the stone coursing and to keep the courses horizontal.

Inside the Temple courtyard stood a great bronze basin, known, because of its size, as "the sea." It rested on the hind quarters of twelve bronze oxen. Ten smaller basins, in two groups of five, were set on elaborate wheeled stands.

Top: Side wall of the Israelite sanctuary at Tel Dan, showing reconstructed beams which (at center left) were placed in the original grooves. The right-hand side is almost completely reconstructed.

Above: The reconstructed Solomonic gateway at Megiddo. Remains of grooves for wooden beams were found in the original gate piers (on the right).

CHAPTER SEVEN: RECONSTRUCTING THE FIRST TEMPLE

View of Solomon's Temple, showing the large "sea" and the smaller wheeled lavers. (photo: Philip Evans)

HISTORY OF THE FIRST TEMPLE

In accordance with the biblical injunction, the Temple in Jerusalem eventually became the sole place for sacrifices and important meetings. In the Book of Deuteronomy there are nineteen references to this particular place of which Moses was told in advance. Deuteronomy 12:5 is the first of these, directing the Israelites exclusively *"unto the place which the LORD your God shall choose out of all your tribes to put his name there, even unto his habitation shall ye seek, and thither thou shalt come."*

Lithograph of ancient Shechem by David Roberts, 19th century.

However, there were also high places in the Land during the time of the Judges which culminated in the period of the monarchy. Shechem, because of its association with the patriarchs, was the place where the children of Israel held their first religious meeting and built an altar on Mount Ebal (Deut 27:5–7; Josh 9.30–31). Solomon's Temple, destined to be the sole center of worship in Israel, took seven years to build and

CHAPTER SEVEN: RECONSTRUCTING THE FIRST TEMPLE

was completed in the eleventh year of Solomon's reign. Prevailing opinion has it that this edifice continued to exist until destroyed by the Babylonians in 586 B.C., although changes were effected by some of the succeeding kings. The first change took place during the reign of Rehoboam, Solomon's successor.

Rehoboam

Upon the death of Solomon, the monarchy was divided between Rehoboam and Jeroboam. Soon afterward, in Rehoboam's fifth year (c. 925 B.C.),[9] Shishak, king of Egypt, sacked the Temple and removed all its treasures (1 Kgs 14:25–28; 2 Chr 12:9), including those collected by David (1 Kgs 7:51) and probably all the gold that was used in the construction of the Temple. With the foundation of Solomon's Temple having been laid in about 967 B.C., it is sad to realize that Solomon's Temple lasted unchanged for a mere forty-two years.

In the meantime, Jeroboam, king of Israel, made two sanctuaries, one in Bethel and one in Dan (1 Kgs 12:28–33; 2 Chr 11:14–15). No remains have been found in Bethel, which may be identified with modern el-Bireh,[10] but the cult site in Dan has been discovered by Biran (1982). This site has a square Temple platform, referred to earlier, with an altar in front of it. Chambers, in which ritual functions were performed, surround the courtyard of this high place. The layout

Fragment of Stele of Shishak, king of Egypt, from Megiddo.

Remains of a cult precinct at Tel Dan with altar in center, 9th to 8th centuries B.C. (NEAEHL)

295

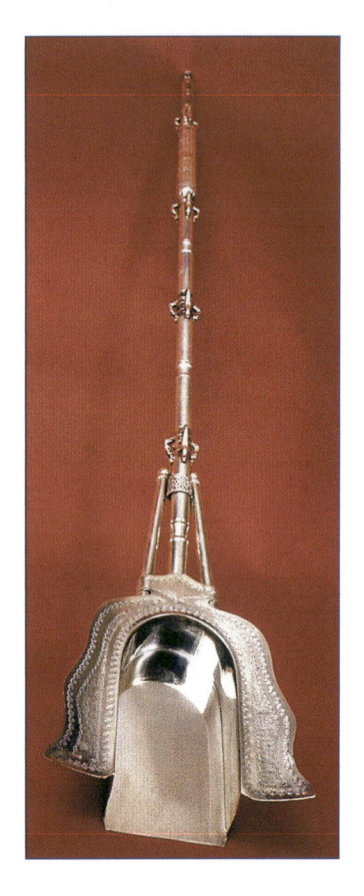

Chapter Seven: Reconstructing the First Temple

of this complex may have been based on that of Solomon's Temple, which was also located inside a courtyard with an altar in front of it. The temple at Dan was built on a 62-foot (19 m), that is, 36 Royal Cubits or 6 reeds, square platform. As stated above (Chap. 2.4.1), it would have been logical for Jeroboam to have built a new Temple complex reminiscent of Solomon's design.

Asa

During the reign of Asa, king of Judah (c. 908–868 B.C.), the Temple treasures were augmented with silver, gold and other vessels that he and his father Abijah (or Abijam in 1 Kgs 15) had collected (2 Chr 15:18). These were soon to be dissipated by the same Asa to buy the services of Ben-hadad, king of Syria, to help him fight against Baasha, king of Israel (2 Chr 16:20). Such passages hint that the Temple treasures were used to finance matters of state.

Jehoshaphat

Asa's son Jehoshaphat (2 Chr 17), who ruled from c. 868 to 847 B.C., was a God-fearing king, who received many gifts from the people of Judah and the surrounding nations. Some of the more valuable gifts may have been stored in the Temple. Jehoshaphat was also a reformer who sent out eight Levites and two priests to teach the people the ways of the Lord. To do so they carried with them *"the book of the law of Yahweh."* This must surely have been the Deuteronomy scroll that was kept beside the Ark of the Covenant inside the Holy of Holies. After a period of teaching, this scroll would have been returned to its place inside the Holy of Holies. There it was later found by Hilkiah the High Priest, during the reign of Josiah (2 Kgs 23:8).

Jehoshaphat was a wealthy king (2 Chr 18:1) who had allied himself to Ahab, king of Israel, by the marriage of his son Jehoram to Ahab's daughter (2 Chr 21:6). After having joined Ahab in battle against the king of Aram and almost lost his life, a prophet told him that Yahweh was not pleased with him. That apparently prompted Jehoshaphat to renew his program of reform, and he appointed judges in every city. They were to judge *"in the fear of Yahweh, faithfully, and with a perfect heart"* (2 Chr 19:9). We are not told that Jehoshaphat added a new court to the existing Temple court, but that appears to have been the case. In the face of enmity by the Moabites and Ammonites, he prayed to God and lamented about his predicament standing before

Reconstructions of silver and gold vessels used in the Temple. (The Temple Institute, Jerusalem)

Above: A silver shovel for removing ashes from the Altar.

Below: A gold mizrak, one of the sacred vessels used in the Temple service to spill the sacrificial blood on the corner of the Altar.

CHAPTER SEVEN: RECONSTRUCTING THE FIRST TEMPLE

the congregation of Judah and Jerusalem *"in the house of Yahweh, before the new court."*

Apparently the old court which Solomon had built had become too small to accommodate the many pilgrims coming to Jerusalem and Jehoshaphat may have added this new court to the existing Temple complex. This would be in harmony with the observation made by Josephus, when he wrote in *War* 5, *"In course of ages, however, through the constant additions of the people to the embankment, the hill-top by this process of levelling up was widened."* The size and location of this additional court is not clear from the text.

Joash

The following sixteen years in Judah saw successive wicked kings—Jehoram, Ahaziah and Athaliah. The sons of Athaliah broke into the Temple and bestowed the looted treasures on the worship of Baal. Even so, the Temple must have functioned with a certain amount of independence, because Joash, the youngest son of Ahaziah, had been hidden in the Temple for six years from the time of birth (2 Chr 22:12).

Enthronement of Joash, 19th century engraving.

Chapter Seven: Reconstructing the First Temple

It is interesting to note that when King Joash (c. 840–801 B.C.) was about to be anointed king, Jehoiada the priest played a major role in the politics of the Kingdom of Judah. According to 2 Kings 11:17, he must have been the high priest:

> *And Jehoiada made a covenant between the LORD and the king and the people that they should be the LORD's people; between the king also and the people.*

Jehoiada divided the Levites into three groups of guards, one of which stood at *"the gate of the foundation."* In 2 Kings 11 (verses 6,19), two gates are mentioned: the Gate of Sur and the gate behind the guards (or runners). This latter gate may have been the Gate of the Guards that led to the king's palace, mentioned later in this chapter. However, this verse 6 is omitted in the Jerusalem Bible, which claims that it is a corrupt verse. The last letter of the Hebrew word *Sur*—*resh*—looks similar to *dalet*, the last letter of the Hebrew for "foundation" *(yesod)* and the beginning of both words are the same Hebrew letters. If a small scribal error occurred, the Gate of Sur and the Gate of the Foundation are one and the same.

We do not know the location of the "Gate of the Foundation." However, its name may hint at the massive work needed to restore the Temple to its original state: 2 Chronicles 24:27 speaks of the great burden laid upon the sons of Jehoiada concerning the *foundation* of the house of Yahweh. The extent of the program of repair (Hebrew: renewal) of the house of the Lord (2 Chr 24:4) is an indication of the amount of neglect and damage the building had suffered in the preceding years. This is supported by the parallel record in 2 Kings 12:5, where we are told that the breaches of the house had to be repaired. These were not just a few cracks to be filled; in the Hebrew the singular—*bedek,* damage—is used, which probably points to a major fissure that may have developed during the ongoing neglect of the building.

During his anointment, King Joash himself stood *"at his pillar"* (2 Chr 23:13), indicating that either a special place was designated next to one of the two pillars, Yachin or Boaz, or that this pillar was a new feature in the Temple not mentioned before. As Yachin means "he will establish," it could have been the pillar where Joash stood when he was *established* king of Judah.

It must have taken several years to restore the Temple, as money

Chapter Seven: Reconstructing the First Temple

Above: A Tyrian silver, two-drachma coin which was the equivalent of a half-shekel, paid as tribute for the Temple.

Left: Joash proclaiming the repairs of the Temple in Jerusalem, 19th century engraving.

was collected from all Israel. The whole nation, not only Judah, was involved *"to repair* (Hebrew, "to strengthen") *the house of Yahweh from year to year"* (2 Chr 24:5). A chest was put outside the gate of the Temple to collect money so that masons and carpenters could be hired *"to repair* (Hebrew, "renew") *the house of Yahweh, and also such as wrought iron and brass to mend the house of Yahweh"* (2 Chr 24:12). Eventually, the house was finished: *"So the workmen wrought, and the work of repairing went forward in their hands, and they set up the house of God in its state, and strengthened it"* (2 Chr 24:13). The Temple must have been restored to its original state and, with the remainder of the money, several gold and silver vessels were made.

When Jehoiada the high priest died, however, Joash forgot his wise counsel and listened to the princes of Judah, and the house of

Chapter Seven: Reconstructing the First Temple

Uzziah struck with leprosy after burning incense upon the altar, 19th century engraving.

Yahweh was once more neglected. Eventually, the King also killed the sons of Jehoiada (2 Chr 24:25).

Amaziah

During the reign of Amaziah (c. 801–773 B.C.), the son of Jotham, the Temple was again plundered, this time by Joash, king of Israel, because the king of Judah had prevented the army of Israel from joining battle against the Edomites (2 Chr 25).

Uzziah

Amaziah's son Uzziah ruled for a long period (c. 787–736 B.C.). Like his grandfather Jotham, he initially prospered when he listened to the advice of a wise man, Zechariah, who *"had understanding in the visions of God"* (2 Chr 26:5). Uzziah strengthened his kingdom and

Chapter Seven: Reconstructing the First Temple

(perhaps after the death of Zechariah) wanted to usurp the right of burning incense on the altar that was in the *heikhal*, a right reserved for the priests only. Azariah, the high priest, opposed Uzziah, who was smitten with leprosy. Both Amos and Isaiah, prophets in the time of Uzziah, mention an earthquake which, according to the prophet Zechariah (14:5), took place in 736 B.C., the year Uzziah died. This earthquake was recorded by Isaiah in Chapter 6, and according to him, the foundations of the thresholds moved. At that time, Isaiah also had a vision of Yahweh of Hosts sitting in the *debir*. The prophecy of Zechariah (14:5) foresaw a latter-day earthquake that will cause the Mount of Olives to split in two.

In 1927 a major earthquake did indeed cause the destruction of many buildings in Jerusalem, including damage to the el-Aqsa Mosque. It has been recorded that this earthquake also caused a crack in the bedrock layers of the Mount of Olives, running east-west, the same direction as implied by Zechariah's prophecy. As we will see later, the earthquake which took place during the reign of Uzziah must have caused considerable damage to the Temple.

The Mount of Olives today, looking southeast.

Jotham

The Temple Mount must have been patched up by the succeeding king, Jotham (c. 756–742 B.C.), who also built the Upper Gate of the house of Yahweh (2 Kgs 15:35; 2 Chr 27:3). This gate was probably built between the court added by Jehoshaphat and the older Temple court. Thus we see continuous building activity on the Temple Mount.

Ahaz

Jotham's son Ahaz (c. 742–726 B.C.) in turn did so much damage to the Temple that after his death, a major refurbishment of the entire Temple Mount was necessary. One of the first things Ahaz did to the Temple is described in 2 Kings 16:8: *"And Ahaz took the silver and gold that was found in the house of the LORD, and in the treasures of the king's house, and sent it for a present to the king of Assyria."* So, all the wealth of the Temple that the previous kings had accumulated was spent by Ahaz to buy the services of Tiglath-pileser III. When Ahaz went to meet him in Damascus, he saw there an altar whose appearance he liked very much and had it replicated to replace the original brass altar which Solomon had made for his Temple. Solomon's altar was moved to the north of the Temple.

Above: Tiglath-pileser III and a vassal king kneeling before him, on relief from the king's palace at Calah. (British Museum)

Below: Conjectural representation of the Sea of Solomon.

This was only one of the many changes made by Ahaz in the Temple:

> *King Ahaz cut off the borders of the bases, and removed the laver from off them; and took down the sea from off the brazen oxen that were under it, and put it upon a pavement of stones. And the covert for the Sabbath that they had built in the house, and the king's entry without, turned he from the house of the LORD for the king of Assyria.* (2 Kgs 16:17–18)

A similar story is told in 2 Chronicles 28:24.

> *Ahaz gathered together the vessels of the house of God, and cut in pieces the vessels of the house of God, and shut up the doors of the house of the LORD, and he made him altars in every corner of Jerusalem.*

CHAPTER SEVEN: RECONSTRUCTING THE FIRST TEMPLE

This "covert" of the 2 Kings verse was probably a covered passageway with a royal entrance in front for use by the king to go to the Temple on the Sabbath. In deference to the king of Assyria, whose vassal he had become, Ahaz had to remove these symbols of royalty. Later on, when we examine the Temple in the time of Hezekiah, we see that Ahaz may have even dismantled the two bronze pillars, Yachin and Boaz, built by King Solomon, in order to pay ransom to the Assyrian king.

Ahaz then closed the doors of the Temple. Much more damage than is actually recorded in the biblical sources must have occurred during the reign of Ahaz, as witnessed by the record of the repair work which his son Hezekiah carried out to make the Temple functional again.

HEZEKIAH'S TEMPLE IN THE BOOK OF CHRONICLES

When Hezekiah (c 725–697 B.C. as sole ruler, and until his death in 686 B.C. with Manasseh as co-regent) began to reign after the death of his father Ahaz, his first act was the re-opening of the Temple doors (2 Chr 29). To do so he first had to repair and strengthen the doors that must have been badly damaged. The priests and Levites then cleared the Temple of all the accumulated filth. The fact that a large number of priests labored a week to cleanse the Temple shows how much rubbish had accumulated, not only in the *heikhal* but also in the *debir*. The rubbish removed by the Levites was dumped in the Kedron Valley. Vessels and furniture that had been dismantled or removed by Ahaz were collected or replaced.

Thus the Temple was rededicated and the services restored. Hezekiah then invited all Israel to come to Jerusalem to keep the feast of Passover. According to 2 Kings 18:4, Hezekiah also removed the high places, broke the standing stones, cut down the Asherah and broke the bronze serpent Moses had made to restrain the people who were making it an object of idol worship. After the Temple was purified, the people went out to the cities of Judah, where the reforms continued and they

Above: Clay cult stand decorated with human and animal figures, from Taanach, 10th century B.C. (NEAEHL)

Below: Silver-plated bronze cult standard decorated with serpents and other religious objects, from Hazor, 14th–13th centuries B.C. (NEAEHL)

Chapter Seven: Reconstructing the First Temple

brake the images in pieces, and cut down the groves (Asherim), and threw down the high places and the altars out of all Judah and Benjamin, in Ephraim also and Manasseh, until they had utterly destroyed them all.

(2 Chr 31:1)

We have already seen in Chapter 2 (p. 189) that Hezekiah enlarged the Temple Mount until it reached a square shape of 500 cubits. In the light of this ambitious undertaking, it seems reasonable to suggest that he would have also restored the Temple, which had suffered so much damage and neglect during the preceding centuries. Initially, he appears to have repaired the Temple in haste to make it serviceable again as quickly as possible. This may, however, have been a mere rescue operation, as we read in 2 Kings 18, that in the fourteenth year of Hezekiah's reign, Sennacherib came to Judah and captured many cities.

To prevent an attack on Jerusalem, Hezekiah paid Sennacherib a ransom, as recorded in verse 16:

At that time did Hezekiah cut off the gold from the doors of the Temple of the LORD, and from the pillars which Hezekiah king of Judah had overlaid, and gave it to the king of Assyria.

The English text reads as though Hezekiah took off the gold from the two famous pillars, Yachin and Boaz, which King Solomon had made. However, in the Hebrew text, the normal word for pillars, *amudim,* is not used but rather *umnot,* which means pilasters (rectangular columns projecting slightly from a wall such as found in the outer walls of the Tomb of the Patriarchs in Hebron; see illustrations, p. 51).

Sennacherib seated on his throne receives booty and prisoners from Lachish, on relief from Nineveh. (British Museum)

It is possible that the two Solomonic pillars, each 18 cubits high, no longer existed. Hezekiah initially may have replaced the original pillars with simple pilasters and overlaid them with gold. It is also an indication that Ahaz, when removing the two bronze pillars, must have also destroyed the *ulam* which the pillars supported.

However, the Temple description in

CHAPTER SEVEN: RECONSTRUCTING THE FIRST TEMPLE

2 Chronicles 3:15 shows that two pillars, 35 cubits high, were made for the edifice. It is possible that Hezekiah restored the Temple after the Assyrian army was destroyed at Lachish. Some scholars believe that the events recorded in 2 Kings 18:17 refer to a second and later invasion.[11] If this was the case, Hezekiah could have rebuilt the Temple in the interlude, at a time when he was also strengthening the walls of Jerusalem. In any event, we believe that the two descriptions of Solomon's Temple differ sufficiently from one another to warrant the suggestion that two different buildings are described. The main core of the later building may still have had original elements from the first building.

Jerusalem in the time of Hezekiah (extension marked in orange), after Avigad.

Comparing the two accounts of the building of the Temple, the first in 1 Kings, chapters 6 and 7, and the second in 2 Chronicles, chapters 3 and 4, many differences become apparent. In the first description, the pillars of brass were 18 cubits in height, while the second records them as 35 cubits high. The height of the first porch is not given; the second one was 120 cubits high. As the porch was probably proportionate in size to the pillars, one may assume that the first porch was lower than the second. In the first account, the Temple is surrounded by three stories of chambers; in the second account these chambers are replaced by upper chambers. The first laver had knobs under the rim; the second had two rows of oxen. The first contained 2,000 baths (12,000 gallons, 44,000 liters); the second 3,000 (18,000 gallons, 66,000 liters).

From the differences between the two records, we must conclude that the Temple destroyed by the Babylonians was not the one constructed by Solomon. During the First Temple period, which lasted more than four hundred years, the Temple had undergone the

Chapter Seven: Reconstructing the First Temple

many changes and repairs which we have mentioned. This then, we believe, is the reason for the two differing descriptions: Solomon's Temple obviously had suffered so much from neglect, wanton destruction and earthquakes that King Hezekiah had it completely renovated and created a 500-cubit-square artificial mount around it in order to restore it to its former glory. This was the Temple that the Babylonians destroyed. However, despite all the alterations and building activities, this last Temple is still referred to as the First Temple. The one built after the Babylonian exile was called the Second Temple. The differences between the two buildings are tabulated below (measurements in cubits).

Above: The table of shewbread in the Sanctuary. (photo: Philip Evans)

Below: The brass laver, situated between the Temple Porch (ulam) and the Altar of Herod's Temple. (photo: Philip Evans)

Differences in Temple descriptions	1 Kings 6–7	2 Chronicles 3–4
Internal dimensions (cubits)	6.2. LxWxH = 60x20x30	3.3. LxW = 60x20
Porch *(ulam)*	6.3. 20 broad, 10 wide	3.4. 20 broad, 120 high
Chambers	6.5,6. 3 side stories high	3.9. upper chambers
Shewbread table	7.48. one table	4.8. 10 tables
Partition between *heikhal* and *debir*	6.31 doors of olive wood	3.14. veil
Holy of Holies	6.20. 20x20x20	3.8. 20x20
2 Pillars of bronze	7.15. 18 high, circumference 12	3.15. 35 high
Capitals	7.16. lower capital 5 high 7.17. 7 nets 7.19. upper capital 4 high	3.15. one capital 5 high with chains
Laver	7.23. 10 diameter 5 high 30 circumference 7.26. 2,000 baths decoration of lilies	4.2. 10 diameter 5 high 30 circumference 4.5. 3,000 baths decoration of oxen

Hezekiah also built chambers—*lesachot*—on the enlarged Temple Mount (2 Chr 31:11). These were initially built as storerooms for the tithes. Later we read that some of these rooms (or additional

CHAPTER SEVEN: RECONSTRUCTING THE FIRST TEMPLE

ones) were used by scribes. Thus we read of the *"chamber of the sons of Hanan, the son of Igdaliah, a man of God, which was by the chamber of the princes, which was above the chamber of Maaseiah the son of Shallum, the keeper of the door"* (Jer 35:4); *"the chamber of Gemariah the son of Shaphan the scribe, in the higher court, at the entry of the new gate of the LORD's house"* (Jer 36: 10); and the chamber of Elishama the scribe (Jer 36:12, 36:20).

Similar chambers are mentioned in the books of Ezra and Nehemiah, indicating that these chambers were rebuilt after the Babylonian exile. Being part of the enlarged Temple Mount, they gave it the character of a *Birah,* the religious-political acropolis of Jerusalem.

Manasseh

After the death of his father in 686 B.C., Hezekiah's son Manasseh undid all the good work done by his father. *"And he built altars in the house of Yahweh, of which Yahweh said, In Jerusalem will I put my name. And he built altars for all the host of heaven in the two courts of the house of Yahweh"* (2 Kgs 21:4–5). Further, in verse 7 we are told that

> he set a graven image of Asherah that he had made in the house, of which Yahweh said to David, and to Solomon his son, In this house, and in Jerusalem, which I have chosen out of all tribes of Israel, will I put my name for ever.

The priests must have feared that Manasseh would remove or destroy the Ark of the Covenant and therefore removed it to a safe location. The Ark was not returned to the Temple until the reign of Josiah, Manasseh's grandson. After spending some time in Assyrian captivity, Manasseh repented and removed the altars he had built and also repaired the *"Altar of Yahweh"* (2 Chr 33:15–16). This means that even the great Altar of Burnt Sacrifices must have been

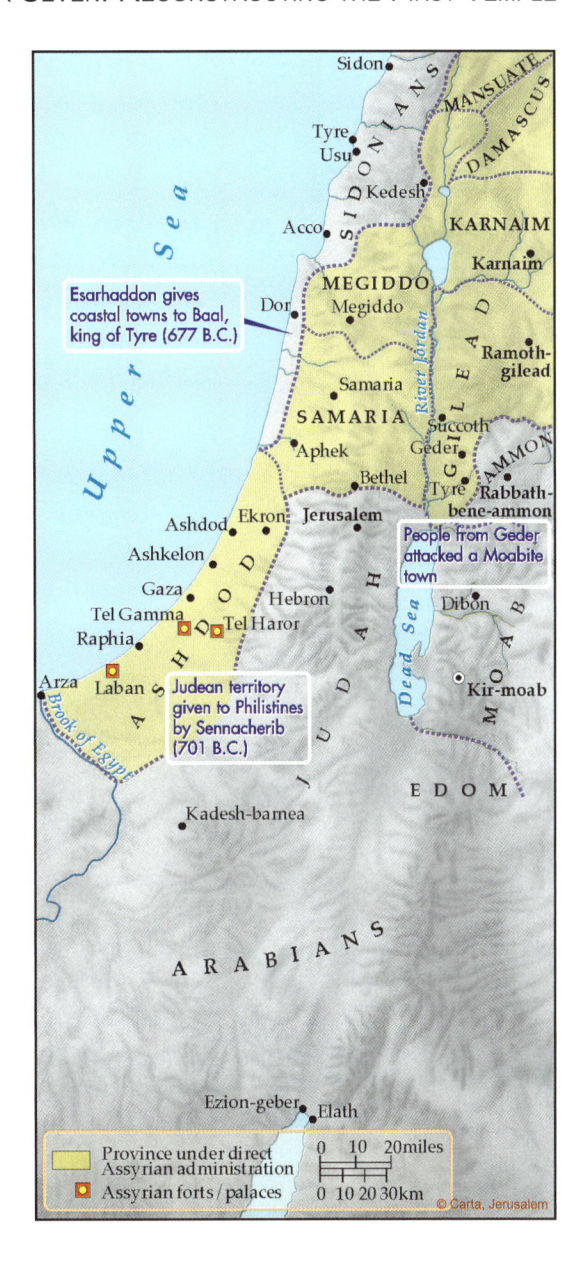

Judah and her neighbors during the reign of Manasseh.

CHAPTER SEVEN: RECONSTRUCTING THE FIRST TEMPLE

either damaged or destroyed during Manasseh's reign. His son Amon continued to worship the idols his father Manasseh had made. An unpopular king, Amon was eventually murdered by his servants.

JOSIAH AND THE ARK OF THE COVENANT

When Josiah (c. 639–609 b.c.) was only a youngster of sixteen, it is recorded that he began to seek Yahweh, and at the age of twenty he began his famous reform to

> . . . purge Judah and Jerusalem from the high places, and the groves, and the carved images, and the molten images. And they brake down the altars of Baalim in his presence; and the images, that were on high above them, he cut down; and the groves, and the carved images, and the molten images, he brake in pieces, and made dust of them, and strewed it upon the graves of them that had sacrificed unto them. And he burnt the bones of the priests upon their altars, and cleansed Judah and Jerusalem. (2 Chr 34:3–5)

Decorated fragment of a cultic stand found in Area G of the City of David, 10th century B.C. (NEAEHL)

Confirmation of the record of his reform was initially thought to have been found in Jerusalem in 1967 by Kathleen Kenyon.[12] Excavating on the slopes of the City of David, she thought to have identified a cultic center with two *masseboth,* or standing stones, and afterwards a *favissa* (a place where discarded religious objects are deposited) containing 1,300 pottery vessels and human or animal figurines, mostly in the shape of horses, some with a sun disc between their ears. The human figurines were mainly female pillar figurines. Kenyon suggested that these figurines may have come from two cultic sites, one associated with fertility rituals and the other with sun worship. Her explanation, however, has been challenged more recently by Franken and Steiner[13], who interpret the site as merely the remains of a common ninth-century B.C. dwelling, whose roof was supported by two monolithic columns. The cave where the discarded figurines were found was apparently part of the dwelling.

The context of this deposit is not yet fully understood. The many broken figurines, especially the horses, remind us nevertheless of the later reform by King Josiah, as mentioned in 2 Kings 23:11, who *"took away the horses that the kings of Judah had given to the sun, at the*

CHAPTER SEVEN: RECONSTRUCTING THE FIRST TEMPLE

Shaphan reading the book of the law before King Josiah, 19th century engraving.

entering in of the house of Yahweh . . . and burned the chariots of the sun with fire."

But to return to Josiah's story—during the cleansing of the Temple, Hilkiah the High Priest made a dramatic find. He alone of all the priests was allowed inside the Holy of Holies and it could only have been there that he found *"the book of the law."* This was the Deuteronomy scroll that was placed next to the Ark of the Covenant inside the emplacement of the Ark, to which we referred in Chapter 6 (p. 268 ff.). Although the Ark of the Covenant had been removed during the wicked rule of Manasseh, when he set up an Asherah image in the Temple, the scroll apparently remained.

After the damage suffered during the time of Manasseh, whether done on purpose or through neglect, the Temple building itself was in need of repair. Money was collected and given to

> . . . *the workmen that had the oversight of the house of*

Chapter Seven: Reconstructing the First Temple

Yahweh; and the workmen that wrought in the house of Yahweh gave it to mend and repair the house; even to the carpenters and to the builders gave they it, to buy hewn stone, and timber for couplings, and to make beams for the houses which the kings of Judah had destroyed.

(2 Chr 34:10–11)

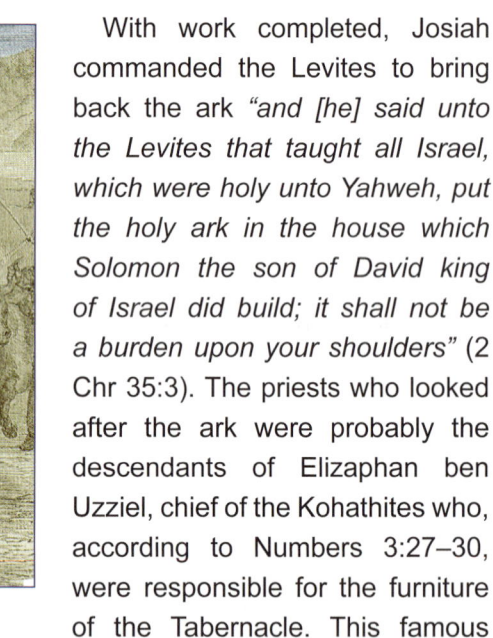

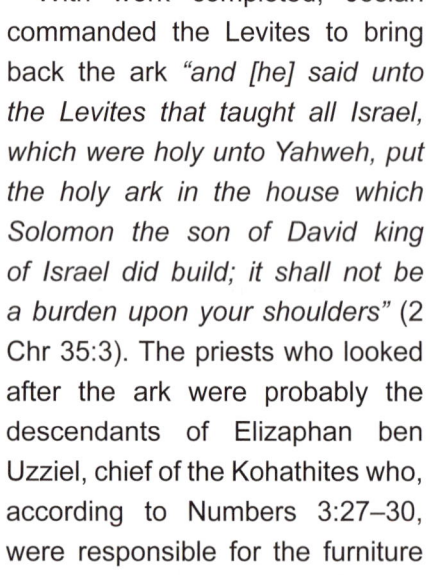

With work completed, Josiah commanded the Levites to bring back the ark *"and [he] said unto the Levites that taught all Israel, which were holy unto Yahweh, put the holy ark in the house which Solomon the son of David king of Israel did build; it shall not be a burden upon your shoulders"* (2 Chr 35:3). The priests who looked after the ark were probably the descendants of Elizaphan ben Uzziel, chief of the Kohathites who, according to Numbers 3:27–30, were responsible for the furniture of the Tabernacle. This famous family is mentioned during the time of David, when Shemaiah was the chief of two hundred of his family (1 Chr 15.8). Much later, during Hezekiah's reign, Shimri and Jeiel are recorded as being the active descendants (2 Chr 29:13). These two men, or their sons, must have removed the Ark from the Temple during Manasseh's rule. They probably kept the Ark near their homes in order to protect it, a task that would have been difficult in Jerusalem.

The Levites bearing the sacred vessels and the Ark of the Covenant, 19th century engraving.

The location of the Ark or the facts concerning its fate during the Babylonian conquest are unknown. It is unlikely, however, that the Ark of the Covenant was destroyed. Such an occurrence would surely have been mentioned in the Scriptures. The same family of Elizaphan may well have removed it from the Temple before it was destroyed by the Babylonians.

In recent decades there has been a surge of interest in finding the Ark of the Covenant. According to the Book of Maccabees,[14] Jeremiah hid the Ark on Mount Nebo in Jordan. In 1993, a book was published which places the Ark in Ethiopia,[15] while many rabbis believe that it is still hidden somewhere under the Temple Mount.[16] This belief is based mainly on 1 Kings 8:8:

> and they drew out the staves, that the end of the staves were seen out in the holy before the oracle, and they were not seen without: and they are there unto this day.

"Unto this day" is supposed to be the key phrase indicating that the Ark is still hidden somewhere under the Temple Mount. In 1981 workers of the Religious Affairs Ministry carried out a dig under the Temple Mount in search of the Ark. However, when this caused disturbances among the Arab population, the project was aborted.

After Josiah, the Ark is not mentioned again until Jeremiah 3: 16–17, which reads,

> And it shall come to pass, when ye be multiplied and increased in the land, in those days, saith the LORD, they shall say no more, The ark of the covenant of the LORD: neither shall it come to mind: neither shall they remember it; neither shall they visit it; neither shall that be done any more. At that time they shall call Jerusalem the throne of the LORD; and all the nations shall be gathered unto it, to the name of the LORD, to Jerusalem….

Although this verse has been interpreted in various ways, it would appear to indicate that if the Ark is ever found, such a discovery will not be by chance but occur in a religious context. It is interesting to note that the name of Elizaphan, the first person ever to be put in charge of the Ark of the Covenant, means "My El (God) has hidden." If his name is at all an indication of what has happened, then God alone knows where the Ark is and He will allow the Ark to be found when the time is right.

Jehoiakim

Josiah died in battle in 609 B.C. while trying to stop Pharaoh Necho from passing through his land to aid the King of Assyria in the conquest of Haran. Upon his tragic death, Josiah's kingdom disintegrated, as lamented by Jeremiah:

> The breath of our nostrils, the anointed of Yahweh, was taken in their pits, of whom we said, under his shadow we shall live among the nations.   (Lam 4:20)

Upon his return to Egypt, Pharaoh Necho replaced Jehoahaz,

Head of Psamtik II, a king of the 26th Dynasty, to which belonged the Egyptian king mentioned in the Bible under the name of Pharaoh Necho.

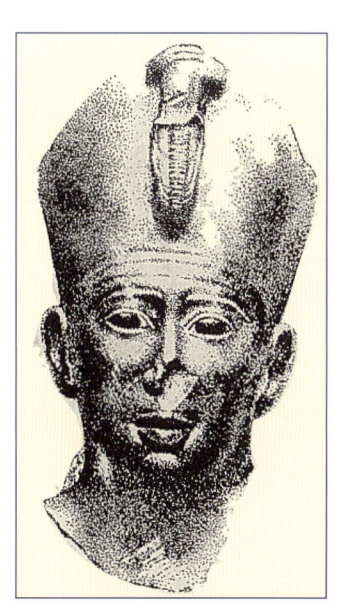

Chapter Seven: Reconstructing the First Temple

whom the people had crowned king three months before, with his brother Jehoiakim. In 605 B.C. Nebuchadnezzar defeated the Egyptian army and the following year he invaded the Kingdom of Judah. Jehoiakim was allowed to continue his rule, but in 598 B.C. he revolted against the Babylonians, who had come to Jerusalem and took some of the Temple treasures away (2 Chr 36:7).

Jehoiachin

When Jehoiakim died he was succeeded by Jehoiachin, who ruled only a few months until he was taken away to Babylon, together with the "goodly vessels" of the House of the Lord (2 Chr 36:11).

Zedekiah

The last king of Judah was Zedekiah. His rebellion against Nebuchadnezzar towards the end of his reign led to the destruction of Jerusalem and the Temple in 586 B.C. Whatever was left of the treasures of the Temple was carried away to Babylon and the Temple was burned down (2 Chr 36:19).

This, then, was the end of the magnificent building which, despite the ravages of time and damage suffered at the hands of men and nature, was called *"the House of God"* till the very end. It took fifty years to lay the foundation of the Second Temple, in c. 535 B.C.

Before we move on to investigate the Second Temple, which was rebuilt after the Babylonian Exile, we would like to establish the earlier connections of David and Abraham with the sacred site of the Temple, especially the location of the altar.

Babylonian Chronicle recording the capture of Jerusalem by Nebuchadnezzar. (British Museum)

ARAUNAH'S THRESHING FLOOR AND THE LOCATION OF THE ALTAR

The location of the First Temple is closely related to the threshing floor of Araunah, the Jebusite king from whom David purchased it, in order to build there an altar to Yahweh his God (1 Kgs 24:18–25). It is generally believed that David's altar was built at the same place that Isaac was bound in preparation for his sacrifice, as related in Genesis 22.

However, we would like to be more precise about the relationship between the Rock, the location of Araunah's threshing floor, the altars erected by Abraham and David, and the place of Solomon's Temple. To do so we must first examine the historical information as preserved

CHAPTER SEVEN: RECONSTRUCTING THE FIRST TEMPLE

in the Hebrew Bible.

The events that occurred toward the end of David's life are recorded in 2 Samuel 24 and 1 Chronicles 21. God had brought a plague upon Israel because David had ordered Joab to count Israel and Judah, having apparently forgotten the injunction recorded in Exodus 30:12 to make provision for paying a ransom for each individual counted. Then David was commanded by God to buy the hilltop of Mount Moriah as a place to offer sacrifices. David first paid 50 silver shekels for the threshing floor (2 Sam 24:24) and later 600 shekels of gold for the whole mountain (1 Chr 21:25), thereby establishing his ownership of Mount Moriah, which was destined to become the Temple Mount.

Let us analyze this event in greater detail. The angel sent by God to bring a pestilence upon Israel was stopped as he stretched out his hand over Jerusalem (2 Sam 24:15–16). It is instructive to note where David saw the angel:

The offering of Isaac as depicted in a 19th century engraving (above) and on the mosaic floor of the Beth Alpha synagogue, 3rd century (below).

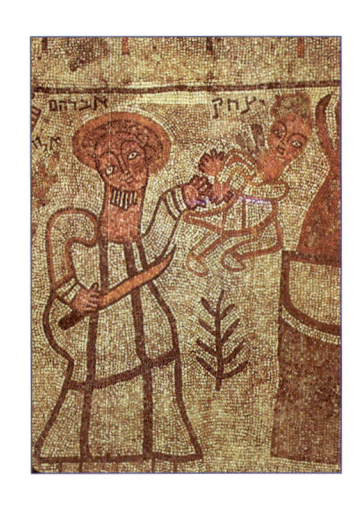

> *And the angel of Yahweh stood by the threshing floor of Ornan [Araunah] the Jebusite. And David having lifted up his eyes, and saw the angel of Yahweh stand between the earth and the heaven, having a drawn sword in his hand stretched out over Jerusalem.* (1 Chr 21:15–16)

Two points should be made here. First, the angel did not stand *on* the threshing floor but *beside* it and, secondly, the angel must have stood on higher ground. We have already noted that threshing floors are not usually located on the tops of mountains but a little lower, so that the wind will carry away the lighter chaff but not the heavier grain. The prevailing wind in Israel blows from the west, so that we would expect Araunah's threshing floor to be located below and to the east of the Rock.

313

Chapter Seven: Reconstructing the First Temple

Artist's impression of King David, having built an altar on the threshing floor he purchased from Ornan (Araunah) the Jebusite, presents an offering in response to the famine that had befallen Israel. "And he [the Lord] answered him from heaven by fire upon the altar…" (1 Chr 21:26). (The Temple Institute, Jerusalem)

The position of the angel beside the floor is identified as being *"between the earth and the heaven."* He was evidently standing at a higher level than David, so that it appears most likely that the angel stood on the top of the Rock, between heaven and earth. This would indicate that, although standing on the earth, he was in direct communication with God in heaven. The sanctity of the Rock was therefore greater than that of the threshing floor. David bought this threshing floor from Araunah and built an altar, not on top of the mountain where the angel stood, that is, the Rock, but on the threshing floor, located lower down and to the east.

The location of the Altar in Herod's Temple can be calculated by using the tables in Chapter 9 (pp. 370–371). Once the location of the Holy of Holies is established, the entire layout of the Herodian Temple complex can be determined. Working backwards, then, the location of the Altar determines the location of the threshing floor.

There is further evidence in the Scriptures showing that the Holy of Holies was located at the highest spot of the Temple. In Chapter 6 (p. 268 ff.), we have already referred to the vision described in Isaiah 6:1, where the prophet sees the Lord sitting in the Temple, *"high and lifted up."* The place reserved for the Deity was undoubtedly the Holy of Holies, where the High Priest alone once a year was allowed to enter on Yom Kippur, the Day of Atonement (Lev 16:29–30), that is, on the tenth day of the seventh month.

The vision, which is also referred to in John 12:41, occurred during the year that King Uzziah died—presumably of the leprosy that he contracted as punishment for offering incense in the Temple, which he was not allowed to do (2 Chr 26:16–21). Although it was only a vision, Isaiah's description was probably based on the actual situation in the Temple, with the Holy of Holies on a higher level than any other part of the Temple.

The angel that David saw was therefore standing in the place

CHAPTER SEVEN: RECONSTRUCTING THE FIRST TEMPLE

destined to become the Holy of Holies, possibly on the very spot where the Ark was later placed in the center of the inner chamber overshadowed by the cherubim. Indeed, this was also the place of the oracle from where God spoke, as we read in Numbers 7:89:

> *And when Moses was gone into the tabernacle of the congregation to speak with him, then he heard the voice of one speaking unto him from off the mercy seat that was upon the ark of the testimony, from between the two cherubim: and he spake unto him.*

ABRAHAM AND MOUNT MORIAH

Notably, both Abraham and David were shown the place where to build their altars by divine instruction. Abraham was sent to the land of Moriah to *"offer him [Isaac] there for a burnt offering upon one of the mountains which I will tell thee of"* (Gen 22:2). After Abraham was prevented by the angel from sacrificing Isaac, he called the name of the place *"Yahweh yira'eh"* as it is said this day *"behar Yahweh yira'eh."* This latter phrase can be translated "in the mountain Yahweh will provide," or "in the mountain Yahweh shall be seen." Both translations have, of course, a prophetic impact, connecting the sacrifice of Isaac to that of the later Messiah.

But where was the exact spot that Abraham built his altar? We are not told in Genesis, but the prophetic meaning of Abraham's words would point to the establishment of a continuous sanctity of this place as an altar. It would have been appropriate for David to build his altar in the place that Abraham had chosen. In that case the location of the Altar of Herod's Temple, which we will show to be 21.6 feet (6.60 m) east of the Dome of the Chain (see p. 357 ff. and plan, p. 362), would indicate the place where King David built an altar. Jewish tradition has always connected the location of David's altar with the one built by Abraham to sacrifice Isaac, so that the place of Herod's altar would be identical with the very place where Abraham bound Isaac.

Plan of the platform of the Dome of the Rock. Araunah's threshing floor was located 21.6 feet (6.6 m) east of the Dome of the Chain. This was the place where David built an altar. The Angel who appeared to David probably stood on the Rock (Sakhra), where the Ark of the Covenant was later placed.

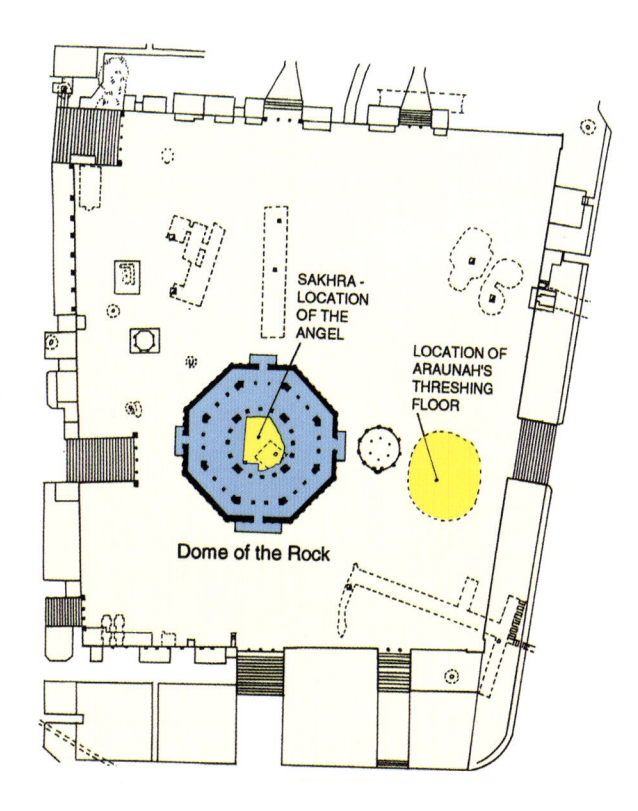

315

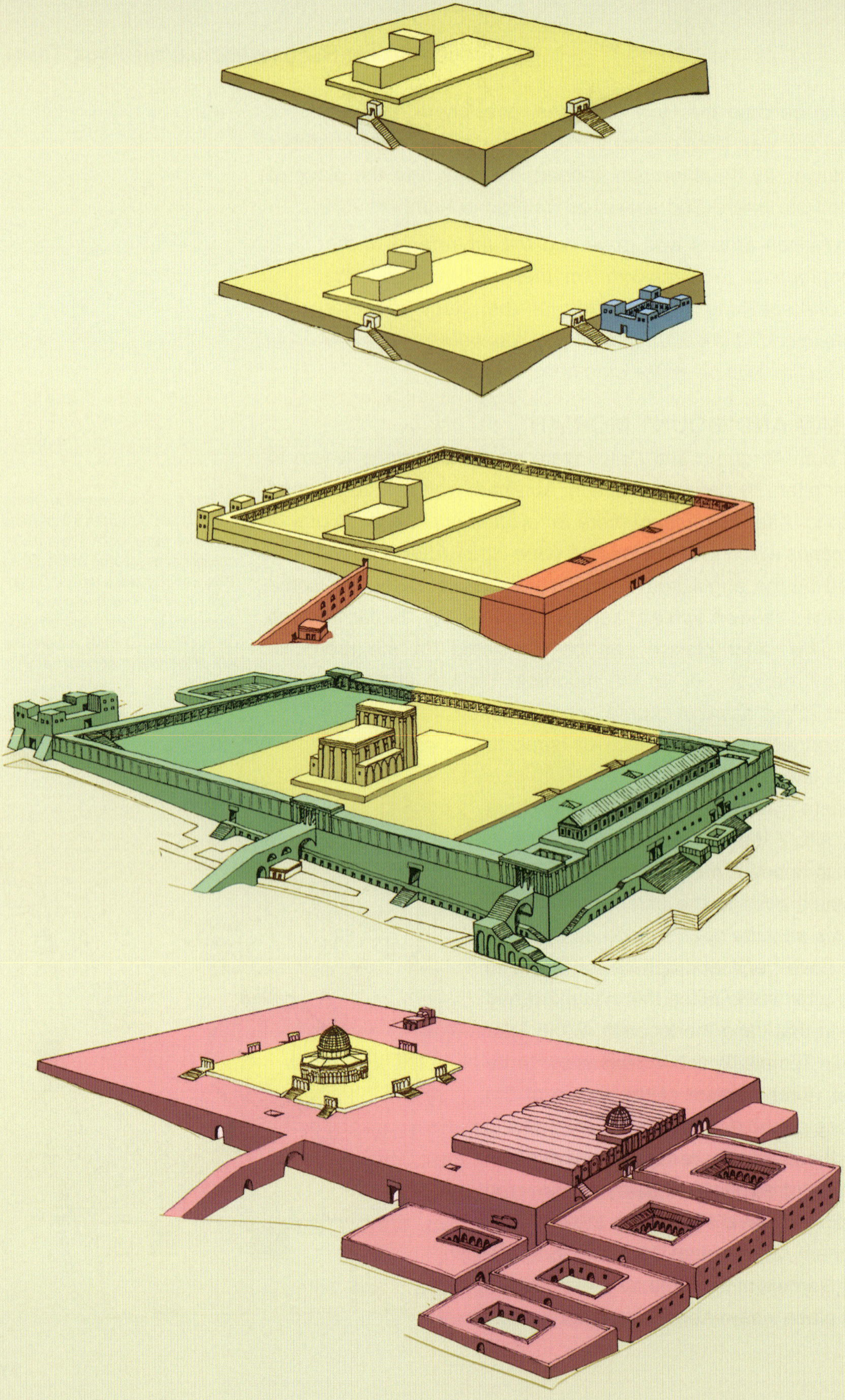

Opposite page: Stages in the development of the Temple Mount, from top to bottom:
1. The square Temple Mount as repaired after the return to Zion.
2. The Akra built to the south of the Temple Mount.
3. The Hasmonean extension.
4. The Herodian Temple Mount.
5. The Temple Mount during the Umayyad period.

Below: The final campaign of Nebuchadnezzar against Judah, 15 January 588 B.C. to 19 July 586 B.C.

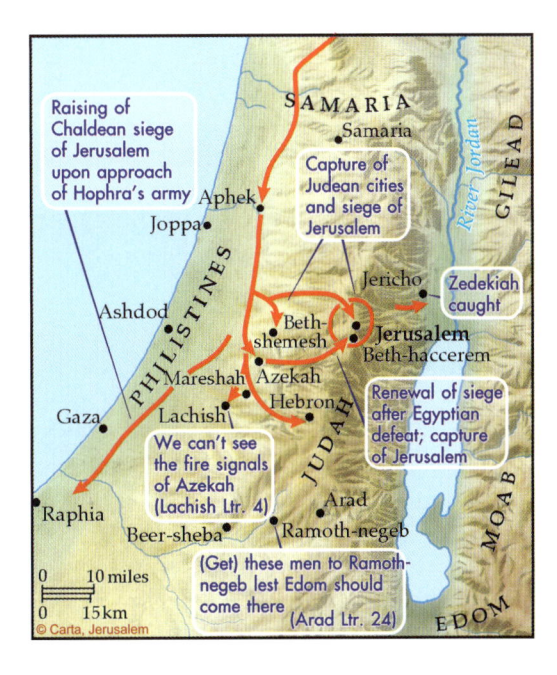

Chapter Eight
Reconstructing the Second Temple

REBUILDING THE TEMPLE IN THE POST-EXILIC PERIOD — Introduction

The Babylonians overran the Land of Israel in 586 B.C., fulfilling Jeremiah's prophecy in Chapter 25:11: *"this whole land shall be a desolation, and an astonishment; and these nations shall serve the king of Babylon seventy years."* The terrible destruction of the First Temple is recorded in 2 Chronicles 36:19–21:

> And they burnt the house of God, and brake down the wall of Jerusalem, and burnt all the palaces thereof with fire, and destroyed all the goodly vessels thereof. And them that had escaped from the sword carried he away to Babylon; where they were servants to him and his sons until the reign of the kingdom of Persia: To fulfil the word of the LORD by the mouth of Jeremiah, until the land had enjoyed her Sabbaths: for as long as she lay desolate she kept Sabbath, to fulfil threescore and ten years.

The rebuilding of Jerusalem's Temple after seventy years of exile is the subject of this chapter. The altar was the first thing to be rebuilt in 536 B.C., exactly seventy years after the first invasion of Nebuchadnezzar during the fourth year of Jehoiakim in c. 606 B.C. Next, the Temple was rebuilt in 515 B.C., seventy years after its destruction in 586 B.C. There

Chapter Eight. Reconstructing the Second Temple

appears therefore to have been a double fulfillment of Jeremiah's prophecy.

Jeshua and Zerubbabel

In Ezra 1:1-3 we read,

> *Now in the first year of Cyrus king of Persia, that the word of the LORD by the mouth of Jeremiah might be fulfilled, the LORD stirred up the spirit of Cyrus king of Persia, that he made a proclamation throughout all his kingdom, and put it also in writing, saying, Thus saith Cyrus king of Persia, The LORD God of heaven hath given me all the kingdoms of the earth; and he hath charged me to build him an house at Jerusalem, which is in Judah. Who is there among you of all his people? his God be with him, and let him go up to Jerusalem, which is in Judah, and build the house of the LORD God of Israel, (he is the God,) which is in Jerusalem.*

Thus begins the history of the construction of the Second Temple, made possible in 536 B.C. by the Edict of Cyrus II (559–529 B.C.). This edict was issued seventy years after the first year of Nebuchadnezzar king of Babylon, in fulfillment of Jeremiah 29:10: *"For thus saith the LORD, that after seventy years be accomplished at Babylon I will visit you, and perform my good word toward you, in causing you to return to this place."* The people who stayed behind in Babylon were urged to help *"with silver, and with gold, and with goods, and with beasts,*

Above: The Cylinder of Cyrus, which tells how he captured Babylon and liberated the prisoners from Babylonia. (British Museum)

Right: The Return to Zion.

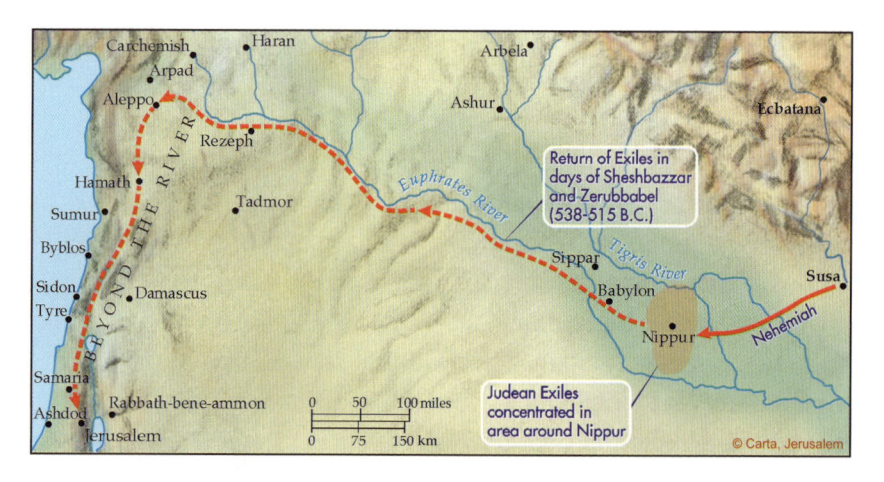

CHAPTER EIGHT: RECONSTRUCTING THE SECOND TEMPLE

Left: The message of Haggai to Zerubbabel and Jeshua was heard: "Who is left among you that saw this house in her first glory? and how do ye see it now? is it not in your eyes in compairson of it as nothing?" (Haggai 2:3).

Below: The traditional tomb of Cyrus at Pasargadae, Iran.

beside the freewill offering for the house of God that is in Jerusalem."

Cyrus also returned the vessels that had been removed from the House of the Lord so that the services could be resumed. In Ezra 1:9–11, we are told that the treasurer of the king's court handed over the 5,400 items to Sheshbazzar, the prince of Judah. (However, Haggai 1:1 tells us that Zerubbabel the son of Shealtiel was the governor of Judah. Scholars agree that Sheshbazzar and Zerubbabel are one and the same person.)

Chapter Eight: Reconstructing the Second Temple

Above: The Persian province of Yehud.

Below: Coin of Yehud.

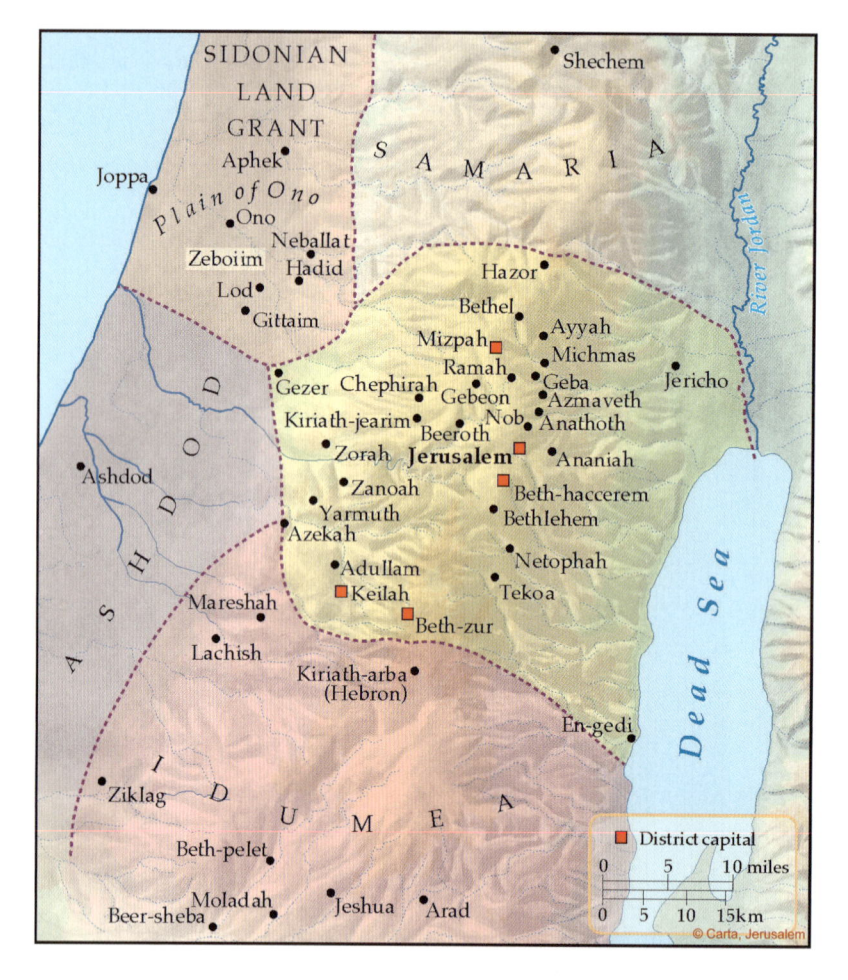

The only information we are given on the dimensions of the building is that *"the foundations thereof be strongly laid; the height thereof threescore cubits, and the breadth thereof threescore cubits"* (Ezra 6:3).

The Altar and the Foundation of the Temple

The first act of the returnees, under the guidance of Zerubbabel and Jeshua the son of Jozadak, was to restore the altar of the God of Israel upon its foundations and to begin offering the continual morning and evening burnt offerings according to Exodus 30:38–42. The Feast of Tabernacles was celebrated together with all its sacrifices. All this was done prior to the laying of the foundations of the Temple, showing that the setting up of the altar and the resumption of the sacrifices had precedence over the building of the Temple.

A year later, in 535 B.C., the foundations of the Temple were laid (Ezra 3:8–10). There is no reason to doubt that the 60-cubit (103 feet or 31.50 m) wide foundations were laid in the same location and had the same orientation as those of Solomon's Temple on Mount Moriah, as the Rock was still in existence and its rocky foundation trenches would have dictated the orientation of the building. Although there was great rejoicing on this occasion, it was mingled with the tears of the older generation of Israelites, who presumably saw these foundations as inferior to those of the previous Temple. Nevertheless, it was an important step towards the restoration of a focal point of worship in this Persian province of Judah (Yehud).

Chapter Eight: Reconstructing the Second Temple

The work was soon suspended due to the opposition of the local Samaritans, who wanted to participate in the building of the Temple, but were rebuffed by Zerubbabel, Jeshua and the heads of the most important families. In 529 B.C., a letter opposing the building of the Temple (Ezra 4:1, 4:6) was sent by the Samaritans to Cambyses II (529–522 B.C.), the Persian king who succeeded Cyrus II and is called by his title Ahasuerus in Ezra 4. Eventually the work stopped in 522 B.C.

The Completion of the Temple

One year later, in 521 B.C., the original Edict of Cyrus was reaffirmed by Darius son of Hystaspes (522–486 B.C.). It was then that Haggai and Zechariah embarked on their prophetic mission and the work was accelerated. In 515 B.C. the dedication of the Temple took place.

About sixty years later, in c. 457 B.C., Artaxerxes (464–424 B.C.) dispatched Ezra on a mission of inquiry to see how further improvements could be made to the Temple and its services. He gave him material, financial support and authority to marshal local provisions for the Temple services. Ezra, a scribe, was determined to teach the people the laws of God and enforce them, especially in view of the assimilation that had taken place.

His mission regarding the Temple was "to beautify the house of the LORD" (Ezra 7.27). This appears to have been the fourth and final stage in the rebuilding of the Temple that had begun with the building of the altar. Next the foundations of the Temple were laid. Finally, after the completion of the Temple structure, and 130 years after

Ezra bringing the law before the congregation, 19th century engraving.

Chapter Eight: Reconstructing the Second Temple

The Return to Zion under Ezra and Nehemiah.

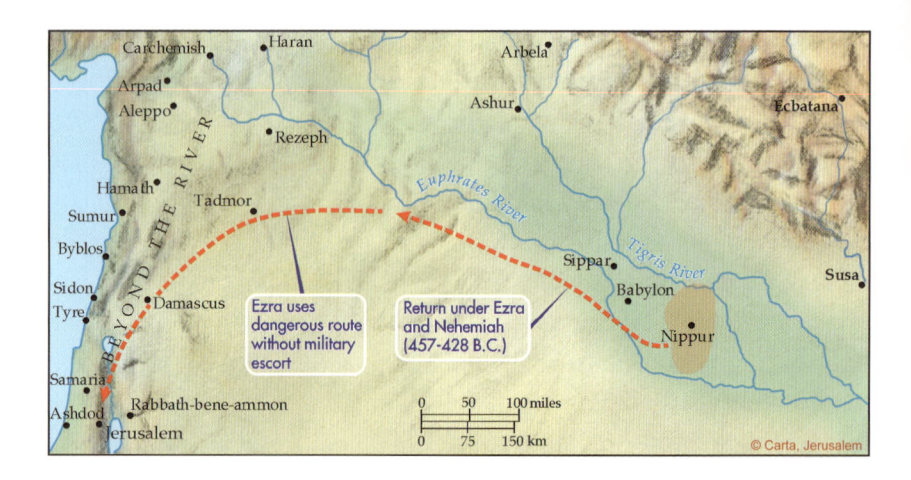

the destruction of the First Temple, the time had come to glorify the building. This brings to mind the prophecy of Isaiah 60:3, *"The glory of Lebanon shall come unto thee, the fir tree, the pine tree, and the box together, to beautify the place of my sanctuary; and I will make the place of my feet glorious."* We have no details about the work that was carried out, apart from the already mentioned fact that the new temple had imposing dimensions of sixty cubits in height and width. One can only speculate on its appearance.

Nehemiah and the *Birah*

Thirteen years later, in the twentieth year of the same king Artaxerxes (that is, in 444 B.C.), a new royal commission was given to Nehemiah. He had asked the king that,

The rock-cut tomb of Artaxerxes I, Naqsh-i-Rostam, Iran.

> *…letters be given me to the governors beyond the river, that they may convey me over till I come into Judah, and a letter unto Asaph the keeper of the king's forest, that he may give me timber to make beams for the gates of the palace which appertained to the house, and for the wall of the city, and for the house that I shall enter into. And the king granted me, according to the good hand of my God upon me.* (Neh 2:7–8)

We have already pointed out in Chapter 2 (pp. 194–197) that the phrase, "the palace which appertained to the house," is *ha-birah asher la-bayit* in Hebrew, and is synonymous with the square Temple Mount which was built for the Temple. Nehemiah therefore repaired the *Birah* and its gates, but apparently had no need to work on the Temple itself as that had been completed earlier.

CHAPTER EIGHT: RECONSTRUCTING THE SECOND TEMPLE

Chambers were built on the Temple Mount for various purposes, as in the time of Hezekiah (see Chapter 7, pp. 303–307). These chambers were for *"for the treasures, for the offerings, for the first fruits, and for the tithes, to gather into them out of the fields of the cities the portions of the law for the priests and Levites"* (Neh 12: 44). Thus, the rebuilt square Temple Mount once more became a *Birah*, the religious-political hub of Jerusalem, over which Hananiah, Nehemiah's brother, was the ruler (Neh 7:2). The concept of a *Birah* must have been familiar to Nehemiah as the citadel of Shushan, where he served the king, was also called a *Birah*.

In Nehemiah 2:13–15, we read about Nehemiah's nocturnal walk around the broken-down walls of Jerusalem. Dramatic evidence of the Babylonian destruction was discovered in the City of David excavations[1].

> *The destruction layer of Stratum 10—the destruction of the entire city of Nebuchadnezzar in 586 BCE—was of similar intensity throughout all the excavational areas in which this stratum was found. The evidence in the Bible (2 Kings 25:8–10; Jeremiah 39:18; 2 Chronicles 36: 18–19) is complemented by the clear-cut archaeological evidence: the total destruction of the various structures, and a conflagration which consumed the various parts of the houses….The final collapse of the structures*

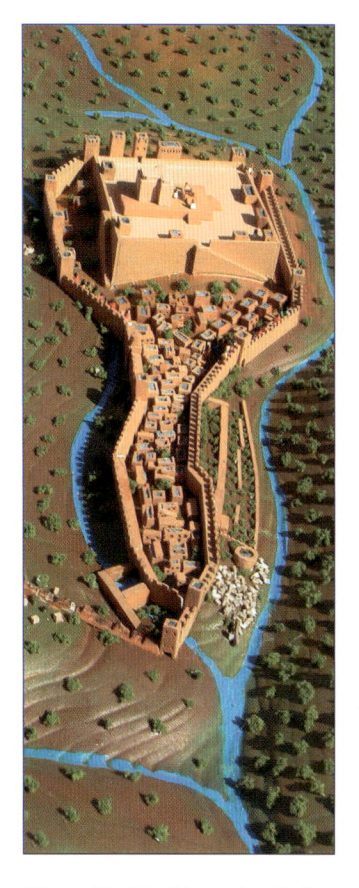

Above: Model of Jerusalem in the time of Nehemiah, looking north.

Left: Lamenting the desolation of the city of Jerusalem after its destruction by the Babylonians, 19th century engraving.

323

Chapter Eight: Reconstructing the Second Temple

Presumed location of Nehemiah's city wall

Jebusite city wall

on the eastern slope came about within a short time, probably during the first winter following the fall of the city, when nature's fury would have been most active with no one present to resist it. The supporting walls, part of buildings and segments of the city-wall collapsed and tumbled down the slope, covering it with a thick layer of stone and earth rubble.

This must have been the scene on the eastern slope of the City of David during Nehemiah's nocturnal survey. Eventually there was no path for his horse to follow and Nehemiah had to retrace his steps and turn back the same way he came (Neh 2:14). Nehemiah then undertook to rebuild the walls of Jerusalem, which at that time were limited to those of the eastern hill. As shown in Chapter 2, the northern wall of the Temple Mount served also as the city wall of Jerusalem at that time. This then is

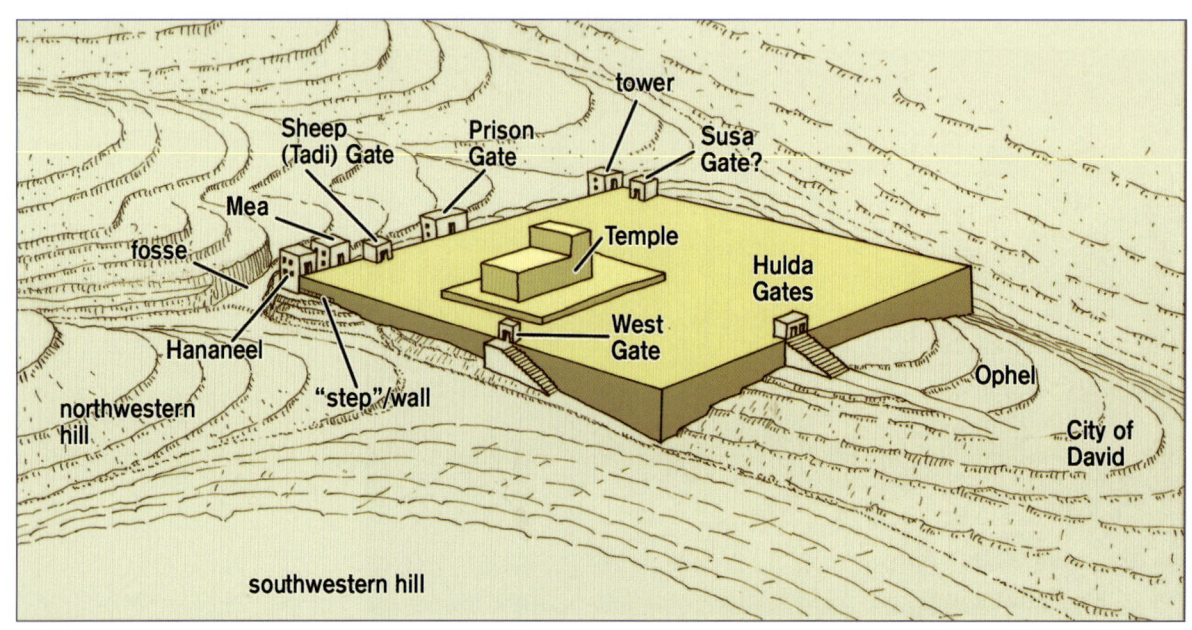

tower — Sheep (Tadi) Gate — Prison Gate — Susa Gate? — Mea — Temple — Hulda Gates — fosse — Hananeel — West Gate — "step"/wall — Ophel — northwestern hill — City of David — southwestern hill

CHAPTER EIGHT: RECONSTRUCTING THE SECOND TEMPLE

the reason that the Temple towers of Meah, Hananeel and Aliyah are mentioned in the description of the walls in Nehemiah 3.

Alexander the Great

The status quo on the Temple Mount apparently prevailed at least to the time of Alexander the Great. Josephus (*Ant.* 11.325–339) has an interesting tale to tell about Alexander the Great visiting Jerusalem, although some believe this story to be a legend.[2] Having captured Gaza, Alexander went to Jerusalem, where he prostrated himself before Jaddua the High Priest, whom Alexander recognized as someone who had once appeared to him in a vision. Alexander, under the guidance of the High Priest, sacrificed in the Jerusalem Temple and allowed the people to continue their religious observances. At the very least, this story shows that the Temple services did, in fact, continue following their reinstitution after the Babylonian exile.

Alexander the Great, detail of mosaic from Pompeii, 2nd–1st centuries B.C.

When Alexander died in 323 B.C., his empire was dismantled. Ptolemy eventually took over Egypt and also occupied the former Persian province of Judea in 301 B.C., while Seleucus ruled the eastern part of the empire, first from Babylon and then from Syria. These two major powers fought many wars, with the land bridge of Israel as their battleground.

CHANGES IN THE SECOND CENTURY B.C.

Our information for this period comes mainly from two sources. One is the book of Ecclesiasticus and the other, the books of 1 and 2 Maccabees. Both works are apocryphal and not included in the Hebrew Bible, although they are found in the Greek and Latin Bibles. Our quotes are from the Jerusalem Bible.[3]

Ecclesiasticus was originally called "Wisdom of Jesus ben Sirach" and is referred to in brief as Ben Sira. According to the foreword, this book is a Greek translation by the grandson of the author. In Chapter 50:1–2 the author writes that

Opposite page (above): The City of David, showing the remains of the Jebusite city wall and the presumed location of the city wall of Nehemiah.

Opposite page (below): Reconstruction of the square Temple Mount or Birah.

325

Chapter Eight: Reconstructing the Second Temple

It was the High Priest Simon son of Onias who repaired the Temple during his lifetime and in his day fortified the sanctuary. He laid the foundations of the double height, the high buttresses of the Temple precincts.

This High Priest was Simon II, son of Onias III, who ruled from about 220 to 195 B.C. The second Temple was apparently in need of repair, which is not surprising considering three hundred years of use since its completion in 515 B.C. It is not clear, however, what exactly the repairs entailed. It seems unlikely that Simon would have replaced the foundations of the Temple with new ones of twice the height, as that would have meant razing the Temple to the ground and reconstructing it on new foundations.

What was needed perhaps was a strengthening of the old foundations to provide greater stability. The location of the high buttresses is also unclear. Verse 3 states that "in his day the water cistern was excavated, a reservoir as huge as the sea." We have already seen in Chapter 4 (p. 222) that, because of its location in the southern part of the square Temple Mount, Cistern 7 is the best candidate for identification with this reservoir. These records, though apocryphal, show the important role that Jerusalem and especially the Temple Mount continued to play in the consciousness of the Jewish people.

The remainder of Ecclesiasticus 50 gives us a unique insight into the way the Temple services were conducted: *"How splendid he was with the people thronging around him, when he emerged from the curtained shrine"* (vs. 5). This evidently is a description of the Day of Atonement when the High Priest entered the *debir* beyond the veil. The author continues to describe the glory of the High Priest, who was to him

> *...like a sprig of frankincense in summer-time, like fire and incense in the censer, like a vessel of beaten gold encrusted with every kind of precious stone...when he put on his splendid vestments, and clothed himself in glorious perfection, when he went up to the holy altar, and filled the sanctuary precincts with his grandeur; when he received the portions from the hands of the priests, himself standing by the altar hearth....When*

The High Priest in the Holy of Holies on the Day of Atonement.

CHAPTER EIGHT: RECONSTRUCTING THE SECOND TEMPLE

all the sons of Aaron in their glory, with the offerings of the Lord in their hands, stood before the whole assembly of Israel, when he completed the rites at the altars, presenting in due order the offering for the Most High, the Almighty, reaching out his hand to the cup, and pouring a libation of the juice of the grape, pouring it at the foot of the altar. (Ecclesiasticus 50:8–15)

This ceremony was accompanied by blowing trumpets and singing hymns of praise, while the people prostrated themselves. The Day of Atonement was the only occasion when the High Priest would pronounce the holy name of Yahweh:

Then he would come down and raise his hands over the whole concourse of the sons of Israel, to give them the Lord's blessing from his lips, being privileged to pronounce his name. (Ecclesiasticus 50:20)

In 221 B.C., war broke out between Ptolemy IV and Antiochus III. It ended with the battle of Paneas (198 B.C.) which Ptolemy lost. When Antiochus reached Jerusalem, the Jews helped him defeat the Egyptian garrison located in the Ptolemaic Akra at the northeast corner of the Temple Mount (see Chapter 2, p. 201). To repay them for their help, Antiochus III made a declaration concerning the Temple and Jerusalem (*Ant.* 12.145): "*It is unlawful for any foreigner to enter the enclosure of the Temple which is forbidden to the Jews, except to those of them who are accustomed to enter after purifying themselves in accordance with the law of the country.*" The Temple services could therefore continue as usual under the new ruler.

This, however, would soon change. In 175 B.C. Antiochus IV Epiphanes took over the Seleucid kingdom.[4] Modeling himself on Alexander the Great, he set out to Hellenize his empire. Many Jews supported him and he allowed them to build a gymnasium at the foot of the Temple Mount. Because the sportsmen who participated in the games performed in the nude, some Jews

The final conquest of Palestine by Antiochus III, 201–198 B.C.

327

Chapter Eight. Reconstructing the Second Temple

The beginning of the Hasmonean revolt, 167 B.C.

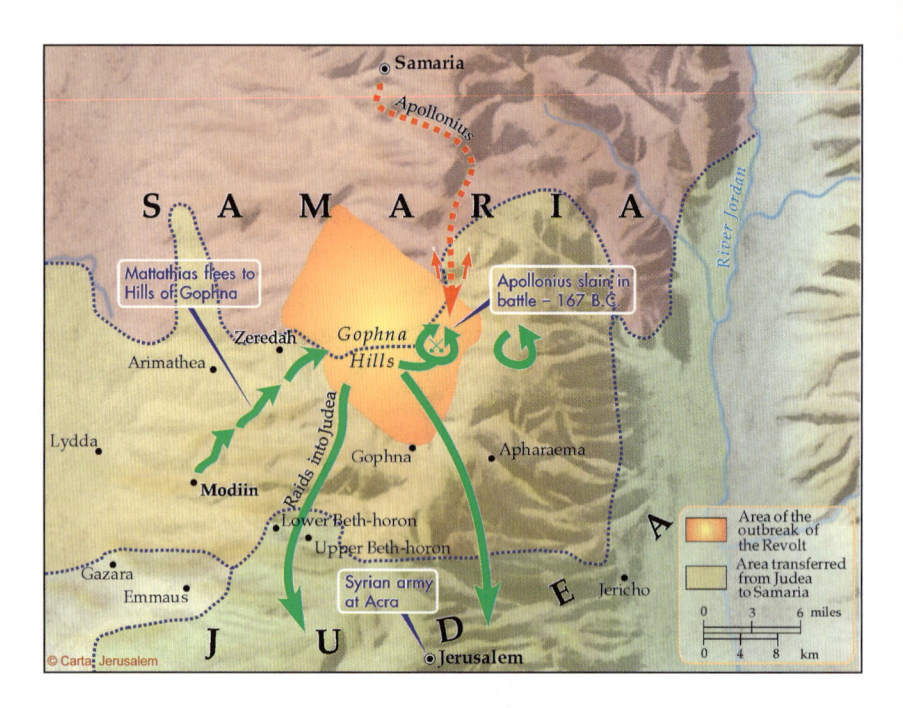

Addition of the Akra to the south of the Temple Mount — a reconstruction.

underwent surgery to remove signs of circumcision. On Antiochus IV's return from invading Egypt, he went to Jerusalem and, according to the First Book of Maccabees, he stormed the city and, breaking

> ...into the sanctuary, he removed the golden altar and the lampstand for the light with all its fittings, together with the table for the loaves of offering, the libation vessels, the cups, the golden censers, the veil, the crowns, and the golden decoration on the front of the Temple, which he stripped of everything. (1 Macc 21–23)

The Temple had again been plundered, although no structural damage was reported. Soon afterwards the Seleucid Akra was constructed south of the square Temple Mount, as we have discussed in Chapter 3. Then followed decrees prohibiting the practice of Jewish religious customs such as the keeping of the Sabbath and the festivals. Circumcision was forbidden on pain of death of the parents, sacrifices in the Temple were banned, new altars were built on which pigs and other unclean animals were offered. On the 18th of

CHAPTER EIGHT: RECONSTRUCTING THE SECOND TEMPLE

December, 167 B.C., *"the king erected the abomination of desolation above the altar"* (1 Macc 1.54). This was an altar dedicated to Zeus built on top of the altar of burnt sacrifices which stood in front of the Temple. When Antiochus IV wished to dedicate the Jerusalem Temple to the Olympian Zeus, it led to the outbreak of a holy war led by a certain Mattathias of the house of Hasmon and his five sons, John, Simon, Judas, Eleazar and Jonathan. The Books of the Maccabees record this struggle between the initially victorious Hellenizers and the resistance movement which fought back and eventually gained religious freedom.

A piglet sacrifice, as depicted on Greek pottery, 5th century B.C.

After three years of struggle, the Temple was recaptured in 164 B.C. The description of the state in which the Temple was found shows the wanton neglect it had suffered. First Maccabees 4:38 reports that *"they found the sanctuary a wilderness, the altar desecrated, the gates burnt down, and vegetation growing in the courts as it might in a wood or some mountain, while the storerooms were in ruins."*

Priests were selected to purify the Temple. A new altar was built of unhewn stones after the removal of the defiled altar. The desecrated rocks were stored in a special place on the Temple Mount as no one knew what to do with them. New furniture had to be made so that the sacrifices could resume. *"They restored the Holy Place and the interior of the house, and purified the courts. They made new sacred vessels, and brought the lampstand, the altar of incense, and the table into the Temple…and hung the curtains"* (1 Macc 4.48–51).

Reconstruction of a harp, played by the Levites in the Temple. This harp, based on an archaeological find in the Megiddo area, has twenty-two strings, corresponding to the twenty-two letters of the Hebrew alphabet. (The Temple Institute, Jerusalem)

Exactly three years after the desecration of the altar to Zeus, the new altar was dedicated.

> They rose at dawn and offered a lawful sacrifice on the new altar of holocausts which they had made. The altar was dedicated, to the sound of zithers, harps and cymbals, at the same time of year and on the same day on which the pagans had originally profaned it. The whole people fell prostrate in adoration, praising to the skies him who had made them so successful. For eight days they celebrated the dedication of the altar, joyfully offering holocausts, communion sacrifices and thanksgivings. They ornamented the front of the Temple with crowns and bosses of gold, repaired the gates and the storerooms and fitted them with doors. (1 Macc 52–57)

Chapter Eight: Reconstructing the Second Temple

Hasmonean priests light the menorah after victory. Because the golden menorah was plundered, the priests made a simple menorah of seven metal poles until they were able to reconstruct the golden lampstand. (The Temple Institute, Jerusalem)

Rebellion of the Maccabees, sculpted by Benno Elkan, from a large menorah in front of the Knesset, Jerusalem.

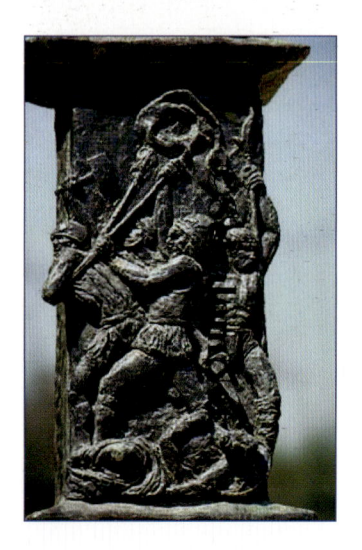

This feast of dedication became known as Hanukkah. It was kept in the time of the New Testament as we read in John 10:22 that it was *"the feast of the dedication, and it was winter."* This feast, also called the Festival of Lights, is still celebrated today. For eight days lights are lit on an eight-branched lampstand or *hannukkiah*—one for each day—to commemorate the miracle believed to have taken place during the original dedication of the altar in 164 B.C. On that occasion, it is recorded that there was only enough oil left for one day's lighting, but it miraculously lasted for eight days.

The neighboring peoples, however, resented the fact that the altar had been rebuilt and the Temple restored, and began to attack the Jewish population. After succeeding his father Antiochus IV Epiphanes, Antiochus V Eupater (164–162 B.C.) besieged Jerusalem. Judas the Maccabee retreated to the Temple Mount and held out until the summer of 162 B.C.

Eventually Antiochus V offered to make peace with the Jews, which they accepted. He then entered the Temple Mount but when he saw *"how strong the place was, he violated his oaths, and ordered his force to go round and pull down the wall to the ground"* (Ant. 12.382–383). This was probably the upper part of the outer perimeter wall of the Temple Mount, the part which stood above the level of the

CHAPTER EIGHT: RECONSTRUCTING THE SECOND TEMPLE

platform. However, the Maccabees apparently held on to the Temple Mount, which they called Mount Zion, while the Hellenizers continued to occupy the Akra. In 141 B.C., the fortress fell to Simon Maccabeus and his forces. They obliterated the Akra and even lowered the mountain on which it was built (as discussed above, pp. 207–211). The whole area was then incorporated into the Temple Mount complex.

Simon established the Hasmonean monarchy in 141 B.C. He took on the role of High Priest, leader of the people and commander of the army, and declared an independent state. Simon's son and successor, John Hyrcanus I (134–104 B.C.), strengthened the new Jewish state and (as mentioned above, pp. 216–219) built the Temple fortress called the *Baris*, at the northwest corner of the square Temple Mount, apparently in the first year of his reign.

Jerusalem began again to expand to the Western Hill in the mid-second century B.C., during which time this hill was probably surrounded once more by a city wall. According to Avigad[5], it was Jonathan who began to build this city wall in order to enclose the new quarter that Simon eventually completed. Many remnants of the ancient wall that were still extant were incorporated in the Hasmonean city wall, called the First Wall by Josephus (*War* 5.142–145).

The new wall followed the line of the city wall first built by King Hezekiah[6]. The northern part ran from the northwest corner of the city, where later the three magnificent Herodian towers—Hippicus, Phasael and Mariamne—were built, to the Western Wall of the square Temple Mount. Josephus tells us in *War* 1.143 that during the siege of the Temple Mount by Pompey, one of the Jewish warring parties—that led by Aristobulus—*"retired into the Temple, and cut the bridge which connected it with the city."* This bridge, which was

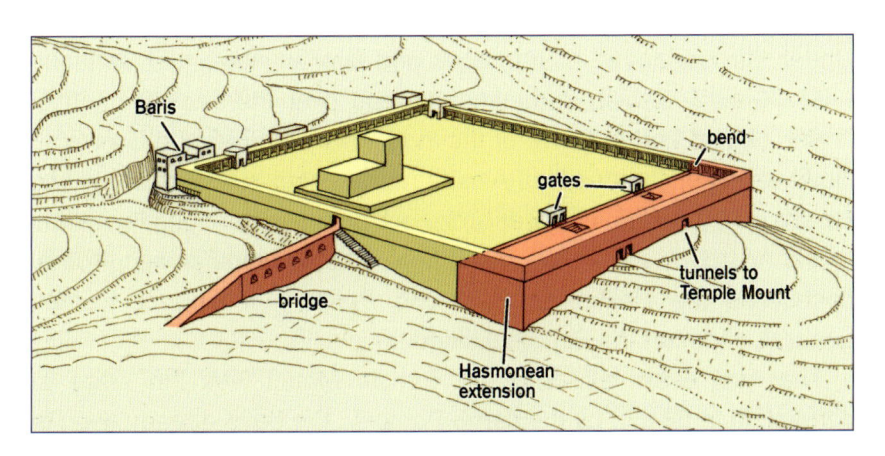

Above: One of the projecting towers of the First Wall, on the crest of the Eastern Hill, with the corner of another tower just beyond it, both of which were built during the Hasmonean period.

Below: Reconstruction of the eastern section of the First Wall and its two towers.

Reconstruction of the Hasmonean extension of the Temple Mount.

CHAPTER EIGHT: RECONSTRUCTING THE SECOND TEMPLE

Right: Reconstruction of the First Wall and towers discovered inside the Citadel courtyard. The present-day walls of the Citadel, shown in a lighter shade, mostly date from the Mamluk or Turkish periods.

Below: The courtyard of the present-day Citadel, the so-called Tower of David next to Jaffa Gate, looking south. In foreground, remains of the First Wall and the two projecting towers on its right, originally built in the Hasmonean period.

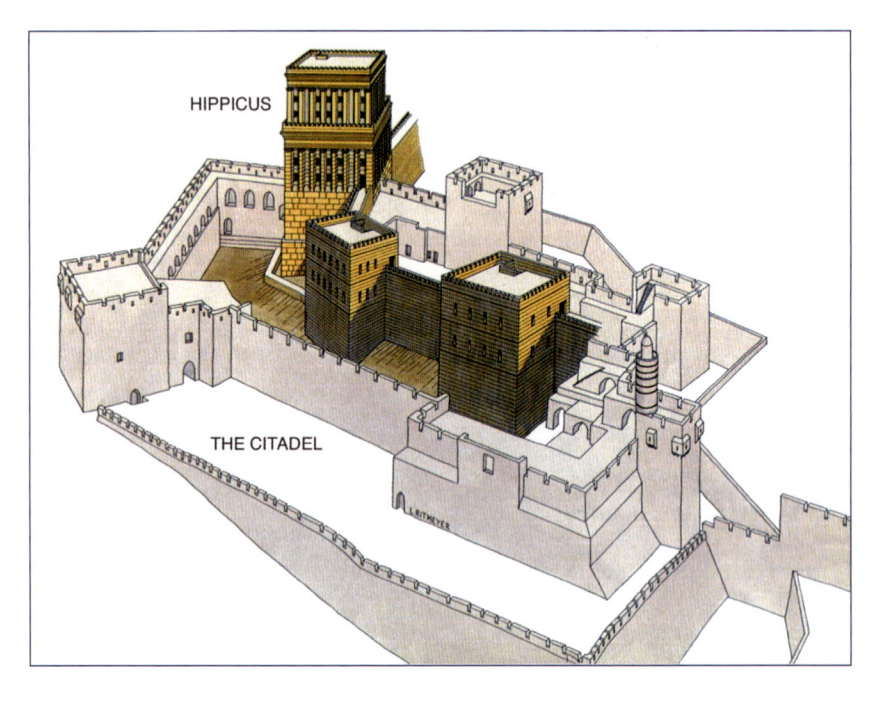

probably built against the city wall, became the forerunner of the later Herodian bridge that was built over Wilson's Arch.

The foregoing makes it clear that the Temple Mount suffered considerable permutations in the second century B.C. After the Hasmonean extension to the south, the Temple Mount was no longer square in shape. Furthermore, a new Baris fortress stood at the northwest corner and a new bridge and city wall joined the newly built quarter on the Western Hill to the Temple Mount. The Temple Mount was also embellished with porticoes and the Temple itself was refurbished with the addition of some golden decorations.

POMPEY'S SIEGE OF THE TEMPLE MOUNT

Under the leadership of Hyrcanus and later of Alexander Janneus (103–76 B.C.), Jewish dominance spread over the ancient Land of Israel, almost to the extent of the kingdoms of David and Solomon. However, after the death of Alexandra, Janneus's widow who ruled for some nine years, civil war broke out between her sons Hyrcanus II and Aristobulus II. In the meantime, a rising world power, Rome, conquered the Hellenistic East and Pompey, a brilliant Roman general, annexed the Seleucid kingdom.

The next event affecting the Temple Mount was the siege of Jerusalem in 63 B.C. by the same Pompey. We have already seen in

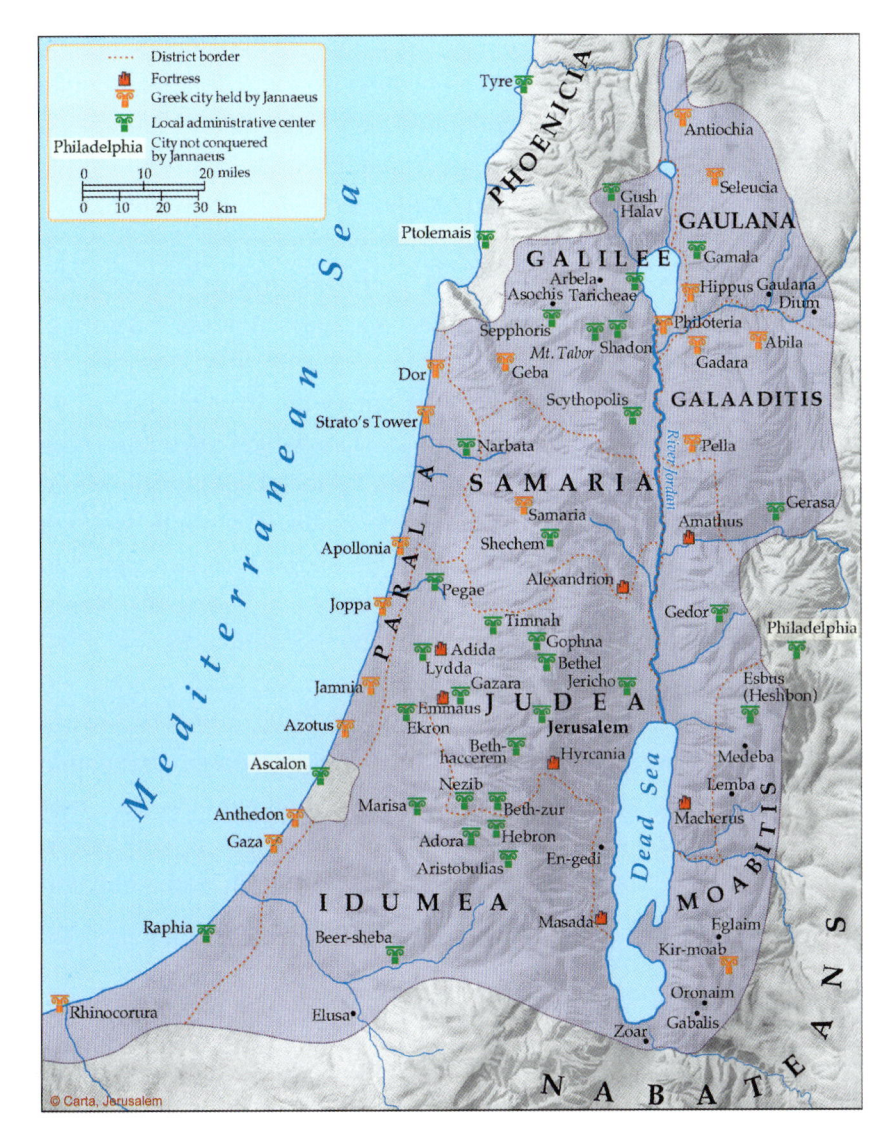

CHAPTER EIGHT: RECONSTRUCTING THE SECOND TEMPLE

Left: *The kingdom of Alexander Janneus, 103–76 B.C.*

Below: *Coin of Alexander Janneus.*

Chapter 2 (p. 168) that the Fosse was filled in by Pompey's soldiers. According to Josephus[7], it was the Jews' adherence to the keeping of the Sabbath day that gave the Romans time to accomplish this task. The Romans then placed siege engines on these earth fills and battered the towers of the *Baris*. They succeeded in breaching one of the towers, thereby allowing the Roman soldiers to pour directly onto the Temple Mount (another proof that the *Baris* was connected to the Temple platform at its northwest corner).

Incidentally, all during the siege the priests continued the services as usual, despite the slaughter of many Jews. Pompey and his

Chapter Eight: Reconstructing the Second Temple

Hasmonean coin, with depiction of a menorah on reverse.

men entered the sanctuary and even went into the Holy of Holies. Nevertheless, he did not remove anything from the Temple, despite having seen there *"the golden table...and the sacred lampstand and the libation vessels and a great quantity of spices, and beside these, in the treasury, the sacred monies amounting to two thousand talents"* (*Ant.* 14.72). The next day Pompey ordered the Temple to be cleansed and the services to resume. From this time on, however, the Jewish state became effectively a Roman province under the control of a proconsul who resided in Syria.

Hyrcanus II was then made high priest by the Romans and in 47 B.C. became Ethnarch of the Jews, a position which gave him more political power. However, Antipater, the father of Herod the Great and son of a rich Idumean of the same name, apparently wielded greater influence in the political arena. He allowed his son Herod to govern Galilee. Antipater was murdered in 43 B.C. Eventually, Herod the Great was proclaimed King of Judah by the Roman Senate in 40 B.C., after having gained the favor of Octavian and Mark Antony. He still had to establish his sovereignty over the Jews, a task he set out to do in the winter of 39 B.C. After a two-year campaign, Jerusalem and the Temple Mount finally fell to him in the summer of 37 B.C. (*War* 1.347–353). When Antigonus, the son of Aristobulus II, was put to death by order of Mark Antony (see also *Ant.* 14.490), Herod became the undisputed ruler of Judea.

HEROD THE GREAT AND THE PROTO-ANTONIA

One of the first things that Herod appears to have done on the Temple Mount was to rebuild the *Baris* fortress. This is clear from *Antiquities* 13.307, where Josephus writes that Aristobulus I *"was lying ill in the castle (Baris) afterwards called Antonia."* However, scholars differ on the historical problem of the Antonia-*Baris* relationship, on the one hand, and the architectural problem concerning the extent of the Antonia and its precise relationship to the Temple Mount, on the other.

As for the historical relationship between the *Baris* and the Antonia, we have seen that the *Baris* was located at the northwest corner of the square Temple Mount. The *Baris* was the successor of the Towers of Hananeel and Meah. This fortress had at least two towers, one of which was called Strato's Tower. In an underground passage of that tower, Antigonus I was murdered by the bodyguards of his brother Aristobulus I (*War* 1.77, 80).

Chapter Eight: Reconstructing the Second Temple

Josephus' description of a subterranean structure would suit our location of the *Baris*, as the site where we have placed it has foundations lower than the Temple courts. This description would be totally inappropriate for a building that was perched high on top of rockscarps. We have also mentioned that the underground passage that connected the *Baris* with the square Temple Mount was most likely Cistern 1 (see plan, p. 332). The *Baris* was destroyed in 63 B.C. by Pompey (*War* 1.147).

The towers of the *Baris*, which according to Josephus had been "extraordinary massive and beautiful," are those which appear to have been rebuilt by Herod after his capture of Jerusalem in 37 B.C. We suggest that this restored fortress was the original fortress, named in honor of Herod's friend Mark Antony. Mark Antony ruled the eastern provinces of the Roman Empire as triumvir from 43 to 32 B.C., but lost the power struggle to his rival Octavian, who later became Augustus. As Herod had supported Mark Antony against Octavian, this rebuilding of the *Baris* and calling it Antonia must have taken place before Mark Antony's naval defeat at Actium in 31 B.C. After this event it is hardly conceivable that Herod would have dedicated any building to him.

For this reason, it has been suggested that Herod's construction of the Antonia preceded his enlargement of the Temple Mount by at least fifteen years, and were therefore separate building activities.[8] We would agree with this, if the site of the original Antonia was, as suggested above, identical with the restored fortress at the northwest corner of the square Temple Mount. However, if the location at the northwest corner of the Herodian Temple Mount is presumed, then this would have been most impractical. In such a situation, both the *Baris* and the original Antonia would have been separated from the square Temple Mount by the Fosse, contradicting Josephus' record of the siege of Pompey.

It is clear, however, from Josephus' description of the Antonia in *War* 5.238–246, which we quoted in Chapter 1 (pp. 124–126), that he refers to the fortress located at the northwest corner of the Herodian Temple Mount. It appears, then, that there were two fortresses in two different locations and that both were called Antonia, one of which had preceded the other. In order to distinguish between the two fortresses, we have called the first one, located at the northwest corner of the square Temple Mount, the Proto-Antonia. The view that

Above: The Herodian tower of Hippicus (today's so-called Tower of David) in the Citadel.

Below: Coin of Mark Antony (left) and of Octavian (right).

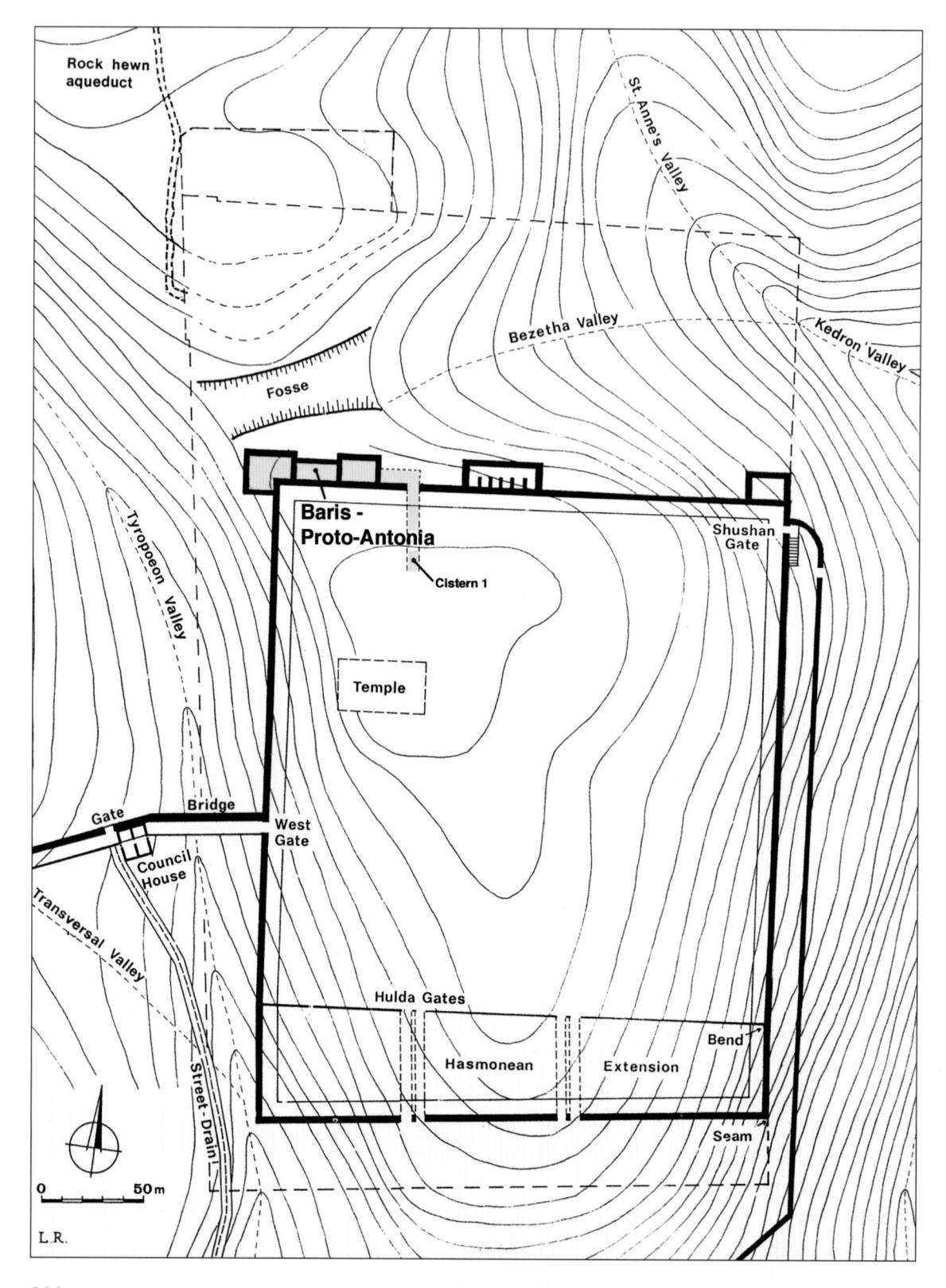

Chapter Eight. Reconstructing the Second Temple

Chapter Eight: Reconstructing the Second Temple

there were two fortresses called by this name, has already been expressed by Warren[9],

> With regard to the Antonia, I still feel in considerable doubt whether it stood on the northwest angle of the present Sanctuary or on the northwest angle of the Dome of the Rock platform, and the only solution I can see to the difficulties is by supposing that it did both.

About twenty years into his reign, Herod began his grandiose project of renewing the Temple Mount by enlarging the square Temple Mount to twice its previous size. It was then that he built the new fortress at the northwest corner of the Herodian Temple Mount. As the name Antonia was originally given by Herod to the rebuilt *Baris*, we suggest that this new Herodian fortress may have inherited the same name, by virtue of popular use.

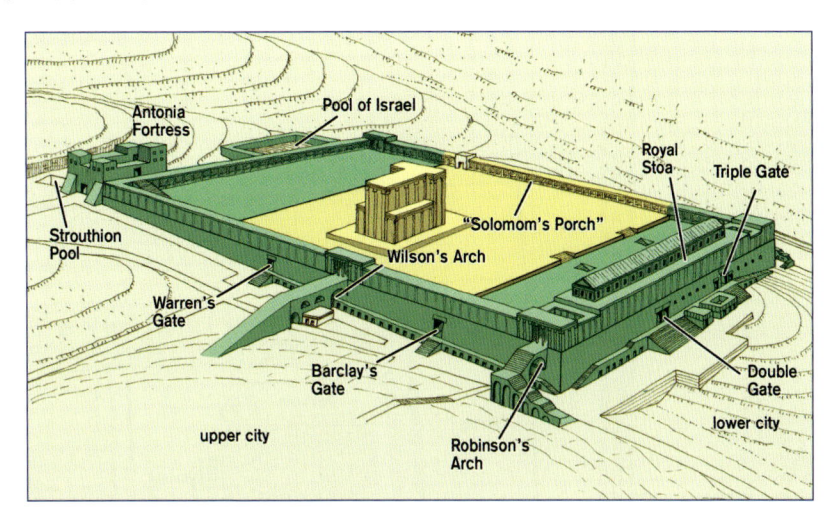

Josephus knew only this fortress, but he also may have remembered that Herod, after having rebuilt it, changed the name of *Baris* to Antonia. The fact that both the *Baris* and the Antonia were located at the northwest corner of the respective Temple Mounts and fulfilled similar functions must have caused this mistake. Josephus' apparent lack of awareness of the transfer of the name Antonia from the old location to the new one has led, in our opinion, to much confusion among scholars.

It is common practice in Israel today to call new settlements after historical towns, even when some distance away from the original site. This also happens with buildings. The Knesset, for example, is the name of Israel's present Parliament building in Hakirya, the Government Center of Jerusalem. The first Knesset building, however, was in Tel Aviv and the second was located on King George Street in Jerusalem, making today's Knesset building the third to bear the same name. A similar carrying over of names to new sites, I conclude, may have happened with the Antonia.

Opposite page: Reconstruction proposal for the location of the Baris–Proto-Antonia Fortress.

Below: Reconstruction of the Herodian Temple Mount.

View of the Knesset building today, Jerusalem.

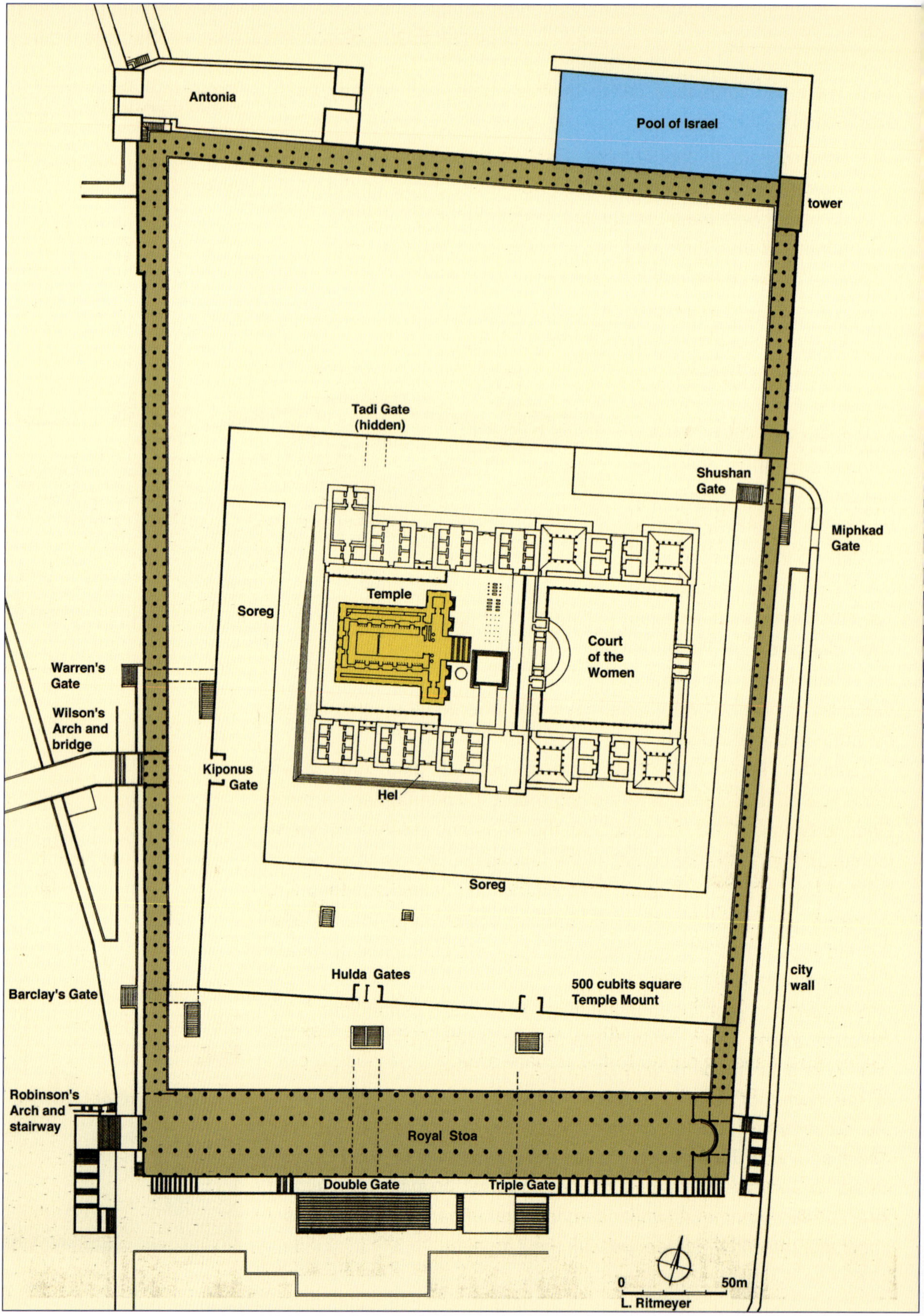
Antonia
Pool of Israel
tower
Tadi Gate
(hidden)
Shushan
Gate
Miphkad
Gate
Temple
Soreg
Court
of the
Women
Warren's
Gate
Wilson's
Arch and
bridge
Kiponus
Gate
Hel
Soreg
Hulda Gates
500 cubits square
Temple Mount
city
wall
Barclay's Gate
Robinson's
Arch and
stairway
Royal Stoa
Double Gate
Triple Gate
0
50m
L. Ritmeyer

Opposite page: Plan of the Herodian Temple Mount.

Below: Model of the Herodian Temple Mount, viewed from the southeast. (photo: Philip Evans)

Bottom: Seal impression with emblem of the Tenth Roman Legion.

Chapter Nine
Reconstructing the Herodian Temple Mount

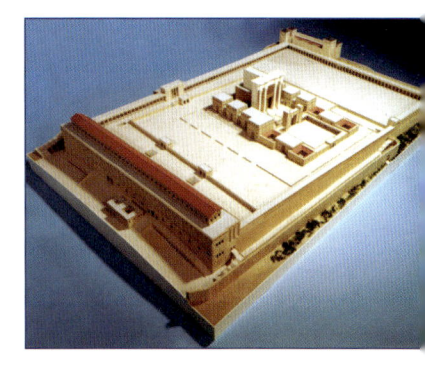

THE HERODIAN PORTICOES AND THE PRESERVED IDENTITY OF THE SQUARE TEMPLE MOUNT

In order to understand the exact layout of the Herodian Temple Mount, we have to investigate the historical record and combine it with the archaeological evidence presented in this book. The Herodian gates which gave access to the Temple platform have been described in great detail in Chapter 1. On reaching the level of the Temple Mount, one would find oneself in a court located between the beautiful Herodian porticoes and the wall of the pre-Herodian Temple Mount. Both these features and the space in between have been described in historical records.

We have already noted that the Mishnah was written and compiled well after the Roman destruction in A.D. 70. The fact that the Mishnah only refers to a Temple Mount which was 500 cubits square indicates that only the old *temenos* was considered to be the *"Mountain of the House"* (see Chapter 2, p. 144). The five gates mentioned in *Middot* 1.3 (two Hulda Gates on the south, the Kiponus Gate on the west, the Tadi Gate on the north which was not in use, and the Eastern Gate) must have belonged to this square area. As there is no point in having gates without a connecting wall between them, it appears that the square Temple Mount preserved its identity on the expanded Herodian Temple Mount, not only as a separate paved area, as some have suggested,[1] but as a completely separate area with its own wall and gates.

In his sixth book of the *Jewish War*, Josephus gives an interesting

Chapter Nine: Reconstructing the Herodian Temple Mount

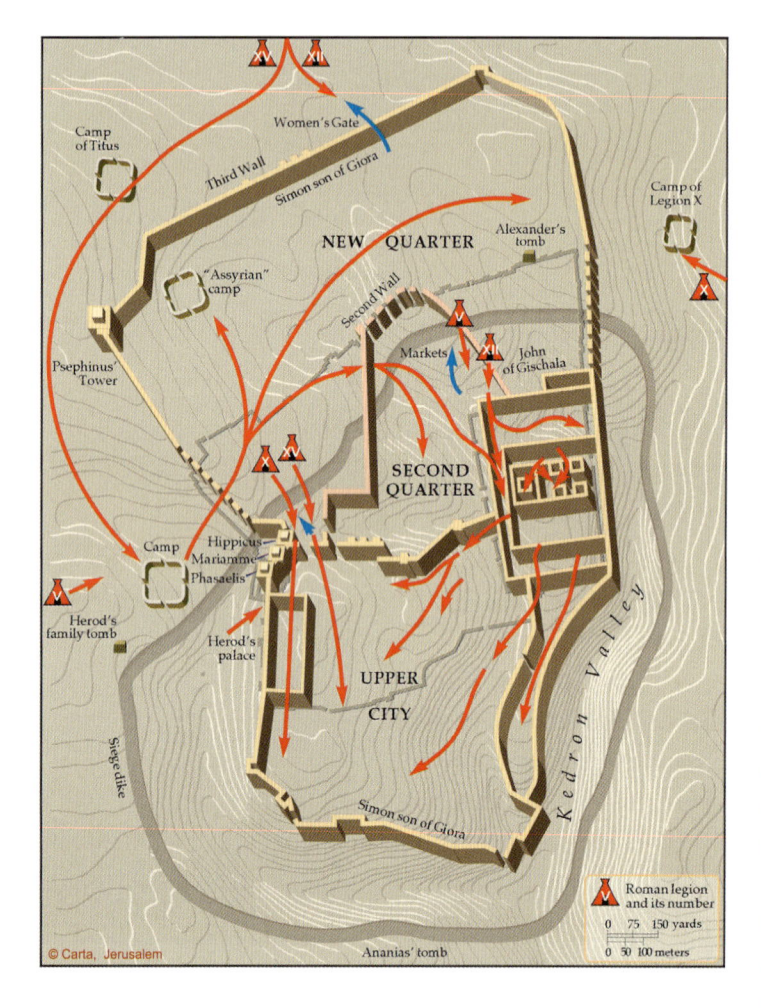

Above: The siege of Jerusalem, A.D. 70.

Below: View of the narrow space between the Herodian western wall and the square Temple Mount. (photo: Philip Evans)

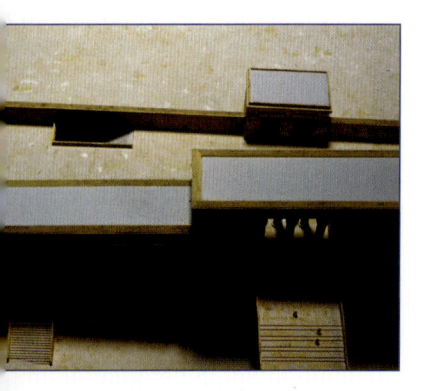

and vivid—though immensely tragic—account of the destruction of the Temple Mount by the Romans, an account that supports a layout for the Temple courts suggested above. The Antonia Fortress was the first part of the Temple Mount captured by the Romans *(War* 6.68–80). When this happened, the Jews fled to the Temple. A battle ensued which took place between the Antonia and the *"entrances"* of the Temple (vs. 74).

The Romans had to retreat to the Antonia (vs. 80), from which they planned their next attack. They could not send in *"the whole force against them owing to the confined nature of the ground; he [Titus] therefore selected thirty of the best men from each century"* (vs. 131) to attack the guards of the Temple. (A century is a company in the Roman army, originally of 100 men.) Josephus again recalls that the battle was *"limited to a narrow space and quickly over; for neither side had room for flight or pursuit"* (vs. 144). As this battle was watched by the rest of the Romans from the Antonia Fortress, the narrow space referred to can only be the area between the square Temple Mount and the Herodian porticoes. In the meantime, the Romans razed the Antonia to its foundations and started to prepare a broad ascent to the Temple (vs. 149). The Jews had retreated behind the wall of the square Temple Mount while also trying to isolate the Romans in the Antonia by setting fire to and destroying *"the northwest portico which was connected to the Antonia"* (vss. 164–165). Eventually, the entire western and northern porticoes were destroyed.

As the inner complex was difficult to assault, Titus ordered the gates to be burnt (vs. 228). A road had to be made through the ruins to those gates so that the Roman soldiers could enter the courts

CHAPTER NINE: RECONSTRUCTING THE HERODIAN TEMPLE MOUNT

surrounding the Temple Court and the Court of the Women. Although completely encircled and cut off, the Jews attacked the Romans while *"they sallied out through the eastern gate upon the guards of the outer court of the Temple"* (vs. 244).

The Roman soldiers now were fighting in the *"inner court,"* or Court of the Women; and then *"routing the Jews and pursuing them right up to the sanctuary"* (vs. 251). One of the soldiers threw a firebrand into the Temple, first destroying *"the chambers surrounding the Temple"* (vs. 261), although Titus and his generals still managed to enter and view the sanctuary and its contents. However, the fire could not be contained and eventually the whole Temple went up in flames. Titus tried his utmost to save the Temple, but he could not restrain his soldiers who were consumed by *"their rage, their hatred of the Jews, and a lust for battle more unruly still"* (vs. 263).

Although these events were indeed dreadful, Josephus' record of the battle has left us with a clear idea of the layout of the Herodian Temple Mount. First of all, the Antonia was captured and the northern and western porticoes burned and destroyed. Earthworks then made it possible for the legions to go up onto the Temple platform. The next line of defense was the walled enclosure of the square Temple Mount, which the Romans could not capture without setting fire to the gates and preparing an assault road through the rubble. After that they entered the Court of the Women, and from there they finally reached the Temple itself.

While reflecting on the battle, Josephus curiously refers to an oracle that was apparently known at that time and according to which, *"The Jews, after the demolition of the Antonia, reduced the Temple to a square, although they had it recorded in their oracles that the city and the sanctuary would be taken when the Temple should become four-square"* (vs. 311). The translator of Josephus, Thackeray, did not know the origin of this oracle (see his note a), but Yadin tentatively connected this oracle with the knowledge Josephus may have had of the Temple Scroll.

This Temple Scroll was one of the Dead Sea Scrolls in which

Above: Triumphal parade of Roman soldiers carrying the Temple vessels, relief on the Arch of Titus, Rome.

Below: Coin of the Tenth Roman Legion.

Drawing of the Antonia Fortress at the northwest corner of the Temple Mount.

341

Chapter Nine: Reconstructing the Herodian Temple Mount

a temple with three concentric square courts was described. The square middle court of the Temple Scroll had internal measurements of 480 cubits, but if the outer walls were included, it could have measured 500 cubits.[2] There is apparently a correlation between the middle court of the Temple of the Temple Scroll and the preserved 500-cubit-square Temple Mount in Jerusalem. Yadin[3] suggested that this "oracle," which Josephus mentioned, may have come from the Temple Scroll:

> *Can it be that the answer is to be found in the scroll, in the context of its absolutely square plan of the Temple with its concentric square courts which, as we have indicated, Josephus may have gleaned from Essene writings or their noted oracle-like commentaries—or perhaps from our very Temple Scroll? He may have arrived at the notion that what they had said or written contained the hint that before the Lord would create his Temple "at the end of days," the earthly Temple had to be square, as set forth in our scroll.*

Reconstruction drawing of the Temple and its courts according to the Temple Scroll. The Temple in the center is surrounded by three concentric courts, the middle one of which measured 500 by 500 cubits.

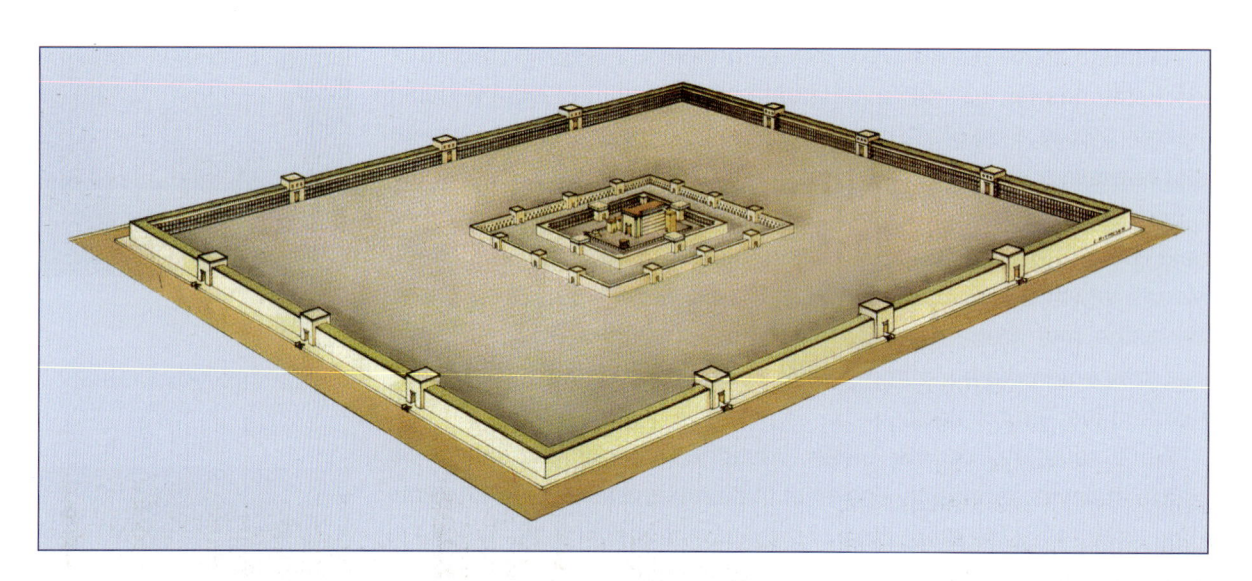

While I was making reconstruction drawings of the Temple based on the Temple Scroll description, Yadin mentioned privately to me that he thought that in their messianic philosophy, the Essene community wanted to build this complex, believing that it would be destroyed upon completion, and be replaced by the Temple of Ezekiel's prophecy.

CHAPTER NINE: RECONSTRUCTING THE HERODIAN TEMPLE MOUNT

For us, however, this oracle supports the theory that the Temple Mount did indeed become a square after the destruction of the Antonia, as the fortified walls and gates of the 500-cubit-square Temple Mount became the next line of defense.

The Herodian porticoes which were destroyed by Jews and Romans alike, stood along the inside of the outer retaining walls that Herod built when he enlarged the platform. The Herodian porticoes, which had double rows of columns supporting a beautifully carved ceiling made of cedar wood, were an impressive sight. Josephus gives the following description:

> The porticoes, all in double rows, were supported by columns five and twenty cubits high—each single block of the purest white marble—and ceiled with panels of cedar. The natural magnificence of these columns, their excellent polish and fine adjustment presented a striking spectacle, without any adventitious embellishment of painting or sculpture. The porticoes were thirty cubits broad, and the complete circuit of them, embracing the Antonia, measured six furlongs. The open court was from end to end variegated with paving of all manner of stone. (*War* 5.190–192)

Section through a Herodian portico, which had two rows of columns.

These rows of columns had corresponding pilasters in the outer wall. One could obviously walk on top of these porticoes, as indicated by Josephus. The gatehouses which were built over the arches of Robinson and Wilson would have been incorporated in these porticoes. As these gatehouses would be higher than the porticoes themselves, there would have been internal staircases to ascend to the roofs of the porticoes. As already noted, the northern portico was built against the southern rockscarp of the Antonia Fortress and a northern gate may have been located in

Computerized view of the Royal Stoa. (Courtesy Slawek Jozwik)

343

Chapter Nine: Reconstructing the Herodian Temple Mount

Opposite page: Plan of the buildings around the Temple Court and the Court of the Women.

Torch-bearing priests on their dawn patrol of the Temple courtyard. One company of priests went in an easterly direction, while the other went towards the west, checking that all was in order for the Temple service.

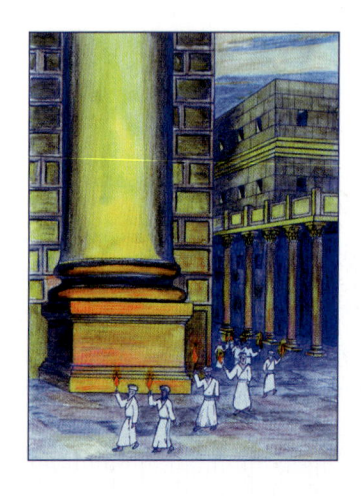

this portico, as intimated by Josephus (*War* 6.222). The magnificent Royal Stoa stood over the Southern Wall of the Temple Mount.

THE GATES OF THE SQUARE TEMPLE MOUNT

As mentioned previously, the square Temple Mount had five gates, namely two Huldah gates on the south, the Kiponus Gate on the west, the Tadi Gate on the north (not in use) and the Eastern Gate (*Middot* 1.3). These were the gates that were burned by the Romans to gain access to the square *temenos.*

We have already described the underground passageway of the Herodian Double Gate, which would have had a staircase at its northern end leading up to the southern Temple court. One can logically assume this exit is opposite the original Huldah Gates. This passageway is located on the same north-south axis as Cistern 1, which was probably the underground passageway of the northern Tadi Gate. We have suggested that the Kiponus Gate stood east of Wilson's Arch and that the monolithic gateposts inside the Golden Gate are the remains of the Eastern Shushan Gate. A connecting wall completed the boundary of the square Temple Mount.

For the layout of the courts and buildings inside the square Temple Mount, we rely mainly on the description of *Middot*. This tractate reflects, of course, the Temple Mount as it existed just before it was destroyed in A.D. 70. We will try and follow the description of the Temple Mount as given in *Middot*.

The first chapter deals with the places where the priests had to keep guard in the Temple. The remainder of the tractate is devoted to a centripetal account of the courts and buildings of the Temple platform. Chapter 2 begins by stating that the Temple Mount measured five hundred cubits by five hundred cubits and then moves inward to the *soreg*. The Court of the Gentiles was the area between the outer walls and the *soreg*. The next element to be described is the rampart, or *ḥel*, located beyond the *soreg* and which could be reached from the south by a flight of twelve steps. The next court is the Court of the Women, located to the east of the Temple. This court had four smaller courts, one at each corner. Moving closer to the Temple, one first encounters the Court of the Israelites and then the Court of the Priests. These two narrow courts were part of the Temple Court in which the Sanctuary stood.

The third chapter is devoted to the Altar, the Place of Slaughter,

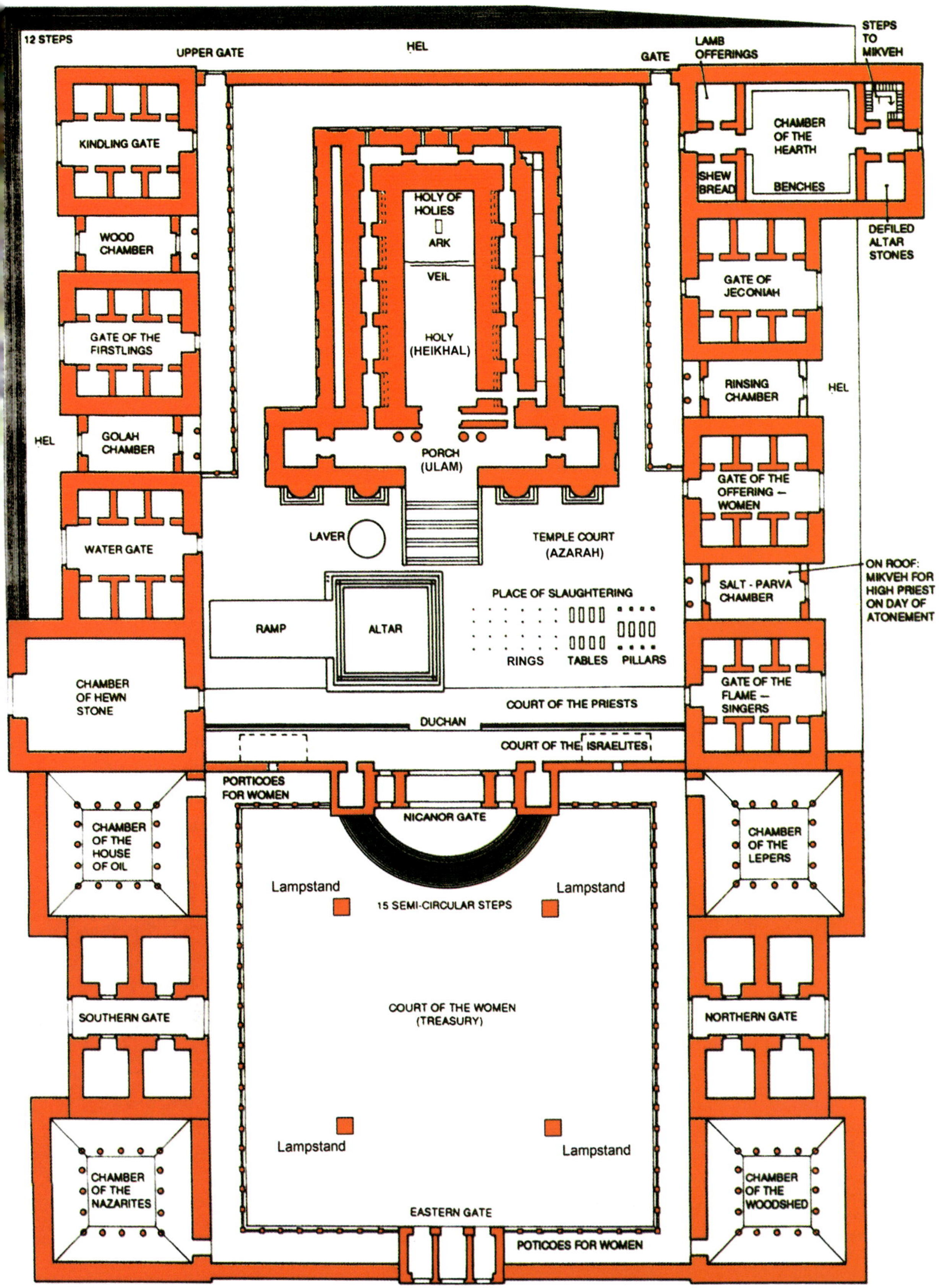
12 STEPS
UPPER GATE
HEL
GATE
LAMB OFFERINGS
STEPS TO MIKVEH
KINDLING GATE
CHAMBER OF THE HEARTH
SHEW BREAD
BENCHES
HOLY OF HOLIES
ARK
VEIL
HOLY (HEIKHAL)
DEFILED ALTAR STONES
WOOD CHAMBER
GATE OF JECONIAH
GATE OF THE FIRSTLINGS
RINSING CHAMBER
HEL
HEL
GOLAH CHAMBER
PORCH (ULAM)
GATE OF THE OFFERING – WOMEN
LAVER
WATER GATE
TEMPLE COURT (AZARAH)
SALT - PARVA CHAMBER
ON ROOF: MIKVEH FOR HIGH PRIEST ON DAY OF ATONEMENT
PLACE OF SLAUGHTERING
RAMP
ALTAR
RINGS
TABLES
PILLARS
CHAMBER OF HEWN STONE
GATE OF THE FLAME – SINGERS
COURT OF THE PRIESTS
DUCHAN
COURT OF THE ISRAELITES
PORTICOES FOR WOMEN
NICANOR GATE
CHAMBER OF THE HOUSE OF OIL
CHAMBER OF THE LEPERS
Lampstand
Lampstand
15 SEMI-CIRCULAR STEPS
SOUTHERN GATE
COURT OF THE WOMEN (TREASURY)
NORTHERN GATE
Lampstand
Lampstand
CHAMBER OF THE NAZARITES
CHAMBER OF THE WOODSHED
EASTERN GATE
POTICOES FOR WOMEN

Chapter Nine: Reconstructing the Herodian Temple Mount

the Laver and the *ulam* of the Temple, while the next chapter gives a detailed description of the Sanctuary itself. The tractate *Middot*'s final chapter describes the chambers that were built around the Temple Court. We will now examine these components in detail.

THE *SOREG*

Inside this square platform of 500 cubits, was a balustrade or railing[4] called *soreg* in Hebrew and δρυφακτοσ in Greek (see plan, p. 338). According to *Middot* 2.3, it was ten handbreadths high and *"had thirteen breaches which the Grecian kings had made; these were fenced up again, and over against them thirteen prostrations were decreed."* Ten handbreadths equals 2 feet 10 inches or 87.5 cm. According to Josephus this balustrade was three cubits high (5 feet 2 inches, 1.57 m). He also tells us[5] that at certain intervals this barrier carried inscriptions in Greek and Latin, forbidding any non-Jew to enter. The text of the inscription reads, *"No Gentile may enter within the railing around the Sanctuary and within the enclosure. Whosoever should be caught will render himself liable to the death penalty which will inevitably follow."*

Despite the fact that Josephus states that the inscriptions were written, *"some in Greek, and some in Roman letters,"* only remains of Greek inscriptions have been found so far. A large stone with a complete Greek inscription forbidding entry to the inner Temple courtyard was found, in secondary use, in the corner construction of a build-

Greek inscription prohibiting Gentiles from entering the inner courtyard of the Temple.

Chapter Nine: Reconstructing the Herodian Temple Mount

ing in a courtyard to the north of the Temple Mount[6]. A fragment of another Greek inscription was found later near St. Stephen's Gate.[7]

As far as the meaning of the inscription is concerned, it has been proposed[8] that in case of trespass, the priestly administrators of the Temple would administer this punishment through summary execution—as was attempted when the Apostle Paul was suspected of bringing Gentiles into the Temple (Acts 21:28–31).

It should be remembered that, under Roman occupation, the Jews were not allowed to execute people. This is clear from the New Testament, where in John 18.31, the Jews said to Pilate, *"It is not lawful for us to put any man to death."* However, according to Josephus' record of the speech of Titus during the siege of the Temple, it would appear that the Jews were apparently granted as a special privilege the right to kill a foreigner who went beyond the *soreg*. War 6.124–126 reports:

> *Was it not you, he said, most abominable wretches, who placed this balustrade before your sanctuary? Was it not you that ranged along it those slabs, engraved in Greek characters and in our own, proclaiming that none may pass the barrier? And did we not permit you to put to death any who passed it, even were he a Roman?*

The *soreg*, therefore, was a screen located inside the 500-cubit-square area (*Middot* 2.3) and not at the outer boundary of this early platform.[9] Beyond the *soreg* was the *ḥel* or terrace (see below), thereby placing the *soreg* between the outer wall of the square platform and this *ḥel*. No dimensions, however, are given to help determine its location. In Chapter 4 (p. 229) we mentioned that Reich (1989) had identified two cisterns (Nos. 6 and 36) as *mikva'ot*, located in the southern court of the square mount. No Gentiles or unpurified Jews would have been allowed through the *soreg*, so this barrier would have stood just to the north of these *mikva'ot*. It is not stated in *Middot* that the *soreg* surrounded all the buildings and courts of the inner Temple complex.[10] As the purpose of the *soreg* was to screen out Gentile visitors, one would expect to find this screen opposite the gates of the square platform. As there was no northern gate, no screen would have been needed in the northern court. *On our plan (p. 338) we have indicated the soreg as a continuous barrier to the west, south and east of the inner Temple complex.*

The Pontius Pilate inscription from Caesarea. (photo Garo Nalbandian)

Illustration of how a mikveh is used.

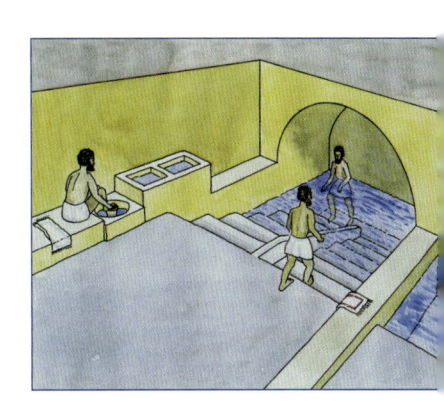

CHAPTER NINE: RECONSTRUCTING THE HERODIAN TEMPLE MOUNT

> **THE HOLINESS OF THE HEL**
>
> *The hel was considered to be holy ground. The following example illustrates this. One of the buildings, the Chamber of the Hearth, at the northwest corner of the Temple Court (Tamid 1.1; Middot 1.6–9), was partially built outside the hel. This building had four rooms, two on either side of the main hall. The two northernmost rooms were located outside the holy ground, because one of them contained the altar stones which were defiled by Antiochus IV Epiphanes (1 Macc 4.44–46) and the other had a winding staircase leading down to a mikveh, used by priests to purify themselves. These two rooms were built outside the hel and a row of flagstones actually indicated the border between holy and unholy ground.*
>
> *In Shekalim 8.4 we are told that if the Veil of the Temple was defiled, it had to be immersed in water and spread out on the hel until sunset for it to be cleansed. It has been suggested that this was also the place where Jesus at the age of twelve sat listening to the teachers and asked them questions (Lk 2:46). Such activity normally only took place inside the Temple Court, but on Sabbaths and festival days the members of the Sanhedrin would come out to the hel to be questioned by the common people and to give them instruction (Babylonian Talmud, Sanhedrin 88b).*

THE HEL OR TERRACE

Middot 2.3 further tells us that the *hel* was 10 cubits (17 feet or 5.25 m) wide and could be reached by climbing twelve steps (see plan, p. 345), although Josephus (*War* 6.195) reports that there were fourteen steps. This discrepancy may have been due to the fact that the platform is not exactly level. It is possible that to the west, where it may have been lower, an extra two steps had to be added. An example of this construction can be seen at the steps leading up to the Double Gate, where, due to bedrock conditions, there are five more steps to the west than there are to the east. Each step leading up to the *hel* was half a cubit (10 inches, 26 cm) high and deep. The *hel* was therefore a paved terrace on top of a stairway from which the gates of the Temple Court could be reached.

THE COURT OF THE WOMEN

To the east of the Temple Court was a 135-cubit- (232.5 feet, 70.88 m) square courtyard, called the Court of the Women. It would therefore have had a surface area of 52,900 square feet or 5,023 square meters. Allowing a square yard per person, this court could easily have held six thousand worshipers at a time. When we recall descriptions of how many people would have visited the Temple during the main festivals, this does not appear too high a figure.

View of the Court of the Women, also called the Treasury in the New Testament. (photo: Philip Evans)

348

CHAPTER NINE: RECONSTRUCTING THE HERODIAN TEMPLE MOUNT

View from inside the Court of the Women looking west toward the Temple. (photo: Philip Evans)

This court was a later addition to the Temple complex. It has been suggested that the construction of the Court of the Women was not completed until A.D. 44.[11]

Court of the Women was so named not because it was reserved for women only, but because this was the farthest women were allowed to enter the Temple precincts. Further alterations took place after its completion. We are told in Middot 2.5, *"Beforetime the Court of the Women was free of buildings, and afterward they surrounded it with a gallery, so that the women should behold from above and the men from below and that they should not mingle together."* This construction is also mentioned in Sukkah 5.2, where it is called *"a great amendment."* The Court of the Women was therefore surrounded with colonnades to keep the men separate from the women.

In these porticoes, thirteen collection boxes for money were placed. These were called *shopharot,* or Shofar-chests. Shofar means a trumpet and this probably refers to funnel-like bronze receptacles which guided coins into the wooden box. From the ensuing sound

Chapter Nine: Reconstructing the Herodian Temple Mount

Trumpet-shaped collection boxes in the porticoes of the Court of the Women. (photo: Philip Evans)

Jewish shekel from time of the First Revolt against Rome (A.D. 66–70). (photo Garo Nalbandian)

one could detect what type of coins were cast inside. No doubt this is how Jesus knew that the poor widow had cast in two mites, as they would have made a faint tinkling noise on touching the trumpet-shaped receptacles (Lk 21:1–4). Other people would have *"of their abundance"* thrown in handfuls of heavy silver shekels, which would have made a great noise. Another of the mishnaic tractates, called *Shekalim,* which deals with the Shekel dues, records that each of the thirteen chests carried an inscription, indicating the object of the offering. There were receptacles for "New Shekel Dues," "Old Shekel Dues," "Bird Offerings," "Young birds for the whole-offering," "Wood," "Frankincense," and "Gold for the Mercy-seat." The remaining six were for "Freewill-offerings." Their placement here in the Court of the Women led to its being called the Treasury in the New Testament.

Another notable feature of the Court of the Women was the presence of four massive lampstands. *Sukkah* 5.2 tells us that

> There were golden menorot there with four golden bowls on the top of them and four ladders to each one, and four youths of the priestly stock and in their hands jars of oil holding a hundred and twenty logs which they poured into all the bowls. They made wicks from the worn out drawers and girdles of the priests and with them they set them alight, and there was not a courtyard in Jerusalem that did not reflect the light of the beth ha-she'ubah.

CHAPTER NINE: RECONSTRUCTING THE HERODIAN TEMPLE MOUNT

This *beth ha-she'ubah* (literally: the place of the water-drawing) was the water-drawing ceremony which took place on the evening of the first day of the feast of Sukkot and thereafter on the remaining days of the feast. It was a joyous occasion, for *Sukkah* 5.1 mentions, *"He that never has seen the joy of the* beth ha-she'ubah *has never in his life seen joy."*

This occasion is referred to in John 7:37–39:

> *In the last day, that great day of the feast, Jesus stood and cried, saying, If any man thirst, let him come unto me, and drink. He that believeth on me, as the scripture hath said, out of his belly shall flow rivers of living water. (But this spake he of the Spirit, which they that believe on him should receive: for the Holy Ghost was not yet given; because that Jesus was not yet glorified.)*

According to a talmudic source, these lampstands were 50 cubits (86 feet or 26.25 m) high, which is half the full height of the Temple! Because of their height, therefore, the ladders which were needed to

One of the lampstands in the Court of the Women. A young priest is climbing the ladder to bring oil to the lamps. (photo: Philip Evans)

reach the golden lamps were probably attached to the stone towers on which the lamps were placed. Each lamp could hold thirty *logs,* which is about 2.5 gallons or 9 liters.

If we assume that the Rock is the place where the Holy of Holies once stood, and we rely on the measurements of *Middot*, we find that the Court of the Women would have been located to the immediate east of the raised platform of the Dome of the Rock, and therefore the pavement of the Court of the Women would have been much lower than the Temple Court. This is one of the reasons that a stairway of fifteen semi-circular steps was built in the western part of this court.

The sources appear to indicate that the court had four gates. We have already mentioned the eastern gate, from which the Jews sallied forth to attack the Romans during the last days of the siege. Here, also, according to the mishnaic tractate Sotah 1.6, the *"water of jealousy"* was given to women suspected of adultery. There were two other gates, one each in the northern and southern walls of the Court of the Women. This is attested in *War* 5.198, where Josephus writes that there *"was one gate on the south and one on the north giving access to the women's court."*

Bird's-eye view of the four chambers of the Court of the Women, looking south (photo: Philip Evans)

On the west stood the magnificent Nicanor Gate, and in the walls on either side of this gate were two openings which gave access to two underground chambers below the Court of the Israelites. According to *Middot* 2.6, the Levites used to play all sorts of musical instruments there.

THE FOUR CHAMBERS OF THE COURT OF THE WOMEN

There were four chambers at the four corners of the Court of the Women (see plan, p. 345). According to *Middot* 2.5, these chambers were 40 cubits (69 feet, 21 m) square and had no roofs. They appear to have been open courts, with the central area open to the sky and porticoes built along the

Chapter Nine: Reconstructing the Herodian Temple Mount

four walls to provide shelter from the hot sun in summer and protection from rain in winter, so that the various functions could be performed regardless of prevailing weather conditions. *Middot* tells us that these four courts were modeled on courts described in the prophecy of Ezekiel's Temple (Ezek 44:22).

Some reconstructions show these chambers as built into the Court of the Women. However, such a layout would have greatly reduced the area for congregational worship, which was the principal function of this court. Hollis[12] suggests that these chambers were located outside the four corners of the Court of the Women, although they could be reached from this court.

The court to the southeast was the Chamber of the Nazarites, where on completion of their vows, consecrated men brought their offerings and cut off their hair and threw it in the fire below the cauldron used for boiling the peace offering. The priest then waved the offering before God, after which the Nazarite was free from his vow of separation and could again drink wine.

To the northeast was the Chamber of the Woodshed, where priests with a blemish had the task of examining logs for woodworm. If woodworm was found in a log, it would be disqualified for use on the Altar.

The Chamber of the Lepers was on the northwest. When a leper was healed, he had to bring offerings according to the Mosaic instructions and was shaved completely. During the next seven days, he was not allowed to enter into his own home or to have marital relations. On the eighth day he had to bring additional sacrifices. He then had to bathe in the Chamber of the Lepers, after which he went to the Gate of Nicanor. Here, the

Above: A Nazarite completing his vow in the Chamber of the Nazarites.

Below: The Chamber of the Lepers, at the northwest corner of the Court of the Women. (The Temple Institute, Jerusalem)

leper thrust his hand into the Temple Court and after the performance of certain rituals, during which blood and oil were put on his body and his sin offering and burnt offering were presented, the leper was considered cleansed from his disease. The leper who was healed by Jesus and to whom he said: *"See thou tell no man; but go thy way, shew thyself to the priest, and offer the gift that Moses commanded, for a testimony unto them"* (Mt 8:4; Mk 1:44; Lk 5:14) would have performed the very same ritual.

The fourth court, on the southwest, was called the Chamber of the House of Oil, where wine and oil were stored.

THE FIFTEEN SEMI-CIRCULAR STEPS

A stairway of fifteen steps was constructed in the eastern part of the Court of the Women so that the Court of the Israelites, which was located on a higher level, could be reached. These steps are lyrically described in *Middot* 2.5 as *"not four-square, but rounded like the half of a round threshing floor."* On these steps the Levites used to sing the fifteen Psalms of Ascents, which are Psalms 120–134.

The Levitical choir on the fifteen semi-circular steps leading to the Nicanor Gate. (photo: Philip Evans)

We have already concluded that the Court of the Women was located to the immediate east of the platform of the Dome of the Rock. As can be seen from the plan (opposite), these fifteen semi-circular steps are located exactly where the present eastern stairway is. This is no coincidence, but supports our location of the Temple courts. According to the existing bedrock levels, it appears that these fifteen steps were cut out of the bedrock or constructed immediately above it. The present-day steps therefore reflect the location of these original fifteen steps, some of which may still be preserved underneath.

We have already referred to the beautiful Nicanor Gate (*Middot*

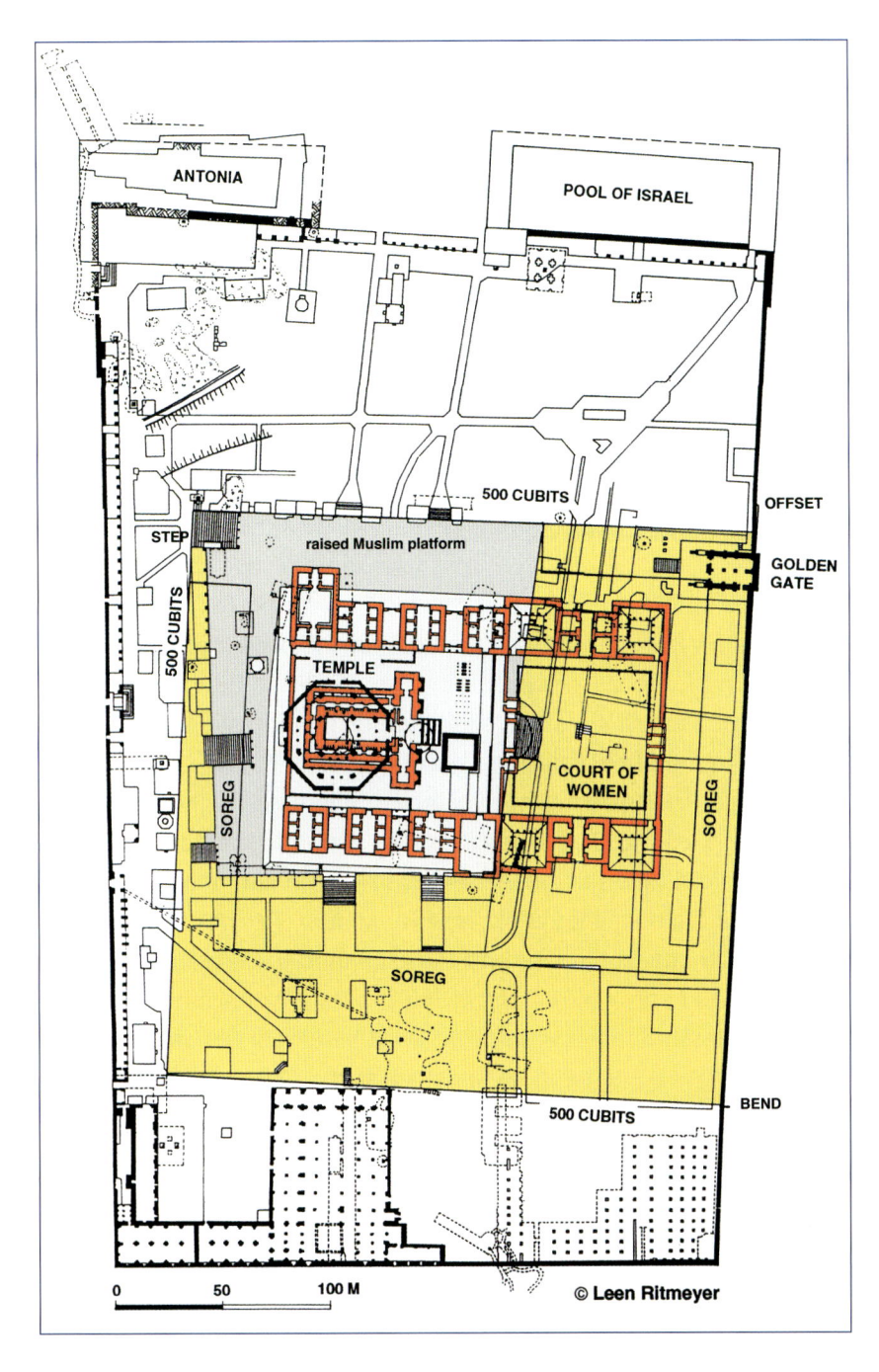

CHAPTER NINE: RECONSTRUCTING THE HERODIAN TEMPLE MOUNT

Plan of the present-day Temple Mount, showing the location of the 500-cubit-square Temple Mount, the location of the soreg and the Herodian Temple complex.

View of the eastern stairway today.

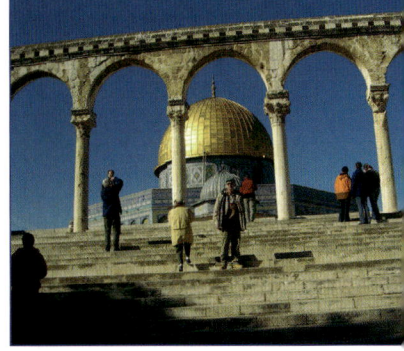

1.4; 2.6), which stood at the top of these steps and which had great doors made of bronze. Many important rituals such as the cleansing of the leper and the purification of women after childbirth were enacted in front of this gate. It was a triple gate, having one massive central opening and two smaller side gates, called wickets in

355

Chapter Nine: Reconstructing the Herodian Temple Mount

Above: Artist's rendition of the Chamber of Phinehas, keeper of vestments. (The Temple Institute, Jerusalem)

Below: Burial cave containing decorated ossuaries, one of which bears an inscription which mentions Nicanor of Alexandria, Mount Scopus, Jerusalem. (NEAEHL)

Shekalim 6.3. This gate structure also had two chambers on either side of the passageway. One was called the Chamber of Phinehas, who was the keeper of the vestments, and the other was for those who made the Leavened Cakes. The central opening could be closed with two massive bronze doors. A legend attached to these doors *(Tosephta* 2.4) says that when these gates were brought from Alexandria by ship, a storm raged. The sailors threw one of the doors overboard in order to lighten the load. While they contemplated throwing the second door overboard as well, the door is reputed to have said to them, "Throw me after it," upon which the storm eased. Upon landing at Jaffa, the other door was found underneath the ship.

According to Josephus, who refers to this gate as the Corinthian Gate *(War* 5.201–206), it was fifty cubits high and the doors forty cubits high. We have used these measurements in our reconstruction of the Nicanor Gate, as they are omitted in *Middot*. The doors of the gate were of *"Corinthian bronze, and far exceeded in value those plated with silver and set in gold."* Interestingly, a large burial cave has been found on Mount Scopus which contained a number of ossuaries, one of which had a Greek inscription stating that it contained the bones of the sons of Nicanor, who had donated one of the Temple gates.

The gates were usually kept open, so that the worshipers could follow the proceedings in the Temple Court from the lower Court of the Women. The High Priest, while burning the red heifer on the Mount of Olives, could also see the opening of the Sanctuary itself through this gate (see illustration, p. 267).

CHAPTER NINE: RECONSTRUCTING THE HERODIAN TEMPLE MOUNT

LEVELS OF THE COURTS OF THE TEMPLE

The examination of the different levels of the Temple Mount is an important factor in our research. These details need to be worked out to complete a picture in harmony with the historical sources and the archaeology of the Temple Mount. Whereas the Holy of Holies was built on the highest point of the mountain, the Herodian Temple itself stood on a foundation, six cubits high, and was reached by a staircase leading up to the *ulam*. In front were courts, each one lower than the other. If the measurements given in the sources are in agreement with the actual bedrock levels on the Temple Mount, they will confirm our proposed location of the Temple.

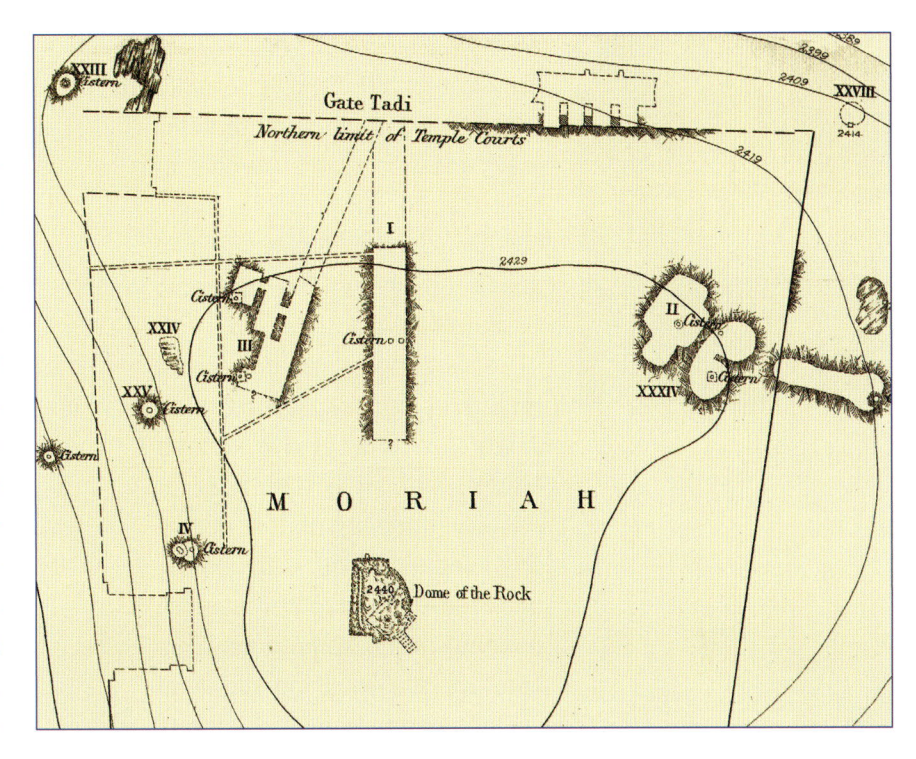

Map of the bedrock contours of the Temple Mount according to Warren.

The crucial part of the process of preparing accurate reconstruction drawings is the making of sections, as these show the various ground levels and the height of the buildings. Drawn to scale, each dimension can thus be measured accurately. In order to draw a section from east to west through the Rock, we have relied again on the levels provided by Wilson and Warren. Their maps[13] give a level of 2,440 feet (744 m, above sea level) for the top of the Rock and a bedrock level of 2,419 feet (737 m) for the bedrock at the foot of the staircase leading up to the raised platform from the east. The fifteen semi-circular steps were also located here. It is important to remember that the difference between these two levels is therefore 21 feet (7 m).

This level of 2,419 feet was the minimum height for the pavement level of the Court of the Women, the same as the bedrock level in the area where the twelve steps leading up to the *hel* on the south

CHAPTER NINE: RECONSTRUCTING THE HERODIAN TEMPLE MOUNT

View of the hel or terrace. (photo: Philip Evans)

HEL: A raised causeway going around the inner precincts.

were built. Steps were necessary to reach the higher Temple Court, from which another stairway leads up to the Temple itself. References to these steps can be found in the writings of Josephus and in the mishnaic tractate *Middot*.

Let us again examine the record in *Middot*, following as it were, a tour of the Temple Mount, starting at the right or eastern opening of the southern Huldah Gates and coming back through the left or western opening of the same gate. This time we are focusing on what we can learn from the various levels. *Middot* 2.2 states, *"whosoever it was that entered the Temple Mount came in on the right and went around and came out on the left."* This can only apply to the Huldah Gates, for only about this gate was it written that it *"served for coming in and for going out"* (*Middot* 1.3).

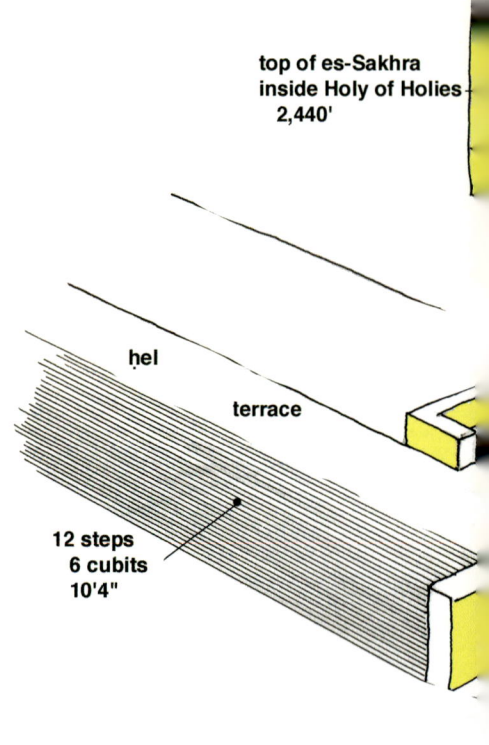

top of es-Sakhra inside Holy of Holies 2,440'

hel

terrace

12 steps
6 cubits
10'4"

The obvious route taken, if one follows the description of the various elements of the Temple Mount, is through the southern *soreg*, then viewing from that southern viewpoint the *hel*, which was located at the top of twelve stairs. The steps that were seen there were all half a cubit high and deep.

The next stop was the Court of the Women (*Middot* 2.5) and the four courts at its corners, then up the fifteen semi-circular steps and through the Nicanor Gate into, first, the Court of the Israelites, then the Court of the Priests, which was two and a half cubits higher, and then the Temple Court or *azarah*, where the Altar and Laver stood. The two-and-a-half-cubit difference in height between the Court of the Israelites and the Court of the Priests was made up of one step

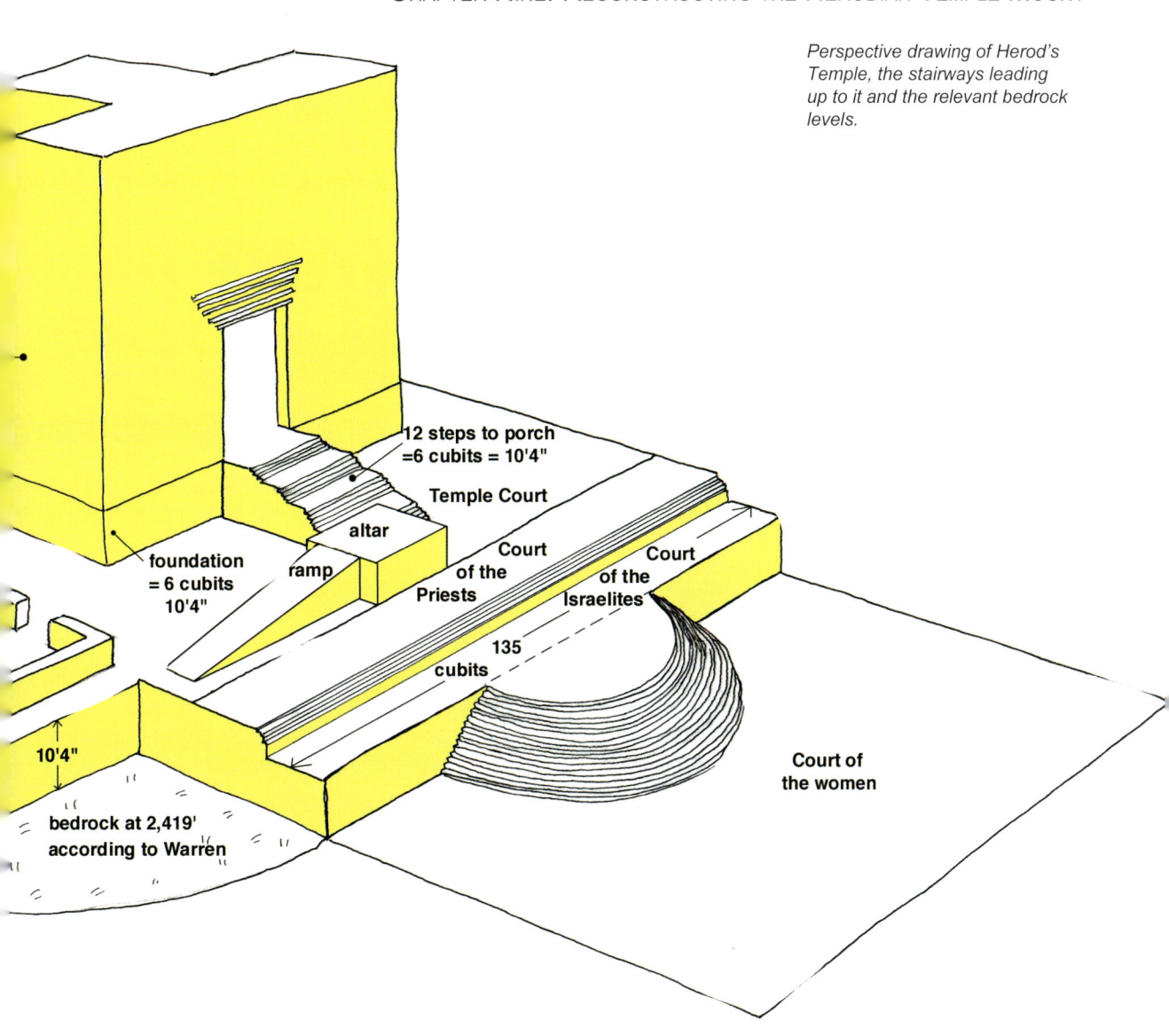

CHAPTER NINE: RECONSTRUCTING THE HERODIAN TEMPLE MOUNT

Perspective drawing of Herod's Temple, the stairways leading up to it and the relevant bedrock levels.

one cubit high and then three steps of half a cubit. These steps were located on either side of a central platform, called *duchan* in Hebrew, where the Levites used to sing the daily psalms (*Middot* 2.6). Another flight of twelve steps led up to the *ulam* of the Temple (*Middot* 3.6).

Then follows a detailed description of the Temple building itself, in *Middot* 4, while the last chapter describes the chambers which were built around the *azarah*. The only other reference to ground level is found in the mishnaic tractate *Yoma* 5.2, where it speaks of the *"Even ha-Shetiyah"* in the Holy of Holies, which *"was higher than the ground by three fingerbreadths."* This term *"Even ha-Shetiyah"* simply means Foundation Stone, indicating that the Rock (es-Sakhra) was

359

Chapter Nine: Reconstructing the Herodian Temple Mount

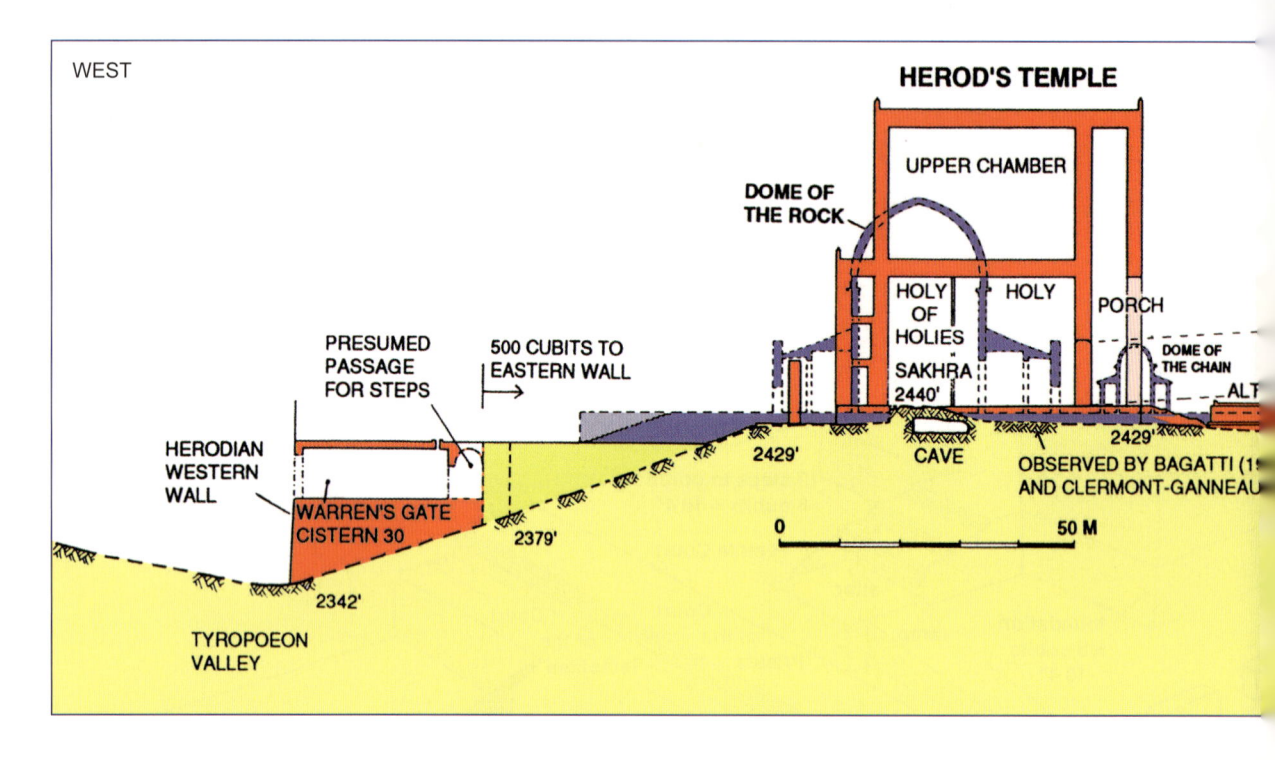

the foundation for the Holy of Holies.

Translating this into actual measurements on the ground, we see that leading up to the *hel* on the south there were twelve steps, having a combined height of 6 cubits (10 feet 4 inches, 3.15 m), and then another flight of twelve steps leading up from the Temple Court to the *ulam* of the Temple. As no other steps are mentioned between these two points, the Temple Court must have been located at a level of 2,429 feet 4 inches. The two staircases have therefore a combined height of twelve cubits, or 20 feet 8 inches (6.30 m). The bedrock level at the foot of the *hel* steps was 2,419 feet, and therefore the level of the *ulam*, which was the same as that of the floor of the Temple, was 2,439 feet 8 inches. To this must be added three fingerbreadths to reach the top of the Rock. As the level of the Rock is 2,440 feet above sea level, we see that these measurements are an exact fit.

Approaching the Temple Court from the east, two different sets of steps needed to be negotiated to overcome the same difference in height. Firstly, from the Court of the Women, the fifteen semi-circular steps led up to the Court of the Israelites, and then another four steps, which together were 2.5 cubits high, led up to the Temple Court. The total difference in height between the Court of the Women and the Temple Court was six cubits, which was the height of the twelve steps

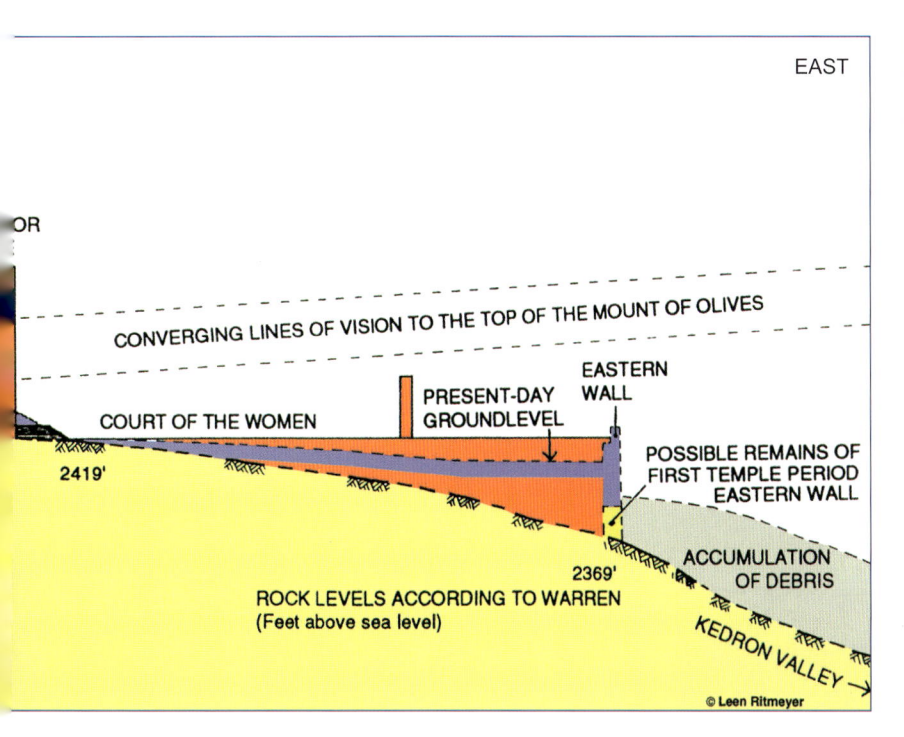

Chapter Nine: Reconstructing the Herodian Temple Mount

East-west section (looking north) through the Temple Mount, showing the location of the Herodian Temple and its courts in relation to existing buildings.

leading up to the *hel*. The fifteen semi-circular steps had therefore a combined height of 6 cubits minus 2.5 cubits, which equals 3.5 cubits (6 feet, 1.84 m). Dividing this height by 15, each step was therefore nearly a quarter of a cubit high (almost 5 inches, or 12.25 cm).

A superficial reading may suggest that this contradicts *Middot* 2.3 which says that all the steps were half a cubit high. However, as we have shown, this statement was made while standing in front of the southern steps. Although this may be surprising at first, it is nevertheless in agreement with the writings of Josephus, where we read that the fifteen steps in the Court of the Women were less steep than all the others *(War* 5.206). In contrast to the information given on the other steps, *Middot* is silent on the height of the fifteen steps, the main purpose of which was to provide a suitable location where the Levites could sing. In any case, the height of almost 5 inches, or 12.25 centimeters, of these steps is not much less than the Herodian steps which were found in the Temple Mount excavations. The steps leading up to Robinson's Arch, for example, were only 6 inches (15 cm) high.

Few researchers have noticed that these steps were lower and have therefore come up with unacceptable conclusions, one of which is that the Rock may be many feet lower today than it used to be[14].

View of the remains of Herodian steps found near Robinson's Arch.

Chapter Nine: Reconstructing the Herodian Temple Mount

Above: View of the Dome of the Chain on the Temple Mount.

Below: Plan of Herod's Temple, courts and altar in relation to the Dome of the Rock and the Dome of the Chain.

Similar difficulties were encountered by those who continue the *ḥel* around the Court of the Women. This terrace was located outside the gates of the Temple Court, at the top of the steps leading up to it. There were twelve steps in the south, but fewer in the north where the bedrock is so much higher. To continue these twelve steps around the Court of the Women is quite impossible, as it would put the floor of the Sanctuary 10 feet 4 inches (3.15 m) above the Rock.

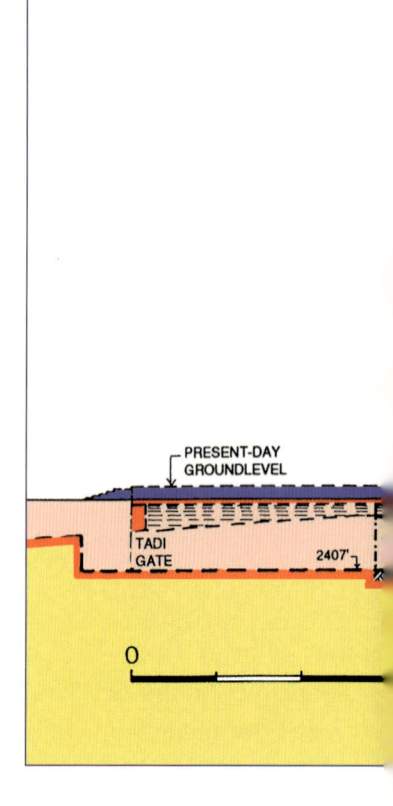

Thus, according to my calculations, the general level of the top of the Rock has remained unchanged since the First and Second Temple periods.

Interesting conclusions can now be drawn from the plan and sections that show the relationship between the Temple, the Dome of the Rock, its platform and the bedrock. The sectional drawings (above and previous pages) show that the raised platform is at present about some 5 feet lower than the Temple foundation, which was 6 cubits (10 feet 4 inches, 3.15 m) high. As far as the Temple is concerned, this indicates that the founda-

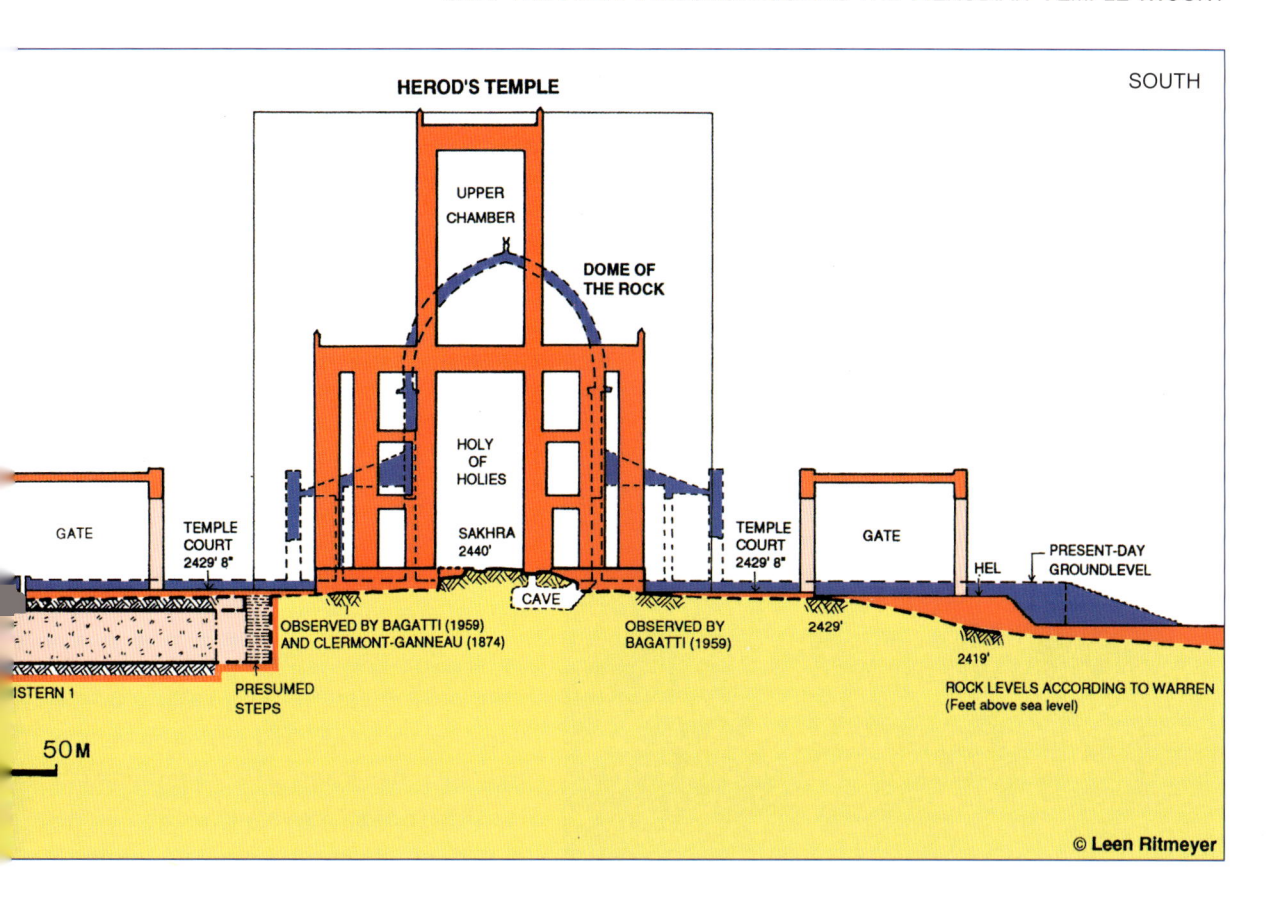

CHAPTER NINE: RECONSTRUCTING THE HERODIAN TEMPLE MOUNT

Above: North-south section (looking east) through the Temple Mount, showing the location of the Herodian Temple and its courts in relation to existing buildings.

Below: Eastern wall of the raised platform incorporated with two Herodian stones.

tion of the Temple was destroyed by the Romans in A.D. 70, or removed at a later date. However, to the east of the Dome of the Rock, the present-day platform is higher than the area where the Altar, the Court of the Priests and that of the Israelites were located. According to my calculations, the Altar would have been located 21.6 feet (6.6 m) east of the Dome of the Chain (see opposite page), leaving open the possibility of some remains surviving there, such as parts of the base of the Altar, the channel through which the blood was drained to the Kedron Valley and the pavements and steps of the courts.

Even more intriguing to contemplate is the fact that the eastern wall of the raised platform follows virtually the same line as the wall which divided the Temple Court from the Court of the Women, although its orientation is slightly different (see plan, p. 355). The present-day eastern steps, which lead up to the raised platform, are located in the middle of this wall. As we have already noted, these steps are built exactly over the fifteen semi-circular steps of the Court of the Women. The section on pages 360–61 shows that these steps were built on

CHAPTER NINE: RECONSTRUCTING THE HERODIAN TEMPLE MOUNT

View of the northeastern corner of the raised platform, showing three courses of ancient masonry.

bedrock or may even have been cut out of it, corroborating the suggestion we made above that some of these steps may have been preserved.

Furthermore, the northeastern corner of the raised platform is built of large stones, set in three horizontal courses. These appear to pre-date the construction of the present platform. This corner is located on the northern boundary of the 500-cubit-square Temple Mount. Here the bedrock rises sharply to the west and, from the topographical data, it appears that the area to the north of the Temple was much higher than the other grounds. The surviving corner may have belonged to a retaining wall which surrounded this higher area and may also have served as a termination for the *soreg* (see plan, p. 355). The high bedrock levels in this area lead to the conclusion that there could not have been twelve steps leading up to the northern *ḥel*. The bedrock being that high, only one or at the most two steps could have been built here.

As we shall see in the last section of this chapter, the southeastern corner of the raised platform coincides with the southeastern corner of an important building that stood here, according to our calculations, namely, the Chamber of Hewn Stone. It is possible that some remains of this edifice still exist.

It appears therefore that the direction of the present-day eastern wall of the raised platform stems from the surviving remains of the Chamber of Hewn Stone, the semi-circular steps in the Court of the Women, and the corner of a retaining wall near the northern wall of the square Temple Mount. In the plan on page 351 we also see that the present-day southern wall of the raised platform is located just at the foot of the Herodian steps that led up to the ḥel. *The northern wall of the platform remained unchanged, as it is built on the ancient rockscarp mentioned before. The northwest corner of the square*

CHAPTER NINE: RECONSTRUCTING THE HERODIAN TEMPLE MOUNT

Temple Mount is still visible in the form of the "Step."

THE TEMPLE COURT (*AZARAH*)

So far, we have seen that the Herodian additions to the square Temple Mount were ignored in the writings of the contemporary rabbis. The square platform was surrounded by a wall with gates. The first area inside the square *temenos* was called the Court of the Gentiles, up to the *soreg*. The *hel* was located in front of the gates of the Temple Court, called *azarah* in Hebrew. Surrounded by gates and other buildings which will be described below, this was the most important court of all because it included the Temple itself. The southern boundary of the Temple Court was located exactly on the east-west axis of the 500-cubit-square platform, as the area to the south of it measured 250 cubits. We have already suggested, in Chapter 2 (p 189 ff.), that this southern area may previously have been occupied by Solomon's Palace and the House of the Forest of Lebanon.

The *azarah* measured 187 cubits (322 feet, 98.18 m) from west to east and was 135 cubits (232.5 feet, 70.88 m) wide. This court, in addition to the Temple, included the Altar, the Place of Slaughter and the Laver.

Model of the original Altar of Burnt Sacrifice in the Tabernacle in the Wilderness. (photo: Philip Evans)

The Altar

The original Altar of Burnt Sacrifice built in the Wilderness of Sinai was made of shittim wood overlaid with brass. It measured 5 cubits (8.6 feet, 2.63 m) long, 5 cubits wide and 3 cubits (5.2 feet, 1.58 m) high. It had horns at the four corners with rings for the staves to carry it when the camp of Israel was on the move.

The Altar in the Second Temple was also square-shaped but, being stationary, was made of unhewn stones, as stipulated in Exodus 20:25: *"and if thou wilt make me an altar of stone, thou shalt not build it of hewn stone: for if thou lift up thy tool upon it thou hast polluted it."* Between the descriptions of Josephus and the Mishnah, however, its measurements are open to

Chapter Nine: Reconstructing the Herodian Temple Mount

The Altar of Burnt Sacrifice in the Herodian Temple Court. (photo: Philip Evans)

Reconstructed horned altar from Beersheba, late 8th century B.C. (NEAEHL)

dispute.

Josephus gives the total dimensions of the Altar as 50 cubits by 50 cubits with a height of 15 cubits. An altar of this size would not have left sufficient space for the twelve steps leading up to the *ulam* (see plan, p. 362).

Middot 3.1 describes the Altar as follows:

> The Altar [at its base] was thirty-two cubits long and thirty-two cubits wide. It rose up one cubit and drew in one cubit: this formed the Base; thus there was left thirty cubits by thirty. It rose up five cubits and drew in one cubit: this formed the Circuit; thus there was left twenty-eight cubits by twenty-eight. The place of the horns was one cubit on every side; thus there was left twenty-six cubits by twenty-six. The place on which the feet of the priests trod was one cubit on every side; thus there was left twenty-four cubits by twenty-four, the place for the [Altar] fire.

There is sufficient space for an altar of this size, and we believe these measurements are correct. The description of the altar in *Middot* does not give its total height, but it was probably 10 cubits high, much like that in Solomon's Temple (2 Chr 4:1). Based on the above quoted description in *Middot*, we believe that this height of the Altar was made up of 1 cubit for the foundation, a solid block of 30 cubits square and 5 cubits high, on top of which was a smaller block, 28 cubits square and probably 3 cubits high (this height is not mentioned in *Middot*; in Ezekiel's Temple description [Ezek 43:14], this part of the Altar is 4 cubits high). Lastly, the four horns at the four corners were 1 cubit in height standing on a cubit-wide ledge. The central area where the sacrifices were burnt was a square of 24 cubits. The "Circuit" was a ledge around the Altar where the priests could walk while they tended the sacrifices.

There is no mention in the Scriptures of a scarlet line around the Altar of the Tabernacle in the Wilderness nor in that in the Temple of Solomon, but according to *Middot* 3.2, a red line surrounded the middle of the Altar that stood in front of Herod's Temple. The Rabbis placed great store by the later laws stipulating where the blood should be sprinkled, with clear distinctions as to when to sprinkle the blood above or below the red line. If done improperly, the sacrifice became invalid, as is mentioned for example in *Zebahim* 8.9.

Middot 3.2 also describes the outlet of *"two holes like two narrow nostrils"* at the southwest corner of the circuit of the Altar where the remainder of the blood was sometimes poured, to go down a water channel into the Kedron Valley. During the feast of Succoth, the priest who carried the flagon of water, which he had drawn from the Pool of Siloam, was joined at the Altar by another priest who carried the wine of the drink-offering. Of the two silver bowls, the one on the western side of the Altar was for the water and the eastern one for the wine. The bowls were perforated on the bottom to allow the liquid to flow, probably through pipes leading to the base of the Altar and then through an underground channel into the Kedron Valley. The bowl for the wine had a wider hole as wine flows more slowly than water.

Two priests pouring water and wine into the silver bowls at the corner of the circuit.

The 32-cubit-long ramp rising up from the south of the Altar is mentioned in *Middot* 3.3. Its construction is based on the stipulation in Exodus 20:26: *"neither shalt thou go up by steps unto mine altar,*

Chapter Nine: Reconstructing the Herodian Temple Mount

Opposite page: The Place of Slaughter, looking south. (photo: Philip Evans)

Below: Artist's rendition of the priestly sanctification of hands and feet at the Laver and preparation of the Altar. (The Temple Institute, Jerusalem)

that thy nakedness be not discovered thereon." The ramp, like the Altar, was built of unhewn stones from the valley of nearby Beth-haccerem and was regularly whitewashed to cover the blood stains left from the Feasts of Passover and Tabernacles. Although the ramp was 32 cubits long, its base was only 30 cubits long, measured along the ground, up to the base of the Altar. The base of the Altar was one cubit deep and there was another one-cubit-deep recess in the side of the Altar. *The length of both the Altar and the Ramp was therefore 62 cubits, as indeed given in* Middot 5.2.

The Laver

The Laver, made of brass, stood between the Temple *ulam* and the Altar. There are a few references in the Mishnah to a special wooden device on the Laver made by a person called Ben Katin *(Yoma* 3.10; *Tamid* 1.4, 3.8). This device could be heard as far as Jericho. Its sound inaugurated the day's service in the Temple.

Before the priest who was chosen by lot to clean the Altar and start up its fires could proceed with his duties, he had to first wash in the Laver. *Tamid* 1.4 records that the other priests admonished him: *"Take heed that thou touch not the vessel before thou hast sanctified thy hands and feet in the laver."* To wash himself, a serving priest would stand below one of the twelve faucets of the Laver and let the water run over his hands and feet while laying the right hand on the right foot and the left hand on the left foot.

The Place of Slaughter

The Place of Slaughter consisted of twenty-four rings, probably attached to short pillars, arranged in four rows of six, into which the heads of the sacrificial animals were placed. The Shambles proper were eight short pillars with marble tables in between upon which rested cedar blocks with hooks on which to hang the slaughtered animals.

Chapter Nine: Reconstructing the Herodian Temple Mount

Chapter Nine: Reconstructing the Herodian Temple Mount

The ritual of slaughter was carefully stipulated. No animal was killed until the great gate leading into the Sanctuary itself was opened. Hearing the noise made by the door, the designated priest tied the animal to the second ring at the northwestern corner of the Place of Slaughter. With legs bound together, the animal's head was put through the ring, facing west. It was dispatched with a knife, its blood was caught in a golden vessel (Heb. *mizrak*) and subsequently sprinkled on the Altar.

Following the ritual slaughter, priests carry the blood to the Altar and, depending on the offering, sprinkle it on the corner of the altar or at its base. (The Temple Institute, Jerusalem)

The Court of the Israelites and the Court of the Priests

On the east of the *azarah* were two narrow strips of 11 cubits (19 feet, 5.78 m) by 135 cubits (232.5 feet, 70.88 m). The westernmost area was called the Court of the Priests and the other, the Court of the Israelites (see plan, p. 362). This latter court was 2.5 cubits lower than the first. Assuming that the Sanctuary was placed symmetrically in the Temple Court, and following *Middot* 4,6, which says that *"the Sanctuary was a hundred cubits square and a hundred cubits in height,"* we see that the spaces on either side of the *ulam* measured 17.5 cubits (30 feet 2 inches or 9.19 m). The back part of the Sanctuary was 70 cubits (120 feet 6 inches or 36.75 m) wide.

Having established the location of the Holy of Holies of the Temple and using the dimensions given in Middot *for the Altar and other areas, we can now project the exact locations of the Temple Courts onto the present Temple Mount.*

According to *Middot* 5.1, the 187-cubit length of the Temple Court from east to west was divided as follows:

1. The Court of the Israelites	11 cubits
2. The Court of the Priests	11 cubits
3. The Altar	32 cubits
4. The space between the Altar and the *ulam*	22 cubits
5. The Sanctuary	100 cubits
6. The space behind the Temple	11 cubits
Total	**187 cubits**

The distance of 135 cubits from south to north, according to *Middot* 5.2, was divided as follows:

CHAPTER NINE: RECONSTRUCTING THE HERODIAN TEMPLE MOUNT

1. The Ramp	30 cubits
2. The base of the Altar	32 cubits
3. The space between Altar and Rings	8 cubits
4. The area of the Rings	24 cubits
5. The space between the Rings and the Tables	4 cubits
6. The space between the Tables and the small pillars	4 cubits
7. The space to the north of the small pillars	8 cubits
8. The remainder (between the Ramp, the wall, and the small pillars)	25 cubits
Total	135 cubits

From these dimensions it is possible to draw the plan (on p. 362) of the Temple Court. Transposing these distances to a plan make it clear that, rather than in the same line, the Altar stood to the south of the longitudinal Temple axis. Thus, the worshipers in the Court of the Women could observe the Blessings of the Priests, which view the 10-cubit-high Altar would have otherwise hidden (see section, pp. 360–361).

THE BUILDINGS AROUND THE TEMPLE COURT

The Temple courtyard was surrounded by gates and other buildings. According to *Middot* 1.4, there were three gates in the north, three in the south and one in the east (see plan, p. 345). In the north, from east to west, were the Gate of the Flame, the Gate of the Offering and the Chamber of the Hearth, with its own gate. In the south, from west to east, were the Kindling Gate, the Gate of the Firstlings and the Water Gate. The Nicanor Gate, with two side chambers, was on the east.

In *Middot* 2.6, however, we read about nine gates, the upper gate being added in the southwest, while the gates in the north, from west to east, are the Gate of Jeconiah, the Gate of the Offering, the Gate of the Women and the Gate of the Singers. There appears to be a contradiction between these two sections of *Middot*. However, these gates had many chambers in which different activities took place, so the same gate may have been called by different names. In the west there were two, apparently nameless, gates (*Middot* 2.6). It has been suggested that the southern one may have been the upper gate and the other that of Jeconiah, mentioned in the same paragraph.

Middot 5.3 mentions three offices in the north, one for the salt

> **DEFINING GATES**
>
> *When reading about gates, we must remember that these were not mere openings in a wall, but two-story high buildings with rooms on both sides of the central passageway. The gates we have reconstructed are based on the plans of such gate buildings, which are also described in Ezekiel's prophecy, chapters 40 and 41. The gates described by Ezekiel are very similar to six-chambered city gates that have been uncovered in Israel.[15] The gates of the Temple Court would have been separate from one another and spaced out. Otherwise, one long gate building would have sufficed. Some names of offices are related to the names of the gates. Each gate having a different function may account for the many offices mentioned in* Middot, Tamid *and elsewhere in the Mishnah.*

Chapter Nine: Reconstructing the Herodian Temple Mount

Model showing the chambers on the north side of the Temple. (photo: Philip Evans)

that was put on the offerings, one for the conservation of hides by salting (Parva Chamber) and one for the rinsing of the intestines of the sacrificial animals (Rinsing Chamber). From the Parva Chamber, a passage led up to a chamber where the High Priest immersed himself on the Day of Atonement. This room was located above the middle office. It is not clear where these chambers were located, but the other rooms must have been located in the two spaces between the three gates and could have been positioned on top of each other. With salt in constant demand, the salt chamber would have been close to the chamber where the hides were being prepared.

The next paragraph in *Middot*, 5.4, mentions a Wood Chamber in the south, an office for the Exile (Golah Chamber) and the Chamber of Hewn Stone. Considering the available spaces between the gate buildings, the Wood Chamber was located in between the Kindling Gate and the Gate of the Firstlings. Between this last gate and the Water Gate was the Chamber of the Golah, which had a water wheel to draw water from a cistern, most likely that called the Cistern of the Golah (Cistern no. 5 in plans on pp. 216, 219), mentioned in *Erubin* 10.14.

The easternmost gate, that is, the Water Gate, was adjacent to the Chamber of Hewn Stone. In this proposal, the present well-head of Cistern 5 falls exactly between the Water Gate and that of the Firstlings, where the Chamber of the Golah was located. This well-head has been preserved up to the present day. Standing beside it,

CHAPTER NINE: RECONSTRUCTING THE HERODIAN TEMPLE MOUNT

one is indeed thrilled to imagine the great wheel that once served to draw water for the altar services. The eastern gate referred to is the Nicanor Gate (*Middot* 2.3), which corresponds to the Corinthian Gate mentioned in *War* 5.201.

According to Josephus (*War* 5.203), the inner measurements of these gates were 30 cubits square and 40 cubits high. Although his measurements in general are not very reliable, in this case and in the absence of any other specifications, we will give him the benefit of the doubt.

In addition to the three gatehouses on the north and south, two important buildings are mentioned: the Chamber of the Hearth and the Chamber of Hewn Stone. The latter was located near the southeast corner of the Temple Court and the former near the northwest corner. In making a plan of these gates and chambers, we have to remember that the walls of the Temple Court must have had a thickness, e.g. of about 5 cubits, in order to agree with the rest of the proportions. The *ḥel,* which was 10 cubits wide, was located in front of the gates. Assuming that the Chamber of Hewn Stone was not a gate building

Model showing the chambers on the south side of the Temple. (photo: Philip Evans)

Chapter Nine: Reconstructing the Herodian Temple Mount

The southern end of the eastern wall of the raised platform, showing a blocking wall which hides the entrance to underground rooms. After Warren's request to explore these rooms, a heap of earth was put in front of the entrance, which was later replaced by the blocking wall.

but a larger structure, like the Chamber of the Hearth, we have drawn it on the plan, with its southern wall in line with the bottom step of the southern staircase that led up to the *ḥel*.

It is interesting to note that the present-day southeast corner of the raised platform is located at this very spot. When Warren was investigating this part of the platform, he noticed that the ground sounded hollow. He eventually discovered that the underground space was called the Cell of Bostam. This name may be derived from the colloquial *bustan*, which means a garden with trees. Some trees are noticeable in this area on pictorial representations of the Temple Mount dating from the Crusader period. Warren wrote the following intriguing report on the area:[16]

> It may be noted that the Cell of Bostam, according to Mejr ed Din, was under the platform on the east. A door, with a window to the north of it and another to the south, is visible on the east wall of the platform, north of No. 5 tank and south of the eastern steps. These three apertures are now closed up, but the levels of the rock in No. 5 tank render it probable that the southeast part of the platform is supported on vaulting. The Cell of Bostam

CHAPTER NINE: RECONSTRUCTING THE HERODIAN TEMPLE MOUNT

was, however, already closed in the time of Mejr ed Din. In 1881 an attempt was made to obtain permission to open this doorway and explore the unknown cells and vaults. This was not only refused, but a large heap of earth was soon piled in front of the closed doorway by order of the architect of the mosque, completely hiding the platform wall on this side. The known levels of the rock render it extremely important that the supposed vaults in this part of the platform should, if possible, be explored in the future.

As can be seen from the photograph (opposite), the blocking wall is still in existence today. Warren was indeed correct in pointing out that an investigation of these underground rooms would be of great interest as they could lead to the discovery of the remains of the southeast corner of the Chamber of Hewn Stone.

The Chamber of the Hearth was located at the northwest corner of the Temple Court. It had four side rooms. The northeastern room had steps leading down to an underground mikveh. This, together with another room to the east, were located outside the holy area, that is, outside the *hel*. A row of stones inside the building marked the beginning of the holy area. According to our plan, this building is located directly above Cistern 3 (see plan, p. 223), which has several chambers, one or more of which may have contained facilities for ritual bathing. Warren noted that the northeast passage was blocked by a masonry wall. Had he been able to excavate a few meters beyond this blocking wall, the steps leading up to the Chamber of the Hearth would probably have been found, as Cistern 3 and the passageway are, apart from the ceiling, completely cut out of the rock.

Here again the archaeological remains which have been preserved on the Temple Mount are in accordance with the written historical sources.

Artist's impression of the Chamber of the Lambs, one of the four side rooms of the Chamber of the Hearth. This chamber housed the animals that were to be offered on the altar. A priest is seen inspecting a lamb for disqualifying blemishes. No fewer than six acceptable lambs are in this chamber at one time. (The Temple Institute, Jerusalem)

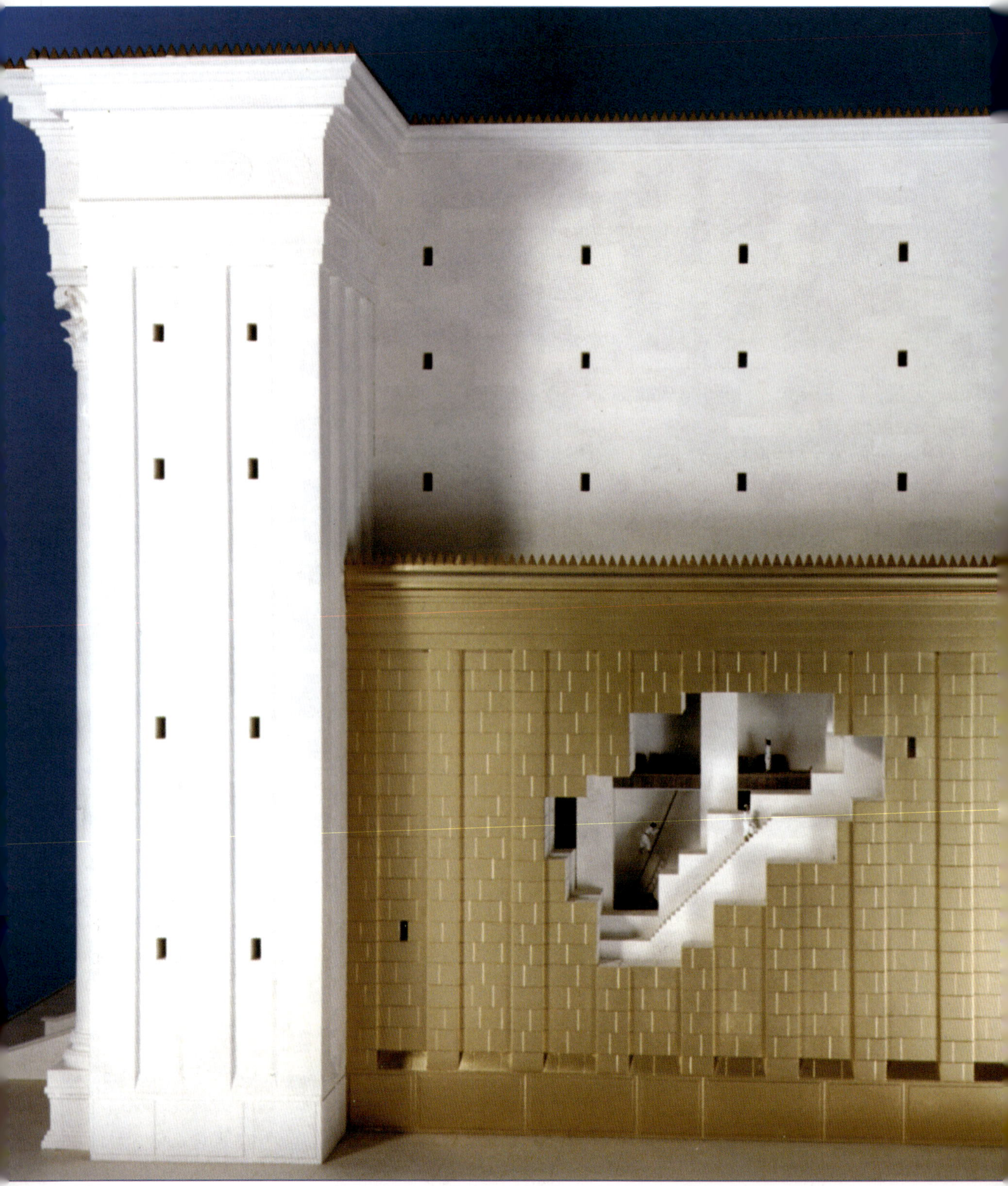

Opposite page: The north side of Herod's Temple, showing, through the hole in the outer wall, the inner cells and stairway. (photo: Philip Evans)

Below: The façade of Herod's Temple. (photo: Philip Evans)

Bottom: Jerusalem in the time of Herod the Great.

Chapter Ten
Reconstructing Herod's Temple

INTRODUCTION

Josephus called Herod's Temple *"a structure more noteworthy than any under the sun" (Ant.* 15.412) and in *War* 5.207–226 he gives a glowing description of the Temple:

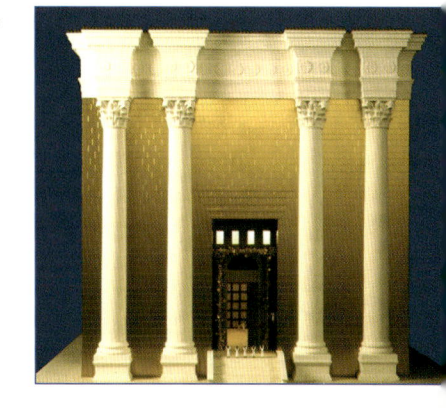

> *The sacred edifice itself, the holy Temple, in the central position, was approached by a flight of twelve steps. The façade was of equal height and breadth, each being a hundred cubits; but the building behind was narrower.… The exterior of the building wanted nothing that could astound either mind or eye. For, being covered on all sides with massive plates of gold, the sun was no sooner up than it radiated so fiery a flash that persons straining to look at it were compelled to avert their eyes, as from the solar rays. To approaching strangers it appeared from a distance like a snow-clad mountain; for all that was not overlaid with gold was of the purest white. From its summit protruded sharp golden spikes to prevent birds from settling upon them and polluting the roof.*

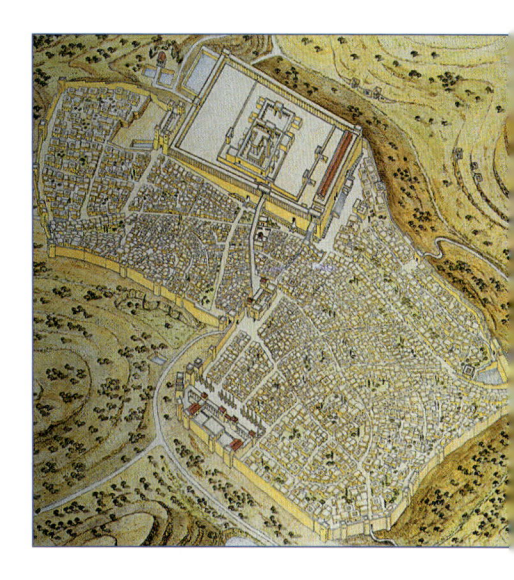

Josephus appears, however, to separate the "façade," or *ulam* of the Temple, from "the first edifice" or the actual Sanctuary, for he writes that through the entrance opening in the façade of the Temple "the first edifice was visible." The more sober account in the mishnaic tractate *Middot* also makes this distinction, describing first the *ulam* in *Middot* 3.7–8 and then the actual Sanctuary in chapter 4. Both accounts apparently

Chapter Ten: Reconstructing Herod's Temple

Plan (right) and sections (below and opposite page) of Herod's Temple.

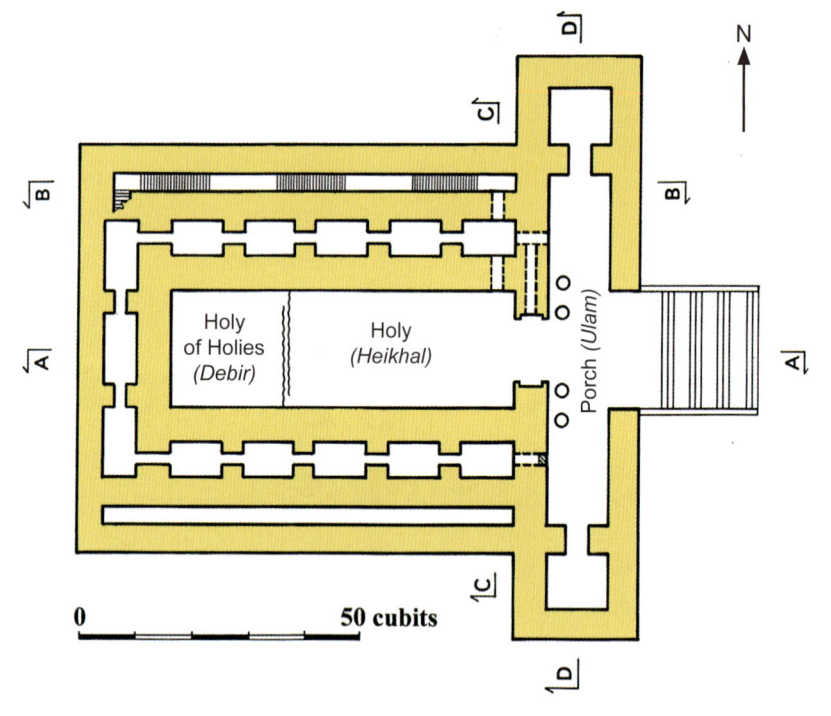

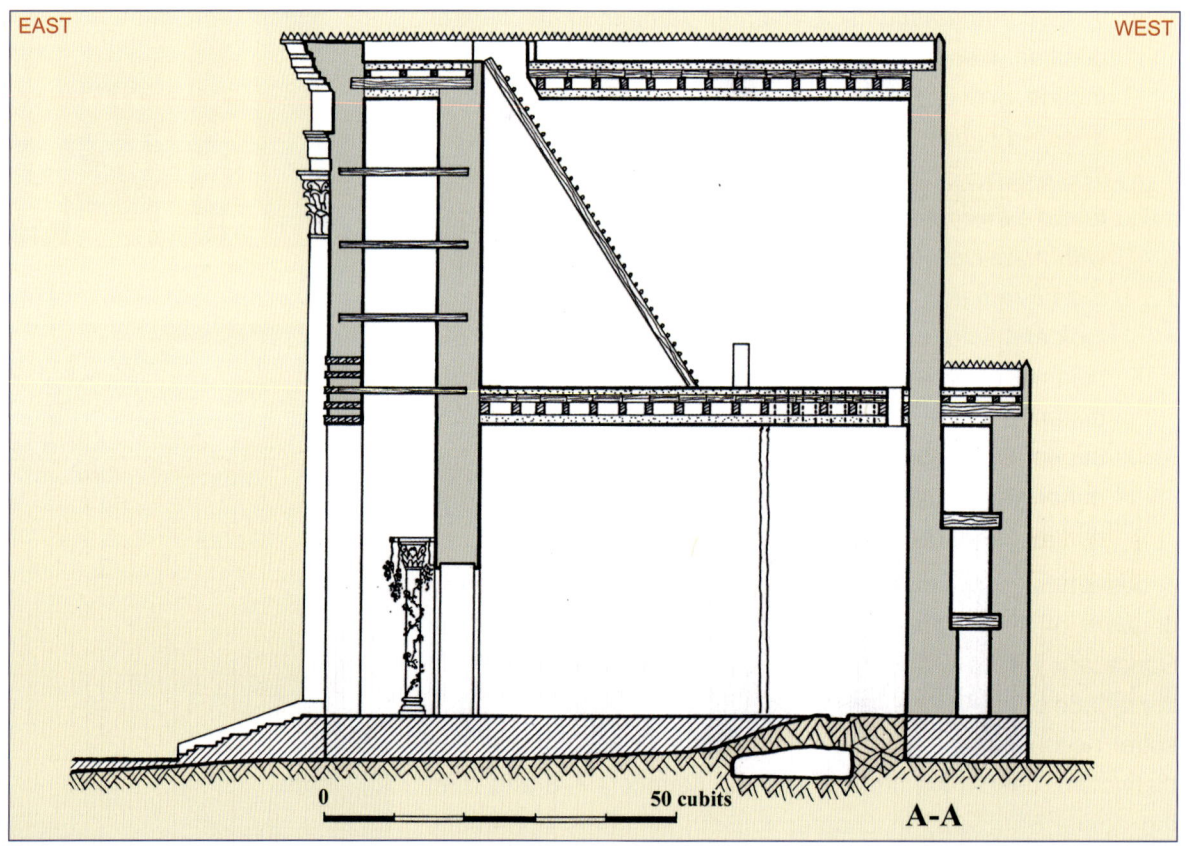

Holy of Holies (Debir)

Holy (Heikhal)

Porch (Ulam)

0   50 cubits

EAST   WEST

0   50 cubits

A-A

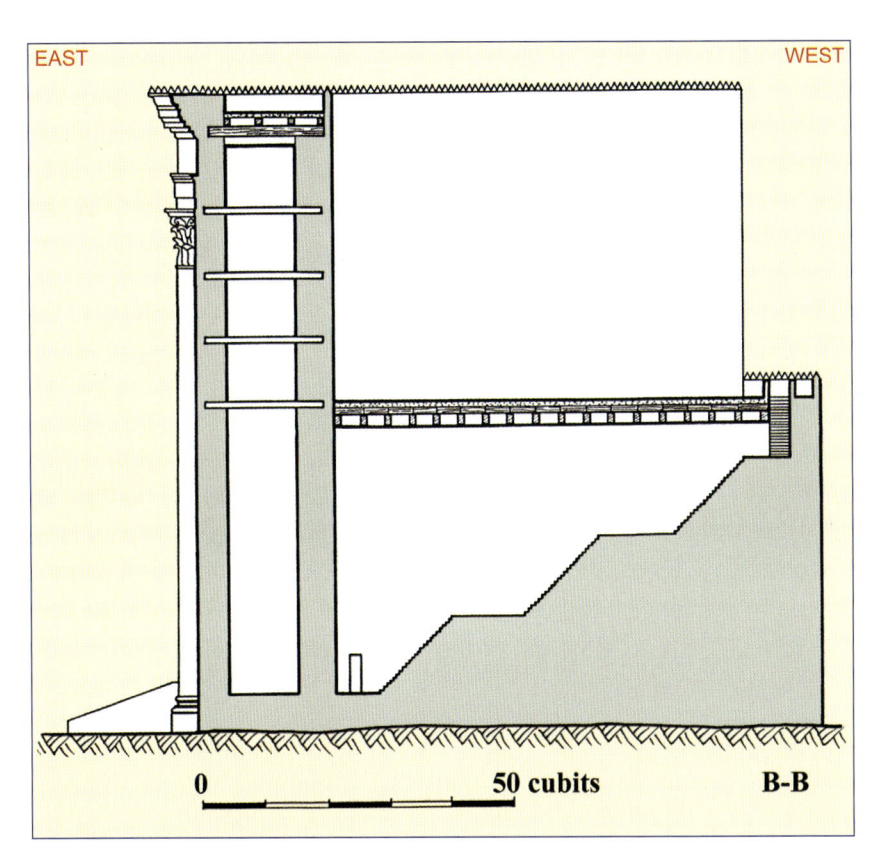

CHAPTER TEN: RECONSTRUCTING HEROD'S TEMPLE

EAST WEST
0 50 cubits B-B

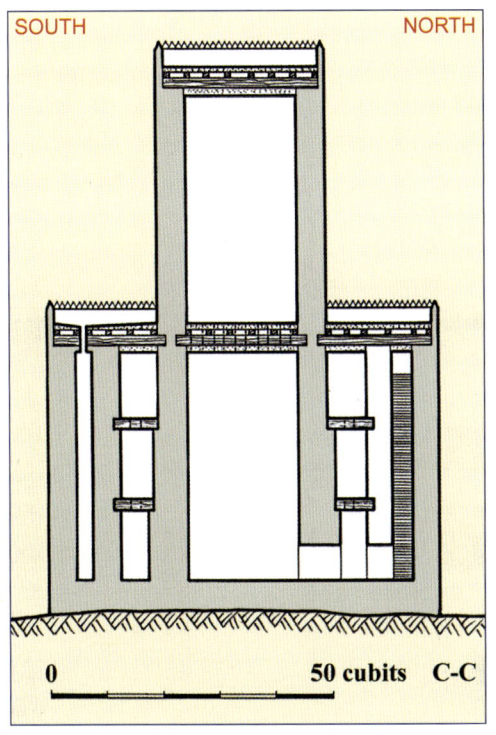

SOUTH NORTH
0 50 cubits C-C

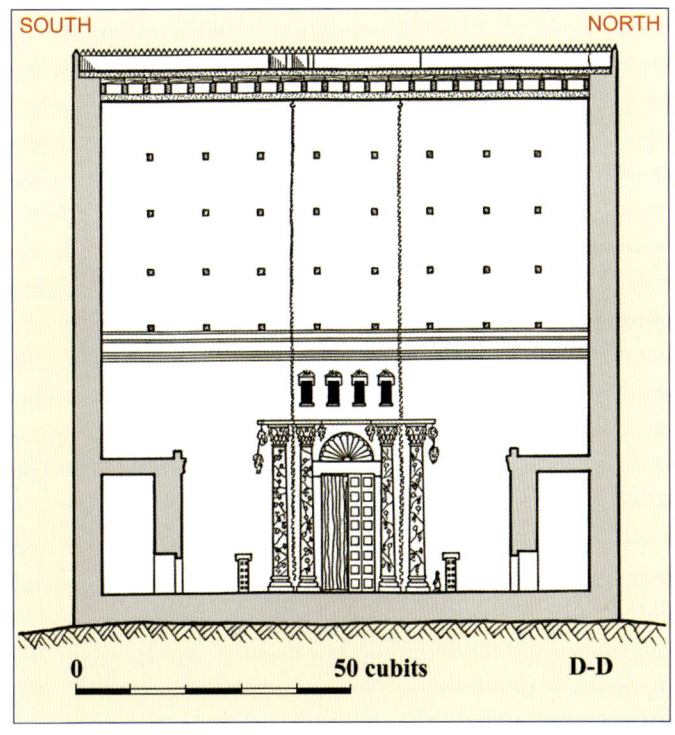

SOUTH NORTH
0 50 cubits D-D

Chapter Ten: Reconstructing Herod's Temple

> **ELEMENTS OF THE ROOF CONSTRUCTION**
>
> *Plaster was usually molded on a bed of bundled reeds, which in this case would be fixed to the underside of the* bet dilfa *(place of dripping or leaking), which was two cubits high. The reconstruction I proposed for the ceilings of Herod's Temple was a layer of two-cubit-high beams, each probably one cubit wide, with a space of three cubits in between. The beams would have to be longer than the interior width of the inner sanctuary, which was twenty cubits. Such large timbers were probably made from cedar trees. Moisture that accumulated in the hollow space between the beams was probably channeled into drains. This may have been the reason why the name "bet dilfa" was given to this roof layer.*
>
> *Another layer of one-cubit-thick crossbeams, laid over the large beams of the* bet dilfa, *formed the* tikra, *which means ceiling. The final top layer was again made of plaster, laid on a bed of sticks and reeds, called the* ma'azivah. *The stone paving was probably made of intricate geometrical designs embedded in the top plaster layer. This was a popular paving technique, called* opus sectile, *of which examples have survived in Jerusalem.[2] Herod the Great must have favored this design because the same paving technique was also used in his palaces at Jericho and Masada.*

viewed the *ulam* as an addition to the actual Temple, although both Temple and *ulam* belonged to one and the same building, namely, the Temple reconstructed by Herod the Great.

Both historical accounts give detailed descriptions of this magnificent building. Apart from some of the measurements, the two accounts are basically in accordance. For greater accuracy, we have used those given in *Middot*.[1]

The Temple was a colossal structure, measuring 100 cubits (172 feet or 52.50 m) long, broad and high. It stood on a 6-cubit-high solid foundation and had two stories, each 45 cubits (77.5 feet or 23.63 m) high, including a ceiling (or roof) of 5 cubits (8.6 feet, 2.63 m). The height of the lower and upper chambers was 40 cubits (68.9 feet or 21 m) each. On the roof was a parapet which was 3 cubits (5 feet 2 inches or 1.58 m) in height, on which were one-cubit-high golden spikes to prevent birds from perching on the roof's edge and fouling the Temple. The total height of the Temple was therefore 100 cubits (172 feet or 52.5 m).

The ceilings were made up of four different elements, according to *Middot* 4.6: *"the wall-frieze one cubit, the place of drippings two cubits, the roof-beams one cubit, and the plasterwork one cubit."* The word translated wall-frieze, *kiur* in Hebrew, means a modeled

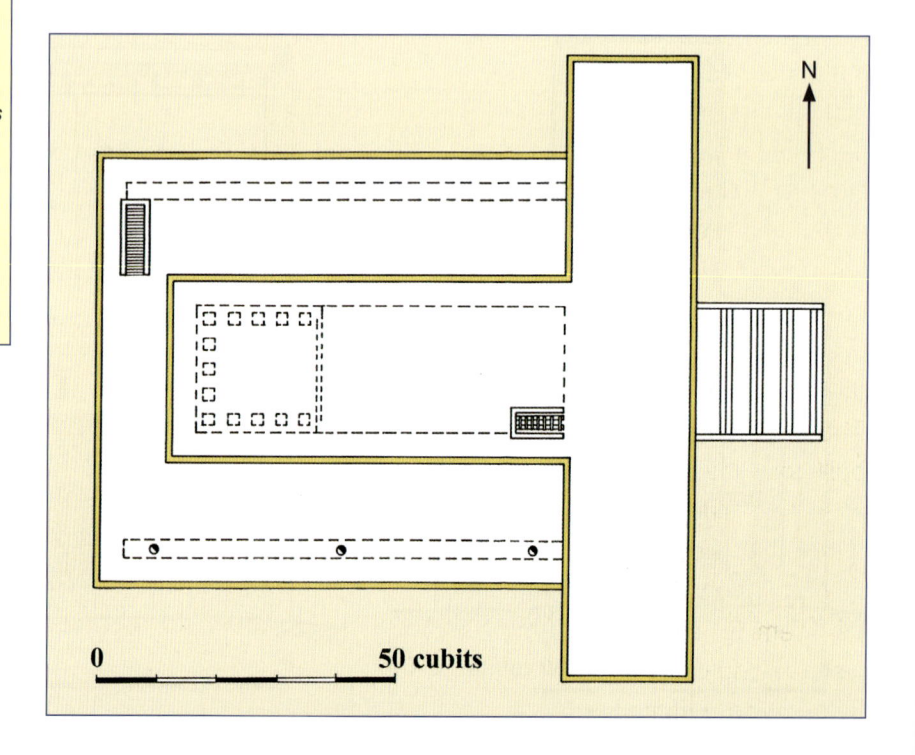

Roof plan of Herod's Temple.

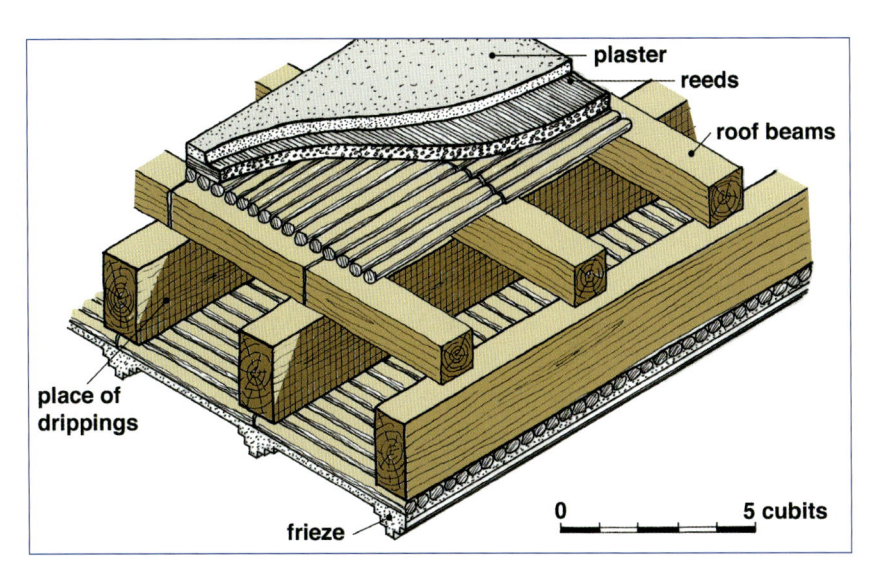

CHAPTER TEN: RECONSTRUCTING HEROD'S TEMPLE

Left: The ceiling construction of Herod's Temple.

Below: The coffered ceiling in one of the outer gates of the Temple Scroll.

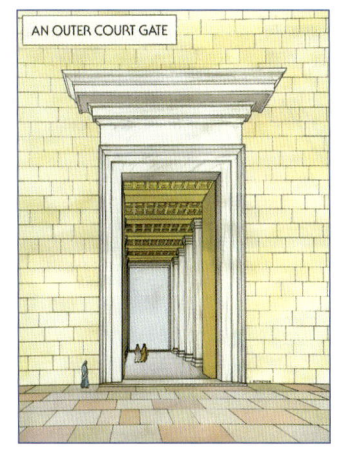

plaster construction, probably like a coffer construction, which was very popular in Roman architecture. I had suggested a similar roof construction for the ceiling of the outer gates in the Temple of the Temple Scroll[3] (see illustration, above).

THE FOUNDATION OF THE TEMPLE

The foundation of the Temple was a six-cubit-high platform of huge stones, with the top of the Rock (Sakhra) barely protruding. After the stone pavement was laid inside the eastern part of the Holy of Holies, the Rock topped it by only three finger-breadths. The walls of the Sanctuary and the *ulam* were built on this massive platform. The foundation was built on the bedrock with the side stones exposed to view.

We will now describe the Temple as if we were visiting it. We start by climbing a staircase

Below: The foundation of Herod's Temple.

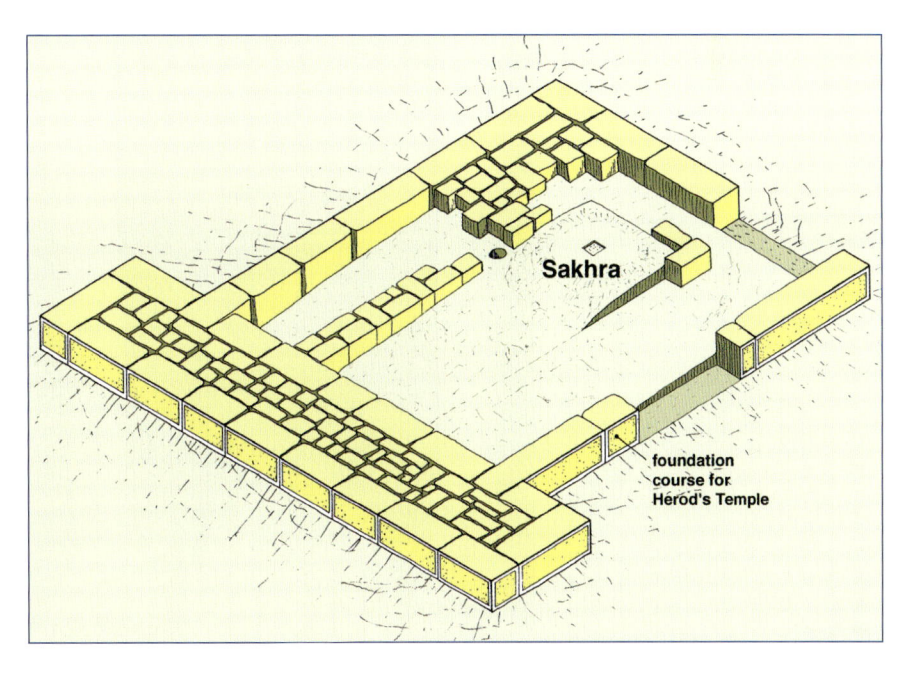

381

Chapter Ten: Reconstructing Herod's Temple

> **A DESCRIPTION OF THE FOUNDATION STONES**
>
> *These massive stones, according to Antiquities 15.392, measured twenty-five cubits in length, eight in height and twelve in width (43x14x21 feet or 13.12x4.20x6.30 m). In War 5.224, however, they were listed as forty-five cubits in length, five in height and six in breadth (77x8.6.3x10 feet or 23.63x2.63x3.15 m). We have seen that the largest stone in the western wall of the Temple Mount measured 45 feet (13.70 m) long and 11 feet 6 inches (3.19 m) high and probably 14 to 16 feet (4.20–4.90 m) deep. The weight of this stone is estimated at 570 tons. We cannot be sure of the original dimensions of the foundation stones, but they must have been enormous. Even if we do not accept the measurements given in the sources at face value, it would safe to assume that these stones may have been six cubits (10 feet 4 inches or 3.15 m) high, the height of the foundation.*

which leads into the *ulam*. We then enter the inner chambers, the *heikhal* and the Holy of Holies, and climb up the inner stairway to reach the intermediate roof level and enter the Upper Chamber. Finally, we ascend a special structure which leads to the roof.

THE PORCH (*ULAM*)

A flight of twelve steps led from the *azarah* to the *ulam* of the Temple or Sanctuary. Each step was half a cubit (10 inches, 26 cm) high and one cubit deep, with a set of three steps separated by landings of three cubits. The floor level of the *ulam* was therefore six cubits higher than the pavement of the *azarah*. As this is the same height as the foundation of the Temple (*Middot* 4.6), we may conclude that the steps were inserted to reach this foundation level. Having climbed these steps, we now enter the *ulam*.

The entrance to the *ulam* was forty cubits high and twenty cubits wide (70x35 feet or 21x10.5 m). It had a curious lintel construction, made of five carved oak beams, each one cubit high, with a row of stones in between. Supposing that the stone layers between the oak beams were also one cubit high, the whole lintel construction had a height of nine cubits (15 feet 6 inches or 4.73 m). The lowest beam, which projected one cubit on either side of the opening, was twenty-two cubits wide. The other four beams also projected one cubit beyond each side of the one below, so that the lengths of the beams from the lowest to the highest were 22, 24, 26, 28 and 30 cubits, respectively. This construction is quite un-

View of the lintel construction of five carved oak beams above the entrance to the ulam. *(photo: Philip Evans)*

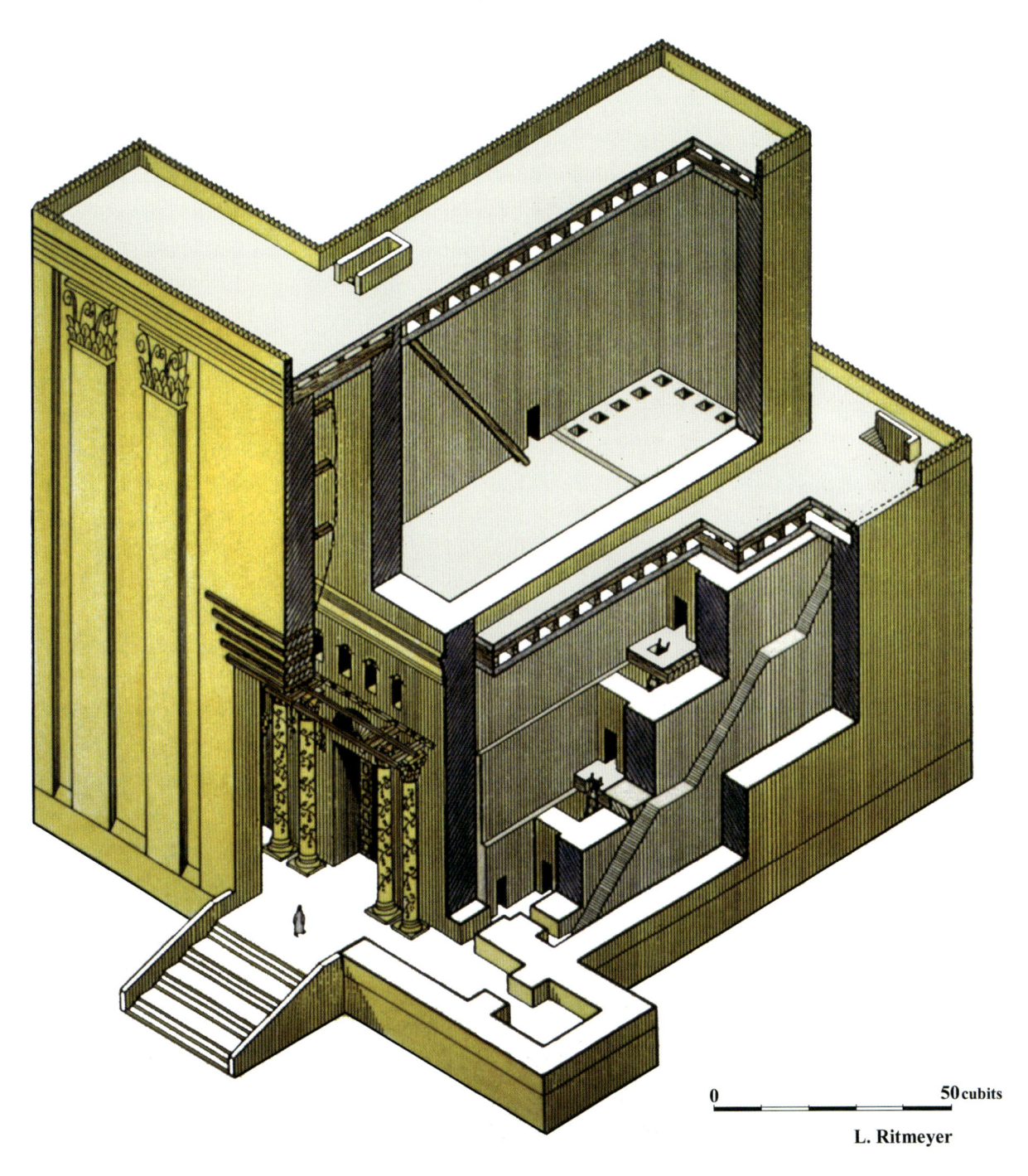

CHAPTER TEN: RECONSTRUCTING HEROD'S TEMPLE

Isometric reconstruction drawing of Herod's Temple according to the mishnaic tractate Middot.

usual and reminds us to be careful not to impose Greek or Roman architectural styles on the Herodian Temple. Although only five carved and most probably gilded beams could be seen from the outside, this construction must have extended the full width of the outer wall of the

Chapter Ten: Reconstructing Herod's Temple

Model of the four "crowns," windows with triangular pediments located above the Golden Vine. (photo: Philip Evans)

Opposite page: View of the golden chains behind the ladder which were used to inspect the four "crowns." (photo: Philip Evans)

ulam, which was five cubits (*Middot* 4.7). As the oak beams were one cubit high and probably square in profile, the lintel construction must have consisted of at least twenty-five beams, that is, five beams for each layer. This was apparently sufficient to carry the weight of the remaining fifty-one cubits (88 feet or 26.78 m) of stone work.

Standing inside the *ulam* and looking up, we see the high outer wall of the *ulam* tied in with cedar beams to the back wall of the *ulam*, which was also the wall of the Sanctuary. We are not told how many of these beams were needed to prevent the outer wall from bulging. Golden chains fixed to the roof construction of the *ulam* hung on either side of the entrance to the Sanctuary. Young priests would climb these chains to inspect the four "crowns" which were located above the entrance to the Sanctuary. These crowns are understood to have been window ornaments, perhaps in the form of ornate and gilded pediments.

Chapter Ten: Reconstructing Herod's Temple

Chapter Ten: Reconstructing Herod's Temple

> **THE MAGNIFICENT GOLDEN VINE**
>
> The most spectacular sight inside the ulam was the Golden Vine, which was trained over posts or pillars.[4] Josephus also wrote about this vine in War 5.210, saying that above the entrance to the Sanctuary itself were "those golden vines, from which depended grape-clusters as tall as a man." Again, in *Antiquities* 15.394–395, we read of "a golden vine with grape-clusters hanging from it, a marvel of size and tapestry to all who saw with what costliness of material it had been constructed." This vine was quite famous and was mentioned by Tacitus (History 5.5) and possibly by Jesus, in John 15, who said in verse 5: "I am the vine, ye are the branches: He that abideth in me, and I in him, the same bringeth forth much fruit: for without me ye can do nothing."
>
> The vine is representative of Israel, for example, as in Psalm 80:8: "Thou hast brought a vine out of Egypt: thou hast cast out the heathen, and planted it," and Jeremiah 2:21: "Yet I had planted thee a noble vine, wholly a right seed." When we contemplate the fact that the entrance to the sanctuary was 20 cubits (34 feet, 10.50 m) high and the Golden Vine was at least that high, we realize how impressive this construction must have been. From the Vine's large scale, we also understand that freewill offerings by the people, whether a golden leaf, a golden berry, or even a whole cluster, must have accounted for a huge quantity of gold. At times it took three hundred priests to remove these offerings, presumably to fill the Temple coffers. It has been suggested[5] that the wavy line above the four columns on the tetradrachm of Bar Kochba represent this Golden Vine. However, according to Barag,[6] the four columns represent the façade of the Temple. I would agree with Barag, for whom I made the reconstruction drawings of the shewbread table and the Temple façade, because the Temple's foundation is clearly marked on this coin in what looks like a horizontal ladder. Other coins show dots above the columns instead of a wavy line. These may indicate rosettes in the entablature of the Temple façade.

The crowns on these windows belonged to, or were dedicated by, four people. The names mentioned are taken from Zechariah 6:14:

> *And the crowns shall be to **Helem**, and to **Tobijah**, and to **Jedaiah**, and to **Hen** the son of Zephaniah, for a memorial in the Temple of the LORD.*

The chains were probably not made of solid gold. To be strong enough to support the weight of a person, they would have had to be extremely heavy and therefore very costly. The links of the "chains" were thus most likely made of iron or bronze overlaid with gold, or possibly were ropes interwoven with golden threads.

Looking sideways, we see two chambers at either end of the *ulam*, called the Chambers of the Slaughter-knives, so called because the knives used for the ritual slaughter were kept here inside the *ulam*.

From its bedrock foundation to the top of the scarecrow,[7] the *ulam* was one hundred cubits high and wide. It projected fifteen cubits on either side of the Sanctuary, which was therefore seventy cubits (120 feet or 36.75 m) wide. The sides of the Sanctuary were lower than the central part of the building; *Middot* 4.7 describes the whole building as a lion, *"narrow behind and wide in front."* The depth of the *ulam* was only eleven cubits and the interior must have looked very narrow compared to the great internal height which was eighty-five cubits (146 feet or 44.63 m).

Above: Coin of Bar Kochba; on obverse, front of a building with four columns and architrave, possibly the façade of the Temple.

Opposite page: The Golden Vine of the Temple. (photo: Philip Evans)

Chapter Ten: Reconstructing Herod's Temple

THE HOLY (*HEIKHAL*)

The entrance to the Sanctuary was overlaid with gold as were the inner walls of the *ulam*. It could be seen through the large entrance opening of the *ulam*, of which Josephus (*War* 5.208) wrote,

> *The entire face [of the* ulam*] was covered with gold, and through it the first edifice was visible to a spectator without in all its grandeur and the surroundings of the inner gate all gleaming with gold fell beneath his eye.*

The opening to the Sanctuary was twenty cubits high and ten wide (34x17 feet or 10.50x5.25 m) and it had two sets of double folding doors. One set of doors was on the outside and the other on the inside, with a space in between when the doors were closed. As the width of the opening was ten cubits, each door must have been five cubits wide. Each door had two folding halves, so that when folded, one door occupied the space of 2.5 cubits, or together five cubits, and would have fitted into the recesses of the six-cubit (10.3 feet or 3.15 m) thick wall. The doorposts were half a cubit (10 inches or 26 cm) wide and deep, so that the recesses measured five cubits long. When folded back, the two doors would fit exactly into these recesses.

On either side of the main entrance were two smaller openings or wickets (see section D-D, p. 379). The southern entrance was never used, but the one on the north led into a narrow passageway, and in turn into one of the cells that were built around the Sanctuary. From

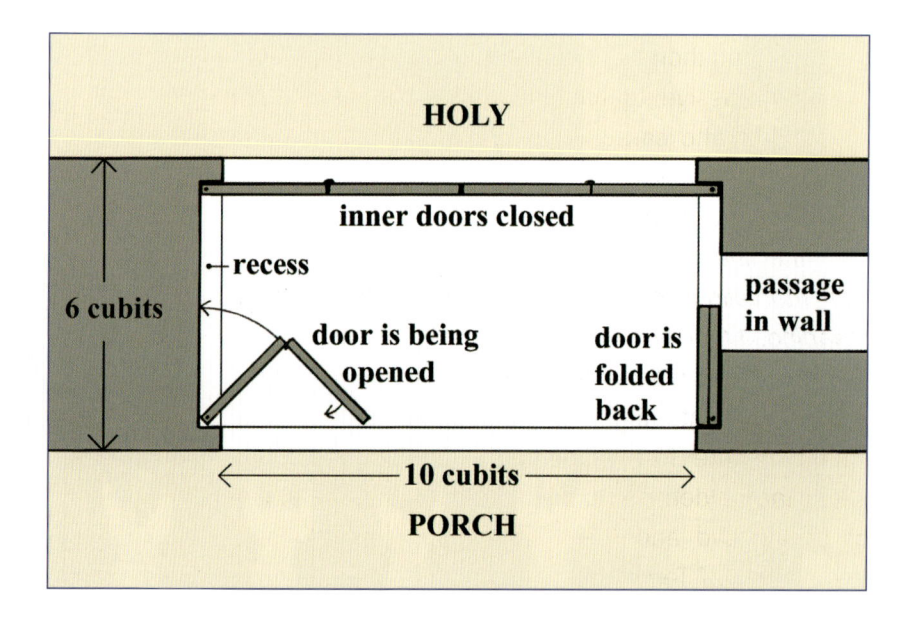

Plan of the two sets of double folding doors of the Sanctuary.

CHAPTER TEN: RECONSTRUCTING HEROD'S TEMPLE

Left: The Altar of Incense. (photo: Philip Evans)

Below: The menorah *in Herod's Temple. (photo: Philip Evans)*

this cell the Sanctuary could be accessed. However, before entering this cell, we would see in the middle of this passageway a side opening on the south leading into yet another passageway. Constructed in the thickness of the wall, it emerged into the recess of the northern double door. When closed, the priest in charge of opening the doors would stand in the space between the two sets of doors, and first open the outer and then the inner doors.

These massive doors were usually not seen by the worshipers who came to the Temple, for, according to Josephus *(War* 5.211–214), in front of the doors hung a *"Babylonian tapestry, with embroidery of blue and fine linen, of scarlet also and purple, wrought with marvellous skill. Nor was this mixture without meaning: it typified the universe."*

The *heikhal* was forty cubits (68.8 feet or 21 m) long and twenty wide (34.4 feet or 10.50 m) and its walls were forty cubits high. Inside this room stood the golden *menorah* or Lampstand, the Table of Shewbread and the Altar of Incense. Although these items of Temple furniture are not mentioned in

389

CHAPTER TEN: RECONSTRUCTING HEROD'S TEMPLE

> **EXCITING ARCHAEOLOGICAL FIND CONFIRMS MENORAH**
>
> *In the Jewish Quarter Excavations, Professor Avigad's team uncovered two plaster fragments in a Herodian fill. Incised on the plaster were a schematic depiction of the menorah, the Shewbread Table and the Altar of Incense.[8] Barag, later,[9] on the same piece of plaster, tentatively identified some lines at the left side of the base of the menorah as the stone out of which three steps were cut, and which stood in front of the menorah to enable the officiating priest to reach the lamps which he had to trim daily. This special stone is mentioned in Tamid 3.9, where it is also recorded that the oil jar was always left on the second step. This exciting find may have originally served as a teaching aid for children to show them the furniture in the heikhal, but for us it provides unique confirmation of the importance of the Jerusalem Temple for people at that time.*

Above: Plaster fragments found in the Jewish Quarter, showing the menorah with its stepping stone, the Shewbread Table and the Altar of Incense.

Opposite page: Drawing of the Veil in the heikhal of Herod's Temple.

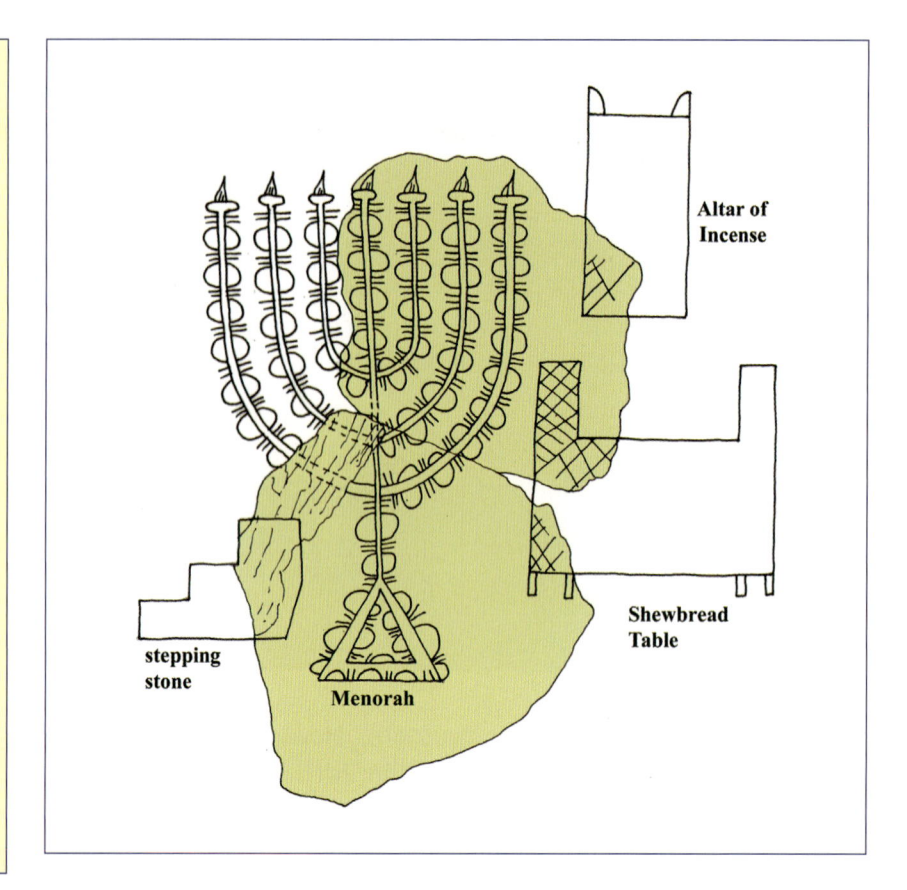

Middot, they are to be found in other parts of the Mishnah, especially in the tractate *Tamid*.

THE VEIL (*PAROKHET*)

Looking west from inside the *heikhal*, one would see a massive tapestry, called the Veil (*parokhet*), which separated the *heikhal* from the Holy of Holies. The mishnaic tractate *Shekalim* 8.5 tells us that,

> *The veil was one handbreadth thick and was woven on seventy-two rods, and over each rod were twenty-four threads. Its length was forty cubits and its breadth twenty cubits; it was made by eighty-two young girls, and they used to make two in every year; and three hundred priests immersed it.*

The veil would have been too large to weave on one loom and therefore it was more likely to have been composed of seventy-two pieces joined together. Because of its enormous size and weight, the veil was probably hoisted up by pulleys fixed to the ceiling

CHAPTER TEN: RECONSTRUCTING HEROD'S TEMPLE

CHAPTER TEN: RECONSTRUCTING HEROD'S TEMPLE

> **TWO VEILS OR ONE?**
>
> It is strange that we read in Yoma 5.1, that there were:
>
> > Two curtains separating the Sanctuary from the Holy of Holies. And there was a cubit's space between them. Rabbi Jose says: Only one curtain was there, for it is written, And the veil shall divide for you between the holy place and the most holy" The outer curtain was looped up on the south side and the inner one on the north side. He went along between them until he reached the north side; when he reached the north he turned round to the south and went on with the curtain on his left hand until he reached the Ark. When he reached the Ark he put the fire-pan between the two bars.
>
> To reach the Holy of Holies, the High Priest would walk through the space between the two curtains. He first encountered the eastern veil, the one visible from inside the heikhal. A gap was left open on the left, or south, side and he entered the Holy of Holies through another gap left on the north side of the inner, or western, curtain. Although the veil is not mentioned in Middot, the supposition that there were two veils is supported by the writer of this tractate, for in Middot 4.7, a "dividing space" (amah traksin) of one cubit apparently separated the forty-cubit-long interior of the Sanctuary from the Holy of Holies. This same space was also accentuated in the upper chamber above by a row of flagstones (Middot 4.5). Although the tradition of one veil dates back to the Tabernacle, indications in the Mishnah point to two veils in the Temple.
>
> Is it possible that initially there was only one veil in Herod's Temple and that a second veil was installed after the rending of the veil at the death of Jesus? The veil that was rent in A.D. 33 had to be replaced, otherwise the Holy of Holies, which the Law of Moses stipulated should only be entered once a year by the High Priest, would be open to view. A second veil may have been added to prevent such a situation from recurring.

construction. Even so, three hundred priests were needed to move it, which shows how massive this veil must have been. If the veil became ritually unclean, or simply dirty, it had to be immersed in the *azarah,* and then laid out to dry on the steps of the *hel.* When a new veil was made, it was spread out on the roof of the portico, so that people could admire its beauty.

The veil is also mentioned by Josephus, *"the innermost recess measured twenty cubits, and was screened off in like manner from the outer portion by a veil"* (*War* 5.219), and in the New Testament, *"And, behold, the veil of the Temple was rent in twain from the top to the bottom"* (Mt 27:51; see also Mk 15:38 and Lk 23:45).

THE HOLY OF HOLIES (*DEBIR*)

The Holy of Holies was a square of 20 cubits (34.4 feet or 10.50 m) and was 40 cubits (69 feet or 21 m) high. It had no windows and was found to be empty at the time of the Second Temple.

We have already quoted *War* 5.219 in connection with the veil. The verse, however, continues to describe the interior of the Holy of Holies, *"In this stood nothing whatever: unapproachable, inviolable, invisible to all, it was called the Holy of Holy."* This does not mean to say that this chamber lacked ornamentation, for *Shekalim* 4.4 says that the surplus of the *terumah* was used to make *"golden plating for bedecking the Holy of Holies."* The *terumah* was originally a heave-offering of agricultural produce, but is used here as a financial

Opposite page: The Holy of Holies in Herod's Temple, showing the High Priest putting incense in the emplacement of the Ark of the Covenant, and a cleaning basket hanging near the walls that were covered with plates of gold. (photo: Philip Evans)

CHAPTER TEN: RECONSTRUCTING HEROD'S TEMPLE

CHAPTER TEN: RECONSTRUCTING HEROD'S TEMPLE

Right: Artist's impression of the Chamber of the Half-shekel. (The Temple Institute, Jerusalem)

Below: Gold plaques from the Sanctuary are displayed before the public, so that festival pilgrims could "observe the beauty and perfection of their (the artisans') work" (Pesachim 57a). (The Temple Instiute, Jerusalem)

contribution which was taken three times a year and put in the Chamber of the Half-shekel of the Temple. If there was enough money available, golden plates of one cubit square[10] were made and hung on the walls of the Sanctuary, for *Middot* 4.1 says that *"all the House was overlaid with gold."* Some of these plates were put on display during the three main pilgrim festivals.

The most important ceremony of the sacral year took place on Yom Kippur. The High Priest went into the Holiest of all to offer incense

AN ANCIENT SOLUTION TO A CLEANING PROBLEM

With golden plates on the walls of the Holy of Holies, access was needed for cleaning purposes. The Holy of Holies, like the rest of the Temple, had to be kept clean. Yet only the High Priest was allowed entry once a year on Yom Kippur, the Day of Atonement (see below). With so many functions to perform on that day, there would have been no time to do the cleaning as well.

The problem was surmounted by having a basket, attached to a rope, descend through the ceiling of the chamber. Closed on three sides, such baskets were lowered with the open side facing the wall. The cleaners standing inside the baskets could only look straight ahead and not into the Holy of Holies.

CHAPTER TEN: RECONSTRUCTING HEROD'S TEMPLE

and sprinkle blood. This is recorded in Leviticus 16:12–14:

> *And he shall take a censer full of burning coals of fire from off the altar before the LORD, and his hands full of sweet incense beaten small, and bring it within the veil. And he shall put the incense upon the fire before the LORD, that the cloud of the incense may cover the mercy seat that is upon the testimony, that he die not. And he shall take of the blood of the bullock, and sprinkle it with his finger upon the mercy seat eastward; and before the mercy seat shall he sprinkle of the blood with his finger seven times.*

As Josephus informed us, the Holy of Holies of the Second Temple was bare and therefore the incense cloud could not cover the mercy seat, which was part of the Ark of the Covenant. However, the exact place where the Ark stood was still visible in the bedrock, as we have seen, and that was the place where the High Priest performed his duties according to *Yoma* 5.2:

> *After the Ark was taken away a stone remained there from the time of the early Prophets, and it was called* shetiyah. *It was higher than the ground by three fingerbreadths. On this he [the High Priest] used to put (the fire-pan).*

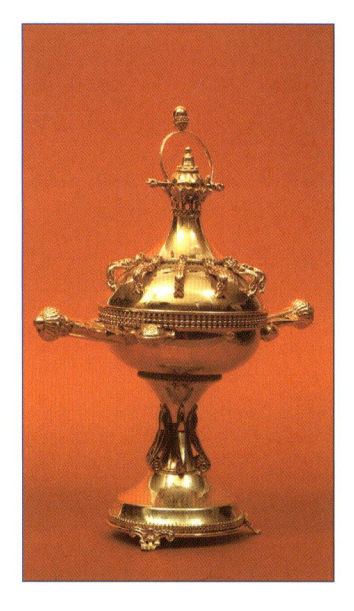

Reconstruction of the censer used by the High Priest in the Holy of Holies. (The Temple Institute, Jerusalem)

THE CELLS SURROUNDING THE SANCTUARY

Leaving the inner chambers of the Temple through the small opening in the northeast corner of the *heikhal*, we find ourselves again in the cell we entered through the small wicket to the north of the main entrance to the *heikhal*. This is one of thirty-eight cells built in three stories around the inner Sanctuary (*Middot* 4.3–4). There were five cells in three layers on the north and also on the south (see plan and section C-C, pp. 378–379, and illustrations, pp. 382 and 396). On the west were two layers of three cells and, as we shall see later, the top layer had two cells only. The lower cells were five cubits wide, the middle one six and the upper ones were seven cubits wide. The wall of the Sanctuary would have been respectively seven, six and five cubits wide, with the floors of the cells resting on the ledges. All the cells were interconnected, each having three openings, two to

Chapter Ten: Reconstructing Herod's Temple

The cells on the north side of Herod's Temple and the inner stairway, visible through a gap in the model's outer wall. (photo: Philip Evans)

connect with the cells on either side and one in the ceiling to reach the cell above.

Stationary or mobile ladders would have been necessary for movement between stories. Josephus also mentions these cells in *War* 5.220–221:

> Around the sides of the lower part of the sanctuary were numerous chambers, in three stories, communicating with one another; these were approached by entrances from either side of the gateway. The upper part of the building had no similar chambers, being proportionately narrower, but rose forty cubits higher in a severer style than the lower story.

As mentioned, the thirty-eight chambers around the inner Sanctuary rested on ledges, like the cedarwood *yatsi'ot* construction of three stories in Solomon's Temple (1 Kgs 6:5). These ledges were one cubit wide. In Herod's Temple, this honeycomb-like structure may have added constructional stability to this huge building complex, and doubles as repositories of vessels and supplies for the Temple ritual. The ongoing ritual in the Temple called for continuous maintenance and much labor.

The distribution of the five cells on the sides of the Temple is unknown. We have arranged them along the inner Sanctuary, which was sixty-one cubits long. The thickness of the walls in between the cells is also not given, but were likely to have been substantial if they also had a structural function to stabilize the high building. In our reconstruction, we have tried to use measurements of whole cubits, and therefore made the walls between the cells four cubits thick and the cells nine cubits long. The cells on the west were slightly longer. The reason why there were only two cells in the upper story on the west will be discussed below.

THE INNER STAIRWAY (*MESIBBAH*)

In the north wall of the cell we just entered and which is located on the lower level at the northeast corner of the cell construction, there is an opening or doorway, which leads to an inner staircase, called the *mesibbah*. This staircase was built in between the northern wall of the cell construction and the outer wall of the Temple building and was three cubits (5 feet 2 inches or 1.58 m) wide (see illustration, opposite page).

The Hebrew word *mesibbah* is usually translated "winding staircase," as this word is derived from *sabab,* meaning "going round" or "turn." This need not indicate that the Temple stairs were circular, but rather that a stepped approach was built around the inner Sanctuary. *Middot* 5.5 describes such a design for the *mesibbah:*

> *A passageway went up from the northeast corner to the northwest corner, whereby they could go up to the roofs of the cells. [The Priest] went up by the passageway facing westward, and went the whole length of the northern side until he reached the west; after he had reached the west he turned his face to the south, and went the whole length of the western side until he reached the south; after he had reached the south he turned his face to the east and went along the southern side until he reached the entrance to the upper chamber, for the entrance to the upper chamber opened towards the south.*

From this description it is clear that two turnings had to be made from the place where the steps began up to the place where the southern opening of the upper chamber was reached. What is not clear is at which point the roofs of the cells are reached. At the request of Patrich, I had initially drawn a straight staircase along the

Chapter Ten: Reconstructing Herod's Temple

Above: View of the exit of the mesibbah *on the west (on the intermediate roof level). (photo: Philip Evans)*

Below: View of the exit on the upper level, where a priest is seen stepping onto the roof after having climbed the cedar beams. (photo: Philip Evans)

northern side only. However, on reflection, this does not constitute a *mesibbah*. I realized later that part of the steps must have turned west. I base my reconstruction on the fact that there were thirty-eight cells in all, arranged over three levels. Thirty cells were located at the two sides of the Temple, leaving eight cells to be divided over the three levels at the west. This number cannot be divided by three and appears to be one cell short. I suggest therefore that the last part of the flight of steps was built into the space set aside for a third cell at the northwest angle of the Temple. This, then, is the reason for our earlier suggestion that there were only two cells in the upper level on the west. In this latest reconstruction presented here (see pp. 374–375) the stairway turns indeed as the word *mesibbah* indicates.

In reconstructing the *mesibbah,* the following details must also be considered. The available length for the staircase on the north was seventy-three cubits (sixty-one for the length of the inner Sanctuary, five for the Sanctuary wall and seven for the cell). If the last flight of steps occupied the place of a western cell, then the length—instead of the width—of this cell must be added to the length of the *mesibbah*, making a total of approximately eighty cubits. Each step was half a cubit high and deep, so that ninety steps would be needed to reach the forty-five-cubit-high roof of the cells. If the steps of the staircase were continuous, then only a forty-five-cubit-long staircase would be necessary.

The fact that more space is available indicates that the *mesibbah* consisted of several flights of steps, interrupted by landings. On the north I have inserted two landings corresponding to the level of the floors of the cells, with another landing at the northwest corner. Similar step/landing constructions have been found in the street complex around the Herodian Temple Mount.

The *mesibbah* was located in the north and west only. On the south there was a similar space of three cubits width, which was called *bet horadat ha-mayim* in *Middot* 4.7. This was a drain which collected all the rainwater that fell on the roofs and also from the *bet dilfa*, and presumably conducted into a cistern.

THE UPPER CHAMBER

The *mesibbah* led up to the intermediate roof level, with its exit probably covered to prevent rain falling on the stairway, and with a parapet around the edges of the roof, like that at the upper roof level.

CHAPTER TEN: RECONSTRUCTING HEROD'S TEMPLE

Crane and pulley in the Upper Chamber above the Holy of Holies. Note the priest inside the basket. (Photo: Philip Evans)

Going south, we enter through the small gate into the Upper Chamber. This was a very large room, the same size as the *heikhal* and Holy of Holies combined; that is, sixty-one cubits long, twenty wide and forty high. In the floor was a one-cubit-wide row of stones laid to mark the space between the two veils. In the floor above the Holy of Holies were *lulin*, large openings through which to lower baskets or boxes for workmen to clean or repair the walls of the Holy of Holies. Only the fronts of these were open, so that the workmen "should not feast their eyes on the Holy of Holies" (*Middot* 4.5).

There must have been a crane or pulley to lower these baskets with the men inside (see illustration, above). In our reconstruction model we have a crane with a treading drum attached to lower or hoist up the basket. This type of lifting device is known from the Roman period and is portrayed on a funerary relief from Syracuse. Cleaning of the Holy of Holies would have been rare. When not in use, the *lulin* were probably closed by trap-doors.

Positioned near the door of the Upper Chamber and on the east side were two slanting cedar beams to reach the upper roof, which was forty-five cubit high. No information is available to explain how these two beams were climbed. We have suggested that notches cut into the beams were used to gain access to the roof and the scarecrow for cleaning. The latter formed the upper part of the four-cubit-high parapet.

I suggested to Patrich that the top cubit was made of pyramid-

Above: A priest can be seen entering the small gate to the Upper Chamber. Through the hole in the wall, the cedar beams leading up to the intermediate roof level can be seen as well. (Photo: Philip Evans)

Below: View of the parapet on the Temple roof. (Photo: Philip Evans)

399

Chapter Ten: Reconstructing Herod's Temple

like stones to make it impossible for birds to find a foothold. These may have been topped by golden spikes. Josephus, in *War* 5.224, doesn't refer to a scarecrow, but to golden spikes only: *"from its [the Temple's] summit protruded sharp golden spikes to prevent birds from settling upon and polluting the roof."* From this great height one would have had a commanding view of the city of Jerusalem and surrounding areas.

In Conclusion

Leaving the Temple the way we entered, we can now look back on this magnificent edifice and the vast esplanade on which it stood with deeper appreciation of both Josephus' passionate description of it and *Middot*'s accuracy of measurement. The history of the Temple will never be recovered in its entirety. Nevertheless, it is my hope that the discoveries recorded in this volume, some based on archaeological excavation, some on careful observation and measurement, some on analysis of the written sources, will help to create for the reader a more vivid picture of the long and turbulent history of the Temple Mount.

The meticulous groundwork for our interpretation of the evidence was long, variegated and arduous. It was needed to lay a strong foundation for our quest for the location of the Temple. As the search unfolded, each new scrap of information has helped to refine our theories and deepen our understanding. Translating this information into visual representations has been of immeasurable assistance in checking and substantiating our proposals. We sincerely believe that the Temple Mount, still the world's most contested piece of real estate, has yielded most if not all its structural secrets.

Reference Section

Abbreviations

General

A.D.	*anno Domini* (in the year of our Lord)
B.C.	before Christ
c.	circa
CA	Carta Archives
cent.	century
chap(s).	chapter(s)
cm	centimeter(s)
ed.	editor; edition; edited by
e.g.	*exempli gratia*, for example
Eng.	English
etc.	*et cetera*, and so forth
ff.	and following
fig(s).	figure(s)
ft.	foot, feet
ibid.	*ibidem*, in the same place
i.e.	*id est*, that is (to say)
in.	inch(es)
m	meter(s)
mm	millimeter(s)
n.d.	no date
n(n).	note(s)
No.	Number
Ph.D.	Doctor of Philosophy
p(p).	page(s)
pl(s).	plate(s)
rev.	revised
sq.	square
vol(s).	volume(s)

Books of the Bible*

Old Testament

Gen	Genesis
Ex	Exodus
Lev	Leviticus
Num	Numbers
Deut	Deuteronomy
Josh	Joshua
Judg	Judges
Ruth	Ruth
1 Sam	1 Samuel
2 Sam	2 Samuel
1 Kgs	1 Kings
2 Kgs	2 Kings
1 Chr	1 Chronicles
2 Chr	2 Chronicles
Ezra	Ezra
Neh	Nehemiah
Esth	Esther
Job	Job
Ps	Psalms
Prov	Proverbs
Eccl	Ecclesiastes
Song	Song of Solomon
Isa	Isaiah
Jer	Jeremiah
Lam	Lamentations
Ezek	Ezekiel
Dan	Daniel
Hos	Hosea
Joel	Joel
Amos	Amos
Obad	Obadiah
Jonah	Jonah
Mic	Micah
Nah	Nahum
Hab	Habakkuk
Zeph	Zephaniah
Hag	Haggai
Zech	Zechariah
Mal	Malachi

New Testament

Matt	Matthew
Mk	Mark
Lk	Luke
John	John
Acts	Acts of the Apostles
Rom	Romans
1 Cor	1 Corinthians
2 Cor	2 Corinthians
Rev	Revelations

Intertestamental Works

1 Macc	1 Maccabees
2 Macc	2 Maccabees

Works/Journals/Reference

Ant.	Josephus: *Antiquities of the Jews*
BAIAS	Bulletin of the Anglo-Israel Archaeological Society
BAR	Biblical Archaeology Review
BR	Bible Review
BS	Bible and Spade
EI	Eretz-Israel
ESI	Excavations and Surveys in Israel
IEJ	Israel Exploration Journal
JBL	Journal of Biblical Literature
MUSJ	Mélanges de l'Université Saint Joseph de Beyrouth
NEAEHL	The New Encyclopedia of Archaeological Excavations in the Holy Land
PEFQS	Palestine Exploration Fund Quarterly Statement
PEQ	Palestine Exploration Quarterly
PJB	Palästina Jahrbuch
PPTS	The Library of the Palestine Pilgrims' Text Society
QDAP	Quarterly of the Department of Antiquities in Palestine
RAr	Revue Archéologique
RB	Revue Biblique
TSBA	Transactions of the Society of Biblical Archaeology
VT	Vetus Testamentum
War	Josephus: *The Jewish War*

* All biblical quotes are from the King James Authorized Version (KJV)

Bibliography

Ancient Sources

Bordeaux Pilgrim. *The Itinerary of the Bordeaux Pilgrim*, translated by A. Stewart and C. W. Wilson, *PPTS* 1 (London, 1887; Reprint, New York, 1971).

Fulcher of Chartres. *A History of the Expedition to Jerusalem, 1095–1127*, translated by F. R. Ryan, ed. H. S. Fink (Knoxville, TN, 1969).

Joannes Phocas. *Pilgrimage of Joannes Phocas*, translated by A. Stewart, *PPTS* 5 (London 1896; Reprint, New York, 1971).

John of Würzburg. *Description of the Holy Land by John of Würzburg*, translated by A. Stewart, *PPTS* 5 (London, 1890; Reprint, New York, 1971).

Josephus, Flavius. *The Jewish War*, translated by H. St. J. Thackeray (London/New York, 1927–28).

Josephus, Flavius. *Jewish Antiquities*, translated by H. St. J. Thackeray, R. Marcus, A. Wikgren and L. Feldman (London/Cambridge, Mass., 1930–65).

Josephus, Flavius. *The Whole Genuine Works of Flavius Josephus* by W. Whiston (London, 1822).

Kamâl al-Din as-Suyûti, *The History of the Temple Mount*, translated by Rev. J. Reynolds (London, Valpy, 1836).

Maccabees. *The First and Second Books of Maccabees* in the *Jerusalem Bible* (London, 1966).

The Mishnah, translated from the Hebrew with Introduction and Brief Explanatory Notes by H. Danby (Oxford, 1933).

Mujir ad-Din. *History of Jerusalem and Hebron* (Paris, 1876).

Nâsir-i-Khusrau. *Diary of a journey through Syria and Palestine*, translated by Guy Le Strange, *PPTS* 4 (London, 1888; Reprint, New York, 1971).

Origen. *Origen of Alexandria. Commentarii in Mattheum,* edited by Erich Klostermann and Ernst Benz. Die Griechischen Christlichen Schriftsteller, vol. 40. (Berlin, 1935).

Saewulf. *The Pilgrimage of Saewulf to Jerusalem and the Holy Land in the Years 1102 and 1103*, translated by W. R. B. Brownlow, *PPTS* 4 (London, 1892; Reprint, New York, 1971).

Strabo. *The Geography of Strabo*, translated by H. L. Jones (London/Harvard, Mass. 1917–32).

Tacitus. *Histories*, translated by C. H. Moore and J. Jackson (London/Harvard, Mass. 1925–31).

Theoderich. *Theoderich's Description of the Holy Places*, translated by A. Stewart, *PPTS* 5 (London, 1891; Reprint, New York, 1971).

Vitruvius. *The Ten Books on Architecture*, translated by M. H. Morgan (New York, 1960).

BIBLIOGRAPHY

Modern Writings

A

Abu Riya, R. (1992). "Jerusalem, Street of the Chain (A)" in *Excavations and Surveys in Israel 1991*, 10, pp. 134–135.

Adler, M. N. (1887). *The Temple at Jerusalem* (London).

Adler, S. J. (1991). "The Temple Mount in Court," *BAR*, 17.5, pp. 60–68.

Aharoni, Y. and M. Avi-Yonah (1968). *The Macmillan Bible Atlas* (New York, London).

Aline de Sion, Sr., M. (1956). *La forteresse Antonia à Jérusalem et la question du prétoire* (Jerusalem).

Amiran, R. and A. Eitan (1970). "Excavations in the Courtyard of the Citadel, Jerusalem, 1968–1969" in *IEJ* 20, pp. 9–17.

Avigad, N. (1980 [Hebrew]; 1983 [English]). *Discovering Jerusalem* (Jerusalem, Nashville).

Avigad, N. (1989). *The Herodian Quarter in Jerusalem—Wohl Archaeological Museum* (Jerusalem).

Avitsur, S. (1976). *Man and his Work, Historical Atlas of Tools and Workshops in the Holy Land* (Jerusalem) (Hebrew).

Avi-Yonah, M. (1975a). *The World History of the Jewish People, The Herodian Period*, vol. 7 (London).

Avi-Yonah, M. (1975b). "Jerusalem of the Second Temple Period" in Y. Yadin, ed., *Jerusalem Revealed*, pp. 9–13 (Jerusalem).

B

Bagatti, B. (1979). *Recherches sur le site du Temple de Jérusalem (Ier–VIIe siècle)*, Studium Biblicum Fransciscanum, Collectio Minor 22 (Jerusalem).

Bahat, D. (1983). *Carta's Historical Atlas of Jerusalem* (Jerusalem).

Bahat, D. (1988). "The Hasmonean Water Conduit near the Temple Mount" in *Ariel* 57/58, pp. 132–142 [Hebrew].

Bahat, D. (1989). *Carta's Great Historical Atlas of Jerusalem* (Jerusalem) (Hebrew).

Bahat, D. (1990). *The Illustrated Atlas of Jerusalem* (Jerusalem).

Bahat, D. (1994). "The Western Wall Tunnels" in H. Geva, ed. (1994), *Ancient Jerusalem Revealed*, pp. 177–190.

Barag, D. (1994a). "The Table of the Showbread and the Façade of the Temple on Coins of the Bar-Kokhba Revolt" in H. Geva, ed., *Ancient Jerusalem Revealed*, pp. 272–276 (Jerusalem).

Barag, D. (1994b). "The Temple Cult Objects Graffito from the Jewish Quarter Excavations at Jerusalem" in H. Geva, ed., *Ancient Jerusalem Revealed*, pp. 277–278 (Jerusalem).

Barkay, G. (1979). "The Cubit of the Old Standard: An Archaeological Consideration of a Problem in Biblical Metrology," *Sixth Archaeological Conference in Israel* (Jerusalem).

Barkay, G. and A. Kloner (1986). "Jerusalem Tombs from the Days of the First Temple" in *BAR* 12.2, pp. 22–39.

Barnabé d'Alsace (1902). *Le prétoire de Pilate et la forteresse Antonia* (Paris).

Ben-David, A. (1970). "The Hebrew-Phoenician Cubit" in *PEQ* 110, pp. 27–28.

Ben Dov, M. (1982). *In the Shadow of the Temple: The Discovery of Ancient Jerusalem* (Jerusalem).

Benoit, P. (1975). "The Archaeological Reconstruction of the Antonia Fortress" in Y. Yadin, ed., *Jerusalem Revealed: Archaeology in the Holy City*, pp. 87–89 (Jerusalem).

Ben-Yashar, M. (1971). "The Admission to the Temple Mount in the Light of Archaeological and Geometrical Discoveries" in *Torah ve-*

Madah, vol. 1, pp. 21–33 [Hebrew].

Berto, P. (1910). *Le Temple de Jérusalem* (Eremo, Italy).

Besant, W. (1886). *Twenty-one Years' Work in the Holy Land* (London).

Bimson, J. J. (1981). *Redating the Exodus and Conquest,* 2nd ed. (Sheffield).

Biran, A., ed. (1985). *Biblical Archaeology Today: Proceedings of the International Congress on Biblical Archaeology, Jerusalem April 1984* (Jerusalem).

Biran, A. (1982). "The Temenos at Dan" in *EI* 16, pp. 15–43 (Hebrew, English abstract).

Broshi, M. and S. Gibson (1994). "Excavations Along the Western and Southern Walls of the Old City of Jerusalem" in H. Geva, ed., *Ancient Jerusalem Revealed,* pp. 147–155 (Jerusalem).

Burgoyne, M. H. (1987). *Mamluk Jerusalem: An Architectural Study* (published on behalf of the British School of Archaeology in Jerusalem by the World of Islam Festival Trust, Buckhurst Hill).

Busink, T. A. (1970). *Der Temple von Jerusalem, von Salomo bis Herodes: Eine archäologisch-historische Studie unter Berücksichtigung des westsemitischen Tempelbaus,* vol. 1: *Der Tempel Salomos* (Leiden).

Busink, T. A. (1980). Ibid. vol. 2: *Von Ezechiel bis Middot* (Leiden).

C

Chaplin, T. (1875). "The Stone of Foundation and the Site of the Temple" in *PEFQS,* pp. 23–28.

Chapman, R. L. (1984). "Masonry in the Late Bronze and Early Iron Ages in the Levant." Doctoral thesis, Institute of Archaeology, University of London.

Charles, R. H. (1913). *The Apocrypha and Pseudepigrapha of the Old Testament,* 2 vols. (Oxford).

Charlesworth, J. H., ed. (1985). *The Old Testament Pseudepigrapha,* 2 vols. (London).

Clermont-Ganneau, M. Ch. (1872). "Une stèle du Temple de Jérusalem" in *RAr* 23, pp. 214–234.

Clermont-Ganneau, M. Ch. (1899). *Archaeological Researches in Palestine during the Years 1873–1874,* vol. 1 (London).

Conder, C. R. (1878). *Tent Work in Palestine,* 2 vols. (London).

Conder, C. R. (1884). See: Warren and Conder (1884).

Conder, C. R. (1909). *The City of Jerusalem* (London).

Corbett, S. (1952). "Some Observations on the Gateways to the Herodian Temple in Jerusalem" in *PEQ* 84, pp. 7–14.

D

Dalman, G. (1909). "Der zweite Tempel zu Jerusalem" in *Palästina-Jahrbuch* 5, pp. 29–57.

Dalman, G. (1912). *Neue Petra-Forschungen und der heilige Felsen von Jerusalem,* Ch. 4: "Der heilige Felsen von Jerusalem" (Leipzig).

Dalman, G. (1935). *Sacred Sites and Ways* (London).

Dalman, K. O. (1939). "Über ein Felsengrab im Hinnomtale bei Jerusalem" in *Palästina-Jahrbuch* 35, pp. 190–208.

De Vaux, R. (1965). *Ancient Israel* (London).

Dunand, M. (1969). "Byblos, Sidon, Jérusalem. Monuments apparentés des temps Achéménides" in *Congress Volume* (Rome, 1968), *VT Supplement* 17, pp. 64–70.

E

Edersheim, A. (1874). *The Temple, Its Ministry and Services as they were at the Time of Christ* (republished 1997, Grand Rapids, MI).

Eliav, Y. (2005). *God's Mountain: The Temple in Time, Place and Memory* (Baltimore, MD).

Eshel, H. (1987). "The Late Iron Age Cemetery of Gibeon," appendix: "The Problem of the Cubit and the Gibeon Tombs" in *IEJ* 37, p. 17.

BIBLIOGRAPHY

F

Fergusson, J. (1847). *An Essay on the Ancient Topography of Jerusalem* (London).

Fergusson, J. (1878). *The Temples of the Jews and the other Buildings in the Haram Area at Jerusalem* (London).

Fleming, J. (1983). "The Undiscovered Gate Beneath Jerusalem's Golden Gate" in *BAR* 9.1, pp. 24–37.

Franken, H. J. and M. L. Steiner (1990). *Excavations in Jerusalem 1961–1967*, Vol. II. *The Iron Age Extramural Quarter on the South-East Hill*.

Fritz, V. (1987), "What Can Archaeology Tell Us about Solomon's Temple?" in *BAR* 13.4, pp. 38–49.

G

Gabrieli, F. (1969). *Arab Historians of the Crusades* (Berkeley and Los Angeles).

Garstang, J. (n.d.). "Jerusalem under Herod the Great" in J. A. Hammerton, ed., *Wonders of the Past*, vol. 3, pp. 999–1020 (London).

Gershuny, L. (1992). "Jerusalem, Street of the Chain (B)" in *ESI 1991*, 10, pp. 135–136.

Geva, H. (1983). "Excavations in the Citadel of Jerusalem, 1979–1980, Preliminary Report" in *IEJ* 33, pp. 55–71.

Geva, H., ed. (1994). *Ancient Jerusalem Revealed* (Jerusalem).

Geva, H., ed. (2000). *Ancient Jerusalem Revealed*, Expanded edition with update (Jerusalem).

Geva, H., ed. (2000). *Jewish Quarter Excavations in the Old City of Jerusalem*, Vol. 1, pp. 37–82.

Gibson, S. and D. M. Jacobson (1996). *Below the Temple Mount in Jerusalem: A sourcebook on the cisterns, subterranean chambers and conduits of the Haram al-Sharif* (Oxford).

Gonen, R. (1985). "On Ancient Tombs and Holy Places: The Cave of Machpela and the Temple Mount" in *Cathedra* 34, pp. 8–14.

H

Hancock, G. (1993). *The Sign and the Seal: A Quest for the Lost Ark of the Covenant* (London).

Herrmann, J. (1882). *Le Temple de Jérusalem* (Paris).

Hollis, F. J. (1934). *The Archaeology of Herod's Temple: With a Commentary on the Tractate Middoth* (London).

Holtzmann, O. (1913). *Die Mishna, Middot* (Giessen).

Hurowitz, V. (1994). "Inside Solomon's Temple" in *BR* 10.2, pp. 24–37.

I

Iliffe, J. H. (1938). "The Thanatos Inscription from Herod's Temple, Fragment of a Second Copy" in *QDAP* 6, pp. 1–3.

J

Jacobson, D. M. (1990–91). "The Plan of Herod's Temple" in *BAIAS* 10, pp. 36–66.

Jacobson, D. M. (1999a). "Sacred Geometry," Part 1, in *BAR* 25.4, pp. 41–53, 62–64.

Jacobson, D. M. (1999b). Ibid., Part 2, in *BAR* 25.5, pp. 54–63.

Jagersma, H. (1985). *A History of Israel from Alexander the Great to Bar Kochba* (London).

Jeremias, J. (1969). *Jerusalem in the Time of Jesus* (London).

Johns, C. N. (1950). "The Citadel, Jerusalem: A Summary of Work Since 1934" in *QDAP* 14, pp. 121–190.

Jones, A., ed. (1966). *The Jerusalem Bible* (London).

K

Kamâl ad Dîn as Suyûtî, *Description of the Noble Sanctuary at Jerusalem in 1470 A.D.* (extracts re-translated by G. Le Strange, London, 1836).

Kaufman, A. S. (1977). "New Light upon Zion: The Plan and Precise Location of the Second Temple" in *Ariel* 43, pp. 63–99.

Kaufman, A. S. (1984–85). "The Meaning of Har Habayit and its Northern Gate" in *Niv Hamidrashia* 18/19, pp. 97–108.

Kaufman, A. S. (1985). Contribution to the Discussion on Session VIII, Revealing Biblical Jerusalem, in A. Biran, ed., *Biblical Archaeology Today: Proceedings of the International Congress on Biblical Archaeology, Jerusalem April 1984* (Jerusalem), p. 484.

Kaufman, A. S. (1991). *The Temple of Jerusalem, Part I, tractate Middot—an ancient version* (Jerusalem) (Hebrew).

Kaufman, A. S. (1997). *The Temple of Jerusalem, Part II (1) tractate Middot—variant readings for chapters 1 and 2* (Jerusalem) (Hebrew).

Kaufman, A. S. (2004). *The Temple Mount: Where is the Holy of Holies? Temple of Jerusalem 3* (Jerusalem).

Kempinski, A. and R. Reich, eds. (1992). *The Architecture of Ancient Israel from the Prehistoric to the Persian Periods* (Jerusalem).

Kenyon, K. M. (1967) *Jerusalem: Excavating 3000 Years of History* (London).

Kenyon, K. M. (1970). "New Evidence on Solomon's Temple" in *MUSJ*, Vol. 46, pp. 139–149.

Kenyon, K. M. (1974). *Digging Up Jerusalem* (London).

Kenyon, K. M. (1978). *The Bible and Recent Archaeology* (Atlanta).

King, J. (1885). *Recent Discoveries on the Temple Hill at Jerusalem* (London).

Kuemmel, A. (1906). *Materialen zur Topographie des alten Jerusalem.* Begleittext zu der "Karte der Materialen zur Topographie des Alten Jerusalem" (1904), (Halle).

L

Laperrousaz, E. M. (1973). "A-t-on dégagé l'angle sud-est du 'Temple de Salomon'?" in *Syria* 50, pp. 355–392.

Le Strange, G. (1890). *Palestine under the Moslems* (London).

M

Macalister, R. A. S. (1900–1903). "The Rock-cut Tombs in Wady er-Rababi" in *PEFQS*, 1900: pp. 101–102, 225–248, 376–377; 1901: pp. 145–158, 215–226; 1903: pp. 170–171.

Magen, Y. (1991). "Elonei Mamre—Herodian Cult Site" in *Qadmoniot* 93–94, pp. 46–55 [Hebrew].

Magen, Y. (1993). "Mamre," in E. Stern, ed., *The New Encyclopedia of Archaeological Excavations in the Holy Land*, 4 vols., pp. 939–942 (Jerusalem).

Maier, J. (1985). *The Temple Scroll: An Introduction, Translation & Commentary* (Sheffield).

Maier, J. (1989). "The Architectural History of the Temple in Jerusalem in the Light of the Temple Scroll" in G. J. Brooke, ed., *Temple Scroll Studies*, pp. 23–62 (Sheffield).

Maier, J. (1990). "The *Temple Scroll* and Tendencies in the Cultic Architecture of the Second Commonwealth" in L. H. Schiffman, ed., *Archaeology and History in the Dead Sea Scrolls*, pp. 67–82 (Sheffield).

Mazar, A. (1975). "The Aqueducts of Jerusalem" in Y. Yadin, ed., *Jerusalem Revealed*, pp. 79–84 (Jerusalem).

Mazar, B. (1969). *The Excavations in the Old City of Jerusalem near the Temple Mount. Preliminary Report of the First Season, 1968* (Jerusalem).

Mazar, B. (1971). *The Excavations in the Old City of Jerusalem near the Temple Mount, Second Preliminary Report*, 1969–79 Seasons (Jerusalem).

Mazar, B. (1975). *The Mountain of the Lord* (New York).

Mazar, B. (1978). "Herodian Jerusalem in the

Light of the Excavations South and Southwest of the Temple Mount" in *IEJ* 28, pp. 230–237.

Mazar, B. (1981). "The Royal Stoa in the Southern Part of the Temple Mount" in *Thirty Years of Archaeology in Eretz-Israel, 1948–1978: The Thirty-fifth Archaeological Convention*, pp. 143–151 (Jerusalem) (Hebrew).

Mazar, B., (1985). "The Temple Mount" in *Biblical Archaeology Today: Proceedings of the International Congress on Biblical Archaeology, Jerusalem April 1984*, pp. 463–468 (Jerusalem).

Mazar, B. (1992). *Biblical Israel: State and People* (Jerusalem).

Meecham, H. G. (1935). *The Letter of Aristeas. A linguistic study with special reference to the Greek Bible* (Manchester).

Merrill, S. (1908). *Ancient Jerusalem* (New York).

Mommert, C. (1903). *Topographie des alten Jerusalem, Zweiter Teil: Das Salomonische Tempel- und Palast-quartier auf Moriah* (Leipzig).

N

Netzer, E. (2005). "What the Courts, Chambers and Gates Which Surrounded the Second Temple Looked Like and How They Functioned" in *Qadmoniot* 38.130, pp. 97–106 (Hebrew).

P

Parrot, A. (1957). *The Temple of Jerusalem* (London).

Patrich, J. (1986). "The *Messibah* of the Temple According to the Tractate *Middot*" in *IEJ* 36, pp. 215–233.

Patrich, J. (1987). "Picturing the Second Temple" in *Eretz Magazine,* Spring 1987, pp. 67–70 (Jerusalem).

Patrich, J. (1994). "The Structure of the Second Temple—A New Reconstruction" in H. Geva, ed., *Ancient Jerusalem Revealed*, pp. 260–271 (Jerusalem).

Peters, F. E. (1985). *Jerusalem: The Holy City in the Eyes of Chroniclers, Visitors, Pilgrims, and Prophets from the Days of Abraham to the Beginning of the Modern Period* (Princeton).

Petrie, W. M. Flinders (1892). "The Tomb-cutters Cubits at Jerusalem" in *PEFQS*, pp. 28–35.

Petrie, W. M. Flinders (1967). In*: Encyclopaedia Britannica,* 1967, Vol. 23, p. 377.

Pierotti, E. (1864). *Jerusalem Explored*, 2 vols. (London).

Price, R. (1994). *The Lost Ark and the Last Days: In Search of Temple Treasures* (Eugene, OR).

Price, R. (1999). *The Coming Last Days Temple* (Eugene, OR).

R

Reich, R. (1989). "Two Possible *Miqwaot* on the Temple Mount" in *IEJ* 39, pp. 63–65.

Reich, R., G. Avni, and T. Winter (1999). *The Jerusalem Archaeological Park* (Jerusalem).

Reich, R. and Y. Billig, "Excavations near the Temple Mount and Robinson's Arch, 1994–1996," in *Ancient Jerusalem Revealed* (2000), pp. 340–350.

Reynolds, J. (1836). *The History of the Temple of Jerusalem* (London).

Rienecker, F. and G. Maier (1994). *Lexicon zur Bibel* (Wuppertal).

Ritmeyer, K. and L. (1989a). "Reconstructing Herod's Temple Mount in Jerusalem" in *BAR* 15, no. 6, pp. 3–42.

Ritmeyer, K. and L., (1989b) 'Reconstructing the Triple Gate', *BAR* 15.6, pp. 49-53.

Ritmeyer, L. (1989c). "Quarrying and Transporting Stones for Herod's Temple Mount" in *BAR* 15.6, pp. 46–48.

Ritmeyer, L. (1990). "The Didactic Approach in Archaeological Restoration," M.A. Thesis (Conservation Studies), University of York.

Ritmeyer, L. (1992a). "The Architectural Development of the Temple Mount in Jerusalem," Ph.D. Thesis, University of Manchester.

Ritmeyer, L. (1992b). "Locating the Original Temple Mount" in *BAR* 18.2, pp. 24–45, 64–65.

Ritmeyer, L. and K. (1994). "Potter's Field or High Priest's Tomb?" in *BAR* 20.6, pp. 22–35, 76–78.

Ritmeyer, L. (1996a). "Where the Ark of the Covenant Stood in Solomon's Temple" in *BAR* 22.1, pp. 46–55, 70–72.

Ritmeyer, L. (1996b). *The Temple and the Rock* (Harrogate).

Ritmeyer, L. and K. (1998). *Secrets of Jerusalem's Temple Mount* (Washington, D.C.).

Ritmeyer, L. and K. (2000a). *From Sinai to Jerusalem: The Wanderings of the Holy Ark* (Jerusalem).

Ritmeyer, L. (2000b). "Ritmeyer Responds to Jacobson" in: "Where Was the Temple?" *BAR* 26.2, pp. 52–59.

Ritmeyer, L. and K. (2002). *The Ritual of the Temple in the Time of Christ* (Jerusalem).

Ritmeyer, L. and K. (2004). *Jerusalem in the Year 30 A.D.* (Jerusalem).

Ritmeyer, L. and K. (2005). *Jerusalem in the Time of Nehemiah* (Jerusalem).

Ritmeyer, L. and K. (2006). *Update: Secrets of Jerusalem's Temple Mount* (in press).

Robertson, D. S. (1971). *Greek and Roman Architecture* (Cambridge).

Robinson, E. (1941). *Biblical Researches in Palestine, Mount Sinai and Arabia Petrea in 1838,* 3 vols. Reprint 1977 (New York).

Robinson, E. (1857). *Biblical Researches in Palestine and Adjacent Countries. Later Biblical Researches, etc.* 3 vols. (London).

Rohl, D. M. (1995). *A Test of Time,* Volume One, *The Bible—From Myth to History* (London).

Rosen, G. (1866). *Das Haram von Jerusalem und der Tempelplatz des Moria* (Gotha).

Rosenau, H. (1979). *Vision of the Temple: The Image of the Temple of Jerusalem in Judaism and Christianity* (London).

S

Saulcy, M. de (1867). "Mémoire sur la nature et l'age respective des divers appareils de maçonnerie employés dans l'enceinte extérieure du Haram-ech-chérif de Jérusalem" in: *Mémoires de l'Institut Impérial de France* (Paris).

Schick, C. (1887). *Beit el Makdas, oder der alte Tempelplatz zu Jerusalem: Wie er jetzt ist* (Jerusalem).

Schick, C. (1896). *Die Stiftshütte, der Tempel in Jerusalem und der Tempelplatz der Jetztzeit* (Berlin).

Schmidt, H. (1933). *Der heilige Fels in Jerusalem* (Tübingen).

Schiller, E. (1975). *The Golden Gate* (Jerusalem).

Schiller, E., ed. (1989). *The Temple Mount and Its Monuments,* Ariel 64–65 (Jerusalem) (Hebrew).

Scott, R. B. Y. (1958). "The Hebrew Cubit" in *JBL* 77, pp. 205–214.

Segal, P. (1989). "The Penalty of the Warning Inscription from the Temple of Jerusalem" in *IEJ* 39, pp. 79–84.

Shanks, H. (1995). *Jerusalem: An Archaeological Biography* (New York).

Shanks, H. (1999). "Everything You Ever Knew About Jerusalem is Wrong" in *BAR* 25.6, pp. 20–29.

Shaw Caldecott, W. (1908). *The Second Temple in Jerusalem, Its History and Its Structure* (London).

Shaw Caldecott, W. (n.d., probably 1911). *Herod's Temple, Its New Testament Associations and Its Actual Structure* (London).

Shaw Caldecott, W. (n.d., probably 1911). *Outline Lecture on Herod's Temple of the New Testament* (London).

Shea, W. H. (1999). "Jerusalem under Siege: Did Sennacherib Attack Twice?" in *BAR* 25.6, pp. 36–44, 64.

Shiloh, Y. (1984). *Excavations at the City of David,* Qedem 19 (Jerusalem).

Shiloh, Y. (1992). "Underground Water Systems

in the Land of Israel in the Iron Age" in A. Kempinski and R. Reich, eds., *The Architecture of Ancient Israel from the Prehistoric to the Persian Periods.* (Jerusalem).

Simons, J. (1952). *Jerusalem in the Old Testament* (Leiden).

Simpson, W. (1872). *Underground Jerusalem. Descriptive Catalogue of the Above Collection of Water-Colour Drawings* (London).

Smith, G. A. (1907–08). *Jerusalem: The Topography, Economics and History from the Earliest Times to A.D. 70*, 2 vols. (London).

Steinberg, S. D. (1983). *The Third Beit Ha-Mikdash* (Jerusalem).

Stern, E. (1992). "The Phoenician Architectural Elements in Palestine During the Late Iron Age and the Persian Period" in A. Kempinski and R. Reich, eds., *The Architecture of Ancient Israel from the Prehistoric to the Persian Periods.* (Jerusalem).

Stern, E., ed. (1993). *The New Encyclopedia of Archaeological Excavations in the Holy Land*, 4 vols. (Jerusalem).

Stronach, D. (1978). *Pasargadae: A Report on the Excavations Conducted by the British Institute of Persian Studies from 1961 to 1963* (Oxford).

T

Tobler, T. (1852). *Denkblätter aus Jerusalem* (St. Gallen-Konstanz).

Tsafrir, Y. (1975). "The Location of the Seleucid Akra in Jerusalem" in Y. Yadin, ed., *Jerusalem Revealed*, pp. 85–86 (Jerusalem).

Tsafrir, Y. (1990). "The 'Massive Wall' East of the Golden Gate, Jerusalem" in IEJ 40, pp. 280–286.

U

Ussishkin, D. (1976). "The Original Length of the Siloam Tunnel in Jerusalem" in *Levant* 8, pp. 82–95.

Ussishkin, D. (1993). *The Village of Silwan: The Necropolis from the Period of the Judean Kingdom* (Jerusalem).

V

Vaux, R. de (1961). *Ancient Israel* (English trans., London).

Vincent, J. H. (1894). *Earthly Footsteps of the Man of Galilee* (New York and St. Louis).

Vincent, L.-H., E. J. H. Mackay, and F. M. Abel (1923). *Hébron—Le Haram el-Khalîl—Sépulture des Patriarches* (Paris).

Vincent, L.-H. (1933). "L'Antonia et le prétoire" in *RB* 42, pp. 83–113 (Paris).

Vincent, L.-H. (1934). "Le Lithostrotos d'après des fouilles récentes" in *RB* 43, p. 157.

Vincent, L.-H. (1954a). "Le Temple Hérodien d'après la Misnah" in *RB* 61, pp. 5–35, 398–418.

Vincent, L.-H. (1954b). "L'Antonia, palais primitive d'Herode" in *RB* 61, pp. 87–107.

Vincent, L.-H. and A. M. Stève (1954–1956). *Jérusalem de l'Ancien Testament*, 3 vols. (Paris).

Vogt, E. (1974). "Vom Tempel zum Felsendom" in *Biblica* 55, pp. 23–64.

Vogüé, M. de (1864). *Le temple de Jérusalem. Monographie du Haram ech-cherif, suivie d'un essai sur la topographie de la Ville Sainte* (Paris).

W

Warren, Ch. (1871). *The Recovery of Jerusalem: A Narrative of Exploration and Discovery in the City and Holy Land* (London).

Warren, Ch. (1876). *Underground Jerusalem: An Account of the Principal Difficulties Encountered in its Exploration and the Results Obtained* (London).

Warren, Ch. (1880). *The Temple or the Tomb* (London).

Warren, Ch. (1881). "The Site of the Temple of the Jews" in *TSBA* 7, part 2.

Warren, Ch. and C. R. Conder (1884). *Survey of Western Palestine: Jerusalem* (London).

Warren, Ch. (1884). *Plans, Elevations, Sections, etc., Showing the Results of the Excavations at Jerusalem, 1867–1870, Executed for the Committee of the Palestine Exploration Fund* (London).

Watson, C. M. (1896). "The Site of the Temple" in *PEFQS*, pp. 47–60, 226–228.

Watson, C. M. (1918). *The Story of Jerusalem* (London).

Watzinger, C. and K. Wulzinger (1921). *Damaskus die antike Stadt* (Berlin and Leipzig).

Wightman, G. J. (1989–90). "Temple Fortresses in Jerusalem, Part I: The Ptolemaic and Seleucid Akras" in *BAIAS* 9, pp. 29–40.

Wightman, G. J. (1990–91). "Temple Fortresses in Jerusalem, Part II: The Hasmonean Baris and Herodian Antonia" in *BAIAS* 10, pp. 7–35.

Wilkinson, J. (1978). *Jerusalem as Jesus Knew It* (London).

Wilkinson, J. (1981). "Architectural Procedures in Byzantine Palestine" in *Levant* 13, pp. 151–172.

Williams, G. (1849). *The Holy City*, 2 vols. (London).

Williams, G. (1864). *Dr. Pierotti and his Assailants, or A Defence of "Jerusalem Explored"* (London).

Wilson, C. W. (1880a). "The Masonry of the Haram Wall" in *PEFQS*, pp. 9–65.

Wilson, C. W. (1880b). *Jerusalem the Holy City, Picturesque Palestine, Sinai and Egypt* (London).

Wilson, C. W. (1865). *Notes on the Survey, and on Some of the Most Remarkable Localities and Buildings in and about Jerusalem* (London).

Wilson, C. W. and Ch. Warren (1871). *Recovery of Jerusalem* (London).

Wood, B. G. (1999). "ABR's Search for the Lost Cities of the Bible, The Search for Ai: Excavations at Kh. el-Maqatir" in *BS* 12.1, pp. 21–30.

Y

Yadin, Y., ed. (1975). *Jerusalem Revealed: Archaeology in the Holy City, 1968–1974* (Jerusalem).

Yadin, Y. (1977 [Hebrew]; 1983 [English]). *The Temple Scroll*, 3 vols. (Jerusalem).

Yadin, Y. (1985). *The Temple Scroll* (London).

Notes and References

Preface
1. Produced by Ritmeyer Archaeological Design, a private firm run by the author and his wife Kathleen.

Introduction
1. The Temple Mount (*birah*) was completed by Nehemiah, but the Temple itself was finished in 515 B.C. See, for example, B. Mazar (1975), p. 61, and Kenyon (1974), p. 176. I prefer this traditional date, although some modern scholars apparently advocate a later date.
2. Simons (1952), p. 381.
3. Watson (1896), pp. 47–60.
4. Mommert (1903).
5. Dalman (1909), pp. 29–57.
6. Hollis (1934).
7. Mazar's contribution was the interpretation of the historical sources, while my part was concerned with the interpretation of the archaeological and architectural data.
8. Mazar (1985), p. 465.
9. Kaufman (1985), p. 484.

Chapter One
1. The quotations from the text of Josephus are taken from Josephus, Flavius, *The Jewish War*, Loeb Classical Library; translation by H. St. J. Thackeray, London, 1961.
Josephus, Flavius, *The Antiquities of the Jews*, Loeb Classical Library; translation by H.St.J. Thackeray, R. Marcus and L. H. Feldman, London, 1976-1981.
The translation of Whiston has also been referred to occasionally, see W. Whiston, *The Whole Genuine Works of Flavius Josephus*, London, 1822.
2. Mazar (1971), p. 2.
3. Warren and Conder (1884), p. 189.
4. Warren and Conder (1884), p. 190.
5. Warren and Conder (1884), p. 173.
6. Warren and Conder (1884), p. 179.
7. Warren, Plans, etc., 31, 32; Warren and Conder (1884), pp. 187–193; Wilson (1880a), p. 17–21.
8. Wilson (1880a), p. 20.
9. Tobler (1852), p. 42.
10. Abu-Riya and Gershuny (1992), pp. 134–136.
11. Kloner, A. The dating of the broad southern street (southern *decumanus*) of Aelia Capitolina and Wilson's Arch, Jerusalem Conference 2006.
12. This tunnel project was begun in 1975 by a team headed by Prof. Benjamin Mazar and later continued by Dan Bahat. The site is now administered by the Western Wall Heritage Foundation. See Bahat (1994).
13. Bahat (1994), p. 181.
14. Wilson (1865), p. 90; Warren and Conder (1884), p. 224; Wilson and Warren (1871), p. 215.
15. Avigad (1983), p. 69, Figs. 30, 38.
16. Warren and Conder (1884), p. 213, Warren, *Plans, etc.,* Pl. 37.
17. Warren and Conder (1884), p. 214; Vincent, Mackay and Abel (1923), pp. 103–107, Figs. 61, 62.
18. Wilson and Warren (1871), pp. 198–201.
19. Bahat (1994), p. 188.

20 Shiloh (1992), pp. 282–285.
21 Robinson, (1867), Vol. 1, pp. 356–364; Vol. 3, p. 251 ff.
22 Warren (1876), p. 316.
23 Schick (1887), p. 122 ff.
24 Watson (1896), p. 59.
25 Dalman (1935), p. 287.
26 This was later corrected, see A Short Guide to the Model of Ancient Jerusalem, Holyland Hotel, Jerusalem, Information Leaflet no. 3, April 1984, Jerusalem, pp. 17–19.
27 Avigad (1983), pp. 81–150; see also Avigad (1989).
28 Mazar (1971), p. 17.
29 Reich, Avni and Winter (1999), p. 14. Reich and Billig (2000), pp. 340–350.
30 Magen (1991, 1993).
31 Vincent, Mackay and Abel (1923), p. 40 ff., Pls. 3, 4, 14, 18, 19, 20.
32 Bliss and Dickie (1898), ch. 4, pp. 132–177.
33 Warren and Conder (1884), pp. 179–183, *Plans, etc.*, Pls. 5, 7, 28–30.
34 Mazar (1971), p. 16, Pls. 12, 13.
35 Mazar (1971), p. 25.
36 Mazar (1971), pp. 8–10.
37 For early descriptions of this gate, see Gibson and Jacobson (1996), pp. 235–259.
38 Burgoyne (1987), pp. 45–46.
39 Corbett (1952), pp. 7–14, Pls. 1–5.
40 Wilkinson (1981), pp. 156, 158.
41 *Plans, etc.* Pl. 26.
42 See also De Vogüé (1864), p. 11, Pl. 6.
43 Macalister (1901), p. 216.
44 Knut Olaf Dalman (1939), pp. 190–208; Gustaf Dalman (1935), pp. 328–334.
45 See Ritmeyer, L. and K. (1994).
46 Wilson and Warren (1871), p. 230 and "Section thro' Western Arch of Triple Gate and Elevation of western side of vault or passage leading from do."; Warren, *Plans, etc.*, Pl. 25. The engaged pilaster referred to is marked C.
47 Warren and Conder (1884), p. 162.
48 Vitruvius, 2.7.5.
49 Vincent and Stève (1956), pl. 128; Ben-Dov (1982), p. 91. This latter drawing shows an impossible reconstruction where the piers of one row of vaults rest on the centers of the vaults below. Such a construction would collapse before it could be completed as the weight of the piers would crush the vaults below. There are no such examples to be found in the entire world of classical architecture.
50 A photograph of the remains of the ancient vault in Solomon's Stables appears on p. 1004 of Garstang (n.d.), pp. 999–1020. As far as we were able to establish, this is the only photograph of the vault that has ever been published.
51 Warren and Conder (1884), p. 129.
52 Wilson (1880a), p. 51.
53 Warren and Conder, (1884), pp. 144, 145.
54 Fleming (1983).
55 For reports on the excavations at the northeast angle, see: Warren and Conder (1884) pp. 126–147; Wilson (1880a), pp. 39–46; Wilson and Warren (1871), pp. 159–188.
56 Warren and Conder (1884), p. 245.
57 Hollis (1934), pp. 50, 58.
58 Simons (1952), pp. 417 ff., 500 and n.2.
59 Warren and Conder (1884), pp. 126–130. Warren, *Plans, etc.,* Pl. 13.
60 Warren and Conder (1884), p. 128.
61 Warren and Conder (1884), p. 141; Wilson (1880a), p. 43; Wilson and Warren (1871), p. 167.
62 The lack of pilasters had been noted by Warren, see Warren and Conder (1884), p. 215. The dissimilarity with the other Herodian walls was used by Jacobson (1990–91), p. 38, to disprove the Herodian date of this tower.
63 Warren and Conder (1884), p. 145.
64 Simons (1952), p. 372, states that, *"there is no break between the 'tower' and the wall, the ancient blocks being properly bonded and the marginal drafts carried round the corner."* We believe that Simons misunderstood Wilson's text (1880a), pp. 24–25, which

reads, *"the appearance of the southern end [of the tower], where the stones are properly bonded and the draft completed round the corner, would seem to indicate that the four lowest courses were 'in situ', if it were not for the irregularity and coarseness of the jointing."*

The corner referred to by Wilson is the southern corner of the tower and not the re-entrant junction of the tower with the city wall. Simons may have been misled by Warren's incorrect drawing of the three courses to the south of the tower *(Plans, etc., Pl. 13)*, which has also been copied wrongly by Vincent and Stève (1956), Pl. 112.

65 Wilson (1865), p. 25.
66 Warren and Conder (1884), pp. 129, 130.
67 Hollis (1934), pp. 58.
68 Wilson (1865), p. 25.
69 Wilkinson (1978), p. 57.
70 Burgoyne (1987), p. 50, n. 8.
71 Merrill (1908), p. 51.
72 Burgoyne (1987), p. 43.
73 Original photograph on glass plate by R. E. M. Bain, published in Vincent (1894), p. 129.
74 Simons (1952), p. 413.
75 This has been confirmed by Burgoyne (1987), p. 44.
76 See for example Bahat (1990), p. 39.
77 Burgoyne (1987), pp. 43, 204, and Figs. 10.4, 14.2.
78 Burgoyne, (1987), p. 178, Fig. 10.3.
79 Vogüé, (1864), pp. 51–52, Pl. 15.
80 Wilson and Warren (1871), pp. 311–312, Fig. facing p. 303; Warren (1880), Fig. opposite p. 95.
81 Schick (1896), pp. 204–207, Tafel 7.
82 Watson (1896), pp. 47–60, Plan 2.
83 Hollis (1934), pp. 95–98, Pl. 4.
84 Simons (1952), pp. 325 ff., 374 ff., 402 ff., 429 ff., 432 ff.
85 Barnabé d'Alsace (1902), pp. 20 ff., Fig. 8.
86 Vincent and Stève (1956), pp. 193–221, Pl. 42.
87 Aline de Sion (1956), Pl. 13.
88 Benoit (1975), pp. 87–89.
89 Bagatti (1979), pp. 48, 49.
90 Wightman (1990–91), p. 15 ff.
91 Burgoyne (1987), p. 44.
92 Robertson (1971), pp. 149, 307, n. 1.
93 Burgoyne (1987), pp. 43, 204.
94 Burgoyne (1987), p. 339
95 This width has been proposed by Warren and Wilson and by Bahat. See Warren and Conder (1884), p. 215; Warren, *Plans, etc.,* Pl. 37; Wilson (1880a), p. 37; Bahat (1988), p. 142, Plan A, 25.

The existence of a 33-foot- (10-m-) wide ditch along the northern scarp of the Antonia plateau has recently been proposed by Wightman. See Wightman (1990–91), p. 18, Fig. 5B:8, 5C.

This hypothesis would, however, need verification. It is difficult to accept that Herod would have replaced the 160-foot-wide excavated ditch to the north of the square Temple Mount with a mere 33-foot-wide ditch to the north of the Antonia, as such a ditch would not have been a great military obstacle for the Romans. However, if the existence of this ditch can be ascertained, it could prove to have been an additional defense to, and part of, the 160-foot-wide fosse, located to the north of the Antonia plateau.

In his article Wightman gives a useful overview of the proposed reconstructions of the Antonia by Vincent, Aline de Sion and Benoit. His interpretation of the water conduit as the *hypogeion* of the *baris* (p. 11), however, would be incompatible with our location of the *baris*.

96 Bagatti (1979), p. 43.

Chapter Two

1 Thackeray (1961), *War* 5.184, note b.
2 See Holtzmann (1913), p. vi, and especially pp. 15–44, *"Der Traktat Middot und Josephus."*
3 The Hebrew Bible (1 Kgs 7:12) states

Notes and References

that Solomon built a "Great Court," which apparently surrounded both the Temple complex and his palace. However, it seems unlikely that this refers to the four stadia square mount, as later (2 Chr 20:5) a "New Court" is referred to, which may have been added before or during the reign of King Jehoshaphat (see discussion in Chap. 2.4.1).

4   Simons (1952), p. 346; Schick (1896), p. 240; Warren and Conder (1884), p. 119.
5   The standard Hebrew text of the *Six Sidrei Mishna* was consulted throughout. The quotations are from Danby (1933).
6   See Chap. 2.3.
7   Abarbanel's comment on *Middot* 2.1 is "The mountain was indeed much larger than 500 cubits would contain either way, but the sanctity did not extend outside this."
8   Chaplin (1875), pp. 23–28.
9   Fergusson (1878), especially Part II, The Temple of Herod, Chap. 1, external dimensions, pp. 71ff. and Part III, Chap. 1, introduction, pp. 193ff.

Although Fergusson's views were widely accepted in the middle of the previous century, and his location of the square Temple Mount therefore included on p. 147, they now seem too outlandish for consideration in this book. This is because his location of the Temple Mount at the southwest corner contradicts the fact that Herodian masonry is found all around the outer walls of the present-day Temple Mount. It is strange, therefore, to see that recently an architect from Tel Aviv, Tuvia Sagiv, has put forward a similar proposal.

10 Warren (1881), pp. 10–12.
11 See Shaw Caldecott (1908), pp. 354–355; (1911a) p. 353.
12 Warren, *Plans, etc.*, Pls. 6, 7.
13 See also Ritmeyer (1992b), p. 64; (1996), p. 73; (1998), pp. 114–116.
14 My photograph of this sill has been published in Adler (1991), p. 64.
15 Danby (1933), p. 604.
16 For a full critique of Jacobson's proposal, see Ritmeyer (2000b), pp. 53–59.
17 Babylonian Talmud, *Yoma* 15a and *Zevahim* 58b.
18 As mentioned in the Preface, this was pointed out to me in 1973 by my predecessor at the Temple Mount excavations, the Irish architect Brian Lalor.
19 This is evident, of course, from the different style of masonry to the north of the seam (see Chap. 3.4). The fact that the eastern wall is pre-Herodian is also supported by Josephus, who in *War* 5.185, states that the eastern wall is Solomonic. In *Ant.* 15.403–417, only the Herodian buildings along the northern, western and southern sides are mentioned. This indicates that Herod did not build the central part of the Eastern Wall.
20 A preliminary plan was published in Mazar (1985), Fig. 2, p. 467.
21 Warren and Conder (1884, p. 215). See also Warren, *Plans, etc.*, Pl. 12, Section O–R. The distance of 52 ft. was measured on this section.
22 This small valley was called "St. Anne's Valley" by Wilson, "Chaphenatha Valley" by Schick (1896), Tafel 4, and "Beth Zetha Valley" by Bahat (1983), p. 11. It was probably named after the new suburb Bezetha; see Josephus, *War* 5.151.
23 Bahat (1983) p.11.
24 Warren believed the "rockscarp" to be the northern limit of Herod's Temple enclosure (1884, p. 224). This scarp also features prominently in the proposals of Mommert and Dalman.
25 During the time of Warren's survey, the northernmost ashlar was also the northern end of the flight of steps; see Warren, *Plans, etc.*, Pl. 4. Sometime later, however, the lowest five steps have been extended farther to the north, up to the Sabil Sha'alam, with smaller stones making up the depth of the steps.
26 For further discussion of these towers, see Chap. 3.

Notes and References

27 Scott (1958), p. 205, n. 1; p. 207, n. 14.
28 Petrie (1892), pp. 28–35.
29 Smith (1907–08), vol. 2, p. 519 and n. 3.
30 Scott (1958), pp. 207–208.
31 Ben-David (1970), pp. 27–28.
32 Jeremias (1969), p. 11.
33 Ussishkin (1976), pp. 93–95.
34 Ussishkin (1986), pp. 250–252. (Hebrew)
35 Barkay (1979), p. 35.
36 See also Barkay and Kloner (1986), p. 37.
37 Eshel (1987), p. 17.
38 Wilson (1880a), p. 47.
39 de Saulcy (1867), Pl. 1.
40 Chapman (1984).
41 Dunand (1969), pp. 64–70.
42 Stronach (1978), p. 62.
43 A small postern was discovered 51 feet to the south of the Golden Gate, but its poor construction gave Wilson the impression of a filled-up hole in the wall, rather than that of a postern in a city wall. See Wilson (1880a), p. 47, and Warren and Conder (1884), p. 145.
44 Warren and Conder (1884), p. 146.
45 Simons (1952), p. 370.
46 *War* 5.145.
47 Warren and Conder (1884), pp. 144–145.
48 The texts from the Books of Maccabees are quoted from A. Jones, ed., *The Jerusalem Bible* (London, 1966), pp. 654–719.
49 Tsafrir (1990) has suggested an Early Islamic date for this wall section, based on the apparently reddish color of the cement in between the stone courses. However, the composition of the cement (lime, oil and virgin soil) given by Warren is based only on the superficial observation of the local workmen of his time, and is inadequate for scientific research.
Tsafrir also pronounced the construction of this wall as "weak," despite the fact that Warren gave up breaking through this massive wall after 5 feet 6 inches. He suggests that this wall was "a low buttress supporting a terrace to carry the approach road to the Golden Gate" in the Early Islamic period. This suggestion, however, fails to take into consideration the following critical points:
a. There would have been no need to build such a support, as there is good reason to believe that the Herodian stairway that led up to the Golden Gate is still in existence today (see Chap. 1, p. 110).
b. A low buttress would not be sufficient to overcome the difference in height of 60 feet between the base of the wall and the sill of the Golden Gate.
c. The nature of the debris encountered by Warren, including the remains of an apparently Herodian column, suggests that the bedrock in this area was covered over after the destruction of the Temple in A.D. 70. It is highly unlikely that the Muslims of the Early Islamic period would have excavated deep down to bedrock to build a low buttress, especially as the foundations for the massive palaces which were excavated by Mazar to the south and west of the Temple Mount do not go down to bedrock.
d. Warren observed a similarity between the stones of this wall and the lower course near the Golden Gate. This should indicate that the stones of this city wall were constructed at the same time as the early masonry on both sides of the Golden Gate. As will be discussed below, we believe that these stones date to the First Temple period.
50 See Warren, *Plans, etc.*, Pl. 24, Section of Ophel Wall at S.E. Angle of the Noble Sanctuary. Here we see that this city wall rests on soil, unlike other Herodian city walls, such as the sections uncovered in the Citadel, see Johns (1950), Amiran and Eitan (1970) and Geva (1983), and along the western wall of the Old City by Broshi and Gibson (1994), which are always built on the bedrock.
51 See Warren, *Plans, etc.*, Pl. 19.
52 On this point alone, Kaufman, in Biran (1985), p. 484, criticized my location of the square Temple Mount, *"To make the 'Ritmeyer*

Notes and References

square' plausible, this archaeological find [the step] should be parallel to the eastern wall of the Temple area. However, these two features digress from the parallel by 1.7 degrees."

According to my calculations, the southern wall is only less than five cubits shorter—less than 1%. This is not at all unusual in building constructions of such enormous size. The much smaller rectangular Herodian structure at Haram Ramat el-Khalil (Elonei Mamre) measures approximately 308 by 213 feet. Despite the fact that this enclosure was laid out on an almost level area, the eastern wall is 1.5% shorter than the western wall. A discrepancy of an even lower percentage at a much larger site does not, in my opinion, make this proposal as to the location of the square Temple Mount any less convincing. The fact that the *step* lines up with the eastern side of the internal passageway of Barclay's Gate is more important than a slightly inaccurate measurement.

53 Simons (1952), p. 405, n. 3. The identification of Coponius with Kiponus depends on the interchangeability of the Hebrew letter *yod* and the Greek letter *omega*. Hollis (*The Archaeology of the Temple*, p. 245), gives two examples, which underline this possibility.
54 *Ant.* 14. 58.
55 *War* 2.49.
56 Biran (1982), pp. 15–43.
57 2 Chr 3.8. The Holy of Holies in the tabernacle was also a square (Ex 26).
58 Ex 25.10.
59 Ex.27.1; 38.1.
60 Ex 30.2; 37.25.
61 Ex 28.15,16; 39.9.
62 Rev 21.16.
63 Schick (1896), pp. 46, 49, 69, Tafel II.
64 Jagersma (1985), p. 54.
65 See 2 Kgs 20.5, 22.4; Jer 26.10, 36.10, 36.12.
66 Mazar (1992), "Jerusalem from Isaiah to Jeremiah," pp. 100–108.
67 Avigad (1983), pp. 46–49.
68 Mazar (1992), pp. 106, 108.
69 Avigad (1983), p. 59.
70 Shanks (1999), pp. 20–29.
71 Mazar (1985), p. 465.
72 Smith (1907–08), Vol. I, p. 424, and n. 4. *"The Mishna mentions two officials: the 'Man of the Mountain of the House,' and the 'Man of the Birah' or Temple proper. 'Ish Har ha-Bayt,' 'Middoth' i, 2, etc. Ish ha-Birah, Orla', ii, 12. Schürer, p. 267, argues that the latter was the Strategos of the Temple, the former a captain who had the charge of the outer court; but in Jer. Talm. 'Pes.' vii, 38a, All Har ha-Bayit = Birah."*

Vol. II, p. 348, *"It is possible that by the Birah Nehemiah meant the separately fortified Temple-Mount, which we know had its own gates."*

Vol. II, p. 461, *"The Birah of Nehemiah had been either the palace of Solomon or the whole fortified Temple Hill. The latter is the more reasonable hypothesis...."*

Vol. II, p. 518, and n. 1, *"The Jews seem, too, to have applied to the Outer Court the name Birah or Castle, yet this may also have been used as in former times for the whole Temple."* ... *"BIRAH 'Middoth' i, 9; from the house Moked on the Hel a winding passage led under the Birah, by which priests who became unclean could pass outside the Temple without treading on consecrated ground. This implies that the Birah here means all outside the Hel. Yet R. Obadiah in his note says that the whole Sanctuary was called the Birah. Cf. 'Tamid' i."*
73 Ritmeyer (1992a), p. 137.
74 Kenyon (1974), p. 111.
75 Smith (1907–08), Vol. I, p. 200, n. 1, translates *aliyah* with "Turret," which he places at the northeast angle of the Temple.
76 Neh 3:1, 12:39. See also Smith (1907–08), Vol. I, p. 201; Vol. II, pp. 261, 348, 460.

77 Simons (1952), p. 429, n. 2.
78 Wightman (1989–90), pp. 29–30.
79 Charles (1913). For a critical evaluation of the *Letter of Aristeas*, see Meecham (1932).
80 Warren (1884), p. 224.
81 Warren (1871), p. 219.
82 Shiloh (1984), p. 21, Pl. 39.1.
83 Warren and Conder (1884), p. 218.
84 Warren and Conder (1884), p. 218.
85 Schick (1887), pp. 84–85.
86 Kaufman (1984–85), pp. 97–108.

Chapter Three

1 Simons (1952), p. 144.
2 Avigad (1983), p. 64.
3 Wightman (1989–90), p. 31.
4 For overviews of the historical and topographical problems concerning the *Akra*, see Simons (1952), pp. 144–157; Tsafrir (1975), pp. 85–86; and Wightman (1989–90), pp. 29–40.
5 A brief outline of our proposal for the location of the *Akra* was first published in 1985, see Mazar, in: Biran, ed. (1985), p. 466.
In the past, some scholars located the *Akra* either on the northwest hill of Jerusalem (see, for example Warren [1880], p. 33) or on the southwest hill (Vincent [1934], *RB* 43, p. 205 ff.; Abel [1926], *RB* 35, p. 520 ff.; Avi-Yonah [1975a], pp.231–232).
We, however, would rather agree with those who place the *Akra* on the southeast hill. See Smith (1908–09), Vol. 1, p. 158; Simons (1952), p. 157; Avigad (1983), p. 65; Tsafrir (1975), p. 85.
A similar location for the Seleucid *Akra* has been suggested by Wightman (1989–90), p. 35, and Jacobson, (1990–91), p. 52, Fig. 2. The location of an oversized *Akra* in this latter proposal would have obliterated, however, the southern approach to the square Temple Mount; and is therefore untenable.
6 Tsafrir (1975), p. 86, has suggested that the bossed masonry to the north of the seam may perhaps be part of the substructure of the *Akra*. This theory, however, contradicts Josephus' record (*Ant.* 13.215), which states that not only the *Akra* was razed to the ground, but the hill on which it stood was leveled. We prefer to explain this masonry as part of the extension of the square Temple Mount in the later Maccabean period. See discussion under section 3.4.
7 Warren and Conder (1884), p. 220.
8 *Erubin* 10.14. The name of this cistern was brought to the attention of Professor B. Mazar by J. Schwartz of Bar-Ilan University, soon after we had suggested the connection between Cistern 11 and the *Akra*.
9 Laperrousaz (1973), pp. 355–392.
10 Dunand (1969), pp. 64–70.
11 Kenyon (1970), p. 144.
12 Tsafrir (1975), pp. 85–86.
13 Avigad (1983), p. 72.
14 Although the words *Birah* (see Introduction) and *Baris* may be etymologically related (see Wightman [1990–91], pp. 7–10), in this book we make a distinction between the two. The *Birah* of the Hebrew Bible refers to the Temple Mount and the *Baris* of Josephus to the Hasmonean fortress at the northwest corner of the Temple Mount.
15 Warren and Conder (1884), p. 218.
16 Benoit (1975), pp. 87–89; Bahat (1994), p. 185.

Chapter Four

1 Warren and Conder (1884), pp. 217–225 (the reservoirs and cisterns are referred to as "tanks"); *Warren, Plans, etc.*, Pls. 6, 7; Wilson and Warren (1871), pp. 204–217. Gibson and Jacobson (1996) have produced a comprehensive sourcebook on the underground structures of the Temple Mount, which includes hitherto unpublished material.
2 C. Muller, *Fragmenta Historicum Graecorum*, 3, p. 228 ff.

NOTES AND REFERENCES

3 R. J. H. Shutt in: Charlesworth (1985), pp. 7–34.
4 Gonen (1985), pp. 8–14.
5 A. Mazar (1975), pp. 79–84.
6 William Simpson, who was known as "Crimea Simpson" because of his experiences in the Crimean War, went out to Jerusalem as illustrator of the Illustrated London News. I would like to thank Dr. Rupert Chapman, secretary of the Palestine Exploration Fund and Shimon Gibson, the photographic officer, for their help and cooperation in obtaining a copy of Simpson's painting of the "Great Sea."
7 Simpson (1872), 9: Watercolour 22.
8 Warren and Conder (1884), p. 218.
9 Reich (1989), pp. 63–65. He suggests, however, that these *mikva'ot* were located outside the early Temple Mount, while in our location of the square Temple Mount they would be placed in the southern court, but outside the *soreg*. The existence of *mikva'ot* within the Temple Mount is not surprising as, according to *Middot* 1.9, another *mikveh* was located in the northern court of the same Temple Mount.
10 Bagatti (1979), p. 27.

Chapter Five

1 Warren, *Plans,* etc., Pl. 31, Section on A–B; Vincent and Stève (1956), Pl. 119.
2 Schick (1896), p. 185.

Chapter Six

1 *War* 5.184; *Ant.* 15.398.
2 Bagatti (1979), p. 27.
3 Avitsur (1976), p. 28.
4 A grant from the Rothschild Foundation made it possible for my family and me to spend considerable time in Jerusalem during the spring and summer of 1994, while I did the post-doctoral research under the supervision of Professor Gideon Foerster of the Hebrew University on Mount Scopus.
5 Pacing out the dimensions of a structure is a method I have used in my surveying for a long time. It gives a very accurate idea of size if one cannot resort to the use of a tape measure. A large step is about 100 cm (3′ 1″ or 95 cm).
6 Tacitus, *History* V, 8, 9.
7 Origen C. Matt. 24.15 and the Bordeaux Pilgrim 591.4.
8 Peters (1985).
9 Peters (1985), p. 350; this reference is taken from Gabrieli, (1969), p. 171.
10 Dalman (1912), p. 110, Fig. 71.
11 Schmidt (1933), Fig. 1.
12 Kamal ad Dîn as Suyûtî, The History of the Temple Mount, Trans. Rev. James Reynolds, London, Valpy, 1836, p. 51. Retranslated by Le Strange (1890), p.136.
13 John of Würzburg, "Description of the Holy Land," *PPTS* 5, p. 13.
14 Mujir ed-Din, *Mines d'Orient* II, p. 88.
15 Saewulf, *PPTS* 4, pp. 16–17.
16 Nasir-i-Khusrau, "Diary of a Journey through Syria and Palestine," *PPTS* 4, p. 47.
17 Le Strange (1890), p. 132.
18 John of Würzburg, "Description of the Holy Land," *PPTS* 5, pp. 13–14.
19 Theodorich's "Description of the Holy Places," *PPTS* 5, pp. 26–27.
20 Le Strange (1890), p. 132.
21 Joannes Phocas, "A Brief Description by Joannes Phocas, of the (Holy) Places in Palestine and Syria," *PPTS* 5, p. 20.
22 Dalman (1912), Fig. 1.
23 Gabrieli, (1969), pp. 168–171.
24 Chartres, Fulcher of (1969): I, 31, pp. 5–10.
25 Wilson and Warren (1971), p. 221; Warren (1876), p. 402.
26 Clermont-Ganneau (1899), Vol. I, p. 217 and Fig. on this page.
27 Dalman (1912), p. 121.
28 Ibn Abd Rabbih, in Le Strange (1890), p. 164.

29 John of Würzburg, "Description of the Holy Land," *PPTS* 5, p. 16.
30 Clermont-Ganneau (1899), Vol. I, pp. 216–217.
31 Bagatti (1979), pp. 28–29.
32 Le Strange (1890), p. 132.
33 Simpson, *PEFQ* 1887, p. 74.
34 Dalman (1912), p. 125.
35 Steinberg (1983), p. 167,168.
36 De Vaux (1965), p. 301.
37 See for example the drawing in Steinberg (1983), p. 168.

Chapter Seven

1 A collection of reconstruction drawings of Solomon's temple appears in: Rosenau (1979).
2 See introductions to these books in The Jerusalem Bible.
3 Many biblical scholars and archaeologists would set the date of the Exodus at 1270–1260 B.C. and the entry into Canaan at 1230–1220 B.C. Nevertheless, the view that the biblical date of 1447 B.C. is correct, is gaining ground among some scholars; see: Bimson (1981); Rohl (1995).
4 Alternatively, the Septuagint gives 25 cubits for the height of the *heikhal*, as does the Lucianic recension. If these texts could be relied upon, then the roofs of the *heikhal* and the *dvir* would be on the same level. See de Vaux (1965), p. 314.
5 Stern (1992), p. 306; Hurowitz (1994), p. 34.
6 Fritz (1987), p. 45.
7 Reich, R., "Palaces and Residencies in the Iron Age: The Integration of Wooden Beams in Stone Construction" in Kempinski and Reich, eds. (1992), p. 213.
8 Biran (1982), p. 20, Pl. 5.1.
9 The regnal dates of the kings of Judah are taken from Rienecker and Maier (1994).
10 Wood (1999), pp. 21–30. *NEAEHL*, 1, "Bethel," pp. 192–194.
11 Shea (1999).
12 Kenyon (1974), pp. 135–143.
13 Franken and Steiner (1990), pp. 19–27.
14 2 Maccabees 2.1–8.
15 Hancock (1993).
16 Price (1994).

Chapter Eight

1 Shiloh (1984), p. 29.
2 Aharoni and Avi-Yonah (1968), p. 111.
3 See Jones (1966).
4 For an overview of the political and religious upheavals that took place between the reigns of Antiochus Epiphanes and Herod the Great, see, Shürer (1980), division I, vol. I.
5 Avigad (1983), p. 72.
6 Avigad (1983), p. 56.
7 *Ant.* 14.61–73.
8 Simons (1952), p. 403.
9 Wilson and Warren (1871), p. 311.

Chapter Nine

1 See Hollis (1934), p. 116.
2 See Yadin (1977), vol. 1, pp. 245, 414; Maier (1985), p. 61.
3 Yadin (1985), p.169.
4 Danby translates it as "Rampart."
5 *War* 5.193–194, 6.124; *Ant.* 15.417.
6 Clermont-Ganneau (1872), pp. 214–234.
7 Iliffe (1938), pp. 1 ff.
8 Segal (1989), pp. 79–84.
9 I had originally suggested that the *soreg* would have been located at the outer perimeter of the 500-cubit-square Temple Mount (Ritmeyer, 1992a, pp. 38–39). However, as shown above, the square Temple Mount retained its outer wall, which played an important defensive role during the Roman conquest. The *soreg* therefore must have been located inside the square Temple Mount. Some scholars still maintain that the *soreg* was the same as the perimeter wall

Notes and References

of the square platform; see most recently Jacobson, (1990–91, pp. 50–51) and Maier (1990, p. 71).

10 Danby wrote a footnote (1933, p. 592, n. 1) about the *soreg* saying that it would be "Surrounding the inner precincts which contained the Court of the Women and the Temple Court," but this need not have been the case.
11 Hollis (1934), p. 276.
12 Hollis (1934), p. 284.
13 Warren, *Plans, etc*. Plates 6 and 7.
14 For example, Jacobson (1990–91), p. 59.
15 Zeev Herzog, "Settlement and Fortification Planning in the Iron Age: The City-Gate," in Kempinski and Reich (1992), pp. 266, 271–274.
16 Warren and Conder (1884), p. 219.

Chapter Ten

1 The first time I worked out the measurements of the Temple was when the editor of *Eretz Magazine*, Yadin Roman, asked me to illustrate an article on 'Picturing the Second Temple' by Patrich (1987). Subsequently, I have worked out more details of the Temple, such as the façade, the layout of the internal staircase and especially the relationship between the Temple and the present-day Temple Mount.
2 See my illustration in Avigad 1983, p. 146.
3 Yadin (1985), p. 144.
4 The fact that the golden vine was draped over four columns was deduced by Patrich (1994, p. 264) from a translation by Leah Di Segni of the Latin version of *Ant.* 15.394–395, "He (Herod) decorated the doors of the entrance… and made flowers surrounding columns, atop which stretched a vine, from which golden clusters of grapes were suspended."
5 Patrich (1994), p. 265.
6 Barag (1994a), p. 276.
7 *Middot* 4.6.
8 Avigad (1983), pp. 147–149.
9 Barag (1994b), pp. 277–278.
10 Patrich (1994), p. 266.

List of Illustrations

Page

1. The Temple Mount today, looking west from the Mount of Olives.
   Map of the land of Israel with Jerusalem at its heart.
2. Benjamin Mazar with author at the excavation site.
   Nahman Avigad with author during restoration work of the Palatial Mansion in the Jewish Quarter.
3. Plate 37 of Warren's *Atlas*, published in 1880, containing a graphic account of his work in Jerusalem during the late 19th century.
   Sir Charles Warren. (CA)
4. Julie Lightburn, modelmaker, with author.
   Model of the Tabernacle in the wilderness. (photo: Philip Evans)
5. Model of the Herodian Temple Mount—overall view from the east. (photo: Philip Evans)
6. Aerial view of Jerusalem and surroundings, looking northwest, early twentieth century. (CA)
7. Model of Solomon's Temple. (photo: Philip Evans)
   Model of Jerusalem during the time of David (lower half) and Solomon's additions (upper half).
8. King Darius I (521–486 B.C.); relief from Persepolis. (CA)
   Map of the return of the Jews from exile.
9. Reconstruction of the Temple Mount based on Ezekiel's vision. (Chipiez, 1887)
   Map of the Temple Mount during the Crusader period.
10. Reconstruction of the Temple Mount and Umayyad palaces to the south. The Dome of the Rock stands on the raised platform.
    The Golden Gate (drawing by de Vogüé) in the eastern wall of the Temple Mount. The gate was closed already in the Crusader period, when it was opened only on two occasions annually. It was later closed permanently, apparently in the Ayyubid period.
11. Roman bust thought to be that of Josephus Flavius. (CA)
12. Limestone, four-horned altar from the Iron Age, found at Megiddo. *(NEAEHL)*
13. The Ark of the Covenant.
    Coin of Herod. (CA)
14. Map of Jerusalem and the Temple Mount by Charles Wilson (1864–65), adapted by Carl Zimmermann, late 19th century.

Page

15. American biblical scholar Edward Robinson (1794–1863). (CA)
    Image of Frederick Catherwood, c. 1840. (CA)
16. Sir Charles Wilson. (CA)
    Cross-section drawing of Warren's Shaft. (S. Cohen)
17. Plan showing the water system on the Temple Mount, indicating the location of 37 water cisterns examined in the 19th century, mainly by Warren and Conder.
18. Aerial photograph showing the beginning of the excavations in 1968.
19. Reconstruction of the Temple Mount complex during the time of Herod.
20. The dimensions of the Temple Mount.
20–21. Reconstruction of the Herodian Western Wall.
21. Close-up view of the Western Wall Plaza.
22. Lowering the area in front of the Wailing Wall in preparation for the construction of the Western Wall Plaza, as this area was subsequently known. (photo: Amihai Mazar)
23. Narrow street in front of the Wailing Wall where Jewish men and women were allowed to pray—1894.
    Complex of houses adjacent to the Western Wall—1894.
24. The Western Wall Plaza plays an important role in the life of the Jewish people today. The site also attracts many tourists.
    Close-up view of a Herodian stone in the walls of the Herodian Temple Mount.
25. The lintel of Barclay's Gate is visible just above the steps that lead into a small chamber below the ramp.
26. The lintel of Barclay's Gate in 1967 before the area was excavated. Note the empty space below the lintel and also the burning of candles, which was forbidden soon afterwards. (photo: Amihai Mazar)
    Drawing of the visible Herodian remains near Barclay's Gate. The sketch shows the original size of the lintel and the gate.
    Sketch of Warren's shaft at Barclay's Gate, showing the remains of the vault and its northern retaining wall built on bedrock
27. East-west section looking south through Barclay's Gate showing the internal stairway and the upper and lower

423

List of Illustrations

Page

street levels connected by steps built over a vault. The Western Wall is built on bedrock.

View of the remains of a row of shops at the southwest corner of the Temple Mount.

Remains of the staircase at the southwest corner of the Temple Mount.

28 Reconstruction drawing of the Herodian remains along the Western Wall near Barclay's Gate, incorporating the shops found along the wall.

29 Rare depiction of Mohammed mounted on his steed. Detail of Arab miniature, c. 1314/15.

30 Wilson's Arch supported a bridge and aqueduct that crossed the Tyropoeon Valley, connecting the Temple Mount with the upper City on the west. The present arch is possibly an Umayyad restoration of the original Herodian arch.

31 Sketch of the southern end of Wilson's Arch. The ashlars of the Herodian Western Wall have been cut to receive the springer and first two voussoirs.

The remains of a stepped street found in the present-day Street of the Chain, which lies above Wilson's Arch.

32 Section through Wilson's Arch and the stepped street found above.

33 Photo of the largest stone found in the Western Wall. It is 45 feet long and weighs 570 tons (according to Bahat).

34 A model of Herod's Temple Mount shows the enormous size of the largest stones found in the Western Wall relative to the scale figures placed in front of them.

View of Warren's Gate.

35 Warren's Gate and master course. The drawing (bottom) shows this portion of the Western Wall as it appears today. Above it is a reconstruction drawing of Warren's Gate and the master course with the beginning of the pilaster construction.

The Western Wall Tunnel. In between the concrete frames Herodian stones can be seen all along the tunnel.

36 The Herodian street at the northern end of the tunnel. The Western Wall, which here is cut out of the rock, continues in an angle behind the large block of bedrock. The vertical quarry channel across the mass of rock shows that the quarrying process was never completed.

37 Warren's sketch of the two pilasters found at the northern end of the Western Wall.

38 View of the western pool of a large twin water reservoir, which was called the Strouthion by Josephus. (photo: Don Edwards)

39 View of the rock-hewn aqueduct.

40 Plan of Herodian and pre-Herodian remains at the northwest corner of the Temple Mount.

Part of the stepped tunnel at Gibeon from the Iron Age. *(NEAEHL)*

Page

41 Reconstruction of the large dam and reservoir near the Pool of Siloam, at the southeastern corner of the city. The outlet of the Siloam Channel can be seen at the top right.

42 Composite section showing the northern end of the Herodian Western Wall, the Strouthion Pool and the northern and southern parts of the rock-hewn aqueduct.

43 View of the northeast corner of the Antonia Fortress and the Strouthion Pool. The part of the fortress walls above the southern end of the pool, seen in the center of the picture, was the least protected and therefore chosen by the Romans as the easiest part to breach.

Roman battering ram. (CA)

The so-called Lithostrotos, today under the Convent of the Sisters of Zion. (photo: Garo Nalbandian)

44 The excavations at the southwest corner of the Temple Mount.

45 Robinson's Arch as depicted in a 19th century engraving.

46 View of Robinson's Arch.

Drawings of the northern and southern ends of Robinson's Arch.

47 Reconstructed elevation of the Pier which supported Robinson's Arch, looking west.

The Pier of Robinson's Arch.

48 Elevation of a relieving arch. The pressure of the weight of the upper courses would break the lintel stone. The arrows indicate the diversion of the pressure away from the lintel to the sides of the door opening.

Several ideas of how to reconstruct Robinson's Arch were put forward before the stairway was found.

49 Pilaster stones found in the debris in front of the pier of Robinson's Arch. In lower center a Herodian wall stone can be seen. This is the bottom course of the pilaster construction of the Temple Mount walls. The right side of this stone is part of the sloping surface and the left side is the beginning of the pilaster with both elements cut out of the same stone. Another pilaster fragment with the typical Herodian margins can be seen lying on its side on top of the debris. This stone shows that part of the pilaster and part of the wall set back in between the pilasters were cut out of the same stone. This demonstrates that the pilasters were not separate wall elements, but were keyed in to the wall construction. A set of three steps still joined together is visible at lower left.

Reconstruction of the stairway leading up over Robinson's Arch to the portal of the Royal Stoa.

50 Pilasters in the Herodian enclosure wall of the Tomb of the patriarchs in Hebron. Note that the sloping surface of the lowest stone in between the pilasters is not the full height of a regular stone course.

51 Pilaster construction at Elonei Mamre.

List of Illustrations

Page

Drawing by de Vogüé of pilasters in the outer walls of the Tomb of the Patriarchs in Hebron.

52 The stepped street ascending to the Upper City over a series of vaults.

Section of the Herodian street excavated during Mazar's Temple Mount excavations close to Barclay's Gate.

53 In the renewed excavations which were carried out between 1994 and 1996, the whole street had been laid open. Both curbstones lining the street are visible.

54 Reconstruction drawing of the Siloam Pool and the adjacent stepped Herodian street.

55 Reconstruction of Herodian Jerusalem. Note the street that begins in the north where the Damascus Gate now stands. It runs through the Tyropoeon Valley, passes under Robinson's Arch and descends into the City of David. A branch of the street leads down by steps to the Siloam Pool, while the street itself ends at the South Gate.

56 Plan of the drain at the southwest corner, as discovered by Warren.

57 Manhole with five slots cut into it found near the western curb below Robinson's Arch.

The Trumpeting Stone as it was found lying on the street.

58 Reconstruction drawing of priest blowing the trumpet while standing in the niche that was cut into the Trumpeting Stone.

The inscription on the Trumpeting Stone, which reads, "to the place of trumpeting to…." The inscription is incomplete, but probably read, "to the place of trumpeting to announce."

During preparatory work for the Jerusalem Archaeological Park, the corner parapet stone has been put right side up and a copy of the inscription has been attached to its original place. The original is on display in the Israel Museum.

59 Silver trumpets were used in the Temple to herald the arrival of the Sabbath, New Month, festivals, etc. The instruments shown here were reconstructed according to Talmudic sources and the Arch of Titus in Rome. (photo: The Temple Institute, Jerusalem)

60 The heavy dashed line indicates the outline of the excavation shaft Warren dug at the southwest corner. The workmen pierced the pavement to be able to dig down to the bedrock. The western side of the Trumpeting stone protruded into the shaft and was most likely broken off by Warren's workmen who for most of the time worked in the semi-dark.

60–61 Reconstruction of the Southern Wall of Herod's Temple Mount.

61 The header and stretcher construction at the southwest corner. The stones are laid alternatively facing west and south.

62 View of the western part of the Southern Wall. The top of the western part of the Southern Wall is dominated by a Crusader construction that today houses the Islamic Museum and the Mosque of the Women. The darker masonry below this lighter-colored building belongs to the Umayyad repair of the Southern Wall. The Herodian stone courses can be seen near the southwest corner.

63 The "high-level aqueduct" to Jerusalem in the Bethlehem area. This part was a pipe composed of interlocking stone segments. *(NEAEHL)*

64 Section through Southern Wall plaza and middle supporting wall.

Artist's impression of the pilgrimage to Jerusalem. (The Temple Institute, Jerusalem)

65 The Double Gate as seen by the explorer Tipping in 1846.

View of the excavated and restored remains of the steps leading up to the Double Gate.

66 Reconstruction plan of the southern part of the Herodian Temple Mount and the adjacent street complex.

67 View of the Double Gate from the outside.

Plan of the Double Gate passageway and the adjacent Crusader tower.

68 Elevation of the exterior Herodian remains of the Double Gate inside the Crusader building and a reconstruction of the Double Gate. The extant Herodian remains are colored in.

Close-up view of the Double Gate lintel.

69 The vaults inside the western and eastern gateways of the Double Gate, viewed from the north.

70 Plan of the Double Gate passageway and domes.

View of the excavations to the east of the Double Gate passageway.

71 Drawing of monolithic column in the Double Gate passageway and the four domes springing from its capital.

Elevation of the eastern wall of the Double Gate passageway with a doorway, known as "Elijah's Standing Place."

Doorway in the eastern wall of the Double Gate passageway viewed from the east.

72 Domed roof of a burial chamber in the Roman Mausoleum at Sebaste (Samaria), late 2nd to early 3rd centuries A.D. *(NEAEHL)*

73 Drawing of the southwest dome in the underground passage of the Double Gate. The black lines indicate the individual stones. (based on drawing by Nili Cohen and Martha Ritmeyer)

Drawing of the decoration of the northwest dome (drawing: Nathaniel Ritmeyer)

List of Illustrations

Page

View of the interior of the Double Gate. (photo: Garo Nalbandian)
74 Reconstructed interior view of the underground passageway of the Double Gate.
The lame man being healed by the Apostles Peter and John, 19th century engraving. (CA)
75 Reconstruction drawing of the buildings in between the Double and Triple Gates.
76 Reconstruction drawing of the Council Chamber, generally identified with the Chamber of Hewn Stone mentioned in the Mishnah.
A Herodian mikveh found next to the Double Gate stairway.
77 Section through stairway of the Triple Gate, the underground passageway and the Royal Stoa above the Southern Wall.
78 View of the Triple Gate.
79 Elevation and section of molding of west doorjamb of the original Triple Gate (after de Vogüé, with corrections).
Herodian ashlar with molding of the west doorjamb of the original Triple Gate. Note that the left side of the ashlar has been carved like a usual Herodian stone and the right side bears the doorframe.
Plan of Triple Gate showing the remains of the Southern Wall, the west wall of the interior passageway and the two-chambered vault.
80 Sketch of the walled compound of the Monastery of St. Onuphrius in the Hinnom Valley. Two first-century tombs, one called the "Refuge of the Apostles" and the other with a notable two-pillared porch (known as *distyle in antis*), located within the monastery grounds, are part of a lavishly decorated tomb complex. The most outstanding tomb—that of Annas the High Priest—lies outside the walls of the monastery.
81 The Hinnom Valley today, looking southeast. In center, the Greek Orthodox Monastery of St. Onuphrius.
82 View of the Monument of Annas.
False doorway in the tomb chamber of Annas.
83 Reconstruction of the triple-gated entrance to the tomb chamber of Annas.
84 Reconstruction of the interior of the tomb chamber of Annas and its domed ceiling.
Reconstruction of the so-called Tomb (or Pillar) of Absalom in the Kedron Valley. Its circular roof is built of finely cut stone, topped by a conical structure with a rosette-shaped calyx.
85 The double gate of Porta Negra in Trier, Germany. (CA)
86 Reconstructed window frame based on excavated remains.
87 Model of the Temple platform—overall view from the southeast. (photo: Philip Evans)

Page

88 General view of the underground passageway of the Triple Gate.
89 The west wall of the Triple Gate passageway. The pilaster stone is located to the right of the arrow.
Close-up view of the pilaster stone in the west wall of the underground Triple Gate passageway, looking west.
Detail of the pilaster, looking southwest.
90 View of the model shows the layout of the 912-foot (278 m) long Southern Wall with the Royal Stoa above. (photo: Philip Evans)
A Corinthian capital found in the excavations of the Jewish Quarter. *(NEAEHL)*
91 Reconstruction of a Corinthian-styled column. (CA)
92 Map of Southern Wall area with dimensions.
93 Computerized depiction of the interior of the Royal Stoa. (Courtesy Slawek Jozwik)
94 Reconstruction of the Royal Stoa.
95 The Knights Templar. (CA)
View of the Single Gate.
96 Interior view of the passageway below the Single Gate.
97 Elevation of the entrance to the passageway below the Single Gate.
Isometric section through Single Gate passageway showing its relationship to the Royal Stoa.
98 View of the remains of an early vault in Solomon's Stables.
99 The inner lintels over the windows in the Eastern Wall near the southeast corner.
100 View of the burnt arch east of the Triple Gate.
View of burnt arches near the southeast corner.
101 View of the model showing the reconstructed eastern end of the Southern Wall. (photo: Philip Evans)
102 Elevation of the Eastern Wall of the Herodian Temple Mount.
View of the southern end of the Eastern Wall.
103 View of the *Seam*.
Elevation of the *Seam*.
104 Reconstruction drawing of the southern part of the Eastern Wall of the Temple Mount.
105 Reconstruction model of the southeast corner, showing the projecting tower, the three windows and the stepped entrance to the small double gateway. (photo: Philip Evans)
106 View of the Golden Gate from the east.
107 View of the Golden Gate from the Temple Mount.
View of the remains of the double entrance gateway, located between the offset of the tower (left) and the *seam* (right).
Detail of Warren's Plate IV, showing the location of the massive wall.
108 Artist's impression of the Yom Kippur ritual of sending the scapegoat into the wilderness. Here, the High Priest

List of Illustrations

Page

is seen presenting the scapegoat to the one responsible for leading the animal into the wilderness. The two stand under the Shushan (i.e. Golden) Gate on the eastern side of the Temple Mount. (The Temple Institute, Jerusalem)

109 Section through the Golden Gate looking north and showing the large northern monolithic gatepost.
Drawing by de Vogüé of southern monolithic gatepost inside the Golden Gate.
Ancient masonry visible in the northern part of the Eastern Wall of the Temple Mount and (below) a proposed reconstruction of this part of the wall during the Herodian period.

110 Arch found in grave in front of the Golden Gate. (photo: Obe Hokansen)
Reconstruction of stairway leading up to the Eastern Gate of Herod's Temple Mount. (photo: Philip Evans)

111 General view of the reconstruction model showing the stairway leading up to the Eastern Gate. (photo: Philip Evans)

112 Artist's impression of the sacrificial ceremony of the Red Heifer and the "causeway" described in the Mishnah. (The Temple Institute, Jerusalem)

113 View of the Pont du Gard in France.

114 Warren's drawing of the east face of the Herodian tower at the northeast corner of the Temple Mount.

115 Masonry types in the Eastern Wall:
A. Herodian masonry with flat, smooth boss;
B. Herodian masonry with unfinished boss;
C. Hasmonean masonry with projecting boss;
D. Early masonry with bulging boss.

116 View of the junction of the south corner of the Herodian tower and the Eastern Wall at the northeast corner of the Temple Mount.
Close-up view. Note that only the lowest course is bonded with the tower.

117 General view of the masonry to the south of the northeast tower of the Temple Mount. Note the projecting bosses of the lowest course, which is Herodian.

118 Reconstruction of the Pool of Israel. As can be seen, its location and depth afforded protection for the Temple Mount from attacks coming from the north. (photo: Philip Evans)

119 Elevation of the Northern Wall of the Herodian Temple Mount.
Reconstruction drawing of the northeast corner of the Temple Mount, indicating the Herodian remains *in situ*.

120 Drawing of the northern face of the Herodian tower at the northeast corner, indicating the Herodian ashlars only and showing where the later repairs which were made with small stones.
View of the north face of the Herodian tower at the northeast corner of the Temple Mount.

Page

121 Old photograph of the Pool of Israel taken in 1894, before the pool was filled in.

122 View of the south wall of the Pool of Israel. The rough stones can be seen below the two windows.

123 Plan (top) and cross section (bottom) of the Pool of Israel.

124 View of the northwest corner of the Temple Mount, showing the rockscarp on which the Antonia was built.

125 Two interior views of the Antonia Fortress. (photos: Philip Evans)

126 View of the re-entrant angle formed at the northwest corner of the Temple Mount.
Coin of Mark Antony after whom the Antonia was named. (CA)

127 Cross section of the Temple Mount from north to south, after Warren. Viewed from the west, it is evident that quarrying from the Herodian period in the natural bedrock in the northwest corner of the Temple Mount was required for construction of the Antonia Fortress. The Ghawanima minaret now stands in the center of this elevated rocky plateau.

128 Close-up view of one of the sockets for the beams of the northern stoa.
Photograph taken in the 19th century, showing the holes, or sockets, for the beams of the northern stoa.

129 Drawing of the Antonia rockscarp with the present-day Umariyya School.

130 View of the L-shaped approach to the Antonia Fortress. (photo: Philip Evans)
Reconstruction drawing of the southern wall of the Antonia Fortress.

131 Reconstruction model of the Antonia and the northern stoa. (photo: Philip Evans)
Herodian paving slabs between the excavated ditch and the Antonia.

132 Cedars of Lebanon, used in the construction of the Temple. (CA)

133 Bedrock layers in the Jerusalem mountains near Yad Vashem.

134 Close-up view of one of the small square projections left by stonemasons.

135 Quarrying stone. The stone cutter at right uses a pickaxe to cut a channel in the rock. The other worker pours water over the wooden beams that have been tightly wedged in the channels. The water makes the wood to swell and the resulting lateral pressure causes the stone to split off from the rock to which it is attached at the bottom.
Transporting stones. At top left the bedrock shows the natural horizontal layering of the bedrock. At top right the quarried stones are waiting to be moved to the stone cutter at bottom left who dresses the stone and leaves a projection so that the stone can be lifted by the crane at

List of Illustrations

Page

bottom right. In the middle of the picture oxen are pulling a very large stone. The men move the rollers from the back of the stone to the front to ease the movement of the stone.

136 Large column found *in situ* in the Russian Compound.
137 The process of building the Herodian Temple Mount walls.
138 Reconstruction model of Jerusalem and the square Temple Mount in the time of Nehemiah.
139 William Makepeace Thackeray (1811–1863), translator of some of Josephus' works. (CA)
140 Josephus Flavius, as pictured in a 19th-century illustration. (CA)
141 Model of the so-called "Porch of Solomon," or eastern portico which faces the Temple façade. (photo: Philip Evans)
142 Lt. C. R. Conder (1848–1910). (photo: Palestine Exploration Fund)
144 Rare title page of the mishnaic tractate *Middot(h)*, printed in Latin in 1630.
145 Plan of the temple at Tell Ta'yinat in northern Syria (today in Turkey), which resembles that of the Solomonic temple as described in the Bible. (CA)
Reconstruction model of the Temple Mount showing a close-up view of the *soreg*. (photo: Philip Evans)
146 View of the northeast corner of the raised platform. The northern wall is to the right of the corner.
147 Schematic plans of various proposals for the location of the square Temple Mount.
148 View of the entrance to el-Aksa Mosque on the Temple Mount.
150 De Vogüé's plan of the Temple Mount.
151 Warren's plans of the Solomonic (left) and Herodian (right) Temple Mount.
152 Details from Warren's Plate XXI, illustrating a drawing of a stone on which were painted two characters (Hebrew letters *Kuf*) and one of the characters (also the letter *Kuf*) that was found on one of the stones on the south side of the southeast corner of the Solomonic Temple Mount.
153 Conder's block plan of Herod's Temple.
154 Schick's plan of the Herodian Temple Mount.
156 Watson's plan of the Temple of Jerusalem.
157 Mommert's plan of the Solomonic Temple and the Palace Court.
158 Dalman's plan of the Second Temple.
159 Hollis's plan of the Mount of the House.
160 The so-called Throne of Solomon, built against the inner face of the eastern wall.
Simon's sketch of the relative positions of Antonia and the northern part of the Herodian Temple area.
161 Vincent's placing of the mishnaic Temple on the Temple Mount.

Page

162 Kaufman's plan of the Temple Mount.
163 Plan comparing the size of the paving stone below the Dome of the Spirits with similarly sized paving slabs in front of the Double and Triple Gates.
Plan of the Dome of the Spirits and the paving slab on which it rests.
164 Jacobson's plan of Herod's Temple.
165 Detail of Warren's Plate 13.
166 Flight of steps at the northwest corner of the raised platform, the lower step of which formed part of an ancient wall.
167 Ashlar with protruding boss in the flight of steps at the northwest corner of the raised platform.
168 Plan of the Temple Mount with indications of the pre-Herodian square Temple Mount.
169 Head of Pompey, from a coin. (CA)
View of the northernmost large stone in the *Step* which is precisely in line with the northern edge of the raised platform.
170 Close-up of the flight of steps at the northwest corner of the raised platform.
171 Egyptian cubit. (British Museum)
Golden cubit exhibited in the Egyptian Museum of Torino. (photo: Francesco Cordero di Pampatarato)
172 The Great Pyramid of Khufu (center) in Giza. (CA)
173 Reconstruction of the Tomb of Pharaoh's Daughter in the village of Silwan.
Reconstruction of the burial caves in the courtyard of the St. Etiénne Monastery, Jerusalem.
174 Stretch of ancient masonry south of the Golden Gate.
175 Detail of ancient masonry south of the Golden Gate.
176 Stretch of ancient masonry north of the Golden Gate.
177 Ancient masonry north of the Golden Gate. Note the deviation in direction from the Turkish city wall above. The *offset* is visible in the foreground. (photo: Alexander Schick)
178 View along the Eastern Wall showing its "bend" at the place where the pillar sticks out from the wall.
Model of Nehemiah's Jerusalem and the square Temple Mount, viewed from the southeast.
179 Schematic plan of the Temple Mount showing the change in direction in the Eastern Wall at the *bend*.
Close-up view of the so-called Mohammed's Pillar.
180–81 View of the eastern wall of the Temple Mount today. (photo: Garo Nalbandian)
182 Reconstruction model of the eastern city wall in the time of Nehemiah.
183 Detail of Warren's Plate 19, showing the "solid red earth."
Reconstruction model of the northeast angle of the square Temple Mount. (photo: Philip Evans)
184 Coin of Coponius (A.D. 6–9). (CA)

List of Illustrations

Page

185 Map of Pompey's siege of Jerusalem in 63 B.C.
187 Reconstruction of the high place at Dan.
Artist's reconstruction of the breastplate of the High Priest. (CA)
188 Signet ring inscribed "(Belonging) to Jotham," thought to be that of Jotham, king of Judah. Found at Tell el-Kheleifeh (biblical Ezion-geber). *(NEAEHL)*
189 Aramaic inscription on stone tablet commemorating the reburial of King Uzziah's remains. *(NEAEHL)*
Reconstruction of the cities of David, Solomon and Hezekiah.
190 "And all nations shall flow unto it" (Isa 2:2). Artist's impression of pilgrims approaching the Holy Temple of Jerusalem. (The Temple Institute, Jerusalem)
View of the excavated remains of the Middle Gate located in today's Jewish Quarter of the Old City.
Reconstruction of the Middle Gate.
191 David instructing Solomon as to the erection of the Temple in Jerusalem, 19th century engraving. (CA)
192 Aerial view of the mound of ancient Susa (biblical Shushan). (photo: Oriental Institute, University of Chicago)
193 Ezekiel's vision of Jerusalem (Ezek 48:30–35). (CA)
194 Rebuilding the walls of Jerusalem in the time of Nehemiah, 19th century engraving. (CA)
195 Artist's impression of the High Priest sanctifying himself in the mikveh before changing vestments. (The Temple Institute, Jerusalem)
196 Map of Jerusalem in the time of the Maccabees.
Antiochus III, king of Syria. (CA)
197 The returning exiles from Babylon construct the altar of the Second Temple—an artist's impression. (The Temple Institute, Jerusalem)
198 Dame Kathleen Kenyon.
199 Reconstruction model of Nehemiah's Jerusalem, from the east, showing the northeast corner of the Temple Mount and the gate Miphkad.
200 Reconstruction model of Nehemiah's Jerusalem from the north, showing the Towers of Meah and Hananeel, and the Sheep and Prison Gates.
201 Seleucid war elephant. (CA)
202 Silver tetradrachm of Ptolemy II Philadelphus. (CA)
203 Dedication of the wall of Jerusalem as described in Nehemiah 12:27–43, 19th century engraving. (CA)
204 Detail of Warren's Plate 6, showing the Tadi Gate.
Reconstruction of Tadi Gate with leaning lintel stones.
205 The only indication above ground of the Tadi Gate is the well head of Cistern 1, photographed here in the 19th century by the Russian photographer Narinsky.
The Cistern today.
206 Plan of the square Temple Mount and the Hasmonean extension.

Page

207 Tetradrachma of Antiochus IV Epiphanes. (CA)
208 Coin with a Seleucid king (unknown) on obverse and Apollo on reverse. (CA)
209 View of the excavation areas in the City of David, looking north towards the Temple Mount. *(NEAEHL)*
210 Plan of the square Temple Mount and the site of the Akra and Cistern 11.
212 Drawing of a Macedonian phalanx. (CA)
Sketch of Cistern 11.
213 View of the *Seam* in the Eastern Wall. (photo: Alexander Schick)
Drawing of Hasmonean stone with projecting boss.
214 Judah's attempt to storm the Akra fortress, as illustrated in the Alba Bible, 15th century.
215 Construction near the Southern Wall of the Temple Mount; these arches lead to Solomon's Stables. (photo: Sam Michelson)
216 Coin of John Hyrcanus I. (CA)
217 Plan of the Temple Mount at the beginning of Herod's reign and the location of the original Antonia.
218 Reconstruction model of the Antonia Fortress (in foreground) at the northwest corner of the Herodian Temple Mount, and Solomon's Porch (in background), on the south. (photo: Philip Evans)
219 Coin of Agrippa II. (CA)
220 Plan of the cisterns and underground structures of the Temple Mount according to the numeration of Warren.
221 Charles Clermont-Ganneau.
Philo of Alexandria. (CA)
222 Deep in the bowels of the Temple Mount, the author looks at the inspection tunnel of Cistern 10, at the right of the picture.
223 Plan showing the development of the Temple Mount with the cisterns and underground structures
224 Painting of the "Great Sea" by William Simpson, 1872.
225 Simon being installed as High Priest, from the Book of Maccabees, 17th century engraving.
226 Artist's impression of the water-libation ceremony during the festival of Sukkot and the celebrants reaching the Water Gate at the Holy Temple. (The Temple Institute, Jerusalem)
227 Artist's impression of the Wood Chamber, one of the chambers in the Temple Court. (The Temple Institute, Jerusalem)
228 This photo shows the two wellheads of Cistern 1. They are in line with the Rock inside the Dome of the Rock.
229 Close-up view of the wellhead over Cistern 1.
Plan showing the north-south alignment of Cistern 1 with the Sakhra (Rock) and the passageway to the Double Gate.
231 The Dome of the Rock on the Temple Mount.
232 Plan of the Temple Mount, showing the location of

List of Illustrations

Page

- the 500-cubit-square Temple Mount and the Herodian Temple complex.
- 233 Topographical map of Jerusalem showing location of the Tyropoeon Valley.
- 234 Plan of the drains at the southwest corner, as discovered by Warren, and their relationship to the square Temple Mount and the subsequent extensions.
- 235 View of the Herodian drainage channel under the street running along the western wall of the Temple Mount. (NEAEHL)
  Sir Charles Warren (1840–1927).
- 236 Dr. James T. Barclay (1807–74).
  Detail of Warren's Plate 31, showing section through Barclay's Gate.
- 237 Hilkiah, Ahikam, Acbor, Shaphan, and Asaiah seek advice from the prophetess Huldah, 17th century engraving.
  Josiah orders the Book of the Law read aloud to the elders, 17th century engraving.
- 238 Perspective drawing showing the stages in the historical development of the Temple Mount.
- 240 Bird's-eye view of a model of the Temple court (center) and the courts surrounding it. (photo: Philip Evans)
- 241 Model of the Herodian Temple Mount showing the space of 11 cubits between the western wall of the Temple and its courtyard. (photo: Philip Evans)
- 242 Plan of the Temple Mount showing the proposed location of the Temple and the Temple Courts, with measurements in cubits.
- 243 View of the Rock.
- 244 View of the cave beneath the Holy Rock, 19th century engraving.
- 245 Araunah the Jebusite offering his threshing floor to David (2 Sam 24:18), 19th century engraving. (CA)
- 246 View of the Rock showing the location of the Holy of Holies.
- 247 Artist's impression of the High Priest making his way through the Sanctuary, walking between the curtains that divided the Holy area from the Holy of Holies during the Second Temple period. (The Temple Institute, Jerusalem)
- 248 The High Priest offering incense on Yom Kippur before the rectangular depression which marked the original emplacement of the Ark of the Covenant. (photo: Philip Evans)
- 249 Judaea Capta engraved on a gold coin minted in Rome in honor of the Roman victory over Judea. (Reuben and Edith Hecht Museum, Haifa)
  The Dome of the Rock, viewed from the southwest. (CA)
- 250 Map of the last stage of the Crusader siege of Jerusalem, 10–15 July 1099.

Page

- 251 Detailed cross section of the Dome of the Rock, drawn by de Vogüé, 19th century.
- 252 Plan of the Rock.
- 253 View of the natural western scarp inside the Dome of the Rock. (photo: Garo Nalbandian)
  Isometric view of the Rock with part of the floor of the Dome of the Rock removed to show the full height of the western and northern scarps.
- 254 The ascent of the Prophet Mohammed on his steed, Buraq, guided by Jibra'il and escorted by angels. A miniature painting from a sixteenth-century Persian manuscript.
  Expulsion of the money changers from the Temple. Fresco by Giotto, 1304–06.
- 255 Philosopher, poet and traveler, Nasir-i-Khusrau (1004–1088).
- 256 Jacob's Ladder by William Blake, 18th century.
- 257 Dalman's plan of the Rock.
- 258 The foundation for the Crusader Church built over the Sakhra. After having reduced it to size, the Crusaders covered the Sakhra with stone slabs and built a flight of steps on the west.
- 259 Interior of the Dome of the Rock, as pictured in Wilson's *Picturesque Palestine* in 1880.
- 260 A reconstruction of the Crusader Church inside the Dome of the Rock.
- 261 Clermont-Ganneau's drawing of the section of the passage just north of the Rock.
  View of the northern side of the Rock, showing its thin horizontal layers of rock.
- 262 Royal Crusader seal with inscription: "the city of the king of all kings," and depictions of (left to right) Church of the Holy Sepulcher, "David's Tower," and the Dome of the Rock. (NEAEHL)
  Entrance to the cave inside the Dome of the Rock. (photo: Garo Nalbandian)
- 263 Angel appearing to Zacharias by Ghirlandaio, 1486–90 (detail).
- 264 The Rock during the Early Islamic period, showing how the inner circle of the Dome was set out. In the drawing, the Crusader cuttings have been eliminated.
- 265 View of the flat areas of the Rock.
- 266 The location of the Holy of Holies in Solomon's Temple.
- 267 Line of vision between the Temple and the highest peak of the Mount of Olives.
- 268 Photograph of the Rock taken directly above the emplacement of the Ark of the Covenant.
- 269 Photogrammetric plan of the Rock.
  The author sitting with a photogrammetrist to create the plan, above, of the Rock.

List of Illustrations

Page

270 View of the rectangular depression (marked by blue rectangle) of the Rock. (Courtesy World of the Bible Ministries)

Moses delivering the Law into the hands of the priests (Deut 31:26), 19th century engraving. (CA)

271 Moses and the burning bush, from a wall painting in the synagogue at Dura Europos, Syria, 3rd century. (CA)

Thoth, the Egyptian god of writing, as depicted on a papyrus from the New Kingdom, c. 1550–1090 B.C.

272 King David bringing the Ark of the Covenant to Jerusalem. (The Temple Institute, Jerusalem)

273 Schematic plan of the Holy of Holies in Solomon's Temple and the removing procedure of the staves from the Ark of the Covenant, as mentioned in 1 Kings 8:8.

274 The harp-playing King David and the High Priest kneeling before the Holy Ark. Painting in the Church of Our Lady of the Ark of the Covenant in Kiriath-jearim.

275 Plan of the Tabernacle.

Reconstruction of the Ark of the Covenant.

276 The Holy of Holies in Solomon's Temple.

277 Section through Herod's Temple.

278 Model of the First Temple, showing the Temple façade and the so-called Sea of Solomon in the foreground. (photo: Philip Evans)

279 Reconstruction of the Ark of the Covenant. (photo: Vic Roberts)

280 The traditional tomb of King Hiram at Tyre. (photo: École Biblique et Archéologique Française, Jerusalem)

Inscription on a bronze bowl at Limassol in Cyprus: "merchant of Carthago, servant of Hiram, king of the Sidonians." (CA)

281 Cedars of Lebanon by James Harding, 19th century.

284 Plan and E-W section of Solomon's Temple.

285 Model of Solomon's Temple—an overall view from the east. (photo: Philip Evans)

Reconstruction drawing of Solomon's Temple.

286 View of the three stories of the *yatsi'a*, the trapdoors (*lulim*) and the ladders connecting the different floors in the model of Solomon's Temple. (photo: Philip Evans)

The so-called Solomon's Quarries underneath the Damascus Gate of the Old City. Tradition has it that this is where Solomon extracted the stones for the Temple.

287 Interior view of the Holy in Solomon's Temple, looking east. (photo: Philip Evans)

288 View of the wooden partition in front of the *debir*. (photo: Philip Evans)

289 View of the wooden partition from inside the *debir*. (photo: Philip Evans)

The acacia or *shittah* tree is one of the most common species found in Sinai. (CA)

Page

A reconstruction of the Ark of the Covenant.

290 Phoenician remains of an ivory carving of winged sphinxes with human faces, reminiscent of cherubim. (British Museum)

The two cherubim standing over the Ark of the Covenant in the Holy of Holies of Solomon's Temple. (photo: Philip Evans)

291 Proposal for the decoration of the inner walls of Solomon's Temple (east-west section).

292 View of Solomon's Temple with the two pillars, Yachin and Boaz. (photo: Philip Evans)

293 Side wall of the Israelite sanctuary at Tel Dan, showing reconstructed beams which (at center left) were placed in the original grooves. The right-hand side is almost completely reconstructed.

The reconstructed Solomonic gateway at Megiddo. Remains of grooves for wooden beams were found in the original gate piers (on the right).

294 View of Solomon's Temple, showing the large "sea" and the smaller wheeled lavers. (photo: Philip Evans)

Lithograph of ancient Shechem by David Roberts, 19th century.

295 Fragment of Stele of Shishak, king of Egypt, from Megiddo. (CA)

Remains of a cult precinct at Tel Dan with altar in center, 9th to 8th centuries B.C. *(NEAEHL)*

296 Reconstructions of silver and gold vessels used in the Temple. (The Temple Institute, Jerusalem)

A silver shovel for removing ashes from the Altar.

A gold *mizrak*, one of the sacred vessels used in the Temple service to spill the sacrificial blood on the corner of the Altar.

297 Enthronement of Joash, 19th century engraving. (CA)

299 Joash proclaiming the repairs of the Temple in Jerusalem,19th century engraving. (CA)

A Tyrian silver, two-drachma coin which was the equivalent of a half-shekel, paid as tribute for the Temple.

300 Uzziah struck with leprosy after burning incense upon the altar, 19th century engraving. (CA)

301 The Mount of Olives today, looking southeast.

302 Tiglath-pileser III and a vassal king kneeling before him, on relief from the king's palace at Calah. (British Museum)

Conjectural representation of the Sea of Solomon.

303 Clay cult stand decorated with human and animal figures, from Taanach, 10th century B.C. *(NEAEHL)*

Silver-plated bronze cult standard decorated with serpents and other religious objects, from Hazor, 14th–13th centuries B.C. *(NEAEHL)*

304 Sennacherib seated on his throne receives booty and

List of Illustrations

Page

prisoners from Lachish, on relief from Nineveh. (British Museum)

305 Map of Jerusalem in the time of Hezekiah (extension marked in orange), after Avigad.

306 The table of shewbread in the Sanctuary. (photo: Philip Evans)

The brass laver, situated between the Temple Porch (*ulam*) and the Altar of Herod's Temple. (photo: Philip Evans)

307 Map of Judah and her neighbors during the reign of Manasseh.

308 Decorated fragment of a cultic stand found in Area G of the City of David, 10th century B.C. *(NEAEHL)*

309 Shaphan reading the book of the law before King Josiah, 19th century engraving. (CA)

310 The Levites bearing the sacred vessels and the Ark of the Covenant, 19th century engraving. (CA)

311 Head of Psamtik II, a king of the 26th Dynasty, to which belonged the Egyptian king mentioned in the Bible under the name of Pharaoh Necho. (CA)

312 Babylonian Chronicle recording the capture of Jerusalem by Nebuchadnezzar. (British Museum)

313 The offering of Isaac as depicted in a 19th century engraving and on the mosaic floor of the Beth Alpha synagogue, 3rd century. (CA)

314 Artist's impression of King David, having built an altar on the threshing floor he purchased from Ornan (Araunah) the Jebusite, presents an offering in response to the famine that had befallen Israel. "And he [the Lord] answered him from heaven by fire upon the altar…" (1 Chr 21:26). (The Temple Institute, Jerusalem)

315 Plan of the platform of the Dome of the Rock. Araunah's threshing floor was located 21.6 feet (6.6 m) east of the Dome of the Chain. This was the place where David built an altar. The Angel who appeared to David probably stood on the Rock (Sakhra), where later the Ark of the Covenant was placed.

316 Stages in the development of the Temple Mount, from top to bottom: 1) The square Temple Mount as repaired after the return to Zion; 2) The *Akra* built to the south of the Temple Mount; 3) The Hasmonean extension; 4) The Herodian Temple Mount; 5) The Temple Mount during the Umayyad period.

317 Map of the final campaign of Nebuchadnezzar against Judah, 15 January 588 B.C. to 19 July 586 B.C.

318 The Cylinder of Cyrus, which tells how he captured Babylon and liberated the prisoners from Babylonia. (British Museum)

Map of the Return to Zion.

319 The message of Haggai to Zerubbabel and Jeshua was heard: "Who is left among you that saw this house in her first glory? and how do ye see it now? is it not in your

Page

eyes in compairson of it as nothing?" (Haggai 2:3). (CA)

The traditional tomb of Cyrus at Pasargadae, Iran.

320 Map of the Persian province of Yehud.

Coin of Yehud. (CA)

321 Ezra bringing the law before the congregation, 19th century engraving. (CA)

322 Map of the Return to Zion under Ezra and Nehemiah.

The rock-cut tomb of Artaxerxes I, Naqsh-i-Rostam, Iran. (CA)

323 Model of Jerusalem in the time of Nehemiah, looking north.

Lamenting the desolation of the city of Jerusalem after its destruction by the Babylonians, 19th century engraving. (CA)

324 The City of David, showing the remains of the Jebusite city wall and the presumed location of the city wall of Nehemiah.

Reconstruction of the square Temple Mount or *Birah*.

325 Alexander the Great, detail of mosaic from Pompeii, 2nd–1st centuries B.C.

326 The High Priest in the Holy of Holies on the Day of Atonement.

327 Map of the final conquest of Palestine by Antiochus III, 201–198 B.C.

328 Map of the beginning of the Hasmonean revolt, 167 B.C.

Addition of the *Akra* to the south of the Temple Mount — a reconstruction.

329 A piglet sacrifice, as depicted on Greek pottery, 5th century B.C. (CA)

Reconstruction of a harp, played by the Levites in the Temple. This harp, based on an archaeological find in the Megiddo area, has twenty-two strings, corresponding to the twenty-two letters of the Hebrew alphabet. (The Temple Institute, Jerusalem)

330 Hasmonean priests light the menorah after victory. Because the golden menorah was plundered, the priests made a simple menorah of seven metal poles until they were able to reconstruct the golden lampstand. (The Temple Institute, Jerusalem)

Rebellion of the Maccabees, sculpted by Benno Elkan, from a large menorah in front of the Knesset, Jerusalem. (CA)

331 One of the projecting towers of the First Wall, on the crest of the Eastern Hill, with the corner of another tower just beyond it, both of which were built during the Hasmonean period.

Reconstruction of the eastern section of the First Wall and its two towers.

Reconstruction of the Hasmonean extension of the Temple Mount.

332 Reconstruction of the First Wall and towers discovered inside the Citadel courtyard. The present-day walls of the

List of Illustrations

Page

Citadel, shown in a lighter shade, mostly date from the Mamluk or Turkish periods.

The courtyard of the present-day Citadel, the so-called Tower of David next to Jaffa Gate, looking south. In foreground, remains of the First Wall and the two projecting towers on its right, originally built in the Hasmonean period.

333 Map of the kingdom of Alexander Janneus, 103–76 B.C.
Coin of Alexander Janneus. (CA)
334 Hasmonean coin, with depiction of a menorah on reverse. (CA)
335 The Herodian tower of Hippicus (today's so-called Tower of David) in the Citadel.
Coin of Mark Antony (left) and of Octavian (right). (CA)
336 Reconstruction proposal for the location of the *Baris*—Proto-Antonia Fortress.
337 Reconstruction of the Herodian Temple Mount.
View of the Knesset building today, Jerusalem. (CA)
338 Plan of the Herodian Temple Mount.
339 Model of the Herodian Temple Mount, viewed from the southeast. (photo: Philip Evans)
Seal impression with emblem of the Tenth Roman Legion. (CA)
340 Map of the siege of Jerusalem, A.D. 70.
View of the narrow space between the Herodian western wall and the square Temple Mount. (photo: Philip Evans)
341 Triumphal parade of Roman soldiers carrying the Temple vessels, relief on the Arch of Titus, Rome. (CA)
Coin of the Tenth Roman Legion. (CA)
Drawing of the Antonia Fortress at the northwest corner of the Temple Mount.
342 Reconstruction drawing of the Temple and its courts according to the Temple Scroll. The Temple in the center is surrounded by three concentric courts, the middle one of which measured 500 by 500 cubits.
343 Section through a Herodian portico, which had two rows of columns.
Computerized view of the Royal Stoa. (Courtesy Slawek Jozwik)
344 Torch-bearing priests on their dawn patrol of the Temple courtyard. One company of priests went in an easterly direction, while the other went towards the west, checking that all was in order for the Temple service.
345 Plan of the buildings around the Temple Court and the Court of the Women.
346 Greek inscription prohibiting Gentiles from entering the inner courtyard of the Temple.
347 The Pontius Pilate inscription from Caesarea. (photo: Garo Nalbandian)
Illustration of how a mikveh is used.
348 View of the Court of the Women, also called the Treasury

Page

in the New Testament. (photo: Philip Evans)
349 View from inside the Court of the Women looking west toward the Temple. (photo: Philip Evans)
350 Trumpet-shaped collection boxes in the porticoes of the Court of the Women. (photo: Philip Evans)
Jewish shekel from time of the First Revolt against Rome (A.D. 66–70). (photo Garo Nalbandian)
351 One of the lampstands in the Court of the Women. A young priest is climbing the ladder to bring oil to the lamps. (photo: Philip Evans)
352 Bird's-eye view of the four chambers of the Court of the Women, looking south (photo: Philip Evans)
353 A Nazarite completing his vow in the Chamber of the Nazarites.
The Chamber of the Lepers, at the northwest corner of the Court of the Women. (The Temple Institute, Jerusalem)
354 The Levitical choir on the fifteen semi-circular steps leading to the Nicanor Gate. (photo: Philip Evans)
355 Plan of the present-day Temple Mount, showing the location of the 500-cubit-square Temple Mount, the location of the *soreg* and the Herodian Temple complex.
View of the eastern stairway today.
356 Artist's rendition of the Chamber of Phinehas, keeper of vestments. (The Temple Institute, Jerusalem)
Burial cave containing decorated ossuaries, one of which bears an inscription which mentions Nicanor of Alexandria, Mount Scopus, Jerusalem. *(NEAEHL)*
357 Map of the bedrock contours of the Temple Mount according to Warren.
358 View of the *hel* or terrace. (photo: Philip Evans)
359 Perspective drawing of Herod's Temple, the stairways leading up to it and the relevant bedrock levels.
360–61 East-west section (looking north) through the Temple Mount, showing the location of the Herodian Temple and its courts in relation to existing buildings.
361 View of the remains of Herodian steps found near Robinson's Arch.
362 View of the Dome of the Chain on the Temple Mount.
Plan of Herod's Temple, courts and altar in relation to the Dome of the Rock and the Dome of the Chain.
362–63 North-south section (looking east) through the Temple Mount, showing the location of the Herodian Temple and its courts in relation to existing buildings.
363 Eastern wall of the raised platform incorporated with two Herodian stones.
364 View of the northeastern corner of the raised platform, showing three courses of ancient masonry.
365 Model of the original Altar of Burnt Sacrifice in the Tabernacle in the Wilderness. (photo: Philip Evans)
366 The Altar of Burnt Sacrifice in Herod's Temple Court. (photo: Philip Evans)

433

List of Illustrations

Page

    Reconstructed horned altar from Beersheba, late 8th century B.C. *(NEAEHL)*

367 Two priests pouring water and wine into the silver bowls at the corner of the circuit.

368 Artist's rendition of the priestly sanctification of hands and feet at the Laver and preparation of the Altar. (The Temple Institute, Jerusalem)

369 The Place of Slaughter, looking south. (photo: Philip Evans

370 Following the ritual slaughter, priests carry the blood to the Altar and, depending on the offering, sprinkle it on the corner of the altar or at its base. (The Temple Institute, Jerusalem)

372 Model showing the chambers on the north side of the Temple. (photo: Philip Evans)

373 Model showing the chambers on the south side of the Temple. (photo: Philip Evans)

374 The southern end of the eastern wall of the raised platform, showing a blocking wall which hides the entrance to underground rooms. After Warren's request to explore these rooms, a heap of earth was put in front of the entrance, which was later replaced by the blocking wall.

375 Artist's impression of the Chamber of the Lambs, one of the four side rooms of the Chamber of the Hearth. This chamber housed the animals that were to be offered on the altar. A priest is seen inspecting a lamb for disqualifying blemishes. No fewer than six acceptable lambs are in this chamber at one time. (The Temple Institute, Jerusalem)

376 The north side of Herod's Temple, showing, through the hole in the outer wall, the inner cells and stairway. (photo: Philip Evans)

377 The façade of Herod's Temple. (photo: Philip Evans)
      Jerusalem in the time of Herod the Great.

378–79 Plan and sections of Herod's Temple.

380 Roof plan of Herod's Temple.

381 The ceiling construction of Herod's Temple.
      The coffered ceiling in one of the outer gates of the Temple Scroll.
      The foundation of Herod's Temple.

382 View of the lintel construction of five carved oak beams above the entrance to the *ulam*. (photo: Philip Evans)

383 Isometric reconstruction drawing of Herod's Temple according to the mishnaic tractate *Middot*.

384 Model of the four "crowns," windows with triangular pediments located above the Golden Vine. (photo: Philip Evans)

385 View of the golden chains behind the ladder which were used to inspect the four "crowns." (photo: Philip Evans)

386 Coin of Bar Kochba; on obverse, front of a building with four columns and architrave, possibly the façade of the Temple. (CA)

387 The Golden Vine of the Temple. (photo: Philip Evans)

388 Plan of the two sets of double folding doors of the Sanctuary.

389 The Altar of Incense. (photo: Philip Evans)
      The menorah in Herod's Temple. (photo: Philip Evans)

390 Plaster fragments found in the Jewish Quarter, showing the menorah with its stepping stone, the Shewbread Table and the Altar of Incense.

391 Drawing of the Veil in the *heikhal* of Herod's Temple.

393 The Holy of Holies in Herod's Temple, showing the High Priest putting incense in the emplacement of the Ark of the Covenant, and a cleaning basket hanging near the walls that were covered with plates of gold. (photo: Philip Evans)

394 Artist's impression of the Chamber of the Half-shekel. (The Temple Institute, Jerusalem)
      Gold plaques from the Sanctuary are displayed before the public, so that festival pilgrims could "observe the beauty and perfection of their (the artisans') work" (*Pesachim* 57a). (The Temple Institute, Jerusalem)

395 Reconstruction of the censer used by the High Priest in the Holy of Holies. (The Temple Institute, Jerusalem)

396 The cells on the north side of Herod's Temple, visible through a gap in the model's outer wall. (photo: Philip Evans)

398 View of the exit of the *mesibbah* on the west (on the intermediate roof level). (photo: Philip Evans)
      View of the exit on the upper level, where a priest is seen stepping onto the roof after having climbed the cedar beams. (photo: Philip Evans)

399 Crane and pulley in the Upper Chamber above the Holy of Holies. Note the priest inside the basket. (photo: Philip Evans)
      A priest can be seen entering the small gate to the Upper Chamber. Through the hole in the wall, the cedar beams leading up to the intermediate roof level can be seen as well. (photo: Philip Evans)
      View of the parapet on the Temple roof. (photo: Philip Evans)

Index

A

Abraham 20, 50
Aceldama 80
Adelman, Benjamin 4
Aelia Capitolina 43
Agrippa II 219
Ahaz 188, 280, 302, 303, 304
Akra 201, 202, 207, 208, 209, 210, 211, 212, 214, 216, 219, 224, 226, 228, 230, 236, 239, 317, 327, 328, 331
Al-Bahr 225
Al-Maghara 231
Alexander the Great 325, 327
Aline de Sion, Marie 127, 128
Altar of Burnt Offerings 146, 155, 187
Altar of Incense 187, 329, 389, 390
Amaziah, king 188, 300
Annas, high priest 80, 83, 84, 85
Antiochus IV Epiphanes 207, 327, 330, 348
Antonia Fortress 15, 22, 32, 42, 43, 113, 119, 123, 124, 125, 126, 127, 128, 129, 130, 131, 136, 145, 155, 170, 217, 218, 230, 239, 337, 340, 341, 343
Araunah 245
Araunah, threshing floor of 7, 244, 312, 313, 314
Ark of the Covenant 13, 17, 247, 248, 252, 261, 268, 269, 270, 271, 272, 273, 274, 275, 277, 279, 283, 286, 289, 290, 296, 307, 309, 310, 311, 315, 392, 395
Artaxerxes 12, 321, 322
Asa 188, 296
Avi-Yonah, Michael 45, 208
Avigad, Nahman 2, 45, 305
Azarah 345, 358, 359, 365, 370, 382, 392

B

Bagatti, Bellarmino 128, 132, 231, 244, 262
Bahat, Dan 32, 41
Bahr al-kebir 224
Barag, Dan 386, 390
Barclay, James 15, 25
Barclay's Gate 21, 25, 26, 27, 28, 29, 34, 35, 37, 52, 104, 216, 230, 231, 235, 236, 239
Baris 41, 126, 169, 200, 201, 207, 216, 217, 218, 219, 230, 331, 332, 333, 334, 335, 337
Barnabé d'Alsace 127, 128
Bayit 7, 282, 283, 284, 285, 286, 322
Bend 161, 175, 176, 178, 179, 184, 186, 207, 213, 239
Benoit, Pierre 128
Ben Sira 225, 226, 230, 325
Beth ha-she'ubah 350, 351
Bet dilfa 380, 398
Bet horadat ha-mayim 398
Bezetha 126, 130
Bezetha Valley 41, 131, 149, 163, 169
Billig, Ya'akov 47, 52
Birah 12, 191, 192, 193, 195, 307, 322, 323, 325
Bir el-Arwah 231
Black Well 230
Bliss, Frederick 17, 54
Bor ha-gola 227
Burgoyne, Michael 68, 121, 127, 128

C

Catherwood, Frederick 15
Cell of Bostam 374
Chambers of the Slaughter-knives 386
Chamber of Hewn Stone 76, 87, 88, 227, 364, 372, 373, 375
Chamber of Immersion 229
Chamber of the Golah 372
Chamber of the Half-Shekel 394
Chamber of the Hearth 205, 229, 348, 371, 373, 374, 375
Chamber of the House of Oil 354
Chamber of the Lambs 375
Chamber of the Lepers 353

INDEX

Chamber of the Nazarites 353
Chamber of the Woodshed 353
Chaplin, Thomas 148, 221
Chapman, Rupert L. 176
Cherubim 247, 273, 274, 283, 288, 289, 290, 291, 315
Cistern of the Akra 207, 211, 212, 224, 230, 239
City of David 55, 100, 173, 188, 189, 190, 204, 208, 209, 210, 308, 323, 324, 325
Clermont-Ganneau, Charles S. 17, 221, 262
Collins, Steven 4
Conder, Claude R. 17, 113, 142, 146, 148, 153, 154, 159, 161, 211, 229
Coponius 184, 186
Corbett, Spencer 71
Corinthian Gate 356, 373
Court of the Gentiles 151, 155, 156, 229, 344, 365
Court of the Israelites 241, 344, 352, 354, 358, 360, 370
Court of the Priests 241, 344, 358, 363, 370
Court of the Women 88, 155, 164, 341, 344, 348, 349, 350, 351, 352, 353, 354, 356, 357, 358, 360, 361, 362, 363, 364, 371
Crusaders 9, 35, 78, 169, 215, 249, 250, 256, 258, 260, 262, 263, 264, 266
Cubit 11, 12, 85, 129, 140, 143, 148, 153, 155, 156, 157, 162, 163, 164, 165, 171, 172, 173, 177, 186, 190, 194, 204, 241, 242, 247, 252, 256, 277, 286, 288, 293, 306, 320, 342, 343, 347, 348, 355, 358, 361, 364, 365, 366, 367, 368, 370, 371, 380, 381, 382, 384, 388, 392, 394, 396, 398, 399
Cyrus, king of Persia 318, 319, 321

D

Dalman, Gustav 11, 45, 81, 146, 158, 159, 251
Dalman, Knut Olaf 81
Darius, son of Hystaspes 8, 321
Day of Atonement   108, 248, 314, 326, 327, 372, 394
Debir 267, 273, 282, 283, 284, 285, 286, 288, 289, 290, 291, 301, 303, 306, 326, 378, 392
De Vaux, Roland 271
De Vogüé, Melchior 10, 16, 51, 79, 109, 127, 142, 146, 148, 149, 151, 161, 251
Dickie, Archibald 17, 54
Dome of the Chain 164, 315, 362, 363
Dome of the Rock 3, 9, 10, 11, 15, 18, 87, 146, 151, 156, 165, 228, 229, 231, 242, 243, 244, 249, 250, 251, 252, 253, 255, 256, 259, 260, 261, 262, 264, 315, 337, 352, 354, 362, 363

Double Gate 29, 50, 51, 60, 63, 65, 66, 67, 68, 69, 70, 71, 72, 73, 75, 76, 77, 79, 82, 84, 85, 86, 87, 89, 91, 92, 93, 94, 103, 104, 152, 155, 205, 209, 213, 229, 231, 237, 253, 344, 348
Dunand, Maurice 213
Dura-Europos 10

E

Eastern city wall ... 107, 179, 180, 182, 183, 198, 199
Ecclesiasticus 139, 221, 225, 226, 227, 230, 325, 326, 327
Edict of Cyrus 318, 321
El Aksa (Aqsa) mosque 69, 148
Evans, Philip 4, 5, 7, 34, 43, 87, 90, 101, 105, 110, 118, 125, 130, 131, 141, 145, 183, 218, 241, 248, 279, 285, 286, 288, 289, 290, 292, 294, 306, 339, 340, 348, 349, 350, 351, 352, 354, 358, 365, 366, 368, 372, 373, 377, 382, 384, 386, 389, 392, 396, 398, 399
Even ha-Shetiyah .... 244, 359 - *See also* Foundation Stone
Excavated Ditch .... 168 - *See also* Fosse
Ezra 8, 194, 197, 198, 279, 280, 307, 318, 319, 320, 321, 322

F

Façade, of the Temple 141, 279, 377, 386
Fifteen semi-circular steps 352, 354, 357, 358, 360, 363
Five hundred cubits 144, 170, 241, 344
Fleming, James 110
Fosse 40, 41, 42, 124, 126, 131, 152, 163, 168, 170, 180, 200, 217, 218, 238, 333, 335
Foundation Stone 25, 136, 163, 244, 359, 382

G

Gate of the Firstlings 371
Gebim 282, 286
Geva, Hillel 5
Golah Chamber 227, 372
Golah Cistern 227, 230
Golden Gate 10, 107, 108, 109, 110, 113, 116, 117, 132, 149, 152, 153, 154, 155, 159, 160, 161, 167, 171, 174, 175, 176, 177, 178, 180, 181, 182, 197, 198, 199, 344
Golden Vine 384, 386
Great Course 32, 77, 93, 100, 152, 155, 159, 160
Great Sea 31, 222, 224, 230

H

Haggai, prophet 319, 321
Hall, Edgar and Marjorie 3
Haram al-Sharif 7
Har ha-Bayit 7, 144, 162
Heikhal 268, 282, 283, 284, 285, 288, 289, 291, 293, 301, 303, 306, 382, 389, 390, 392, 395, 399
Hel 145, 195
Herod, king 8, 9, 10, 13, 19, 20, 30, 32, 50, 51, 61, 85, 94, 103, 105, 109, 123, 124, 126, 127, 133, 142, 144, 145, 146, 149, 152, 153, 155, 156, 157, 158, 159, 161, 188, 204, 211, 213, 216, 219, 229, 233, 234, 239, 277, 286, 334, 335, 337, 343, 377, 380
Herod's Temple 4, 10, 18, 21, 32, 34, 44, 61, 110, 122, 132, 139, 141, 149, 152, 153, 160, 161, 163, 164, 165, 230, 233, 242, 248, 277, 291, 306, 314, 315, 359, 362, 367, 377, 378, 380, 381, 383, 389, 390, 392, 396
Hezekiah, king 41, 188, 189, 190, 191, 193, 237, 280, 303, 304, 305, 306, 323
Hilkiah, high priest 237, 296, 309
Hokansen, Obe 110
Hollis, Frederick 11, 127, 142, 146, 148, 159, 160
Holy of Holies .... 11, 25, 146, 148, 153, 154, 160, 163, 187, 229, 242, 244, 245, 246, 247, 248, 256, 261, 263, 265, 266, 267, 268, 269, 273, 274, 275, 276, 277, 279, 284, 288, 290, 296, 306, 309, 314, 315, 326, 334, 352, 357, 359, 370, 381, 382, 390, 392, 394, 395, 399 - *see also Debir, Kodesh hakodashim*
Hulda(h) Gates 85, 87, 144, 184, 209, 210, 212, 216, 229, 237, 339, 344
Hurley, Joseph 2
Hypogeion 216, 230

J

Jacobson, David 164
Jaddua, high priest 325
Jehoiachin, king 188, 312
Jehoiakim, king 188, 311, 312, 317
Jehoshaphat, king 188, 296, 297, 302
Jeremiah, prophet 201, 279, 310, 311, 317, 318, 323, 386
Jeshua, son of Jozadak 8, 10, 194, 197, 225, 318, 319, 320, 321
Jewish Quarter 2, 5, 35, 45, 90, 188, 189, 190, 246, 390
Joash, king 188, 297, 298, 299, 300

Josephus, Flavius 8, 11, 13, 20, 34, 35, 38, 42, 45, 52, 55, 58, 61, 80, 81, 83, 90, 91, 92, 94, 100, 113, 118, 123, 124, 126, 129, 131, 133, 139, 140, 141, 142, 143, 144, 145, 146, 148, 149, 152, 153, 155, 156, 157, 158, 159, 160, 161, 163, 169, 170, 171, 180, 184, 186, 187, 188, 200, 201, 207, 208, 209, 212, 216, 217, 218, 219, 225, 235, 238, 242, 268, 280, 281, 289, 297, 325, 331, 334, 335, 337, 339, 340, 341, 342, 343, 344, 346, 347, 348, 352, 356, 358, 361, 365, 366, 373
Josiah, king 188, 237, 247, 275, 296, 307, 308, 309, 310, 311
Jotham, king 188, 300, 302
Juvelius, Walter 17

K

Kane, John 2
Kaufman, Asher S. 149, 162, 163
Kedron Valley 84, 113, 169, 244, 303, 363, 367
Kenyon, Kathleen 198, 308
Kindling Gate 371
Kiponus Gate 144, 184, 339, 344
Kodesh hakodashim 282, 293

L

Lalor, Brian 2, 48
Lampstand .... 328, 329, 330, 334, 350, 351, 389 - *See also* Menorah
Laperrousaz, Ernest-Marie 213
Laver 302, 305, 306, 346, 358, 365, 368
Letter of Aristeas 139, 201, 221
Liebi, Roger 87
Lightburn, Julie 4
Lithostrotos 43, 128
Lulim 282, 286

M

Macalister, Stewart 17
Maccabees, First Book of 182, 328
Maccabees, Second Book of 201
Manasseh, king 188, 189, 247, 275, 303, 304, 307, 308, 309
Mancini, John 4, 5
Marwani Mosque 214
Mazar 12
Mazar, Amihai 22, 26
Mazar, Benjamin 1, 2, 17, 18, 22, 55, 59, 65, 193, 195
Megiddo 12, 293, 295, 329

Index

Menorah (Lampstand) 330, 334, 389, 390
Merrill, Selah 121
Mesibbah (winding staircase) 397, 398
Mikveh, mikva'ot 76, 77, 195, 229, 230, 231, 347, 348, 375
Miphkad Gate 198, 199, 200
Mishnah, *Erubin* ... 212, 221, 224, 227, 230, 239, 372
Mishnah, *Kelim* 108, 163
Mishnah, *Middot* 11, 12, 13, 85, 86, 108, 139, 140, 143, 144, 145, 146, 148, 149, 152, 153, 154, 155, 156, 157, 159, 160, 161, 162, 163, 164, 167, 171, 173, 177, 184, 195, 204, 222, 227, 229, 238, 241, 242, 244, 261, 266, 267, 277, 339, 344, 346, 347, 348, 349, 352, 353, 354, 356, 358, 359, 361, 366, 367, 368, 370, 371, 372, 373, 377, 380, 382, 383, 384, 386, 390, 392, 394, 395, 397, 398, 399
Mishnah, *Sanhedrin* 76, 87, 348
Mishnah, *Shekalim* 112, 246, 348, 350, 355, 390, 392
Mishnah, *Sukkah* 59, 349, 350, 351
Mishnah, *Tamid* 348, 368, 371, 390
Mishnah, *Yoma* 108, 112, 246, 277, 359, 368, 392, 395
Mommert, Carl 11, 146, 148, 156, 157, 164
Monastery of the Temple 169, 231
Mountain of the House 7, 140, 144, 145, 148, 149, 152, 153, 155, 156, 157, 158, 161, 162, 173, 238, 339
Mount Moriah 1, 8, 20, 137, 243, 277, 313, 315, 320
Mount of Olives 1, 81, 108, 112, 113, 132, 144, 267, 284, 301, 356
Murphy O'Connor, Jerome 2, 268

N

Nehemiah . 8, 12, 139, 177, 182, 192, 194, 195, 197, 198, 201, 203, 279, 307, 322, 323, 324, 325, 335
Nicanor Gate 352, 354, 356, 358, 371, 373

O

Oesterly, William O.E. 11, 159
Offset 105, 107, 113, 115, 117, 132, 175, 177
Ophel 100, 225

P

Parapet 57, 58, 60, 380, 398, 399
Parker, Montague B. 17, 18, 251, 261
Parokhet see Veil
Parva Chamber 372

Patrich, Joseph 397, 399
Paul, apostle 127, 347
Philo 221
Pilgrim of Bordeaux 221, 263
Place of Slaughter 344, 365, 368, 370
Place of the water-drawing 351
Pompey 169, 184, 200, 217, 218, 239, 248, 331, 332, 333, 334, 335
Pont du Gard 113
Porch (*ulam*) 80, 82, 159, 164, 186, 277, 284, 293, 305, 306, 346, 357, 359, 360, 366, 368, 370, 378, 382
Porch of Solomon 141
Prison Gate 200, 202, 203, 222, 231
Proto-Antonia 334, 335
Ptolemaic Akra 201, 202, 219, 327

R

Raised Platform 10, 11, 146, 152, 155, 157, 158, 161, 163, 165, 167, 169, 170, 177, 184, 202, 204, 205, 238, 239, 288, 352, 357, 362, 363, 364, 374
Ramp (of the Altar) 368, 371
Red Heifer 108, 112, 267, 356
Rehoboam, king 188, 295
Reich, Ronnie 47, 52, 229, 347
Rings 71, 134, 365, 368, 371
Rinsing Chamber 372
Ritmeyer, Kathleen 2, 5
Ritmeyer, Martha 73
Ritmeyer, Nathaniel 73
Roberts, Vic 4, 279
Robinson, Edward 15, 44, 79, 208, 343
Robinson's Arch 21, 22, 31, 44, 45, 46, 47, 48, 49, 50, 52, 54, 55, 57, 72, 83, 107, 110, 133, 136, 236, 361,
Rock, The (*es-Sakhra*) 3, 11, 146, 151, 153, 154, 155, 156, 157, 159, 160, 163, 205, 222, 228, 229, 231, 242, 243, 244, 245, 246, 247, 249, 250, 251, 252, 253, 254, 255, 256, 258, 259, 260, 261, 262, 263, 264, 265, 266, 267, 268, 269, 270, 277, 288, 312, 313, 314, 315, 352, 354, 357, 359, 360, 361, 362, 363, 381
Rock-hewn aqueduct 38, 42, 230
Royal Cubit 171, 172, 173, 239, 246, 296
Royal Stoa .... , 45, 49, 50, 51, 58, 61, 69, 70, 72, 77, 83, 89, 90, 91, 92, 93, 94, 97, 102, 103, 104, 129, 164, 230, 237, 343, 344
Russian Compound 134, 136

INDEX

S

Sakhra, es- (The Rock - *See* Rock, The (*es-Sakhra*)
Scapegoat 108, 112
Scarlet line 367
Schick, Alexander 177, 213
Schick, Conrad 17, 127, 146, 148, 154, 155, 177, 205, 221, 231, 237
Seam 102, 105, 149, 160, 162, 174, 175, 177, 179, 186, 207, 213, 214, 216, 239
Sederot 282, 286
Seleucid Akra 201, 207, 208, 328
Shanks, Hershel 3
Sheep Gate 199, 202, 203, 205
Sheshbazzar, prince of Judah 319
Shopharot 349
Shushan, citadel 108, 144, 192, 195, 323
Shushan Gate 178, 344
Simon, son of Onias 225, 227, 326, 331
Simons, Jan 127, 148, 160, 161, 201, 208
Simon Maccabee 209, 211, 214, 331
Simpson, William 224, 227
Single Gate 61, 95, 96, 97, 103, 137, 179
Sisters of Zion convent 43
Solomon's Pools 62
Solomon's Stables 18, 61, 86, 88, 95, 97
Solomon's Temple 20, 30
Solomon, Davia 2
Solomon, king 7, 8, 10, 17, 20, 62, 102, 110, 140, 141, 153, 155, 160, 161, 171, 186, 187, 188, 189, 190, 191, 192, 219, 247, 256, 261, 270, 273, 275
Solomon's Pools 31, 222
Solomon's Porch .... 113, 218, 219 - *Also* Porch of Solomon
Solomon's Stables 18, 61, 86, 88, 95, 98, 99, 101, 108
Solomon's Temple 4, 7, 11, 141, 149, 152, 153, 157, 161, 187, 194, 246, 266, 273, 274, 276, 279, 280, 281, 284, 285, 286, 290, 291, 292, 294, 295, 296, 305, 306, 312, 320, 367, 396
Soreg 145, 153, 164, 229, 344, 346, 347, 355, 358, 364, 365
Square Temple Mount 11, 12, 13, 91, 123, 126, 139, 140, 141, 143, 144, 145, 146, 148, 149, 152, 153, 154, 156, 158, 162, 165, 168, 170, 173, 174, 177, 178, 180, 182, 183, 184, 186, 190, 193, 194, 195, 196, 198, 199, 200, 201, 202, 204, 207, 208, 209, 210, 211, 213, 215, 216, 218, 219, 222, 224, 227, 228, 229, 230, 231, 233, 234, 235, 236, 237, 238, 239, 241, 252, 267, 317, 322, 323, 325, 326, 328, 331, 334, 335, 337, 339, 344
St. Anne's Valley 118, 131, 169
Step 13, 165, 169
Straton's Tower 216
Strouthion Pool 22, 42, 43, 128, 129, 130
Sukkot 226, 351

T

Table of Shewbread 306, 389
Tadi Gate 144, 163, 204, 205, 216, 221, 229, 230, 339, 344
Tell Ta'yinat 145
Tel Dan 186, 293, 295
Temenos 1, 164, 238, 339, 344, 365
Temple Court (*azarah*) 68, 86, 122, 132, 148, 152, 153, 164, 188, 216, 227, 231, 236, 237, 241, 242, 293, 296, 302, 335, 340, 341, 344, 346, 348, 352, 354, 356, 357, 358, 360, 362, 363, 365, 366, 370, 371, 373, 375
Temple Scroll 341, 342, 381
Thackeray 139, 143, 341
The Antiquities of the Jews (*Ant.*) 9, 20, 35, 61, 126, 129, 133, 140, 142, 143, 152, 169, 188, 196, 200, 201, 208, 209, 212, 216, 219, 235, 325, 327, 330, 334, 377
The Jewish War (*War*) 339
Titus 59, 100, 340, 341, 347
Tomb of the Patriarchs 37, 50, 51, 116, 161, 304
Tosafot Yom Tob 148
Tower Meah 201
Tower of Hananeel 200, 201
Transversal Valley 34
Triple Gate 30, 61, 63, 70, 75, 76, 77, 78, 79, 80, 82, 83, 85, 86, 87, 88, 92, 93, 94, 95, 97, 98, 99, 100, 104, 158, 160, 163, 184, 209, 211, 212, 230, 236, 237, 239, 355
Trumpeting Stone 57, 58, 60
Tsafrir, Yoram 213
Tsela'ot 282, 285, 286
Tyropoeon Valley 20, 21, 26, 27, 30, 31, 41, 45, 52, 54, 55, 56, 65, 164, 169, 233, 234, 235

U

Ulam (Porch) 282, 284, 293, 304, 306, 377, 380, 381, 382, 384, 386, 388
Upper City 21, 30, 31, 45, 52, 214
Ussishkin, David 173
Uzziah, king 188, 280, 300, 301, 314

439

Index

V

Veil (*parokhet*) 246, 258, 273, 291, 306, 326, 328, 348, 390, 392, 395
Vincent, Louis Hugues 17, 127, 128, 146, 161, 162, 208, 269

W

Waqf 214
Warren, Charles 3, 12, 17, 21, 25, 26, 27, 28, 29, 31, 34, 40, 45, 47, 55, 56, 57, 60, 75, 95, 96, 101, 102, 107, 113, 114, 115, 116, 118, 121, 127, 142, 146, 148, 151, 152, 153, 155, 159, 164, 168, 169, 178, 179, 180, 182, 183, 184, 199, 202, 204, 205, 208, 211, 212, 213, 216, 221, 229, 230, 231, 234, 235, 237, 238, 239, 261, 357, 374, 375
Warren's Gate 21, 29, 32, 34, 35, 221, 231, 235
Warren's Shaft 16, 60, 204
Water Gate 226, 227, 371, 372
Watson, Charles 11, 45, 127, 146, 148, 155, 156
Well of the Abyssinian 230
Well of the Leaf 230
Well of the Pomegranate 230
Well of Souls 231
Western Wall tunnels 21, 32, 34, 37, 38
Wightman, Gregory J. 128, 201, 208
Wilkinson, John 119
Wilson, Charles 15, 16, 17, 30, 31, 79, 174, 221, 343, 357
Wilson's Arch 21, 22, 30, 31, 32, 37, 45, 62, 149, 151, 184, 236, 332, 344
Wood, Bryant 4
Wood Chamber 227, 372

Y

Yadin, Yigael 341, 342
Yatsia 282, 285, 286
Yehud, Persian province of Judea 320
Yom Kippur 108, 248, 276, 277, 314, 394

Z

Zechariah, prophet 201, 300, 301, 321, 386
Zedekiah, king 188, 312
Zerubbabel, son of Shealtiel 8, 10, 158, 194, 197, 198, 225, 248, 318, 319, 320, 321